Liem Sioe Liong's
Salim Group

Liem Sioe Liong's Salim Group

The Business Pillar of Suharto's Indonesia

RICHARD BORSUK • NANCY CHNG

INSTITUTE OF SOUTHEAST ASIAN STUDIES

Singapore

First published in Singapore in 2014 by
ISEAS Publishing
Institute of Southeast Asian Studies
30 Heng Mui Keng Terrace
Pasir Panjang
Singapore 119614

E-mail: publish@iseas.edu.sg
Website: <http://bookshop.iseas.edu.sg>

© 2014 Institute of Southeast Asian Studies, Singapore
First Reprint 2014
Second Reprint 2014
Third Reprint 2014

*The responsibility for facts and opinions in this publication rests exclusively with the
authors and their interpretations do not necessarily reflect the views or the policy of the
publishers or their supporters.*

ISEAS Library Cataloguing-in-Publication Data

Borsuk, Richard.
    Liem Sioe Liong's Salim Group : the business pillar of Suharto's Indonesia /
Richard Borsuk and Nancy Chng.
    1.   Liem, Sioe Liong, 1917–2012.
    2.   Salim Group.
    3.   Businesspeople—Indonesia—Biography.
    4.   Chinese—Indonesia—Biography.
    5.   Conglomerate corporations—Indonesia.
    6.   Family-owned business enterprises—Indonesia.
    7.   Indonesia—Politics and government—1960–1998.
    I.   Chng, Nancy.
    II. Title.
HC446.5 L71B73   2014

ISBN 978-981-4459-57-0 (soft cover)
ISBN 978-981-4519-82-3 (hard cover)
ISBN 978-981-4459-59-4 (e-book, PDF)

Photo credits:
Front cover photo — from Salim archives, reproduced with kind permission
from Anthony Salim.
Back cover photo — reproduced with kind permission of *Tempo*/Rully Kesuma.

Typeset by Superskill Graphics Pte Ltd
Printed in Singapore by Markono Print Media Pte Ltd

CONTENTS

PREFACE

This project on Liem Sioe Liong and the Salim Group was undertaken as an independent venture — neither authorized nor financed by the group or the Liem family. The root was our interest to document the life and times of Liem, a pivotal figure in Asian business who founded a conglomerate that in its heyday was by far the largest in Southeast Asia. As Liem was Suharto's main *cukong* — a Chinese businessman providing funds for Indonesia's military and political leaders while receiving patronage and protection — his story provides an insight to how Suharto was able to stay in power for more than three decades.

There have been a few books published in Indonesian and Chinese about Liem, mostly hagiographies. Significantly, none included the tycoon's direct inputs. Given Liem's desire for a low profile, he had declined previous requests from prospective biographers. Historically, the Salim Group has been highly averse to publicity despite its very public participation in a wide range of businesses during the Suharto regime. Indeed, in many cases, the group chose to ignore inaccuracies in news reports and was content to allow errors in stories to go uncorrected.

Years after Suharto fell from power, we approached Liem's youngest son, Anthony Salim, and said we wanted to write a book on his father and the group. By the mid-2000s, Indonesia had found its footing in the post-Suharto period and Liem had long ago left the driving to Anthony. Currently CEO of the Salim Group, Anthony spent years after Suharto's fall working to avert a collapse of the group due to the massive debts incurred from events in 1997–98.

We requested Anthony and his father to help us tell as accurate and comprehensive a story as we could. We made it clear that we had to retain full control of the manuscript; it was clearly understood that the family and Salim executives could not see any of the text prior to publication.

Keeping the writing project independent and credible was of paramount importance to us. Anthony agreed to our requests. His father talked to us between 2006 and 2007, whenever his health permitted. Anthony, who did not vet our questions to himself or to his father, spent many hours with us over a period of years. This was the first time that both father and son talked to writers on a wide range of topics. Conversations took place in Singapore.

While we started with the idea of a biography of Liem, it made sense to widen the scope to encompass the history of the group, which was important for context. Because of Liem's intricately woven ties with Suharto, and indeed with the top military generals from the beginning of the New Order, his story, in a sense, reflects slices of the country's history.

As journalists, we tried to be even-handed in writing about the business conglomerate so closely tied to the political and economic fortunes of Indonesia under Suharto. Regretfully, by the time we started our conversations with Liem, he was already nearly 89 and in declining health. His memory was weakening, and his recall of recent events was patchy. He seemed to remember the old days better and preferred to talk about the distant past. He was usually in good humour, chatting with us on Saturday afternoons in his old Singapore office, Permanent, in Clifford Centre. No business had been conducted there for some time, but Liem wanted it kept open as it was supposed to live up to its name. Long after the 1998 riots which ended his living in Indonesia, Liem still could not get out of the habit of going to an office. Often, food was brought in for a late lunch, which he insisted we shared. On a few occasions, he was disinclined to answer our questions, preferring to make small talk instead. During the initial sessions, he had long-time Salim executive Benny Santoso sit in with us. When he became more comfortable with us, he was content to chat in private. We conversed in Indonesian and Mandarin, although sometimes, he would break into his Hokchia dialect, which was not understood by us.

Since this project was not a Salim initiative, not all family members and executives wished to talk to us. Even an old friend of Liem, in our presence, warned him about disclosing too much information. Several Salim executives we approached made themselves unavailable.

Although Suharto was no longer the strongman when we started our research, the power he and his cronies were perceived to hold lingered. We encountered instances when people asked if we were afraid of repercussions, if Salim didn't like what we wrote. The group naturally made enemies over the years. To try to get their side of the story, we approached some Salim business rivals but many of them declined to meet us.

Research was conducted in Jakarta, Singapore, Kudus, Semarang, Hong Kong and Fuqing, Liem's hometown in China. Most of Liem's friends had passed away so we didn't have the benefit of their input. We talked to former business partners and politicians. Liem's Indonesian partners, Sudwikatmono and Ibrahim Risjad (both since deceased), were cooperative and pleasant. The fourth member of the "Gang of Four", Djuhar Sutanto (Liem Oen Kian), fell out with Liem and Anthony after the 1997–98 financial crisis. His son Tedy Djuhar declined to give an interview. We are well aware that there are gaps in this narrative, and some readers may have a different opinion of certain events mentioned. We are responsible for any errors or shortcomings.

This project could not have gotten off the ground were it not for Anthony Salim. We thank him for accepting our conditions and for meeting us many times. Benny Santoso, Executive Director of the Salim Group was always responsive to our requests to chase down information. We thank the Salim staff (both current and former) as well as members of the Liem family in Indonesia, China, Hong Kong and Singapore who provided input or helped in some capacity or other. We'd like to make special mention of Hindarto Budiono in Jakarta; his kindness and friendship will always be remembered. We hope we did not place too great a burden on the Salim staff in Jakarta, in particular, Susan Tan and Sandra Setiadi. For access to Liem family photos, our thanks to Mira Salim, Anky Handoko, Benny Santoso and especially Anthony, for permission to use them.

Two academics, Yuri Sato and Marleen Dieleman, who have done extensive and valuable research on the Salim Group, have been generous in sharing information with us. Marleen made available her doctoral thesis to us before it was published. Masya Spek shared with us her equity reports of listed Indonesian companies. Thee Kian Wie willingly provided us with many of his research papers. We enjoyed his fine company and were deeply saddened to learn of his passing in early February 2014. Our thanks to Keetie Sluyterman of Utrecht University for sending us her impressive volume (co-authored with Joost Jonker) documenting the history of Dutch international trading companies.

We are particularly indebted to our good friends in Jakarta and elsewhere for their unwavering support and encouragement. Roosniati

Salihin deserves special mention for her kind hospitality over the years; we enjoyed her good humour and insights on the Indonesian business scene. On top of other help, Puspa Madani hunted down old Indonesian company registrations and provided valuable translation help for official documents. We are also grateful for the help and amity of Windrati Selby, Manggi Habir and Cesar de la Cruz. Many old friends from our Jakarta days continue to welcome us warmly on our return visits and kept us well plied with delicious Indonesian food and excellent conversation. We would like also to express our gratitude to the many individuals — some mentioned in the text by name, others who requested anonymity — who agreed to be interviewed or simply, met us for chats; we have learnt a lot from them. We apologize for not naming everyone who have provided us with information, assistance and support.

At the Institute of Southeast Asian Studies in Singapore, Ambassador K. Kesavapany (director from 2002 until 2012) approved our proposal for this research. We would like to thank him as well as current Director Tan Chin Tiong. We would also like to acknowledge the friendship and kind assistance provided by the ISEAS staff, particularly in the library and in the publications unit, where senior editor Rahilah Yusuf helped transform the manuscript into a book. Our sincere appreciation goes to the two anonymous reviewers for their helpful and insightful comments.

Last but not least, we thank our family for their forbearance. We honestly did not know this project would take this long, but we learnt much about Indonesian history along the way. A special note of appreciation to Denise: Her assistance, endless patience and understated humour helped sustain us all these years.

Richard Borsuk and Nancy Chng
February 2014

INTRODUCTION

Fifty years after he reached Java's shores from China in 1938 with barely more than the clothes he wore, Liem Sioe Liong was boss of Indonesia's biggest conglomerate and was showing up in magazine lists of the world's wealthiest people. This reflected how much the Salim Group he founded flourished during the long presidency of his friend and patron, General Suharto. At the height of his success, Liem sat atop a vast business empire, estimated by some to encompass 600 affiliated companies — Liem said he didn't know the exact number — and was a force in many strategic industries, including wheat-milling, cement-making and banking.

In the mid-1990s, more than 200,000 people worked for Salim companies in Indonesia and overseas. In 1996, the year before the Asian financial crisis hit Salim — and Indonesia — hard, revenue from group operations was estimated at US$22 billion, nearly three times as large as the second-ranked group, Astra.[1] Liem noted in a Salim corporate profile published that year — the last one issued: "Today, our companies are intimately involved in the day to day lives of literally millions of Indonesian families."[2] Liem's Bank Central Asia grew to become the country's biggest private bank. Indocement, an agglomeration of Salim's cement plants, became Indonesia's dominant cement producer; Bogasari, its flour processing unit, expanded a Jakarta plant into the world's largest mill; and Indofood overtook Nissin Foods of Japan as the world's leading instant noodle manufacturer.

Liem himself didn't like to dwell on indicators of wealth — he was uncomfortable with portrayals of himself as the richest businessman in Southeast Asia (but he didn't object to rankings issued by the Finance Ministry showing him as the No. 1 taxpayer in Indonesia, as he wanted it be known that he paid his dues). In a country where the Chinese have historically been subjected to discrimination and periodic violence, the tycoon understandably preferred to keep a low profile. Liem liked to quote a Chinese proverb: "Tall trees attract the wind. We don't want to talk about how big we are; people get jealous."[3] Until a foreign journalist for the Associated Press mentioned Liem's Salim Group in 1971,[4] very few people outside the country had heard of the man who became Suharto's most important business pillar.

Liem and Suharto (who came into power following the 1965 abortive coup) had much in common, including an abiding interest in making money. For the strongman, money equalled power, and he needed to build his power base. The Chinese businessman stumped up whenever Suharto or his generals needed funds, for political or personal needs. Liem stepped up to the plate whenever he was called on, and was able to deliver. Both men saw their role as vital to the building of a country that was both broken and broke when Suharto claimed the helm in the mid-1960s. The mutual benefits were substantial. Thanks to the patronage he received, Liem become extremely wealthy, while his success helped keep the authoritarian leader in power more than thirty years.

The practice of patronage was not started by Suharto, the republic's second president. Under Sukarno, businessmen — and not limited to the Chinese — also enjoyed special favours. But Suharto honed the practice into an art. His bestowing of favours to cronies was done in the understanding that there was a payback. In some businesses, that meant shares given straight out to family members. In others, *yayasan*, or foundations, under his control benefited. The foundations, which did not publicly publish accounts, received contributions often to the tune of millions of dollars, ostensibly for the benefit of charities, but sometimes funnelled to projects or private enterprises linked to members of Suharto's family. Liem never complained about helping Cendana (as the interests of the First Family were commonly referred to, Cendana being the name of the street where the president lived). Indeed, Liem readily offered shares to the president and his family members, including 30 per cent of his flagship bank. For him, it was the price of doing business in Indonesia, his adopted homeland.

Liem built the Salim Group into one of Southeast Asia's first multinational enterprises. He had an uncanny ability to pick capable partners and was able to tap the extensive network of fellow overseas Chinese to obtain capital as well as expertise. At first, links were with his dialect group with roots in Fujian, the Hokchia community, then with the Indonesian military and of course, the most powerful of them, Suharto. His personality traits stood him in good stead — he combined humility with generosity — two qualities appreciated by Suharto and others who benefited from his largesse. Because of skilled partners, Liem was able to expand into businesses in which he had little if any expertise. He also worked hard to prove his trustworthiness. He was a risk-taker, and emerged from a coterie of wannabe cronies to become Suharto's top financier.

Liem reckoned he first met Suharto in the hills of central Java during the struggle for independence, when Republican units fought the Dutch who were intent on reasserting control on their colony after World War II. Then, Liem was just one of the Chinese traders running supplies of basic goods to the soldiers. Suharto's posting in 1956 to Semarang as commander of an army division rekindled the acquaintance, although by that time Liem had moved to Jakarta. The trust that Liem earned with some of Suharto's top aides came in handy after Suharto became president and was looking for businessmen to work with. In the early days of their link-up, Liem told the president of the Chinese saying that a good leader has to provide his population with the four basic needs — clothing, food, shelter, and transportation. It dovetailed with the Javanese concept of *sandang-pangan* (food and clothing). Liem said to Suharto: You need the funds; I can help raise it. Of his relationship with the president, Liem said: "We were like brothers."[5] Indeed, they were kindred souls. During Suharto's early days as a leader, he conversed often with Liem, who was a frequent visitor to the president's Cendana home. But Liem had the foresight to grow his group beyond his Cendana links. In this, the lead was taken by his capable son Anthony Salim, who pushed beyond the shores of Indonesia. As academic Richard Robison pointed out in 1986 in his seminal work *Indonesia: The Rise of Capital*:

> The Liem group has been able to take advantage of policies designed to protect and nurture domestic capitalists, particularly in import substitution, because of its capacity to secure monopolies and access to the financial and organisational resources of international capital. But the Liem group can no longer be regarded as a client or comprador group hanging onto the coat-tails of Indonesian generals and foreign bankers; it is a major regional and international financial and industrial group with a substantial capital base.[6]

More than a decade after Robison's writing — during which time Salim's size and scope widened — Liem's Jakarta home was burned amid deadly riots and Suharto was toppled. A backlash quickly arose that threatened to crush the Salim Group, which had huge debts. Suharto's enemies bayed for Liem's blood and assets. Before the convulsions of 1998, Liem had handed over the reins of his empire to his youngest son Anthony, who after Suharto's fall shrewdly relinquished chunks of assets to secure Salim's food business, for survival and eventual expansion. Liem's rag-to-riches tale — from poor village migrant to business titan — is interwoven with Indonesia's economic narrative. The Salim Group's journey, explored in this text, aims to tell part of the story of how business was done in Suharto's New Order, and in the early post-Suharto period.

Notes

1. Yuri Sato, "The decline of conglomerates in post-Soeharto Indonesia: The case of Salim Group", *Taiwan Journal of Southeast Asian Studies* 1, no. 1 (2004), p. 25.
2. Salim corporate profile, Jakarta, 2006.
3. Interview with Liem Sioe Liong, 23 September 2006.
4. Frank Hawkins, "Indonesia's own military-industrial complex", *Bangkok Post*, 28 January 1971.
5. Interview with Liem, 12 August 2006.
6. Richard Robison, *Indonesia: The Rise of Capital* (Sydney: Allen and Unwin/Asian Studies Association of Australia, 1986), p. 297.

Liem Sioe Liong, once described as "*cukong* extraordinaire", in his office, with the Indonesian flag flanked by ones for Bogasari flour mill and Indocement.
Source: Unless otherwise stated, all photos are from Salim archives, reproduced with kind permission from Anthony Salim.

Liem, flanked by his sons who were involved in his businesses, Anthony, the youngest, is on the left, and Andree, the second son.

The "Gang of Four", comprising (from left) Liem, Sudwikatmono, Djuhar Sutanto (Liem Oen Kian) and Ibrahim Risjad.

Helping launch Liem as one of the region's biggest tycoons was Chin Sophonpanich (middle), of the Bangkok Bank, who provided crucial financial support and introduced Liem to important Asian tycoons. With them is Taiwanese tycoon and diplomat C.F. Koo.

President Suharto (right) presided at the opening of Salim's flour milling factory, Bogasari, in 1971. Suharto's cousin Sudwikatmono (in white) held the title of Director I.

The sprawling Bogasari flour-milling complex in Jakarta, as seen from the air.

Liem met the girl of his dreams in Kudus and, after a brief courtship, married her in 1944. Java was still occupied by the Japanese, but they managed to hold an elaborate ceremony.

The young Liem boys — Albert, Anthony, and Andree — in the early 1950s.

An early family portrait: Mr and Mrs Liem and their four children — Albert, Anthony, Mira and Andree.

Liem (right), with elder brother Sioe Hie (next to him), younger brother Sioe Kong and their youngest sister, Yue Ying.

Liem's home in Kudus, Central Java, where he lived before moving to Jakarta in 1952. He and his uncle and brother ran their coffee business from here.
Source: Nancy Chng.

Gen. Sudjono Humardani (right) an important "financial general" and one of Suharto's closest aides, was instrumental in linking Liem with Suharto. Admiral Sudomo, former security chief, is on the left.

Dubbed the "banking doctor", Mochtar Riady helped build Liem's Bank Central Asia into the country's largest private bank, then left to develop his Lippo Group.
Source: Tempo/Ronald Agusta.

The Liems, visiting the United States in the early 1980s, met Bill Clinton when he was Governor of Arkansas.

Liem gave his first interview to an Indonesian media in 1984, talking to *Tempo*'s Fikri Jufri.

Suharto summoned tycoons to his Tapos ranch in March 1990 to urge them to "share their wealth" with cooperatives. With Liem are Prajogo Pangestu of Barito Pacific and Astra International's William Soeryadjaya (bowing).
Source: Tempo/Bambang Harymurti.

Suharto and Liem being shown plans for a development in Karimun, Riau islands, in March 1997. Also present were Singapore Prime Minister Goh Chok Tong (centre, behind Liem) and Minister for Information and the Arts George Yeo (on right). Indonesian Minister for Research and Technology B.J. Habibie is second from right, and Tunky Ariwibowo, Minister of Industry and Trade (partly hidden) is behind him.

Posing for a photo in 1999 with Madam Wu Yi, who had been Chinese Minister for Foreign Trade and Economic Cooperation. She later became China's Vice-Premier and was ranked by *Forbes* as one of the world's most powerful women. She retired in 2008.

In 1991, a year after diplomatic ties were restored between Indonesia and China, Xi Jinping, who in 2013 became China's President, led a delegation to Jakarta that visited Liem's office. Xi held various positions in Fujian, Liem's home province, and was Governor from 2000 to 2002.

Liem and Xi kept up their friendship; Liem made one of his last visits to Beijing in 2009, and met with Xi, who by then was China's Vice-President.

A fan of Min opera from his province, Liem became a lifelong patron of the troupe from Fuqing. He and his wife pose with some performers at the Singapore Futsing (Fuqing) Association.

Students at a Fuqing middle school — named for Liem's father — awaiting the arrival of their principal benefactor during a visit in February 2006. Liem was a regular donor to educational and other causes in Fujian province.
Source: Nancy Chng.

Ancestral photos in Liem's home in Fuqing, China. His parents are on extreme left and second from right, flanking his grandparents;
his uncle is on extreme right.
Source: Nancy Chng.

Liem paying respects to his ancestors during a 2006 visit to his home village.
Source: Nancy Chng.

Liem and his wife at a ceremony marking the 35th anniversary of Bank Central Asia in 1992. *Source: Tempo* / Hidayat Surya Gautama.

In 1996, Liem Sioe Liong travelled to the United States to receive the prestigious Dean's Medal from the Wharton School in Philadelphia.

The Liem family at Liem's 50th wedding anniversary celebration in Singapore in 1994.

First Pacific's 25th anniversary in 2006 was celebrated with a lavish party in Hong Kong, hosted by Anthony Salim and Manny Pangilinan.

Queue forming in front of BCA's head office in the May 1998 run on the bank.
Source: KOMPAS/Arbain Rambey.

Liem's single-storey house in Jalan Gunung Sahari, Jakarta. He had resisted renovating the house so as not to disturb the *feng shui*, or balance of elements that he believed had brought him luck.
Source: Nancy Chng.

The outside of Liem's torched mansion, adjoining his old bungalow. During the May 1998 riots, Liem's Jakarta home was targeted by what appeared to be an organized mob.
Source: Nancy Chng.

A 2006 photo of the charred living room of the home that was burned during the 1998 riots.
Source: Nancy Chng.

Old friends meet again: Visiting former strongman Suharto at his Cendana home with Anthony Salim in 2004.

Albert, Mira, Andree and Anthony — with their parents.

Liem Sioe Liong died on 10 June 2012 in Singapore. His wake was held at Mt Vernon Funeral Parlour.

Former Indonesian President Megawati Sukarnoputri, daughter of Indonesia's founding president Sukarno, being greeted by Anthony Salim at Liem's wake. Her grandfather, Hasan Din, was an early business partner of Liem's.

Orders for floral wreaths for Liem's funeral temporarily depleted supply of fresh flowers in Singapore.

Liem was one of the founders of Prasetiya Mulya Foundation; a building at its Jakarta management school is named after him.

The gigantic statue of Mi Le Fuo (sometimes called "Laughing Buddha") in Haikou. Liem's clansmen compare him to the Laughing Buddha, who represents luck and plenitude.
Source: Nancy Chng.

Anthony Salim in January 2014. He kept control of key parts of the Salim Group after a backlash against cronies following Suharto's fall.
Source: Nancy Chng.

1

A JAVANESE "KING" AND HIS *CUKONG*

One hankered after power, the other after money, and when they paired up they made a potent team that kept them on top in Indonesian politics and business respectively for three decades. President Suharto and Liem Sioe Liong worked very closely together, building a symbiotic relationship that resulted in huge benefits for both. Liem, founder of the colossal business conglomerate known as the Salim Group, proved himself to be a reliable businessman and became Suharto's main *cukong*[1] — a Chinese financial backer who is given protection by powerful political or military leaders. In his rise from an itinerant peddler to Indonesia's wealthiest businessman, Liem received patronage from several generals, but most importantly from Suharto himself. The strongman acquired unchecked and, for a long time, uncheckable power and until his shocking resignation in May 1998, was one of the world's longest-serving heads of government. In 1983, sycophantic parliamentarians conferred on him the title *Bapak Pembangunan* — "Father of Development", which Suharto cherished, as he liked to claim that all his endeavours were for the good of the "common man". But while he claimed to identify with the "*wong cilik*" (Javanese for "little people"), Suharto saw himself as possessing the *wahyu*, sort of a divine right, to be the country's ruler. An Indonesian historian once commented: "Like a Javanese monarch, Suharto always equated his self-control and harmony in relation to the spiritual world with the well-being of the nation and the state."[2]

He surrounded himself with people who could serve faithfully and unquestioningly. To stay at the apex of power, Suharto relied on several pillars. One was the military — which the general used effectively. He used money to keep the armed forces loyal to him and used them to suppress political opponents — both real and perceived ones. The military had stepped in to run companies of the colonial Dutch that Sukarno, the first president, nationalized in 1957, and top generals became used to having opportunities to enrich themselves. They became an even bigger player in Suharto's New Order. Another crucial prop for Suharto was financial and other aid from the West. Indonesia was in dire straits when he came into power, and the way he and his team of Western-trained technocrats opened the country for foreign investment was vital for economic growth. But the nation also needed to generate wealth domestically, and here is where Liem made substantial contributions to the New Order. The *cukong* and his Salim Group became a pillar for Suharto.

A BEAUTIFUL FRIENDSHIP

During Suharto's authoritarian regime, politics and business were closely intertwined. Throughout his military career, Suharto had shown a keen interest in business, stemming from the days when he, like all regimental commanders, was expected to secure additional income to supplement the meagre pay of the soldiers. From as early as the 1950s, he had several trusted military aides and businessmen such as Sudjono Humardani and Mohamad "Bob" Hasan engage in ventures to raise funds. An early endeavour involved bartering sugar from Java for rice. Suharto's overzealousness in generating money later earned him a rebuke and a transfer out of active command in 1959. The need for extra-budgetary funds predates the New Order; during President Sukarno's time, the government also leaned on businessmen to fund his projects. Sukarno had a so-called "Revolution Fund", from which he could dip into for his pet projects. But that paled in comparison to the fund-raising endeavours of his successor. Suharto was a master at squeezing money, which he needed to cement political support. These "unscrutinized off-budget sources of income" amounted to perhaps one-half of actual government expenditures in the New Order's formative years, said an academic.[3] One of his early prime contributors was Ibnu Sutowo, boss of state oil company Pertamina. This was one reason the president was so hesitant to hold the oil honcho accountable when he nearly bankrupted the country in the mid-1970s. Suharto's early group of advisors included the influential "financial generals" who helped him network with Chinese businessmen, among whom was Liem.

After the Japanese Occupation ended in 1945, Chinese traders such as Liem scrambled to revive their interrupted businesses. They started provisioning soldiers of the new republic, who sometimes camped in the hills of Central Java in their fight with the Dutch troops. Liem was one of the suppliers to Suharto's unit and managed to impress the soldiers with his eagerness, diligence and personable nature. One officer in charge of logistics, named Sulardi, was a cousin of Suharto. Some twenty years later, Sulardi's younger brother Sudwikatmono would become Liem's business partner. According to Sudwikatmono, it was his brother who introduced Liem to the man who became the second president of the republic.[4] It was shortly after Sukarno relinquished power to Suharto in March 1966 that the seeds of the Liem-Suharto collaboration began to germinate. The following March, Suharto became Acting President, and he took an active interest in exploring business ventures with Chinese businessmen as well as members of his family.

In 1952, Liem moved to Jakarta, capital of the young republic, to hunt for opportunities. He left his business in Kudus to be looked after by his two brothers, although he still regularly travelled there as well as to Semarang. In 1956, Suharto was appointed commander of the Diponegoro Division, based in Semarang, and several of his aides in charge of finance continued their friendship with Liem. A few of them went on to assume important roles in the Suharto presidency; at least one recommended Liem as a worthy *cukong* for Suharto. Over time, Liem became what journalist David Jenkins called a *"cukong extraordinaire"*.[5] He evolved into the president's top "go-to guy" in money matters, transplanting other Chinese businessmen who jostled for proximity. Suharto, his limited formal education notwithstanding, was as wily as a fox when it came to making use of people, discarding those who could not consistently deliver the results he sought.

Although Liem and Suharto were born in different countries, they shared many attributes and character traits. Foremost was their humble backgrounds: Both were born to rural families and had limited access to formal education. They were superstitious and ascribed to mysticism. Character-wise, both men were usually unstintingly polite who hid their true feelings behind a pleasant countenance. This, however, belied the steeliness of their character. The Liem-Suharto partnership sustained each man's ambitions. The Chinese migrant who arrived penniless in Java in 1938 became one of Asia's wealthiest individuals, thanks to a combination of his character, link with the president, his business instincts and his networking skills. Liem, a big believer in *feng shui*, or Chinese geomancy, attributed his good fortune to *hokie*, or luck.

Suharto and Liem had a classic patron-client relationship, with the president "protecting" Liem, and ensuring his formative ventures succeeded by allowing him monopolies and preferential treatment. The payback was funds channelled the president's way — either to family members, senior generals, the Golkar[6] political machine or Suharto's many foundations. Liem gave shares in his companies to Suharto's family, starting with the president's cousin Sudwikatmono, who was the designated partner for the Chinese businessman. He gave equity to Suharto's two older children in his bank, Bank Central Asia. The conglomerate that Liem founded became known as the Salim Group, after the Indonesian surname he adopted in 1967, when Chinese in Indonesia were exhorted to adopt Indonesian-sounding names to facilitate their integration. Liem's Indonesian name was Soedono (sometimes spelled Sudono) Salim. The "Soedono" part was picked for him by the president. It was an apt choice: the prefix "soe" means "good" in Javanese (and many Javanese names, such as Suharto's own start with that). It also jelled with Liem's Chinese name, Liong, actually spelled Liang in *hanyu pinyin*,[7] which also means good. The "dono" part is Javanese for *dana* — the Indonesian word for funds or money. Salim, an Indonesian-sounding name indeed, resembled the Chinese for *san* Lin, *san* being the Chinese for three. It stood for the three Lins, Liem and his two brothers who migrated to Java. The fact that Suharto chose Liem's Indonesian name in 1967 indicated how fully he came to trust Liem early in his tenure.

Liem withstood the test of time, proving his usefulness to the president over many years. He and Bob Hasan were Suharto's closest cronies to the end. Bob was a foster son of Suharto's ex-commanding officer Gen. Gatot Subroto. Aside from carrying out Suharto's business assignments (since the 1950s), Bob was more of a chum to Suharto — his lifelong fishing and golfing partner. He was long-time chairman of the Indonesian Wood Panel Association, known as Apkindo, which operated in effect as a cartel. His companies received preferential treatment over the course of the New Order. A Chinese convert to Islam, Bob was given the Trade and Industry portfolio in Suharto's last Cabinet in March 1998; the government lasted less than ten weeks (instead of the intended five years) when riots culminated in Suharto's resignation. Never one to shy from controversy, the moustachioed Bob once declared he was "proud" to be a Suharto crony.[8]

Like Bob Hasan, Liem admitted to being the president's crony, despite the negative connotations the term had. In a 2006 interview with the authors, he said: "Yes, I was an *antek* (crony, or lackey), but I was not a bad one."[9] Over the years, Liem was the one the president turned to as his main milk cow. He was trustworthy and could be counted on rallying fellow Chinese Indonesian tycoons to cough up contributions for Suharto's many foundations — his "spigots" as Jusuf Wanandi called them.[10] Wanandi, an important behind-the-scenes political player and co-founder of the Jakarta-based Centre for Strategic and International Studies, wrote in his memoir that Liem was the coordinator for donations by the Chinese tycoons for the president. Before each election, for instance, Suharto would summon Chinese tycoons to his ranch at Tapos, and drum up money for his political machine, Golkar. "We must make sure Golkar wins. For that I will ask Liem Sioe Liong to ask donations from you," Wanandi quoted the president as saying... "He [Liem] would decide (how much each would give) because he knew how much they were worth. And they wouldn't dare not to give. They would transfer the money to Sioe Liong and he would give it to Suharto."

In the early days of Suharto's presidency, there were several Chinese businessmen who enjoyed closer links to the general, and got chances to do business for him. One was a Peranakan[11] businessman, Jantje Liem, whose Chinese name was Lim Poo Hien. He later adopted the Indonesian name Yani Haryanto. Jantje's father was a motorcycle distributor, but the son had an engine business. Jantje was introduced to Suharto by one of his generals, and soon won over the trust of the new president. His Indonesian name — Haryanto — was picked by Suharto, who injected Yan (which is how Jan is pronounced; the "tje" is Dutch for "little") into the contraction of his own name — Harto. The Dutch-educated Jantje was debonair and mingled easily with Westerners. His fondness for hunting brought him in close contact with another wild game aficionado, Ken Crane, who worked at the U.S. embassy, and a firm and lifelong friendship developed. Jantje lived on Jalan Cendana in Jakarta's Menteng district, and got Suharto to move there from his house on Jalan Agus Salim. Jantje became wealthy from his sugar plantations and became a business partner with various members of Suharto's family, including Mrs Tien Suharto's brothers and later, with the president's children (who grew up with his own kids). Suharto's suggestion that Jantje partnered Liem in business did not work out due to the different personalities, styles and cultural backgrounds.[12]

Among the Totok (more recent arrivals of the Chinese) preceding Liem as having close links with Suharto were a small group of Hokchia, including Djuhar Sutanto, who were already supplying uniforms to the navy. But Liem came highly recommended by some of Suharto's closest advisors including Maj. Gen. Sudjono Humardani, one of the financial generals, whose special relationship with Suharto was enhanced by his role as mystical advisor. Through him, Liem won Suharto's confidence. When Liem became the *cukong* closest to Suharto and the one the president tended to turn to for getting big schemes started, one major factor may have been that Liem was spectacularly successful in getting capable partners to work with him. Also, he was able get capital from outside the country — hard to come by in the early New Order, when foreign banks were not making loans to the country.

Liem's trustworthiness stood him apart; once he gave his word to undertake a mission, he would fulfil it, even if he had to make a loss. It was the way that Liem could be depended on, that was the glue for the strong bond that developed between the two men. In 1967, Suharto asked Liem to take Sudwikatmono as a partner, which signalled the start of what became referred to as "Cendana's business interests", Cendana being the name of the street where Suharto lived in Menteng, central Jakarta. Suharto tried to pair Liem with his wife's brother, but that did not work out. The winning partnership turned out to be Liem, Sudwikatmono and two others — Djuhar Sutanto, who brought with him his associate, Ibrahim Risjad. These four formed the foundation of the Salim Group. The Indonesian media dubbed the four men *"Empat Serangkai"*, meaning a quartet, but the moniker which stuck was "the Gang of Four".

THE JAVANESE "KING"

"Serving his master is the religion of the Javanese." — *Multatuli's Max Havelaar*

The earliest English language biography of Suharto, published in 1969, was written by journalist O.G. Roeder, who aptly described him as *The Smiling General*. Like the quintessential Javanese, Suharto sought to mask his feelings behind a smile (although there were occasions during his presidency when he showed flashes of anger). His cousin Sudwikatmono once noted that the word *sabar*, meaning calm or patient, is often associated with Suharto. It is one of three "S" words in the motto Suharto displayed on his office door: "*Sabar, Sareh,* and *Soleh*". The motto, Sudwikatmono said, represented "Pak Harto's [as Suharto was called] philosophy of life. The words stood for patience; thoughtful consideration; and piety or virtue." He wrote:

> If, for example, a staff member reports something in a hasty and nervous manner (Suharto) as a supervisor would accept it with "*sabar*", not become excited himself. With "*sareh*", a matter must be considered thoroughly before making a decision. Further, once a decision is taken, it should not be changed. As for "*soleh*", we must always pray for HIS blessing as God will ultimately decide everything. For the Moslems, this is done by praying five times a day.[13]

Because Suharto was so understated compared with his flamboyant predecessor, it was easy to underestimate him. When he took over the presidency from Sukarno, the U.S. embassy in Jakarta sent a cable to headquarters describing him as a "devious, slow-moving, mystical Javanese". Another embassy report filed later called him inscrutable — "a contradictory mixture of modernizer, single-minded military officer and Javanese traditionalist".[14] Brian May, a journalist living in Jakarta in the 1970s wrote in his book *Indonesian Tragedy*:

> there were rare occasions when the man who overthrew Sukarno, and then brought to heel all the generals who helped him, shows himself for a second or two. The soft features suddenly sharpen and the kindly eyes glint menacingly. Few people have seen this steely transformation, but those who have, are struck by it. I saw it only once, when Suharto suddenly turned and fixed his glance on a suspected general who was talking to a European at a reception. At this moment he immediately appeared as a man who could not only lead, but rule, Indonesia.[15]

Suharto was Javanese to the core — circumspect and deliberately slow to act, like a chess player pondering his next moves. The Javanese are polite and frown on emotional displays and flamboyant conduct. Retnowati Abdulgani-Knapp, author of an authorized biography of Suharto, commented on the nation's second president: "His reserved approach and reluctance to make anyone feel uncomfortable or to embarrass anyone in public makes it hard to understand or guess what he is really thinking … there are hints in his expression and gestures but they are not easy to decipher."[16] R.E. Elson, in his 2001 biography on Suharto, said "patience, stubbornness and calculation were Suharto's watchwords — pushing forward when he saw openings, holding ground when opportunities closed, orchestrating the isolation and departure of potential obstacles or troublemakers."[17] On Suharto's deceptively calm demeanour, Elson wrote:

> It took many of the Jakarta elite some time to realise that the cool, restrained, taciturn and ever-smiling Suharto had grown into a devastating, ruthless, manipulative politician, who had managed by shrewd calculations of timing, bluff and threat to dethrone the father of nationhood and himself attain the highest office in the nation within thirty months of the October 1 (1965) affair.[18]

American political scientist Ben Anderson, banned for many years by the government from entering Indonesia for implying in his writings that Suharto might have had advance knowledge of the coup attempt launched the night of 30 September 1965, wrote after the strongman's death: "Resentful, suspicious and cunning, the dictator made sure that no potential rivals, military or civilian, could develop any independent social or political base."[19] The late Mangunwijaya, a respected Catholic priest, once contended that Suharto felt he owned and *was* the state, remarking: "Suharto combines in himself the attributes of a King of Mataram, a Japanese military commander and a Dutch plantation lord."[20]

As a young man, Suharto did not stand out as someone destined for great things. He showed no burning ambition. He did not speak Dutch and was not fluent in English, unlike Sukarno who could converse in seven languages. And unlike promising officers in his peer group, Suharto was not picked for a training course overseas. Compared to Sukarno, who was university educated, suave and charming, Suharto was dull and rather wooden. Elson related the time Suharto nearly hung up his uniform; in 1950, when he was reprimanded by his divisional commander, Gen. Gatot Subroto, for starting a transport business to benefit his veterans, Suharto became so disheartened that he "almost decided to quit military service and pursue another profession; if need be [he] was prepared to become a taxi driver." His wife quickly disabused him of the idea: "I told him that I did not marry a taxi driver; I married a soldier."[21] Despite his apparent lack of ambition, Suharto demonstrated that he was capable of seizing opportunity, something that Liem was also good at in business. And unbeknown to many in the early days, Suharto had a streak of ruthlessness in him. In the uncertain days following the attempted coup, his superior, Gen. Nasution (himself the target of the coup plotters) also underestimated him. While Nasution wavered (he was said to be traumatized by his daughter's death, from gunshot wounds sustained the night of the coup), Suharto did not, and forced Sukarno to sign over power to him on 11 March 1966. Those who had their doubts about Suharto's staying power would be proven wrong.

When Suharto spoke — unlike Sukarno, he could not excite or inspire crowds — he regularly used the word "framework" (*rangka*). His personal framework heavily reflected how the feudal traditions of Javanese culture were firmly embedded. In politics, Suharto proved to be a masterful *dalang* — the puppeteer who control the characters in the Javanese shadow puppet play, *wayang kulit*. Liem's youngest son Anthony Salim, who after his return from studies in the United Kingdom often accompanied his father to meet Suharto, noted that there were multiple characters on Suharto's screen, and "we are just only one of the players". The president, he added was "a very strong man... He took advice from various sources but he made his own decisions."[22] Often trying to weigh in were Suharto's team of technocrats, led by economist Widjojo Nitisastro, and dubbed "Berkeley Mafia" as most were graduates of the University of California at Berkeley. But they had to compete for the president's ear with a big cast, including *cukongs*, army generals and a group called the "nationalists", led by influential Research and Technology Minister B.J. Habibie, whose big-spending national aircraft programme the technocrats hated but Suharto loved. (Habibie was Suharto's last vice-president; he was sworn in as president when Suharto resigned on 21 May 1998.) Like the *dalang*, Suharto adeptly directed the political theatre. He masterfully played rivals off against each other and balanced competing interests. He would summon his advisors to see him individually — leading to people dubbing the process "KISS", for *ke-Istana sendiri-sendiri*, or "going to the palace one by one". People seeking time with the president often bumped into each other at Cendana. Anthony recalled multiple occasions when he and his father would bump into Widjojo coming out of meetings with Suharto. "He didn't like us very much," Anthony said of Widjojo.[23]

Once his confidence grew, Suharto had his technocrats, politicians and military running scared. He brooked no dissent, and effectively sidelined those advisors deemed too big for their boots, or who were perceived to pose possible threats to his power. An early rare public display of anger was manifested after student protesters in 1971 slammed his wife's grandiose plans to build a multimillion dollar theme park, Taman Mini Indonesia Indah (for which Liem and other tycoons were squeezed for donations). Armed toughs bashed the students while Suharto threatened to use the military to "pummel anyone who tries to violate the constitution".[24] Later, when a group of disaffected distinguished retired generals and former ministers signed a petition to parliament (referred to as *Petisi* 50) criticizing the president's "self-serving" interpretation of the national ideology Pancasila, an enraged Suharto made their lives miserable for years, banning them from overseas travel, cutting off their credit and impeding their business activities.

AN IDEAL *CUKONG*

If Suharto needed a crony, there couldn't be a better one than Liem. The Chinese businessman had a natural entrepreneurial flair, a pleasant personality and a charming mannerism that was an advantage when it came to networking. Moreover, he was generous, discreet and trustworthy. Liem's credibility with the president grew when he was able to consistently deliver the goods. (Reliability was of paramount importance to Suharto. Long-time Singapore leader Lee Kuan Yew wrote in his memoirs of his Indonesian counterpart: "I found him to be a man of his word … his forte was his consistency."[25]) Being Chinese, Liem posed no political threat to Suharto. Their relationship — formed from mutual need — became a real friendship. In 2006, when asked what kind of man Suharto was, Liem replied: "Kind and compassionate… He set up charities to help people; I told him, I have money, we can work together."[26] Kindness and compassion are not words normally associated with the country's second president, as his political enemies would attest. Naturally, Liem viewed the president from a different perspective, being beholden to Suharto. On his part, Liem could have been called "the genial tycoon". People close to Liem describe him as even-tempered. His cousin Djoni Prananto said he never once saw Liem get angry or raise his voice. "Om [using the Dutch word for 'uncle', which is how most people address Liem] is *sabar* (calm or patient); he never got mad. Everyone liked him. And if someone crosses him, he doesn't seek revenge. If he ever got angry, he was quick to forget", added Djoni.[27] Suharto quickly got comfortable with the Chinese businessman, who became a frequent visitor, dropping by casually some evenings without prior appointment at the residence on Jalan Agus Salim, and then at Jalan Cendana No. 10 after Suharto moved there. Unlike some of the leader's relatives and aides, who treated him with condescension and occasionally even disdain, Suharto was always courteous with Liem. Liem recalled: "Pak Harto would stand up when I entered the room. Once I said to him, 'Please don't do that; we only stand up for our seniors ... but he laughed and replied: 'I am an ordinary person'."[28]

Both Liem and Suharto had good instincts about people, and valued loyalty. Liem lined up an impressive array of partners who enabled him to achieve his goals. Suharto, thrown into decision-making at the highest level when he was ill-prepared, initially relied heavily on advice from a coterie of trusted aides and technocrats. But as they gained confidence and experience, both trusted their own judgements most of all. Suharto's long list of advisors in the early days of the New Order got whittled down, and by early 1990s, he seemed to be listening only to a handful of sycophantic people and his immediate family. In the early years of his presidency, Liem and Suharto frequently exchanged ideas on business, with the *cukong* offering suggestions, but these would have been raised in the only way Javanese would do it — carefully, indirectly and in private. Later, Liem was the conduit for feedback from the private sector.

In dealing with Suharto, it was prudent to know one's place. The president let it be known in no uncertain terms that he was the ultimate decision-maker. Anthony Salim made this comment about Suharto: "When speaking to any boss, you know where you stand. He is *the* boss. In any organisation, the boss is still the boss, whether you think the boss is stupid or [is] right or wrong ... it doesn't matter — he is the holder of power."[29] His father's decades-long relationship with Suharto was predicated on Liem knowing where he stood in relation to the president. Only then could he continue to be in Suharto's good graces and receive protection for his businesses.

Suharto and Liem both wanted to make money and that desire helped fuel their friendship. Although money made them powerful, and they lived for decades with the trappings of wealth and prestige associated with their station in life, both men clung to the nostalgia of their village childhood — the president was most relaxed being around the folksy-ness of farmers and Liem was content to have a simple breakfast of porridge and fried tofu with his family. Throughout his presidency, Suharto lived in the same unpretentious house on Jalan Cendana. His chief weakness was his indulgence in his children, and allowed them to enjoy the privileged life he never had when he was young. Although after his fall, many allegations were made about Suharto's ill-gotten wealth (in a May 1999 issue, *Time* magazine claimed its correspondents found indications that at least US$73 billion passed through the family's hands between 1966 and 1998),[30] but Elson wrote that he believed Suharto was "not personally a greedy man … he was interested in money because it was central to his capacity to maintain power and to move Indonesia in the directions he desired."[31] Liem never publicly criticized the president, but years after Suharto's resignation, the *cukong* opined that the president "indulged his children too much".[32] On his part, Suharto almost never publicly talked about Liem, even when the Indonesian media were critical of favours accorded the *cukong* and his group. On one occasion he directly addressed these criticisms — meeting with *pribumi* (indigenous) bosses of small and medium-sized enterprises at his Tapos ranch in September 1995, he denied that he was in "collusion" with the Chinese financier. The reason Liem enjoyed big positions in cement and flour-milling was that he had been asked to invest in industries needed by the state, the president said.

Liem said Suharto enjoyed listening to stories about Chinese history and folktales, even if initially he did not understand everything Liem said. Speaking in a mixture of Indonesian and Javanese but with a very heavy Chinese accent, Liem could not always make himself understood to the president. Sudwikatmono once half-jokingly said whenever he was present at their meetings, he had to be translator for Liem. Liem said he introduced Suharto to Chinese herbs, and made sure the president was supplied with ginseng, bird's nests, cordyceps and other expensive herbs and tonics.

So intertwined were the fortunes of the two men that it was inevitable that Suharto's fall in 1998 imperilled Salim. Just as Suharto had a long list of enemies that grew over his thirty-two-year rule, Liem attracted a host of business rivals and foes, both Chinese and *pribumi* who resented Salim's special position. May 1998 opened payback and backlash time. Liem's time as strategist and deal-maker was over; it fell to Anthony to prevent the crushing of the empire. In retrospect, Anthony said, one of

Suharto's main failures was that he did not embrace change because he became too powerful and stopped listening to things he did not want to hear. "Suharto ruled the country based on [the concept of] Javanese king and philosophy ... Society could accept that, at the time. But it takes two hands to clap. [Over time], the situation changed, the social structure changed, expectations changed ... So you have to embrace change in order to adapt, otherwise you become a dinosaur."[33] The close association that Liem had with Suharto came at a price — enmity. When the strongman fell, the knives came out for all those associated with him. Naturally, Liem was a prime target. During the frenzied May 1998 rioting, mobs (thought to be organized) broke into Liem's Jakarta residential compound, setting fire to his house and cars. Liem would never live in Indonesia again.

SHARED BELIEF IN MYSTICISM

Another common ground shared by Liem and Suharto was their interest and belief in mysticism. Liem was deeply superstitious, often seeking advice from Buddhist monks and Taoist fortune-tellers before embarking on ventures. Before he became more overtly Muslim, Suharto was a practitioner of *kebatinan* — Javanese mysticism — and often consulted with *dukun*, or spiritual advisors. For a period in his youth, he studied under a Javanese mystic Kiai Daryatmo, from whom he "absorbed a great deal of spiritual backboning".[34] He learnt meditation in his quest to attain inner development and spiritual wisdom. He meditated in holy caves in Java. The late Indonesian historian Onghokham wrote:

> If former President Sukarno became a dictator because he was the Great Leader of the Revolution, Suharto became one because, like the old Javanese kings praised in song and myth, he was Paku-Buwono, the "Nail of the Universe." If you take the nail away, the universe collapses.[35]

Suharto surrounded himself with sacred heirlooms of power, noted the historian. Called *pusaka*, these objects helped leaders maintain their hold on power. Among them were a gong from the palace of Surakarta (Solo) and the Gajah Mada masks of Bali, dating to the thirteenth century Majapahit empire.[36] Of course, the most dominant *pusaka* in his possession was his wife, Ibu Tien, a descendant of the Mangkunegara royal family. From her, he derived his *wahyu*, the God-given right to rule. To many observers, it was no coincidence that after her death in 1996, things went downhill.

It was said that Suharto identified with Semar, the clown-god from Javanese mythology, who entertained audiences in the *wayang kulit* shadow puppet performances. Although Semar was a comical figure, he was actually wise and powerful and was regarded as the guardian spirit of Java. According to an anthropologist, Semar represents the common folks, and their suffering.[37] Semar was in effect, Suharto's alter ego. In 1974, the year before Indonesia invaded East Timor, Suharto took the highly unusual step of inviting Australian Prime Minister Gough Whitlam to a cave in Central Java called Gua Semar (Semar's cave) where he used to meditate. The occasion was significant for the Indonesians and interpreted as Suharto's taking the Australian leader into his confidence.[38]

Liem, too, was familiar with Javanese holy sites. He often made pilgrimages to a sacred area in East Java called Gunung Kawi, where he consulted fortune-tellers before undertaking substantial business commitments. Gunung Kawi, said to be the burial site of two Javanese saints, is revered by worshippers of different faiths. It gets more than 100,000 pilgrims each year, many of them Indonesian Chinese — but quite a few Javanese — seeking blessings or favours. Believers maintain that meditating under the "goddess tree" (Dewa Ndaru in Javanese) enhances prospects of having one's dreams realized. Many believers sit under the tree with hopes that a leaf may drift onto their laps, an indication that their prayers would be answered. For years, Liem was a regular pilgrim, making the three-hour drive from Surabaya four or five times a year. Chinese temples coexist with a mosque, and it is at one of the temples located here that Liem used to seek divination about his business plans. Liem must have had many prayers answered, as he donated heavily for upkeep of the area, paying for road improvements and building a dormitory for worshippers. He also donated towards construction of a Goddess of Mercy statue in the area. According to him, Suharto had also visited the site. Liem adhered closely to the advice proffered by monks.

At temples where he worshipped, Liem often resorted to divination methods to help him decide on what course to take. One commonly used involved the shaking of inscribed sticks from a bamboo cylinder until one falls out, which is then read and interpreted by a monk or fortune-teller. The timings of the inauguration of factories were all calculated to the minute, using the time and date of his birth according to the Chinese calendar. His divine consultations even reached the more mundane levels, such as whether the timing was right for his banks to obtain a foreign exchange licence.[39]

His adherence to the principles of Chinese geomancy, or *feng shui*, led him to be extremely cautious about undertaking unnecessary changes. He would often keep things as they were, just so that his *hokie*, or luck, would not be compromised. Thus, the decrepit-looking house in Kudus where the peanuts were pressed and the weekend bungalow in the hills in Central Java where he sometimes sought solitude still look quite unchanged. His modest single-storey home in Jalan Gunung Sahari was hardly renovated, although the soothsayers did not object to his building a modern double-storey mansion right next door (this was the one that was attacked and burnt by rioters in May 1998). He would not even dare touch the very simple headstones that marked his ancestors' graves in his hometown in China, never mind that they were so small they could barely be seen.

He consulted monks and seers often about a whole range of subjects. He said he once asked a clairvoyant about the duration of Suharto's presidency and was told it would last no more than seven terms.[40] (Suharto resigned less than three months into his seventh term.) In 1998, while recuperating in the United States from eye surgery during the darkest days as Jakarta burned and the Suharto regime was collapsing, Liem visited a Buddhist temple in Los Angeles. The monk told him to be patient. While it was "winter" for him now, the "Sakura" (spring) season would arrive, the monk said.[41]

ESTABLISHING BIG BUSINESS

In the early days of his presidency, Suharto was advised by Liem to strive to fulfil people's "four basic needs" — *yi, shi, zhu, xing*, in Chinese, namely, clothing, food, shelter, and transportation. Only then, Liem said, citing a Chinese belief, would society become more stable and the population more content (and presumably, more pliant). The Javanese equivalent of these basic necessities is encapsulated in the expression *sandang pangan* — meaning food and clothing. Liem indicated that he was ready to do the president's bidding, and Suharto did, in some cases, effectively assign him to build a factory or enterprise. When Liem entered a new area such as flour-milling, it was not exactly risky as Suharto ensured the investor would have a sole or dominant position in the market.

Besides helping to fulfil the "four basic needs", Liem added a fifth. For many Indonesians, taking a puff of their clove-infused cigarette, called *kretek*, was almost a basic need. Liem — and Suharto's half-brother — got exclusive rights for years to import cloves from Zanzibar and Madagascar.

Getting the balance right between supply and demand for cloves had always been tricky, and although cloves were native to Indonesia, the country had in the past resorted to importing the spice from those two African countries. Smuggling of the commodity from the entrepôt centre of Singapore also earned some individuals a pretty penny.

Clothing was the area in which Liem would have a very small role. Because textiles was a highly competitive area in much of Asia and not one in which Suharto could make him dominant, Liem switched attention to other areas. Japanese researcher Yuri Sato, the first to look at the Salim Group in detail, wrote in 1993 that after receiving early on lucrative profits from government-licensed businesses that it could dominate, "pursuing monopolistic and oligopolistic market positions became a cornerstone of the group's corporate behaviour".[42] Being in privileged positions helped put Salim on a fast growth track. In 1992, Sato wrote, Salim "accounted for 39 per cent of the total sales of the 10 largest Indonesian business groups, making it by far the largest conglomerate in the country and the largest in Southeast Asia, ahead of those in Singapore, Taiwan and Hong Kong and just behind the Republic of Korea".[43]

To the public, the Salim Group became huge because of monopolies, which gave it the cash-flow to invest in businesses where there was competition. Before it branched out into a vast array of businesses, the group had three main pillars which gave it a solid foundation:

Food: Bogasari Flour Mills was the first substantial investment for Salim. Established in 1969, it was to become the world's biggest miller. It was a crucial pillar of his empire, with its history illustrating some aspects of Suharto's Indonesia: while it was a privately owned company, its articles of association stipulated that 26 per cent of profits go to two foundations linked to Suharto. The company's position was controversial throughout the New Order. Suharto maintained its business position until the International Monetary Fund (IMF) forced him to end the protection, but through the years the president could not stop the milling company from being a significant target for criticism. Indofood Sukses Makmur in the 1990s became the world's biggest maker of instant noodles, even overtaking the Japanese manufacturer that invented it. In 1995, the company had captured 90 per cent market share in Indonesia.

Cement: Another pillar was cement, a business in the area of "shelter". It had an oligopolistic position although there were state-owned manufacturers, and, in 1985, its company Indocement received a state bailout that was essential to the group's survival.

Banking: Liem became a kingpin through PT Bank Central Asia (BCA). With help from seasoned banker Mochtar Riady, it became a behemoth and the country's largest privately owned bank. Liem allocated 30 per cent shares for Suharto, put in the names of his two older children, Sigit Haryoyudanto and Siti Hardiyanti Hastuti Rukmana, better known as Tutut. The bank suffered a massive run in May 1998 after Suharto's resignation and Liem lost his flagship financial institution.

In the area of transport, Salim was not in the dominant position in Indonesia, though it rose to become number 2, behind Astra International, founded by William Soeryadjaya. Financial woes of the Soeryadjaya family led to Salim owning stakes in Astra (for a few years) as well as its own Indomobil. Liem entered property primarily in partnership with Ciputra, a savvy developer who also worked with the Jakarta government. Salim expanded into scores of other areas, including chemicals, sugar and oil palm plantations, mining, forestry, pharmaceuticals, shipping, distribution and retail, communications and the leisure industry. The group described itself as "opportunity-driven" and there was no shortage of opportunities, especially as Suharto pushed import-substitution policies for many years. Anthony Salim, who became the group's chief executive, was quoted as saying: "In the 1990s, it was as if every business you touched turned into gold."[44] As Liem was close to Suharto, many business people sought partnerships with Liem.

Salim was not content simply to be a large domestic player. In the early New Order years, Liem registered companies in Singapore, where he could take loans more easily than in Indonesia (until he obtained Indonesian citizenship). But it was only after Anthony's return in 1971 from studies in England, that Salim actively pursued geographic expansion beyond Indonesia so that not all eggs were in one basket. With Salim money, Anthony and Filipino banker Manny Pangilinan, in 1981 started First Pacific, an investment company in Hong Kong. In the first of waves of asset acquisition and shuffling, First Pacific bought a Dutch trading company, Hagemeyer (founded in Java during the colonial days), and a California bank, Hibernia Bank. At one time, First Pacific had operations in more than forty countries. In 1996, it became a component stock in Hong Kong's Hang Seng Index. After Suharto fell in 1998, Salim's eggs outside Indonesia proved very helpful to efforts to deal with debts and keep Salim in Indofood.

A combination of risk-taking, winning personality and the willingness to share the spoils contributed to Liem's emergence as the best-suited

Chinese-Indonesian crony for Suharto. Many Chinese entrepreneurs had to latch onto senior military figures for their businesses to grow — and it could be said vice versa, for the benefits were mutual. After laying claim to power in the aftermath of the 1965 abortive coup, Suharto wasted no time in using his *cukongs* to raise funds for the military, whose full support he needed to consolidate his position. But it was not just a strong relationship with the president that propelled the Salim Group. Liem exhibited excellent intuition and foresight, demonstrating an uncanny ability to pick good managers and partners. Also, his successor, Anthony, born a month after Liem survived a horrific car collision, possessed needed skills and tried to steer Salim to go global. However, as pointed out by an academic, the effort did little to change the group's image in the eyes of the public, "which interpreted the business of the group as an extension of the Suharto family".[45]

Responding to charges that the Salim Group became synonymous with Cendana (the president's family) interests, Anthony admitted: "We know too, but unfortunately we had no choice ... we had to have two feet on the accelerator, not because we wanted to, but we cannot be separated. How can you move away when all the major industries of the country are with you? All the important commodities — food, banking, construction — [we were] the nerve and muscle."[46] He added: "The main thing is knowing where you put yourself. You get burned if you're too close to the fire; when you're too far away, you get cold and die. That's very important ... Just to be close enough [to] feel the heat, but you don't get burned."[47]

Notes

1. *Cukong* is derived from a Hokkien term meaning "boss" (*zhu gong*). See Leo Suryadinata, ed., *Ethnic Chinese in Contemporary Indonesia* (Singapore: Chinese Heritage Centre and ISEAS, 2008), p. xiii.
2. Onghokham, "Soeharto and the Javanese tradition of monarchy", *Indonesia and the Soeharto Years: Issues, Incidents and Images* (Jakarta: Lontar, 2005,) p. 320.
3. R.E. Elson, *Suharto: A Political Biography* (Cambridge: Cambridge University Press, 2001), p. 151.
4. Interview with Sudwikatmono, 8 August 2006.
5. David Jenkins, "The quiet, bald moneymaker of Jakarta's elite", *Sydney Morning Herald*, 10 April 1986.
6. Abbreviated for Golongan Karya, meaning functional groups. It later became in effect, Suharto's political party.

7. *Hanyu pinyin* is the official romanization system of Chinese characters adopted by China and other nations.
8. Interview with Bob Hasan, 29 May 2003.
9. Interview with Liem, 3 June 2006.
10. Jusuf Wanandi, *Shades of Grey: A Political Memoir of Modern Indonesia, 1965–1998* (Jakarta: Equinox, 2012), pp. 236–37.
11. A Peranakan was an assimilated Chinese whose ancestors may have arrived in Indonesia several generations ago. Usually unable to speak Chinese, the men were sometimes referred to as "Baba" and the women as "Nonya".
12. Given his U.S. embassy connections — which Liem did not have — Jantje expected to play a part in milling the American wheat that Washington gave Suharto as aid. But Jantje found himself cut out of a role in flour milling, which went to Liem. According to a confidential source, Jantje got lucrative sugar plantations as a consolation.
13. Sudwikatmono, "Manajemen 3 Sa: (catatan seorang pengusaha)", in *Manajemen Presiden Suharto: Penuturan 17 Menteri*, edited by Riant Nugroho Dwidjowijoto (Jakarta: Yayasan Bina Generasi Bangsa, 1996).
14. Bradley Simpson, *Economists with Guns: Authoritarian Development and US-Indonesian Relations, 1960–1968* (Stanford: Stanford University Press, 2008), pp. 214, 219–20.
15. Brian May, *The Indonesian Tragedy* (Routledge & Kegan Paul, 1978), pp. 156–57.
16. Retnowati Abdulgani-Knapp, *Soeharto: The Life and Legacy of Indonesia's Second President* (Singapore: Marshall Cavendish, 2007), p. 329.
17. Elson, *Suharto: A Political Biography*, p. 166.
18. Ibid.
19. Benedict Anderson, "Exit Suharto: Obituary for a mediocre tyrant", *New Left Review*, no. 50 (Mar–Apr 2008).
20. Theodore Friend, *Indonesian Destinies* (Cambridge, MA: Belknap Press of Harvard University, 2003), p. 258.
21. Elson, *Suharto: A Political Biography*, p. 50.
22. Interview with Anthony, 22 July 2007.
23. The authors tried on several occasions to talk with the ailing Widjojo, one of modern Indonesia's most important planners, but were told that the time was not suitable or that he was not feeling well. He died in March 2012.
24. Elson, *Suharto: A Political Biography*, p. 199.
25. Lee Kuan Yew, *From Third World to First: The Singapore Story: 1965–2000* (New York: Harper Collins, 2000), p. 305.
26. Interview with Liem, 3 June 2006.
27. Interview with Djoni Prananto, 6 May 2006.
28. Interview with Liem, 6 May 2006.
29. Interview with Anthony, 22 July 2007.

30. "Indonesia: It's All In The Family", *Time*, 31 May 1999.
31. Elson, *Suharto: A Political Biography*, p. 281.
32. Interview with Liem, 6 May 2006.
33. Interview with Anthony, 14 October 2007.
34. Elson, *Suharto: A Political Biography*, p. 6.
35. Onghokham, "Soeharto and the Javanese tradition of monarchy".
36. Ibid.
37. Niels Mulder, *Mysticism in Java: Ideology in Indonesia* (Amsterdam: Pepin, 1998), p. 31.
38. Lee Khoon Choy, *Indonesia: Between Myth and Reality* (Singapore: Federal Publications, 1977), p. 147.
39. Confidential interview, Jakarta.
40. Interview with Liem, 6 May 2006.
41. Ibid.
42. Yuri Sato, "The Salim Group in Indonesia: The development and behavior of the largest conglomerate in Southeast Asia", *Developing Economies* XXXI, no. 4 (December 1993), p. 437.
43. Ibid., p. 408.
44. Marleen Dieleman, *The Rhythm of Strategy: A Corporate Biography of the Salim Group of Indonesia* (Amsterdam: ICAS/Amsterdam University Press, 2007), p. 59.
45. Ibid., p. 126.
46. Interview with Anthony, 4 March 2007.
47. Interview with Anthony, 22 July 2007.

2

ROOTS

Nothing in Liem's childhood gave any indication of how illustrious his future would be. He was born to farmers in a small village of some 600 people in Fujian province, China. Like many village children in China in those days, he lived a hardscrabble existence. His village was located in a region considered inhospitable for farming — surrounded by mountains and bordered by the sea, there was a scarcity of arable land. The soil, tainted by the sea's high saline content, allowed only hardy plants such as peanuts and sweet potato to be cultivated. There was no system of irrigation. Still, farmers coaxed rice to grow. (When Liem became wealthy and wanted to help his homeland, one of the early projects he initiated was the construction of a reservoir, feeding an extensive irrigation canal system. This enabled the entire area of Fuqing to develop and indeed, prosper.)

The disagreeable conditions of the region were pithily encapsulated by the local adage: *"jiu nian han, yi nian zai"*, which translates to "nine years of drought, one year of disaster [meaning floods.]" It was no surprise that many young men from the area left in droves in search of a better life elsewhere. Liem became one of them. In 1937, the Japanese invaded China. The weak and corrupt Kuomintang Nationalist government, facing a growing threat internally by the Communists led by Mao Zedong, were no match for the invaders. Law and order disintegrated in many parts of the country, with local warlords and bandits claiming power over many areas. By 1938, war had reached Liem's doorstep. He had lost his father the previous year, and now faced certain conscription. He was as reluctant to leave his recently widowed mother as she was to have her favourite son leave her side. Confronted with the realities, they agreed he should join his elder brother Sioe Hie, already in Java with their uncle. Thus began Liem's journey to become one of the wealthiest men in Nanyang, as Southeast Asia was then called.

BACKGROUND

Liem was born Lin Shaoliang, in 1917, the Year of the Snake, on the seventh day of the seventh month of according to the Chinese zodiac.[1] Official records in Indonesia listed his birth as 1916, and the family used that to calculate his age. For those who believe in Chinese mythology and horoscope, many of the characteristics associated with those born in the Year of the Snake fit Liem perfectly. As one source notes, those born in the Snake Year have "a strong, charismatic presence and a charm which has been described by some astrologers as 'bewitching' or 'beguiling.' With a penetrating eye and attention to the desires of their conquests, they're known as experts in the art of seduction."[2] Those who made Liem's acquaintance could certainly attest to his charm, his persuasive power, and the magnetism he possessed. In the area of business and finance, many Snakes are successful; they excel in finding solutions to complex problems. They can be shrewd, "biding their time in making a deal only to strike like lightning and make a killing when they judge the moment is right". A Snake, so the belief goes, has a strong, almost obsessive desire for fame, money and power.

Despite being a Snake child, Liem said he was always terrified of snakes.[3] His home village, called Niuzhai [meaning cow shed] is in the Haikou area, about 12 kilometres east of Fuqing city, Fujian province. People in this area speak the Fuqing dialect, commonly referred to as Hokchia. Fujian is said to be home to more than 100 dialects — not all mutually understood — and there is a local saying that villagers separated by a blade of grass may not even understand each other. The Hokchia consider anyone speaking the same dialect as being related; to them being *"tongxiang"* — being from the same village — was akin to being related. They also accord special affection or closeness with residents from

Fuzhou (Hokchiu speaking) and Putian (Henghua speaking). His father, Lin Yuanzai, was an only son born to farmers, who subsequently adopted another boy. This was Liem's uncle, Lin Jinzai, who went to Java where his name was rendered as Liem Kiem Tjai.[4] Liem's family although not well off, was not among the poorest in the village, as his mother, Chen Guisong, came from a family that owned some land in the village, about 70 *mu* (equivalent to 4.6 hectares). Many villagers didn't have any land of their own and they had to work on other people's plots. Liem's parents had a total of eleven children: Liem was preceded in birth by four siblings — eldest brother Sioe Hie[5] was five years his senior. He was followed by three girls, one of whom died in infancy; the other two were given away. A third son, Liem Sioe Kong,[6] was born two years after Liem.

REMINISCENCES[7]

According to Liem, he was his mother's favourite child. "I was a clever boy — some people described me as *lihai* [a description that conjures a combination of being smart, talented, formidable and wily]. But sometimes I was quite naughty," he related. "My mother doted on me. When I was very young, she called me by a girl's name to confuse the 'fox spirit' haunting the village." (At that time, several male infants in the village had died mysteriously and the superstitious villagers believed there was a female spirit who took the form of a fox and preyed on them.) Liem remembered his mother as an extremely kind and gentle person: "She was good natured and helpful to everyone. She was known in the village for her compassion. Many people often asked for help and she would always do whatever she could. She never had a harsh word to say about anyone." Life in the village was harsh and unpredictable, Liem recalled. A typical day for him meant getting up very early and working in the fields with his father, and sometimes helping out in the kitchen. He did not have a lot of time playing games during his childhood, but sometimes, he and his friends caught birds and crickets. An indulgence he had was watching street (Min) opera. He would be spellbound by the free performances, which often spun historical-based tales where good inevitably triumphed over evil. Once, he got into trouble with his father for getting home late after a night at the opera and for telling a lie. He recounted:

> During New Year and on certain festivals, there would be performances
> held in the village; I was very excited whenever there was an opera and

would watch until it ended, past midnight. Once, I got into trouble with my father. I was about 15 years old. I had sneaked off to a nearby village to watch an opera performance without telling my parents. By the time I reached home, it was quite late. The door was locked. Father let me in. He didn't shout at me, but quietly asked: "Have you eaten?" I lied that I had, but he simply said: "You didn't have any money with you." Then he took out a cane, and said, "I've never had to hit you before but now you have to be taught a lesson, and I will have to cane you hard." And he caned me until my skin broke. Mother stopped him from hitting me further, saying: "Do you want to kill him?" Father turned to me and said: "Some people beat their children to take out their unhappiness and frustration, but I never did that. This caning is a lesson to you and I have to make sure you never forget it." I never did, and he never caned me again.[8]

What stuck in his memory was the daily effort to put food on the table. Liem recounted:

You had to work very hard, but it didn't mean you have enough to eat. We could only think of getting by day to day. We ate mostly what we grew — mostly sweet potato, rice and vegetables. We seldom had meat on the table. That was only for special occasions, like at New Year. And even when we had meat, it wasn't a lot of it. And even if you owned land, it didn't mean you were able to till it. There were times when nothing would grow. Everyone seemed to be always short of money. If you needed money, you had to borrow from relatives or neighbours. If they couldn't lend you or if what you borrowed wasn't enough, you had to go to the loan sharks. They were charging sky-high interest rates — up to 20 per cent a month. The luckier villagers were those who had children or family members overseas, who send money back home. So many people in the village try to send at least one or two sons overseas.[9]

Liem's parents and grandparents were kind and generous people. Though they were not of any means themselves, they would always try to help anyone who sought their assistance. From their Buddhist belief, Liem learnt about compassion and the importance of honesty. From the Confucianist tradition they practised, he had the concept of filial piety and loyalty drilled into him. (Decades later, when he travelled to China, Liem made it a point to visit his ancestors' graves to honour them.) His father, although kind-hearted, was a stern man who would not tolerate dishonesty, Liem said.

During his adult life in Indonesia, detractors liked to point out that Liem was poorly educated, with some even describing him as uneducated. Although he did not have the opportunity to attend a regular school, he and several village kids were taught in an informal setting by a teacher hired by their parents. He recalled that until at least the age of thirteen, he studied under a teacher whose name he gave as Liu Kaiming. Teachers in those days were held in high esteem. This teacher, who had a relative in the village, was "a knowledgeable person", Liem recalled, adding:

> He knew a lot about many subjects, but he especially liked teaching us Chinese history. We learnt *guwen* (the Chinese classics), and *kong yi* (Confucianism). He made us study *sishu wujing* (The Four Books and Five Classics, the authoritative books of Confucianism, said to be written before 300 B.C.) and history of *chun chui zhanguo* (the Spring and Autumn period and Warring States period.) It was customary in those days for students to run errands and perform chores for their teachers. We cleaned Teacher Liu's house and cooked for him. Studying under my teacher gave me a solid foundation. I realized from a young age that education is of great benefit; it's like an investment for a person's future. I believe the lessons I had in the village helped made me what I am today. That's why when I had children of my own, I tried to make sure they had a good education and I sent them overseas for school.[10]

As a child, Liem said, he had a good memory and a good head for figures. He liked to ask questions, and was open-minded (which served him well later in life when he entered the business world, where he was receptive to new ideas and quick to embrace technology for his banks and factories. When he was in his late eighties, he said he regretted not having the chance to learn how to use a computer.) His favourite subject was Chinese history and when he was young, he enjoyed the stories of legendary Chinese heroes. (Many years later, he regaled Suharto with tales of Chinese folklore. "He enjoyed them immensely", Liem recalled.) As a teenager, Liem had a brief stint as an entrepreneur when he and a friend started a small noodle-making business. They made raw noodles, the fine, thin variety popular among the Fujianese called *mien sien*, which is often served at celebratory occasions. The business lasted two years. Family life took a turn in 1937 when Liem was not quite twenty with the sudden death of his father. As Liem recounted:

> Father came home one day carrying some sweet potatoes. He looked very tired and said he didn't feel well. There had been a bad drought

and many people in the village had fallen ill. We rushed to look for the *sinseh* (the village traditional Chinese medicine practitioner), but he didn't come that day. I remember he was a fat guy. He showed up only on the following day. He didn't do very much for my father; only took his pulse, and there was no injections given at that time. Father quickly got weaker and weaker, then he went into a coma and on the third day of his illness, he died.[11]

The family later concluded that he might have contracted pleurisy. The death was so sudden and the family so unprepared, Liem recalled they had trouble finding a photograph to use for the funeral rites. His father's untimely death, at age forty-nine, placed Liem as the "man of the house". It was time for him to get married and be a family man, his mother decided. Actually, at the time of his father's death, he was already betrothed to a young woman in the village, the niece of a brother-in-law. Her name was Zheng Fenglai. It was a match made by his parents, and Liem said he had no feelings for her: "She was the same age as me. I didn't want to marry her. I did not find her attractive. She was plain looking, with large ears and a big nose." Still, his mother was determined to hold the wedding ceremony, and tradition dictates that it had to be within 100 days of a parent's death, or withhold a wedding until three years later. Liem said he initially refused to go ahead with the wedding, upsetting his mother. He did not want to be called unfilial, so he eventually agreed. He claimed, however, that he never developed feelings for the woman he married, and once he got to Java, considered himself as an eligible bachelor. His arranged marriage was not widely known by many outside his immediate family. When he fell in love with a young girl in Java and married her in 1945, he certainly did not tell her he had a wife in China, and it was years later before she was told. For many others, it was not until his mother's death in Hong Kong in 1972 when his "first" wife claimed her position as daughter-in-law that many business associates realized Liem had a previous marriage. However, Liem said he was always grateful to Madam Zheng, who spurned his advice to remarry but took good care of Liem's mother until the end of her days. Madam Zheng later adopted a daughter, and Liem took care of them financially.

LEAVING HOME

In 1938, Japanese troops were marching towards Fujian. The Nationalist government was losing control of many parts of the country; chaos was descending. For the young men left in villages, the choice became increasingly stark: leave or fight. Liem's brother already sent enough money to cover a passage to Java. But the debate about leaving his mother raged in Liem's mind. Unwilling though she was initially "lose" him, Liem's mother was convinced it was the right thing to do when faced with the prospect of her son going to war. "In the end she convinced me to leave. When news came that Japanese soldiers had already arrived in Fujian, it hastened my departure", Liem recounted. His mother cooked *mien sien* for his farewell dinner and gave him a lucky charm to wear. It was a talisman she had sewn together with a few pieces of the precious ginseng root, with instructions to chew on the ginseng should he ever feel hunger. His journey did not get off to a smooth start. He made it as far as Xiamen[12] then called Amoy, to catch a cargo ship bound for Surabaya. He joined other young men bound for Java. The port city was crowded with many people waiting for ships headed to various places. He recalled:

> We had to hang around and wait for days until we were processed for leaving. I remember using a pillow made of stone. When my turn came, the officials took a look at me and refused to believe I was 21 although I showed them my papers. I even produced a letter of permission from military government. But they said I was no more than 17 and wouldn't let me board the ship."[13]

Liem said he had no choice but to return to the village, where he waited a few more weeks before making another attempt to leave. This time, in Xiamen, he bribed an official and was finally allowed to board an 800-ton cargo ship (operated by Holland Lines) bound for Surabaya. He recalled his journey:

> The voyage took about two weeks. We slept on the open deck of the ship. The sea was quite rough; we were rolling about a lot of the time. Sometimes, we were hungry but too seasick to eat. When food was brought out — often it was just rice, served in bamboo baskets, with cabbage and occasionally, dried pieces of beef — some of the passengers would rush for the food. Sometimes, by the time I got to it, there was nothing left. During the trip, my bag with my money was stolen. So when I arrived in Java, I only had the clothes I was wearing. The ship docked at Surabaya on the 21st of the seventh month, 1938. I noted that the numbers for 1938 also added to 21. And I was 21 at the time. So I thought the number 21 would be my lucky number.

On arrival at Surabaya harbour, Liem failed to be met by a family member and was put in a holding centre by Dutch officials. Three anxious days passed before his brother-in-law Zheng Xusheng showed up. He explained that he was delayed by the unexpected early arrival of a baby at Kiem Tjai's home in Kudus. Said Liem: "I didn't understand why that affected him, and I was angry with him … We then took the train headed for Kudus, where Sioe Hie and my uncle were waiting for me.[14]

JAVA DAYS

Kudus is an old Islamic town in Central Java; its name, derived from Arabic, meant Holy City, but it is better known as the home of the *kretek*, the distinctive and popular clove-scented cigarette favoured by millions of Indonesian smokers. One of the nine holy men of Java — the *Wali Songo* as they were called — lived and died here in the mid-sixteenth century. These men, interestingly of Chinese origin, were credited for the conversion of Java to Islam. A monument still stands in Kudus that bears testament to the religious significance of yore — the old mosque, called *Menara* Kudus. It is a distinctive reddish brick and stone building, and three-tiered roof. Kudus lies 50 kilometres east of Semarang, an important port in those days. These two towns were the stomping ground for itinerant Hokchia peddlers, of which Liem, initially was one.

These peddlers, moving between cities or towns, were called *danbangke* in Chinese. Historian Twang Peck Yang, in his seminal work on Chinese traders in the pre-independence period, defined the term as "a travelling trader working on his own".[15] When Liem arrived in Kudus, he started by selling clothes, carrying them in baskets suspended between a pole. When he saved enough, he "graduated" to a bicycle. Then he would hop on a train and travelled to Semarang to sell his goods. Liem found Kudus a very pleasant town, relaxed and different from his village in China. Although his work days were long, he revelled in the welcoming spirit and the friendliness of the Javanese. Unlike in his home village, Liem saw immediate rewards to his diligence, even though they were small in the early days. He did not have to worry about starving. There were many hawker stalls offering a variety of cheap foods, many of which Liem initially found too spicy, but later got accustomed to. He developed a fondness for the local heavily spiced soup called *soto* Kudus.

Although Kudus was his base, it was in Semarang where Liem developed important contacts that helped him decades later. After the country achieved independence, Semarang became the base of a territorial command of the new republic's army, and Liem made became acquainted with senior officers, including its commander, Lt. Col. Suharto. In the late 1930s, Semarang was a bustling city. It was the capital of Central Java and the second busiest port on the island after Surabaya, surpassing even Batavia (the old name for Jakarta) in maritime importance. According to a population census taken in 1930, it was the third city in the Dutch East Indies with the most Chinese (numbering 28,423), after Batavia and Surabaya, and just ahead of Medan.[16] A journalist writing in 1980 described the city thus:

> Semarang is unlike the gentle royal cities of Solo and Jogjakarta near the south shore of Java. It sits on Central Java's hot northern plain, and has the only port open to large ships on that stretch of coast. Under the Dutch it became a busy trading and administrative centre. Joining the Muslim entrepreneurs of the north coast came great numbers of Chinese traders and their families. Even in the depressed 1950s great wealth flowed through the city: sugar and other agricultural produce going out, industrial raw materials and finished goods coming in.[17]

Semarang was one of the ports visited by the legendary Chinese admiral and explorer Zheng He (also known as Cheng Ho, and commonly by the locals as Sam Po Kong). A Muslim eunuch from the Ming court of China, Zheng He landed in Java in the fifteenth century when it was still under the Majapahit empire. In Semarang, a temple, called the Sam Po Kong temple to honour him is at the place where he was believed to have first dropped anchor. (There is also one of the same name in Malacca, Malaysia.) Zheng He has been the object of worship and reverence by the Chinese community throughout Southeast Asia. At the temple in Semarang, an anchor said to be an original from his ship is prominently displayed in the grounds. The original temple was built in the early eighteenth century. (It has since undergone massive renovations funded by generous donations from the public, with a prominent contributor being Liem.) In the late nineteenth century, it was purchased by a wealthy businessman Oei Tjie Sien, who opened it to the public for free. Oei was the father of Java's "Sugar King" Oei Tiong Ham, probably Indonesia's first locally born businessman who built a transnational empire known as The Oei Tiong Ham Concern, with offices in Southeast Asia, China, Europe and the United States. That he accomplished what he did during the Dutch colonial era, with his trading company surpassing the established Dutch ones, was regarded as a tremendous feat. (Decades later, with Liem establishing himself as the region's wealthiest businessman, comparisons were inevitably made between the two.)

During Liem's early days, he and his brother Sioe Hie made frequent trips to Semarang, extending credit to customers for goods, a business described as *mindering crediet*, which is considered a form of money lending. Liem made good use of his dialect clan support to obtain capital. *Singkeh*, the Hokkien dialect term for recent arrivals from China, relied heavily on the support of their dialect groups on multiple levels, but mainly financial and emotional in the early days of settling in.

Many started with the occupation they were familiar with, for example, the Hokkien, from the southern region of Fujian centred around Xiamen, tended to be shopkeepers; the Henghua operated bicycle shops; the Hainanese opened coffee shops. The Hokchia, being latecomers, often found themselves at the bottom of the totem pole. They took work as rickshaw-pullers in Singapore or as timbermen in Borneo. In Indonesia, they started as the poorest and most despised of the Chinese petty traders , noted the writer Lynn Pan, "earning a peripatetic living in the rural areas, engaged in something between hire-purchase and money-lending, a line of business that few other people found attractive, involving as it did high risks and minute profit margins".[18]

Hokchia peddlers often had to travel to rural areas to sell their wares. This itinerant existence resulted in one benefit — they established close contacts with the *pribumi*, or indigenous people. As Twang noted about the Hokchia: "There was no other Chinese group more intimate and familiar with Indonesians ... Trust was established in many cases."[19] Indeed, trust was the hallmark of Hokchia business operations, and it was certainly Liem's *modus operandi* all through his life. Twang wrote that these Hokchia *danbangke* were cliquish and tended to live as a group. In a description that fitted Liem's work routine, Twang wrote that the *danbangke* "rode bicycles loaded with textiles out into the villages in the morning, returning in the afternoon, or in some areas, only a few days later ... The job required hard physical labour as well as 'cajoling intimacy' with the indigenes, both qualities the *baba* [Peranakan] — the Malay/Indonesian-speaking as well as the Dutch-speaking — did not possess."[20] Unlike another Chinese dialect group, the Hakka, who ran *warung* (small shop or stalls) or were *klontong* (peddler), the Hokchia moneylenders "tended to penetrate deep into the rural areas".[21]

The start of Liem's working life in Java mirrored the established pattern of other new migrants. From his arrival until the Japanese Occupation began in 1942, he worked diligently, first selling clothes, then starting a coffee grinding business with his brother and uncle. They also produced peanut oil from their shophouse in Kudus after the War. Liem recalled that during his initial days following his arrival he helped Sioe Hie to sell clothes, which he carried in baskets suspended from a pole, until he saved enough to buy a bicycle. It did not take him long to realize that there was strong competition from others offering similar wares, and he quickly decided he had to stand out. He admitted to shamelessly capitalizing on his personal charm to win customers:

> I developed a *mulut pintar* (sweet tongue) to persuade customers to buy from me instead of from someone else. Most of my customers were Javanese, mainly women. When I first started selling things, I didn't speak their language so I would just smile at them. They were nice to me; maybe they felt sorry for me. I was young and strong, and also quite handsome. The *nonyas* (married women) seemed especially to like me. I picked up the Javanese language from them. There was one *nonya* who was very fond of me. She always bought something from me and usually overpaid me. Her husband was a district official. Once, she even invited me into her house, but I was afraid. I said: 'Oh no, your husband would cut off my head!' But she replied, 'Don't worry. My husband is afraid of me! If I ordered him to kneel, he would kneel'![22]

If there was one lesson that Liem learnt early on about business it was this: sometimes you have to spend money to make money. A quick learner, Liem decided that a savvy salesman could not afford to "think small" or focus simply on petty money-saving ways if he were to grow his sales. He gave the example of Sioe Hie, his older brother who had arrived in Java much earlier but seemed stuck in the same groove. Liem thought his brother was a penny-pincher who concentrated on saving his money and was reluctant to part with it. Sioe Hie did not share his younger brother's business philosophy, it seemed. Liem cited an incident to illustrate this:

> Sometimes to sell our wares, we had to go up a hill. It was not easy to push our bicycles loaded with things. Once, I suggested to Sioe Hie that we pay a truck driver to load our bicycles on his truck on the way up. 'Then you can ride downhill after you finished selling the things,' I said to him. But he didn't want to spend the money and insisted on pushing his heavy bicycle up the hill. Not me! I paid the driver. We quickly passed

Sioe Hie — I could see he was huffing and puffing. By the time he arrived
at the top of the hill, I had already sold all my goods! My brother was not
clever in business. He worked so hard but earned so little. Within a short
time of my arriving in Kudus, I was making more money than him.[23]

By his own reckoning, Liem was already doing "quite well" two years
after his arrival. He recalled having saved enough to buy the equivalent
of five new cars, about 2,600 Dutch guilders at the time. But for him,
it was just a teaser. He yearned for more. And this was his second lesson
in doing business: Trading was too dependent on margins. Simply selling
his wares would not catapult him to the ranks of the wealthy. "You can
never make very much", he reasoned to himself. Better profit may be
obtained in manufacturing, he thought. He claimed it was his idea to
make and sell peanut oil. It started as a home business. Joined by his
uncle and Sioe Hie, he laboriously pressed peanuts to extract the oil.
"It was a dirty business", he recalled. "I devised a better way to filter the
peanut oil so our oil was of good quality." He revealed that he had an
inventive side, experimenting with extracting other types of oil, such as
from cotton seeds. Although the oil was clear, he said, that did not sell
well and it was quickly discontinued. By this time, his younger brother
Sioe Kong also arrived from China, and they moved to a house on Jalan
Bitingan Lama (now called Jalan Mangga) in Kudus. This was where they
started a coffee business after the War. They dried and processed coffee
beans and packed them for sale. But their livelihood was disrupted by
the Japanese Occupation in 1942.

THE HARDY HOKCHIA

Liem's headstart in business was immensely helped by the strong solidarity
his dialect clan is well known for. The help they rendered each other helped
new arrivals overcome many of the adversities they faced. The Hokchia
clan association, for instance, would provide assistance to the newly arrived
migrant, and soon he would qualify to participate in a loan scheme called
arisan. This pool of money from clan members is available each month for
someone who won the bid to use it. The Hokchia have built a reputation
of being tough, resourceful, and courageous. They are natural risk-takers.
Generations of Hokchia youth have ventured to distant shores, fuelled
with not much more than a dream of striking it rich — or at the very least,
fare better than the dim prospects they faced at home.

The adventurous spirit of the Fuqing people is legendary. They even have a saying for their wanderlust: In any spot in the world where the sun shines, you can find a Hokchia. They can be found toiling in the sweatshops in New York's Chinatown, or running a small business in a South Pacific island. Liem once commented on his clansmen: "Hokchia people go everywhere in search of money. Even when they turn into ghosts, they will still be looking for their fortune. They are willing to brave death as long as there's money to be made."[24] Tragically, this has been borne out even as recently as within the last decade. In 2004, a group of illegal Hokchia workers were swept out to sea by a rogue wave at England's Morecambe Bay while gathering cockles. A few years earlier, a truckload of them — all illegal migrants being smuggled in through Europe — were found suffocated to death in England. A British academic researching migration from Fujian between 1999 and 2001 concluded that the province had established a sophisticated infrastructure of smugglers — from goods to human beings — and that the tradition of migration had become a normal way of life in that area. "It has nothing to do with desperation and poverty ... it has to do with opportunity", the academic noted, pointing out that in the same way that middle class families in the United Kingdom aspire to send their children to university, Fujianese aspire to working abroad.[25]

According to Michael Backman writing in his book *Asian Eclipse*, people from the Fuzhou area, comprising the Hokchia-Henghua-Hokchiu grouping, probably account for less than 5 per cent of the world's total overseas Chinese population, "but can count many of the biggest and most successful overseas Chinese entrepreneurs among them".[26] Given their small numbers, he added, "the Fuzhou are probably the most successful trading minority the world has ever seen". Just prior to the 1997–98 Asian financial crisis, the top thirty of the Fuzhou group controlled more than 1,500 companies between them (with) net combined assets of at least US$26 billion, he noted. "Their success is a remarkable achievement considering that most started out with little capital and by doing menial jobs such as repairing bicycles or selling cooking oil door to door", he wrote. The commercial power of the Fuzhou-Hokchia group in Indonesia is summarized by a research report by a brokerage firm; it surveyed its high net-worth clients and found that more than 80 per cent of them happened to be not only Chinese but also Hokchia.[27]

In Indonesia, other "Fuzhou group" prominent businessmen include Liem's long-term business partner Liem Oen Kian — also known by his

Indonesian name, Djuhar Sutanto, a Hokchia from a nearby village. Two other well-known Hokchia were the late founders of two *kretek* (clove-scented cigarette) manufacturers. One was Oei Wie Gwan of Djarum, whose sons Michael Bambang Hartono and Robert Budi Hartono in 2012 occupy the top spot of the Forbes Asia's wealthiest Indonesians list.[28] (Djarum ended up owning Liem's flagship bank, BCA, after the 1997–98 financial crisis.) The second was Surya Wonowidjojo (Tjoa Ing Hwie), who established Gudang Garam in 1956; by the 1980s, Gudang Garam, based in Kediri, East Java, was the largest *kretek* producer in Indonesia, employing 42,000 workers.[29] Well-known Indonesian banker Mochtar Riady, Liem's partner credited with building up BCA and founder of the Lippo Group, is a Henghua (his father migrated from Putian).

Liem's early partner in the flour milling business was illustrious Malaysian businessman, the sugar baron Robert Kuok, who is Hokchiu. Kuok's father left his hometown Fuzhou for what was then Malaya. Another well-known Indonesian Hokchia is The Ning King of the Argo Manunggal Group, which has diversified from its textile manufacturing roots into mining, steel, property and plantation. In the Malaysian province of Sarawak, many of the Chinese millionaires are also originally from Fuzhou. Despite their wealth, these people are infamously frugal. A Sarawak-based Hokchiu millionaire once had this to say about his kinsmen: "They are notoriously thrifty people; food and education are just about the only things that can pry open a Fuzhou wallet."[30] Alex Ling, the son of another prominent Malaysian Hokchiu, once remarked to a reporter: "They are very, very hardworking people … They can live anywhere — on boats, in the jungle. My father ate monkeys when he worked in logging camps. These things mean very little to them."[31]

HARD TIMES

Liem might have thought he had escaped war when he left Fujian in 1938, but less than four years later, the Japanese showed up again in his neighbourhood, this time in a different country. The Japanese Occupation of Indonesia from 1942 to 1945 would be described by Liem as the most difficult period in his life. With credit-purchasing activity banned, he had to find other sources of income. Still, there was a bright spot during this trying time: he met and married the girl of his dreams.

In 1942, when the Japanese invaded Indonesia, they did so with such lightning speed and well-planned strategy they caught the Dutch off guard. Much like their invasion of Malaya and Singapore, the Japanese attacked where they were least expected. The event was recounted by a Chinese Indonesian woman:

> The Dutch had assumed that the Japanese would invade Java through the two major port cities of Surabaya and Jakarta and therefore concentrated their defences in those locations. They were taken completely by surprise when, on the night of 1 March 1942, the Japanese launched simultaneous amphibious landings along the poorly-defended north coast of Java instead. From these beachheads, the Japanese quickly spread out across Java before the Dutch could react and within days had surrounded the Dutch forces, still struggling to reorganise themselves out of their port cities. It was a hopeless situation, reminiscent of the method used to defeat the Allies in Malaya and Singapore. The expected Battle of Java was effectively over before it had begun ... The prevailing mood was one of stunned disbelief that the Dutch in Indonesia had capitulated so quickly...[32]

The woman's father had a straightforward theory for how swiftly the Japanese overcame the Dutch defences. Weeks before the invasion, he had observed that "the Dutch loved their wives and families, whereas the Japanese loved their country and Emperor ... In the coming showdown between the two countries, the Japanese would win as they would sacrifice everything to achieve victory, even themselves."[33] The invasion heralded an era of great confusion and chaos, with the Dutch colonial masters finding the tables turned on them, becoming prisoners of war of an Asian race. Many indigenous Indonesians initially welcomed the Japanese as liberators who held out promise to help free them of their 350-year colonial shackles. For many Chinese in the Dutch East Indies, however, it was a period of great suffering. The Japanese were merciless in their treatment of anyone who stood in their way of establishing their goal of building the Greater East Asia Co-Prosperity Sphere. Anyone suspected of aiding China's resistance was hunted down and summarily executed. The Japanese had cause for concern: the Singapore-based rubber magnate and Chinese patriot Tan Kah Kee had been successfully raising funds for the Chinese war effort. As chairman of the Southeast Asian Chinese Anti-Japanese National Salvation Movement, he became a focal point for rallying anti-Japanese sentiments among the overseas Chinese communities.

The Dutch had watched with great apprehension the ignominious and quick surrender of Singapore by the British in February 1942. Writing about this period, Twang noted that "major Chinese businessmen in the big cities moved their stockpiles to secondary cities or towns in the interior". In some cases, they were ordered by the Dutch to evacuate (presumably with their goods) from major cities, partly to facilitate a "scorched earth policy" — to not leave anything of value or use to the Japanese.[34] Many businesses were disrupted when perfectly functioning factories were destroyed at the hands of the Dutch demolition corps and retreating Dutch soldiers. "Of the 130 sugar mills in Java in 1940, only 32 escaped destruction. The Oei Tiong Ham Concern, the largest non-Dutch trading firm operating in the East Indies, had a sugar factory in Semarang blown up and a rubber plant in Palembang burnt. Retreating Dutch troops also destroyed roads and bridges, paralyzing transportation between cities."[35] During the early days of the Occupation, some Chinese shops were looted by *pribumi*, who exploited the chaos of the War to give vent to their resentment of perceived economic predominance of the Chinese. But the huge warehouses and factories of the Dutch trading companies were also not spared.

Meanwhile, the Japanese forces rounded up European staff and managers of plantations and offices and sent them to concentration camps set up in different areas in Java and the outer islands. Even women and children were imprisoned. The suffering of the Dutch at the hands of the Japanese was duly recorded by staff of Dutch trading houses. A report to shareholders by one of the "Big Five"[36] Dutch trading companies, Lindeteves, spoke of "the personal misery, the material damage, and the complete disruption of everything intentionally and systemically wrought by the Japanese occupation regime on the Dutch East Indies, in disregard of all laws of civilization and humanity, and surpassing all that had happened in the Netherlands itself". For most of the Dutch trading houses, World War II proved to be "a nadir in their existence".[37] The harsh rules imposed by the Japanese extended to every aspect of daily life. One of the first official orders they laid down after assuming control of Indonesia was to close all Chinese and Dutch-speaking schools, sending students home or in some cases into internment. Any Chinese who could not give his name in Chinese or who was caught speaking Dutch could be slapped, kicked or arrested by the military police. Any Chinese who had Dutch names had to stop using them and they had to learn how to write their names in Chinese characters to comply with Japanese regulations, even if they were Peranakan and never learnt the Chinese language.[38]

The Japanese also carefully monitored Chinese associations and businesses, many of which were ordered to close. Although they banned all money-lending and the practice of credit-extending, they tolerated the smuggling of certain goods and essential commodities in dire shortage. Many Hokchia, who by nature were risk-takers, were quick to seize this opportunity. As noted by the writer Sterling Seagrave: "Many ordinary Chinese suffered in Java during the war. Those who thrived were the foxes who smuggled rice, medicines and strategic commodities, which they sold to the Japanese at a fat profit."[39] Those "foxes" include the Hokchia-Henghua who were among those Chinese Totok groups "which fared relatively well under the Japanese Occupation and which during the years of the revolution contributed significantly to the republican forces", wrote academic Peter Post.[40] He commented that while the three-year period of Japanese military rule was "disastrous for the pre-War colonial power structure and harsh for the larger part of the indigenous peasantry", it also offered possibilities for "new business forces within Indonesian society who under Dutch rule played only marginal roles. For Liem Sioe Liong and his brothers, the Occupation disrupted their *crediet mindering* livelihood. Ever resourceful, they got together with a few friends to sell whatever they could, which included fermented tofu called *oncom*, peanut oil, rice wine and fruits."[41]

A WAR-TIME ROMANCE AND MARRIAGE

Although the war was a nightmarish period for most, there was one bright spot for Liem: that was when he met and married the girl of his dreams. So smitten was he by the sweet smile of the young, pretty student playing netball with her school friends, he vowed to himself he would make her his bride. Never mind that he was supposed to be a married man — that was conveniently forgotten. That was his past. (It was not until 1961, when Liem took his Indonesian-born wife to visit his mother in China that she learnt about his first wife in the village.) Liem recalled the occasion when he first set eyes on Lie Kim Nio:[42]

> She was 17 at the time, 10 years younger than me. When she saw me, she smiled — a very sweet smile. I thought she was the prettiest girl in her school. A mutual friend introduced us. I passed a note to her, and I was thrilled when I got a reply. It meant she was interested in me![43]

The daughter of a Peranakan Chinese batik trader, Lie had moved to Kudus from Lasem, a coastal town in Java. The family did not speak any

Chinese dialects. Her father, Lie Chuan Nok, was at first suspicious of Liem, a recently arrived Totok, and objected to Liem's courtship of his daughter, fearing the possibility of "losing" her if Liem married her and took her to China. The cultural divide between Peranakan and Totok was wide in those days between the Chinese who have lived in the country for multi-generations and the new arrivals. Liem said he understood his father-in-law's initial wariness. "I had a reputation as a playboy at the time, and had many girlfriends!" he said, chuckling.[44] Despite having his livelihood disrupted by the Japanese Occupation, Liem came across as a self-possessed young man. He was confident and had an air of determination. Plus, he had stashed away enough savings for a wedding ceremony. For his marriage plan, there was one other factor working in his favour — it was widely perceived that young and single women were still vulnerable to being preyed on by Japanese soldiers. Thus it was almost compelling for the pretty seventeen-year-old Lie to get married. The constraints of living under the Occupation notwithstanding, Liem used his savings and arranged for a lavish wedding. The memorable three-day ceremony started on 15 April 1944, with the entire Hokchia community in Kudus invited. A wedding photo showed the bride and groom surrounded by huge bouquets and arrangements of flowers. The wedding feast featured sixty tables filled with food — an impressive display, considering the lean war times. Liem took his bride home in a horse-drawn carriage. The newlyweds moved into the house he was renting. There was an incident a few weeks after the wedding that demonstrated how living under the Japanese was still fraught with danger. He was arrested on suspicion of hiding weapons and beaten. He recounted the incident:

> I was detained by the Japanese soldiers. They were searching for hidden weapons. There was a ban on keeping weapons. You could be executed if they found you concealing a weapon. Somehow, there was a rumour that I had a gun hidden in my house. So the Japanese soldiers searched the house and compound. Eventually they found a rusty pistol in the well. I didn't know how it got there; maybe someone had thrown it in there a long time ago. They arrested me and kept me for days. They questioned me but I said I didn't know about the pistol. They beat me until I coughed up blood. This happened about two weeks after I got married. My new wife and family members managed to bribe someone to help get me released. It was a frightening time.[45]

Notes

1. Liem gives his date of birth according to the Chinese calendar. Some biographies state his birthday as July 1916, which was how it was recorded in his Indonesian passport. Because the Chinese calendar follows the lunar cycle, the corresponding date in the Gregorian calendars moves every year. When he became a tycoon, he decided on marking his birthday on 7 September, which, he says, is less confusing for his Indonesian friends and business associates.
2. <http://www.metaphysicalzone.com/china/snake4.shtml>.
3. Interview with Liem, 15 April 2006. Some of the transcriptions of the interviews with Liem have been edited by the authors to enhance readability.
4. Kiem Tjai's son, Liem Sioe Djwan, who chose the Indonesian name Djoni Prananto, also became active in business, and entered several ventures with Liem's partner, Sudwikatmono.
5. *Hanyu pinyin* name: Lin Shao Xi; Sioe Hie was the Indonesian spelling. He later took the Indonesian name Soehanda Salim.
6. *Hanyu pinyin* name: Lin Shao Gen; Indonesian name: Soedarmo Salim.
7. This section is based on various interviews with Liem conducted between April 2006 and April 2007.
8. Interview with Liem, 3 June 2006.
9. Interview with Liem, 16 September 2006.
10. Interview with Liem, 14 April 2007.
11. Interview with Liem, 16 September 2006.
12. About 200 kilometres away from Fuqing, directly opposite Taiwan, Xiamen was the main staging point for would-be emigrants from Fujian.
13. Interview with Liem, 15 April 2006.
14. Ibid.
15. Twang Peck Yang, *The Chinese Business Elite in Indonesia and the Transition to Independence, 1940–1950* (Kuala Lumpur: Oxford University Press, 1998), p. 97.
16. Ibid., p. 53.
17. Hamish McDonald, *Suharto's Indonesia* (Australia: Fontana, 1980). p. 30.
18. Lynn Pan, *Sons of the Yellow Emperor: A History of the Chinese Diaspora* (New York: Kodansha, 1990), p. 230.
19. Twang, *The Chinese Business Elite in Indonesia*, p. 59.
20. Ibid., p. 57.
21. Ibid., p. 56.
22. Interview with Liem, 14 April 2007.
23. Ibid.
24. Interview with Liem, 15 April 2006.
25. Frank Pieke, a lecturer in Chinese politics and society at Oxford University.

Story from BBC News:<http://news.bbc.co.uk/go/pr/fr/-/2/hi/asia-pacific/3472691.stm>. Published 9 February 2004, 14:24:37 GMT.

26. Michael Backman, *Asian Eclipse: Exposing the Dark Side of Business in Asia* (Singapore: John Wiley, 1999), p. 224.

27. Ibid., pp. 224–26.

28. The Hartono brothers of Djarum occupied the top position in the November 2011 issue of "Indonesia's 40 Richest", *Forbes Asia*. 18 November 2011, p. 74. They also topped the 2012 Forbes listing, with estimated combined assets of US$15 billion. Gudang Garam's Susilo Wonowidjojo came in at no. 3 with US$7.4 billion; Anthony Salim ranked fourth, with US$5.2 billion.

29. Leo Suryadinata, *Prominent Chinese Indonesians: Biographical Sketches* (Singapore: Institute of Southeast Asian Studies, 1995), p. 227.

30. Raphael Pura, "A breed apart: Stamina and success mark Fuzhou Chinese diaspora", *Asian Wall Street Journal*, 8 June 1994.

31. Ibid.

32. Stuart Pearson, *Bittersweet: The Memoir of a Chinese Indonesian Family in the Twentieth Century* (Singapore: NUS Press, 2008), pp. 68–69.

33. Ibid.

34. Twang, *The Chinese Business Elite in Indonesia*, p. 70.

35. Ibid., p. 101.

36. The Dutch "Big Five" are: Internatio, Borsumij, Geo. Wehry, Lindeteves, and Jacobson & Van den Berg.

37. Joost Jonker and Keetie Sluyterman, *At Home on the World Markets: Dutch International Trading Companies from the 16th Century Until the Present* (The Hague: Sdu Uitgevers, 2000), pp. 259–60.

38. Pearson, *Bittersweet*, p. 69.

39. Sterling Seagrave, *Lords of the Rim: The Invisible Empire of the Overseas Chinese* (London: Bantam, 1995), p. 183.

40. Peter Post, "On bicycles and textiles: Japan, South China and the Hokchia-Henghua entrepreneurs", in *South China: State, Culture and Social Change during the 20th Century*, edited by L.M. Douw and P. Post (Amsterdam: Royal Netherlands Academy of Arts and Sciences, Verhandelingen, Afd, 1996), p. 147.

41. Interview with Liem, 29 April 2006.

42. Sometimes spelled Lie Las Nio; her Chinese name as rendered in *hanyu pinyin* is Li Shuzhen.

43. Interview with Liem, 15 April 2006.

44. Ibid.

45. Ibid.

3

ESTABLISHING A FOOTHOLD

The end of the Japanese Occupation in 1945 was universally celebrated but brought fresh challenges. As the Japanese were surrendering, nationalist leader Sukarno proclaimed independence on 17 August, raising a red and white flag hastily stitched by his young wife Fatmawati. The declaration of independence, however, was not recognized by the Dutch, who were keen to reassert control over their colony and all its resources. The tussle between the colonial forces and the independence fighters went on until 1949. During this time, the Dutch tried to choke off supply lines to the revolutionary soldiers, imposing sea and land blockades. Suppliers had to sneak through Dutch controlled areas, turning them effectively into smugglers. For those willing to take the risks, smuggling was a lucrative activity.

For small itinerant traders like Liem, it was a chance to start recouping his lost income. His hard-earned savings in Japanese Occupation-issued notes — stashed in sacks — were wiped out overnight when it was declared worthless. As he recalled: "The new government compensated every household by the number of occupants living there: regardless of how much money you had, each person was entitled to only one rupiah. There were eight of us living in our house, and we received a total of eight rupiah. That was all. The Occupation ended but I had to start all over again."[1] Adding to his responsibilities as a family man was the arrival of his first-born, Albert, that year. Although he was back to square one, Liem was luckier than most; he was once again able to capitalize on the strong Hokchia kinship, borrowing capital from his clansmen to restart his business. There was even a new customer base — the independence fighters. He joined others in smuggling basic necessities to them, laying the groundwork for a role that would reach far beyond being just a supplier. It was during this time that he established important contacts that later helped put him on the road to riches.

STRUGGLE FOR INDEPENDENCE

After the Japanese surrender, the Dutch, aided by British and other allied forces, waged a bitter war with the nationalists in their attempt to recover their colony. The independence fighters were led by Sukarno and Mohammad Hatta, and the struggle to rid the Dutch colonialists lasted until 1949, when international politics played a significant role in getting The Hague to cease attempts to lay claim over their "Dutch East Indies". Many of the new republic's senior military officers cut their teeth during this period, including Suharto, who headed a regimental command in Central Java. The soldiers of the republic were often in need of provisions and ammunition, and running supplies to them was often a risky business. Many of these "smugglers" who scored impressive runs were Chinese, especially the Totok, and among them the Hokchia, the most daring risk-takers of all.

Liem saw in this a great opportunity to relaunch his shattered business and he plunged in it enthusiastically. He worked hard as he noted the soldiers of the republic bought from whoever got supplies to them first. He sold essentials such as soap, coffee, sugar, rice and tobacco. Some reports later alleged that he smuggled guns and ammunition; one such allegation appeared in a 1978 profile of Liem — by then a tycoon; it was his first interview to the media. Written by the Hong Kong-based editor of *Insight* magazine, Ian Verchere, it claimed that Liem was a gun-runner, citing "British intelligence" as its source of information. But Liem vehemently denied it, stating: "I was never involved in supplying arms."[2]

Liem was comfortable doing business with the Indonesians, especially the Javanese, who were his customers since his arrival. Supplying victuals to the Republican troops was not something he viewed as onerous.

He preferred dealing with the Indonesians rather than the Dutch, for whom he had no special sympathies; he never learnt their language nor been exposed to their culture. As he put it: "From the time I arrived in Java, I had few contacts with the Dutch. I could not speak their language. But I picked up some Javanese and Indonesian language and I felt quite comfortable with the people."[3] During the four-year independence struggle, running provisions for the Republican soldiers in Central Java was the mainstay of his business. He became familiar with the hills around Gunung Muria, an extinct volcano east of Semarang, where the guerrilla units of the republic were sometimes holed up. He loved the cool air and the forested hills. (Some time later, he was able to purchase a bungalow in the hills, which he used occasionally as a weekend retreat.)

SMUGGLING AS ECONOMIC ACTIVITY

The word "smuggling" evokes negative connotations; it implies an illegal activity that brings retribution or punishment by the authorities. For most Indonesians, however, it was how goods had to travel from one part of the sprawling archipelago to another. It was during the four years when the Dutch were trying to reassert control that the transport of goods and commodities had to be authorized. To try to choke off supplies to the Republican soldiers, the Dutch blockaded both sea and land. To many, during the struggle for independence, breaking the Dutch blockades was deemed a patriotic act.

Smuggling became an important "economic activity", enabling many of the Chinese traders to get back on their feet after World War II. Strong links were forged between Chinese suppliers and Republican forces during that time. "That Chinese businessmen and Indonesian revolutionaries joined forces was significant for the political and economic structure of independent Indonesia", noted the historian Twang Peck Yang. The partnership had a natural synergy: the Chinese knew where to source for goods and had the means to pay for them; the Republican military could ensure passage. Twang continued: "It was easy for the military to perceive or justify the importance of their role in the economy in a war situation. The maintenance and operation of trade required army and navy personnel. The military's hand in the economy was, in some circumstances, the policy of the Republic."[4] This was evident in the various business activities undertaken by military officers.

Several state-owned trading companies also had their roots in the smuggling of goods, which were usually bartered as cash was in short supply. The nest of islands in Sumatra that formed the Riau province provided excellent cover for "smugglers" who courageously ran the Dutch sea blockade between Singapore and Indonesia. The new government set up several companies ostensibly to do import-export businesses, but a main goal was to procure arms for its nascent armed forces. Among them were N.V. Trading, based in Madiun, East Java, and Tiga Mas, headquartered in Yogyakarta,[5] which served as the capital of the republic when the Dutch chased the independence leaders out of Jakarta. In 1947, the Central Trading Company (CTC), was set up in Bukit Tinggi, the republic's capital in Sumatra. One of its founders was a *pribumi* entrepreneur from Aceh, Teuku Mohamad Daud, who explained that an English name was chosen for the company to give it "prestige". Daud had joined the fledgling Indonesian National Army (TNI) right after the proclamation of independence. In 1947, he was assigned to the Sumatra command based in Bukit Tinggi and tasked with procuring military equipment. Recounting his experience, he wrote:

> We were forced to finance acquisitions by smuggling agricultural commodities from Riau; this proved very difficult because we lacked expertise in what was essentially barter trade. We tried to collect exportable commodities of all kinds, including tea, coffee and rubber; in this way we became traders. We established CTC as a government-owned trading company in Bukit Tinggi in 1947 ... In this way our smuggling activities were legalised.[6]

According to Daud, the idea behind CTC was to break the monopoly of the existing Dutch trading monoliths operating in the Netherlands Indies — the so-called "Big Five" — Internatio, Borsumij, Geo. Wehry, Lindeteves, and Jacobson & Van den Berg.[7] Daud, who died in 1999, provided an illuminating account of CTC activity, and recounted the daring exploits of a Chinese naval officer named John Lie — a rare instance of an ethnic Chinese who served in the Indonesian military:

> Sometimes by way of an injection of capital we received chests of raw opium sent from Java in a small plane. We sold this and other commodities to Chinese merchants in Pekanbaru (in the Riau islands), who then smuggled them to Malaya. In Aceh, we had some shipping at our disposal, mostly *prahu*, but also the speedboat PT58 commanded by the naval officer Admiral John Lie. Although the Dutch tried several times to

blockade us, they could not locate us because there were so many inlets in Aceh from which we could carry out our operations. Products such as rubber from Langsa were smuggled to Penang, where CTC had a branch office. With the proceeds we purchased much needed uniforms, shoes, vehicles and weapons for our military. We needed goods, not money, so our smuggling was really barter trade.[8]

The heroic exploits of John Lie — also known as Jahja Daniel Dharma — are legendary. He conducted his smuggling exploits dodging Dutch blockades with a missionary-like zeal. He provided guns, weapons and ammunition for the Republican troops from all over Southeast Asia. His network of operations stretched from Singapore to Penang, Manila, Bangkok, Rangoon and New Delhi. Young (he was in his thirties) and daring, Lie was a major source of arms for the Republican cause. He bought five ships from the British but all were shelled, strafed, and bombed, leaving one that was never caught. When people marvelled at his derring-do, Lie provided this explanation:

When I was a boy, I did wrong. The Lord told me to move on, and I went to sea. I spent 15 years on Dutch ships sailing between Durban and Shanghai. But I saw the Dutch did wrong, so once again I moved on. I went to the Holy Land. There, God told me to go home and help make Indonesia a Garden of Eden — where there would be no Dutchmen.[9]

It was said that Lie's activities were "the most outstandingly successful" among the many smugglers operating at the time. John Lie died in 1988. In 2009, twenty-one years after his death, he was officially declared a 'National Hero' by President Susilo Bambang Yudhoyono. Historian Yong Mun Cheong, who provided the John Lie story in his book *The Indonesian Revolution and the Singapore Connection: 1945–1949*, detailed the large-scale smuggling during the independence struggle:

Economic dislocations during those trying years gave rise to a group of traders who worked on a small scale as individuals ferrying goods in boats from one place to another. The kind of goods depended on demand … Capital was small, trading journeys were irregular, and a lot depended on traders' personal contacts. The traders were mainly Chinese (engaged in) *danbang* activity (an itinerant trader who carried the goods from one place to another). Only a thin line separates this means of livelihood from its later metamorphosis, smuggling. Boats of all shapes and sizes were used to carry a wide variety of goods, from rubber, oil, quinine and copra from Sumatra, to tea, coffee, batik, sugar and peanuts from Java.

Other commodities included tin ore, pepper and even opium. Many of those engaged in smuggling activities probably didn't even consider what they were doing as illegal, but as something that some authority or other didn't approve of, and that usually meant forking over some money to someone to look the other way. Smuggling was an ambitious term packed with emotions during those days of the Indonesian revolution. Much of its meaning depended on the perspective taken to describe the movement of goods. To the traders in Singapore, free market forces determined the direction of the flow of goods. To the Dutch, smuggling was an act of evasion. Trade was regarded as smuggling when the activity lay outside Dutch control. But whatever the meaning and attributes, smuggling played a crucial role in advancing the Republican cause.[10]

Yong related an amusing incident about smuggled uniforms:

> The Republican army in Pekanbaru was well supplied with military material from Singapore. At a parade in 1946, some one thousand Republican army personnel were able to don British uniforms, all sequestered from Singapore. There was a report that men dressed in British military garb attacked a Dutch post, and this was extremely confusing to the defenders, who were not sure about the identity of their opponents.[11]

In 1949, the Dutch finally bowed to international pressure and signed what was called the Roem-Royen Agreement, ending efforts to reclaim their colony. The nationalists could finally claim victory, and savour real independence. With the Dutch gone, that was the end of "smuggling" for the Republic, but the bartering of goods persisted, continued by regimental commanders needing to raise funds.

SUKARNO'S PRESIDENCY

Indonesia's first president belonged to the league of supremely charismatic leaders. He was highly educated (trained as an architect and engineer) and spoke several foreign languages. His charm, usually directed at attractive ladies, was renowned. His public speeches could electrify a crowd. The late Cornell scholar George Kahin described his first exposure to Sukarno's magnetism in Yogyakarta in 1948:

> I had heard that Sukarno was an excellent orator, but I was totally unprepared for the extent of his rapport with that crowd. He had a

sort of magnetic charisma that quickly established a bond with it. He modulated his voice skilfully, used gestures at just the appropriate places in the rhythm that he developed, and within a few minutes the crowd seemed silently to interact with him ... he travelled through much of the Republic making such speeches and, in the process, giving his audience the feeling that they were part of an historical enterprise predestined for success. It was as if he was a heart pumping oxygen into and animating the Indonesian body politic.[12]

Skilled orator though he was, Sukarno found that it took more than words to overcome the problems of building a nation from a highly diverse patchwork of ethnic groups and creating an administration from scratch. The years following 1949 were highly challenging. On the gaining of independence, he commented:

Thus ended our period of struggle. And thus began our struggle for survival. The deed to the house called Indonesia was now securely in our hands, but it was a badly damaged house. It leaked aplenty. Its windows, doors, roof, and walls were broken. Our economy, government administration, transportation systems, communications media, methods of production were all damaged. Even morally and mentally, we needed repairs.[13]

Politically, and economically, the new republic was woefully weak and debilitated. With the departure of the colonial administration, there was almost no infrastructure in place to govern the sprawling archipelago, which stretched from Sumatra to the islands just short of West New Guinea. (That resource-rich territory, later renamed Irian Jaya, remained under Dutch control until a Sukarno campaign — in which Suharto played a key role — wrested it away in the early 1960s.) Indonesia faced huge challenges, including crippling inflation. A foreign journalist once described some of the challenges the new country faced:

The economic and social dislocation caused by the Japanese Occupation and the wars with the Dutch would in themselves have presented an enormous problem even for a government supported by a united and suitable trained people... The first Republic at one stage issued currency unbacked by any receipts at all, and note-printing presses ran on uncontrolled when the unitary Republic was formed ... the largely illiterate nation was divided into 366 ethnic groups ... cutting through some of these were religious sects, secular nationalists of various kinds, Communists of every kind, bandits and petty warlords with military rank, who, after fighting the Dutch, established enclaves in which they alone were the law.[14]

The atmosphere of distrust, detrimental to attracting badly needed foreign capital for investments, was to last until after the abortive coup in 1965. There was neither money nor expertise to develop an industrial base in infrastructure and manufacturing. Academic Richard Robison noted that by 1957, "it had become clear that private domestic capital was unable to provide the basis for capital formation and the leaders of the new Republic began to turn towards state capital".[15] This also would not succeed. The political picture, too, was daunting. Independence spawned a plethora of parties, each championing its own agenda, and rebellions against Jakarta, including one backed by the Central Intelligence Agency (CIA), broke out. Sukarno had to work within the constraints of the political system which landed him with multiple governments during that fractious period. He faced six assassination attempts and multiple revolts. As time wore on, Sukarno started ranting about a continuing revolution. As he became increasingly suspicious of the West, Western leaders were growing uneasy with his increasingly pro-socialist polemic and growing dalliance with Indonesia's communist party, PKI. He famously told the United States "to hell with your aid" and instead of tackling economic woes, he built monuments.

THE CHINESE "ISSUE"

Governments under Sukarno were also faced with a lingering issue that needed urgent attention — how to handle the Chinese population. The Dutch attempt to recolonize the country resulted in split loyalties among the Chinese. Some Peranakans who had allied themselves with the Dutch left for the Netherlands. Others were staunch supporters of the republic, but became disillusioned when they found themselves targeted by anti-Chinese violence and failed to receive adequate protection from the revolutionary government. In 1946, the new nation's leaders convened what they named the Yogyakarta Conference on the Chinese at which Vice-President Mohammad Hatta[16] declared that the economic position of the Chinese after the Japanese occupation (which was said to still remain higher than that of the Indonesians in general) was the crucial reason for the anti-Chinese activity during the revolution.[17] That year, a citizenship law was passed automatically conferring Indonesian citizenship to all Chinese born in Indonesia "who had resided there for five years unless they repudiated it within a given period." As noted by Charles Coppel: "This law demonstrated the desire of the Indonesian government to show its acceptance of Peranakans, while permitting the Chinese nationalists among them to reject local citizenship."[18]

The latent hostility held by many *pribumi* for the Chinese was analysed by Pramoedya Ananta Toer, Indonesia's best-known writer. Later incarcerated by Suharto for his leftist thinking, Pramoedya in the late 1950s wrote extensively — and rather sympathetically — about the Chinese in Indonesia. He blamed the Dutch for fomenting the hatred and distrust that the *pribumi* developed for the Chinese, pointing out that the Chinese who settled in Java and elsewhere before the Dutch period had no problems integrating. Pramoedya noted that the Chinese had been in Sumatra long before the Dutch arrived — since the year A.D. 942 — and brought with them agricultural tools that they introduced to the local farmers. They perfected the techniques for growing pepper and introduced tea cultivation. They improved the productivity of sugar cultivation by bringing in better techniques.[19] But the Dutch treated the Chinese as "aliens" and made them live in their own enclaves, requiring permission to travel out of those designated areas. In his 1960 book *Hoakiau di Indonesia* (The Chinese in Indonesia), a compilation of letters to a Chinese friend (the book was banned by Suharto), Pramoedya wrote about the prevalent anti-Chinese sentiments:

> Before the arrival of the VOC [Vereenigde Oost-Indische Compagnie, or the Dutch East India Company, founded in 1602] the Chinese had been absorbed by the Indonesian society. But as the colonialists began to understand that there was a continuing, spontaneous migration of Chinese to Indonesia, the colonialist began to fear the growing number of Chinese. They felt threatened. So the VOC introduced all kinds of regulations to limit the migrations ... since then, the Chinese have been treated like a rubbish bin into which every kind of filth has been thrown: insults, humiliations, degradation, agitation, torture, murder. They were never in a position to resist. They had no army. They were just peaceful people not after anything else but a bowl of rice.[20]

But resentment against the Chinese continued to fester in post-colonial Indonesia, with periodic outbursts of violence, culminating in May 1998, the worst outbreak in modern history. The various governments under Sukarno paid considerable attention to giving a leg up to the native population to chip away at the perceived dominance of the Chinese in business and introduced policies that discriminated against them. Economic planners put in place policies to narrow the perceived gap between *pribumi* and "aliens". Some of these specifically targeted the Chinese and foreign competition, including providing state credit as well as protection for *pribumi* businessmen. In rice, for example, the government restricted membership of the boards of milling companies to Indonesian citizens, which at the time excluded most Chinese. Similar protection was granted in other fields, including stevedoring and bus transportation.[21] One of the more controversial policies was launched in 1950. Called Benteng — meaning fortress — it aimed to foster indigenous traders by reserving import licences exclusively for them and gave them loans and facilities. Licences were supposed to generate for the *pribumi* enough capital to move into other sectors. In reality, however, many who got them knew next to nothing about importing, nor how to document and finance imports. They therefore turned to experienced Chinese traders, selling them the coveted licences instead. What this succeeded in doing was to create what was dubbed an "Ali Baba" relationship between the *pribumi* and the Chinese. (The Ali was the *pribumi*, and the Baba, the Chinese. Straits-born Chinese or Peranakan were often called "Baba".) Even successful *pribumi* businessmen such as Soedarpo Sastrosatomo, who built up a wide-ranging business that encompassed shipping, finance and importing, described the Benteng Programme as a disaster. "Licences were given to people who were not even remotely businessmen but who believed that they were entitled to enjoy these facilities as the fruits of the Revolution", he commented.[22] The result of this flawed programme saw *pribumi* businessmen who enjoyed close ties with the power-holders and the military being granted licences. They were dubbed "briefcase importers" as they were merely puppet traders, carrying documents which they sold to real Chinese traders. Indonesian economic historian Thee Kian Wie commented: "Instead of building a strong *pribumi* business class, the Benteng Programme had fostered a group of socially unproductive rent-seekers."[23] Robison added: "What was being consolidated was not an indigenous merchant bourgeoisie but a group of licence brokers and political fixers."[24] Acknowledging the programme's failure, the government dismantled it in 1957.

Many years later, in 1986, Professor Sumitro Djojohadikusumo,[25] one of the principal architects of the country's post-independence economic policy, defended the Benteng Programme, asserting it was created as a counterforce to Dutch interests. "I had no illusions about what might happen but I thought that if you gave assistance to ten people, seven might turn out to be parasites but you might still get three entrepreneurs", he wrote.[26] In the early days of the republic, Sumitro played a significant role in crafting many economic policies. He was a nationalist, favouring support for *pribumi* interests and was very much opposed to the kind of special position that Liem later assumed. Sumitro tried to thwart, or at least reduce, some of the privileges Suharto accorded Liem, such as a plan to give him a monopoly for clove imports.

The Chinese in the new republic who were not citizens faced further restrictions. In 1954, the government imposed rules curtailing the movements and activities of these "aliens", including the levying of hefty taxes on the breadwinner, and supplementary ones on their dependants. Remittances to China were barred, and only 15 per cent of foreign credit was permitted to go to firms owned by them. To get around these regulations, Chinese business owners had to allocate 50 per cent of the equity to Indonesian partners. Three years later, "aliens" were forbidden to establish or expand enterprises. Liem and many of his Hokchia businessmen friends, all migrants in the 1930s, were affected. This would explain the reason official registrations of Liem's companies during that period did not list his name. Writing about the consequences of these restrictive regulations, academics Jusuf Panglaykim and Ingrid Palmer observed:

> Excluded from importing new equipment they (the "aliens") tended to move into smaller, un-mechanised enterprises such as theatres and hotels. This was only a tendency because industries such as the textile industry expanded and mechanised under Chinese ownership during the 1950s. This was largely achieved by using an Indonesian for his name, by lobbying officials, or by playing on their supposed Indonesian citizenship from past, doubtful legislation. But the confusion surrounding the definition of an Indonesian citizen until 1958 added to the risks of investment. This brought home to them just how uncertain was the future of people of non-Indonesian origin.[27]

An even more draconian measure was adopted in 1959, which spurred the departure of an estimated 120,000 Chinese to China. In what was referred to as regulation PP10 (Peraturan Pemerintah No. 10 of 1959), "alien Chinese" were banned from retail trade in rural areas. According to one estimate, at that time 83,783 out of 86,690 retail shops in villages were owned by Chinese. Following this ban, there was an "exodus of the poorest Chinese traders from the countryside into the cities".[28] The "poorly conceived and sometimes crudely implemented" policy led to the mass exodus on ships which the Chinese government sent.[29] As in the Benteng Programme, PP10 failed to achieve its desired aim of giving the *pribumi* a boost. By that time, many Chinese capitalists had already filled the void progressively left by the Dutch in the cities and towns between 1945 and 1958. Those still in the rural areas established joint ventures with former *pribumi* employees. But the indigenous capitalists were simply unable to replace the Chinese retailers. Even though it was Sukarno's government which had introduced PP10, the president himself was not entirely in favour of it and had been unable to prevent its promulgation due to support for the ban from business interests and the military. Sukarno was only able to campaign publicly for a mild form of implementation, which was left largely to local military commanders. Some local commanders were overzealous in carrying out the policy. One colonel in West Java removed Chinese traders practically at gunpoint from villages under his command. The army "literally threw hundreds of Chinese families into trucks and took them to hastily constructed relocation camps. Not infrequently, resistance met with harsh punishment."[30]

A LEASE ON LIFE

The year 1949 was a historic one for Indonesia — when the Dutch finally accepted the nation's sovereignty. For Liem, it was a momentous year. That was the year he escaped death in a horrific car accident. It happened just weeks before the birth of his third child. Grateful to be alive to see the newborn, Liem broke with tradition that dictated the naming of his son according to the family tree.[31] He named the child Fung Seng, meaning "meeting a new life", as that was what he felt he had been given. Liem Fung Seng later assumed the name Anthoni (also spelled Anthony) Salim, and as detailed later, lived up to his name by rescuing the Salim Group in the post-Suharto era.

In the post-War years, Liem often travelled between Kudus and Semarang to source for supplies. He was by then able to ditch his bicycle in favour of shared taxi rides. According to Liem's account of the accident, it happened one September day in 1949, when he had to rush to Semarang to head off a likely confiscation of a shipment of goods by the Dutch. He hopped on a taxi in Kudus, together with friends also headed to Semarang. He related:

> I didn't have my own car; very few people had private cars in those days. To get to another town, you shared a rented taxi — what was called *mobil umum* (public car). A few of my friends were also going to Semarang, so we decided to share the taxi. When we were getting into the car, I got in front with the driver. My friend in the back seat asked if he could sit in front instead, and I obliged him. I got in behind him, by the window. Some time after we started off, the older man sitting in the middle, next to me, said he was feeling hot and needed air. He asked if he could switch places with me so he could be by the window. I was a little annoyed, but I agreed and ended up in the middle seat. About 20 minutes before we reached Semarang, the taxi driver overtook two cars. Then we saw an oxcart ahead. Just as the driver was pulling out to overtake it, a Dutch military truck suddenly appeared, heading straight towards us! It was a big vehicle, one of those 10-tonne trucks. Our taxi smashed headlong with the truck.
>
> The driver and the friend in front who had asked to switch seats with me were killed instantly. The man who asked for my window seat was seriously injured and spent months in hospital. The third person in the car also died. I was found unconscious, with a broken left leg and some head abrasions. I was taken to St Elizabeth Hospital in Semarang, run by the Dutch. It was supposed to be only for Dutch people, or for those with some connection with the Dutch. I think I was admitted because the collision was with a Dutch military truck. They had to operate on my leg. Until today, my left leg is about 1 cm shorter than my right. It took a few days before my family found me. I spent a total of three months in the hospital. During that time, my wife had delivered our baby. I was so thankful to be alive for the birth of my third son that I decided to name him Fung Seng. I said to my son: "This is because your father is still alive".[32]

It may have been that traumatic incident that gave Liem more courage to take big business risks later. A biographer of American tycoon Cornelius Vanderbilt once noted: "Close encounters with death have a reputation for transforming lives, for starting dramatic new departures."[33]

MOVING TO JAKARTA

In 1952, when Anthony was a toddler, Liem decided that the capital of the new republic offered better business opportunities. He relocated his family to Jakarta, leaving his brothers to look after their businesses in Kudus. Scores of Hokchia traders in Kudus, including friends of his, were already packing their bags for Jakarta. For Liem, his action was driven by a desire to make more money than simply relying on the slim margins in the trading business. For a Chinese trader who had not yet been allowed to acquire citizenship and who faced racial discrimination in his adoptive country, it was not an easy task. Moving to Jakarta did not guarantee success. He was just another struggling businessman. In the 1950s, Liem was a nobody. As his son Anthony acknowledged, his father was a "very small potato" in the Sukarno era.[34]

Their first "home" in Jakarta was the Hotel Chiao Tung (meaning communications) on Jalan Hayam Wuruk, in the heart of Chinatown (the hotel name was later changed to Wisata Dharma). At that time, it was considered one of the best hotels in the Pasar Pagi and Pintu Kecil area of Glodok, where many of the Chinese shops and businesses were located. From there, he moved to a house in Petojo and later, bought a one-storey house in Jalan Gunung Sahari VI. This was the house he kept largely unchanged over the years, so as not to disturb the *feng shui* — the elements that ensured his luck. Even after Liem became wealthy and he built a two-storey mansion beside the original house, he never undertook renovations of the old house.

Jakarta in the 1950s was a chaotic city. The author James Michener visited in 1951, the year before Liem moved there. He was researching the subject of the Chinese in Indonesia for *Life* magazine, in particular on the Chinese-owned trading firm, the Oei Tiong Ham Concern. In his piece, he described Jakarta as "a crowded, short-tempered city where some 3,000,000 persons are jammed into quarters intended for only 500,000. Of the 3,000,000 some 250,000 are Chinese". In his inimitable style, Michener wrote about the bustling activity along one of Jakarta's main streets, called by its Dutch name Molenvliet in those days (now Jalan Gajah Mada heading north and Jalan Hayam Wuruk heading south), which he described as one of the world's most distinctive:

> The street consists of two very spacious avenues separated by a wide, colourful, *café-au-lait* canal. It is a remarkable stretch of water, serving as sewer, bathing beach, laundry, playground and garbage repository ... At the foot of Molenvliet, where the canal jogs eastward, the Chinese-owned *tokos* [little shops] become a fascinating jungle called Glodok, one of Asia's memorable Chinatowns. Under broad awnings petty merchants

sell absolutely anything up to and including last year's model of the atomic bomb.[35]

The author noted the plethora of Communist books found in the many bookshops in Glodok, pointing out a "startling" one in Indonesian entitled *How to take over the land*, that had on its cover an enormous red arrow pointing crushingly down on a map of Indonesia. This was two years after the Communist victory in mainland China, and the nationalists (Kuomintang) had been driven out to Taiwan. The Totok community in Indonesia had conflicting loyalties. Liem was not ideologically driven and felt no affinity to the Kuomintang but he was not a supporter of the Communists either. During World War II, he was purely concerned about survival and did not take part in political activism. His ties were parochial; his attachment to his homeland was primarily to his village where his mother lived.

Liem's relatively unknown stature in Indonesian business circles in the 1950s — in fact, until the mid-1960s — is confirmed by prominent Chinese Indonesian businessman Sofyan Wanandi (Liem Bian Koen),[36] at one time the trusted aide of close Suharto advisors. According to Sofyan, "up until when Suharto came to power, Liem was nobody — he was a small fry."[37] As part of his ambition to branch out from trading, Liem acquired the licence of a knitting company in Semarang, which, not so strangely for those times, had a provision in its articles that allowed it to conduct banking activities. Liem quickly turned that company into a bank. He also started small factories producing nails and bicycle parts. He bought over a textile plant in Kudus named Muliatex, which started making a brand of singlet called "777" — digits adding up to Liem's lucky number of 21. (Anthony Salim says he still wears this brand of undershirt.) It was not until 1968 that he started Tarumatex, his other textile factory, in Bandung.

THE "NEW ORDER" IS ESTABLISHED

From the second half of the 1950s, political turmoil and tensions between competing parties and groups rose. There were major rebellions against Sukarno, one in Sumatra (PRRI, which stood for Revolutionary Government of the Republic of Indonesia) and another in Sulawesi (Permesta, a contraction of the Indonesian for '"Charter of Total Struggle").

The President accused the CIA, with cause, of backing them because of his opposition to the United States and his dalliance with China, the Soviet Union and the world's "Nefos" — short for "newly emerging forces". At home, Sukarno came under attack, especially from August 1957 when he announced the start of "Guided Democracy", which he would lead through enhanced powers. Three months later, in one of the six assassination attempts, eleven people were killed and at least thirty seriously injured in an attack while he was visiting his children's school in Cikini, central Jakarta. "An aide saved Sukarno's life by pushing him to the ground as the first of many hand grenades exploded", historian George Kahin wrote.[38] When investigations a few months later established that the CIA was supporting the PRRI rebellion, Sukarno became convinced that the agency was plotting his assassination.

By the early 1960s, Sukarno was seriously weakened by the deepening economic crisis and political conflict that plagued the republic. Academic Richard Robison summed up the situation leading to tumultuous 1965:

> The vacuum of power at both the social and the political level and the resulting entropy throughout the 1950s culminated in a political revolution from above, led by Sukarno with the support of the military. Parliamentary government was supplemented by an authoritarian regime, populist in style and corporatist in structure. However, the chaos was not over. Sukarno's political authority rested upon a highly personalised brand of patronage and charismatic populism that had neither an organisational nor a social base to sustain it. It led to a military takeover in 1965, and to the elimination of both Sukarno and the growing Communist Party (PKI).[39]

The murky events of the 30 September 1965 attempted coup, blamed by counter-coup leader Suharto on the communists, have been written about at length and hotly debated, particularly on why Suharto, then commander of the Army Strategic Reserve (Kostrad) was not on the coup-makers' list of targets. The murder of seven senior military officers, including six generals, was followed by the decimation of the PKI and the killing of hundreds of thousands of people accused — often by neighbours and acquaintances — of being leftists. The wave of killings that started after Suharto took charge continues to traumatize many Indonesians.[40] A combination of factors including a politically weakened Sukarno, confusion about the masterminds of the attempted coup, divisions in the armed forces, and a climate of fear and uncertainty contributed to Suharto's ascendancy to power. With surprising meekness — cowed perhaps by the unanswered questions of the brutal killings of the generals, the uncertainty of the political situation and the intimidating presence of three generals who appeared at his Bogor residence, Sukarno signed a letter on 11 March 1966 effectively transferring power to Suharto. This document is popularly referred to as Supersemar, a contraction for *surat pemerintah sebelas maret* (which stood for Letter of Instruction of 11th March). It was apt, as everyone knew that Suharto identified with Semar, the mythical god who was bumbling, but wise. The transfer of power from Sukarno to Suharto created a new government led by Suharto, Adam Malik and the Sultan of Yogyakarta, Hamengku Buwono IX.

Suharto, the consummate Javanese, adopted a typically Javanese approach in handling Sukarno — he was patient and guarded. The Javanese have a phrase that best describes this approach — *alon-alon asal kelakon*, which basically means, slowly but surely. Initially uncertain of the extent of support he had in the armed forces, he did not want to be too hasty in unseating the popular Sukarno.

There were factions in the military still considered loyal to the charismatic first president. Moreover, the PKI had grown roots in many areas. Thus Suharto would not be rushed. He consolidated power over the next two years: In March 1967, he was appointed Acting President by the MPRS (Provisional People's Consultative Assembly), and on 27 March the following year, he was sworn in for a five-year term as full president. Sukarno was put under house arrest. A sick and broken man, Sukarno died in June 1970.

Once in power, Suharto displayed cunning and ruthlessness in dealing with opponents. As historian John Legge wrote: "In the beginning, the New Order may have been cautious in establishing its authority, but within a few years the conciliatory approach it had adopted to all but the communists had begun to give way to a more authoritarian style."[41] Over time, Suharto turned more towards his close aides for advice, the military men who served with him in the Diponegoro command. Legge noted:

> The trend was plain enough by 1969. [Adam] Malik and the Sultan continued to hold ministerial office ... but their position as close confidants of Suharto was gone, and their places were taken by the circle of officers surrounding the President — his personal staff (Aspri) — especially Maj. Gen. Ali Murtopo, the head of OPSUS (Special Operations) and Maj. Gen. Sudjono Humardani who advised the President both on financial affairs

and personal, mystical ones. In a regime where constitutional procedures were only vaguely defined, the informal influence of a group of this kind with regular and easy access to the President became more important than the influence of those holding formal government office.[42]

Apart from getting a grip on political power, Suharto was poised to exert influence over another area close to his heart: getting into business. For Liem, who got acquainted with Suharto many years earlier but was not a friend at the time of the dramatic 1965–66 events, the creation of the New Order was real serendipity.

Notes

1. Interview with Liem, 6 May 2006.
2. Ian Verchere, "Liem Sioe Liong: Suharto's secret agent", *Insight*, May 1978.
3. Interview with Liem, 16 September 2006.
4. Twang Peck Yang, *The Chinese Business Elite in Indonesia*, pp. 254–55.
5. Also spelled Jogjakarta.
6. Teuku Mohamad Daud, "Recollections of My Career", in *Recollections: The Indonesian Economy, 1950s–1990s*, edited by Thee Kian Wie (Singapore: Institute of Southeast Asian Studies, 2003), pp. 254–55.
7. For details on the Big Five, see the excellent volume by Joost Jonker and Keetie Sluyterman, *At Home on the World Markets*.
8. Daud, "Recollections of My Career", p. 255.
9. Yong Mun Cheong, *The Indonesian Revolution and the Singapore Connection: 1945–1949* (Leiden: KITLV, 2003), pp. 122–23.
10. Ibid., p. 102.
11. Ibid., p. 118.
12. George McT. Kahin, *Southeast Asia: A Testament* (London and New York: Routledge, 2003), p. 45.
13. *Sukarno: An Autobiography*: As told to Cindy Adams (Hong Kong: Gunung Agung, 1965), p. 264.
14. Brian May, *The Indonesian Tragedy*, p. 74.
15. Richard Robison, *Indonesia: The Rise of Capital* (Sydney: Allen and Unwin/Asian Studies Association of Australia, 1986), pp. 36–37.
16. Among Hatta's relatives was prominent indigenous businessman Haji Ning (his stepfather), the grandfather of Hashim Ning. The West Sumatran family had a small trading business dealing with rubber, tea and coffee. Hashim Ning was an early *pribumi* beneficiary of political patronage, starting from his automotive dealership in the 1950s. He later became a partner of Mochtar Riady.

17. Twang, *The Chinese Business Elite in Indonesia*, p. 133.

18. Charles Coppel, "Patterns of Chinese Political Activity in Indonesia", in *The Chinese in Indonesia: Five essays*, edited by Jamie Mackie (Hong Kong: Heinemann, 1976), p. 41.

19. Pramoedya Ananta Toer, *The Chinese in Indonesia* (English edition) (Singapore: Select Books, 2008), pp. 177–78.

20. This translation is from the English edition, ibid., p. 89.

21. Robison, *Indonesia: The Rise of Capital*, p. 42.

22. Soedarpo Sastrosatomo, "Recollections of My Career", in *Recollections: The Indonesian Economy, 1950s–1990s*, edited by Thee Kian Wie, p. 154.

23. Thee, ed., *Recollections: The Indonesian Economy, 1950s–1990s*, p. 12.

24. Robison, *Indonesia: The Rise of Capital*, p. 45.

25. Sumitro was considered the "father" of Indonesian economists. His sons Hashim Djojohadikusumo and Prabowo Subianto became notable players in business and politics in the New Order. Hashim had interests in cement, coal-mining and other areas while Lt. Gen. Prabowo — at one time married to Suharto's second daughter — was for years commander of Kopassus (the "Red Berets"). His leadership ambitions were publicly known and became a source of tension with some of his superiors. As commander of the Army's Strategic Reserves (Kostrad) in 1998, he was accused of masterminding the violence in May 1998, which included the killing of protesting students at Trisakti University by snipers. Prabowo denied any role in the mayhem that contributed to the downfall of Suharto. In 2009, he ran unsuccessfully as a vice-presidential candidate under Megawati, the daughter of Sukarno.

26. Sumitro Djojohadikusumo, "Recollections of My Career", in *Recollections: The Indonesian Economy, 1950s–1990s*, edited by Thee Kian Wie, 2003, p. 59.

27. J. Panglaykim and I. Palmer, "Entrepreneurship and Commercial Risks: The Case of a Schumpeterian Business in Indonesia" (Singapore: Institute of Business Studies, Nanyang University Occasional Papers 2, 1970), pp. 32–33.

28. Robison, *Indonesia: The Rise of Capital*, p. 86.

29. David Jenkins, "Giving credit where it is due", *Far Eastern Economic Review*, 21 September 1979.

30. Sumit Mandal "Strangers who are not foreign", in *The Chinese in Indonesia*, by Pramoedya Ananta Toer, p. 38.

31. According to the Liem family tradition, the generation of Liem's sons should bear the given name starting with "Sin" (*Xin* in *hanyu pinyin*) as was the case for Anthony's two older brothers.

32. Interview with Liem, 22 April 2006.

33. T.J. Stiles, *The First Tycoon: The Epic Life of Cornelius Vanderbilt* (New York: Alfred Knopf, 2009), p. 93.

34. Interview with Anthony, 4 November 2007.

35. James Michener, "Chinese success story: In Southeast Asia, where communists are now trying to exploit old hardships, the Oei family is a monument to free enterprise", *Life*, 31 December 1951.

36. Sofyan and his brother Jusuf Wanandi were former student activists in the 1960s who became aides to Suharto's close advisors, generals Sudjono Humardani and Ali Murtopo in the early New Order period. Together with the two generals, they founded the influential think-tank Centre for Strategic and International Studies (CSIS). The brothers exercised significant clout in policy-making until they made the mistake of telling Suharto he should start thinking about grooming a successor, and they quickly fell into disfavour. Currently head of the business concern Gemala Group and others, Sofyan has been an informal spokesman for the Chinese Indonesian business tycoons.

37. Interview with Sofyan Wanandi, 17 September 2006.

38. Kahin, *Southeast Asia: A Testament*, p. 155.

39. Richard Robison, "Authoritarian states, capital-owning classes, and the politics of newly industrializing countries: The case of Indonesia", *World Politics* 41, no. 1 (October 1988): 52–74.

40. See Theodore Friend, *Indonesian Destinies* (Cambridge, MA: Belknap Press of Harvard University, 2003), pp. 111–13, for various estimates, including the U.S. embassy's figure 300,000; Ben Anderson's range of 500,000 to 1 million, and his own: half a million, give or take a couple hundred thousand.

41. John Legge, *Indonesia*, 2nd ed. (Sydney: Prentice Hall, 1977), p. 168.

42. Ibid.

4

CRUCIAL LINKS

Liem Sioe Liong never read Dale Carnegie, but for his ability to make friends and win the trust of influential people, he could have been a poster boy for Carnegie's best-selling work *How to Win Friends and Influence People*, first published in 1936, two years before Liem set foot in Java. Although he was not fluent in the language and knew little about Javanese culture, within a short time of his arrival, Liem was able to attract customers with his winsome smile and charming ways. As a supplier first to the independence fighters in the foothills of Central Java, then to the Diponegoro Division commanded by Suharto, Liem impressed his customers with his honesty and reliability. Among his Hokchia clansmen, he had a reputation for being trustworthy and discreet. Within a few years of his arrival in Java, he was entrusted with the responsibility of harbouring a political fugitive hiding from the Dutch when they were asserting their claim on the country after the Japanese surrender. It turned out that the fugitive was Hasan Din, a father-in-law to the republic's first president, Sukarno. Liem and Hasan Din became friends as well as business associates, of which more would be written about later.

Thirty years after Liem set foot on Java, he was scouting for big money to fund plans for his first huge venture, the flour milling business. Soon after, he needed fresh funds for the planned cement manufacturing. For this,

Liem had to go beyond the country's shores to obtain it. Two overseas Chinese tycoons played important roles in channelling funds as well as expertise. For flour, he turned to Malaysian Chinese Robert Kuok; for cement it was Thai-Chinese banker Chin Sophonpanich, a self-made tycoon who knew a thing or two about the importance of having powerful patrons. But to get to that stage, where he could undertake the role of the country's first industrialist, he would have had to earn the trust of the country's new leader Suharto, who became full president in 1968. Although Liem and Suharto had been acquainted since 1949, the Chinese businessman did not have steady contact with the general until after 1966, when Suharto seized power. For Liem's "anointment" into the privileged position of a *cukong*, he had members of the senior military men belonging to a group dubbed "Financial Generals" to thank.

THE MILITARY AND BUSINESS

In Suharto's New Order period, every Indonesian general worth his salt would have at least one *cukong* to partner with. The top brass needed the business acumen of the Chinese entrepreneurs to get funds, and in return gave them protection and privileges. It was a mutually beneficial relationship. Not that this was a uniquely Indonesian practice: all over Southeast Asia where the Chinese were a minority, close relationships with the military and bureaucratic elite had to be forged for survival and growth. Even in the Dutch colonial period, savvy Chinese businessmen such as Oei Tiong Ham knew the importance of cultivating the good graces of senior Dutch officials and officers. Oei's descendants in the post-colonial period failed to do likewise with emerging leaders in the new republic, and paid a heavy price for their negligence. They lost the company and all its assets in Indonesia when the government abruptly nationalized the firm.

Like other regimental commanders in the 1950s, Suharto was forced to be inventive to raise funds needed to make up for budget shortfalls. He proved particularly capable at this, reflecting his interest in business, but he was far from the only military officer who spent time mulling money-generating opportunities. The involvement of the "men in green" in business enterprises dates back to the 1957–58 period, when Indonesia kicked the Dutch out and seized their companies. With few bureaucrats to fill the managerial vacuum, the military was called on. Officers, despite their lack of experience, were mobilized to run appropriated companies, and the armed forces became associated with everything from shipping firms and airlines to hotels and timber concessions. When Sukarno declared the start of "Guided Democracy" in 1957, divisional commanders gained martial law powers, and one result was an open-door for generals to raise money for themselves or their units. With martial law in place, a journalist noted, "direct entrepreneuring became possible ... often a Chinese partner provided the bulk of the capital while the 'baju hijau' (green shirts, i.e. those in uniform) gave easy progress through or around bureaucracy and taxes."[1]

Business enterprises were the means for the military to augment its perpetually under-funded budget, and also a way to channel funds to the pockets of the underpaid soldiers and high-ranking officers. A Western military attaché was quoted by journalist David Jenkins as saying: "Somewhere over there at Hankam [Defence Ministry], there is a pot of gold which they dip into to meet their extra-budgetary needs."[2] Suharto proved particular adept at establishing foundations, or *yayasans*, to accept donations and channel funds for his various causes. Suharto had a special bond with those officers in charge of finance and economic sections (often referred to as Finek) in the military. Each regiment had its own Finek division. Officers who held these positions (usually assigned to the 7th Assistant) were not only in charge of the accounting but had to be inventive at developing ways to get money. Many of Suharto's financial generals held 7th Assistant positions.

Their growing role in the economy earned the armed forces accusations of abuse and scandals. An early case that warranted an investigation concerned Ibnu Sutowo, who was to become the powerful head of oil company Pertamina. In 1958, when he was still a colonel and the army's operations chief, Sutowo ordered the clearance of goods through the port of Tanjung Priok in order to effect payment in Singapore for military supplies. When Army commander Gen. A.H. Nasution, learnt about this, he temporarily suspended Sutowo from office. Nasution had appointed Sutowo, a medical doctor, to head the state oil firm Permina (established in 1957 and precursor of Pertamina) after the Dutch were kicked out. Despite his suspension from his army position, Sutowo was allowed to stay in his Permina job.[3] After Suharto came to power, Sutowo succeeded in turning the petroleum industry into his personal fiefdom, and used Pertamina money to fund much of the military's "extra-budgetary" needs, in the process making quite a few generals beholden to him. He became virtually untouchable. It was not until the mid-1970s, when he nearly bankrupted the country, that Suharto reluctantly dismissed him.[4] After that, Suharto turned more to his *cukongs*, and Liem in particular, to help fund his projects.

Suharto was not spared Nasution's critical eye. The Sumatra-born Nasution had a reputation of being less tolerant of financial shenanigans. In August 1959, Nasution ordered an investigation of regional commands for cases of corruption or illegal activities. It turned up evidence that Suharto, then commander of the Diponegoro Division, had been conducting barter trade, which was considered illegal. His "punishment" involved a transfer out from his command to the Army Staff and Command School in Bandung. Suharto's military career appeared not to have been damaged. Just a few months later, he was promoted to the rank of Brigadier General, and in 1962, to Major General and appointed to head the Mandala command, Sukarno's effort to "liberate" West Irian,[5] then still under Dutch control. In 1963, Suharto assumed command of Kostrad (Army Strategic Reserve Command) which had its own Finek section. This opened up more opportunities for the business-minded Suharto. He started a foundation at Kostrad the following year called Yayasan Dharma Putra Kostrad (YDP). YDP was particularly active in business after Suharto became acting president, partnering with Liem in various ventures. After 1966, with no one more senior than himself, Suharto had free rein to explore new horizons in business. To help consolidate his power, Suharto relied heavily on his coterie of "political" and "financial" generals. These officers exercised great influence over the patronage system. Academic Harold Crouch noted:

> They played a major role in determining appointments in both the military hierarchy and the government administration. Furthermore, they concerned themselves with the implementation of policy, particularly in such fields as foreign investment, the allocation of construction contracts, and the opening of other business opportunities that had implications for the smooth functioning of the patronage machine. Thus many officers were beholden to them for important appointments or profitable business opportunities, while officers still active in the military field looked to the president's advisors to ensure for them a bright future.[6]

SUHARTO'S GENERALS

To help anchor his hold on power, Suharto tapped multiple sources, but for advice, he relied heavily on those he knew well and trusted. His ascendency to the topmost office in the country was so sudden that he was ill-prepared. A political neophyte then, he had to surround himself with people mainly officers who had served with him. In August 1966, he created a circle of advisors dubbed Spri, short for *staf pribadi* (personal staff). Members were assigned different functions — politics, intelligence, finance and economy. Suharto biographer Elson noted that the formation of the trusted group was an organizational style closely attuned to his long experiences of military life, "when he had surrounded himself with a small and constant group of close associates, most of whom shared his Central Java heritage."[7] Spri members included generals Ali Murtopo and Yoga Sugama, who were responsible for intelligence gathering and political advice. The leader of the group was Gen. Alamsjah Ratu Prawiranegara, who cut his teeth in finance when he was in the Army Central Command. A wealthy officer, he was described by an academic as the "epitome of the military entrepreneur", for his string of ventures with Chinese businessmen.[8] Alamsjah cultivated good ties with the Japanese, who were keen to invest in Indonesia after the fall of the left-leaning Sukarno. Working under him and handling finance and economic matters were Maj. Gen. Sudjono Humardani and Maj. Gen. Suryo Wiryohadiputro, who later became one of the most active "business" generals working with the Chinese. Alamsjah, Sudjono and Suryo, together with a few others, were dubbed the "financial generals".

The one among them who had a special link to Suharto was Sudjono. He was said to have developed a relationship so close to the president that an aide once remarked that he was the only person besides Ibu Tien to be allowed into Suharto's bedroom.[9] Sudjono assumed an extra role — he was the president's spiritual advisor, his personal *dukun*. For the power and influence he exerted, he was dubbed "Rasputin" by the press. His endorsement of Liem — someone he knew from the 1950s — as a worthy candidate to become Suharto's *cukong* carried a lot of clout. Thereafter, Liem also became close to other senior military men, including generals Suryo and Sofjar (another important financial general of his day).

One of the most powerful of the political generals was Ali Murtopo, who worked closely with the financial generals as well as the major money-spinner in those days: Ibnu Sutowo. Murtopo played a big role in helping Suharto consolidate his power base. Head of Special Operations (called Opsus for short, a contraction of its Indonesian name), Murtopo was the president's ear on the ground. He gathered intelligence reports and devised political strategies — not hesitating to use thugs and strong-arm tactics to thwart and threaten any opposition or potential rivals. In the process, he earned a reputation of being one of the most feared men in the Suharto regime. Murtopo and Sudjono Humardani retained Suharto's trust and were reappointed to the president's inner circle called Aspri, or "personal assistants" after Suharto disbanded the earlier version, Spri, in 1968. (Gen. Alamsjah was dropped.) Detractors accused them of being a "kitchen Cabinet". Warranted or not, Murtopo acquired a reputation for being ruthless and manipulative. He was the president's "henchman extraordinaire" — the mastermind behind many of the New Order's political, strategic and military manoeuvres.[10] Murtopo stayed as Suharto's right-hand man for nearly twenty-five years. His close aide, the Catholic activist Liem Bian Kie, now better known by his Indonesian name, Jusuf Wanandi, defended his former boss as "bright and brave and unorthodox". Wanandi, his brother Sofyan and fellow activist Harry Tjan Silalahi got the backing of Murtopo and Sudjono to establish the think-tank Centre for Strategic and International Studies (CSIS). CSIS played an important role in formulating some early New Order policies, especially with regard to Irian Jaya and East Timor. Wanandi and his colleagues helped Murtopo plot the campaign to win the support of tribal leaders in Irian, as losing a U.N.-mandated plebiscite in 1969 on integration into Indonesia would have seriously damaged Suharto's credibility. They organized missions to help improve living conditions, and Murtopo sent to the remote region "tobacco, beer, food stuff, prefab houses, everything".[11] Journalist Bill Tarrant, who chronicled the history of the *Jakarta Post*, an English-language daily started by Wanandi with Murtopo's approval, said it was Wanandi who persuaded the general to abandon the tinted glasses that made him look like a "tinpot generalissimo".[12]

Sudjono Humardani — "Minister of Magic"

Among Suharto's clutch of advisors in the early New Order, few were as trusted as Maj. Gen. Sudjono Humardani. Born in Sunan Palace, Solo in 1919, Sudjono was of "true royal blood", wrote Suharto biographer Retnowati Abdulgani-Knapp.[13] One foreign journalist described him as a "slim, elegant figure with a fine, aquiline face under a great bush of hair", and possessing a "kind and serene nature". Sudjono, he wrote, "epitomised the elegant conjunction of mystic, economic and political skills aspired to by the Javanese statesman and courtier".[14] Many foreign journalists who did not understand the significance of Javanese mysticism in Suharto's mind — disparaged Sudjono as a "*dukun*" or shaman. He was described as "weird", greeting guests barefoot in a room lit with candles. One reporter wrote: "He once received a Western ambassador in darkened room, with objects that appeared to have occult significance looming in the dimness; he was wearing a kind of Javanese costume and glided about in bare feet".[15] One of the epithets given to him was "Minister of Mystical Affairs". His strong links to the Japanese were also panned.[16]

Sudjono's special relationship with the president stemmed from their shared spiritual guru, or master, Romo Diyat. This guru once told Sudjono to look after Suharto as it was predicted that one day he would become a great man.[17] Thus, it was said, Sudjono became 100 per cent loyal to Suharto. Abdulgani-Knapp commented: "It was easy to understand why a person like Suharto often listened to his spiritual advice. Sudjono believed that 'God gave a few humans *daya luwih* or greater ability, some to heal and a few to rule'."[18] Sudjono believed Suharto possessed that *daya luwih*, and served his senior loyally as Suharto rose through the ranks.

The *kebatinan* that Sudjono and Suharto practised is a search for the inner self, a search enhanced by prolonged periods of meditation, and in so doing, attain inner harmony.[19] Not a true religion, it is more a way of life "in which an individual seeks a more harmonious relationship with God, either alone or through a school. By developing inner powers, followers believe a man will be able to reach a higher state of consciousness. He will then be able to use this power for the ultimate good of the community," wrote a journalist.[20] Sudjono would take trips on Suharto's behalf to consult mystic priests in Java. Sofyan Wanandi, the general's close aide, told a journalist: "They would go to sacred spots, a cave or special lake. The mystic would go into a trance and tell the future ... Sudjono would make notes and report back to Suharto."[21]

Besides being a spiritual mentor, Sudjono also served Suharto well in the area of business. His proven track record in organizing the barter trade and running Suharto's foundations in the Semarang days put him in good stead as an invaluable member of the new president's team. Sudjono also had established strong bonds with several Chinese businessmen, including Liem, whom he had befriended from Central Java. Sudjono's strong interest in business dovetailed nicely with Liem's aspirations. He trusted the Chinese businessman whose sincerity and reliability left a good impression. Sudjono was the one who signed a letter of recommendation for Liem's application for citizenship. A friend of Liem said Sudjono never directly asked for money but accepted sacks of rice for the soldiers.[22] (As members of the board of Bank Windu Kencana, Sudjono and Gen. Suryo were entitled to a share in the bank's profits.[23])

Sudjono attended a Dutch business school in Semarang and in 1964, was sent to the United States for a ten-month course in finance at Fort Benjamin Harrison in Indiana. His strong tie to Suharto was established when he served under Suharto in the Diponegoro Division in the 1950s. At Suharto's behest, Sudjono worked with Bob Hasan in various business schemes, starting with the successful barter trade between Central Java and Singapore, exchanging the region's sugar for much-needed rice from Thailand, via Singapore. The profits were used to help farmers obtain fertilizers and seeds. In 1957, Suharto had set up two foundations — Fourth Territory Foundation (YTE) and the Fourth Territorial Development Foundation (YPTE) — to improve conditions for his troops and to help the region's farmers. At the end of that year, Sudjono returned from a stint in Bandung to become deputy head of Diponegoro Division's Finek section. Under him, the foundations developed rapidly.

Sudjono's skills in running the foundations cemented his ties with Suharto. These "fund-raising" apparatuses characterized the rent-seeking behaviour associated with much of the Suharto New Order. As noted by Elson: "the foundations placed levies on goods and services (such as ownership of a radio or use of electricity) and solicited contributions from companies and businesses." He noted that "under Suharto's prompting and Sudjono's tireless attention, the foundations began a rapid process of investment into private companies concerned with the distribution of primary commodities, in association with prominent business figures."[24] In 1957, Sudjono and fellow officers established ventures with interests in marketing, transportation and industry, and the next year, collaborated with Bob Hasan in setting up an inter-island shipping line, Pangeran Lines. "In such activities", continued Elson, "Sudjono and his military and civilian associates were allocated positions which entitled them to percentages of profits".[25]

Sudjono had been Alamsjah's deputy at Finek, Army Central Command, from 1963 to 1965. Six months after Suharto assumed control (following the March 1966 "Supersemar" letter signed by Sukarno transferring power to him), he dispatched Sudjono to the Netherlands, the United States and

Japan to seek "assistance in economic stabilisation".[26] Sudjono made Sofyan Wanandi manager of the Defence Ministry (Hankam)'s business venture, PT Tri Usaha Bakti (TUB). (Sofyan later established his own business ventures, among them the Gemala Group.) TUB was the largest military business enterprise at that time. Incorporated in 1969, it was the umbrella "to consolidate military business holdings".[27] Sudjono served as a director. At its peak, TUB had at least thirty companies, including a battery factory, an automobile assembling plant, clothing and shoe factories, rice mills, and forestry projects. It also operated a bank, Bank Gemari (later absorbed into Liem's PT Bank Central Asia or BCA), and owned an airline, Zamrud Airlines.[28] Profits were earmarked for the benefit of servicemen, retired military men and army widows. An example of TUB's activities was the building of 2,000 homes for low-ranking soldiers.[29] TUB made liberal use of Chinese partners to obtain capital for its ventures, and Liem was a principal one. According to Sofyan Wanandi, Sudjono was responsible for linking Toyota with William Soeryadjaya, whose Astra International became the country's largest car assembler. Sofyan said the general also facilitated the joint venture between Matsushita and *pribumi* Sulawesi businessman Thayeb Gobel, who was a pioneer in the electronics business.[30]

Sudjono later usurped Alamsjah's role as the go-to person for Japanese businessmen. Alamsjah's downfall was precipitated by a faux pas he committed shortly after Suharto was confirmed as full president in 1968. Suharto made Japan his first overseas destination. Briefed by Alamsjah, he expected his hosts in Tokyo to announce a massive financial aid package during his visit, but it did not happen and Suharto left, embarrassed. The blame fell on Alamsjah, who was responsible for the wrong signals. He was packed off to the Netherlands as ambassador. Sudjono stepped into his former superior's shoes. An embittered Alamsjah suspected Sudjono of planting doubts in Suharto's mind about him. He later passed a remark about his former protégé: "That Sudjono is crazy ... he is not intelligent ... he is just a *dukun*".[31]

One of Sudjono's first acts as the "anointed" Japanese intermediary was to negotiate for the release of two Indonesians arrested in Japan for violating currency regulations. The men were working for a subsidiary of PT Mantrust, whose founder, a Chinese Indonesian by the name of Tan Kiong Liep, enjoyed the patronage of Sudjono and other senior generals.[32] But Sudjono's influence extended beyond business; he was closely allied with political strategist Ali Murtopo. Their legacy lives on in the think-tank

CSIS. Until it fell out of favour with Suharto in 1988 (when Jusuf Wanandi wrote a memo suggesting that the president think about grooming a successor), CSIS played a vital role as a conduit to the "outside world". Jusuf Wanandi and Harry Tjan were the intermediaries to the international community, often explaining the country's positions to foreign diplomats and journalists. They also regularly sent Suharto memos with feedback and advice. Suharto read them faithfully until he was angered by the broaching of the taboo topic of succession.[33]

The Japanese, who became Indonesia's largest source of aid and investment, were enamoured of Sudjono, whom they quickly grew to trust. Prime Minister Eisaku Sato, Japan's leader from 1964 to 1972, described him as "the bridge between the two countries".[34] Sudjono was instrumental in getting construction restarted at the controversial US$2 billion Asahan aluminium smelting project in North Sumatra. The project, which also generated hydroelectricity, had been discontinued in 1963 after the withdrawal of the Russian team that was meant to help build it.[35] Sudjono's close links with the Japanese lasted until his death in a Tokyo hospital in 1986. High-ranking Japanese officials came to pay their respects to the man they considered "an intermediary without equal". For his funeral, the Japanese ambassador to Indonesia accompanied his body to its burial place outside Solo.[36]

In the arrogance of his later years, Suharto denigrated the contributions of Ali Murtopo and Sudjono. Of Murtopo, he wrote:

> When he was alive, some people thought that Ali Murtopo was the man who decided everything. Why? Perhaps because he was a good speaker, courageous, and as my special assistant, he was supposedly very close to me and they thought that everything depended on him. Thinking along these lines, people thought that the government could make no decision without him.... this just wasn't true. The proof? After Ali Murtopo died, the government went on as usual. If we had been dependent on him, then after his death, the government would have come to a halt. It was not true that everything depended on him.[37]

As for Sudjono, the president commented:

> I had heard people say that he knew more about mysticism than I did, but Djono himself used to do the *sungkem* (pay his respects) to me. He regarded me as his senior who had more knowledge about mysticism ... Some people say mysticism is doing this or that which you can learn

from a guru. But to me, mysticism is a way to be near the One Almighty God. It is true Djono often came to see me with a book full of notes. He believed in spiritual teachings and in that capacity, he often gave me advice. I just listened to make him feel good, but did not take in everything he said. I analyzed it and thought about it to see if it made sense or not. If it was reasonable, if it made sense, I would accept. If it didn't, I would not follow his advice. So those who thought that Djono was my guru in mysticism had it wrong.[38]

Jusuf Wanandi, an early supporter of Suharto and Murtopo's right-hand man, found the president's remarks about his two loyal military aides ungracious and dishonourable. He defended Murtopo, often portrayed as a "mere hatchet man", someone without scruples with only blind loyalty to his boss, whereas in fact, he wrote, the general was a man "committed to Indonesia, who saw Suharto with all his faults, and who had a conscience … He had one obsession: how to make the Indonesian people modern, progressive and well-developed."[39] Murtopo and Sudjono, said Wanandi, thought only about the state and the nation, nothing for themselves. "For Pak Djono, it was all for Pak Harto", he wrote.[40]

Suryo — A Friend to All *Cukong*

Maj. Gen. Suryo had long experience in finance from the days of the revolution when he was in charge of army finances. His links with the president were forged in the early 1960s when he served under Suharto in the Mandala command to "liberate" West Irian. Suryo was friendly to the *cukongs*, including Jantje Liem, and became an early patron of Liem Sioe Liong. "Whenever Liem was short of money in the early days, he would call Gen. Suryo, who would make arrangements to help him out", said someone who knew Liem well.[41] Suryo was reappointed to Aspri and made in charge of Finance and Economy. His responsibilities increased after the sudden death in 1973 of another financial general, Brig. Gen. Sofjar, taking over the latter's position as 7th Assistant at Kostrad. He was also chairman of State Audit and director of the President's "Team to Regularise State Finances", a body tasked with supervising the redistribution of the assets of confiscated enterprises.

Another *cukong* who was very tight with Suryo was Ong Seng Keng, a Jakarta businessman whose Indonesian name was Arief Husni. Ong, a Hokchia like Liem,[42] had good ties to Gen. Yani, the army commander killed in the 1965 abortive coup. Suryo was said to have introduced Ong to Suharto in 1966. At the opening of Ong's Ramayana Bank in 1970, Suryo read a speech on the president's behalf, reflecting the good relationship he had established with Suharto.[43] Ong, who died in an accident in 1974, was implicated together with Suryo, in a fraud case in 1970–71 over a shipment of fertilizers ordered, and allegedly paid for, from Taiwan, but which never arrived in Jakarta. Suryo was also close to oil czar Ibnu Sutowo, and to Achmad Tirtosudiro, head of the revamped state logistics agency Bulog from 1967 until 1973 (when scandals and mismanagement led Suharto to send him to Germany as ambassador). Suryo served as president-director of government-owned Hotel Indonesia, and was given permission to build two hotels in Jakarta — the Mandarin and Hilton.[44] Liem became a shareholder in the Mandarin, while the Hilton (more recently called the Sultan) was owned by Sutowo's family.

Sofjar — Kostrad's Money Man

Suharto's last position before becoming president as head of Kostrad meant he gave special attention to its foundations. Richard Robison wrote that of all the military units in the post-1965 period, Kostrad was "most closely associated with that group of officers which came to dominate the positions of real power and influence under the New Order". Robison noted that with Suharto's rise, YDP, as well as the Chinese businessmen most closely associated with him during his period as commander of the Diponegoro Division and Kostrad, notably Liem and Bob Hasan, "were to experience a rapid rise".[45] It was Suharto who assigned Kostrad's Finek chief Brig. Gen. Sofjar to work with Liem. A Minangkabau from Sumatra, Sofjar was responsible for the activities of two foundations, YDP and a smaller one called Trikora. YDP's coffers received a substantial boost after the establishment of Liem's wheat milling plant, PT Bogasari, as the foundation, together with Suharto's wife's Harapan Kita (Our Hope) foundation, were stipulated by Bogasari's articles of association to receive 26 per cent of the profits of the company.[46]

Not all of the military-run companies were successful; in fact, many stalled. A bank called Windu Kencana was established in May 1967 under the ownership of military-linked foundations, with an authorized capital of Rp10 million. The four "financial generals" at the time held the top positions: Sofjar (then a colonel) was President Director; Alamsjah was

Director; Suryo and Sudjono were the Chairman and Vice-Chairman respectively. The shareholders were listed as the foundations YDP, Trikora, and Jayakarta.[47] Later, Liem was asked by Suharto to get involved. Liem subsequently injected capital in the bank, and he and his younger brother and their families became the principal shareholders. Windu Kencana was able to capitalize on its "impeccable political connections", and channelled funds to the foundations for business development, including airlines (Seulawah and Mandala) and forestry, as well as a small trading company and even film production.[48] Sofjar's business reach was further extended when he became chairman of the Indonesian Chamber of Commerce and Industry, known as Kadin. While he was still a colonel, Sofjar was allocated a 25 per cent share in the Volkswagen sole agency, PT Garuda Mataram, a company formed from assets appropriated from a Guided Democracy period business. The company was a joint venture involving Kostrad and Opsus together with the Mantrust group, and was the largest company in the YDP stable. Holding the position of Director at Garuda Mataram was Sudjono's right-hand man, Sofyan Wanandi (Liem Bian Koen).[49] Sofjar's important business role came to an abrupt end in 1973 when he fell ill and died. The fortunes of the YDP group waned shortly after.

THE MALARI INCIDENT

Ali Murtopo's position as one of the most powerful men in the early New Order was dented following a highly public rivalry with another ambitious general, which led to the first serious political challenge to Suharto. The rivalry between Murtopo and Gen. Sumitro, deputy commander of the armed forces, culminated in riots in January 1974 during the visit of the Japanese Prime Minister Kakuei Tanaka, in what became known as the Malari[50] incident. Unhappiness over rising food prices, rice shortages, and the growing power of Suharto's personal assistants had been stewing for more than a year. The number of business ventures undertaken by Chinese businessmen with high-ranking military men continued apace, and it was apparent that the president was clearly taking no action at the widespread corruption. At the same time, foreign capital was flowing in, most visibly by the Japanese, who were courted by Suharto's financial advisors.

The Japanese had been taking a more high-profile role in the country, providing up to one-third of Indonesia's foreign economic assistance. An academic noted: Japanese aid was "large and visible, and that much of it was tied to the purchase of goods manufactured in Japan was widely known and criticised. It was assumed ... that the principal aim of the aid was to develop markets for Japanese products."[51] The growing presence of the Japanese in Indonesia sparked resentment against the influx of foreign capital. The fact that many Japanese firms partnered Chinese businessmen in ventures gave critics added fuel.

But the Malari Incident had its roots in the intra-military struggle between Ali Murtopo and Sumitro, who also held the position as head of the powerful and feared public security agency Kopkamtib (Operations Command for the Restoration of Order and Security). Sumitro was a stocky, in-your-face military man. From East Java, he had never been accepted in Suharto's inner circle, which comprised mainly officers from Central Java. He was said to have become resentful of the growing influence of the Aspri group and in particular, of Ali Murtopo and Sudjono. He aligned himself with reform-minded officers in the Defence Ministry and courted students protesting against corruption. While touring a campus at the end of 1973 he had declared that "a new style of leadership was needed".[52] Meanwhile, some media kept up the drumbeat against corruption and the Japanese lobby (now personified by Gen. Sudjono). *Indonesia Raya* and *Tempo* ran critical articles. Mochtar Lubis, editor of *Indonesia Raya*, who had been leading the charge, wrote in an editorial: "We feel that it is extremely damaging and dangerous for Indonesia to allow Sudjono Humardani to continue to play his role as this unofficial channel."[53]

While Malari had no direct impact on the Chinese *cukongs* such as Liem, in Indonesia, public anger is often easily channelled into protests against the Chinese, and it was no different this time. Anti-Chinese riots broke out in Bandung, where some 1,500 shops and houses were damaged. As tensions escalated, Suharto summoned Sumitro and the Ali Murtopo group to a meeting at the Palace on New Year's eve. A chastised and emotional Sumitro denied he was mounting a challenge to Suharto's leadership. The president had Sumitro and Murtopo appear at a joint press conference two days later to deny a rift in the armed forces. If that quelled the public rivalry between the two factions, it failed to dampen the whipped-up emotions of the students who continued with their demonstrations. They protested outside Murtopo's office, calling him a "political pimp" and burnt an effigy of Sudjono.[54] On 15 January, coinciding with Tanaka's visit, a huge crowd demonstrated rowdily near the state guest house where the Japanese leader was staying. Rioters targeted Japanese cars, Toyota showrooms and a Japan Airlines operated hotel. Eleven people were killed and nearly 200 seriously injured in the riots. Tanaka had to be flown by helicopter to the airport.

The government arrested more than 800, many of them students. But fallout to both Sumitro and Murtopo was lasting. Two weeks later, Sumitro was dismissed as Kopkamtib chief and later forced to resign his armed forces position. In the showdown with his rival, he had lost. Ali Murtopo's standing took a beating as well. He would later be appointed Minister for Information, which although a Cabinet position, did not accord him the power he was accustomed to having. The president abolished Aspri in late January and moved to address some of the complaints raised, including corruption. In a meeting with senior journalists, he denied that his wife had dealings with large businesses.[55] Soon after Malari, Suharto introduced regulations that were more nationalistic in orientation and stiffened requirements for foreign investments. He also sought to rein in the ostentatious lifestyle of the wealthy.

The incident led to the rise of another general who would undertake a significant political and advisory role until the late 1980s. It was Benny Murdani, once Murtopo's assistant and intelligence protégé. Suharto had him recalled from his posting in South Korea, and installed him in the Defence Ministry. Murdani would supplant Murtopo as the president's top henchman. Murtopo's dominance over politics suffered a further blow after the downfall of his good friend and chief financial supporter Ibnu Sutowo, who is said to have funded Opsus and other operations. Murtopo died of a heart attack in 1984. Jusuf Wanandi, who worked for Murtopo, wrote in his memoirs, that "just how close Malari came to open war has never been fully explored. But I know for a fact it came closer than most people assume."[56] After the incident, Wanandi said, Suharto trusted no one but himself.

CRUCIAL LEG-UP FROM OUTSIDE INDONESIA

To become a real big-wig in the business world, Liem realized, he could not merely be content to rely on the patronage of Indonesian generals. Access to capital is also essential. And if a businessman were to start in manufacturing, he would need expertise. Liem's ability to use his network to get both was the crucial factor in determining his success. Having the backing of the Indonesian president was an effective calling card for the network of Overseas Chinese tycoons. Critical among them was Thai-Chinese banker Chin Sophonpanich, who opened his bank vault and made vital connections for Liem, and Malaysian Robert Kuok, who provided him with know-how as well as took a share in Liem's flour business.

Chin Sophonpanich acquired a legendary status as godfather to many Southeast Asian Chinese tycoons. As chairman of the Bangkok Bank, he provided loans that enabled entrepreneurs like Kuok and Thai-Chinese Dhanin Chearavanont (a fellow Teochew) of the giant agribusiness — later telecommunications — Chareon Pokpand Group to become multinationals. Another early 1970s era businessman who received Chin's assistance was Singapore-based shipping tycoon Robin Loh, who got lucrative shipping contracts due to his friendship with Ibnu Sutowo. For Chin, Liem was a natural bet, a sure winner. What Liem had going for him was his proximity to power. And Liem was close to the very top. Chin Sophonpanich picked his beneficiaries carefully. They went on to become the richest men in their respective countries at one time or another. Chin, who knew the importance of having patronage and building links, came upon Liem when he was sniffing opportunities to grow the bank beyond Thailand's shores. With the instincts of a seasoned and successful gambler, he placed bets on those who impressed him with their business acumen. Businessmen who had strong ties with important or powerful figures were also a good bet. Chin became a pivotal figure in a network of ethnic Chinese business moguls in Southeast Asia, connecting one to another. The number of member moguls was not large, but the clout was. In 1991, *Institutional Investor* magazine said of the "fellowship": "This extraordinary group constitutes a powerful regional network — informal though pervasive, with local variations but essentially stateless, stitched together by capital flows, joint ventures, marriage political expediency and a common culture and business ethic."[57] Liem, who became good friends with the Thai banker, acknowledged the invaluable assistance that Chin provided in the early days.[58] His son Anthony added:

> I think a lot of people's success was due to Chin's help. Robert Kuok was also close to Chin, in the beginning. Then everybody took off ...
> [In those days] they were not eligible to borrow from Citibank or Bank of America. I remember my father told me he started to borrow a few hundred thousand dollars from Bangkok Bank at that time.... In 1967 when we bought our first house in Katong [in Singapore], I think for

S$42,000 — I was studying in Singapore. It had seven or eight rooms, the old house, not the one now that we have now — we borrowed money from Bangkok Bank.[59]

Chin, better known in the Chinese community as Tan Piak-chin, was born in 1910 in Thonburi, across the Chao Phraya River from Bangkok. He rose from proverbial humble roots to become a real wheel of fortunes in Southeast Asia. Like the majority of Thai Chinese, Chin was a Teochew; his father, a clerk, migrated to Thailand from the Swatow (Shantou) area, on the coast of China's Guangdong province. At age five, Chin was sent to Hup Sua, the father's home village for education, returning to Bangkok when he was 18. A diligent worker, he took on all kinds of work in the early days, starting as a shop apprentice, cook, and then clerk. His sharp mind did not escape his superiors, and it destined him for greater glory. He eventually started a lumber company. Chin's flair for numbers pivoted him towards the field of finance. In 1944, he helped found Bangkok Bank and became its president in 1952. Chin was smart and a natural numbers guy. His son Chatri once remarked: "You could give him a set of figures today and in a few years later he could still recall them."[60] Long-time Bangkok Bank executive and director, Vira Ramyarupa, labelled Chin a mathematics "genius". Chin's instincts told him he needed to build connections to political power to fulfil his ambitions. And in those days, that was equated to the generals. He became an important ally of the Thai military clique led by Field Marshall Phin Choonhavan that seized power in a 1947 coup. Chin was very close to Phin's son-in-law, the feared director-general of the police, Phao Sriyanonda, who many believed ran an opium-smuggling syndicate. Phin lost power in 1957 when a rival, Field Marshal Sarit Thanarat staged a coup. Vulnerable after his patron was pushed out, Chin exiled himself to Hong Kong and stayed out of Thailand until 1963. (In 1954, he opened a Bangkok Bank branch in Hong Kong, which became his base during his years in exile.)

Driven by his desire to grow the bank, Chin didn't sit around twiddling his thumbs in Hong Kong. He used his time to travel around the region, broadening his network and expanding business with Chinese traders. He made loans to people that state-owned or foreign banks would not have anything to do with at the time, often simply based on his instincts. Bangkok Bank opened a branch in Jakarta in 1968 and Liem met the Thai banker shortly after. Liem remembered Chin fondly, describing his friend as a "good man".[61] Kuok once described Chin's modus operandi: "He didn't wait for you to go see him ... he wanted to see how you operated, how you placed your desk, the sense of drive in the office."[62] Liem and Chin shared many attributes of the typical Chinese tycoon and got on well. Both were amiable and liked mixing business with pleasure. Knowing Liem's almost nightly jaunts to the Blue Ocean nightclub in Jakarta's Hayam Wuruk district, Chin supplied a steady stream of beautiful singers from the region. Liem recalled visiting Bangkok in the early 1970s, accompanied by his wife and mother-in-law. The Thai banker insisted on taking Liem out for a night of carousing, to somewhere he deadpanned, which was "not a place to take wives". What should I do with my wife and mother-in-law, Liem asked his Thai host. "Order *mee goreng* (fried noodles) from room service!" came the reply. Liem exclaimed: "Are you joking!" to which Chin half-jokingly retorted: "Never be afraid of your wife!"[63]

Chin played an instrumental role in Liem's cement business, introducing him to a Taiwanese cement manufacturer who provided the technical know-how. Chin himself also took a stake in one of the cement plants, and had a seat on the board. "I am indebted to Chin", Liem acknowledged.[64] When Chin died in January 1988, at age seventy-seven, Liem and a contingent of Chinese tycoons from the region went to Bangkok to pay their respects. Attending the last day of Chin's elaborate funeral rites were Thailand's King Bhumibol and Queen Sirikit, signalling the important role Chin played in Thai business.

The other entrepreneur who had a long relationship with Liem was Robert Kuok Hock Nien. Now a regional businessman with a slew of ventures from the luxury hotel brand Shangri-La to the diversified Kerry Group and Hong Kong's *South China Morning Post*, Kuok started off as a commodities guy in Malaysia.[65] A *Forbes* magazine cover once described him as "the world's shrewdest businessman".[66] Kuok provided Liem with the crucial expertise in getting wheat-miller Bogasari started. He took equity in the venture, though in the names of others, as he was not Indonesian. Kuok's point man in Liem's enterprise was Sumatran-born Piet Yap, who recalls Liem seeking him out to help fulfil a rice order by Suharto in 1967.[67] It was the beginning of a long-lasting relationship between Kuok and Liem. Kuok's father was Hokchiu, being from Fuzhou, the capital of Fujian province.

Unlike Liem and Chin, Kuok received high-quality formal education, with a Bachelor's degree from the prestigious Raffles College in Singapore where his fellow students included future Singapore leader Lee Kuan Yew as well as future Malaysian prime ministers Tun Abdul Razak and Hussein Onn. Kuok spoke eloquent English, which helped his career. He was born in 1923 in Johor Baru, the Malaysian city that is separated from Singapore by a one-kilometre causeway. His father migrated from China to British-run Malaya, and eventually became a rice and sugar trader in Johor. When World War II ended, the British who reasserted control of Malaya, gave Kuok's father a contract to supply fresh produce to Japanese prisoners-of-war interned at a rubber estate in Johor. The family later was appointed distributor of essential foodstuffs for part of Johor. The diligent and serious Robert was given the job to manage its warehouses. In 1948, when Robert was twenty-five, his father died. The following year, family members created Kuok Brothers, which traded rice, sugar and flour. Robert, the youngest of three brothers, soon took charge. Eldest brother Philip became a diplomat and, after Malaysia became independent in 1957, was its ambassador to several countries. Middle brother William took a very different path, joining the Malayan Communist Party to try to liberate the Malayan Peninsula from British colonialists. He was killed by British troops in the jungle in 1952.

Kuok went to London for a period of years during the 1950s and later based himself in Singapore, an entrepôt for commodity trade. He decided to give most attention to sugar, which he worked on in Britain and which was in greater demand than local supply in Southeast Asia. For dealing with British-controlled sugar trading companies, Kuok had an advantage over many Chinese traders in Asia. "The sugar trade was conducted in English, which put me in a stronger position", he once said. "I was reading Reuters."[68] In 2011, Kuok threw light on why, very early on, he saw sugar as a good opportunity. In a rare interview — Kuok almost never talked to the media — he explained his attraction to sugar to China Central Television (CCTV). "If children threw tantrums at night, the adults just needed to give them some sugar and they would remain quiet", he said. Unlike with petrochemicals, Kuok added, there was always demand for granulated sugar, which was so cheap that it could easily be profitable. "So the simplest and wisest business to get rich in was the sugar refinery business", Kuok said.[69]

For his dominance in sugar refining and trading in Southeast Asia — work that put him in contact with Liem and Indonesia's commodity regulator Bulog — Kuok was billed "the Sugar King". But he told CCTV that he did not like that epithet, preferring the other more contemporary one of "Hotel King". But even then, he said, "the word 'king' is just a fake one".[70] The title comes from Kuok's creation of the Shangri-La hotel chain in Asia and beyond, including London and Paris. Salim, which had benefitted greatly from Kuok's help in getting Bogasari flour mill up and running, was a co-investor in the Shangri-La Jakarta, which opened in 1994. Kuok, who was much liked by Beijing after completing the World Trade Centre in the Chinese capital following the 1989 crushing of pro-democracy protests in Tiananmen, made China his biggest horizon for expansion. According to the Shangri-La website, in 2012, there were 108 hotels worldwide under the Shangri-La umbrella; 55 were in China.[71]

Before building up Shangri-La, Kuok moved his base from Singapore to Hong Kong. Kuok bought out Rupert Murdoch's controlling share of the *South China Morning Post*, a business move that had to have pleased Beijing. One major factor behind Kuok's success was that he felt at home wherever he was. "I adapt like a chameleon to the particular society where I am operating at the moment", he told *Forbes* in 1997. In that article, he also shared some of his business philosophy. "You think you're a smart businessman, but you must realise that many people are smarter than you", he said. "If there are smarter people — stronger, better horses running [then] why aren't you putting some of your money on them and not all of it on yourself?"[72] Anthony Salim, who eventually had some friction with Kuok over Bogasari, praised him as a gentleman. "I really respect him, and I learnt a lot from him, as a person and businessman", Anthony said. "A lot of people have money; he has a lot of wisdom. There aren't many people like him."[73]

Notes

1. Hamish McDonald, *Suharto's Indonesia* (Australia: Fontana, 1980), p. 30.
2. David Jenkins, "Military Budgets: The Military's Secret Cache", *Far Eastern Economic Review*, 8 February 1980.
3. McDonald, *Suharto's Indonesia*, p. 31.
4. See Box 7.1 on Pertamina in Chapter 7.
5. Now called Papua in the Reformasi (post-Suharto) period.
6. Harold Crouch, *The Army and Politics in Indonesia* (Ithaca, NY: Cornell University Press, 1978), p. 308.
7. R.E. Elson, *Suharto: A Political Biography* (Cambridge: Cambridge University Press, 2001), p. 145.

8. Crouch, *The Army and Politics in Indonesia*, p. 243.

9. Related by Sofyan Wanandi, and quoted in Bill Tarrant, *Reporting Indonesia: The Jakarta Post Story, 1983–2008* (Singapore and Jakarta: Equinox, 2008), p. 43.

10. See Ian Chalmers and Vedi Hadiz, eds., *The Politics of Economic Development in Indonesia: Contending Perspectives* (London: Routledge, 1997), p. 73.

11. Tarrant, *Reporting Indonesia*, p. 41.

12 Ibid., p. 33.

13. Retnowati Abdulgani-Knapp, *Soeharto: The Life and Legacy of Indonesia's Second President* (Singapore: Marshall Cavendish, 2007), p. 87.

14. McDonald, *Suharto's Indonesia*, p. 131.

15. Brian May, *The Indonesian Tragedy* (Routledge & Kegan Paul, 1978), p. 293.

16. See Michael Malley, "Soedjono Humardani and Indonesian-Japanese Relations, 1966–1974", Indonesia Issue, Cornell, No. 48 October 1989, p. 61.

17. Jusuf Wanandi, *Shades of Grey: A Political Memoir of Modern Indonesia, 1965–1998* (Jakarta: Equinox, 2012), p. 229.

18. Abdulgani-Knapp, *Soeharto*, p. 88.

19. See Lee Khoon Choy, *Indonesia: Between Myth and Reality* (Singapore: Federal Publications, 1977), pp. 180–90.

20. David Jenkins, "Power of the Mystic Lobby", *Far Eastern Economic Review*, 31 March 1978.

21. Tarrant, *Reporting Indonesia*.

22. Confidential interview, Singapore, 10 August 2006.

23. Elson, *Suharto: A Political Biography*, p. 162.

24. Ibid., p. 63.

25. Ibid.

26. See Malley, "Soedjono Humardani and Indonesian-Japanese Relations, 1966–1974", p. 48.

27. Richard Robison, *Indonesia: The Rise of Capital* (Sydney: Allen and Unwin/Asian Studies Association of Australia, 1986), p. 259.

28. Crouch, *The Army and Politics in Indonesia*, p. 283.

29. Paul Handley, "Onward business soldiers", *Far Eastern Economic Review*, 24 October 1985.

30. Adam Schwarz, *A Nation in Waiting: Indonesia's Search for Stability*, 2nd ed. (St Leonards, NSW: Allen & Unwin, 1999), p. 108.

31. Malley, "Soedjono Humardani and Indonesian-Japanese Relations, 1966–1974", p. 53.

32. Mantrust, founded in 1967 by Tan (also known as Teguh Sutantyo) and a partner, was a major supplier of goods to the army. In 1970, it was one of several companies investigated by an anti-corruption panel, the Commission of Four, set up by Suharto under pressure from students and activists.

33. See Wanandi, *Shades of Grey*, pp. 230–33.
34. Malley, "Soedjono Humardani and Indonesian-Japanese Relations, 1966–1974", p. 58.
35. See Elson, *Suharto: A Political Biography*, p. 217.
36. Malley, "Soedjono Humardani and Indonesian-Japanese Relations, 1966–1974", pp. 61–63.
37. *Soeharto: My Thoughts, Words and Deeds; An Autobiography*, as told to G. Dwipanyana and Ramadhan K.H. English translation (Jakarta: Citra Lamtoro Gung Persada, 1991), pp. 378-79.
38. Ibid.
39. Wanandi, *Shades of Grey*, p. 226.
40. Ibid.
41. Confidential interview, Singapore, 10 August 2006.
42. Leo Suryadinata, "Chinese economic elites in Indonesia", in *Changing Identities of the Southeast Asian Chinese since World War II*, edited by Jennifer Cushman and Wang Gungwu (Hong Kong: Hongkong University Press, 1988), p. 275.
43. May, *The Indonesian Tragedy*, p. 220.
44. David Jenkins, *Soeharto and His Generals: Indonesian Military Politics 1975–1983* (Ithaca: Modern Indonesia Project, Cornell University, 1984), p. 25.
45. Robison, *Indonesia: The Rise of Capital*, p. 263.
46. State Gazette, 7/8 1970, No. 258.
47. State Gazette No. 74, 1968.
48. Elson, *Suharto: A Political Biography*, p. 193, and see Robison, *Indonesia: The Rise of Capital*, p. 263.
49. Robison, *Indonesia: The Rise of Capital*, p. 248.
50. A contraction for *Malapetaka Lima Belas Januari*, meaning the "January 15 Disaster".
51. John Bresnan, *Managing Indonesia: The Modern Political Economy* (New York: Columbia University Press, 1993), p. 148.
52. McDonald, *Suharto's Indonesia*, p. 136.
53. David T. Hill, *Journalism and Politics in Indonesia: A Critical Biography of Mochtar Lubis (1922–2004) as editor and author* (London: Routledge, 2010), p. 105.
54. McDonald, *Suharto's Indonesia*, p. 137.
55. Elson, *Suharto: A Political Biography*, p. 201.
56. Wanandi, *Shades of Grey*, p. 118.
57. Henny Sender, "Inside the Overseas Chinese Network", *Institutional Investor*, 1 September 1991.
58. Interview with Liem, 16 September 2006.
59. Interview with Anthony, 14 October, 2007.
60. *Chin Sophonpanich: In memoriam, 1910–1988; The Man and His Dream* (Bangkok: Business Review (*The Nation*), 1988).

61. Interview with Liem, 13 May 2006.

62. Andrew Tanzer, "The Amazing Mr Kuok", *Forbes*, 28 July 1997.

63. Interview with Liem, 13 May 2006.

64. Interview with Liem, 16 September 2006.

65. The country was still called Malaya when he got started in business.

66. *Forbes*, 28 July 1997.

67. Piet Yap, *The Grains of My Life* (Singapore: Piet Yap, 2010), p. 44.

68. Tanzer, "The Amazing Mr Kuok".

69. The interview, in Mandarin, was posted by a viewer on YouTube. The interview's content was reported by *The Star* newspaper in Malaysia. (Ng Si Hooi, "Down-to-earth tycoon", *The Star* (Malaysia) 18 September 2011).

70. Ibid.

71. <http://www.shangri-la.com/shangrila/find-a-hotel> (accessed 3 September 2012).

72. Tanzer, "The Amazing Mr Kuok".

73. Interview with Anthony, 17 October 2010.

5

THE SCENT OF MONEY

Clove, the aromatic spice used to flavour the popular Indonesian *kretek* cigarette, may resemble a nail, but over this humble flower bud, wars have been fought, and fortunes made or lost. For Liem, it was trade in this spice that helped him lay the groundwork for the path to riches. Called *cengkeh* in Indonesian, cloves were found originally in the five remote islands in Eastern Indonesia known as the Spice Islands. In the late eighteenth century, some seedlings were smuggled to Africa, where they flourished in the soils of Madagascar and Zanzibar (today part of Tanzania). Ironically, cloves that were grown there yielded buds of a preferred quality for use in the production of *kretek,* the clove-infused cigarette beloved by Indonesian smokers. But importation for the spice was tightly controlled by the government, and suppliers had to be purchased from middlemen in Singapore and Hong Kong, making them immensely wealthy. When Indonesia was not producing sufficient quantities for domestic demand, politically connected companies were granted permission to import from the African countries, starting in the Sukarno era. In 1965, using a company founded by his partner, Hasan Din, a father-in-law of President Sukarno, Liem secured a one-time permission to bring in 3,000 tons from Africa. That single import helped ease his debt burden, and he became convinced there was big money to be made in this business.

Traditionally, *kretek* have been hand-rolled; the fragrance of the clove said to be further enhanced when rolled by young women using the sides of their hips. *Kretek* consumption surged in the 1970s following the introduction of machines to roll the sticks, bringing down price per stick. Around 90 per cent of the cigarettes consumed in Indonesia are *kretek*. From being an industry that was in doldrums in the 1950s, *kretek* manufacturing began its resurgence and in the last decade or more, the owners of the largest *kretek* manufacturers consistently rank among the wealthiest in the country. The cigarette industry is the largest contributor to the country's excise coffers. So addicted are Indonesian smokers to their *kretek* that at the height of the 1997–98 financial crisis, sales of the scented cigarette actually rose — an indication that people were willing to forgo other luxuries but not their puff, or that they felt they needed it more, to soothe their woes. Until the 1980s, when Indonesia once again became self-sufficient, and improved the quality of the spice, licensed clove importers stood to make a very handsome profit, even if the margin they were allowed to make was modest. Liem, who in the late 1960s was one of two people permitted to import cloves, recalled years later that it was easy money, even though by regulation, the profit margin for importing cloves was set by the government at 2 per cent.

HISTORY

In the late 1960s, when *kretek* consumption was burgeoning, domestic production in Indonesia was less than 10,000 tons, far behind demand of between 30,000 to 40,000 tons.[1] Indonesia — the world's largest clove consumer — dictated global prices of the spice. A foreign journalist in 1987 noted: "Indonesians used to call cloves the gamblers' crop. Such was the price that a farmer could earn more in one year from 20 mature trees than the national per capita income."[2] In 1981, when clove prices were 9,000 pounds sterling a tonne, Zanzibar and Madagascar supplied US$120 million worth of cloves to Indonesia. Up until the mid-1980s, clove shipments to Indonesia from those two countries accounted for up to 70 per cent of their foreign exchange earnings. At the time, clove cultivation was the livelihood of more than a million small-holders in Indonesia, and two million farmers in the two east African countries.

During the "Guided Economy" under Sukarno, *kretek* factories faced unreliable supplies of cloves and extreme price fluctuations due to unpredictable import controls set by the government and poor distribution. So tightly regulated was the industry that even moving shipments within the country needed official permission. Enter the droves of clove smugglers, on the hunt for a fast buck. Some reports say Liem was also involved in smuggling cloves from the Moluccas, where they were grown, to Kudus, the home to *kretek* production.[3] Liem was no stranger to cloves and *kretek*. From 1938 to 1952, he lived in Kudus. In the late nineteenth century, a local resident by the name of Haji Jamhari, suffering from chronic asthma, discovered that clove oil helped relieve his cough.[4] An inveterate smoker, he hit on the idea to crush some cloves into the tobacco that he rolled in dried corn husks. Tobacco and corn grew plentifully around Kudus. The corn husks used for wrapping the tobacco and crushed cloves crackled as they burned, giving rise to the name *kretek*, which is said to resemble the crackling sound. The fragrance of the cloves soon found a following and a cottage industry sprung up in Kudus.

However, sourcing the needed cloves from another part of the archipelago was no easy street. The business of supply was never cut and dried. In the 1950s, at least three separate bodies were given a monopoly to import cloves, at different times.[5] Licences to import cloves were granted to politically well-connected individuals. Until October 1953, supporters of the Wilopo Cabinet held it, and subsequently those who supported the Ali Sastroamidjojo Cabinet got it.[6] It was common for government ministers to use the existing import licensing system to buy political support.[7] The import and distribution of cloves during this period was so unreliable that a large amount was smuggled to Java not only from the Moluccas, but also from Sumatra and North Sulawesi, where the spice had also been introduced. A researcher noted that the average price soared ten times between 1949 and 1953.[8] From the 1950s, indigenous *kretek* producers in Kudus were gradually displaced by Chinese manufacturers in Semarang, Surabaya and Malang, who also ventured into production of non-clove sticks known in Indonesia as "white" cigarettes. The Chinese were able to capitalize on their connections and easier access to credit — therefore they were able to create a better distribution network. Another factor in their favour, as pointed out by an academic, was the "greater trust within the Chinese group, which is related in turn to the fact that the Chinese are more committed to business as a way of life. The Chinese ethical code makes it easier for the Chinese *kretek* manufacturers to borrow the funds necessary to tide them over periods of high clove prices and other adverse conditions."[9] In Suharto's New Order, especially in the 1970s, the *kretek* industry was given a boost by various factors — a government policy to push transmigration, which relocated thousands of Javanese to the outer islands, thus spreading the taste for *kretek* throughout the archipelago; an oil boom, and importantly, the introduction of machinery to enable *kreteks* to be machine-rolled. With a duopoly created for clove imports, supplies to the *kretek* industry stabilized, enabling a more efficient production schedule.

Until the 1970s, hand-rolled *kreteks* were a cottage industry. Most of the Kudus-based *kretek* manufacturers were small. An exception was PT Djarum — one of the "Big Four" manufacturers.[10] Djarum's founder, Oei Wie Gwan, was a friend of Liem's. As Liem recalled, during the Dutch days, Oei operated a factory producing firecrackers. According to Liem, the Dutch, having difficulty differentiating between enemy fire and exploding firecrackers, banned their production and shut the factory down.[11] Oei turned to *kretek* manufacturing in 1951 after buying the licence to the brand. Starting with just ten workers, he built Djarum to become a successful *kretek* maker until his death in 1963. The company was left to his two sons, Michael Bambang and Robert Budi Hartono. (In an interesting twist of developments, Djarum later bought control of Salim's flagship Bank Central Asia (BCA) in the aftermath of the 1997–98 financial crisis.) Liem was also friends with the late Surya Wonowidjojo (Tjoa Ing Hwie) who in 1958 founded PT Gudang Garam, in Kediri (170 kilometres from Kudus). Surya, also a Hokchia, was born in China in 1925 and arrived in Indonesia when he was still a child.[12] His father ran a small provision shop in Madura, but after his death, Surya moved to Kediri to work in his uncle's *kretek* factory. When he set up his own factory, it was in a former salt warehouse, hence he named his company Gudang Garam, literally "salt godown". Thanks to his business savvy, Gudang Garam fairly quickly established itself as the largest *kretek* producer.

Before Liem and Suharto's half-brother were granted the duopoly to import cloves, CV Berkat, a company run by an Indonesian Chinese named Yap Swie Kie held the import monopoly. Yap (Soetopo Jananto) was close to one of Suharto's generals. (Yap's loss of the clove monopoly was compounded by his loss of the Mercedes sole agency to Ibnu Sutowo, but they did not dent his fortunes as he had extensive forest concessions.[13]) Those fortunate enough to be granted the rights to import cloves were virtually ensured of an easy fortune; it was no wonder many lobbied to have a piece of the pie. After Indonesia became self-sufficient, fortune-hunters still racked their brains to think of money-making schemes from the *kretek* industry. The last, most egregious attempt was made by the youngest son of President Suharto, Hutomo Mandala Putra (Tommy), in 1990. His clove monopoly, BPPC (described in a later chapter) was a debacle, causing havoc to *kretek* producers, suffering to farmers, and costing the government millions of dollars.

THE DUOPOLY

In the 1960s, African cloves were being imported into Indonesia mostly by way of Singapore and Hong Kong. Indonesia was taking up to 90 per cent of the clove output of the two Indian Ocean islands, and paying the middlemen handsomely. Then Trade Minister Sumitro Djojohadikusumo[14] sought to create a direct trade link with the African suppliers and thus enhance Indonesia's bargaining power by consolidating its buyers. He felt that there was no reason that traders in Singapore and Hong Kong should profit from Indonesia's clove trading. Sumitro favoured a monopoly to be given to a *pribumi*-owned company. He had made it a personal mission from the 1950s to promote *pribumi* interests. In the matter of the clove import, he wanted to give the import monopoly to PT Mercu Buana, a company started by Suharto's half-brother Probosutedjo and even lobbied against giving Liem a role in the clove import business. But Liem had influential Suharto advisor Sudjono Humardani on his side. An added plus for Liem was his previous experience in importing the spice. In the end, Suharto placated both sides by allowing both to import, effectively creating a duopoly, with Mercu Buana sharing import rights with Liem's PT Mega.

In 1968, Sumitro signed a decree designating the two companies as exclusive importers of cloves for Indonesia. The import price and their selling price in the domestic market would be set by the government, with both companies guaranteed a 5 per cent commission of what they brought in. The rest of the profits were to be funnelled into a special fund administered by the president for contributions to hospitals and other personal philanthropy. The commission to the two companies was subsequently adjusted to 2 per cent.[15] The profit obtained from the import of the spice, plus the other licence Liem obtained — that of flour milling in 1969 — "served as the stepping stone for Liem's spectacular rise in the mid-1970s as the richest tycoon in Indonesia".[16] The initial clove imports provided Liem "with stable annual revenues averaging US$340,000 between 1968 and 1970, and US$1.2 million between 1971 and 1980".[17] Official statistics from data collected (from Indonesia's statistics office) showed that clove imports amounted to US$654.2 million from 1971 to 1982. A 1978 feature on Liem by *Insight*, a Hong Kong magazine, claimed that he "even imported from China some Zanzibar cloves in 1975, which the Chinese government had earlier received as payment-in-kind for its construction of the Tazara (Tanzania to Zambia) railway. China being Indonesia's sworn enemy, this affair indicates how special Liem's privilege was."[18]

PT Mega

Liem's clove trading vehicle was PT Mega, a trading firm founded in 1950 by Hasan Din. Liem's contact with Hasan Din came during the revolutionary years, when he was asked by the Hokchia clan association in Kudus to provide shelter to an unnamed political figure hiding from the Dutch. Liem had by then already built a reputation among his fellow clansmen as a reliable and discreet businessman. He readily agreed despite not knowing the identity of the guest. It turned out to be Hasan Din, the father of Sukarno's young bride, Fatmawati. Liem got on well with the "Datuk" (the honorific Hasan Din was called) and they became firm friends.

Hasan Din was born in the West Sumatra city of Padang in 1905. He became a religious leader in the Sumatran town of Bengkulu; from 1939 to 1952, he was chairman of board of Muhammadiyah, an Islamic education organization started in Yogyakarta, and a director of Indonesian Muslim Bank (Bengkulu 1946). Hasan Din ran a school in Bengkulu, where the Dutch exiled Sukarno in 1938. Hasan Din enlisted Sukarno to teach at his school, where one of the students was his own teenage daughter, Fatmawati. Sukarno, at that time married to his former landlady who was much older than him, fell in love with the pretty student who was twenty-two years his junior. In 1943, he married her. It was Fatmawati who stitched the red-and-white Indonesian flag that was hoisted when her husband proclaimed independence in August 1945. Sukarno considered her Indonesia's first First Lady, though she was far from his last wife. (She died in 1980, from a heart attack as she was returning home from performing the *hajj* in Mecca.) Hasan Din introduced Liem to his son-in-law, but the Chinese businessman only had a cordial acquaintance with the country's first president and did not enjoy any special favours. Liem recalled that

Sukarno loved entertaining and said he was a guest at several functions.[19] Contrary to popular belief, it was Liem who introduced Hasan Din to the military officers of the Diponegoro division who served under Suharto, and not the other way around. Of his friendship with Hasan Din, Liem had this to say: "Datuk was a nice man. When I met him, I felt *senang* (happy). He brought me *hokie* (good luck)."[20] Hasan Din became Liem's first *pribumi* business partner, and held board or director positions in several of Liem's companies, including BCA. Hasan Din remained a business partner until his death in 1974. PT Mega, Hasan Din's trading company, was set up with a friend named Oei Tjeng Hien, a Chinese Peranakan Muslim from Bengkulu also known as Haji Abdul Karim.[21] The company was named after Hasan Din's young granddaughter, Megawati — the eldest daughter of five children Sukarno and Fatmawati had. (In 2001 — more than fifty years after Liem sheltered Hasan Din from the Dutch — Megawati Sukarnoputri became Indonesia's fifth president.) Liem eventually bought over Hasan Din's share in PT Mega. Liem's close relationship with Hasan Din did not secure Liem special privileges from Sukarno, except for a special single clove import shipment which he was allowed in 1965. Still, that single deal made a difference to his cashflow.

Liem's involvement in PT Mega was not officially recorded until the 1970s, when he and his two brothers Sioe Kong (Soedarmo Salim) and Sioe Hie (Soehanda Salim) became citizens and could be officially listed in company records. Official records in 1974 listed Liem and his two brothers as President Commissioner and directors of PT Mega, respectively, while Hasan Din was President-Director and Abdul Karim remained a Director.[22] It was not until 1979 that an official listing was made of the original two shareholders as having sold all their shares to Liem and his brothers.[23] A state gazette in 1982 listed Abdul Karim as president director of the company, with Liem retaining the position of President Commissioner (equivalent to chairman) while his younger brother Soedarmo (Sioe Kong) and older brother Soehanda (Sioe Hie) were director and commissioner, respectively. The company's authorized capital was increased from Rp10 million to Rp1 billion. The shareholders were listed as Liem and his two brothers.[24] Liem always regarded PT Mega as having brought him luck. He refused to have the company deregistered even after it became almost dormant following changes in the 1990s to the clove import regulations and increased domestic production brought to imports to zero in 1986.

Probosutedjo's Mercu Buana

PT Mercu Buana was established by Suharto's half-brother Probosutedjo (Probo for short), his wife and associates in 1967.[25] Probo had moved his family to Jakarta when Suharto became de facto President. (He and Suharto shared the same mother.) Born in Yogyakarta in 1930, Probo moved to Medan, North Sumatra, in 1951 where he worked as a teacher. While in Medan, he set up two companies with friends, but it was not until Suharto became acting president that Probo's business fortunes rose dramatically. Probo was personally not close to Suharto, but as a family member of the president, he became a sought-after candidate for the Ali-Baba (Chinese plus *pribumi*) business arrangement; some Chinese entrepreneurs hoping to have doors opened for lucrative government contracts saw an advantage in having him as a partner. One long-time business partner of Probo's, from the early 1970s, was Agus Nursalim of the Kedaung Group. One of Asia's largest glass and ceramic-ware manufacturers, Kedaung also owned companies engaged in shipping, stainless steel manufacturing, packaging and animal feed production. Probo was once also involved with the late Hokchia businessman Ong Keng Seng (Arief Husni) in Bank Ramayana. He also had an automotive venture, started in 1977, with General Motors in PT Garmak. Later business associations included Eka Cipta Widjaja's Sinar Mas Group and the Jan Dharmadi Group. In 1984 he joined Gudang Garam's Surya Wonowidjojo[26] to establish a joint venture producing cigarette paper.

Despite partnering multiple Chinese Indonesians in business, Probo was a vociferous critic of what he considered the privileged position enjoyed by ethnic Chinese tycoons. He stepped up the rhetoric especially after he became head of Kadin (Chamber of Commerce and Industry). He was believed to be jealous of the cozy relationship Liem had with his half-brother, but refrained from openly antagonizing the Salim Group. However, Probo showed his prickly side whenever it was implied that he got special favours for being related to the president or when his exclusive rights to import cloves was called a monopoly. In a 1976 interview with *Kompas*, a leading Indonesian newspaper, he asserted: "No, the import rights was not instructed by the president, but by the then Trade Minister [Sumitro].... in fact, Pak Harto said: 'better not to give it to Mercu Buana, because it belongs to my brother, or people will presume that I facilitated it'."[27]

In his autobiography published in 2010 entitled *Saya dan Mas Harto* (Me and Brother Harto), Probo relates how he got into the clove import duopoly:

> It seems Mas Harto [Suharto] had directed Liem Sioe Liong to be the importer. However, Pak Soemitro [the trade minister] felt there shouldn't just be one party as licensed importer. In the end, he proposed me. At the beginning, Harto rejected me to be a part. He had more trust in Liem, seen as able and experienced in clove imports. Mas Harto knew Liem was a clove importer while he [Suharto] was in Semarang. It seems Liem's success was still in Mas Harto's mind. Nonetheless, Pak Soemitro firmly [backed me] as I'm also capable. In the end, Mas Harto agreed. According to Pak Soemitro, I and Liem are considered to already understand the channels and in-and-outs of clove-importing activities.
>
> This trust was not without limits. Our scope of work was only as an importer, temporarily the right to trade cloves was in government's hands. We just collect a fee from purchasing services to Madagascar and Zanzibar of 2 per cent. We agreed. Then officially PT Mercu Buana, which I led, and PT Mega, Liem's company, became official clove importers in the name of Indonesia. The guidance for this formally came through Minister's Decision No. 332/Kp/XII/70 of 31 December 1970. In that said letter, it is divided that Mercu Buana becomes the handling agent for cloves in East Java, and Mega becomes the handling agent for cloves for Central Java. All the performance that we do was monitored tightly by the Trade Department on the basis on Minister's Instruction No. 45/M/INS/XI/70 that came out 27 November 1970.
>
> This opportunity sounds like a gift from God. However, look at the heavy responsibility behind it. It wasn't easy to negotiate clove imports from Zanzibar and Madagascar ... also, there was a need to urgently develop clove plantations domestically so that there's sufficient supply for the needs of cigarette factories, and the price can be put under pressure.[28]

In 1990, Probo filed a Rp50 billion defamation suit against business analyst Christianto Wibosono after the latter stated at a university seminar that Probo "became rich because the government gave him a special licence to import cloves."[29] Probo stated that he merely received a 2 per cent fee for the imports, which in 1986 amounted to only Rp116 million (US$63,000) out of a total of Rp9 billion (US$4.8 million) profit, the rest being channelled to what a paper called "the presidential war-chest to finance the so-called presidential aid".[30] Wibisono apologized, ending the case. The following year, Probo also threatened to sue an Indonesian academic Yahya Muhaimin, whose doctoral dissertation for the Massachusetts Institute of Technology also stated that PT Mercu Buana had exclusive rights (together with PT Mega) to bring in cloves from Africa. The thesis entitled "Business and Politics: Indonesia's Economic Policy 1950–1980" was translated into Indonesian and published by a social research institute, LP3ES (Lembaga Penelitian, Pendidikan dan Penerangan Ekonomi dan Sosial). A journalist reporting on the complaint said: "Probo focused on the description of his licence as a 'monopoly' — which surprised observers given that his exclusive licence to import cloves is a matter of historical record. According to Probo's lawyer, his client believed he was performing a 'mission' for the country by importing cloves, not capitalising on a business monopoly."[31] "How do you distinguish between a mission and a monopoly in a court of law?" asked the publisher who was also being sued. The issue was settled after the author agreed to modify the wording in future editions and made an apology. Although his readiness to settle before the case reached the courts was criticized by some fellow academics, it was said that Muhaimin was worried that "going to court against Probosetudjo would eventually pit him against Suharto".[32] (Probo stayed in the news before and after Suharto's fall. In November 1997, his Bank Jakarta was one of sixteen banks closed by the government, enraging Probo, who started an action to sue Finance Minister Mar'ie Mohammad.)

During the presidency of Susilo Bambang Yudhoyono, Probo came under investigation for corruption. Probo's case centred on the misuse of government reforestation funds. An audit of forestry taxes in the Reforestation Fund undertaken in 1998 found that in the preceding five years, some US$5.2 billion was lost to corruption (including inflated budgets for projects funded by the fees, and overstating areas to be planted in order to receive larger subsidies from the fund), inefficiency, and tax evasion.[33] A court case against Probo involving alleged losses of US$10 million grabbed public attention not only because of his high profile, but because he unabashedly stated that he had disbursed Rp16 billion (about US$1.6 million) in bribes to pay off judges and court officials, including those at the Supreme Court who were handling his appeal against conviction.[34] Probo, who never faced a charge for bribing the court, was sentenced to a four-year jail term in the forestry case, ordered to pay a Rp30 million fine, and to return the funds to the state.[35] In 2008, shortly after Suharto's death, he was released after serving two-thirds of his sentence.

SUHARTO DEFENDS THE DUOPOLY

The clove duopoly was a lightning rod for critics. Academic Ross McLeod, discussing the topic of corruption during the New Order, had this to say:

> Early on, [Suharto] realised the effectiveness of private sector monopoly privileges for generating rents. The earliest prototype emerged in 1968 — the first year of the New Order... (with the government giving rights of imports to just two firms)... such monopolies usually had some spurious national interest rationale for the sake of appearances, but in the absence of a free press and an effective parliament, few voices were raised in opposition to them.[36]

Profits from the clove imports, minus the commissions for the two companies, were channelled to the scheme called Banpres, a contraction for Bantuan Presiden, meaning literally, presidential help, for Suharto to dispense as he pleased. This was one of the ways he generated extra-budgetary funds and kept people beholden to him. When the criticisms of the duopoly persisted, Suharto eventually felt compelled to defend it. He wrote in his autobiography that it did not bother him that people blamed him for creating the duopoly considering the large amount it raised for Banpres. The funds were deposited in state banks and only the interest was used by Banpres, he clarified. He added: "if only the public knew [of the small percentage of profit that the companies were allowed to retain] their reaction [anger] would be different ... the two companies each received only two per cent of the profits, while the rest went to Banpres. From each company, Banpres was able to get hold of Rp250 billion."[37] The biggest recipient from the Banpres largesse was a Jakarta military hospital, which received Rp40 billion. Other beneficiaries included a motley mix comprising small-scale agricultural schemes, livestock farming, and even political parties (other than Golkar, which received funds directly from another Suharto foundation).

Suharto dwelt on the subject of the duopoly at some length in his autobiography. In an attempt to quell speculation that he enriched himself with the funds generated from the clove imports, he wrote: "I myself do not keep the money; I only make the decisions."[38] He elaborated:

> From each of these two enterprises, we have received Rp123 billion, or a total of Rp246 billion. This money is also deposited and the interest

used. As long as we continue to import cloves, the fund will continue to grow ... Once, the clove project was made an issue. 'That's a monopoly,' people said. I just let them talk. We knew that profits from the clove trade were substantial, but the two companies only received a 2 per cent fee. The companies — Mercu Buana and Mega — had invested their own capital for the projects, mostly from bank loans which had to be paid back with interest.

In 1985, we ran short of cloves and had to import 10,000 tons. Only 300 tons were sold. Previously the price was $8,000 a ton; then the price dropped to $3,000 a ton. We had to protect the people's clove market. So I ordered to sell the imported cloves for Rp10,000 per kilogram, minus expenses; the total cost became Rp5,000. We were able to deposit Rp5,000 per kilogram in the Presidential fund. The imports of 3000 tons brought in three million times Rp5,000, or Rp15 billion ... using money from the fund, we were able to purchase equipment for hospital ICU units ... I am convinced that these methods have helped the government's financial position and thus aided in accelerating the development process ... It is true this is possible because of my [presidential] position. But I have to find the way. What is clear is that this is not for me personally. All this is for development.

From the Presidential Fund alone, we have spent Rp250 billion, not a small amount. And perhaps this is why some people are suspicious and wonder how much I get, whereas, in fact, I have never touched this money, let alone asked for it. It is I who have established the foundations. It is I who have looked for the money. I have not received any fee whatsoever from these foundations. Instead, sometimes I use my own money for some project. What for? Well, for example, when meetings are held in my home, I have to bear the costs.[39]

By 1986, soaring domestic production effectively put an end to clove imports by PT Mega and PT Mercu Buana, although the decree creating the duopoly was never officially rescinded. By 1990, the limelight on the clove industry turned to Tommy Suharto.

Notes

1. Sudharmono's contribution in *Di antara para sahabat: Pak Harto 70 tahun* [Among Friends: Pak Harto's 70th], edited by G. Dwipayana and Nazaruddin Sjamsuddin (Jakarta: Citra Gung Lamtoro Persada, 1991), p. 17.
2. John Murray Brown, "Commodities and agriculture: The politics of Indonesian cloves", *Financial Times*, 20 August 1987.

3. Shin Yoon Hwan, "Demystifying the capitalist state, political patronage, bureaucratic interests, and capitalist-in-formation in Suharto's Indonesia", Ph.D. thesis, Yale University, 1989, p. 330.

4. For a comprehensive history of *kretek*, see Mark Hanusz, *Kretek: The Culture and Heritage of Indonesia's Clove Cigarettes* (Jakarta: Equinox, 2000).

5. Richard Robison, *Indonesia: The Rise of Capital* (Sydney: Allen and Unwin/Asian Studies Association of Australia, 1986), pp. 49 and 58.

6. Ibid.

7. Sumitro Djojohadikusumo, "Recollections of my career", *Bulletin of Indonesian Economic Studies* (Canberra) 22, no. 3 (December 1986): 27–39.

8. Shin, "Demystifying the capitalist state", p. 330, fn 182.

9. Lance Castles, *Religion, Politics and Economic Behavior in Java: The Kudus Cigarette Industry* (New Haven: Yale University, 1967), p. 88.

10. The others were Gudang Garam, Sampoerna, and Bentoel.

11. Interview with Liem, 23 December 2006.

12. Leo Suryadinata, "Chinese economic elites in Indonesia", in *Changing Identities of the Southeast Asian Chinese since World War II*, edited by Jennifer Cushman and Wang Gungwu (Hong Kong: Hongkong University Press, 1988).

13. Robison, *Indonesia: The Rise of Capital*, p. 279.

14. Educated in the Netherlands, Sumitro was regarded as the "Father of Indonesian economists". He started the Faculty of Economics at the University of Indonesia. Sumitro was exiled after throwing support behind a rebellion against Sukarno. He was invited back from exile and appointed trade minister by Suharto in 1968. Sumitro died in 2001.

15. Keputusan Menteri Perdagangan No. 332/Kp/XII/70, dated 31 December 1970, appointed Mercu Buana as handling agent for cloves in East Java; and PT Mega for Central Java. Accessed from <www.tokohindonesia.com>.

16 Shin, "Demystifying the capitalist state", p. 351.

17. Yuri Sato, "The Salim Group in Indonesia: The development and behavior of the largest conglomerate in Southeast Asia", *Developing Economies* XXXI, no. 4 (December 1993), p. 411.

18. Ian Verchere, "Liem Sioe Liong: Suharto's secret agent", *Insight*, May 1978.

19. Sukarno's love for a good time is legendary; he acknowledged as much in his autobiography: "I perform best in front of an audience and often one visitor will share some gossip, or another offer the latest joke ... My capacity for joy is boundless. I can sing and dance until three a.m. and I can outplay anyone..." (*Sukarno: An Autobiography*: As told to Cindy Adams (Hong Kong: Gunung Agung, 1965), pp. 290–91). Liem recalled being present at one of the many parties hosted by Sukarno, when he was made to sing. "I couldn't sing, and didn't know any Indonesian songs. Luckily, there I had a lady singer friend also present and I asked her to sing with me. We sang the song *Burung Kakatua* [a well-known Indonesian children's song about the cockatoo]."

20. Interview with Liem, 22 April 2006.

21. See Michael Backman, *Asian Eclipse: Exposing the Dark Side of Business in Asia* (Singapore: John Wiley, 1999), p. 114.

22. State gazette 352/1974 for PT Mega.

23. "Kuasa dan risalah rapat PT Mega", No. 145, 19 January 1979; see also TBN RI, 23 April 1982.

24. State Gazette No. 491/1982 on minutes of meeting of PT Mega.

25. State Gazette No. 137/1968; Akta Notaris No. 14, 13 June 1967; cited in Yahya Muhaimin, *Bisnis dan Politik: Kebijaksanaan Ekonomi Indonesia, 1950–1980* (Jakarta: LP3ES, 1991), p. 252.

26. Surya died in 1985.

27. "Keterangan Probosutedjo mengenai usahanya", *Kompas*, 29 September 1976.

28. Probosutedjo, *Saya dan Mas Harto: Memoir Romantika Probosutedjo* [Me and brother Harto], With Alberthiene Endah (Jakarta: PT Gramedia Pustaka Utama, 2010), pp. 400–401.

29. *Indonesian Observer*, 10 March 1990.

30. *Indonesian Observer*, 12 March 1990.

31. Adam Schwarz, "Raising the stakes," *Far Eastern Economic Review*, 6 June 1991.

32. Ibid.

33. "Wild Money: The Human Rights Consequences of Illegal Logging and Corruption in Indonesia's Forestry Sector", Human Rights Watch Report, 2009, p. 11.

34. "Probosutedjo admits to bribing judges", *Jakarta Post*, 12 October 2005.

35. "Probosutedjo put behind bars", *Jakarta Post*, 1 December 2005.

36. Ross McLeod, "Suharto's Indonesia: A better class of corruption", *The Indonesian Quarterly* 28, No. 1 (2000), p. 100.

37. *Soeharto: My Thoughts, Words and Deeds; An Autobiography*, as told to G. Dwipanyana and Ramadhan K.H. (English translation) (Jakarta: Citra Lamtoro Gung Persada, 1991), p. 292.

38. Ibid.

39. Ibid., p. 250.

6

"GANG OF FOUR"

The partnership that became the most powerful business group during Suharto's time started from very modest premises. In the late 1960s, when the four men — Liem, Sudwikatmono, Djuhar Sutanto and Ibrahim Risjad — began working together, their office was a non-airconditioned room measuring 8 × 6 metres on the top floor of a nondescript building in the heart of Jakarta's Chinatown. One had to hoof it up four storeys to get to the austere office at Number 20 Jalan Asemka, as there were no elevators. Initially, the room had only one desk and two chairs. There was a single telephone, and even that line was shared with another office. Sudwikatmono, or Dwi, as he was often called, recalled that in the early days, when the four partners had their meetings, two of them would be standing while two sat. Dwi remarked that the highly superstitious Liem was always reluctant to make changes that might affect his luck or disturb the good *feng shui* of a room or building.[1]

IN THE BEGINNING

The conglomerate that arose from those humble beginnings, usually simply called the Salim Group, was essentially a Suharto creation. At the very least, he played the role of midwife in its birth. After all, he put Liem together with Dwi, and suggested Liem team up with Djuhar. Match-making business partners seemed to be an activity the new leader liked to make time for. He got his financial generals working on ventures with Chinese businessmen. In 1967, a Sukarno-era trading company, Hanurata, got new shareholders — two of his *yayasans*, Trikora and Harapan Kita. Liem Sioe Liong provided the capital and was asked to run it. Suharto also installed his brother-in-law in the company and arranged for his cousin Dwi to be there. The successful pairing of Liem and Dwi was a Suharto initiative, but other business match-making propositions did not work out so well.

Liem Sioe Liong was a relative newcomer to the Suharto inner sanctum; as mentioned earlier, two other Liems preceded him: Jantje Liem and Liem Oen Kian (Djuhar Sutanto). Suharto suggested that the three Liems joined forces. They tried but it didn't last. The two Totok, Liem and his compatriot Djuhar, both Hokchia who knew each other from Central Java, did not find the Peranakan Jantje Liem compatible to work with. Their personalities, cultural background, and business visions were different. Jantje Liem was Dutch educated and non-Chinese speaking. "Jantje was happy doing trading while Liem wanted to go into manufacturing", said a Jakarta business consultant, who knew all the parties.[2] The Totok Liems and Jantje then decided to part company. Liem and Dwi got on fine, but encountered problems working with Ibu Tien's (Mrs Suharto) brother in Hanurata. Djuhar, meanwhile, split with his Hokchia partners and joined Liem and Dwi, bringing along his *pribumi* associate Ibrahim Risjad. This quartet formed what became known in the Indonesian media as the "Four Friends" or "Four Pillars", but the moniker that stuck was "the Gang of Four", an epithet made famous by Mao Zedong's wife, Jiang Qing.

Djuhar was already in partnership with four Hokchia friends and they had a trading company called CV Waringin. When Liem Sioe Liong entered the picture, Djuhar's business partnership was fraying from a scandal involving a bank it operated. In 1968, Liem injected capital into Waringin, took it over and reorganized it as a limited liability company, PT Waringin Kencana (meaning "golden banyan tree"). *Waringin*[3] is a Javanese word for the thick-trunked banyan tree, a symbol of strength and longevity in Southeast Asia as it offers shelter from rain and the intense tropical sun. The Buddha attained enlightenment while sitting under a banyan tree. In Indonesia, it took on a political association after Golkar, the organization that became Suharto's political machine, adopted it as its symbol. (Formed in 1964 while Sukarno was still president, Golkar — a contraction of Indonesian words that translate as the awkward-sounding "Functional Groups" — was started by army brass who wanted to consolidate non-government bodies that opposed the Communist Party. Suharto resurrected it in 1971 and made it into a tool to help him remain in office. Civil servants were required to belong to Golkar, which guaranteed it millions of votes.)[4] Waringin Kencana was further recapitalized the following year, with shareholders including Liem's son Andree Halim and family members of Djuhar, including his wife and son. Sudwikatmono and Ibrahim Risjad each received 50 shares out of a total of 1,000.[5] Djuhar split from the partnership with his Hokchia friends (and had a legal dispute with one of the founding members later), effectively dissolving the *kongsi* with them, and the new "Gang of Four" associates began their journey to great wealth.

The four brought different contributions and strengths. Liem was the overall leader, the glue that held the group together. Dwi, viewed by many as Suharto's proxy, had links to the very top and had good connections with the president's close aides. Risjad proved a capable trader. Djuhar was an energetic manager and hands-on facilitator. In a 1994 interview with the Indonesian magazine *Warta Ekonomi*, one of the few occasions he consented to speak to the press, Liem likened the four partners to the four legs of a chair — all four were essential for ensuring stability. The article quoted an unnamed Salim executive as describing the partners as the four elements of nature — earth, wind, fire, and moon. Liem, he said, was the earth, while Djuhar represented fire — a "flame that could not be extinguished"; Risjad was the moon — "good at lobbying and harmonizing", while Dwi was the wind, "effective at penetrating bureaucracy".[6]

Writing in a festschrift for Dwi's sixty-third birthday in 1997, Risjad used a more down-to-earth explanation in describing the gang's initial division of labour: Dwi acted as liaison with the government, while Risjad himself was in charge of marketing; Liem took care of all "finance problems" while Djuhar managed the operations. "Uncle Liem acted as the chairman being in charge as the umbrella for all of us ... Om Liem was the leader in every meeting," wrote Risjad.[7] In the same volume, Dwi marvelled at how easily Liem could get money just by picking up the phone. Reflecting on their roles, Djuhar wrote that he and Risjad "were strong in rubber and yarn, while Om Liem and Pak Dwi were strong in crops and trading networks".[8] According to Risjad, the Gang of Four's strong sense of solidarity was what made the group "quite solid" even when it entered what he called its "successful era". He expressed the opinion that usually companies in Indonesia fell apart "when they enter their successful era. They cannot maintain the spirit of cooperation, tolerance and the strong feeling of togetherness."[9] The solidarity among the four was strongest in the early days. With a touch of nostalgia, Djuhar recalled "staying in cheap hotels, eating at food stalls, riding *becak* (pedicabs) and walking under the sun to find the land for our business".[10] Risjad said a normal day at the Jalan Asemka office meant leaving every morning "to do our tasks; in the afternoon we returned and discussed the work. We had meetings every Friday. It's not a formal meeting; just got together to have lunch after Friday prayers. We discussed all the matters together … we formed what people describe as synergy."[11] When Dwi was asked decades later about the chemistry among the four, he replied that they got on well. Djuhar, he conceded, tended to get emotional at times, while Liem always remained calm. "I've known Om Liem for so long", Dwi said in an interview, "He's always wise. He doesn't discriminate against anyone … I have never seen him angry."[12]

The early camaraderie was also acknowledged by Liem's son Anthony, who said the gang enjoyed good harmony in the beginning. Each partner undertook a separate role. Anthony noted: "Pak Ibrahim was working on outside relationships; Pak Dwi was in contact with the boss [Suharto]. My father had been sort of the umbrella, and Oen Kian worked with the factory people and the construction projects … This [formula] worked well for many years."[13] Suharto's "matchmaking" of this business group hit the jackpot. Liem and his three new partners, all from humble beginnings, formed a relationship that generated great wealth for each. For nearly three decades, they acted in concert, with little public evidence of discord. According to Anthony, though, there was nearly a split in the early 1970s when Djuhar was not happy about an arrangement and complained about Liem. "Djuhar probably thought he was much smarter than my father", said Anthony, adding that Liem then offered to split the partnership up and divide the businesses, but Djuhar backed down.[14] (After May 1998, there was serious friction between the Djuhar and Liem families, leading to a lawsuit, as written about later.)

In the early days, Liem and Djuhar each had 45 per cent shareholding in the partnership, and Dwi and Risjad were allocated 5 per cent each; later that was amended to 40 per cent each for Liem and Djuhar, and 10 per cent each for Dwi and Risjad. Dwi confirmed that his share was given by Liem as he had no money of his own in those days.[15] According to Anthony, his father provided most of the seed capital for the early ventures, while the group received credits from state banks. Waringin Kencana continued the commodity trading activities of CV Waringin, and expanded its rubber processing in Sumatra. Waringin Kencana built a crumb rubber factory in Palembang, which opened in October 1970 and sold most of its production to Goodyear. A second factory, in Jambi, was inaugurated in June 1971. That opening was attended by Trade Minister Sumitro Djojohadikusumo, who was friendly with Risjad but not particularly with Liem. Also in attendance was then Bank Indonesia governor Radius Prawiro, who later held economic portfolios in the Cabinet, and stayed on very friendly terms with Liem. A photograph from the Jambi opening, published in the *Straits Times* (Singapore) showed Sumitro, Radius and Liem in attendance, as well as one of the financial generals, Maj. Gen. Suryo Wiryohadiputro, identified in the caption as Suharto's Personal Advisor (Finance). Risjad described Waringin Kencana as the foundation for bigger companies the gang went on to operate, such as Bogasari and Indocement. Waringin was able to expand rapidly, thanks to generous government credits and export licences that were "far in excess of its formal quota".[16] The company was one of several investigated by a commission on corruption that Suharto (under pressure) set up in 1970. Called the Commission of Four, its members found that Waringin had in fact flouted coffee export quotas, but no action was taken against the company.[17] Waringin Kencana was the foundation for Salim operations. Soon after, the group moved on the much larger ventures, with flour miller Bogasari and cement companies.

SUDWIKATMONO: "KING MIDAS"

The stars must have been in the right alignment when Sudwikatmono was born on 28 December 1934. That, believers would say, could explain the astronomical ascent of a village boy to become one of the wealthiest men in Indonesia. The story of Dwi, Sudwikatmono's nickname, has more of a fairy-tale touch to it than the "rags-to-riches" tale of many entrepreneurs. His was a case of manna falling from heaven — he did not actively solicit or start new ventures but literally found himself being offered a partnership in a burgeoning business and a starting salary 2,500 times his existing one.

His story prompted the local media to dub him Indonesia's King Midas.[18] Without putting up a single rupiah of his own in the early days, he became a shareholder in many lucrative businesses.

A civil servant working for a state firm, Dwi's life took a dramatic turn when he was tapped in 1967 by his cousin Suharto — then Acting President — to be Liem's business partner. Over time, he held top positions in Salim's pivotal money-spinners: flour miller Bogasari, Indocement and Indofood. Besides being given shares in Liem companies, he also got appointed to top corporate positions despite lacking experience. In Bogasari, which got registered in 1969 and started production in 1971, Dwi was given a 5 per cent share and appointed "Director No. 1", the equivalent of the president-director title that later came into use. Later, he also assumed the position of president-director at two other large Salim corporations — Indocement and Indofood. As his positions in the corporate world increased, he found himself a hot commodity — investors, both foreign and domestic, seeking a *pribumi* partner beat paths to his door. Evidently, all they needed to know about his credentials was his relationship to the president: trusted cousin and foster brother. It helped that Dwi had an agreeable personality. Until Suharto's children were old enough to start asserting their claim on monopolies and preferential treatment (their share of "rent" collection), Dwi was the Cendana face in business. It was never publicly stated, of course, but he was the sanctioned representative of the interests of the First Family. Easy-going, unpretentious and instantly likeable, Dwi got on with almost everybody. Partners such as Liem found it easy to deal with the stocky man with a squarish face and a quick smile.

Liem did not discourage his partners from starting ventures of their own or forming partnerships outside the "gang". Dwi entered scores of new businesses. According to business research firm PT CISI Raya Utama, by the mid-1990s, he was estimated to have had interests in about 300 companies, many of them subsidiaries of his two groups Astenia and Subentra. Business activities spanned petrochemicals, plastics, property and banking to forestry, supermarkets and media (movie distribution, broadcasting and print). In 1995, CISI calculated his net worth at between Rp500–550 billion.[19] He was quoted by Indonesian business magazine *SWA* that year as estimating his monthly income — comprising salary, bonuses and dividends — at "not less than 10 billion rupiah". The magazine gave its own estimate including interest income: Rp25 billion a month.[20] In January

1998, a newspaper, citing analysts' estimates, put his total assets at close to Rp6 trillion.[21] Whatever the figures, Dwi belonged to the stratosphere of the very wealthy Indonesians. Home was a sprawling 10,000 square metres mansion, with a private 9-hole golf course in Pondok Indah, a tony housing development in south Jakarta that Salim money helped build. One of Dwi's hobbies was collecting paintings, and he was especially fond of home-grown artists, including famous names such as Basuki Abdullah, Affandi and Raden Saleh. He owned so many even the huge amount of wall space of his mansion was not adequate to display all of them. Dwi also bought houses in other parts of Jakarta, and in Bali as well as in the weekend hill resort of Puncak and owned homes in Singapore and in Beverly Hills, California.

Dwi's name became synonymous with movies, as he owned a chain of cinemas and had a virtual monopoly on film distribution in Indonesia, which naturally irked many in the country's struggling movie industry. He liked the nickname given him by the press — *Raja Bioskop*, meaning Cinema King — as watching movies was a lifelong favourite pastime. During his high school years, he and some classmates befriended employees at a cinema and snuck in to watch movies for free. His favourite stars included Zsa Zsa Gabor, Cary Grant, Humphrey Bogart and James Dean.[22] His movie business was run under his venture Subentra Group, started with long-time associate Benny Suherman. It was the dominant importer of Hollywood movies and distributor of local films, and decided how long films would be screened. Local filmmakers had to wait until the New Order was over to enjoy more openness in the industry. Subentra cinemas, mostly small cineplexes and nicely appointed, were operated as Cinema 21, the figure being Dwi's special number, which coincidentally was also Liem's lucky number. Among the Javanese, the number 21 (*selikur*) is regarded as sacred, and is believed to bring luck. During the financial crisis, Dwi had a falling out with Suherman and another partner, Bambang Sutrisno, with whom he had started the Golden Truly supermarket chain.

With time, Dwi's business interests got increasingly high-tech. He didn't need to understand the business nor have the experience; his name was what his partners sought. The government, acting under orders from "higher up", granted concessions and awarded tenders to companies owned by Salim, Dwi and others politically well-connected — especially those owned by Suharto's children when they came of age to enter business. In 1982, for example, despite not having any experience in the area, a company majority owned by Dwi was awarded a US$600 million tender to build a large section of an olefin petrochemical complex in North Sumatra. Company officials admitted they didn't have any expertise in petrochemical plants and the company had been formed to undertake this project.[23] In 1986, foreign investors in Indonesia's plastics industry were outraged by the erection of a "toll-gate" that meant higher costs for producers and easy revenue for Dwi and others. Foreign firms were shocked by the unexpected government announcement to channel all basic materials for the manufacture of plastic products through a private Hong Kong-based company named Panca Holdings. At the time, industry players had never heard of the firm. It turned out that Panca's directors included Dwi and two of Suharto sons — Sigit Haryoyudanto and Bambang Trihatmodjo. Downstream manufacturers in Indonesia complained that their costs were raised by at least 20 per cent — for nothing more than "paper shuffling" by an added middleman.[24] A lack of experience in specific industries did not deter Cendana-connected business groups from making multimillion dollar investments. Until Suharto's children started businesses of their own, Dwi was the most obvious "front man" for the president. Later, he also partnered Suharto's children in several substantial investments. His Astenia Group, for example, obtained a 44 per cent share in plastics manufacturer Tri Polyta Indonesia together with another businessman, Prajogo Pangestu, as well as with Suharto's second son Bambang — who by then had established his diversified Bimantara Group.[25]

Humble Beginnings

Like his cousin Suharto, Dwi came from humble roots. He was born in Wuryantoro, a village in the regency of Wonogiri, near Solo, in Central Java. His father, Prawirowihardjo, a minor land official, was married to the younger sister of Kertosudiro, Suharto's father. Suharto's parents were divorced and when Suharto was eight years old, his father "kidnapped" him one day and deposited the boy at his sister's to enable him to get a better education in Wuryantoro.[26] Suharto's entry into his aunt's household happened five years before Dwi was born, and Dwi grew up thinking Suharto was his real brother.[27] It was not until he was a teenager, Dwi said, that he found out the relationship was actually that of a cousin. (In Suharto's authorized biography, Dwi and his siblings are listed as Suharto's brothers and sisters.) According to Dwi, his parents treated Suharto as one of their children and his mother had a special place in her heart for him. He recounted: "My mother always said there was something unique about Harto. She thought he was especially clever and she had a hunch he was destined to be 'somebody' one day."[28]

When he was growing up, Dwi was not as close to Suharto as his older brother Sulardi was, due to their thirteen-year age difference. Sulardi and Suharto were almost inseparable during their schooling years: they played, rode bicycles, and went to school together.[29] In 1931, Suharto and Sulardi moved to Selogiri to attend school at nearby Wonogiri. There, they stayed with Sulardi's eldest brother. Two years later, the daughter of the newly-arrived district chief joined Sulardi's class. Two years younger than Suharto, her name was Siti Hartinah. Her parents became friendly with the Prawirowihardjos. In 1947, when Suharto was contemplating marriage, his foster mother suggested a match with Siti Hartinah, a distant descendant from the royal family of Surakarta (Solo). Both sides agreed, and on 26 December that year, Suharto married her in Solo.[30] His wife became better known by her nickname, Tien.

Suharto and Sulardi continued their close links during the revolutionary struggle against the Dutch, who were trying to regain control of Indonesia after the Japanese surrender, serving in the same unit in the hills of Central Java. Sulardi was in charge of logistics and had direct dealings with the suppliers, among whom was Liem. According to Dwi, it was his brother who made the first introduction between Suharto and Liem: "My brother said there was a Chinese supplier who stood out from the rest. He was friendly and earnest. His name was Liem. In those days, there wasn't a tender system; whoever came first, fulfilled the orders. Liem's supplies usually reached them first."[31] Liem continued his business of provisioning Suharto's troops when the latter was based in Semarang as commander of the Diponegoro Division. Dwi said Suharto was impressed with Liem's honesty and reliability. "Liem is the right person to supply us", he recalled Suharto as once saying. "He's always committed and never lies to us; he tells us the coffee he supplies is mixed with corn — he doesn't pretend it is pure coffee. He tells us that it can be stored for three months and he is right. Moreover, his price is cheap, and our men never complained."[32]

Of Prawirowihardjo's sons, Dwi was the only one who did not serve in the military. Dwi said his father nixed the idea of him joining, saying as all his other sons were in uniform, he didn't want to risk losing all of them. He urged Dwi to get a government job instead. When he was growing up, Dwi said he didn't have any burning ambitions. While at school, he earned some money by learning to repair discarded Singer sewing machines and then reselling them. He did well enough in his high school examinations to earn a place to study economics at Yogyakarta's Gadjah Mada University, but lacked money for fees and textbooks. He decided to look for work in Jakarta instead. "It was tough in those days", he recalled, "you had to work very hard before you were able to save anything".[33] In 1958, he used his savings to buy a train fare to Jakarta, boarding with just 50 rupiah in his pocket and "a head full of dreams".[34] In the capital, he landed a clerical position at the headquarters of the navy. His office was on Jalan Gunung Sahari; coincidentally, Liem's house was on a lane coming off the same street. In 1960, Dwi joined PN Jaya Bhakti, state-owned trading company formed from a merger of three entities. It was headed by Gen. Suhardiman, head of the anti-communist workers union, Soksi.[35] Dwi was assigned to the export-import section, where his duties included arranging the import of raw materials for the textile industry. "I handled woven yarn, raw material for textiles, and even flour from Australia — I remember it was Frog brand", he recalled.[36] Within four years, Dwi was promoted to section head. As raw material imports were controlled by the government, private sector orders had to be done through Jaya Bhakti. Dwi said he often had contact with businessmen who needed permits from his office. Among the buyers who came through Dwi's door was Liem's younger brother, Liem Sioe Kong, who had also moved to Jakarta from Kudus. The Liem brothers had, at that time, established two textile plants. As recounted by Dwi:

> Sioe Kong often came to the office and would ask for textiles bearing such and such code. I was asked to write the D.O. (delivery orders) Sometimes, he would hand me envelopes. When I opened them, I found a lot of money inside. I was nervous. I refused to accept them; I was afraid of being fired. He wanted me to accept the money by saying "I gave money to your friends," but I still refused it. Once, he introduced me to his brother, whom everyone called Om[37] Liem. This was about 1963. He invited me to lunch. Om Liem asked me if I had a brother named Sulardi. I said "yes." He said he knew Sulardi in Jogjakarta.

But there was no further contact between Dwi and Liem until Suharto put them together in 1967, by which time, Dwi said, Liem had no recollection of having met him before. Another frequent visitor to his Jaya Bhakti office was Ibrahim Risjad, then working with Djuhar Sutanto at CV Waringin. Risjad got on well with Dwi. Around 1963, Risjad said, he sensed that Dwi was a little restless in his job and he suggested that Dwi quit to join the private sector where "opportunities abound".[38] But Dwi, unsure of what he wanted, dithered. He was not doing too badly, he reasoned to himself, as he was able to supplement his monthly income. In his memoir, Dwi said he got decent profit from selling used gunny sacks, sourced from the port at Tanjung Priok. He would wait for ships to dock and collect the used sacks, then take them to the nearby market, Pasar Pagi, to sell. For each sack, his profit was Rp5.[39] His wife Sri Sulastri added to the family income by selling soap (*Cap Tangan*, or "Hand" brand), which she bought directly from the factory, and peddled to small shops and neighbours for a small margin. She also sold sandals and plastic shopping bags. She continued to do this even after Dwi joined Waringin in 1968. Naturally, after the money started rolling in for her husband, she did not have to sell sandals anymore. Instead, over the years, she took on the role as advisor to her husband.[40]

Becoming a Business Honcho

While Dwi was working at Jaya Bhakti, his foster brother Suharto was moving up the ranks in the army. In 1963, Suharto was promoted to commander of Kostrad, the army strategic reserve command. By that time, he was living in a house on Jalan Agus Salim in the elite Menteng district in central Jakarta. Whenever he had to leave the capital, he would ask Dwi to keep an eye on the house. While fulfilling that duty, Dwi became acquainted with many senior military associates of Suharto. It was in that house that he was officially introduced to Liem in 1967. He recounted the occasion in an interview:[41]

> One day in 1967, Pak Harto asked me to go to his house. He said he was expecting a guest at 5 p.m. and he wanted me to personally escort him in. I wrote down the guest's name: Liem Sioe Liong. I realised that it was the *cukong* I had met before. At 4.45 p.m., Om Liem arrived in a Volkswagen Beetle. The guards — I think they were from *Kopassus* [Special Forces Command] — let him into the compound. I looked at

him and thought to myself: 'So this is the man they call a *cukong*; well, he does look like one — he's *botak* (bald), has a potbelly and speaks very confidently. Oh, he is bold'!

(In those days, Liem was often called Botak Liem. When he became wealthier, the pejorative was dropped in favour of Om [uncle] Liem.)

He asked where he could park his car. When I welcomed him, Om Liem asked me how I knew his name. He seemed to have forgotten that I had met him before. I replied I had been asked by Pak Harto to greet him. He reminded me of one of my former teachers in Yogya,[42] who was clever and bold, and also bald. Then Om Liem entered the house and Pak Harto received him. Their meeting lasted about one hour. When he was leaving, Om Liem passed me his name card and asked me to go to his office the next morning at 10 a.m. I looked at the card. It said: Bank Central Asia. The office was on Jalan Asemka. I said I would be there. The next day, I arrived in a taxi at 9.45 a.m. I met Pak Hasan Din,[43] and another director of the bank named Gunardi. Om Liem just chatted with me; he never took notes. He said he was looking for a good *pribumi* to join in his business and that Pak Harto had suggested me. I was offered a (monthly) salary of 1 million rupiah and a share in the company.

Dwi's shocked and bewildered look did not go unnoticed. But it was misinterpreted. As Dwi was leaving the office, Liem's legal advisor pulled him aside and said the offer was open to negotiations if it was considered insufficient. Dwi chuckled when he recalled the episode: "They offered me one million rupiah! At that time, my salary at Jaya Bhakti was only 400 rupiah a month. The rent for my room in Jalan Lengkeng in Menteng, was 150 rupiah. I felt I was in a dream."[44] He said he couldn't sleep that night and laid in bed thinking. He decided to call on Suharto the next day. He recounted the conversation with his cousin:

Pak Harto explained to me that he had asked Om Liem to take me as a business partner, because at the time Om Liem was not yet an Indonesian citizen.[45] Pak Harto said: "If Liem asked for a loan from the state bank for his business ventures, he would only be able to get Rp10 million at most ... whereas in fact, I assigned him to import cloves[46] for the welfare of Kostrad soldiers ... so I suggested that he takes you as his partner. Can you do that? It's fine if you can't. I will not force you".[47]

It was indeed an offer Dwi could not refuse. All that was left was to tell his boss. He continued: "I had to tell Pak Suhardiman, my boss at Jaya

Bhakti, that I was resigning. He was shocked. He asked me to stay, saying he had plans to promote me to become general manager. But I told him I had no choice as it was an order."

Dwi's first entry into the corporate world came in the form of a 10 per cent share in the Suharto foundation-owned trading company PT Hanurata, which had been passed to Liem to run after he injected capital in it. Originally established in 1954, Hanurata imported steel, flour and sugar, among other things, and exported copra, coffee, pepper and rubber. After faltering in the late Sukarno days, the company was reconstituted under Suharto in 1967 and put under the ownership of two of his *yayasans* (foundations). The principal shareholders of Hanurata were Yayasan Harapan Kita ("Our Hope" foundation, headed by Suharto's wife, Ibu Tien) and another foundation, which later ceased operating: Yayasan Bantuan Beasiswa Yatim Piatu Trikomando Rakyat, also known as Yayasan Trikora.[48]

Suharto took a direct role in the attempt to revive Hanurata, installing his wife's younger brother, Ibnu Widojo, as a director in 1968. Ibnu Widojo turned out not to be a good match for Liem. As brother-in-law of the president, he expected privileged treatment. He had an inflated ego and felt his ancestral ties to the royal palace of Solo meant he deserved to be treated like royalty. He was arrogant and disdainful towards Liem and created a lot of tension for the *cukong* and Dwi. According to Dwi, Widojo was jealous that Dwi was appointed Director No. 1 (in those days the position of President Director was not created yet) in Hanurata while he was Director No. 3. Dwi said: "Widojo wasn't happy at all about that. He considered himself a blue blood, being from the palace."[49]

On his part, Liem found Suharto's brother-in-law overbearing. His patience was stretched. The last straw was triggered by a small incident. Recounted Dwi: "One day, in front of Pak Harto, Widojo asked Om Liem for a cigarette. Om Liem was in the middle of talking to Pak Harto, and without thinking, he pulled out a stick from the pack and handed it casually to Widojo. He failed to offer the whole pack. Widojo flew into a rage, and threw it away."[50] Soon after that episode, Liem decided that he would not continue to have Widojo as a partner. He wanted to avoid further confrontation and unpleasantness. The best option, Liem thought, was to cut his losses and walk away from Hanurata. It was a reflection of Liem's approach: don't continue an unhappy business relationship; be prepared to split up even if it meant incurring a loss. He decided to leave the company to Widojo. When he told Dwi of his decision, Dwi wanted out as well. However, he was afraid to broach the subject with his cousin. Said Dwi: "It was Om Liem who told Pak Harto: 'The atmosphere is not good; I feel offended too. The rules are too aristocratic'. Liem then asked me how come I was so different from Widojo. I replied, 'it's because I came from the village, not a palace'."[51] When Liem left Hanurata, some members of the senior staff also decided not to stay in the company. They tendered their resignation en masse. Widojo found that he was unable to run Hanurata himself. Subsequently, Widojo wrote to Liem, telling him he was returning the company to him. Suharto then stepped in to revamp the management, bringing in his half-brother, Probosutedjo and some officers from Kostrad. A few years later, he appointed a son-in-law, Indra Rukmana (husband of his eldest daughter Tutut), to the board. But Hanurata never became a business success.

When Dwi became part of the Gang of Four, he had no funds of his own to inject in the projects. He admitted to not having to pay for any of his "investments" for some twenty years. "I didn't have the money then", he admitted.[52] Later, though, he said, he paid for his shares in new ventures. Dwi's strength was his Cendana connection, and he was honest enough to concede that. He readily acknowledged that for doing business in Indonesia, having the right connections was the most important factor for success; next came trust. Dwi was ideally suited for his role as liaison person with government officials. Among the Gang of Four partners, Dwi was the most agreeable and hence, the peacemaker. He described himself as a mediator, whenever disagreements arose. In the festschrift for Dwi's sixty-third birthday, Liem praised his partner as a "sincere, professional and honest person" who was easy to get along with.[53] Djuhar remarked that Dwi was disciplined, punctual and persevering.[54] Ibrahim Risjad listed the following attributes of Dwi:

> He's modest, practical, pragmatic, and cooperative; he's a wise person. This is what makes him an efficient professional. Pak Dwi respects others, regardless their titles or their stature ... this is extraordinary, considering that he's a member of President Suharto's family. And in business, he never insists on getting his way; he always tries to follow the existing procedures. [Over the years] he has become an efficient CEO and is a figure respected by everyone, from the shareholders, employees, officials, businessmen, journalists to the common people.[55]

Having an even temperament served Dwi well. It often produced the desired results, even if it sometimes taxed his patience. He recounted an experience in the early days when he was tasked to seek a higher quota for coffee exports. Even his Palace connection cut little ice with crusty Trade Minister Sumitro. The minister had been behind policies which benefited *pribumi* businessmen and made it known he was not in favour of granting concessions and privileges to Chinese businessmen. When Dwi showed up at his house to discuss the quota issue, he was curtly told to seek an appointment at the office. He was given a time, at 8 a.m. the next morning. Dwi arrived at 7.45 a.m. But Sumitro didn't receive him. By noon, Dwi recounted, he was hungry and wanted to leave, but was told to wait. It was not until 4 p.m. that he was allowed in for his appointment. The minister eventually acceded to the request. Although annoyed, Dwi said he reminded himself to follow Liem's usual calm approach and did not show his irritation. "No matter how unhappy Om Liem was with a person, he didn't show it", Dwi said.[56]

It was Liem who taught him the virtue of keeping one's word — *"kalau janji sama orang selalu tepat"*, Dwi said. Liem's honesty and straightforwardness impressed many. "When he says A; he means A", continued Dwi.[57] For Dwi, increased exposure to the corporate world helped him outgrow his unsophisticated bearing. In the early days, he looked and dressed like a country bumpkin. A senior military officer who later became a cabinet minister recalled meeting Dwi for the first time — at the opening of Bogasari Flour Mill in 1971. Suharto was officiating at the ceremony. Dressed in a white suit, with hair slicked back and wearing big spectacle frames, Dwi stood out like a sore thumb. The general said he asked someone standing nearby who that was and was astounded to learn that the man was not only Suharto's foster brother but he was the company's Director No. 1.[58]

The Indonesia media appreciated Dwi's relative approachability. *Eksekutif* magazine, for example, commented that Dwi was always accessible to the press and "was not stingy with information … he's comfortable with publicity; Liem and Djuhar won't allow the press to come close [to them]."[59] When Dwi's four children — three daughters and a son — grew up, each went into businesses with his help. Dwi said that he suggested to them to either join with the second generation of the Salim Group — in particular with Anthony Salim, or to go down their own path. They chose their own path. He helped finance his daughters' investments in U.S. restaurant franchises such as Lawry's, Planet Hollywood and Tony Roma's (the last through a Singapore company called Mas Millennium, a

50-50 venture between Dwi and Djoni Prananto, a cousin of Liem). Before Suharto's fall, Dwi's daughter Martina was the Jakarta representative of Sotheby's. His son Agus Lasmono became head of a coal, oil and gas group named Indika Energy, which got listed on the Jakarta exchange in 2004. When the financial crisis hit in 1997, Dwi's businesses teetered. He had disputes with several long-time partners including Henry Pribadi (Liem Oen Hauw) of the Napan Group, a cousin of Djuhar. Their capital-intensive projects, with loans denominated in dollars, contributed to huge losses. Another falling out was with Bambang Sutrisno, his partner in the supermarket chain Golden Truly and Bank Surya, who fled Jakarta in 1997. The dispute was acrimonious. (In 2002, a Jakarta court tried Sutrisno *in absentia* and sentenced him to life imprisonment for stealing Rp1.5 trillion from Bank Indonesia.)

In April 1998, seven weeks before Suharto resigned, the Indonesia Bank Restructuring Agency froze the licences of Dwi's Bank Surya and Bank Subentra, most of whose loans were to bank shareholders, in violation of banking regulations. Together, they had chalked up debts of Rp1.88 trillion to the state. His two banks collapsed. In September, Dwi signed an agreement with the government on settling Surya's debts, and pledged some assets to be sold, as Anthony Salim did on a far larger scale. Dwi received a "release and discharge" statement from the government saying he had resolved all his debt issues before Anthony got one in March 2004.

In his later years, he was prone to illnesses after suffering a stroke. In August 2010, looking frail but cheerful, he attended the wedding reception held in the Capella Hotel in Singapore of fellow "Gang" member Ibrahim Risjad. Dwi died in a Singapore hospital on 8 January 2011, from kidney problems. He was seventy-six.

DJUHAR SUTANTO, THE "NUTS AND BOLTS" MAN

For over three decades, Liem Sioe Liong worked closely with his Hokchia clansman Djuhar Sutanto, whose late father was a friend from their days in Central Java. Djuhar is more commonly known in the Indonesian Chinese community as Liem Oen Kian, his Chinese name.[60] Djuhar's father, Lin Hongkuan, hailed from a neighbouring village in Fuqing. According to Liem, Lin Hongkuan died of cancer at age forty-nine. Before he died, he asked Liem to help take care of his family, as his youngest child was only an infant.[61] Liem said had regarded Djuhar as a member of his own family. From the early days of their working relationship, Djuhar assumed the role of the operations man who took care of the nuts-and-bolts in implementing projects undertaken by the Salim Group. The tall, bespectacled Djuhar earned a reputation among his fellow Hokchias as ambitious and shrewd. A business consultant in Jakarta who used to do work for the Salim Group observed: "You always see Om Liem being hounded for money by the generals and others, but very few people went after Djuhar."[62] Djuhar deliberately kept a low profile in Indonesia and was the least accessible of the Gang of Four to the Indonesian media. In the mid-1960s, Djuhar's close link with Suharto was due to a Hokchia business partner who was friendly with a senior Suharto aide.

Some Indonesian media erroneously reported that Djuhar was born in Indonesia. He was born in China in 1928 in a village called Xi Tou Chun in the Fuqing district of Fujian province. In 1936, he left China with his mother to join his father who was then making a living as a moneylender in Kudus. The young Djuhar was a natural athlete, excelling at volleyball, basketball and badminton. In 1953, he was picked to head an Indonesian volleyball team going to China. However, due to flight problems, he did not get to Beijing, but he was able to arrange a visit to his home village. That trip, he said, made him realize how dire conditions still were in his village, with hardly any improvements from the time he left. He vowed then that he would try to help conditions in his ancestral home. According to a commissioned biography of Djuhar, his father was a chauvinist who insisted his children spoke not only their Hokchia dialect but learnt Mandarin and be imbued with traditional Chinese values. When his children made their new home in Java, he wanted them to remember their Chinese roots. Djuhar recalled: "My father always said we should be a Chinese who people can respect. He preached the importance of cultivating responsibility and trust. He said 'even if you die of hunger, you should not owe anybody one cent'."[63] When the Japanese occupied Java, they banned the teaching of the Chinese language. Students enrolled in Chinese schools were forced to learn the Japanese language from Japanese teachers. An infuriated Lin pulled his son out of school and kept him home so he would not have to learn Japanese. "I don't want the killers of Chinese to be my son's teachers", he privately declared. Before the war ended in 1945, however, his father contracted cancer. According to Djuhar, his dying father vowed to live long enough to see the Japanese surrender.

"He said if he could not see that day, his eyes would not close in death. His will was strong. Not long after the Japanese surrendered, he passed away", recounted Djuhar.

The eldest of four children, Djuhar was sixteen when his father died, while the youngest was still an infant. With the burden of providing for the family on his shoulders, Djuhar decided to join some Hokchia clansmen who had a batik printing business in Pekalongan, along the north coast of Java. In the early 1950s, with the departure of the Dutch, business opportunities opened up — nowhere more than in the new republic's capital, Jakarta. Many of the *singkeh* (recently arrived migrants from China) packed their bags from different parts of Java and headed there. Liem had moved to Jakarta in 1952. In 1956, Djuhar decided he would follow in the footsteps of Hokchia friends and head for the capital too. His close friend Liem Ngie Hoo was already there and had joined a business with another Hokchia emigrant partnership. (In 1967, when the Chinese were urged to assume Indonesian-sounding names — to help them assimilate — Liem Ngie Hoo took the name Imin Sugiono.) Imin had been best friends with Djuhar, being from the same hometown and arriving from China on the same ship. They shared a room in Djuhar's uncle's house in Kudus. About forty-five years later, ironically, this close-knit relationship ended in a bitter court battle in Singapore (See Box 6.1).

"Four Seas" and "Five Stars" *kongsi*

Djuhar's rise to business prominence was rooted in help from his Hokchia friends, although initially not involving Liem Sioe Liong. Djuhar joined a business partnership that comprised three other Hokchia clansmen in Jakarta, but would later separate with them when he linked up with his father's friend Liem Sioe Liong. Djuhar's doorway to Jakarta business was via Imin, who had joined the business of another Hokchia by the name of Liem Lay Duan (who took the Indonesian name Ridwan Halim). Liem Lay Duan was a fairly recent *singkeh*, having left Fuqing only in 1950. He spent four years in Kudus in his uncle's furniture business before striking out on his own in Jakarta. When Imin asked to join his small trading business, Lay Duan readily agreed and they informally incorporated their 50-50 partnership as a *kongsi*,[64] allowing them to conduct business, even though they were not citizens at the time. Shortly after, Lay Duan invited his nephew, Tan Ie Lok, to join them, giving him 10 per cent share from his holding. Then Djuhar arrived in Jakarta and wanted in. Imin offered him 10 per cent from his shares. As there were now four of them in the business, they decided to call their venture Four Seas *kongsi*. In 1961, the Four Seas partners entered a contract with the Indonesian Catholic Party headed by I.J. Kasimo to manage a bank owned by the party, called Bank Pembangunan Ekonomi Indonesia (BPEI), or Economic Development Bank of Indonesia.[65]

The following year, the Four Seas partnership received a boost when a fifth Hokchia came on board. The newest member of the *kongsi* was a man by the name of Liem Chin Song who was to play a pivotal role in the group. Invited in by Lay Duan, Liem Chin Song — whose Indonesian name was Yacob Sulaiman but was better known by his nickname Yacovan (also spelled Yacofun) — cultivated the friendship of a close aide of Suharto when the latter was appointed commander of Kostrad in 1963. Thanks to the friendship with the aide, this group of Hokchia businessmen had a good inside track to Suharto. Yacovan's entry into Four Seas necessitated a name change for the group, as there were now five of them. The *kongsi* decided to call itself Five Stars. Apart from his connection, Yacovan brought value by injecting additional capital of Rp2 million. More of consequence to the Salim story, Yacovan brought into the new venture his trusted and capable *pribumi* employee, Ibrahim Risjad, whom he had hired for clerical work in his trading firm, CV Waringin.[66]

With his capital injection, Yacovan assumed a 40 per cent share in Five Stars. His job was to handle commodity trading. Imin and Lay Duan had 20 per cent each and were in charge of provisioning the navy. Djuhar had 10 per cent and was the office manager. Tan held the remaining 10 per cent and despite his lack of banking experience, was appointed general manager of BPEI. The following year, the partners agreed to divide the *kongsi* shares equally so that each of them held 20 per cent. The partnership took over the operations of Yacovan's CV[67] Waringin, which was exporting coffee and had an exclusive contract to supply uniforms to the fledgling navy. As the company was registered under the Indonesian Commercial Code, it could participate in government tenders.[68] The Five Stars office was located diagonally across from BCA on Jalan Asemka in Kota, Jakarta's Chinatown. At that time, BCA — whose licence Liem bought in 1957 — was smaller and less established than BPEI. According to a person knowledgeable about the operations, at that time BPEI had substantial deposits from Kostrad as it offered very high interest rates on deposits; the bank was paying about 9 per cent a month to Kostrad.[69]

The Unravelling of the Partnership

In 1966, the year after the abortive coup that precipitated Sukarno's fall, the military under Suharto started more aggressive forays into businesses, often working with Chinese businessmen, and banking was an area of interest. Five Stars *kongsi* entered more direct cooperation with the military with the purchase of the licence of Semarang-based Bank Timur NV (at the time, no licences were being issued for new banks). It was renamed Bank Gemari, a name chosen by Suharto himself and a contraction for *Gemah Ripah*, meaning "very prosperous" in Javanese. Bank Gemari was officially owned by the Defence Ministry's foundation, Tri Usaha Bhakti. The powerful head of Suharto's select private staff, Gen. Alamsyah, sat on the Board of Commissioners of Gemari. Together with BPEI, Gemari had military-connected foundations as major depositors. (Bank Gemari faltered after a few years and was later absorbed by Liem's BCA.) None of the Five Stars partners had any experience running a bank, and in those days, many banks were run based on personal relationships rather than proper practices. There were unfettered cross-borrowings between the two Five Stars-operated banks. Loans were freely made to bank owners; according to Imin Sugiono, BPEI loaned Rp200 million to Five Stars, "which in turn used the funds as its contributions to the working capital of the joint venture with Liem Sioe Liong's Group."[70]

In mid-1968, BPEI manager Tan Ie Lok was investigated by police after it was reported that certain unauthorized transactions had been made. Suharto's close aide Ali Murtopo was kept apprised of the situation as the bank held sizeable military deposits. The bank was closed without prior notice, for two weeks. Tan, who maintained that all his activities were undertaken with the good of the military in mind, was never charged. However, the bank's reputation never recovered. One consequence was that the Hokchia friends started to doubt one another; the level of distrust became such that it was only a matter of time before their partnership unravelled. In due course, Tan quit the *kongsi*, together with Liem Lay Duan, who had brought him into the partnership.[71] Yacovan also became embittered and exited.[72] Liem Sioe Liong, who had been watching from the sidelines, was distressed to see his fellow Hokchia clansmen at each other's throats. He tried to mediate, but without success. Years after the episode, Imin Sugiono unsuccessfully sued his once-best friend Djuhar, whom he brought into the original Four Seas partnership (see Box 6.1). Djuhar, in the end, succeeded in stealing the thunder from his Hokchia partners, becoming the most successful and wealthiest among them after Suharto picked him to work together with Liem Sioe Liong. The other members of the Five Stars *kongsi* mostly faded into obscurity, underscoring the truism that it was nearly impossible to be spectacularly successful in the New Order period without political or military patronage. The original principals were only merely able to watch from the wings as control of their old company passed to the new grouping comprising Liem, Sudwikatmono, Djuhar and Ibrahim Risjad — the quartet that grew from strength to strength.

Djuhar and Liem took over CV Waringin and registered it as PT[73] Waringin in 1968. Their names do not appear in the State Gazette, but their *pribumi* partners, Ibrahim Risjad and Sudwikatmono, were shown to hold 250 shares each, out of a total of 1,000 issued shares. (The rest were held by two other Indonesian associates.) Sudwikatmono was appointed Director I, while Risjad was listed as Director II.[74] The following year, the company's name was changed to PT Waringin Kencana, and a new shareholding was recorded. Records show that Liem, under his Indonesian name Soedono Salim, and Djuhar became listed as shareholders in October 1969, after they obtained citizenship. Barely two months later, there was a restructuring of the shareholding and more names were added, including Liem's second son Andree Halim and Djuhar's son, Tedy Djuhar. Djuhar's cousin, Henry Pribadi, who was to become an industrialist, also became a shareholder. Another shareholder was Djuhar's wife, Christine Arifin. Waringin Kencana's principal activities were listed as trading in coffee and primary products and producing crumb rubber in Sumatra.[75]

IBRAHIM RISJAD: "THE MAN FROM U.N.C.L.E."

Ibrahim Risjad, the fourth member of the "Gang" has been described by some of his peers as one of the shrewdest *pribumi* businessmen in the country. Born in Sigli, Aceh province, in 1934, Risjad was the son of a small textile trader. The family lived above his father's shop. He moved to Medan for secondary school but didn't finish it. He started working life as a young journalist in north Sumatra. In an interview with the co-author, he revealed that his early ambition was to become a first-rate journalist and had set his sights on winning a Colombo Plan fellowship so he could study overseas. But then he discovered there was no funding for the study of journalism. His career path took a turn when he accompanied a friend on a trip to Jakarta in 1956. There, he saw the potential for business opportunities and resolved to move to the capital city.[76] Risjad said it was his father who imbued in him an interest in business: "I was taught how to do business by my father when I was still a little boy; that's how I developed my sense of business," he once said.[77]

In Jakarta, he found clerical work in CV Waringin, a trading company owned by Yacob Sulaiman (Yacovan). When Yacovan teamed up with the Four Seas partners, he brought Risjad with him. Risjad's abilities and keen business instincts impressed his Chinese bosses, including Djuhar Sutanto. When Djuhar broke away from Five Stars to join Liem Sioe Liong, he invited Risjad along. Often low-keyed, the diminutive Sumatran possessed a sharp intellect and a good memory. He has a sense of humour which undoubtedly helped in the rough and tumble world of business in Indonesia. In a 2006 interview, he chuckled as he dubbed himself "The Man from U.N.C.L.E.",[78] in reference to the popular American action spy TV show from the 1960s.[79] This was because of his long association with Liem, who was commonly addressed as "Om Liem", "Om" being Dutch for uncle.

Risjad acknowledged that in Indonesia, being very successful in business required more than smarts. Having the right connections was vital. "Business was born from politics.... It means connections. If you don't have it, [and depend] on the capital business only, it will not be enough. So my business was born from politics", he stated.[80] In the course of his work, Risjad said, he came across Liem Sioe Liong's name even before 1960, having had dealings with Liem's younger brother Sioe Kong as early as 1957. The company Risjad worked for, CV Waringin, sold and exported commodities. According to Risjad, the company hit a bad patch in the mid-1960s. Liem Sioe Liong then bought the company, which was revamped and renamed Waringin Kencana in 1967. As Liem had become close to Suharto by that time, business opportunities grew dramatically.[81] After Suharto attained power, Risjad said, there was also a change in the business from licences to "real business". He said: "There weren't any dollar subsidies anymore for imports so that it [became] impossible to continue the licence business. That's the time when we began with the export business. Then I was invited [by Uncle Liem's group to join them] because those people knew that I was capable."[82] Risjad confirmed that the partnership of Liem's Gang of Four was initiated by Suharto.

The preferential treatment accorded the group by Suharto's government was what allowed Salim to grow by leaps and bounds, but each member of the Gang also capitalized on his particular expertise. Risjad told *Eksekutif* magazine: "I am strong in marketing. For example, when we produced cement, none of the four of us [were] experts in the field ... But we have the plus point compared with other people: we know marketing orientation.... People often forget that the industry survival is caused by its strong marketing."[83] Describing himself as a "master in international trade", he said he honed experience in trading from living in Medan, an important trading centre in the colonial days. As the two *pribumi* members in the team, Risjad and Dwi had more frequent contacts with government bureaucrats. The two had different sets of friends, which helped expand the ties of the group. While Dwi was close to Suharto's military aides, Risjad was close to Trade Minister Sumitro Djojohadikusumo, with whom he had contact almost every day, so that the minister "could get market information and education."[84]

While the Gang of Four had its hands full with the continually growing stable of companies under the group, it did not limit each person's investments and business activities to only those firms. The development of independent businesses by members of the Gang did not have any impact on the group, Risjad said, adding:

> Uncle Liem has quite a big business on his own. Although it's small, Pak Djuhar has also his. Pak Dwi is also having his private business. So do I. All [have] become successful; the group stays in harmony [and] the private businesses run well... it's because there is willingness. Of course, family life is another thing. But for the business matter, as collective power, we're united.

As for the second generation, he noted: "there is already mutual understanding. Actually, Uncle Liem is the most influential one as the parent at present. Uncle Liem is involved in the guidance (*pembinaan*) of our children."[85]

Risjad started his own business group, Risjadson, in 1989 with two of his sons. By the mid-1990s, the group had sixty companies, with operations encompassing property, aluminium industry, banking and finance, agribusiness, tyre cord and packaging film. Risjad and Dwi partnered each other in various investments outside the Salim umbrella, several of them with extended family members of Liem and Djuhar, including Henry Liem, a nephew of Liem, and Djuhar's cousins, the Pribadi brothers — Henry, Andry and Wilson. Henry Pribadi's Napan Group was a co-investor in the plastic packaging industry with Risjad in a listed company called Argha

Karya Prima. Risjad was also with them and another Chinese Indonesian businessman by the name of Robby Sumanpow (of Batara Indra Group) in listed tyre cord manufacturer, Branta Mulia. Risjad held the position of president director in that company. Robby was known as Gen. Benny Murdani's *cukong*, and at one time held the monopoly in coffee exports from East Timor, when it was still under Indonesian control. (Murdani was the powerful commander of the armed forces in the mid-1980s before he fell out of favour with Suharto.) In 1994, it emerged that Risjad, together with Henry Liem and Andry Pribadi, were the mystery buyers of a Medan-based British plantation company PT London Sumatra. They agreed to pay Harrisons & Crosfield US$273 million for the firm it had owned since 1904. The firm operated nineteen oil palm and rubber plantations covering 46,000 hectares.[86] Lonsum had an initial public offering (IPO) in 1996 and later faced serious management problems. The company eventually moved out of Risjad's hands, and in a twist, was purchased by Anthony Salim in 2007.

Like Dwi, Risjad went into banking. His bank was called RSI, for Risjad Salim International. It opened in July 1989, and had assets of Rp733 billion in June 1997, just before the financial crisis.[87] It started off being 100 per cent owned by him and his family. Risjad maintained that the "Salim" part of the bank's name did not have anything to do with Liem and the Salim Group but was named for his late wife, Zakiah Salim.[88] Ironically, Salim did have a role in the bank during the Asian financial crisis after Liem and Anthony had to step in when RSI had liquidity problems. Despite the lifeline from Liem, the bank was subsequently closed.

From 1990, the Gang of Four partners stopped making new investments as a group, in line with Liem's belief that it was a good thing for the partners to pursue their own interests beyond the group's activities. Liem acknowledged as much when he was asked about the blooming of businesses by the partners independently. In a rare interview to the Indonesian press, he told Tempo magazine in March 1990: "Our holdings are already too big ... so we [should] break it up ... but our offices remain on the 20th floor of Indocement building. So we can often meet and talk." Asked if it was better if things were "broken up", he replied:

> The responsibility of each one will be lighter. If all the big capital is put together as one, the responsibility will be even bigger. For me, it's better if I, for example, help Pak Ibrahim and Pak Dwi. Like in Ibrahim's bank (RSI), I don't have shares, I'm only a commissioner. So, the relationship

between us is better. If you get into difficulties, I can help; and if I'm in difficulty, you can give assistance. This is my business philosophy.[89]

Risjad wrote in 1997 that in the early days, the four members of the Gang were "not allowed" to leave the team. "Our commitment was 100 per cent... We have the commitment that this business partnership of four will never been broken. How could it be; we're always together since we were young and when our business was still small. We hold on to it [our commitment]. We were even still sharing the same office room, as being advised to us by someone (keeping to the advice by a *feng shui* master)."[90] The *feng shui* was certainly good for as long as Suharto lasted as president. The businesses that the four engaged in over time encompassed many of the strategic sectors in Indonesia's economy, and all four partners became wealthy in their own right by the early 1990s. But following the financial crisis and Suharto's resignation, the partnership did fall apart. Like many conglomerate bosses in Indonesia, Risjad had financial woes, but managed to work out a debt repayment programme that cleared his Rp639 billion in debts and allowed him to obtain his MSAA[91] clearance in 2002. Later, Risjad and his sons catapulted to the ranks of the wealthy once again, thanks to their interests in coal mines. (Risjad passed away on 16 February 2012, in Singapore following a battle with cancer.)

BOX 6.1
Close Friends Face Off in Court

Two migrants from Fuqing were childhood friends and literally had been in the same boat, travelling to Java after leaving their homes in China. They had roomed together and considered themselves as close as brothers. But sixty-five years later they ended up as bitter foes, fighting in court. One was Djuhar Sutanto, who teamed up with Liem Sioe Liong. The other was Imin Sugiono (Liem Ngie Hoo), who was in a Hokchia *kongsi* with Djuhar before Liem entered the picture. In a suit filed in the Singapore High Court in 2001, Imin alleged that Djuhar owed him money from decades earlier, in connection with how the partnership that linked with Liem Sioe Liong operated. Djuhar contested the allegations. Imin's suit contended that Djuhar was a member of a group named Five Stars and did not act as he was supposed to on behalf of the five people in that group when entering a venture with Liem Sioe Liong. Imin also described Djuhar as "like a brother". According to an affidavit Imin filed, he and the other partners agreed to take a backseat while Djuhar acted as a "trustee" for the Five Stars members. This statement was denied by Djuhar, who told the court: "I do not recall what we called our business, and I most certainly do not remember it being called Five Stars Company."

After Djuhar started working with Liem Sioe Liong in Waringin, the Five Stars *kongsi* fell apart and the other members missed out, basically, on being part of the business the Gang of Four profited from. In 1992, Imin asked Djuhar to pay him for his share in the now-defunct Five Stars. Djuhar refused, and to prevent the ugly dispute from escalating, Liem stepped in to help settle the issue between Hokchia kinsmen and paid Imin $500,000 even though it had nothing to do with him.[92]

After the Asian financial crisis in 1997–98, Imin tried again to get money from Djuhar. He filed his lawsuit in Singapore, seeking compensation for his share in Five Stars, which he calculated to be worth $500 million. Djuhar vigorously fought the case, which came up about the same time that the Liem and Djuhar families were having disagreements about what assets the Salim Group could pledge to settle its debt to the Indonesian government. In his statement submitted 25 September 2001 to Singapore High Court, Djuhar said of Imin, himself and others who worked together before the teaming up with Liem, "We started together

continued on next page

BOX 6.1 — *cont'd*

when we were all young and poor and we were all happy to be able to get all the work that we could get our hands on."[93] Imin's lawyer submitted to the court a letter to Djuhar dated 8 August 2001 which summarized the Five Stars relationship with Liem Sioe Liong this way:

> Sometime in or about 1964, (Five Stars member) Yacob Sulaiman was introduced to Suharto. Through Yacob, Suharto started having business dealings with Five Stars. Five Stars had a good relationship with Suharto … Sioe Liong's Group also enjoyed a good relationship with Suharto. After Suharto became President, it was proposed that Five Stars and Sioe Liong Group teamed up to benefit from the new regime. It was eventually agreed that you (Djuhar) would represent the interests of Five Stars and Sioe Liong would represent the interest of Sioe Liong Group in this joint venture. Our client had suggested that you be the representative and the other parties of Five Stars went along with his suggestion.[94]

However, Djuhar not only rejected any payout to Imin, he demanded that his former close friend and partner return the $500,000 disbursed in 1992, claiming it was only a loan. However, the case went nowhere. The High Court agreed with Djuhar's lawyer that Singapore was not the appropriate venue for Imin's lawsuit. On 11 December 2001, the Judicial Commissioner ruled that "All future proceedings in the action herein be stayed on the grounds of *forum non convenienus*". He wrote:

> The contract was made by Indonesians in Indonesia in the 1960s, and that generally indicates that Singapore is not the natural forum… The matter is one that clearly emanated from Indonesia almost or about 25 years ago. The applicable law would be Indonesian law; the claim itself is not straightforward and the apparent entanglement of fact and law virtually dictates that the trial be held in its natural forum. The appeal [for a "stay", meaning no trial would proceed] is therefore allowed."[95]

The disintegration of the Five Stars *kongsi* illustrated the weakness of the informal business partnerships of the old days among Chinese friends, and the dependence of many businessmen on political patronage in the New Order. Those who did not enjoy political patronage risked disappearing into obscurity, as experienced by the several Hokchia businessmen mentioned here.

Djuhar, together with Liem Sioe Liong, went on to develop new ventures under the aegis of Suharto.

Notes

1. *"Kelompok 4 serangkai"* [group of four friends] in Lazuardi Adi Sage, *Dari Wuryantoro ke Sineplek: Biografi popular kisah sukses Sudwikatmono* (Jakarta: Trendi Media, 1994), p. 103.
2. Private conversation, Jakarta, 14 February 2008.
3. Called *beringin* in Indonesian.
4. For history and explanation of Golkar, see Michael Liefer, *Dictionary of the Modern Politics of Southeast Asia*, 3rd ed. (London and New York, 2001), pp. 123–24.
5. State Gazette No. 275, 1970.
6. "Kami besar bukan karena dekat dengan Pak Harto" [We're big not because we're close to Pak Harto], *Warta Ekonomi*, 21 February 1994.
7. R.N. Dwidjowijoto, ed., *Sudwikatmono: Sebuah Perjalanan di antara Sahabat* (Jakarta: Yayasan Pendidikan Hanurita, 1997), pp. 146–54.
8. Ibid, p. 112.
9. Ibid.
10. Dwidjowijoto, *Sudwikatmono*, pp. 111–15.
11. Ibid., pp. 146–54.
12. Interview with Sudwikatmono, Jakarta, 8 August 2006.
13. Interview with Anthony, 2 January 2007.
14. Interview with Anthony, 2 January 2007.
15. Interview with Sudwikatmono, 8 August 2006.
16. Richard Robison, *Indonesia: The Rise of Capital* (Sydney: Allen and Unwin/Asian Studies Association of Australia, 1986), p. 302.
17. See Theodore Friend, *Indonesian Destinies* (Cambridge, Mass.: Belknap Press of Harvard University, 2003), p. 164.
18. "Sudwikatmono, pensiunan raja Midas. Nasib konglomerasi Cendana" [Sudwikatmono, the retired king of Midas. The fate of the Cendana conglomerate.], *Tempo*, 16 January 2000.
19. "Jalinan lobi dan bisnis: Sudwikatmono" [Sudwikatmono's Interwoven Lobby and Businesses], *SWA magazine*, 1/XI April 1995.
20. See *SWA's* special report on Dwi, in April 1995, "Sudwikatmono mungkin orang yang hidupnya paling nikmat di Indonesia" [Sudwikatmono, possibly the person with the most comfortable life in Indonesia].
21. "Sudwikatmono: Becoming a giant through partnership", *Sunday Observer* (Jakarta), 11 January 1998.
22. Dwidjowijoto, *Sudwikatmono*, p. 5.
23. Joseph Manguno, "Half brother of Suharto wins project", *Asian Wall Street Journal*, 20 September 1982.
24. Stephen Jones, "Suharto's kin linked with plastics monopoly", *Asian Wall Street Journal*, 25 November 1986.

25. Richard Borsuk, "Japanese group, Jakarta banks join in credit", *Asian Wall Street Journal*, 31 May 1990.

26. Retnowati Abdulgani-Knapp, *Soeharto: The Life and Legacy of Indonesia's Second President* (Singapore: Marshall Cavendish, 2007), p. 22.

27. Interview with Sudwikatmono, 8 August 2006.

28. Ibid.

29. O.G. Roeder, *The Smiling General: President Soeharto of Indonesia* (Jakarta: Gunung Agung, 1969), p. 87.

30. R.E. Elson, *Suharto: A Political Biography* (Cambridge: Cambridge University Press, 2001), p. 6.

31. Interview with Sudwikatmono, 8 August 2006.

32. Ibid.

33. Ibid.

34. Dwidjowijoto, *Sudwikatmono*, p. 7.

35. Suhardiman was also Director of the state corporation Berdikari until 1972 (Robison 1986, p. 252). Before Suharto's financial generals took centre stage, Suhardiman was considered Indonesia's most powerful military entrepreneur of the time; Robison, *Indonesia: The Rise of Capital*, p. 361, quoting *Sinar Harapan*, 11 January 1968.

36. Interview with Sudwikatmono, 8 August 2006.

37. Om, also spelled "oom", is the Dutch word for "uncle".

38. Eddy Soetriyono, *Kisah Sukses Liem Sioe Liong* [The success story of Liem Sioe Liong] (Jakarta: Indomedia, 1989), pp. 89–91.

39. Dwidjowijoto, *Sudwikatmono*, p. 15.

40. See ibid., pp. 16 and 44; also Soetriyono, *Kisah Sukses Liem Sioe Liong*, p. 94; and "Mereka termasuk pengusaha terkaya ASEAN" [They are among the wealthiest ASEAN entrepreneurs], *Warta Ekonomi*, 24 February 1992.

41. Interview with Sudwikatmono, 8 August 2006.

42. Contraction for Yogyakarta, also spelled Jogjakarta.

43. Hasan Din, the father of Sukarno's wife Fatmawati, was taken by Liem to be a business partner; he was the grandfather of Megawati, who became the country's fourth president in 2001.

44. In Sudwikatmono's memoir, he was said to be earning Rp1,600 a month at that time.

45. Liem obtained his Indonesian citizenship later that same year, with Gen. Sudjono Humardani signing his recommendation.

46. If Dwi's memory was correct, this implied that Suharto and Liem discussed the importation of cloves as early as 1967. Liem's company, PT Mega, and a company owned by Suharto's half-brother Probosutedjo were officially granted the licence to import clove in 1968.

47. Interview with Sudwikatmono, 8 August 2006.

48. Trikora was a contraction for Tri Komando Rakyat, or Triple Command of the People, a Sukarno-initiated campaign in West Irian. The foundation was established in 1962 by Suharto to aid orphans and widows of soldiers killed during Indonesia's military campaign to wrest the area from the Dutch.

49. Interview with Sudwikatmono, 8 August 2006.

50. Ibid.

51. Ibid.

52. Dwidjowijoto, *Sudwikatmono*, p. 31.

53. Ibid., pp. 189–92.

54. Ibid., p. 115.

55. Ibrahim Risjad, "Sahabat istimewa" [Special friend], in Dwidjowijoto, *Sudwikatmono*, pp. 145–54.

56. Interview with Sudwikatmono, 8 August 2006.

57. Dwidjowijoto, *Sudwikatmono*, p. 49.

58. Confidential conversation in Jakarta, 24 April 2008.

59. "Tragedi bisnis Sudwikatmono", *Eksekutif*, May 1999, pp. 64–67.

60. *Hanyu pinyin* spelling: Lin Wenjing.

61. Interview with Liem, 28 November 2006.

62. Private conversation, Jakarta, 2 May 2006.

63. Xiao Liu, *Lin Wen Jing: Ta gai bian le jia xiang* [He Changed His Home: Fuqing's Lin Wen Jing Returns After 18 Years] (Hong Kong: Takungpao Publishing, 2005).

64. The term *"kongsi"* refers to business arrangements common among the Chinese in Indonesia at the time. Taken from the Chinese word meaning "to share", the *kongsi* operated much like a limited liability company, or what the Dutch called *naamloze vennootschap*. According to historian Onghokham, this was the common practice among the Chinese during the colonial period. Among the *singkeh*, businesses with friends as partners tended to operate what was referred to as *kongsi mulut* — literally, ventures sealed by mouth (or oral agreements). As they considered each other kinsfolk, the partners often did not formalize their companies, basing their agreement purely on trust. See Onghokham, "Chinese capitalism in Dutch Java", *Southeast Asian Studies* 27, no. 2 (Kyoto University) (September 1989).

65. Material on the background of the *kongsi* obtained from confidential interviews in Jakarta and Singapore between December 2006 and August 2007.

66. Confidential interview. Jakarta, December 2006.

67. CV: *Commanditaire Vennootschap*, a limited partnership. According to Yuri Sato, CV Waringin was set up in 1953 (Sato 1993, p. 411). At that stage, however,

Liem Sioe Liong had nothing to do with the company. When Liem entered a partnership with Djuhar, they reorganized the company and registered it in 1968 as a limited liability company, PT Waringin (Perseroan Terbatas). In 1969, the company was renamed PT Waringin Kencana.

68. Affidavit filed by Imin Sugiono to Singapore High Court, 10 September 2001.
69. Confidential interview in Jakarta, December 2006.
70. Imin statement to Singapore High Court, 11 October 2001.
71. Confidential source.
72. Yacovan eventually resettled in Canada, where he died in 2005.
73. Perseroan terbatas, a limited liability company.
74. State Gazette No. 189, 1969.
75. State Gazette, No. 275, 1970.
76. Interview with Risjad, 15 September 2006.
77. *Indonesia's Economy — Entering the Third Millennium* (London: International Quality Productions, 1997).
78. U.N.C.L.E. in the TV series stood for "United Network Command for Law and Enforcement". Two secret agents, played by Robert Vaughn and David McCallum, fight the enemies of peace.
79. Interview with Risjad, 15 September 2006.
80. "Ibrahim Risjad: 'Dalam international trade, saya masternya' ", *Eksekutif*, April 1990, pp. 20–22.
81. Interview with Risjad, 15 September 2006.
82. "Ibrahim Risjad", *Eksekutif*, April 1990.
83. Ibid.
84. Ibid.
85. Ibid.
86. Richard Borsuk, "Plantation deal raises profiles of investors", *Asian Wall Street Journal*, 30 September 1994.
87. "Risjadson Group: Expansion step blocked by crisis", *Indonesian Commercial Newsletter*, 27 April 1998.
88. "Bila prospek sedang cerah", *Tempo Interaktif*, 5 August 1989.
89. "Liem bicara lagi: 'Saya masih kuasa penuh'", *Tempo*, 10 March 1990.
90. Risjad contribution in Dwidjowijoto, *Sudwikatmono*, pp. 146–54.
91. MSAA: Master Settlement and Acquisition Agreement, which regulated the transfer of assets from ailing conglomerates that had their banks recapitalized by the government to IBRA.
92. This was in a statement to the Singapore High Court made by Djuhar on 27 September 2001 in response to the suit initiated by Imin. Describing the $500,000 as a "loan", Djuhar said it was disbursed by Liem Sioe Liong to the

plaintiff (Imin) on the defendant's (Djuhar) behalf. There was no indication the loan was ever repaid.

93. Documents on file at Singapore High Court examined on 30 July 2008.
94. Affidavit of 26 September 2001 containing the 8 August 2001 letter from Harry Elias Partnership to Djuhar Sutanto.
95. Documents on file at Singapore High Court examined on 30 July 2008.

7

A "NEW LIFE"

Anthony Salim, once described by a journalist as a Ferrari-engined executive, has been helming the Salim Group in the post-Suharto era. He very nearly didn't get a chance to know his father. In 1949, just weeks before he was born, his father came close to losing his life in a car accident. Thankful to be alive, Liem named his newborn Fung Seng,[1] literally meaning "meeting a life". (Decades later, Anthony lived up to his name by resuscitating the conglomerate his father founded, preventing a near-death of the companies under the Salim umbrella, in the aftermath of the 1997 financial crisis that also ultimately led to the overthrown of Suharto, Salim's main patron.)

Anthony's stewardship of the business group was a gradual process, at least in the eyes of the public. If indeed Liem noticed early that the youngest of his three sons was the brightest, the boldest and the hungriest to get into business, he would not acknowledge it to the world. It is a credit to Liem, though, that he was wise enough to break from the traditional Chinese thinking that the eldest son is automatically the heir apparent and thus entitled to inherit the business. In his early teens, Anthony often accompanied his father to his factories; when he returned in 1971 from his studies overseas, he was impatient to learn the ropes of Salim's growing stable of businesses. Nurturing his youngest son's curious mind,

Liem frequently took Anthony along to meetings with Cabinet ministers, officials, other businessmen, as well as with Suharto. Those meetings gave the young man an opportunity to learn by observing. For a long time, Liem refused to be drawn into speculation about who among his children would take over the reins of the group. His older sons Albert and Andree were also assigned to Salim businesses, but Anthony showed keenness to get into every pie.

Asked in 1984 if Anthony was the group's "crown prince", Liem was purposely non-committal, commenting: "All the children are the same. What's needed here is teamwork. Those who say that Anton will replace me are outsiders."[2] The year Anthony returned from a two-year course in the United Kingdom, Suharto officiated at the opening of the Salim's first huge industrial venture, Bogasari Flour Mills. By 1975, when he was not yet twenty-six, Anthony was being entrusted by his father with increasing responsibilities. He had a part in negotiating with banker Mochtar Riady to join Bank Central Asia. Two years later, he acted as translator for his father when he was asked by Suharto to get involved in the Pertamina tanker case (see Box 7.1). In 1984, the year his father was asked about who would succeed him in running the group, Anthony was already holding the title "Managing Director" of Salim Economic Development Corporation, an unofficial umbrella company (that did not hold any equity) for the group's many ventures. Anthony's approach to corporate management was straightforward; he liked to keep things clear cut and separate. To him, the old Chinese style of *kongsi* ownership was a relic of the past. He urged his father to part ways in business with his brothers Sioe Hie and Sioe Kong and their families. In the 1980s, he led the push to grow the business empire beyond Indonesia's shores — to be less dependent on the patronage of Suharto.

BACKGROUND

Liem Fung Seng was born in Kudus on 15 October 1949 (his birth date in official documents was recorded erroneously as 25 October 1949). When he was seventeen, Chinese Indonesians were being urged to adopt Indonesian names and drop their Chinese-sounding ones. He wanted a name that started with "A", in keeping with the names chosen by his two older brothers, Albert and Andree, so he picked "Anthony". The registration clerk recording the name change suggested that he spelled it with an "i" at the end so it would look less "Western". Years later, he said, a secretary preparing his name cards wrote it as "Anthony" instead of Anthoni Salim and he was fine with it. Friends call him Anton, and at home he's often just "Seng". When he was born, Anthony sported a highly unusual feature: on the top of his head he had three "crowns" (the section where the hair parted). For the Chinese — and the Javanese too — this feature held special significance as most people have only one crown. Believers said it was a sign of extraordinary intelligence. For someone to possess two crowns on the head was already an indication of greatness. In his 1860 classic *Max Havelaar*, Multatuli (pseudonym of the Dutch anti-colonialist writer Eduard Douwes Dekker) wrote:

> The *Adhipatti* [a titled Javanese nobleman] examined the head of the little boy [Max], and to be sure, he too saw the *user-useran*, the double crown of hair which, according to Javanese superstition, means that its owner is destined eventually to wear a royal crown".[3]

Anthony was neither Javanese royalty nor a Chinese prince, but anyone who's had dealings with him over the years, whether they liked him or not, would agree on one thing — that he is sharp and intelligent. As with his father, he is described as *"lihai"* — connoting a combination of being clever, amazing, wily, capable and cunning. His father said of his son: "Anton's mind is like a computer; he processes things very quickly."[4] A self-admitted poor student at school, Anthony relied on his sharp instincts, tenacity, courage and excellent memory to hone his business skills.

Liem's four children were born two years apart, starting with Albert, whose Chinese name is Liem Sien Pin, in 1945. Second son Andree (Liem Sien Tjong) was born in 1947. Through quirks in registration, the surnames of the two older sons were recorded as Halim instead of Salim, when Liem chose that as his family name in 1967. Youngest child and only daughter Mira was born in 1951. The following year, Liem moved to Jakarta, staying temporarily at hotels until a suitable house was found. Even after they moved into the house, it was hard to feel at home initially, as the military was known to appropriate houses belonging to the Chinese, and the owners were forced to move into an annex, called a pavilion. Anthony recalled that on one occasion in the 1950s, the family had to do just that, but they got the house back in due course. The Liem children grew up in a close-knit family. As a young boy, Anthony was precocious and hyperactive, always on the look-out to play a trick on friends and siblings. He had little patience for school, preferring to spend time flying kites with friends or holding cricket fights. One of his acts of mischief resulted in a fire in the living room of their Jakarta home when he was playing with matches, but luckily, damage was minimal.

With their father spending much of his time pursuing business opportunities, the Liem children depended on the calm and inner strength of their mother, who raised them with the help of a maid. Anthony said his mother "was always quiet; she didn't talk much. But we felt her presence, her warmness and caring. We didn't communicate much, but we were close."[5] Liem said he and his wife tried to treat their sons equally, but Albert had a special place in her heart. Anthony, the mischievous one, exasperated her at times and sometimes got his ears pulled as punishment, but corporal punishment was generally not practised at home. Liem described his wife as an ideal partner, as she focused on raising the children and handled family matters, allowing him to pay full attention to business. It probably also helped family harmony that she was discreet and refrained from grilling him on matters outside the home.

A SCARY INCIDENT AT HOME

There was one event in the days of the nascent friendship between Liem and Suharto that rattled the family. That was when a uniformed man showed up at the house asking for Liem. Not finding him, he shot his wife, nearly killing her. Anthony recalled that it happened in June 1966. His father was part of an unofficial delegation visiting Singapore — diplomatic relations had not been re-established and Suharto was putting an end to the Confrontation policy his predecessor had adopted.[6] As recounted by Liem:

> I was in Singapore at the time. One afternoon around 4.30 p.m., a man wearing the uniform of the Marines went to my house looking for me. My wife thought he had come for money, and invited him in. He took off his cap and sat down and was told that I was in Singapore. Tante [Dutch for aunt, it is also how some people address older non-*pribumi* ladies] went into the bedroom to get some cash. There was a screened mosquito door leading to the room, but one of the door hinges was broken so it didn't swing properly. The man followed Tante into the room but his entry was hampered by the broken hinge. Tante heard the door and turned around; she was startled to see that the man had a gun in his hand. She shouted:

"*Jangan, pak!*" [don't, sir]. He fired two shots, one hit her arm; the other her stomach. It seemed the bullet missed the heart and exited through her back. It was a lucky thing; otherwise, she would have been dead, for sure. But God and Buddha must have been protecting Tante. She started screaming. The man ran off; in his hurry, he left his cap behind. Albert was in the house at that time; he ran to his mother... They rushed Tante to hospital. No one was able to reach me immediately, but strangely, that night of the incident, I could not sleep.

At that time, it was still *Konfrontasi* and there was no direct communication between Indonesia and Singapore. My family didn't know where I was staying. It took me three days after the shooting before I was able to return to Jakarta. I rushed straight to the hospital from the airport. When I saw Tante, I cried. I thought surely there was no hope for her, but Tante was brave. She told me she was alright and said I should go home first to get some rest. It was clear to me that someone was trying to kidnap or harm me. If I had been home, I think I would have been killed for sure. After that incident, we hired a *satpam* [guard] for the house."[7]

Anthony, who was on his way home from school when the assault happened, said it was a miracle his mother didn't die. "The bullet just missed her heart; it went in one side of the body, and somehow came out the other, so no bullet was lodged in the body. Another bullet had pierced her arm," he related.[8] He said his mother didn't panic. She managed to staunch the bleeding while Albert and the family chauffeur rushed her into the family car to take her to the hospital. It was fortunate, too, that by this time Liem had already established good credentials with Suharto, who was de facto president (Sukarno was still nominally president). According to Anthony, the political situation was still chaotic and uncertain at that time, but the army was in control. Anthony said he had to race to a blood bank to get supplies for his mother, who had lost a lot of blood. He recounted:

> We drove the VW; we put a sten gun on the roof of the car to help clear the way — to let people know this was an emergency. We went against traffic. That probably saved her life. When Pak Harto was informed of the incident, he immediately arranged to send us the best doctor — his name was Dr Imam Santoso. I stayed with my mom in the hospital for three weeks.[9]

It was fortunate, he added, that the bullets used were the smaller 32mm calibre or "the consequence could have been a lot worse". Theories about the shooting abound. The family wanted to believe the man might have been trying to get money from Liem and was confused after finding him overseas. Still, if it were a simple case of asking for money, he didn't need to be armed; Liem and his family were used to giving to people who asked for help. At that time, Liem was not yet the wealthy crony he would become, but he was already a successful businessman. The fact that the perpetrator was in Marine uniform added to the confusion, as it was widely known that the Marines had more Sukarno loyalists than the other services in the armed forces. According to Anthony, the police later apprehended the shooter, but the family decided not to press charges against him. Asked why, Anthony replied: "We felt there was no point. Why create more problems? Things already happened. Seeking justice sometimes doesn't pay. He was jailed for two years for some other crime."[10]

SCHOOLING

Denied the chance of formal schooling, Liem encouraged his children to pursue tertiary education. But none of them were outstanding students. The three sons enrolled in college, but not all graduated. Albert's college studies were interrupted by the chaotic situation prevailing in Jakarta in the mid-1960s. Andree, like Anthony, studied in the United Kingdom after high school. Anthony's school experience was nothing memorable; his performance less than sterling, often struggling to pass year-end examinations that determined whether a student moved up to the next grade. "I was always on the borderline of passing", he admitted.[11] He was often bored at school, looking forward to recess, when he could escape the confines of the classroom and eat his favourite snacks. He loved *perkedel,* a deep-fried potato croquette. As soon as the school day was over, he would race home to play with friends. Too slightly built to take on bullies, he cultivated friends who served as his protectors. "Although I was not the ringleader, I had influence, and they protected me", he said, with a smile.[12]

In his third year at a Chinese middle school named Sin Hua (New China), he failed the finals and had to repeat the year. His education got interrupted following the failed 30 September 1965 putsch. Anti-communist demonstrations organized by the two largest student groups KAMI and KAPPI[13] had disrupted schooling. Eventually, all Chinese schools in the country were forced to close. Anthony's parents, like many others during that chaotic period, pondered what to do. His father thought that sending his playful youngest son to China might be a good option, but his mother was appalled at the idea. She had made her first visit there in 1961, and remembered being horrified at the conditions she saw. Anthony related: "My mom said 'no' to the idea. 'Why should I send my son to be tortured there?' she said. So she told the travel agent not to issue the ticket. It was a lucky thing, or else I would have been caught in the Cultural Revolution!"[14]

Instead, he was sent to Singapore in late 1966, enrolling first at the Seventh Day Adventist School then located at Serangoon Road. Many Indonesian Chinese students were also enrolled there. Much of the early time was spent learning English. A year later, Anthony switched to St Joseph's Institution which he also attended for a year. One of Anthony's legal guardians in Singapore, the late Peter Fong,[15] once told a friend that he lost count of the number of visits he had to make to the school to persuade administrators not to give a failing grade to his charge. Just before Anthony was due to take his "O" Levels[16] examinations, administered to students in Singapore after four years of secondary school, he decided to continue his education in the United Kingdom. Friends found him a business course offered by Ewell County Technical College (since renamed North East Surrey College of Technology), located outside London. Upon graduation, he tooled around Europe in the two-door Mercedes Benz sports car his proud father bought him. It cost £15,000. It was Anthony's first indulgence in luxury. He also travelled to the United States for a few weeks but was soon chomping at the bit to return home and become involved in his father's businesses. Anthony recalled, "I was not married yet. I was engaged when I was 21 and I got married four years later." His bride, Siti Margareth Jusuf, whom he met in school, was the daughter of a Hakka Chinese businessman. "It was pretty simple", Anthony said coyly of his courtship, "it wasn't anything too romantic".[17] He recalled, though, that the wedding celebrations went on for five days.

SIBLINGS

Albert and Andree do not have the intensity of their youngest brother. The eldest, Albert, is easy-going and good-natured; Andree is polite but reserved. Both older brothers are dapper dressers, while Anthony is more casual and prefers a batik shirt to a business suit. Liem mused about the different characters of his three sons. Albert was laid-back, he said. "He was his mother's favourite. He's fun-loving … a bit lazy. He didn't like to work too hard. He loved guitars and fast cars. Andree was an asthmatic child. He's a hard-worker, but he's not a risk-taker. Anthony was the naughty one. He is daring. When he grew up, he worked all the time."[18] On his relationship with his two brothers, Anthony said: "I was close to my two brothers when we were young. Later, Albert went to a local university; Andree and I went off to the UK. I went first, and Andree came after me. That's when we [Albert and I] started drifting apart. But Andree and I remained close."[19] Among his father's acquaintances, Albert is considered friendlier and more approachable. "Albert would make small talk with us; he is easy to chat with, unlike Anthony," said a family friend.[20] As his father became wealthier, Albert acquired a taste for the good life and developed a love for motorbikes.

Albert has not played an active role in the Salim companies since he parted ways with the group in the mid-1980s; the reasons for his departure from the group appear to be sensitive. According to sources, Albert had a disappointing performance at the Volvo auto business that he was asked to run. He was said to be frustrated that his father seemed to be giving more responsibilities to his two younger brothers. Some sources close to the family said Anthony pressured his father to restrict Albert's participation in Salim, but Anthony denied it. "We didn't kick him out. He just walked away and left us — my father, Andree and myself in the family businesses," Anthony said in reply to our question.[21]

Albert declined to be interviewed, but agreed to answer a list of submitted questions. An intermediary indicated he would not answer "touchy" issues. He provided brief written answers to the authors' questions. However, he invited the co-author to lunch at the tastefully decorated Kembang Goela restaurant, located in the Plaza Sentral office building in Jakarta, both partly owned by his family. Albert was a gracious host, but he was cagey about revealing his businesses. He said he owned several properties around the world but wouldn't say where. After leaving Salim, a patron whose identity he would not disclose, gave him substantial help. Since then, he has partnered different "well-connected individuals" in various ventures. (According to the Jakarta rumour mill, Gen. Sudharmono, a former state secretary, who was Suharto's Vice-President from 1988 to 1993, was one of Albert's main patrons.) Albert's exit from Salim left Liem family interests in the hands of Anthony and Andree and their father. Much later, in 1998 after the violence that led to the fall of Suharto, second brother Andree also exited the group's operations in Indonesia and relocated to Singapore.

Albert was more forthcoming when talking about his childhood. Born in Kudus, he was named Sin Pin (also spelled Sien Pien). Kudus, he recalled, was a beautiful small town. He had fond memories of weekend visits by his maternal grandmother, bearing cakes, bananas and delicious snacks. She ran a small food stall where Albert would occasionally help out. One memory that stayed in his mind, he said, was the time the family had to seek refuge in a factory as some planes were bombing the area. (These were presumably Dutch planes strafing what they thought were rebel positions, although Albert would have been not more than four years old at the time.) He also recalled that his father played the drum at a parade in the town square in Kudus at Chinese New Year. He was nine before he joined his father in Jakarta. When he was a student, Albert represented his school in basketball and table tennis competitions. He also loved swimming and was a keen sportsman. In Jakarta, Albert attended two Chinese schools — Sin Hua, where his younger brothers would also enroll, and Pa Tjung. He was admitted to study Economics at Uraika University (now called Trisakti) but his education was interrupted when the university was burned down in the aftermath of the 30 September 1965 coup.

Until Liem became a business partner with Suharto, his capital was stretched. He had ambitious plans but, not being an Indonesian citizen yet, did not qualify for bank loans. Albert described that period as one of "difficult capitalization", and everyone at home chipped in whatever way they could to help. He said his mother and aunt raised money by selling bread and pastries. Even in the mid-1960s, Albert said, he often worked without pay when he delivered goods such as textiles to customers. He added that he worked for a year — also unpaid — when his father was granted rights to import cloves from Africa, together with a company belonging to Suharto's half-brother Probosutedjo. "I helped my dad in the clove warehouse; every day I had to check and note the weight of the incoming and outgoing stocks. I checked everything at the warehouse, to prevent 'leaks'. I spent many long hours at the clove warehouse," said Albert. "That was a tough time. … it was my national service. I worked hard and waited for my turn to be more involved in my father's business, but I was told to wait further," he added.[22]

Helping out in his father's businesses yielded one important benefit for Albert — it allowed him to get to know "powerful" individuals, including Gen. Sofjar, Pertamina boss Ibnu Sutowo, Adam Malik (Vice President 1978–83), Radius Prawiro, B.J. Habibie, Ginandjar Kartasasmita (who became Coordinating Minister for the Economy in the last Suharto Cabinet in 1998) and Sudharmono. With some help, he was able to strike out on his own and set up businesses independent of his father. According to Albert, he met his wife Liliani during his school days and dated her for eight years before they got married. Albert was assigned by his father to run PT Salim Jaya Motor, a company Liem started for the assembly of two models of Volvo, the Swedish marque. The auto business was difficult to break into and assembling just two models did not allow the company to develop the critical mass it needed. Although the company won an order to supply cars to senior government officials, it proved difficult to collect payment. The Volvo venture was not considered a success.

Many years later, when the Salim companies sprouted like wild mushrooms after a rain, Albert wanted to go back in but found the door shut. Anthony likened Albert's departure to a train leaving the station — "there's no turning around", he said, "Once the train has left the structure doesn't allow you to come back."[23] Asked if Albert's departure from the group caused friction in their relationship, he replied: "No, there is no friction. Basically, [there was some] unhappiness. It's two different things … friction means that you have a problem; unhappiness is a result. When you have a claim, you have friction. But being unhappy is — if you don't like what you see… So Albert belongs to the second category."[24]

On his part, Albert claimed he was content with his life. Aged sixty-two at the time of the 2007 lunch at Kembang Goela, Albert said: "Now I am running my business in property, factory, mining, etc. In the meantime, I try to teach my children in work and social life. At this age, I am happy with my life. I am enjoying the time I can spend with my wife and my grandchildren."[25] Albert has four children, two sons and two daughters. His wife is involved in charity work and is active in a Buddhist association. A hint of bitterness is evident from the comment he made: "It is sad to see my parents have grown really old. After passing by half of a century, I think I had not done much. I am saddened when I think that I could have contributed a lot towards my dad's group of companies but I had no chance to do so. I am an optimist. With all these, I am becoming more mature to face the difficulties on my own. I just feel that there are inequalities in our group, not like other big family groups in Indonesia."[26]

Liem's second son Andree spent much of his time at the family's flagship bank, BCA, where he earned a reputation as a caring boss and was well-liked and highly regarded by the staff. His father assessed him thus: "Andree is careful and thrifty. When he was at BCA, he used democratic practices; he was a professional."[27] A naturally cautious person, Andree did not like taking huge risks. A senior Salim executive commented: "Andree isn't an entrepreneur like Anton; he was not looking to grab available opportunities."[28] Andree also studied in Singapore, enrolled at the Chung Cheng School in Katong. Like Anthony, he also did a two-year course in the United Kingdom, graduating with a diploma in Business Studies from the South East London Technical College. Andree's principal management role was at BCA, although he held board positions in various Salim companies. At BCA, he worked alongside Mochtar Riady, who served as a mentor and teacher to both Andree and Anthony. Years after his exit from the bank which grew meteorically under his leadership, Mochtar Riady was asked to compare the capabilities of the two brothers. He replied: "There is no comparison. Anthony is very sharp."[29]

Andree politely declined a request to be interviewed or answer any questions for this book. Some family friends say he became more withdrawn after the sudden death of his first wife. She left him with two children. Andree remarried an attractive woman with three young children of her own. After the May 1998 riots that saw his father's house thrashed and burnt and many Chinese Indonesians attacked, Andree and his family moved to Singapore. According to Liem, his second son was traumatized by the violence. Andree subsequently withdrew from many Indonesian board positions, and concentrated on business ventures in Singapore, Hong Kong and China. His primary vehicle in Singapore is QAF Ltd, a food production and distribution company. (In 2010, the company reported S$856 million in revenue and after-tax profit of S$48.7 million.[30]) He has majority shares in Hong Kong-listed Peaktop International Holdings Ltd., principally a home and garden product manufacturer.

At BCA, Andree and Anthony worked harmoniously as a team, especially after the departure of Mochtar. Although the three brothers have gone their separate ways after 1998, Anthony maintained there is no ill will among them. As family members, he said, "we are always there for each other". But, he added:

> We keep business separate [from personal matters]. When [someone in the] family is having a problem, we're always there, for whatever reason. But when we do business, there is a clear distinction; it's better that way. It's the same with my uncles. They were partners with my dad.

Then my father [separated]; he said: ok, you take everything, we don't want anything. So whatever is my share, I give you that. No hassle ... because we can seek new things. We are more opportunity-driven; we don't want to dwell on what we have. It's very clear-cut. The philosophy and principle of the family is very clear. It started with my dad, and I continue it, and hopefully, the next generation will too ... because the business will be affected if you have no straight code and conduct. This is probably something a lot of families cannot do when the founder and the creator pass away ... Then they start to quarrel, and then all these break-ups happen.[31]

Mira, the baby in the family who everyone called "mei-mei" (little sister) had no active role in the Salim group. She had chosen to pursue a secretarial course in the United Kingdom but did not complete it and instead got married to Franciscus Welirang, a Chinese Indonesian from Padang, Sumatra. Franky, as he is called, cut his teeth in the wheat milling business — initially with Bogasari's textile weaving mills and worked with Piet Yap to build up the operations of the wheat miller. Franky rose to become CEO of Bogasari as well as a director of several other Salim companies, including Indofood.

LIVING AND BREATHING BUSINESS

An observation about the single-mindedness of the Chinese about business was once made by one of Indonesia's leading *pribumi* executives, Julius Tahija. It was a comment that fits Anthony to the T. Writing in his memoir, the late Tahija, the first local boss for the Indonesian operations of oil giant Caltex, said he got to know some Chinese boys in his English language classes during the Dutch colonial days. Spending time with them and getting to know them better "made me appreciate what business meant to the Chinese ... the boys lived, walked, slept, and ate business 24 hours a day. Their most frequent thought was, 'How can I get the next guilder'?" Tahija wrote.[32] He also observed the strong camaraderie and great emphasis on trust that the Chinese possessed:

> The great strength of the Chinese, I concluded, came from their mutual loyalty. It went far beyond family. Once they trusted you, they would help you and stand by you through anything ... however, you only had to be dishonest once and they would never trust you again. ... the Chinese had a wonderful capacity to be stimulated by their mistakes. If a textile

merchant had to take a loss on a deal he would say, "Forget about it. Let's see how we can recover by finding new opportunities".[33]

Anthony certainly has shown this zeal for business. He has eschewed the relaxed, spoiled lifestyle of a rich man's son. Although he had fun zipping around in his sports car after graduation, his persona has been more of a scrappy entrepreneur — always thinking how to make the next big bucks. Liem once described his youngest son as wise beyond his years, and Anthony showed that quality by never trying to outshine his father or take credit away from him. He said it was his father's ability in picking capable and trustworthy partners and managers that allowed the Salim Group to build a strong foundation. Even after years of being in the driver's seat, Anthony continued to brief his father on all aspects of business plans. Asked if he tried to step out of his dad's shadows and make his own mark, like some scions of business tycoons in Asia, Anthony asserted in an interview in 2007: "I would never try to compete with my dad. That would be stupid." He said it was his father who taught him a lot about business. But he pointed out, "I also had the keenness to learn. It's [like] both hands clapping; it's not only one side. If you want to learn, you have to do it like that. You're never on a single track. If you're single-tracked, it doesn't work."[34]

Businessman Sofyan Wanandi, who was close to early New Order advisors and a friend of Liem's, credits Anthony with spearheading the push into many of the new ventures undertaken by the Salim Group starting in the 1980s. Said Sofyan: "Liem didn't have many business ideas (of his own) until Anthony came back from school in UK ... Anthony uses a lot of professionals; he is super-smart; he can make quick decisions ... he's no-nonsense."[35] An Indonesian journalist, Bondan Winarno, commissioned to research the history of BCA, also commented on Anthony's management style, saying that once Anthony has been armed with facts, he liked to make decisions quickly, "so discussions with him were usually intense".[36]

Anthony's grasp of the intricacies of the financial world was rooted in his ability to absorb information and inputs. Soon after his return from the United Kingdom, he started to tune in to his father's mindset. "Yes, after several years [of being with him], I think we have a lot of similarity in thinking, the way we arrive at a decision", Anthony mused.[37] In a December 2006 chat with the authors, Liem remarked of his son: "He's a quick learner. He can remember and process everything. Making money is now his responsibility; he works all the time. He runs here and there; I can't keep up with him."[38]

Like his father, Anthony understood the workings of the insidious patronage system of the New Order. He gave support not only to Salim's patrons, but to some who sought or needed assistance. Government salaries are extremely low in Indonesia — one root of the country's endemic corruption — and many officials do not view receiving gifts as bribery. The Liems and many other businesspeople considered sharing the "spoils" as part of the price of doing business in Indonesia — which could be a highly lucrative place to do business. But Anthony was well aware that the political patronage enjoyed by his father had a limited shelf-life, and globalization was changing the world. As early as in the late 1970s, he convinced his father of the advantages of investing offshore and pushed for the Salim Group to explore opportunities outside Indonesia.

Besides a passion for business and a good head for figures, Anthony shared some other of his father's attributes: Courteous and cordial outside, determined and steely inside. But some in the business community in Indonesia are more wary of the son, who is considered less compassionate by nature and far pushier in character. Both father and son were disciplined in their exercise regimen; Liem used to wake up early and took brisk walks each morning, usually around his factory compound for seven kilometres. Anthony does a gym routine at home before heading to the office. Unlike his father, however, who liked to frequent a nightclub where he mixed business with pleasure, Anthony stays late into the night at office. It is common for him to work well past midnight. Anthony and his father place a high value on loyalty; they remained loyal to Suharto even after his fall. Liem said he admired former Armed Forces commander Gen. Benny Murdani, who even after many years of faithful service to Suharto, was shunted aside after he tried to caution his boss about the excesses of his children. Despite his demotion from his position as trusted aide and advisor, Murdani never publicly criticized his boss, Liem pointed out.

Anthony's curiosity and desire to learn helped him be a quick understudy. He gives this appraisal of himself: "I was very independent from young; I dared to try things ... I can get along with people quite OK. That's because of my character — I'm able to mix [easily]."[39] While his course in England helped provide him with some groundwork for his business career, he described it as "very basic stuff — they touched on statistics, basic law, accounting, financial stuff … But when you come back, you don't know how to bring them together. Then you have to assemble them … make them act as one." He probably succeeded quite well in figuring out how to "bring them together", as he became known later in the Group as someone who devours the weekly reports sent by the company's executives. "You can't pull wool over his eyes", commented one of them.[40]

People who have had dealings with Anthony over the years conclude that he is someone you don't trifle with. Even after the passing of Suharto, many people remain guarded about Anthony and the Salim Group. They include business rivals, former associates, and ex-company executives. Some declined to be interviewed for this project, reasoning that there was nothing to be gained by it. The fear factor may have diminished somewhat with the passage of time, but the guardedness lingers. In Indonesia, it is not uncommon that powerfully linked cronies are viewed with apprehension. Asked about the perceived fear that some people have of him, Anthony appeared bemused. Reflecting for a moment, he remarked:

> I think there are two types of businessmen: shrewd or nasty. People sometimes cannot distinguish between the two … When you are shrewd, you are very calculating, and you know exactly what you want. But being shrewd, [the question is then] are you fair or unfair? That's another consideration. If you are shrewd but "not fair", that is the bad side. You could be shrewd but [act] with certain principles … We are not nasty. We cannot afford to be nasty because we don't want to do harm to people … So there are some principles, at least for the Salim family — things you want to do, or what you don't want to do … so that is something [where] you have to exercise self-discipline.[41]

On first impression, one could be forgiven for not being initially bowled over by Anthony. Slight of build, often casually dressed and sometimes even a little unkempt looking, he doesn't exactly cut an imposing figure. He shuns branded shirts and wears outdated owl-like spectacle frames. His mop of hair covering his forehead adds to his boyish looks. His sartorial preference trends towards the comfortable fit of a long-sleeved batik shirt, which he normally wears to the office. Over that, he sometimes slip a sleeveless dark vest. He grins when he divulges that he still uses the 777 brand undershirt manufactured by his father's early textile factory.

He certainly does not fit the profile of a corporate predator. A *New York Times* journalist who once interviewed him wrote: "He looks very much like a product of the central Javanese town of Kudus, where he was born."[42] But Anthony possesses a self-confidence that allows him not to give a hoot what people think of him. The banker Mochtar Riady, who joined BCA in 1975 and was credited with building the bank to become the country's largest private bank, recalled being underwhelmed by the "hippie-looking" young man when he was first introduced to Anthony. (Their meeting is recounted in Chapter 10.) Anthony dons a suit and tie for formal occasions, but he looks most in his element in his beloved batik shirts, of which he estimates he has at least 200. Asked about his penchant for batik shirts, he said:

> I wear batik because I like batik. Some people wear Gucci because they want to be seen in it ... It's their choice. When Indonesians buy a lot of Gucci bags and everything else, they just want to have people see that "I wear Gucci". For me, I wear batik for comfort. But if you need expensive stuff, so be it. Because you buy what you want.[43]

In a lighter vein, he compares the intricate designs of batik to how business is done in Indonesia — the designs can be complicated and there can be many different shades of one colour. "Batik is not like a Burberry [design] which is very clear-cut, where you can easily see the lines, the squares ... See, (pointing to his shirt), the batik motif here is always rather dark ... how can you distinguish this? It's basically a blur! The batik colours [to me, means] ... whatever the situation, you can survive!"[44]

While Anthony may not be debonair, he is clearly respected in the corporate world. Some foreign CEOs visiting Jakarta seek him out and come away impressed with his analytical mind. Though he fared poorly in school, his curiosity and his thirst for knowledge turned him into a voracious reader after he entered the business world. His inner sanctum on the nineteenth floor of the Indocement building is cluttered with books, stacks of newspapers and reports, and magazines. Papers are strewn everywhere — on his desk, on shelves, even on the floor. He says he doesn't have enough time to read what he wants. Still, he is reluctant to discard old newspapers. Along the walls of his Singapore home are bundles of yellowing newspapers neatly tied with strings, some going back a few years. They are not allowed to go to the recycling bin until he gives the nod. At home, Anthony speaks Indonesian and Javanese, and says he understands Hokchia, his father's dialect. His Mandarin has improved a great deal in recent years, thanks to increased business activities in China. He speaks good English, but perhaps his best "language" is business talk — his partners in China, the Middle East and the English-speaking world have no problems understanding him.

"A BLACK WIDOW"[45]

Liem's management mantra has always been: "Pick the right horses to run for you. Once you pick them, trust them. If you don't trust them, don't pick them." Benny Santoso, Anthony's lieutenant since the mid-1990s, (he currently sits on the boards of various Salim companies including Indofood and First Pacific), has been with the Group since 1981. He says his boss takes the father's motto a step further: "According to Anthony, trust is good, but control is even better!" said Benny half-jokingly: "Pak Anton doesn't trust anybody 100 per cent — not even me!"[46] A long-time senior executive at Indofood noted Anthony's tendency to micro-manage. "He has so many things to work on … he may have been too aggressive when Suharto was strong. But he's a real entrepreneur — he grabs opportunities."[47] Manuel (Manny) Pangilinan, the Managing Director and CEO of First Pacific and a partner with Anthony since 1981, described him as "an engaging type of character, who is performance-driven".[48] One of the Philippines' top entrepreneurs, John Gokongwei, once commented to a journalist about Anthony: "We talk the same language. I like the way he does things, the way he decides and follows through."[49]

Anthony can be more direct and confrontational than his father. He is also far less reluctant to cut people loose if he feels they are not working out. Manny jokingly said of Anthony: "I call him a Black Widow [for the way he] 'kills' his advisors and peers."[50] High-profile exits of Salim senior executives include Johannes Kotjo, in the early 1990s, and Eva Riyanti Hutapea from Indofood. Anthony denies that he "pushes" people out, but he says, if "we think [someone's] service has already reached maturity, we ask him to retire. We don't fire people, as a principle — unless you do wrong. If you are totally wrong, [then] we ask you to resign."[51] Anthony has not been shy about ending partnerships, even long-time ones, and that has made some view him as a hard-nosed businessman, with less compassion than his father had. His preference for control meant he has had few reservations about disengaging partners, even long-time ones (see Robert Kuok's comments about changes in Bogasari in the "Noodle King" chapter). In the mid-1970s, when Liem wanted to get Mochtar Riady to manage his bank, Liem's younger brother Sioe Kong apparently objected. Foreseeing the likelihood of more complications arising with participation of his cousins in the family businesses, Anthony nudged his father to part ways with his uncles. Anthony's hand was also evident in the break-up between Salim and the Sinar Mas Group in the palm oil business in 1990.

It has been said that one can tell a lot about people from the way they handle a crisis. The financial crisis of 1997 and its aftermath showed Anthony in his true mettle. He spent several tough years hammering out solutions to salvage what he could of the group, in an atmosphere that had turned outright hostile. Anthony doggedly plodded on in negotiating with bankers, the IMF, and the team set up by the government to handle the massive loans poured into private banks to keep them afloat, better known by its acronym, IBRA (Indonesian Banking Restructuring Agency). The survival of the Group hinged on him. Those at the opposite end of the negotiating table with him knew they had to do their homework diligently or be prepared to be outmanoeuvred. His reputation as a tenacious negotiator precedes him. A member of the IBRA team who asked not to be named said that those participating in meetings with Anthony were forewarned of his presence, so that they had to arrive fully prepared and "well-armed with figures".[52] Dutch academic Marleen Dieleman, who did her doctoral dissertation on the Salim Group, cites another unnamed IBRA staffer as saying:

> Within IBRA, Anthony Salim laid down his cards on the table, but it was still a poker game. He is smart ... Asks us for our conditions first. We would like to have the liquid assets, like Indofood shares, but it turns out there is a condition, that if he has less than 51 per cent ownership, his bank loans become immediately payable. Obstacles arise. Instead he offers Indomobil. Anthony Salim is very tough to negotiate with.[53]

Anthony's hands-on management style is evident from his insistence on detailed briefings by group managers. One said:

> Every week we report on sales to Anthony Salim, he likes to concentrate on market share. He is very detailed. One day, he asked for the profitability of each product. So we submitted a pile of papers, and he actually read it all. He even pointed out that product such and such was not profitable. He has very good and creative ideas and made insightful remarks.[54]

Another person Dieleman spoke to, described as being close to the Group, offered this comment:

It is very difficult to get along with him. His personality makes him want to meddle in things. Anthony Salim is energetic, intelligent and has a dazzling breadth of knowledge; the level of detail is very high. He has the illusion that he knows enough to run all businesses.[55]

First Pacific's Manny Pangilinan agreed that Anthony was a "details person" but thought he gave trusted Salim executives a long leash in running the show. On his relationship with Anthony, which became severely tested in 2002, Manny commented: "There will always be some collisions. In the first 15 years, we would talk twice or three times a day, even for just five minutes. There was a great deal of communication. But not a great deal of interference. He would judge from context and tone of voice [in phone calls] if things are ok."[56]

Imbued with Confucian values when he was growing up, Anthony is the epitome of a filial son. "Anthony will never go against his father's wishes", remarked a family friend.[57] He admired his father, and shared his father's tradition of consulting Buddhist monks and *feng shui* (geomancy) masters before determining the time for important events, such as the official launch of a company or the opening a factory. For calculating his propitious time, he gives geomancers his real birthday — 15 October 1949 — and not the date erroneously recorded in his birth certificate. Asked if he believes in fate, he answered: "[It's] a given. The Indonesians believe in *takdir*, the preordained, and *nasib* (luck). These two words are very important. Whether you're hardworking or not, these two determine your success; luck — you can have, but *takdir* is something else — that's it ... [you] can't do anything about it."[58] He said he believes that everything is connected to the time of one's birth:

From your birth day and time ... should be able to predict some things;... from that, you can know your lucky time.... maybe it's something illogical, but the Chinese have been using it for 5,000 years, so something must be right. [Then you can set] the direction and time; that's very important, especially for things like ground breaking; you have to get it right — the push of the button is the most important. At this point, every single second affects your decision, one or the other ... you make a choice, and you make a decision."[59]

A workaholic, Anthony rarely takes a day off. He doesn't have any hobbies; work is his life and pastime. Asked if he's ever taken up golf, he replied: "No, I don't want to talk to a ball!" There were some family vacations, but he rarely is able to get business out of mind. Another Salim executive remarked that Anthony expects his senior managers to be always "on call". He cited an example of returning from the United States at 11 p.m. one night from a business trip, only to be put on an 8.30 a.m. flight the next morning to Australia, then having to spend the next few days running ragged. He wryly observed: "[Our] wives have to be very patient and understanding."[60]

Asked how he keeps up with his gruelling work schedule, Anthony replied: "If you enjoy it, it's ok." Benny, however, notes that his boss has sacrificed family life for work. During the dark days, when Anthony was battling for the survival of the Group and fending off legal challenges, he had an inner circle of friends and staff who helped sustain him. He said he was especially moved by Salim staff members, of whatever religion, who held prayer sessions for him and his father. These days, he is philosophical about many of the past events, even with those who tried to bring down the Group. He tries to stay focused on the future, and exploring business possibilities. "I'm having fun", he said, adding: "The most important thing is, in your life you do what you think is best and you're happy. Maybe some people are unhappy with us, but that's ok ... I don't consciously do things to make people unhappy. I sleep well at night."[61]

LEARNING THE ROPES

Over the course of the years, Anthony has made plenty of mistakes, as he readily admits, starting with his first business initiative. Eager to prove himself after his return from the United Kingdom, he was initially brash and aggressive. It was his father, he said, who stepped in to keep him in check. "When I made a mistake, my father corrected me but he was supportive. This was most important." One example he gave of an early business blunder was his decision to import cement from North Korea:

> It was in 1971 and I wasn't yet familiar with the business. I committed three errors in that decision: firstly, North Korea was a communist country, so it was not popular with Suharto at that time. Secondly, it was considered a pariah state by the international community. Thirdly, I didn't know enough about the cement business. While most manufacturers used five layers of Kraft paper for transporting cement, the North Koreans used only three. When the cargo ship docked, the Indonesian workers handling the cement were quite rough. They threw the bags about. Many of the

cement bags broke — about 70 per cent were ripped. It was so messy; we had to repackage them on board. After that, we had to clean the ship. In addition, we had to pay extra demurrage charges. Then the cement had to be sold as "contaminated" second-hand cement. We lost a lot of money on that load. That was an expensive lesson. My dad merely said to me: "You know, this is your first experience." So I never forgot that.[62]

He also admitted to misjudging people. "Sometimes I think I am more often wrong than I am right about people ... but the important thing is to learn from your mistakes."[63] When he was young, Anthony said, he was hungry "to do things" but had no particular target in mind. As he put it:

I didn't set out to achieve a goal ... because you don't know what it [your goal] is. My dad had ambition — he wanted to be big, but without necessarily knowing what to do. That was the starting point. When I came back from the United Kingdom, things were already established ... the foundation was laid. But to build from ground to level 5 — that's harder.[64]

On his approach to establishing himself as a businessman in his own right, Anthony said he did not want to take advantage of his father's wealth, acquired on the coat-tails of Suharto. Although he was born with the proverbial "silver spoon in his mouth", Anthony had the fire in the belly of someone at the bottom of the ladder. His father had already created a solid foundation and Anthony wanted to build on that. "It's a matter of choice," he reflected. "You have to have a willingness to engage; a willingness to take responsibility and a willingness to commit yourself. It's like being in a kitchen — you can have all the tools, utensils, a good set in the kitchen, but you still have to be a good cook ... If you're good, you can work with less equipment, but can still turn out good food..."[65] Unlike some scions of business dynasties, who have tried to step out of their fathers' shadows, Anthony had been content to work alongside his father. His self-assuredness helps him be inured to criticisms and he said he's not bothered by allegations reported in the media. Always careful to give credit to his father, he noted, with some modesty: "Observing my father's accomplishment — I think he must have [done] something right ... compared to me, he's much, much higher; he had no reference point. I would never compete with my old man ... [if I did] maybe I would only get 5–10 per cent of his results."[66]

Among Liem's three sons, Anthony was not only regarded as having the sharpest mind, he was also the most willing to stick his neck out. Liem often used the Indonesian word *pintar*, meaning "smart" or "clever", and the Chinese word *lihai*, meaning very capable, when talking about his youngest son. He also often took Anthony's advice, though on one occasion probably regretted it. In 1978, Anthony talked him into giving their first ever exclusive media interview. It was with Ian Verchere, the editor of Hong Kong-based business journal called *Insight*. At the time, Anthony thought the Group was ready to have a profile outside the country. Several months earlier, he had been the translator for his father in sensitive negotiations with Swiss-based tanker magnate Bruce Rappaport to settle a lawsuit out of court. Liem had been asked by Suharto to step in to help bring closure to the multimillion dollar case that had nearly bankrupted state oil firm Pertamina (see Box 7.1). The *cukong* would have preferred to have kept his role very low keyed, considering that two Cabinet ministers were already tasked with handling the case. Verchere's story appeared in the May issue with Liem on the cover, appearing as a caricature dressed in Napoleonic uniform, posing in front of a portrait of Suharto. The headline read: "Liem Sioe Liong: Indonesia's Imperial Cukong".

Anthony said later they were not happy with the portrayal. He maintained that the article contained some inaccuracies and added that had he known of Verchere's decision to focus on the Pertamina case, he would not have urged his father to agree to the interview.[67] Nevertheless, the *Insight* feature was the most comprehensive profile about Liem in those days. Even at that early stage, Verchere already described the twenty-nine-year-old Anthony as a "skilled businessman in his own right", and called him the "heir apparent". He noted that Anthony was the one who accompanied his "non-English speaking father on all overseas missions and participates in major negotiations". Verchere also remarked that some of Anthony's cousins — the children of Liem's brothers Sioe Hie and Sioe Kong — "resent his succession" and noted "signs of growing inter-family strife".[68] It would be several years later, in 1984, that both father and son sat down for another interview, this time with news magazine *Tempo*, and the first session with a domestic media organization. It was arranged by Liem's good friend and fellow business tycoon Sofyan Wanandi. The interview was done by experienced journalist Fikri Jufri. It was so unprecedented for Liem to grant interviews that the demand for the magazine necessitated a reprint within hours.

Liem agreed with Anthony that for the Salim group to become more professional and to attain its goal to go international, it was probably best to part ways with the families of his brothers. Anthony explained that the split, effected in the early 1990s, was necessary to avoid possible complications or unhappiness arising from ownership and decision-making issues as his generation came of age. "There were some of the old companies from the early days ... my father told his brothers they could have his shares in those; we could always start new companies; in fact we were already doing that," he said. In settling the separation, Liem let Sioe Hie and Sioe Kong have textile manufacturer Tarumatex and Bank Windu Kencana (which Liem had originally hoped to make his flagship financial institution but it didn't turn out that way).

Joining his father's vast array of business operations meant Anthony had to know something about everything. He learnt about banking from Mochtar and about property from Ciputra, Salim's partner in several real estate projects. He started with the basics; in the early New Order period, when Waringin Kencana built two crumb rubber factories in Sumatra — Salim's first foray into industry — Anthony went to observe firsthand the construction process. "I even bathed in the river", he recalled.[69] (The crumb rubber business was never profitable, Anthony said; "The traders in Singapore were smarter than us ... the profit margin for processing was so small." After being in the business ten years, Anthony said he made the decision to sell the factories.[70]) When Salim was entering the palm oil business with Sinar Mas and Raja Garuda Mas (RGM), it was the boss of RGM, Sukanto Tanoto, the Medan businessman, who taught him what he needed to know, Anthony said. Sukanto was named by *Forbes* as the richest man in Indonesia in 2007. Anthony described him as "very intelligent and very articulate" who built his business from ground up.[71] Based on learning from experienced people who excelled in their fields and getting exposure to different businesses, Anthony said he was able to lay the groundwork for the Group to become international. Anthony summarized his business philosophy this way:

> Learning by doing and by being involved ... plus the willingness to get outside help; having an open mind and heart; trying to create the environment based on your needs and requirement ... all those are factors that helped a lot. You have to force yourself to learn new material, plus make contacts. At that time, foreign investment was coming into Indonesia, so I had exposure to the international players — small, medium, big; then I started to assemble a team.[72]

BOX 7.1
The Oil Tanker Case: A Secret Role

In the mid-1970s, Liem was still enjoying Suharto's trust, while Anthony was making rapid inroads to earning his father's confidence. When the scandal over Pertamina's debts blew up and the government was dragged into a highly public lawsuit over tankers ordered by Ibnu Sutowo, Suharto turned to Liem to help negotiate with the Swiss magnate who brought about the suit. Liem turned to his youngest son to act as translator in the highly confidential talks, which were kept out of the public eye. They took place in Singapore in August 1977. Although senior government ministers were already engaged in negotiations, Suharto signalled Liem to get involved to work out an out-of-court settlement with Bruce Rappaport, the Swiss-based tanker magnate who was suing Indonesia over unpaid ships ordered by Pertamina, to the tune of US$1.55 billion, an amount nearly equal to Indonesia's total foreign exchange reserves at the time. The case was one in which Anthony first cut his teeth in the world of international business intrigue. Liem's little-known role in the high-profile case prompted Ian Verchere in his 1978 piece to dub him "Suharto's Secret Agent."[73]

The oil tanker scandal centred on Ibnu Sutowo, the long-time Pertamina boss and considered by some as the second most powerful man in the country after the president for his contributions to the government's coffers. During the early days of the New Order, Sutowo, who ran the oil firm as his personal fiefdom, was the most important source of patronage money. A cunning, flamboyant and inventive administrator, the former general, trained as a medical doctor, answered to no one except the president. Even though Pertamina was put under the administration of the Ministry of Mining, Sutowo consistently circumvented it. There were no public accounts, much less accountability. He dispensed money from the oil firm liberally to whomever he saw fit, to all levels of government. He was a major contributor to the military (including helping fund Ali Murtopo's Opsus), to Suharto's foundations, and provincial administrations, which bought him loyalty. It was understandable that many dared not risk killing the goose that laid the golden egg. As John Bresnan pointed out:

> Ibnu's free-handed patronage had won him many friends. It is known that
> he helped provincial governors with projects that were locally significant in
> the late 1960s. He sat on the Golkar board and was reliably reported to have
> been the main source of its funds for the 1971 election campaign.[74]

continued on next page

BOX 7.1 — *cont'd*

When times were good for Pertamina, Sutowo called the shots. In the early 1970s, said a journalist who wrote an expose on the tanker affair, "the name of the game was oil, and the prince of that domain was Gen. Sutowo".[75] Foreign bankers fell over each other to lend huge money to the oil firm, with many loans at "extremely high interest rates", which made Pertamina an "exceptionally lucrative customer".[76] Few knew of the mounting troubles at the company until one day in February 1975, Pertamina failed to pay a short-term syndicated loan of US$40 million, led by a U.S. bank. Then one after another, outstanding debts surfaced — no one knew exactly the total, but the minimum total officially published was said to be US$6.2 billion, with "additional obligations" boosting the figure to more than US$10 billion.[77] As the government scrambled to settle Pertamina's massive debts, Rappaport demanded payment of the promissory notes in the supertanker deal that Sutowo had committed to. It turned out that Sutowo had signed 1,600 promissory notes to Rappaport to provide collateral of US$1.266 billion — notes he had signed, he said, without reading — that committed Pertamina to buying (in a hire purchase deal) thirty-four tankers for US$3.3 billion. The Indonesian government balked, charging that the magnate had overinflated the rates for chartering the vessels. To force payment, Rappaport initiated legal action in July 1976.

Rappaport was not someone to be trifled with. The Haifa-born wheeler-dealer cultivated powerful friends in many countries and counted among his golfing buddies political leaders such as then Thai Prime Minister Chatichai Choonhavan and Israeli politician (and later President) Shimon Peres. He was said to be close to U.S. and Israeli intelligence agencies. Besides being an oil and shipping magnate, Rappaport was also a banker — he founded Geneva-based Inter Maritime Bank in 1966, and owned 7.5 per cent of the Bank of New York.[78] A *Wall Street Journal* reporter described him as "a balding, heavy-set shipping tycoon with a garrulous manner [who] liked to wear expensive double-breasted three-piece suits, smokes Cuban cigars, is addicted to golf and travels in a chauffeured Cadillac".[79] Another journalist writing for the *New York Times* said people who know him "say he built his empire by knowing how to charm the right people, by being tough with his subordinates, and by knowing how to use litigation."[80]

Rappaport and Sutowo had developed a firm friendship. They were reported to have met in a Geneva nightclub in the mid-1960s when the general was looking to buy an oil tanker for Permina, Pertamina's predecessor. That led to years of lavish entertainment of each other. The lawsuit that Rappaport launched was nothing personal; he said he too, was being squeezed by his creditors. For a person who headed the largest state company in the country, Sutowo was shockingly nonchalant about bookkeeping and management practices. One astonished American banker visiting Sutowo's office recalled seeing promissory notes simply stuffed in an open filing cabinet "just like someone would throw papers in a drawer" ... "the enormity of it!" he was quoted as exclaiming; "I saw a promissory note on top for $50 million ... I was dumbstruck by the chaos."[81]

Sutowo conveniently left it to the government to deal with Pertamina's financial problems. On the tanker case, Indonesian government officials who later investigated the company concluded that Pertamina made "speculative commitments in the hopes of profiting on the spot tanker market."[82] Discussions about what to do about Sutowo and his financial transgressions at Pertamina involved the president and his top military aides. When pressure mounted on Suharto and it looked like he had no choice but to get rid of his main financial backer, the president still thought it prudent to consult Army Chief of Staff, Gen. Maradean Panggabean. As recounted by Bresnan:

> Panggabean said he wanted to clear the plan to drop Ibnu with his commanders, with the heads of 10 or so major units ... They agreed, on the understanding that Ibnu would never go to jail. Suharto accepted these terms but added another of his own: "provided he never talks".[83]

It was speculated that the last straw for Suharto was a faux pas made by Sutowo that angered the president. At the first meeting of the Association of Southeast Asian Nations (ASEAN) heads of government in Bali in February 1976, the oil honcho — not a guest at the session — whisked Philippine President Ferdinand Marcos off in a helicopter to play golf and caused him to be late for an appointment with Suharto. The next month, Mines Minister Mohamad Sadli, who was also chairman of Pertamina, summoned Sutowo to his office for the first time ... and dismissed him "with honour". Even after he was fired, Sutowo refused to take responsibility for the mess he made. Throughout the affair, Suharto was hesitant to act against his ally and financial backer Sutowo, a man he had greatly admired. Born in Yogyakarta in 1914, Ibnu Sutowo was a son of a regency head near Semarang. Sutowo graduated from medical school in Surabaya in 1940. He also attended Sorbonne in France and Leiden in Holland; in short, he was highly educated while Suharto was not. When oil revenue peaked in the early 1970s, Sutowo's status was akin to a celebrity's; he was hailed as the country's first indigenous Rockefeller. That he financed much of the armed forces budget and campaigns made him all the more "untouchable".

continued on next page

BOX 7.1 — *cont'd*

Over the tanker case, however, Suharto eventually compelled the oil magnate to make an affidavit accusing Rappaport of fraud. In the 1976 court affidavit, Sutowo acknowledged a range of "misdeeds". Among them, he confessed that less than four months after signing the promissory notes, he "had requested and received a US$2.5 million loan from Rappaport. He placed the money in his personal checking account at Chase Manhattan's Jakarta branch, and lost the receipt."[84] The loan was not repaid. In November 1976, Suharto appointed two ministers, Trade Minister Radius Prawiro and J.B. Sumarlin (Minister of State for Administrative Reform), to handle the tanker case.

In December, Rappaport offered to settle for about 20 per cent of his claim. Under his proposal, Indonesia would pay US$254 million plus US$31.3 million in interest. But then the Indonesians produced the affidavit signed by Sutowo admitting to serious personal wrongdoings while at Pertamina's helm. Accusing his friend of "deviousness, deception and fraud", Sutowo swore that in late 1974, Rappaport had come to him, explained he was experiencing "personal difficulties" and asked for a series of promissory notes so he could soothe his business associates. Sutowo said Rappaport told him the notes would be kept in a bank vault and never be enforced against Pertamina. By trying to cash the notes, "Mr Rappaport has engaged in a reprehensible act of personal deception to me and has made a fraudulent claim upon Pertamina", Sutowo stated.[85]

If the Indonesians thought Sutowo's affidavit would cow Rappaport into a quick settlement, they were wrong. The tanker magnate's intransigence threatened to bring Pertamina to the brink of bankruptcy. The Indonesian government, wrote Ian Verchere of *Insight* magazine, was "desperate to pay off the mercurial banker with minimal expense and publicity".[86] Continued Verchere: "Political muscle having failed, it was now obvious to President Suharto and his financial advisors that only the shrewdest negotiating skills could out-manoeuvre the blustering tactics of Monsieur Rappaport. What Indonesia needed was a faceless intermediary endowed with the same entrepreneurial talents … to the head of state, only one man of 135 million could possibly fit that bill — Liem Sioe Liong, the president's secret friend…"[87]

Unlike William Soeryadjaya of the Astra Group, who was close to Sutowo, Liem had little to do with Pertamina and its powerful boss, so he was in effect, an outsider. The only credential he was armed with was the trust accorded him by the president. So Liem stepped in to play a brief but apparently important role in helping end the Pertamina imbroglio. The meeting between Liem and Rappaport in mid-1977 was held in Singapore. Verchere wrote that the meeting was at one of Liem's

Singapore offices. Also present was Liem's close partner Djuhar Sutanto as well as Anthony. By the time Liem met with Rappaport, the Swiss magnate had agreed to settle out-of-court for US$150 million. Liem indicated the government was prepared to pay US$120 million. But the shipping tycoon held his ground, explaining that he had his own debts to settle. Rather than try to push him further down, Liem sensed a deal was at hand, and opted to help close it. After their talk, according to *Insight*, Liem "discreetly advised the government to pay US$150 million and avoid further rancour and press coverage". On 11 August 1977, ministers Radius and Sumarlin announced the settlement at a press conference in Jakarta. Indonesia would pay US$150 million to cancel contracts on the fifteen ocean-going tankers on which it was facing claims totalling US$1.55 billion. The Indonesians paid Rappaport's firm US$75 million immediately and the remainder in interest-free instalments over three years. In return, Rappaport returned the US$1.266 billion in promissory notes. Government officials never publicly acknowledged the intermediary role played by Liem. In a 1998 book, Radius, a long-serving minister in the New Order, wrote about Sutowo and the Pertamina episode but made no mention of Liem's involvement:

> Ibnu transformed it [Pertamina] from a collection of third-world businesses to a multinational conglomerate that topped out in the mid-1970s as the 200th largest international corporation. For Indonesia, this was an astonishing accomplishment. Despite its size and importance, Pertamina had only the veneer of a sophisticated multinational corporation. It was however, a multibillion-dollar veneer, and that was enough to convey a very favourable impression. Beneath the surface, however, Pertamina lacked systems, controls, management, and experience. Pertamina was an accident waiting to happen.[88]

On his version of the tanker case, Radius commented:

> Indonesia's case looked progressively more grim, though. Things improved when Ibnu was confronted with the weight of evidence. He then agreed to make an affidavit in which he implicated Rappaport of fraud. The case remained deadlocked, but Indonesia believed that the cost of stalemate was greater for Rappaport than for the country. The tankers could not be used while the various cases were pending. Therefore, while Rappaport was paying an expensive team of lawyers to execute his legal strategy, he was losing potential revenues that could have been gained by releasing the tankers. Furthermore, Indonesia believed it was better prepared to fight a global battle than Rappaport, especially since it seemed that world opinion was turning against him. In August 1977, Pertamina and Rappaport reached

continued on next page

BOX 7.1 — *cont'd*

> a settlement. Pertamina agreed to pay US$150 million to cover US$1.55
> billion in contracts with Rappaport — both those that had been fulfilled
> and those still pending.[89]

Radius had good relations with Salim and remained a friend of Liem
until his death in May 2005 at age seventy-six. He had attended the
cukong's lavish fiftieth wedding anniversary celebration in 1994 as well
as the sixtieth in 2004, both held at the Shangri-La Hotel in Singapore.
For Liem, playing a backroom broker suited him just fine as he couldn't
be seen to play a role in matters in which the state had to decide. It was
a vote of confidence in him by Suharto. The *Insight* article commented
that "once again, this personification of the self-made Chinese millionaire
had faithfully served his political masters and proved the inestimable
value of the local Chinese community to the generals of the Indonesian
army."[90] In his article, Verchere said that Liem got a financial dividend
from his negotiations, alleging that the Salim founder "pocketed"
US$8 million from Rappaport, which was deposited into an account in
Bangkok Bank.

When the article was published, Liem and the Salim Group did
not issue a denial — keeping in line with the group's policy of ignoring
media reports. Decades later, asked by the authors on separate occasions
about the payout allegation in *Insight*, Anthony flatly denied it.[91] He said
indeed a payment had been made to a Bangkok Bank account, but that
was one of the six or seven accounts worldwide that Rappaport had
specified for the Indonesian government to deposit into as part of the
agreed settlement. People assumed a payment to a Bangkok Bank account
was for Liem because of his friendship with then Bangkok Bank chairman
Chin Sophonpanich, Anthony said. Asked if his father had received any
remuneration or favours from the Indonesian government for his role in
the negotiation, Anthony replied no, though he acknowledged that "we
get other things" from the government as the group at the time had the
clove duopoly, the licence to mill flour for state logistics agency Bulog
and other privileges. In answer to a question why Suharto felt it necessary
to involve Liem, a private businessman and relatively unknown at that
time in international business circles, to help out on a settlement of the
Pertamina debts when two ministers were already on the job, Anthony
replied: "What we were doing was shadowing those two ministers, to
make sure the case is settled. Pak Harto assigned Pak Radius and Pak
Sumarlin to handle the matter ... I think at that time it was very chaotic,
because Suharto was disappointed with Ibnu Sutowo."[92]

As for Sutowo, he never had to worry about being prosecuted. After a brief period of "informal house detention" from 1977 to 1978, he went on to enjoy a "prosperous and busy retirement as a successful businessman", never once expressing remorse or taking responsibility for Pertamina's or the country's woes.[93] The Attorney General's Office conducted a perfunctory pro forma investigation over the Pertamina affair, and more than two years later announced that Sutowo would not be facing any charges. A year after Suharto was forced out of power, Sutowo acceded to an interview with the *Jakarta Post*, in which he made the highly dubious assertion that Suharto fired him "because I turned down his proposal for a business I thought was wrong". Asked why he remained silent for so long, he replied: "Had I openly revealed it to the public, I would have gone missing. At the very least, my children might have been in danger."[94]

After his dismissal, Sutowo went on to become president of the Indonesian Red Cross, and his family remained active in business. A family bank, PT Bank Pacific, ran up huge debts by 1997, in spite of an earlier bailout by the central bank, and authorities had to liquidate it. Sutowo's son Ponco owned the Hilton Hotel (later Hilton pulled out from its franchise agreement and the hotel was renamed Sultan Hotel), where his younger brother Adiguna on New Year's day in 2005 shot dead a waiter over a bill. Prosecutors asked for a life sentence, and a court handed down a seven-year jail term. Ibnu Sutowo died on 12 January 2001, at age eighty-seven. However, his son Ponco has continued to thrive as a successful businessman with his Nugra Sentana Group investing in hotel and property. He was listed by Globe Asia magazine of Indonesia as ranked 109th of the country's richest in 2012, with a net worth estimated at US$185 million.[95]

While Sutowo castigated Rappaport in his 1976 court affidavit that Indonesia used to fight the financier's claims, the Pertamina chief seemed to harbour no ill will about his long-time friend. Just like Suharto, Sutowo valued personal loyalty. When a *Wall Street Journal* reporter found the former Pertamina boss at a California golf tournament in February 1977, he blamed the grief over the tanker episode not on Rappaport (who died in January 2010), but on bad economic conditions. "If you make a deal with someone, you're partners in both good and bad times", he asserted.[96] On his part, Suharto described the Pertamina affair as "a bitter experience and a lesson for us all". Referring to the episode in his autobiography and defending his slow response in moving against Sutowo, he wrote: "I kept quiet until the boiling water had cooled down sufficiently for me to drink it."[97]

Notes

1. Feng Sheng, in *Hanyu Pinyin*.
2. Fikri Jufri, "Liem buka suara: 'Orang banyak salah sangka'", *Tempo*, 31 March 1984.
3. Multatuli, *Max Havelaar, or the Coffee Auctions of the Dutch Trading Company* (London: Penguin, 1987) (first published 1860), p. 125.
4. Interview with Liem, 9 December 2006.
5. Interview with Anthony, 26 November 2006.
6. Confrontation, or *Konfrontasi*, the campaign launched by Sukarno to challenge the legitimacy of the recently formed Federation of Malaysia, which included Singapore at the time.
7. Interview with Liem, 13 May 2006.
8. Interview with Anthony, 26 November 2006.
9. Ibid.
10. Ibid.
11. Ibid.
12. Ibid.
13. KAMI = Kesatuan Aksi Mahasiswa Indonesia, or Indonesian Student Action Front; KAPPI = Kesatuan Aksi Pemuda dan Pelajar Indonesia, or Indonesian Youth and Student Action Front.
14. Interview with Anthony, 26 November 2006.
15. Conversation in Singapore on 28 June 2008 with Murray Clapham, ex-Australian diplomat and a close friend and business associate of Fong's. Peter Fong had business interests in Southeast Asia. A colourful character, he was a Kuomintang pilot and worked with the Flying Tigers, a group of mercenary pilots mainly comprising American military personnel led by the legendary Gen. Claire Lee Chennault. They were used to help defend China against Japanese forces just before the start of World War II. According to Piet Yap, who became Salim's main wheat purchaser, it was Fong who appeared at his hotel door in Jakarta one day in 1967 saying that his boss, Liem Sioe Liong, wanted to meet to discuss business opportunities. Peter Fong died in April 2008. (Clapham passed away in 2011.)
16. The "O" level examination is usually taken by students after four years of secondary school by sixteen or seventeen-year-olds; this was based on the British system. Anthony would have been older than his peers in Singapore as his schooling was disrupted in Jakarta, and when he got to Singapore, he had to spend time learning English. Students who pass the "O" Level would be admitted to two more years of pre-university classes and sit for an "A" level exam before they can apply to university or other tertiary institutions.
17. Interview with Anthony, 18 September 2011.
18. Interview with Liem, 9 December 2006.

19. Interview with Anthony, 26 November 2006.

20. Private conversation in Fuqing, China, 8 February 2006.

21. Interview with Anthony, 23 December 2007.

22. Conversation with Albert at lunch in Jakarta, 4 December 2007.

23. Interview with Anthony, 23 December 2007.

24. Ibid.

25. Conversation with Albert, 4 December 2007.

26. Written communication with Albert, Jakarta, 4 December 2007.

27. Interview with Liem, 10 June 2006.

28. Private conversation with a senior Salim executive, 21 March 2007, Jakarta.

29. Interview with Mochtar Riady in Singapore, 24 January 2007.

30. QAF company website <http://www.qaf.com.sg/launch.asp>.

31. Interview with Anthony, 4 March 2007.

32. Julius Tahiya, *Horizon Beyond: Entrepreneurs of Asia* (Singapore: Times Books International, 1995), p. 14.

33. Ibid., p. 15.

34. Interview with Anthony, 2 January 2007.

35. Conversation with Sofyan Wanandi, Singapore, 17 September 2006.

36. Conversation with Bondan Winarno, Jakarta, 6 December 2007.

37. Interview with Anthony, 25 March 2007.

38. Interview with Liem, 9 December 2006.

39. Interview with Anthony, 18 March 2007.

40. Conversation with a Salim executive, Jakarta, 23 March 2009.

41. Interview with Anthony, 14 October 2007.

42. Mark Landler, "Year of living dangerously for a tycoon in Indonesia", *New York Times*, 16 May 1999.

43. Interview with Anthony 24 June 2007.

44. Ibid.

45. The name of a very venomous American spider; the female has a black body and a habit of eating her mate.

46. Conversation with Benny Santoso, 4 May 2009.

47. Private conversation, Jakarta, 21 March 2007.

48. Interview with Manny Pangilinan, 20 April 2007.

49. Cris Prystay, "Philippine Tycoon Can Cap a Career with PLDT Deal", *Asian Wall Street Journal*, 7 June 2002.

50. Interview with Manny Pangilinan, 20 April 2007.

51. Interview with Anthony, 18 March 2007.

52. Confidential interview, Jakarta, 15 July 2010.

53. Marleen Dieleman, *The Rhythm of Strategy: A Corporate Biography of the Salim Group of Indonesia* (Amsterdam: ICAS/ Amsterdam University Press, 2007), p. 94.

54. Ibid., p. 119.

55. Ibid.
56. Interview with Manny Pangilinan, 20 April 2007.
57. Confidential conversation, Jakarta, 30 November 2007.
58. Interview with Anthony, 25 March 2007.
59. Interview with Anthony, 3 December 2006.
60. Confidential conversation, Jakarta, 23 March 2009.
61. Interview with Anthony, 14 October 2007.
62. Interview with Anthony, 25 March 2007.
63. Interview with Anthony, 18 March 2007.
64. Ibid.
65. Ibid.
66. Interview with Anthony, 15 July 2007.
67. Interview with Anthony, 24 December 2006.
68. Ian Verchere, "Liem Sioe Liong: Indonesia's Imperial Cukong", *Insight*, May 1978.
69. Interview with Anthony, 3 December 2006.
70. Ibid.
71. Interview with Anthony, 4 March 2007.
72. Interview with Anthony, 18 March 2007.
73. Ian Verchere, "Liem Sioe Liong: Suharto's secret agent", *Insight*, May 1978.
74. John Bresnan, *Managing Indonesia: The Modern Political Economy* (New York: Columbia University Press, 1993), p. 185.
75. Seth Lipsky, *The Billion Dollar Bubble and other stories from The Asian Wall Street Journal* (Hong Kong: Dow Jones, 1978), p. 4.
76. Ibid., p. 11.
77. Ibid., p. 16.
78. Steven Greenhouse, "A secret emperor of oil and shipping", *New York Times*, 4 February 1988.
79. Lipsky, *The Billion Dollar Bubble*, pp. 19–20.
80. Greenhouse, "A secret emperor of oil and shipping".
81. Lipsky, *Billion Dollar Bubble*, p. 2.
82. Ibid., pp. 23–24.
83. Bresnan, *Managing Indonesia*.
84. Lipsky, *Billion Dollar Bubble*, p. 30.
85. Ibid., pp. 28–29.
86. Verchere, "Liem Sioe Liong".
87. Ibid.
88. Radius Prawiro, *Indonesia's Struggle for Economic Development: Pragmatism in Action* (Kuala Lumpur: Oxford University Press, 1998), p. 104.
89. Ibid., p. 109.
90. Verchere, "Liem Sioe Liong".
91. Interviews with Anthony, 24 December 2006 and 2 March 2008.

92. Interview with Anthony, 24 December 2006.

93. R.E. Elson, *Suharto: A Political Biography* (Cambridge: Cambridge University Press, 2001), p. 215.

94. Johannes Simbolon, "Ibnu Sutowo speaks up about graft charges", *Jakarta Post*, 10 May 1999.

95. "150 richest Indonesians", *Globe Asia*, 2012.

96. Earl Gottschalk, "Teed Off? Sutowo Defends Role at Pertamina's Helm, Retreats on Rappaport", *Asian Wall Street Journal*, 14 February 1977.

97. *Soeharto: Pikiran, ucapan dan tindakan saya: otobiografi seperti dipaparkan kepada G. Dwipayana dan Ramadhan K.H.* (Jakarta: Citra Lamtoro Gung Persada, 1989), pp. 305–306.

8

FLOUR POWER

In the film *The Year of Living Dangerously*, a main character, Billy, falls to
his death after unfurling from a high-rise window a banner declaring:
"Sukarno, Feed Your People". The message was similarly applicable to his
successor Suharto, who in 1966 was in the process of easing the country's
first president out of office. The new leader had yet to consolidate his power,
but he was well aware that he badly needed to keep people fed if he was
to be accepted. The country was seriously short of rice, the staple and the
fulcrum of Indonesian life. The grain was the lifeblood of Indonesians, and
at the time, soldiers and civil servants received part of their salary in rice.
Inadequate food supplies were fuelling runaway inflation, which by some
calculations topped 500 per cent. Supplying food to help prop the nascent
anti-communist Suharto regime became an important part of a massive
effort by Western nations, led by the United States. Suharto demanded
huge aid, sending emissaries to Washington. In September 1966, after
meeting Indonesian Foreign Minister Adam Malik, U.S. Vice-President
Hubert Humphrey wrote President Lyndon Johnson:

> Indonesia requires large amounts of rice and is attempting to obtain rice
> not only from the U.S. but also from Burma, Thailand and some from
> Taiwan. They need much more from the U.S., however, than they now

have reason to believe they will receive ... I suggested increased uses of wheat and bulgar (cracked wheat), but was told that there was a consumer resistance due to a lack of understanding and custom. Mr Malik agreed that it would be in the long-term interest of Indonesia for wheat and bulgar to be increasingly introduced... Mr Malik emphasized that his country's urgent rice and cotton needs were also essential to feed and clothe the troops. With the ending of confrontation on the Malaysian border and to keep the military from becoming restless, it was necessary to keep the large numbers of troops in Indonesia satisfied and occupied.[1]

Washington donated some rice but Suharto kept pushing for more, given Indonesians' attachment to the grain. The United States, however, wanted to promote wheat, of which it had stockpiles. Over time, Suharto signalled that wheat would be okay if there really couldn't be more rice. A 7 July 1967 telegram from U.S. Ambassador Marshall Green to the State Department, written after a three-hour session with Suharto, said that the Indonesian leader reiterated a message sent earlier through Maj. Gen. Sudjono Humardani that while Indonesia "critically" needed as much rice as possible, he was "even interested eventually in [the] possibility of wheat... he [is] hoping to change national diet habits, starting with Djakarta, so that bread is substituted for rice on [the] breakfast menu." (Intriguingly, Green noted he was developing a personal rapport with Suharto "though I do not wish to exaggerate where this could lead, bearing in mind that it may take some time for Suharto to break out of his Javanese mold which includes doing things through intermediaries and by indirection. A responsive reaction to his reasonable requests would, however, do much to assist in our problem with communication with Suharto.")[2]

In November 1967, with the United States in the midst of the Vietnam War, National Security Advisor Walter Rostow wrote Johnson about aiding Indonesia: "If Suharto is to stay afloat, he must have $325 million." Rostow recommended that Washington supply one-third of that, and other governments the rest. Four days later, Johnson replied: "Walt, I want to do everything I can for Indonesia — as quickly as I can. Send me a program."[3] It included sending wheat, which was milled mainly in Singapore, as Indonesia had no milling capacity at the time. Johnson got a chance to directly press for acceptance of wheat when he went to Australia in December 1967 for the funeral of its prime minister, Harold Holt, who drowned while swimming. Johnson had hoped to meet Suharto at the funeral, but the general sent his foreign minister to represent him.

Malik gave Johnson a letter from Suharto that apparently asked for more food aid; after the meeting. Rostow reported: "We expect the Indonesians, like India, will learn to use wheat. We are short of rice. We shall increase the rice acreage by 20 or 30 per cent but we could send wheat right now. President Johnson believes the Indonesians will like wheat when they get used to it."[4] Within months, the effort to get the Indonesians to accept — and consume — wheat was bearing fruit. In February 1968, a National Security staff member, Marshall Wright, informed Rostow: "We no longer have a problem pushing wheat. Everybody is a believer... our problem is to make sure we don't choke this promising infant to death before he develops a man-sized appetite."[5]

GETTING A FIRST SLICE OF FOOD SUPPLY

In 1967, as just a few well-off Indonesians were eating bread made with U.S. wheat, Liem was starting his first foray into food — which involved rice. Liem, who grew up with hunger in China, told the authors that early in the New Order, he shared with Suharto a Chinese saying that a leader would be considered a success if he was able to provide the four basic needs to his people — food, shelter, clothing and transport. Over time, Liem would have some involvement in all four areas, though his role in clothing — starting with Tarumatex, a textile factory in Bandung (and Muliatex in Kudus) — was never large. (Not coincidentally, there were no monopolies in that business.) In food, by the mid-1970s Liem was in a sweet spot from which wealth flowed, thanks to an effective monopoly position for milling wheat.

Liem's first stab at the food business came when the newly-formed state commodities agency, Badan Urusan Logistik, or Bulog, in 1967 assigned him to import 35,000 tons of rice. Before looking at his foray, it is instructive to look at the background of Bulog, an agency that would play a vital role for Salim. Amid a flurry of decrees that helped build a power-structure dependent on him, Acting President Suharto created Bulog in May 1967 to control the price and distribution of "basic staples". It replaced an ineffective National Logistics Command (Kolognas), which Suharto himself "commanded". The head of the revamped agency was Gen. Achmad Tirtosudiro, a former Kostrad officer said to be "personally and professionally close" to Suharto and the Kostrad financial general, Suryo.[6] Over time, Bulog would join Pertamina as Indonesia's most powerful and lucrative state operations. Bulog was given control over a growing number of foodstuffs, the central one being rice. It operated a buffer stock and massive warehousing programme designed to let people from all over the country pay the same price for their rice.

As with Pertamina, Bulog's massive scale and bureaucracy meant plenty of opportunities for theft and graft. In 1978, an Australian academic wrote that the agency "quickly acquired considerable notoriety as a centre for corruption".[7] Bustanil Arifin, who replaced Tirtosudiro as boss in 1973, acknowledged as much, saying: "After Pertamina, many people believe it is here you can earn money. But if we cannot take action [against corruptors], then the whole institution will collapse."[8] Bulog did not collapse, despite significant corruption, and over decades it won some plaudits for maintaining stable rice prices, which Sukarno couldn't provide. Asked about Bulog and its tainted reputation, Anthony Salim said it was "correct" policy by Suharto to have an agency that made essentials such as rice available at the same price everywhere. He added: "Of course there is some [corruption]... but Bulog was very good as a stabiliser, politically... on the whole, it is a very good establishment. Bulog has a lot of obligations.... Without Bulog, who wants to bring rice to Irian Jaya or Ambon?"[9]

Soon after its creation, Bulog became embroiled in scandal, stemming from how state funds were handled. At 3 per cent annual interest, the central bank lent money to Bulog, which then deposited some in private banks paying 10 per cent or more. Garnering interest that high was too good to last, and those banks collapsed. The biggest case, in December 1968, was Bank Duta Ekonomi, a unit of trading company PP (for Pilot Project) Berdikari,[10] which was formed in 1966 from the melding of several Sukarno-era state firms. Later, Suharto reorganized Berdikari under the control of three of his foundations: Dakab, Dharmais and Supersemar.[11] In 1970, a Commission of Four on Corruption appointed by Suharto (under pressure) was "extremely critical of Bulog's performance" and recommended that its regional agencies be disbanded.[12] Nothing was done. In 1972, the agency was in shambles, and its incompetence was exposed after it wasn't prepared for a disastrously bad rice harvest. Severe shortages made prices spike more than 100 per cent. This spawned widespread discontent that threatened to become a political crisis for Suharto.

In early 1973, Suharto packed Tirtosudiro off to Germany as ambassador, and recalled Bustanil Arifin from the United States. The trouble-shooting, one-star general had been Bulog's deputy chief from 1969 until 1972, when Suharto sent him to New York as Indonesia's consul-general. The forceful and burly Bustanil, whom Indonesia expert David Jenkins called a free-wheeling military entrepreneur who enjoyed the good things in life and "had a certain notoriety as a ladies' man", was one of Suharto's most important and loyal aides.[13] Many people incorrectly believed his wife Suhardani was related to the president's spouse Tien, but their common ground was their hometown, Solo. Bustanil, who was born in West Sumatra in 1925 and had a law degree from a Bandung university, was yanked back to deal with the food crisis because he knew Bulog — and he got things done. In 1965–66, he had secured rice from Thailand and Burma to deal with shortages.[14]

Upon his return to Jakarta, Bustanil managed to lasso rice prices and get Bulog functioning smoothly. Suharto kept Bustanil atop Bulog for twenty years, and put him in the cabinet between 1978 and 1993. Bustanil won some praise for his tenure at the agency. John Bresnan, a Ford Foundation staff member in Jakarta, wrote that the "dynamic" Bustanil turned Bulog into a "much more competent organization, possibly the most powerful food agency in Asia".[15] In 1978, The *Far Eastern Economic Review* headlined an article about him "The man who gets things done".[16] Walter P. Falcon, then director of the Institute for International Studies at Stanford University, lavished praise on him in a book published in 1995 for Bustanil's seventieth birthday. Falcon wrote:

> I pay tribute to him as a wise strategist; a committed educator; an effective leader of men and women; a savvy politician; a caring person, especially for the poor; an instinctive economist; an efficient administrator; and the best damned rice trader in the world.[17]

When Liem got his Bulog rice contract in 1967, he did not know about rice-trading. The inexperience could have cost Liem dearly, according to an Indonesian commodity trader who helped fulfil the contract. The trader was Piet Yap, who was working for rising commodity king Robert Kuok of Malaysia. The gregarious Yap was born in 1929 in Padang, where Bustanil was born four years earlier, though they did not know each other there. In 1967, Yap was working largely in sugar — the foundation of Kuok's fortune — but he had acquired good knowledge of other commodities. (Yap, who went to work for Kuok in Singapore in 1959, wrote: "My first love is in sugar and it blossomed when I met Robert Kuok."[18]) At the time that Liem needed rice, Thailand was the world's dominant exporter. But when Liem found out that Thai rice cost a lot more than he thought it would, he asked an associate to look for Yap, whom he had not met but who had a reputation as a savvy commodity trader. Yap, then living at the Hotel Indonesia in Jakarta, had a chat with Liem. If Liem had gone ahead and bought Thai rice, Yap wrote in his memoir decades later, "he would incur a huge loss". Yap asked Liem for forty-eight hours to investigate the market from Singapore. On his return to Jakarta, Yap proposed to take over Liem's contract and pay him a small profit. The trader could do this because he found rice available from Egypt, which Liem did not know grew it. Sticky, short-grain Egyptian rice was not what Indonesians were used to but "we had no choice and had to lay our hands on any type of rice", Yap wrote. Liem, he declared, "was extremely delighted and relieved that this rice deal gave him a profit instead of a large loss".[19] For Yap, the deal generated a dividend in giving him a chance to work with Liem. Over time, the extroverted trader would gain a big post in Liem's empire and become the world's biggest buyer of wheat. Yap wrote about formation of his Salim link: "After a few rice deals, Liem gained confidence in me and we ventured into regular rice and sugar deals, growing the Kuoks' business substantially."[20]

Yap's trading helped build an alliance between Liem and Kuok, which was critical for the start of milling wheat into flour in Indonesia. Historically, wheat was absent from Indonesian diets, but this would change in the New Order, in part because of food aid from Western governments. The bulk of the food from the United States came via Public Law 480 (PL 480), passed in 1954 when Dwight D. Eisenhower was president and renamed Food for Peace by President John F. Kennedy. Eisenhower said the aim was to "lay the basis for a permanent expansion of our exports of agricultural products with lasting benefits to ourselves and peoples of other lands".[21] The United States got Suharto to begin receiving food aid in the form of wheat. Most of it was processed in Singapore, where a private company named Prima opened a mill in 1963. At the end of the 1960s, Prima's owner — like Liem, a migrant to Indonesia from Fujian — battled Liem for approval to mill flour in Java, as written about later. Before Indonesia was able to mill wheat, imported flour often reached Indonesian customers spoiled, due to the poor conditions in which it was shipped or stored on arrival. Liem said he complained to Suharto about the poor quality of the flour, urging him to report to the United States. It's better, the cukong said, "to import wheat directly and mill it ourselves".[22] While flour usage was small in the late 1960s, moving into milling was mutually attractive for Liem's group, who would get into a new business, and for Suharto, who wanted to promote industrialization and raise money.

THE BIRTH OF BOGASARI

There are different accounts of the birth of Bogasari Flour Mills. Yap wrote that the idea was a "simple suggestion from Liem in 1968".[23] Ibrahim Risjad, the youngest member of Liem's Gang of Four and, in the late 1960s, a member of a government committee deciding how to use U.S. aid, said the gang simply submitted a proposal to the government to process flour, and it won approval.[24] A source close to Jantje Liem, another *cukong* who was tight with Suharto in those days, claimed it was Jantje who first suggested the idea of milling wheat domestically. But when the "edict" to start the mill came, it did not include him.[25] Bustanil Arifin, in a 2009 interview with the authors, described himself the *bidan* (midwife) for Bogasari's birth. By his account, in the late 1960s Indonesia wanted multiple sources of flour, and not just Singapore, so he went to Malaysia to see Robert Kuok and "ask him if he can process" for Jakarta. According to this account, Kuok replied "Pak Bustanil, why don't you build your own mill?". Bustanil recounted that when he reported this to Suharto, the president immediately said yes and the next day called Liem to talk about getting it built.[26] At the time, Liem possessed two important things, according to Bustanil — Suharto's trust and a piece of land along Jakarta Bay, which Yap later called a "swamp". Liem, when the authors asked him, was unable to recall details of Bogasari's creation. Anthony, who was twenty and studying in Britain when Bogasari was registered, salutes Kuok as instrumental to its success. "Without Robert Kuok, maybe we don't have Bogasari", mused Anthony, "because he was the one who understood the business. He's the originator of the flour mill, not us; we didn't know the business during my dad's time."[27]

Asked by the authors about Bogasari's creation, Kuok, in a written reply, said that in the second half of 1969 or early 1970, he met Liem and Djuhar and told them their "best business opportunity" was to try to get a licence from Suharto to build flour mills. Within two weeks, they told him Suharto had approved and given full support, and they proposed a joint venture between Salim's Waringin and the Kuok family. According to Kuok, the paid-up capital was US$5 million, with the Kuoks putting in 75 per cent and Waringin 25 per cent, while the shareholdings were the other way around, with 25 per cent for the Kuok family and 75 per cent for the Indonesians. Also, according to Kuok, the joint venture had to be "unofficial" as Suharto "had decided that the flour milling business had to be owned by Indonesian nationals".[28]

In 1995, Suharto gave his version of Bogasari's roots. While vigorously defending his friendship with Liem, he claimed credit for getting it going. He said that after Liem, who wanted to help the nation, affirmed he had access to foreign capital, the president instructed him "it's good if you can set up a flour mill ... because the government has wheat assistance credits from America. But you only process (the wheat), the reins stay with Bulog." Suharto also insisted that it was not Liem who "*mendirikan*" (got things going) as "he acts like a tailor only".[29] Suharto never acknowledged that a non-Indonesian, Kuok, played a big part in Bogasari's creation.

In line with the project getting registered and being portrayed as a domestic investment, Kuok's name never was on any documentation about shareholders. In May 1969, Liem's group had registered a company named PT Boga Sari — initially spelled as two words — with authorized capital of Rp500 million. "Boga" means food, while "sari" is essence. Later, when Suharto approved the project, the name was amended to Bogasari Flour Mills. Early on, shareholders of record included Sudwikatmono (4 per cent), Ibrahim Risjad (4 per cent) and Liem's eldest son Albert Halim (22 per cent). Christine Arifin, the wife of Djuhar Sutanto — wrongly identified by several academics as Bustanil Arifin's wife — had 12 per cent. It was clear early on what benefits Suharto could reap from the establishment of Bogasari. Its 1970 articles of association said that 26 per cent of the profits would go to the Harapan Kita Foundation, headed by Suharto's wife Tien, and the Dharma Putra Foundation owned by the Army Strategic Reserve Command, or Kostrad, which Suharto had led in 1965.[30]

Shortly after Bogasari started building the Jakarta mill, it broke ground for a second one in Surabaya. Anthony credited Kuok for proposing construction for Indonesia's two biggest cities at the same time, describing the Malaysian as "the one with the sharp eyes" and as well being "10–20 years ahead of us in trading".[31] The government helped with the funding. Some specifics remain unclear. Australian academic Richard Robison said that only five days after PT Bogasari was registered with capital of only

Rp100 million, it received credit from Indonesian state banks of Rp2.8 billion.[32] In a 1990 interview, Ibrahim Risjad acknowledged government involvement, though gave no details. He said the Indonesian private investors provided 25 per cent of the company's equity, which fits with what Kuok said (Risjad made no mention of him).[33] A Bogasari advertisement that ran in *Kompas* the day after Suharto opened the Jakarta mill on 29 November 1971 confirmed the central bank assistance. The text said investment costs up until then had been Rp1.8 billion, and that the bulk of that money came from a credit given by Bank Indonesia and channelled through state-owned Bank Negara Indonesia 1946.[34]

Tempo magazine reported some buzz at the opening about the state credit. It quoted an unnamed businessman as saying Bogasari got Rp2.2 billion, not Rp1.8 billion, in a five-year loan from BNI with annual interest of just 1 per cent. Asked about the loan, BNI's chief executive E. Soekasah Somawidjaja only said that the mill would not have any repayment problem as "demand for flour will rise and with people coming from overseas to put up factories, cakes will be popular". Bogasari director Sudwikatmono — who *Tempo* did not identify as a Suharto relative — commented if the mill produced at full capacity, the loan could be repaid in four years and "if the government stops flour imports from overseas, repayment can be even more smooth". (The government did halt imports.) Liem was not mentioned in the *Tempo* article; the only other Bogasari person named was Ibrahim Risjad, who the magazine labelled *"lihai"* (sly or cunning).[35]

The Jakarta mill's original capacity was 650 metric tons of flour a day (and, by the mid-1990s, soared to 9,500 tons). The grinding machinery came from West Germany. Later, Bogasari switched to Italian equipment. Bogasari's first bulk import of wheat — 8,000 tons from Australia — was a donation to Indonesia from Canberra. "We were very grateful for the generous gesture that was not forgotten", Yap wrote. "Ever since then, we imported large quantities of our wheat requirements from Australia."[36] Bogasari appears to have been one of the first factories that Suharto officially opened. While he was still identified as "General Suharto" on a plaque unveiled at the mill opening, he ditched his uniform for a suit-and-tie at the opening ceremony. In his speech, Suharto promised that the government would help domestic investors obtain capital in line with "prevailing regulations". He added that state help would not be a gift, as the cash had to be returned. Suharto, who eight months later opened the Surabaya mill, appealed to Indonesians to use local products and declared that development should be "for us, from us and by us". Liem, who was Bogasari's chairman, did not address the audience at the ceremony. That was left to "Director I" Sudwikatmono, who announced that the mill would save Indonesia US$3.3 million a year in foreign exchange while exports of its by-products would bring in US$2 million annually.[37]

Before Bogasari's official opening, the government put in place regulations that kept the miller dominant and assured Bulog monopoly control of the flour business. The agency became the sole importer of wheat and the sole seller, for wholesale trade, of flour. Bogasari got the right to mill all flour sold in the big markets of Java and Sumatra, which had about 80 per cent of Indonesia's population, and received a fee per ton from Bulog. To ensure Bulog's dominance and Bogasari's profitability, Indonesia banned anyone else from importing flour. The system effectively allowed Bogasari and Suharto to assert that Bogasari technically was not a monopoly, but was — as Suharto said in 1995 — like a tailor who received fabric from a customer and got a fee for making it into a dress. However, the way the system worked, customers could not go to any other tailor, and Bogasari got more than just a fee for services. It was allowed to sell the by-products of flour milling, pollard and bran, which are used in animal feed. Flour usually accounts for about 75 per cent of wheat grain, and the rest — from the kernels — is available for other use. So as a tailor, Bogasari could keep and sell the equivalent of about 25 per cent of the raw material it got and, over decades, that generated Bogasari a significant side income.

Aside from tailoring, Bogasari played an instrumental role in buying the raw material: Bulog depended on Yap to make contracts for the wheat Indonesia bought. This gave Salim the foundation for a very solid relationship with Bulog and, given Suharto's strong backing of Bulog, bolstered Salim's position as a reliable partner for the president. In 1999, two academics summed up what the monopoly on flour meant for the miller:

> It helped accelerate the growth of the private Salim Group ... the Group's astounding expansion and growth into many unrelated industries — from shipping to banking — all started with flour. Ever since 1969, Salim subsidiary Bogasari has monopolized the import, milling and distribution of wheat. It became the largest domestic wheat flour producer, and one of the largest instant noodle producers and exporters in the world. It achieved this prominence because cf support from Bulog. In return, the

Salim Group became one of the strongest private supporters of the New Order's high economic growth.[38]

Milling flour was an attractive business. Calculating mill margins for Indonesia is complex, as at times consumers got subsidized, and in other ways and times they got effectively taxed via a surcharge paid by local flour distributors (and passed on to consumers). When the surcharge exceeded the subsidy, as it sometimes did, Indonesian consumers were paying more than world prices for flour. In a 1992 report, the World Bank said that in 1988, the mill margin in Indonesia was US$35.70 a ton compared with about US$10 a ton in the United States. When that margin was measured another way, the Indonesian level worked out to 31 per cent, or five times the 6 per cent level in the United States that year, the bank found.[39] Indonesian mill margins bounced around widely. The World Bank said mill margins were 24 per cent in 1980. An academic who worked on the subject put the 1979 margin at 35 per cent, and in a range of 19 per cent to 24 per cent for 1976–80. He also calculated the 1988 margin as 24 per cent of the international price of wheat, compared with about 7 per cent for U.S. millers.[40]

Most U.S. mills use the flour they produce to make their own foods, thus receiving benefits from vertical integration. In Bogasari's early years, Liem was not making instant noodles or any other food, and would not have had a big income, as flour consumption was relatively small. But the business was poised for growth, as it was securely protected from competition. Also, when a bad rice crop translated to a shortage, the Suharto government promoted consumption of flour-based food such as bread and noodles. After Salim became an instant-noodle giant, wheat became part of the Indonesian diet. Indonesia catapulted to second place in global noodle consumption, after China.

A RIVAL IS MUSCLED OUT

Whenever Salim wanted to expand operations, in many cases it did so by purchasing additional capacity, or by funding a project carried out by a new partner. That was what happened, for example, when Liem bought Indomobil to expand Salim's then-insignificant auto business, and when Metropolitan Development, a company involving property honcho Ciputra, launched real estate projects. But not all expansion came by one of these two avenues. In the early 1980s, Salim's expansion in the flour business triggered charges that the government resorted to strong-arm tactics to muscle a competitor out. The rival, Prima Flour, started its milling operations in Indonesia in the 1970s. Headquartered in Singapore, Prima was founded by Cheng Tsang Man, a Fujian-born migrant who was taken to Makassar in Sulawesi (then called Celebes) when he was eight.

Born in 1916, Cheng had minimal formal education; he got ahead, according to Prima's website, thanks to "relentless hard work, discipline and determination".[41] After World War II, he moved to Jakarta and started a trading business, but later decided to leave because times were bad, for Chinese and for business. "When strong anti-Chinese sentiments were high in Indonesia in the late 1950s, I decided to find a new base for my family and business," he once wrote in *Petir*, a publication of Singapore's ruling People's Action Party.[42] Cheng went first to Hong Kong, but after finding no worthwhile investment project after two years, he relocated to Singapore, setting up a company called South Grand Textile with another Indonesian Chinese businessman.

The ambitious Cheng wanted to do more than textiles. When the Singapore government sought proposals from private companies wanting to build a flour mill, Cheng competed and won, beating out foreign investors despite lacking experience in that industry. He impressed Singapore's then-Finance Minister (later deputy prime minister) Goh Keng Swee, who in 1963 officiated at Prima's commissioning. (Cheng named his company after the Latin word for "first".) According to Cheng, Singapore banned the import of flour until 1973, which gave Prima and a second local miller, Khong Guan, "time to strengthen and consolidate our operations".[43] In 1977, Prima's enterprising founder started tapping another income stream by opening a revolving restaurant on top of his mill's wheat silo. Cheng later wrote that he made Singapore his base as his experience in the island state "convinced me that it was a good government with sound economic policies". When Goh Keng Swee died in 2010, Cheng's son Primus, who became the company's CEO after his father retired in 1998, wrote that the late deputy prime minister, who provided support and set rational policies, was instrumental to Prima's success.[44]

After Prima started production in Singapore, it sold some of its flour to Indonesia. Cheng never considered rebasing there — the 2000 *Petir* article said Singapore gave his family "a sense of safety and stability"[45]

— but he remained interested in Indonesia. Until the mid-1960s, there were no real opportunities to invest, due to tumultuous times. In 1963, when Prima opened its plant, Singapore joined the newly formed Federation of Malaysia, and Sukarno launched his military campaign *Konfrontasi* (Confrontation) in a bid to crush Indonesia's neighbour. By 1966, Sukarno was elbowed out, and Suharto took charge. As part of realigning Indonesia with the West and capitalism, Suharto ended *Konfrontasi* and repaired relations with the world. The period when investors gave Indonesia a wide berth was beginning to end, and Cheng became keen to mill wheat there. He shaped a plan to build three mills with a total investment of S$72 million. One would be in Jakarta, the second in Surabaya and the third in Cheng's former home Makassar. (The city was renamed Ujung Panjang under Suharto and, after his fall, reverted to Makassar.) PT Prima Indonesia was incorporated in January 1970, eight months after BT Boga Sari was registered.

Even though Suharto pitched Indonesia as a place foreign investors were welcome, in some cases they were not. There was a long list of sectors in which foreigners were barred, and the president saw them as needed only for what the government or domestic businesses could not do. Also, even early in the Suharto era, when outside capital was badly needed, prospective foreign investors were often usually bedevilled by Indonesia's intractable and venal bureaucracy. So they required a powerful backer in government to surmount obstacles and navigate a jungle of official permits. Cheng's three-mill plan had a strong government supporter in Trade Minister Sumitro Djojohadikusumo. Sumitro, who Suharto brought into his government to show his emphasis on economic development, had supported PRRI, a CIA-backed separatist movement in West Sumatra during Sukarno's time. As a result, the economist went into exile for years, spending some of that time in Singapore, where he and Cheng became friends. Back in Jakarta and installed as Suharto's Trade Minister, Sumitro gave Cheng the green light for his three-mill plan.

But Cheng soon found his plans stymied, as Suharto wanted to preserve the big potential markets on Java for Liem and his group, especially because some profits would be shared by two foundations, one owned by the Army Strategic Reserve and another linked to his wife. Not surprisingly, the people who set up Bogasari wanted the choice sites of Jakarta and Surabaya, and Suharto ensured they got both. Cheng secured approval only for Sulawesi — a consolation prize — so his scale of milling would be far smaller than he wanted. As late as January 1971 — as Bogasari was constructing its Jakarta mill — Cheng still hoped for permission to build mills for the two biggest cities. Applications for Jakarta and Surabaya "are pending", he told the Singapore *Straits Times*. "We are aware that Indonesian national firms are vying for the same location but the decision rests with the Government."[46]

Whatever its milling bona fides, Prima never stood a chance against Liem's Bogasari. Long afterwards, Anthony Salim assessed the competition this way: "Sumitro lost to Suharto, of course … we are a friend of Pak Suharto, he [Cheng] is a friend of Pak Sumitro. And we are a friend also of the minister of industry at that time, Gen. Mohamad Jusuf. Of course we [would] win."[47] As a foreign investor, Cheng got a four-year tax holiday for the Sulawesi mill, which started grinding wheat in 1972. As a foreign investor, Cheng was also vulnerable to bureaucratic pressure and harassment that an Indonesian, especially someone well-connected like Liem, never faced. Cheng, under Jakarta's rules at the time, was required to sell 25 per cent of his mill to Indonesian interests after ten years of production. For Prima, milling in Sulawesi was profitable, but the sailing was anything but smooth. There were plenty of petty rules to cope with, and they could change without notice or recourse. With flour considered a "strategic" commodity, domestic trade was managed by Bulog, which was progressively getting closer to Liem's group. Lacking the top-tier link that Bogasari had, Cheng was not competing on a level playing field.

Prima faced problems from the start. There was little flour demand in the only areas where it was allowed to sell — Sulawesi, Moluccas, West Irian, Nusa Tenggara and East Kalimantan — which accounted for only 15 per cent of Indonesia's population. In those regions, rice was still king. Years later, the *Asian Wall Street Journal* wrote that Bogasari received better quality wheat from Bulog than Prima did.[48] In December 1979, nearing the deadline to divest 25 per cent of his mill to an Indonesian citizen, Cheng struck a deal to sell the stake to a businessman named Wirontono. Prima Ltd announced that the Jakarta businessman would buy 2.25 million shares for US$3.50 each in a deal the Singapore-listed company said was done to comply with divestment rules for foreign investors. The deal never took effect, as the Indonesian investment board did not give needed approval. (Until Suharto fell from power, he signed every board approval letter, no matter how small the amount involved.) At first, it seemed officials were just sitting on Cheng's proposal but then about one year after submission, the board rejected it, saying that because flour was "strategic", the 25 per cent stake would have to be bought by a state-owned company, not an individual. Prima also found that the rules had changed — it would have to divest at least 50 per cent of the mill, not 25 per cent. In late 1980, Prima told the Singapore Stock Exchange that as a sale to Wirontono had not been approved, it was talking with another party.

Meantime, Prima's operating problems increased. Bulog cut its wheat allocation while Prima's licence to distribute flour was limited to just Sulawesi instead of all of eastern Indonesia. Some members of parliament accused Bogasari of being behind Prima's woes, which Bogasari director Ibrahim Risjad denied in testimony to a committee.[49] Prima eventually resolved its problems in Indonesia by exiting from flour-milling there altogether. A detailed article about events leading to Prima selling 100 per cent of the Sulawesi mill ran in the 23 November 1981 *Asian Wall Street Journal*, headlined "Suharto Relatives, Officials Gain Control of Indonesian Flour Trade". Prima did not sell directly to Suharto relatives, but Suharto-linked parties gained what the *AWSJ* called "a long-sought monopoly of the lucrative flour trade in Indonesia". It quoted an "industry official" describing the flour trade as a "licence to print money". Ultimately, the buyer was PP Berdikari, a state trading firm now whose president director was none other than Bulog chief Bustanil Arifin. The *AWSJ* article detailed negotiations in Singapore with Prima, which it said had rejected earlier proposals to sell to a team made up of Berdikari, Bogasari, Bustanil and Suharto's oldest son Sigit. According to the report, the Indonesian proposal was to have PP Berdikari itself buy 30 per cent of the Prima mill, while other stakes would go to Sigit (20 per cent), Bogasari (45 per cent), and Bustanil himself (5 per cent). (Four months later, after Berdikari bought all of Prima's mill, Bustanil said the *AWSJ* report saying he, Suharto's son Sigit and Bogasari were part of the group buying Prima was "a lie". He said "It's against the law for me to hold shares in the company (Prima) and the President's son was never involved."[50])

Whether or not Berdikari itself was paying for the mill-purchase, it was the buyer-of-record. The per-share purchase price was the same one that Wirontoro was going to pay Prima Ltd two years earlier. Prima Ltd told its shareholders it considered Berdikari's price "fair", and they approved the sale. A column in *Business Times* Singapore complained that "Not only was Prima Ltd under pressure to sell this subsidiary to local interests but, for some inexplicable reasons, the Indonesian plant could not obtain sufficient and regular wheat supplies for milling." The column also said Prima had expected to get a significantly higher price than it did for the whole mill. While the Singapore company was now free of the "trouble-ridden" plant, if conditions there were not so difficult, it would have wanted to retain a controlling interest to get a steady earnings stream, the column noted.[51] Thanks to the lost Indonesia work, Prima Ltd's turnover fell 66 per cent in 1982 to S$50.3 million.

In a report on the formal transfer of the mill in March 1982, the *AWSJ* cited a knowledgeable source quoting a view from Cheng, who had other businesses in Indonesia, on why he did not publicly complain about his exit from milling: "What's to be gained by it? We wound up with a $20 million profit on the sale. And we have to look at the political realities. We have to live with them as they are, if we hope to continue doing business there."[52] Decades after being pressured into selling the Sulawesi mill, Prima still did not want to talk about it. Eldest son Primus, who took over from the founder, declined a request by the authors in 2006 to discuss the subject. (While facing growing headaches working in Indonesia, the enterprising Cheng found another country that worked out much better, long-term, for a milling investment: Sri Lanka. In the late 1970s, Cheng made a deal with authorities in Colombo to build a mill to supply all the island nation's needs. At one stage, Prima's complex at Trincomalee was the biggest in the world under one roof. In 2013, during which Cheng died, Prima still had hefty business in Sri Lanka.)

The transfer of the Sulawesi mill's shares took place on 11 March 1982, at a ceremony in Jakarta at which Bustanil announced the plant's new name: PT Berdikari Sari Utama Flour Mills. At the share transfer ceremony, Berdikari signed an agreement assigning "temporary management" of its new asset to Bogasari. So Bogasari obtained effective control of Indonesia's flour business, which the *AWSJ* estimated to then be worth US$400 million a year.[53] After the signing, Bustanil said that at the Sulawesi plant, Bogasari's contract would only last "until we can get a professional flour-mill executive in to run it", and that Bogasari's fee would be 0.5 per cent of Berdikari Sari Utama's gross sales.[54] Bogasari was still managing the mill when Suharto fell sixteen years later.

Not publicized was that on the very same day the mill ownership formally changed, Salim bought 40 per cent of PT Berdikari Sari Utama Flour Mills from PP Berdikari.[55] The purchaser of that stake wasn't PT

Bogasari, which let Salim maintain that its milling business didn't have
a monopoly on flour-milling, as another company owned the Sulawesi
mill. But because Bogasari managed the former Prima plant, Indonesia's
flour industry fit this 1992 World Bank summary: "The mills are owned
and/or managed by a single company."[56]

After Suharto's fall, Salim's 40 per cent ownership of the Sulawesi
plant came to light when the group pledged that stake to the government
along with more than 100 others in a bid to cover its debts. And in 2004,
Salim returned as part-owner of the greatly-expanded Sulawesi mill, which
now was named PT Eastern Pearl Flour Mills.

Notes

1. Foreign Relations of the United States, 1964–1968: Volume XXVI, Indonesia;
   Malaysia-Singapore; Philippines, Document 222. (Johnson Library, National
   Security File, Name File, Vice President, July 1, 1966, Vol. II. Document posted
   on website of the U.S. Department of State Office of the Historian, <http://
   history.state.gov/historicaldocuments/frus1964-68v26/d222>, accessed on
   23 July 2011.

2. Telegram from National Archives and Records Administration, RG 59, Central
   Files 1967–69, POL 15–1 INDON. Secret. On website of the U.S. Department of
   State Office of the Historian, <http://history.state.gov/historicaldocuments/
   frus1964-68v26/d236>, accessed on 23 July 2011.

3. Johnson Library, National Security File, Indonesia, Vol. VIII, 6/67-6/68, cited
   on the website of U.S. Department of State Office of the Historian, <http://
   history.state.gov/historicaldocuments/frus1964-68v26/d249>, accessed on
   23 July 2011.

4. Johnson Library, National Security File, Indonesia, Vol. VIII, 6/67-6/68, found
   on the website of U.S. Dept. of State Office of the Historian, <http://history.
   state.gov/historicaldocuments/frus1964-68v26/d250>, viewed on 23 July
   2011.

5. Johnson Library, National Security File, Indonesia, Vol. VIII, 6/67-6/68, cited
   on website of U.S. Dept. of State Office of the Historian, <http://history.state.
   gov/historicaldocuments/frus1964-68v26/d252>, accessed on 23 July 2011.

6. Richard Robison, *Indonesia: The Rise of Capital* (Sydney: Allen and Unwin/Asian
   Studies Association of Australia, 1986), p. 229.

7. Harold Crouch, *The Army and Politics in Indonesia* (Ithaca, NY: Cornell University
   Press, 1978), p. 278.

8. Guy Sacerdoti, "Bulog archipelago under fire", *Far Eastern Economic Review*,
   24 February 1978.

9. Interview with Anthony, 17 December 2006.

10. Berdikari was a contraction of the phrase *berdiri di atas kaki sendiri*, meaning standing on one's own feet. It was a concept promoted by President Sukarno, who urged economic self-sufficiency.

11. Dakab (Dana Abadi Karya Bakti) was founded in June 1985 to coincide with Suharto's sixty-fourth birthday. Funds were used to support Golkar. According to Elson, it was "a money printing machine" for Golkar, donating Rp200 million per month to various levels of Golkar. By 1985, Suharto boasted, its assets amounted to Rp43 billion. (R.E. Elson, *Suharto: A Political Biography* [Cambridge: Cambridge University Press, 2001], p. 252). Dharmais, established in 1975, was meant to help orphans and poor families, and provided assistance to the physically and mentally disabled. Supersemar was formed in May 1974 to grant scholarships to bright and talented students from deprived families. As acknowledged by Suharto's authorized biographer, "this *yayasan* became something of a mystery and was often looked upon as an instrument to support Pak Harto's political ambitions" (Retnowati Abdulgani-Knapp, *Soeharto: The Life and Legacy of Indonesia's Second President* [Singapore: Marshall Cavendish, 2007], p. 247).

12. Robison, *Indonesia*, p. 230.

13. Jenkins, *Soeharto and His Generals: Indonesian Military Politics 1975–1983* (Ithaca: Modern Indonesia Project, Cornell University, 1984; republished by Equinox, Singapore, 2010), pp. 177–78. Suharto's unwavering support for Bustanil was shown by an episode Jenkins reported. In 1973, a daughter of a higher-ranking general, Army Deputy Chief of Staff Mohammad Jasin, wrote to her father that Bustanil misbehaved with her on a flight to London. (She used the phrase "*kurang ajar*", which translates as "less than educated" and means behaved badly.) Jasin asked Suharto to discipline Bustanil, but nothing was done, and the enraged father was also refused an appointment with the president about the incident. Jasin later summoned Bustanil to his home and struck him in the face, according to Jenkins. Later that year, when the chief of staff's job was vacant, Jasin did not get it.

14. Alwin Arifin et al., *Mengelola Dengan Hati: Pelajaran Sederhana Seni & Praktik Manajemen Bustanil Arifin* (A book written and published by Bustanil's family to mark his 85th birthday in October 2010) (Jakarta: privately published, 2009), p. 21. Bustanil died in February 2011.

15. John Bresnan, *Managing Indonesia: The Modern Political Economy* (New York: Columbia University Press, 1993), p. 127.

16. David Jenkins, "The man who gets things done", *Far Eastern Economic Review*, 20 October 1978.

17. In Fachry Ali, *Beras, Koperasi dan Politik Orde Baru: Bustanil Arifin 70 tahun* [Rice, Cooperatives and New Order Politics; For Bustanil Arifin's 70th birthday] (Jakarta: Pustaka Sinar Harapan, 1995), p. 460.

18. Piet Yap, *The Grains of My Life* (Singapore: Piet Yap, 2010), p. xiv.

19. Ibid., p. 44.
20. Ibid., p. 45.
21. <http://www.usaid.gov/our_work/humanitarian_assistance/ffp/history.html>, accessed 2 April 2011.
22. Interview with Liem, 9 December 2006.
23. Yap, *Grains of My Life*, p. 59.
24. "Ibrahim Risjad: 'Dalam international trade, saya masternya'" ["Ibrahim Risjad: 'In international trade, I am the master'), *Eksekutif*, April 1990.
25. Private conversation, Singapore.
26. Interview with Bustanil, 5 November 2009.
27. Interview with Anthony, 20 May 2007.
28. Written communication from Robert Kuok, 7 December 2010.
29. "Presiden bicara soal kolusi dan monopoli" [President discusses issue of collusion and monopoly], *Kompas*, 25 September 1995.
30. State Gazette No. 258 of 1970.
31. Interviews with Anthony, 17 December 2006 and 17 August 2009.
32. Robison, *Indonesia*, p. 232.
33. "Ibrahim Risjad", *Eksekutif*, April 1990.
34. "Kredit PMDN harus dikembalikan", *Kompas*, 30 November 1971.
35. "Awal Biru", *Tempo*, 25 December 1971, p. 42.
36. Yap, *Grains of My Life*, p. 67.
37. "Kredit PMDN harus dikembalikan".
38. Jeremy Mulholland and Ken Thomas, "The Price of Rice", *Inside Indonesia*, No. 58, April–June 1999. <http://www.insideindonesia.org/edition-58-apr-jun-1999/the-price-of-rice-2209696>, accessed 28 October 2010.
39. World Bank, "Indonesia: Agricultural Transformation Challenges and Opportunities", Report No. 10504-IND, 1 September 1992, pp. 101–102.
40. Stephen Magiera,"The Role of Wheat in Indonesia's Food System", U.S. Department of Agriculture, Foreign Agricultural Economic Report, No. 170, Economic Research Service, 1981. Also see Magiera, "Grain Quality as a Determinant of Wheat Import Demand: The case of Indonesia", U.S. Department of Agriculture, April 1993.
41. <http://www.prima.com.sg/abt_us/founder.htm>.
42. Cheng Tsang Man, "Why Prima came to Singapore", *Petir* magazine, May/June 2000.
43. Ibid.
44. "Legacy of a captain of industry", *Business Times* (Singapore), 20 May 2010.
45. Cheng, "Why Prima came to Singapore".
46. "Prima's Flour Mills in Indonesia: How Many?", *Straits Times*, 29 January 1971.
47. Interview with Anthony, 17 August 2009.

48. Joseph Manguno and S.K.Witcher, "Suharto relatives, officials gain control of Indonesian flour trade", *Asian Wall Street Journal*, 23 November 1981.
49. Ibid.
50. Joseph Manguno, "Indonesian-run Firm Buys Flour Mill, Stirs Controversy", *Asian Wall Street Journal*, 12 March 1982.
51. "Hock Lock Siew" column, *Business Times*, 3 March 1982.
52. Manguno, "Indonesian-run Firm Buys Flour Mill, Stirs Controversy".
53. Manguno and Witcher, "Suharto relatives, officials gain control of Indonesian flour trade".
54. Manguno, "Indonesian-run Firm Buys Flour Mill, Stirs Controversy".
55. E-mail communication from Salim head office, Jakarta, 11 August 2009.
56. World Bank Report No. 10504-IND, 1992, "Indonesia: Agricultural Transformation Challenges and Opportunities", p. 101.

9

CEMENT BUILD-UP AND BAILOUT

During his thirty-two-year regime, Suharto seldom spoke publicly about Liem. This is not surprising, as the strongman presumably felt no need to defend his relationship with his main *cukong*, who was supposed to be there to give financial support but not talked about. Also, the Indonesian media never had the chance to directly ask about Liem, as Suharto hardly ever gave press conferences. The few interviews he granted always required the media to submit questions in advance, and if the keepers of Suharto's door didn't like a question, the media requesting the interview was informed that the president's busy schedule made one impossible. Still, there was no way to shut people up completely, and the Suharto-Liem link continued to be a matter of public discourse, with some bolder media commenting on it. Suharto broke his silence one day in 1995, when he surprisingly responded to persisting public discussions about the greatly slowed pace of economic reform by launching an unexpected, robust defence of his ties with Liem.

"CARRYING OUT AN ASSIGNMENT"

One of the major topics in Suharto's unscripted remarks was cement. This was surprising, too, as the subject getting heavy attention at that time was

Bulog's continuing monopolies, in particular over wheat imports, and Bogasari's domination of flour-milling; in the preceding months, Salim's position in flour had come under renewed public criticism. Little if any attention was paid then to cement, where there was no monopoly. A decade earlier, though, Suharto had bailed out Liem when his cement business was overextended, and now that he had decided to speak on his pal's behalf, cement was the key subject, along with flour. Suharto told 200 small- and medium-sized *pribumi* executives at his Tapos ranch that where critics saw the *cukong* as a big crony in collusion with the President, he saw a capable businessman who dutifully carried out whatever "national service" he was instructed to do. People had the wrong notions about how Salim became big in cement, Suharto declared to the assembled audience, jabbing the air with a finger to emphasize his point. "Everything has been mistaken, as if there was collusion between me and Liem. No. It was for the sake of the country and the nation," he proclaimed. Suharto then put his spin on how Indonesia's cement industry got a big private investment. He complained that once — he did not specify when — an American investor who he did not identify promised to build two plants as long as Suharto agreed not to issue any other licences for cement-plants. If that plan was followed, Indonesia would have to rely on imports from the U.S. company and "we would never be independent [in cement]", Suharto declared. "Then I summoned Liem and asked him: 'Are you capable of building cement plants?' and he replied: 'Yes, I am'."[1]

The "American investor" must have been Kaiser Cement & Gypsum, which began building a cement factory in Indonesia in 1971. (In the late 1980s, Kaiser sold out of its joint venture, named Semen Cibinong ("*semen*" is the Indonesian spelling of cement), and its main shareholder became Hashim Djojohadikusumo, son of former minister Sumitro and the brother of army general Prabowo Subianto, then married to Suharto's middle daughter Siti Hediyati Haryadi, known as Titiek.) In Suharto's mind, cement was a good example of how Liem proved a reliable "go-to guy" — when Suharto wanted something, the *cukong* delivered. In cement, as in many strategic areas, Suharto did not want to rely on a foreign investor. Unlike Bogasari, whose profits were shared directly with Suharto-linked foundations, Liem's cement plants did not directly contribute to the *yayasans* but they provided good income for Suharto's foster brother Sudwikatmono. Also, cement could not be attacked as a Salim monopoly, as state-owned plants always produced a significant share of national output. But there was effectively a cartel of domestic producers, with Liem's investments in a protected position and, crucially, he was able to get a bailout when overreaching made one necessary. In cement, Liem was far from Indonesia's pioneer. Dutch authorities opened the colony's first plant in 1910 in West Sumatra. The Japanese ran it during World War II and, after Indonesia declared independence, the Dutch regained it until Sukarno nationalized the plant, later called Semen Padang, in 1958. One year earlier, Sukarno opened the first plant built by independent Indonesia, state-owned Semen Gresik, in East Java. Under Suharto, Kaiser Cement was the first private investor in cement, then in 1973 Liem entered with PT Distinct Indonesia Cement Enterprise, after which he gained a moniker — "cement king".

OVERSEAS CONNECTIONS

Cement exports were never substantial, but being in the business opened and deepened links between Liem and the outside world. Cement plants cost more than flour mills, and Liem needed capital from outside Indonesia. His important link with Thai-Chinese banker Chin Sophonpanich supplied crucial seed money. Bangkok Bank had made good money at home, and was a major creditor to the country's leading cement company, Siam Cement. Indonesia, which in 1973 became Asia's only member of OPEC, received attractive windfalls from the 1973–74 world "oil shock" and offered a promising market for lending, especially when the local investors were friends of the president. In Liem's first cement company, Chin served as vice-chairman of the supervisory board. Money and technical assistance also came from a Taiwanese businessman, Chen Yu Hao, founder of the Taiwanese conglomerate Tuntex Group, by way of an introduction from Chin. "I bought his know-how", said Liem. But Chen, who decades later fled Taiwan when he came under investigation for allegedly siphoning off company funds to invest in China, exited earlier than expected from the Indonesian joint venture when his cashflow was stretched. Chen was "smart but slippery", Liem commented later about his brief Taiwan business partner.[2] Chin Sophonpanich, however, remained a lifelong friend until his death in 1988. Anthony Salim saluted Chin for his immense help, especially in cement. "We owed him big time. Without him, the face [of Salim] would not have been the same … he was pivotal."[3]

Cement manufacturing is a capital-intensive business. For expansion, long-term funding on top of what was provided by Chin was needed.

Anthony's bonding with Filipino banker Manny Pangilinan, after they met in 1977, led to syndicated loans for cement expansion that helped establish Salim's creditworthiness outside Indonesia. Later on, it was easy for Salim to get foreign loans, but in the late 1970s offshore borrowing remained very difficult because Indonesia's name was mud in Western banking circles after the Pertamina honcho Ibnu Sutowo's actions in the mid-1970s nearly bankrupted the country. By the start of the 1980s, this was changing. After Liem became established in cement, export-credit agencies in Western countries wanted to secure contracts for their companies by lending money to Salim for the purchase of equipment and services. In 1981, Liem received US$120 million in French government export credits for cement expansion. "Although the loan doesn't carry an Indonesian government guarantee, banks appear eager to participate to strengthen their ties to Liem and his businesses", the *Wall Street Journal* reported, quoting a source as saying the "politically-connected" Liem Group had become a "prime target" for many banks.[4]

The timing looked good for a Liem thrust in cement. The government's five-year "Repelita" development plan — despite Suharto's fervent anti-communism, he took socialist-style central planning seriously — targeted huge increases in cement production. Liem jacked up capacity at his base at Citeureup, 45 kilometres south of Jakarta. .The site, located close to Kaiser's plant, was near vast limestone, clay and sand deposits. (Limestone constitutes about 80 per cent of the raw material for making clinker, the main ingredient in Portland cement.) The Citeureup complex eventually covered 200 hectares and became, for a time, the world's biggest cement-making facility.

PT Distinct Indonesia Cement Enterprise was known as DICE, but the business was not much of a gamble. Indonesia was growing, and a private cement-builder could seize the moment in a way that bureaucratic, underfunded state producers could not. In 1975, two years after DICE was created, Phase 1 — for 500,000 metric tonnes — was completed. An additional 500,000 tonnes from Phase II was ready a year later, and Phase III kicked into operation in 1979. Salim set up a different company for each kiln, a route that provided financial benefits not possible if the added capacity came under one corporate roof. This was because Indonesia's laws allowed each new company to be eligible for lower duty rates for imported equipment plus tax holidays. Details on tax holidays granted by the government were not publicized. For DICE, some specifics were contained in a 1985 document prepared by First Pacific Ltd, Salim's in-house financial advisor, for cement-business creditors. It was titled "Recommended Proposals to the Lenders of the Indocement Group for the Acceptance of the Restructuring and Merger of the Indocement Group of Companies". It said that from July 1981, DICE had been given a tax exemption on five years' profits for an amount totalling Rp60 billion on the condition that the money be reinvested in the company within a year. DICE's tax-holiday benefits between 1975 and 1981 were not stated.[5]

In 1979 and 1980, as the world's second "oil shock" was filling Jakarta's coffers, Liem and his partners hit the accelerator, anticipating large new demand for construction and infrastructure projects. Liem's Kilns 6, 7, and 8 — each with 1.5 million tonnes capacity — went into production between 1983 and 1985.[6] Thanks to the blistering expansion, Liem's plants now had more capacity than the state did. By 1985, his capacity reached 8.9 million tonnes a year, compared with only 500,000 tonnes a decade earlier. Yuri Sato, who in 1993 published the first academic research focusing on Salim, wrote that within that decade, Liem's business overtook Siam Cement as Southeast Asia's leading producer.[7] As part of Salim's expansion, it created a company named Perkasa Indonesia Cement, which teamed up with Spanish contractors Technicas Reunidas and Centunion, who played the biggest part in building Salim's plants and received export credits from the Spanish government. It was access to such foreign credits that would encourage Suharto to turn to Liem to help get built an oil refinery expansion that Pertamina had long planned but which got derailed by its financial disaster. The goal was to add a hydrocracker in an oil refinery at Dumai, in central Sumatra, so the refinery could break petroleum into simpler forms of energy such as kerosene and gasoline. Scores of potential builders from around the world eyed what was expected to be a US$500 million piece of work.

However, the path to signing a contract to build the hydrocracker proved complex. Controversy stemmed from the role played by Salim, whom Suharto brought in because he wanted the project done without Indonesian government guarantees for loans. Thanks to Salim's link to the Spanish contractors, the construction was awarded to a Spanish-Taiwanese consortium that competing bidders initially had not taken seriously. The reason was they did not know that Salim, with no previous involvement in oil, had been tapped for a role in the hydrocracker. After the Spanish-Taiwan group was picked to negotiate with Pertamina, the *Far Eastern Economic*

Review wrote that because of the links to Liem, "government favouritism has become the charge most frequently heard among competitors, bankers, diplomats and even certain well-placed government officials". Environment and Development Minister Emil Salim defended state actions. "It's not favouritism to any particular group, but the ability to come up with the financial availability", he said. "The standard was the same for all. Whether the standard was right, that is another question."[8]

Eventually, the plan to have the project operated by the builders, rather than Pertamina, was dropped. The Spanish-Taiwan consortium linked to Liem still got the work, for which the price tag had doubled to US$1 billion — a sizeable chunk of which the Spanish government did finance. Salim did not again play a role in energy, which remained the jealously-guarded turf of Pertamina and its group of preferred, *pribumi* partners. The main lesson from the convoluted path to a hydrocracker did not involve Salim, but Suharto: after Ibnu Sutowo's fall, Suharto would never again give a Pertamina chief or even a highly trusted official any real decision-making ability. *FEER* wrote of the Dumai contract saga:

> The key to any major project is Suharto himself. While top-level sources say he has a high regard for the selection process of tenders and bids for projects, they also stress that when that system gets bogged down, he "turns to his entrepreneurial instincts." According to one of these sources, "he just gets impatient".[9]

INDOCEMENT'S BIRTH AND RESUSCITATION

In the early 1980s, Salim and Suharto shared a desire for break-neck cement growth. While PT Indocement Tunggal Prakarsa, in which Salim's cement interests would be consolidated, was not created until 1985, for years prior to that, the collection of plants was informally called the Indocement Group. Cement products made by the different companies shared a common logo, carried by Salim's main brand, Tiga Roda, which meant three wheels. The logo showed three circles shaped like a pyramid inside three larger circles. Indocement said the logo was "intended to symbolize the unity and harmony between people, performance and product".[10] By 1985, however, there was nothing harmonious between Salim's cement capacity and its sales volumes. On the contrary, there was a great mismatch; aggressive expansion was completed at a time demand dropped like a rock. When world oil prices tumbled by 1984, the Indonesian economy reversed gears and went into recession, imperilling the state budget, as oil accounted for the bulk of revenue. Some infrastructure projects were cancelled or delayed, cutting cement demand just after Salim's sixth kiln, the biggest yet, added 1.5 million tonnes a year to capacity.

Prior to this setback, Salim was giving thought to listing its cement business to raise money. In early 1984, Anthony was quoted in Jakarta media as saying the group would "eventually" sell shares in the cement business. But in March, Liem gave his first interview to an Indonesian media, in which he didn't give any indication of wanting to sell shares. The interview, with *Tempo* magazine, created a sensation as there was a big appetite to see what the low-profile Liem said. Asked about shares in Liem businesses remaining strictly with the family and its partners, unlike in advanced countries, the tycoon replied that in the East, "the father must give to the children, and children give to the grandchildren. If the children aren't capable, it's dangerous."[11] Despite Liem's comments, the *Far Eastern Economic Review* reported a month later that a share-offering involving the group's cement business was "scheduled" for the end of 1984. Such an IPO, the magazine said, "will also, no doubt, help clear up some of the misconceptions and mystery surrounding the Liems by forcing the group to open up to public scrutiny". Going for a listing, it added, "has been interpreted as an attempt by the group to diversify away from its present political dependence on the government in the hope of strengthening its position in the longer term".[12]

But then there were political problems. In September 1984, the army crushed a protest by Muslims in Jakarta, leaving dozens dead, and the following month small bombs exploded outside two Bank Central Asia branches, as written about in the next chapter. Any chance for an IPO now was gone. After 1984, cement was far from the "growth story" underwriters needed for a share-sale as the supply-demand mismatch was acute. By 1985, Liem had nearly 60 per cent of national capacity — and about 60 per cent of that capacity was unutilized. Salim was learning that the sky definitely was not the limit. That year, with capacity at 8.9 million tonnes, Indocement produced 3.9 million tonnes and sold only 3.34 million tonnes domestically and exported 516,000 tonnes.[13] Anthony acknowledged later that Salim was probably over-ambitious in adding cement capacity. "We were probably supposed to be only flying 727s, not 747s", he mused.[14]

To escape from his bad spot, Liem needed money, and it was not going to come via Jakarta's sleepy little stock exchange. Instead, he got a large injection from the best new shareholder he could possibly get — the Indonesian government — and on great terms. It supplied cash without wanting any say in the business. In a bailout ordered by Suharto, the state took a 35 per cent stake and effectively guaranteed Indocement could survive and later thrive. Indeed, in the years after the bailout, the Indonesian economy started performing better, thanks to deregulation moves that unshackled industries and spurred non-oil exports. Domestic demand for cement rose 13 per cent in 1989 and 21 per cent in 1990. Suharto, who could make any decrees and rules he desired, always wanted to be able to say his actions had a legal basis. For the cement bailout, it came in the form of Government Regulation No. 32, dated 25 June 1985. Typically, it was not announced. Word of its existence began circulating in Jakarta in early July. The text labelled cement as a "vital commodity for national development" and declared the government had a "duty to maintain the stability of cement prices and smooth supply for domestic consumption". Hence, the decree said, it was necessary for the state to invest, adding that it was putting Rp364.33 billion — equivalent then to US$326 million — into a company whose name was given as PT Indocement Tunggal Prakarsa. This was a new firm that consolidated Salim's string of cement plants. At the time of the decree, Liem had been making cement for more than a decade, though PT Indocement had been a legal entity only a short time. The company was incorporated on 16 January 1985, while the Ministry of Justice had approved its deed of incorporation on 17 May and amendments to its articles of incorporation on 15 June — only ten days before the decree about pumping in money.

The agreement between the government and Indocement was signed by a Finance Ministry official and ten shareholders of Indocement — including Liem, Anthony and Liem's younger brother Soedarmo Salim (Liem Sioe Kong), according to a document given to Indocement's creditors. The pact said that the government accepted shares to meet its obligation to maintain stable prices and consistent supply. One line stated: "In order to have everything running properly, Indocement shall be managed by professionals."[15] Thus, the government confirmed that bureaucrats would not enter along with the money.

According to a cabinet minister at the time, the regulation was adopted without it ever being discussed in cabinet. "The president did not ask what others thought of the idea", he said.[16] Even if the technocrats had been in the picture, they could not have done anything. They had very limited lobbying power whenever Suharto's inner circle was involved. Also, in mid-1985, the technocrats had just scored a big victory, and would have been loath to pursue a case they would lose. Their victory came in their successful persuasion of Suharto to deal with Indonesia's infamously corrupt customs service, which was stifling production and thwarting efforts to increase exports. The president agreed to one of his boldest moves ever — removing half of the department's staff and bringing in Swiss surveillance firm SGS to value imports and collect duties. Rather than being fired, the officials who were shunted aside were made "*non-aktif*" so they were still able to collect their salaries, but were removed from soliciting or getting bribes. The injection of cash for Indocement, made at a time the government was promoting austerity, came from a Finance Ministry budget designed for investing in the state's productive capacity. Critics were upset by the bailout's precedent of helping a private business working with a "vital commodity", and for reason. Six years later, cloves were labelled "vital" in new rules that blatantly favoured Suharto's youngest son Tommy.

Soon after the cement bailout, Salim received a second dose of state aid. Four Indonesian state-owned banks lent Indocement money so it could pay off US$120 million in foreign debt, effectively swapping a costly dollar-denominated loan for one that was, like most of Indocement's revenue, in rupiah.[17] The refinancing was handled by First Pacific Finance, part of Liem's wing in Hong Kong. The US$120 million syndicated credit that got replaced, signed in November 1981, had been led by American Express Bank, where First Pacific co-founder Manny Pangilinan had worked before teaming up with Anthony. In order to make the credit refinancing from the state banks comply with Indonesian central bank rules, an amendment in Indocement's ownership structure was needed so that the two *pribumi* shareholders teamed with Liem, Sudwikatmono and Ibrahim Risjad, jointly owned 15 per cent instead of 13 per cent.[18] After the rearrangement, Indocement's shareholders were:

Government of Indonesia: 35 per cent
PT Mekar Perkasa (half owned by Liem's side, half by Djuhar Sutanto's
    side): 50 per cent
Ibrahim Risjad: 7.5 per cent
Sudwikatmono: 7.5 per cent

The Liem side's half-ownership of Mekar Perkasa broke down as follows: Soedono Salim (Liem himself) (25.38 per cent), Anthony Salim (14.62 per cent), Andree Halim (7.69 per cent) and Liem's younger brother Soedarmo Salim (2.31 per cent). For the 50 per cent of Mekar owned by the Djuhar side, four individuals had holdings that mirrored the Liem side: Djuhar (25.38 per cent), son Tedy Djuhar (14.62 per cent), son Johny Djuhar (7.69 per cent) and cousin Henry Pribadi (2.31 per cent).[19]

On the state's entry into Indocement, the *Asian Wall Street Journal* wrote, bankers assumed "the government is 'paying back' the Liem group for spearheading a government drive to build a cement industry and reduce dependence on imports".[20] It was payback, driven by the Suharto-Liem bond and by how when one of them needed aid, the other came through. An Australian economist, writing about Indonesia's tough economic period, remarked that "even the mighty Liem Sioe Liong group seems to have run into liquidity problems" though in his case there was a "helping hand".[21] The government did not talk about giving a helping hand. Liem's partner Sudwikatmono said in July that the government "apparently sees us [Indocement] as too big in controlling the market".[22] In August, Finance Minister Radius Prawiro defended the decree as necessary to "pre-empt the possibility of monopoly production of cement by Indocement" — though it is hard to see how government funds going into Liem's business would promote that goal.[23] When asked about the cash injection in 1989, one technocrat motioned towards the official portrait of Suharto on his wall and said "Please ask him."[24] All that Suharto ever said on the subject came in his 1995 defence of Liem. The president insisted that the money given Indocement was an "investment loan" that was "needed because of the difficulties that happened in a strategic industry".[25]

By the time Suharto mentioned the cement aid, he could contend that helping Indocement — which he did not name — had benefited the government. He told the audience at Tapos that the value of the US$350 million injection had become about US$660 million following Indocement's 1989 IPO, discussed in the next section; as Suharto spoke in 1995, the government had a paper profit from its stake. Its 35 per cent was reduced to 30 per cent by the IPO, and then to 26 per cent in the company's 1992 restructuring. During the 1997–98 crisis, shares of Indocement plummeted. Academic Shin Yoon Hwan, who did a 1989 thesis on Indonesian conglomerates, said the sparse state justification for the injection in 1985 reflected how involved parties ...

did not admit that the government meant to help Liem's company out of its financial trouble, thus avoiding any suggestion that Liem has special privileges. But Indocement's financial trouble became obvious later when four state banks decided to loan the company US$120 million to convert its foreign debt into a rupiah loan.[26]

First Pacific Ltd's October 1985 document for lenders, who had to approve Indocement's restructuring, projected that Indocement would make a net profit in 1986, with the projections increasing in each of the next four years.[27] This proved way too optimistic. For 1987, the company reported a loss of Rp95 billion rather than the projected Rp25 billion rupiah profit, and 1988 saw a Rp78 billion loss instead of a forecasted Rp31 billion gain. In a 1994 interview with the *Asian Wall Street Journal*, Anthony Salim defended the help Indocement received, calling it "strategic" for the government and paying it a good return. He asserted that the government had instructed Salim to expand heavily in cement, so it had an obligation to help tackle the problem. Anthony steered away from using the word "bailout" but drew parallels with the U.S. government's bailout of Chrysler in 1979. "Chrysler was strategic for the U.S. and Indocement was strategic for Indonesia", Anthony pointed out.[28] However, Chrysler just got loan guarantees; Indocement got a big bundle of cash.

Speaking to the authors years later, Anthony likened the Indocement rescue to President Ronald Reagan's action to help Harley-Davidson, which in the early 1980s suffered a huge loss in market-share for super-heavyweight motorcycles (more than 850 cc) to Honda and other Japanese manufacturers. In 1982, Harley won anti-dumping judgements from the U.S. International Trade Commission, which led Reagan to levy an extra 45 per cent tariff on imported Japanese models. Harley snatched back market leadership in the United States. Anthony gave the authors this account of what happened when Salim's cement production reached 7 million tonnes:

> It was just equal to the demand… We'd be able to make so much money as the capacity and the production just fits. And then one day Pak Harto [Suharto] and Hartarto [Industry Minister from 1983 to 1988] said that the target (in the state five-year plan) is going up, there will be more cement required. Virtually they said you need to purchase [capacity for] another five million tonnes.[29]

Asked if he was saying Salim was instructed to expand further, he replied: "Well, almost that this is the necessity — that you have to construct five million tonnes… So [we went from] from 7 to 12 million tonnes." On top of that, he added, another 3 million tonnes was done as if "by accident because we thought we could export".[30] Luckily for Salim, when its supply dangerously exceeded demand, the state supplied a mountain of aid.

A LITTLE HELP SPAWNS A BIG LISTING

Thanks to receiving funds to pay off some short-term, high-interest debt, Indocement sailed into better financial straits. Still, the company sought additional capital and, for a brief time, it looked like the party stepping up to the plate would be the Sultan of Brunei. In 1987, after Sultan Hassanal Bokiah met Suharto in Jakarta, State Secretary Sudharmono reported that the visiting ruler expressed interest in Indocement. If he bought 20 per cent, Sudharmono pointed out, "he has the right to sit on the board of directors. And that can be very attractive if Brunei does not want to buy cement from anywhere else."[31] It's not clear whether the Brunei leader was serious. He also expressed interest in buying a Bali hotel, and that was serious; he teamed with Suharto's daughter Tutut to acquire the Nusa Dua Beach Hotel from a state company, for an undisclosed but almost certainly highly attractive price.

The late 1980s paved a new way for Indonesian companies to raise money, as reforms kick-started the moribund Jakarta Stock Exchange. For the first time, foreign fund managers were flying in and pushing some companies to "go public". Many were particularly hopeful for a listing by Astra International, flagship of Salim's much bigger car industry rival, William Soeryadjaya. He had a far better public image than Liem did, partly because he was born in Indonesia, perceived to be well-integrated and not closely linked to Suharto. He also had in place a professional public relations department. William, whose grandfather had migrated to Java from Fujian, was born in 1922 about 80 kilometres east of Bandung. (He died in 2010.) He had a Chinese name, Tjia Kian Liong, but virtually nobody used it or even knew it. While rising in business, William had significant ties with Pertamina chief Ibnu Sutowo, but was not directly linked with Suharto. When Astra got listed, the company stayed popular for its responsiveness. Anthony conceded Astra's public relations superiority: "I think the PR of Pak William is very good", he commented.[32] Salim, he acknowledged was poor in public relations and added: "we consciously don't want to do it … we've been branded as cronies for such a long time anyway."[33]

Even though there was stronger interest in an Astra initial public offering, Indocement moved to go public earlier in the biggest IPO to date. In the second half of 1989, Indonesia's stock market became hot, and Salim wanted to move while the going was good. However, there was a major obstacle: the Finance Ministry had a rule that any company going public had to have been profitable for the two preceding years. Indocement said it lost Rp95 billion in 1987 and Rp78 billion in 1988, plus another Rp15 billion in the first seven months of 1989. The losses, the later prospectus for the IPO explained, were "mainly due to high financial changes, coupled with the imbalance between increased installed capacity and sluggish demand of cement".[34]

Given Indonesia's rule requiring two years of profits, authorities should have blocked the IPO. But as happened in 1985 when Indocement was squeezed, Salim found a way to work around the problem because it was Salim. Indocement was issued a waiver for the rule. Its application for an IPO was approved on 16 October 1989. From critics' point of view, rules were blatantly changed to benefit Salim. From Salim's point of view, the waiver was legal, so there was full compliance. "We always work according to the prevailing set of rules, the established rules", Anthony told the authors later.[35]

Until just before Indocement's IPO licence came through, the company was tinkering with its shareholding. One change was to convert debentures issued to three Suharto-linked foundations, which had provided Rp20 billion each to Indocement in early 1989. The conversions meant that before the IPO, each foundation owned 1.19 per cent of Indocement. Between 30 October and 10 November, the public was offered 10 per cent of Indocement. Shares were sold at Rp10,000 each (US$5.60 at the time) and Anthony took the roadshow to Hong Kong, London, Edinburgh and Amsterdam. He touted how Indonesian manufacturing was then growing at 20 per cent to 30 per cent a year, and Indocement plants were running at 94 per cent capacity. "As the market leader, we are well-positioned to take advantage of this growth rate", he stated. One consequence of the IPO was that it allowed the large shareholders to cash in some of their stakes. Liem received about US$20 million and Sudwikatmono got US$6 million. The government, whose stake was trimmed to 30.4 per cent from 35 per cent, collected US$28 million.[36] Some fund managers felt compelled to subscribe to the IPO, as Indocement would be the biggest Indonesian stock. The manager of Jardine Fleming's Indonesia Fund, Simon Hallett, said he thought the shares were expensive but "I don't want to be seen ducking a major issue". Eric Sandlund of Tyndall International (Asia) steered clear, citing two reasons. First, the issue is "too big for a market at this early stage of development". Second, "we're concerned about the earnings history — there isn't one".[37] Another concern, for some, was Indocement's distribution system, done through a Salim company not part of the cement maker, Semen Tiga Roda Prasetya. They thought this could impede tracking financial performance and let profits get parked with the unlisted distributor, which Indocement denied. One Indocement director predicted the IPO would be at least two times subscribed, but it just barely succeeded and was only 0.5 per cent oversubscribed. Danareksa, the state-owned lead underwriter, put on a brave front, with director Yannes Naibaho, arguing that a full subscription was "a good achievement for such a small market".[38]

In 1992, Indocement strangely also became a food company, as there was an asset-shuffle (written about later) in which Bogasari was injected. In the years leading to Indocement's purchase of Bogasari, Indonesia's cement industry had zero deregulation and zero new capacity; no plant was built between 1987 and early 1992. This meant that by 1994, thanks to the booming economy, there was a cement shortage and some parties began to hoard it. Still, producers such as Indocement could not cash in as might be assumed during a supply shortage. That's because the Indonesian government still controlled prices, using a mechanism called "guiding" prices (*harga pedoman semen*, or HPS) for main cities. When introduced in 1979, a securities analyst observed years later, the HPS "ironically was not meant to curb rising prices but set a minimum price at a time of oversupply to ensure better returns for privately-owned cement companies".[39] The HPS prices were taken as fixed ones by the national industry, which had an elaborate system of delivery quotas. It was not called a cartel, of course, but that essentially was how it functioned. That was the conclusion of three foreign economists, who wrote: "The full participation of producers and regulators in this process creates a 'cartel-like' arrangement in which competition between producers is 'controlled'."[40]

During the 1994 cement shortage, demand in Jakarta, accounting for 20 per cent of national consumption, soared 31 per cent from a year earlier. National consumption that year reached 21.5 million tonnes — almost double 1989's 11.4 million tonne figure. In October 1994, Suharto instructed the cabinet to resolve the cement crisis. Indocement did not want to increase its market-share, as that would open Salim up to new criticism. At the peak of the shortage, Jakarta was awash in rumours that a reason for it was that Indocement was diverting production to Manila for a project there that Tutut had invested in. Suharto's daughter was a major BCA shareholder and Indocement owned 8.8 per cent of her toll-road company. The rumours were so strong that Indocement denied repeatedly that cement was being diverted to the Philippines. "It is a big, big lie", insisted Executive Director Daddy Hariadi. Even if it were true, he said, the amount of cement said to be going to Manila would be only five hours of Indocement production time per month.[41]

STEEL: THE SECOND BAILOUT

A second episode of state help to Liem came in the late 1980s. While the Salim Group could say the government got a good return on its Indocement investment, it is unclear if the state later did well from bailing out Salim from involvement in making steel-sheets known as cold-rolled steel. Indonesia, like many developing nations, wanted to make its own steel as a symbol of industrial ability. But it costs a lot to produce steel, and the process often requires pricey government cosseting. Indonesia's effort to add steel to its list of import-substitution industries was, for decades, an expensive failure. Suharto once called the subsidies the government paid for domestic steel a "sacrifice by the people". As with some other Indonesian investments, there have been winners — but it often meant builders and suppliers, plus any parties they colluded with to mark up costs.

The history of Indonesian steel development is intriguing because while the first two presidents had diametrically different views and style, they shared the opinion that the nation must make its own steel. Suharto, despite often following technocrat advice in his early years, continued to champion expensive policies promoting import substitution. His determination to continue funding Research and Technology Minister B.J. Habibie's extravagant project to have Made-in-Indonesia airplanes is just the costliest example among many. The flamboyant Sukarno, in the late 1950s, declared that Indonesia had to produce its own steel. Home-grown production fit the mercurial leader's bent and anti-West stance. But his government had no money to build a mill. So, the left-leaning Sukarno asked the Soviet Union to put up a complex as part of its foreign aid and Moscow — competing fiercely with fellow-communist capital Beijing for his affection — agreed. The chosen site comprised ricefields near the small town of Cilegon, in the northwest corner of Java, almost directly opposite Krakatau island, which unleashed one of the world's most powerful volcanic eruptions in 1883. The site, it seems, was picked in the belief that there were good deposits of iron ore, the critical raw material for making steel, just across the narrow Sunda Straits in southern Sumatra.

Astonishingly, no money was spent studying the feasibility of the site or the project. So when the Russians made some preliminary moves towards building in Cilegon neither they nor the Indonesian government knew that Sumatra did not have any significant iron ore. After a Cilegon visit in 1975, Australian economist H.W. Arndt concluded: "The Soviet authorities, in conformity with their policy of 'non-interference' in their clients' choice of aid projects, appear not to have investigated this matter until after construction had begun in the early 1960s."[42] On fields where work was not ready to commence, Sukarno in May 1962 officially broke ground for the "Trikora Steel Project", named after his campaign launched a few months earlier to wrest West Irian from Dutch control. (Trikora was an abbreviation of Tri Komando Rakyat, or the People's Threefold Command, the name of Sukarno's campaign.) But four years later, when Sukarno lost power, no meaningful work had been done on the complex and the Russians packed their bags and went home. Steel was low on Gen. Suharto's early agenda, especially with inflation running amuck and government coffers almost bereft of money. In 1967, the Trikora Project was shelved and its rusting equipment abandoned. But once the economy stabilized and the West was giving large aid, Suharto did pay attention, as he saw steel as a backbone for domestic industry. In 1970, the programme was revived under the name Krakatau Steel. To build what the Russians never did, Suharto turned to his pal at Pertamina, Ibnu Sutowo.

Even before the first world oil shock of 1973–74 gave him big money to play with, Ibnu Sutowo threw his energy into reviving the steel project. He used Krakatau Steel to burnish his reputation for getting things moving, whatever the cost or rip-offs. Elaborate feasibility studies were completed, and construction contracts awarded to German companies Kloeckner, Siemens and Ferrostal. Hundreds of German engineers and technicians descended on Cilegon, and construction began. However, not everything was going smoothly — though this time money was flowing in. Arndt, the economist, noted that at Indonesia's "Steel City" in 1975, the most striking impression "was the contrast between the advanced stage of construction of housing, offices and social amenities, on the one hand, and the embryonic stage of industrial plan and infrastructure, on the other". He also noted that a fine club was nearing completion while a golf course and smart restaurant were already in business.[43]

Liem did not have any links with the steel project, as he did not have direct business dealings with Ibnu Sutowo. Coincidentally, though, disputes rooted in work done at Krakatau Steel led to Liem's name getting into a document submitted during a seventeen-year court battle in Singapore between the Indonesian government and the widow of Sutowo's long-time assistant Gen. Achmad Thahir over US$35 million that the aide left in a Singapore bank account when he died. In one affidavit filed for the widow, Kartika Ratna Thahir, who was Thahir's second wife, she asserted that her husband had been a business partner of Liem in a Jakarta property deal and in supplying 5,000 jeeps to the Indonesian army, partly through Liem's auto business Central Sole Agency. In the affidavit, Kartika's lawyers stated that through deals like the alleged jeep sale:

> Liem obtained knowledge of Thahir's financial resources, including the said ACU (Asian Currency Unit) deposits... Liem was at all times, and is, the closest business associate, the personal advisor and treasurer of the President of Indonesia. (Kartika) will contend that in all circumstances, the knowledge of... Liem is the knowledge of the President of Indonesia.[44]

Kartika also asserted that Thahir was collecting money with the approval of Sutowo and the government, not on his own. Given his low official salary — never more than US$9,000 a year — it was "not a term of Thahir's employment as general assistant to Sutowo that he should serve exclusively in that capacity. Thahir was free to supplement his said very small salary by remuneration earned in his private capacity," she contended. His extra income "was not secret", she said, alleging that both Sutowo and the Indonesian government knew about it and "consented thereto".[45] Liem, who did not have to make a deposition in court, denied all Kartika's allegations. In August 1994, the marathon fight over the Thahir deposits ended with the Singapore Court of Appeal dismissing Kartika's last appeal to get the money, which the judges said belonged to Pertamina.

Whatever amounts went into private pockets from contracts to build Krakatau Steel, the complex finally started producing steel and Suharto opened one part in 1977. Even then, the project was a mess, as there were too many cooks near the furnace. The complex, *FEER* reported, "has involved at least 10 foreign countries and two dozen manufacturers, which makes its management and coordination more than usually difficult". The magazine said that critics saw Krakatau Steel as "by far the biggest of the industrial white elephants owned by the Indonesian government".[46] Earlier, Indonesian newspapers obtained financial accounts done by Price Waterhouse which, they said, showed accumulated losses at Krakatau of about Rp250 billion (US$400 million then) from January 1977 through June 1980.

But Suharto, who was partial to any programme demonstrating Indonesia's ability to manufacture something it used to import, remained undeterred. He expanded the size and scope of the complex, which made slabs of what's called hot-rolled steel. To establish an integrated steel industry, plans were made to add a process called cold rolling to transform slabs into thin sheets and coils used for making auto bodies and pipes. In the late 1970s, Indonesia's imports of cold-rolled steel were about US$400 million a year. The government was Krakatau Steel's sole owner, so it was natural that the plans were for it to build the cold-rolling process. It formed a company, Cold Rolling Mill Indonesia (CRMI), and the mill's cost was estimated at US$800 million. But in the early 1980s, plummeting oil prices meant the government needed help to do the project. It was time for Suharto to call on his main cukong. Liem brought in Ciputra, his partner in property. The two set up PT Kaolin Indah Utama, which took a 40 per cent stake in CRMI. Krakatau Steel kept 40 per cent, and the remaining 20 per cent share was held by a foreign investor who was not really a foreign investor, Sestiacier S.A. of Luxembourg. The company involved some Liem money. The private investors put US$245 million into CRMI and arranged financing for the rest.

Because CRMI was no longer fully state-owned, the government could not guarantee foreign loans taken to build the cold-rolling mill. In spite of that handicap, an arm of Citibank arranged a US$218 million syndicated commercial loan. Financing was also sought from Spanish and French export credit agencies, for their contractors. The agencies, in turn, unsuccessfully sought loan guarantees from Krakatau Steel and the Indonesian government, though the Finance Ministry wrote what bankers call a "comfort letter" that supported the project. Such a letter was good enough to get the export credit agencies to give needed loans. Significant work for CRMI was undertaken by two Spanish engineering firms, Centunion and Technicas Reunidas, which Liem had helped get to work on the US$1 billion Dumai refinery project in Sumatra. Two French companies were primary contractors, and their involvement brought US$250 million of credits from France.[47]

In the interview he gave *Tempo* in 1984, Liem said foreign creditors gave commercial loans for the cold-rolling mill "with the condition that 40 per cent should be in private hands well-known to the banks". Talking with Tempo soon after the CRMI deal was done, Liem and Anthony portrayed their entry into steel as performing national service. Liem said "We moved into Krakatau Steel to help the government", while Anthony asserted, "If you want to invest up to US$800 million, it is easier to invest in other factories that make profit more quickly. But this is a special task."[48]

Suharto ensured that for undertaking a "special task", Liem and his partners received compensation. In April 1984, a month after mill construction began, the government gazette contained a Trade Ministry decree awarding sole rights for the import of cold-rolled steel sheets and coils to Krakatau Steel and a private company acting on its behalf, PT Giwang Selogam. Corporate records obtained by the *Asian Wall Street Journal* showed that Giwang Selogam's shareholders included the private investors in CRMI. Liem owned 20 per cent while Ciputra had 11.1 per cent. Others included Anthony Salim and Sudwikatmono. Suharto's foster brother was president-director of both Giwang Selogam and Kaolin Indah Utama, the company with 40 per cent equity in CRMI.[49]

The government decree that gave Giwang Selogam a monopoly said the set-up would "ensure a smooth implementation" of the import of cold-rolled steel. For customers, the arrangement translated to higher costs. A separate decree fixed the selling prices of the imported products, which were above what companies in Indonesia had been paying. In his dissertation, Shin summed up the steel deal between Liem and the state this way:

> Because of the overrated purchasing power of the domestic consumers and the high production costs and thus limited export capability of its products, Krakatau Steel was undergoing an underutilization of capacity and a large amount of loss. Both sides agreed upon a deal that Liem would take the loss by buying Krakatau's hot-rolled steel at high domestic prices and selling at low prices in the international market, and that, in return, Giwang Selogam would control the US$300 million a year market of the cold-rolled sheets and coils by importing and pricing them.[50]

Giwang Selogam got a guaranteed processing fee; it worked out to a commission of US$20 per metric ton and a handling fee of 2.5 per cent of total value. It also got flak. A 1986 World Bank report estimated the arrangement raised domestic steel prices by 25 per cent to 45 per cent.[51] Users of cold-rolled steel complained sheets were much more expensive, and said the lead-time on orders was twice as long as when they freely imported. Shin noted there were complaints "from all corners of downstream industries" and that Suharto's half-brother Probosutedjo, partner in a glassware factory, moaned: "Why does the government protect an industry which does not yet exist?"[52] John Bresnan of Columbia University commented that the monopoly "worked badly for all parties but the monopolists".[53] In Salim's view, building CRMI performed the service of giving Indonesia production of cold-rolled steel. Suharto opened the plant in 1987, and Giwang Selogam's import licence ended that same year. The plant did not fare well financially. One factor was a 31 per cent devaluation of the rupiah in September 1986 that increased its debt-repayment burden. Equipment imported for CRMI was priced in dollars or other foreign currencies, while its revenue was in rupiah.

Another factor was poor integration, at the start, between CRMI and other parts of Krakatau Steel. CRMI received a smaller volume of hot-rolled steel products from another part of the complex than expected. Krakatau estimated it would make 490,000 tonnes of hot-rolled steel in 1988, but produced only 330,000 tonnes. CRMI had to import about 30 per cent of its needs from Japan, which raised costs. Then CRMI could not sell as much as it aimed to, due to a weak, post-devaluation domestic economy and low oil prices. "After we completed [CRMI], there was recession… we couldn't sell, couldn't pay debt", Anthony admitted.[54] To maintain production, somebody had to put in more money into CRMI, and it was not going to be the private investors, who saw no chance for the mill to break even any time soon. According to Adam Schwarz, a study by banking advisors to the state concluded that by 1988, CRMI had accumulated losses of US$610 million and said that Liem had proposed to the government the private shareholders get bought out for US$290 million and absolved of debt commitments. The advisors, he wrote, contended that shareholders' interests in CRMI "are in fact without value".[55] CRMI finances were not publicly available, and for decades until it went public in 2010, Krakatau Steel did not publish accounts. Anthony Salim, who later acknowledged that Giwang Selogam "made good money", estimated Salim's net loss for involvement in CRMI at about US$100 million.[56]

Whatever losses the private parties took, they were able to cut them. In March 1989, the government made a US$75 million loan to CRMI, which was converted into equity. That was a first step for merging CRMI into Krakatau Steel, which took over the 60 per cent in non-state hands. The merger formally took place in September 1991. First, Liem and Ciputra helped the government build a mill it could not afford, and later it was the government's turn to help the businessmen. In the CRMI case, unlike with Indocement, Anthony agreed to call the state action a bailout. But to him, the government was fulfilling a contractual agreement. "With CRMI, we had a written agreement," he pointed out, "They had to bail us out."[57]

A Golkar member of parliament, Ben Messakh, mildly criticized the US$75 million injection, which is notable because under Suharto, MPs almost never did anything other than endorse government policies. "If the injection is to help the private shareholders, we don't agree", Messakh said, but conceded that CRMI was a "very essential industry" so if state action was "to make the industry sound, we support it". The MP tempered his criticism, noting that some government aid was justified because it had encouraged Liem and Ciputra to join CRMI. If the rescue was costly, he added, "some people will say the government helps the richest man in Indonesia but for us in the Parliament, the question is whether CRMI is needed or not — and it's needed."[58] In 1992, an economist commented that the cold-rolling mill "continues to generate problems for many parts" of the steel industry. He said the cost of supporting the complex

> is being borne through the invisible taxes imposed on the Indonesian community by high compensating tariffs and surcharges on a number of downstream products whose main market is inevitably domestic... High-cost cold-rolled steel feeds a state-owned tin plate mill whose output is reputedly 40 per cent more costly than imports.[59]

Liem's role in cement and steel forged extra strong bonds with Suharto. In his dissertation analysing the development of Salim and Astra, Shin wrote:

> While Astra responded actively and positively to industrial policies the state formulated, the Liem group colluded with the state through joint ownership of companies. The participation by Liem in the state's steel project and that by the state in Liem's cement companies demonstrate

that these industries retain *national* significance, removed from his earlier ventures, which power-holders used for their factional interests... he was willing to demonstrate that he also contributed to the industrialisation of Indonesia. Despite the apparent cause his large-scale joint ventures may have, Liem was, after all, a money-maker par excellence. He made the state come to the rescue of Liem's cement factories, not vice versa; for CRMI, he did not fail to grab the recompense; and in both, he projected himself to be seen as a national industrialist".[60]

There was one significant side dividend for Salim from the work with Krakatau Steel — Liem forged a close friendship with Tunky Ariwibowo, a senior government official who later became Industry Minister. A Canadian-educated metallurgist, Tunky had been assigned to the Trikora steel project in 1964 when he was twenty-eight. Sukarno was still president at the time, and the Russians were in West Java. The following decade, after Krakatau Steel was formed to replace Trikora, Suharto tapped Tunky to try to fix the mess surrounding the unbuilt plants. He became Krakatau's president-director in 1975, in the middle of the Pertamina crisis when contractors that Ibnu Sutowo had done dicey deals with were screaming for payment.

In a book honouring Tunky published after his death in 2002, J.B. Sumarlin — former Finance Minister and one of the technocrats who worked on the Pertamina debt debacle — commended Tunky for playing an essential role in resolving crises at Krakatau Steel.[61] Tunky remained Krakatau's CEO until 1993, when Suharto made him Industry Minister. For fostering progress at Krakatau and helping improve Indonesia's investment climate, Tunky won plaudits from investors, though his standing took a knock in 1996 when he had to be main public defender of Tommy Suharto's unpopular "national car" project. Tunky became close to Anthony through the cold-rolling mill chapter, and the friendship was enhanced by their cooperation on the three-nation Growth Triangle, written about later. In the memorial book, Anthony wrote that Tunky possessed a "cold hand" (*tangan dingin*), an Indonesian idiom meaning someone is highly skilled and successful.[62] The close ties between Tunky and Anthony prompted a joke among some pundits that Tunky had an MBA, which in this case stood for "management by Anthony". The two bailouts received in the 1980s — one in cement and one in steel — positioned the group to spend on projects like the Growth Triangle. After the bailouts, it was boomtime for Salim.

Notes

1. Various Indonesian newspaper reports, 25 September 1995.
2. Interview with Liem, 13 May 2006.
3. Interview with Anthony, 17 December 2006.
4. "Indonesia cement plant owners line up US$120 million bank loan", *WSJ*, 13 October 1981.
5. First Pacific Ltd, "Recommended Proposals to the Lenders of the Indocement Group for the Acceptance of the Restructuring and Merger of the Indocement Group of Companies", 15 October 1985, p. 29.
6. Yuri Sato, "The Salim Group in Indonesia: The development and behavior of the largest conglomerate in Southeast Asia", *Developing Economies* XXXI, no. 4 (December 1993), p. 419.
7. Ibid, p. 418.
8. Guy Sacerdoti, "High oil profits permit a change in financing strategy", *FEER*, 4–10 April 1980.
9. Guy Sacerdoti, "A Made-in-Indonesia Controversy", *FEER*, 15 February 1980.
10. Company brochure for Indocement's 1989 IPO.
11. Fikri Jufri, "Liem buka suara: Orang banyak salah sangka", *Tempo*, 31 March 1984, pp. 68–69.
12. Manggi Habir, "Only a few brave the public arena", *FEER*, 19 April 1984, p. 83.
13. Prospectus for Indocement initial public offering, 1989, p. 34.
14. Interview with Anthony, 21 January 2007.
15. First Pacific Ltd, "Recommended Proposals", p. 87.
16. Confidential conversation, 23 March 2007.
17. Steven Jones and Cheah Cheng Hye, "Indocement Replaces US$120 Million Loan", *AWSJ*, 15 July 1985.
18. First Pacific, "Recommended Proposals", p. 18.
19. Ibid., p. 20.
20. Jones and Cheah, "Indocement Replaces US$120 Million Loan".
21. Howard Dick, "Survey of Recent Developments", *Bulletin of Indonesian Economic Studies* XXI, no. 3 (December 1985), p. 18.
22. "Indikator", *Tempo*, 6 July 1985.
23. "Pembelian Saham PT Indocement, Bukan Untuk Membantu Dana", *Kompas*, 14 August 1985.
24. Private conversation, Jakarta, 25 October 1989.
25. Various Indonesian newspaper reports, 25 September 1995.
26. Shin Yoon Hwan, "Demystifying the capitalist state, political patronage, bureaucratic interests, and capitalist-in-formation in Suharto's Indonesia", Ph.D. thesis, Yale University, 1989, p. 375.

27. First Pacific, "Recommended Proposals", p. 57.
28. Richard Borsuk, "Salim Group Steels Itself For Life After Suharto", *AWSJ*, 25 February 1994.
29. Interview with Anthony, 21 January 2007.
30. Ibid.
31. "Brunei offers 100-million-dollar loan to Indonesia", Reuters, 10 September 1987.
32. Interview with Anthony, 24 December 2006.
33. Interview with Anthony, 8 April 2007.
34. Indocement prospectus, 1989, p. 46.
35. Interview with Anthony, 14 January 2007.
36. Steven Jones, Christopher Hunt and Richard Borsuk, "Fund officials cool on Indocement offering", *AWSJ*, 8 November 1989.
37. Ibid.
38. Richard Borsuk, "Indonesia's biggest-ever share offering succeeds but falls below expectations", *AWSJ*, 17 November 1989.
39. "Grey but never dull", Smith New Court report on Indonesian cement, July 1995.
40. H.H. Plunkett, W.E. Morgan and J.L. Pomeroy, "Regulation of the Indonesian Cement Industry", *Bulletin of Indonesian Economic Studies* 33, no. 1 (April 1997).
41. Mark Clifford, "Hard Times Ahead", *FEER*, 3 November 1994.
42. H.W. Arndt, "PT Krakatau Steel", *Bulletin of Indonesian Economic Studies* 11, no. 2 (1975), p. 120.
43. Ibid.
44. Guy Sacerdoti, "Litigation: The revelations of a widow", *FEER*, 1–7 August 1980.
45. Ibid.
46. Susumu Awanohara, "Krakatau's production is coated in confidentiality", *FEER*, 23 June 1983, pp. 60–66.
47. Richard Borsuk, "Jakarta's Steel-Mill Rescue Sparks Dispute", *AWSJ*, 5 July 1989.
48. Jufri, "Liem buka suara", *Tempo*.
49. Borsuk, "Jakarta's Steel-Mill Rescue Sparks Dispute", *AWSJ*.
50. Shin, "Demystifying the capitalist state", p. 373.
51. William Frederick and Robert Worden, eds. *Indonesia: A Country Study* (Washington, D.C.: U.S. Library of Congress, 1993), accessed at <http://countrystudies.us/indonesia/>, on 20 August 2010.
52. Shin, "Demystifying the capitalist state", p. 373.
53. John Bresnan, *Managing Indonesia: The Modern Political Economy* (New York: Columbia University Press, 1993), p. 250.
54. Interview with Anthony, 4 November 2007.

55. Adam Schwarz, *A Nation in Waiting: Indonesia's Search for Stability*, 2nd ed. (St Leonards, NSW: Allen & Unwin, 1999), p. 112.

56. Interview with Anthony, 4 November 2007.

57. Interview with Anthony, 4 March 2007.

58. Borsuk, "Jakarta's Steel-Mill Rescue Sparks Dispute", *AWSJ*.

59. Ross Chapman, "Indonesian Trade Reform in Close-Up: The Steel and Footwear Experiences", *Bulletin of Indonesian Economic Studies* 28, no. 1 (1992): 80–81.

60. Shin, "Demystifying the capitalist state", pp. 377–78.

61. J.B. Sumarlin, "Ir. Tunky Ariwibowo: Seorang pekerja keras, jujur, loyal dan tekun mengabdi tugas" [Tunky Ariwibowo: A hardworking, honest, loyal and diligent, dutiful 'servant'], in Astuti R. Ariwibowo, comp., *Dalam Kenangan Tunky Ariwibowo: Pekerja Keras*. [In Memoriam: Tunky Ariwibowo, a Hardworker] (Jakarta: Privately published, for his 1000th day memorial, 2005), p. 91.

62. Anthony Salim, "Pak Tunky", in ibid, p. 125.

10

A BANKING BEHEMOTH

One of the crown jewels in the Salim stable was Bank Central Asia (BCA). Its transformation to the country's leading private bank from one that was barely breathing in the early 1970s could be credited to the efforts of one person — Mochtar Riady, who Liem brought on board in 1975. Prior to Riady's entry, Liem's banks (including Bank Windu Kencana, co-owned with a Kostrad foundation) were in dire need of professional help. Both were nowhere able to offer fully fledged financial services. In 1973 Salim had two flour mills in operation and was constructing a cement plant. Big factories required huge funding, and Liem was one of the few individuals in Indonesia at that stage — still early in the New Order — who was able to line it up. His immediate rapport with Chin Sophonpanich of Bangkok Bank was critical for channelling seed money into his cement venture. Although he could tap into outside funds, Liem knew that gaining long-term strength hinged on developing his own banking capability. When Suharto came to power, Liem was already a "banker" in the sense that he partly owned banks, but this meant just possession of a licence, not any real accumulation of assets. In the late Sukarno period, Indonesia had scores of minuscule private banks, many of which were owned by politicians or their pals, but they were weak.

BCA started life as a textile company called NV Semarang Knitting Factory. Curiously, its articles of association allowed it to conduct banking activities. As the company was not doing well, Liem and a Hokchia friend named Tan Lip Soin purchased the licence in 1957 from the owner, a businessman in Semarang named Gunardi.[1] Liem wanted the company for its banking licence, and changed its name initially to Bank Asia N.V. and subsequently to Bank Central Asia. He also moved its operations to Jakarta from Semarang.[2] Liem, who was not yet an Indonesian citizen, installed his good friend Hasan Din as a director. When Suharto tapped Liem to be his *cukong*, he assigned Liem to cooperate with his generals at the Kostrad Foundation (Yayasan Dharma Putra Kostrad) that he headed. Bank Windu Kencana had been incorporated in 1954, but in 1967 it was reconstituted with several of Suharto's financial generals on its board. Liem and his two brothers were listed as co-owners. According to Liem, he offered equity in BCA to Suharto himself, who declined having his name there, so in 1974, 30 per cent of the equity was placed in the names of the president's older children, Sigit Haryoyudanto (20 per cent) and Siti Hardiyanti Hastuti, known as Tutut (10 per cent). The stakes were later amended to 16.7 per cent for Sigit and 13.3 per cent for Tutut.[3]

MOCHTAR RIADY, THE "BANKING DOCTOR"

Liem's financial experience was limited to selling goods on credit in Central Java. In 1975, once again, Lady Luck was smiling on him. A chance encounter early that year spawned the transformation of BCA. The bank's meteoric growth, which helped propel Liem into the ranks of Asia's wealthiest men, had its roots in an airplane ride. Liem and an Indonesian banker he was acquainted with, Mochtar Riady, happened to be on the same flight to Hong Kong. For Liem, it presented a good opportunity to talk with a man with a reputation of turning around troubled banks. Mochtar, then in his mid-40s, earned his moniker "banking doctor" after resuscitating three institutions: Bank Kemakmuran, which he ran from 1960 to 1963, then Bank Buana until 1971, and finally, Pan-Indonesian Bank, better known as Panin Bank, which he built into the largest private bank at the time, with a sixty-branch network. In the mid-1970s, BCA had no foreign exchange licence, just two branches and was ranked a lowly twenty-third place out of fifty-eight private commercial banks in assets. At most, according to academic Yuri Sato, BCA "was only able to handle receipts and payments in rupiah within the group".[4] Bank Windu Kencana stayed insignificant after the death of Gen. Sofjar, who headed the Kostrad foundation. Liem knew that he needed to tap into the expertise of those who had experience in the field if he were to grow his banking ventures. The timing for both men was fortuitous. Shortly before that flight to Hong Kong, Jakarta's then-small banking circle was abuzz with rumours that Mochtar was planning to part ways with his brothers-in-law (who were also his cousins), the majority owners of Panin Bank. For Liem, there was no better time to pop the question to Mochtar: "Do you want to build up my banks?" he inquired. The banker expressed interest, and the two agreed to continue the conversation back in Jakarta.

Mochtar Riady (Li Mo Tie, spelled Li Wenzheng in *hanyu pinyin*) said ever since he was a boy, he had wanted to be a banker. Not having a finance background didn't faze him. He once told an interviewer that when he started at Bank Kemakmuran, he "couldn't tell the left from the right of a balance sheet".[5] He set goals for himself and then applied himself to fulfilling them. Mochtar Riady was born in Batu (meaning stone), a small town near Malang, in East Java, in 1929. By the Chinese zodiac, it was the Year of the Snake, and he was one cycle, or twelve years, younger than Liem. But Mochtar, who converted to Christianity later in life, dismissed any significance to it, saying he did not give much credence to Chinese mythology. Mochtar's parents had migrated to East Java from Putian, a town in Fujian province, from about 120 kilometres south of Liem's birthplace, and which later became known as the "sports shoes capital of the world", for its contract production of shoes for some of the well-known brands. Mochtar's parents spoke the Henghua dialect. When they migrated, they had to make the painful decision to leave three daughters behind in China. In Batu, they started a small shop selling batik. Mochtar was the couple's sixth child. When Mochtar was nine, his mother died giving birth to her ninth child. The baby, a girl, did not survive.[6] His father, who never remarried after his wife's death, looked after the surviving children.

Mochtar's ambitious character showed early. He was a bright and determined young boy. A photo of him at age nine shows a serious-looking child with slicked-down hair staring piercingly at the camera. Around age 10, Mochtar became fixated with the idea of becoming a banker. When he was old enough, he thought to himself, he would move to Jakarta and work in a bank. Asked what brought on this obsession, he couldn't explain, though, he recalled, on his way to school he used to pass a Dutch bank, and was impressed by its neatly dressed, professional looking staff. He imagined himself as one of them, but working in a more "happening" city like Jakarta, not the quiet town of Malang. Given the family circumstances, it seemed an improbable dream. One day, Mochtar shared his vision with his father. Instead of encouraging the boy to follow his dream, his father tried to disabuse him of such lofty aspirations. "He thought I was crazy", Mochtar recalled. "He said, 'just look at yourself in the mirror. Do you see a banker?' But I said to him, 'for a plant to grow big, it cannot stay indoors'."[7]

While Mochtar was in high school in Malang, World War II ended, and the country became embroiled in the independence struggle against the Dutch. Although he was a son of immigrants, Mochtar felt strongly enough about the Independence movement to get actively involved in the struggle. He became president of the East Java Overseas Chinese Student Association, demonstrating against the Dutch.[8] In 1947, he was arrested for anti-Dutch agitation and deported to China, where his older sisters still lived. There were only two choices for him at the time, he recalled — agree to be deported (even though he was born in Indonesia), or go to prison.[9] He went to Nanjing (Nanking), then capital of Nationalist China under the Kuomintang, and enrolled at its Chung Yang University, which later became the University of Nanjing. In 1949, when the Communists gained control of China, Mochtar fled to Hong Kong, from where he returned to an Indonesia now finally free of the Dutch. He settled in Surabaya, got married and worked in a department store owned by his mother-in-law. He moved to Jakarta in 1956 — the first step towards fulfilling his childhood dream. In 1960 he was asked to help resuscitate a fledgling bank called Kemakmuran (meaning prosperity), that his cousins partially owned. He plunged into the task, demonstrating an aptitude for it, and helping turn the bank around in less than three years.

Subsequently, he repeated his success at Bank Buana. When his brothers-in-law started Panin Bank, created in 1971 from the merger of several small ones, including Kemakmuran, Mochtar joined them. Mochtar took to banking like a fish to water. But his working relationship with his relatives was not without disagreements. After a few years, he decided to part company. In 2007, asked by the authors about the reason behind the split, Mochtar replied with a wry smile: "It's a very long story." He alluded to a "difference of concept" with Mu'min Ali Gunawan (Li Mo Ming),[10] the oldest brother-in-law. He summarized the issue from his viewpoint:

> A banker has to be very conservative and concentrate on banking but not other [activities]. Mu'min [had] conflict of interest with customers... [We] fought all the time ... incurred two runs on the bank... I told them if you still want to go with this approach, I don't think I can continue to work... Bad decisions end up on my shoulder. I was CEO. I say I will go out myself. Had difference of opinion ... the owners wanted to do a lot of different businesses... I wanted to stay focused... No hard feelings.[11]

On his part, Liem had a good feeling about Mochtar from their chat and sensed the banker was just what he needed. However, not everyone was convinced. Liem's younger brother Sioe Kong was opposed to having Mochtar come on board. A close friend warned Liem about Mochtar, comparing him to the clever and wily fabled Monkey King (Sun Wu Kong) in the Chinese literature classic *Journey to the West*. In the story, the Monkey King, accompanying the Buddhist monk Tang Sheng (Xuanzang) in his quest to acquire Buddhist scriptures, loved to trick whoever he met. No one except Tang Sheng was able to control the Monkey King. To seek reassurance, Liem made a trip to Gunung Kawi in East Java to consult the soothsayer, as he often did before embarking on bold ventures. The prophecy was good. On his return, he confidently told his detractor, "I will be Tang Sheng to Mochtar."[12]

Negotiations happened quickly. Within a month of his in-flight chat with Liem, Mochtar was keen to come on board. Liem offered him a choice of banks to run: Windu Kencana or BCA.[13] Without hesitation, the "banking doctor" picked BCA as his new patient. Both institutions could do with professional help. Mochtar later said BCA was "on the verge of bankruptcy". At the time, BCA had at most US$1 million of assets, and just twenty-seven staff. Among them, Mochtar stated later, "no one knew anything about banking". Perhaps more importantly, BCA had no Liem family members who were involved in day-to-day matters. "I prefer to start from zero. Easier to build [BCA] up rather than go into Windu Kencana," he explained years later. At Windu Kencana, Mochtar noted, Liem's younger brother Sioe Kong was involved and "many others" were inside, adding that this could be "not easy to handle".[14]

Mochtar recalled being grilled by Liem during their initial talks. One of the questions Liem asked the banker was the target for BCA's growth. Liem had been impressed at the stellar growth of Panin with Mochtar at the helm. Mochtar recalled their conversation on this topic:

He [Liem] raised one question: "You took two and a half years to grow
Panin; how long will it take you to grow BCA from zero to largest private
bank?"

I told him: "maybe two and a half years to make BCA the largest."

He asked: why are you so confident?

I answered: you have something more than Panin. What Panin had,
we have.

Pak Liem says: Panin is a forex bank. BCA is not; Panin has 60 branches,
BCA only one office. Panin has US$200 million in assets, BCA only US$1
million. So what is it they have that we don't?

I answered: You're talking about quantity. I'm talking about quality.
That's the difference. I have access to [your] 3 golden keys. Panin doesn't
have [them].

When Liem asked what he was referring to, Mochtar said he replied:

The first golden key is Liem Sioe Liong, to open the door to the *kretek*
cigarette industry, with your clove monopoly. Much depends on him.
I will use the Liem Sioe Liong connection to get the cigarette business.
The second golden key is Liem Sioe Liong, to open the door to flour mill
customers through Bogasari. They have a lot of customers. The third
golden key is Liem Sioe Liong, to open the door to cement and building-
materials customers. I am using you to open these three areas.[15]

Mochtar believed he was on the right track with the experience he gained
from working with the three previous banks, and he had confidence he
could duplicate the formula for success with BCA. He had learned to
identify the niche markets to focus on, and that strategy had worked.
For instance, at Kemakmuran, he focused on the Fujian immigrants who
dominated the bicycle trade; at Buana it was the textile and agricultural
sectors, while at Panin, he zoomed in on the import market. When it came
to Liem's bank, Mochtar was confident Liem's privileged position would
allow him access to sectors his previous banks did not. Anyone could open
branches and add banking assets, he reasoned, but only Liem had those
"golden keys", and with them it "would be very easy to grow the bank
with my experience".[16] Mochtar's entry into BCA met mutual needs. As
Anthony Salim summed up years later, the banker "needed a house [new
workplace] and my dad needed a partner, so they got married".[17] It was,
for fifteen years, a highly successful marriage by any measure — one in
which Liem gave his partner tremendous scope and freedom.

With Mochtar agreeing to take on the challenge of building up BCA, all that remained to discuss was what he would get in equity of the bank. According to Liem, Mochtar initially asked for 30 per cent equity, which was his shareholding at Panin. "I told him it was not possible; that would have meant he would have more shares than me", Liem said.[18] Liem had already given a total of 30 per cent to Suharto's two oldest children. If Liem had agreed to give Mochtar 30 per cent, only 40 per cent would be left for Liem, his two brothers and uncle, who were also shareholders at the time (they would later be bought out). Asked to confirm that he sought 30 per cent, Mochtar denied it. They agreed on 17.5 per cent, which Mochtar said already made him the largest single shareholder.[19] Liem, as an individual shareholder, owned just 5 per cent according to BCA records, but his family retained majority control.

The negotiation between Mochtar and Liem was a good indication of the personalities of the two men who would become giants in Indonesian business. After sizing each other up, they determined that they trusted each other. That was the key to the relationship. The banker liked to say that the business of banking is not about money, but trust. And so it was with the new industrialist Liem. "When [Pak Liem] trusts somebody, then he really trusted [him] ... and he trusted me 100 per cent," Mochtar said. After the initial "interrogation", Liem never interfered with Mochtar's decisions at BCA. Nearly two decades after their "marriage" ended, the banker remained full of praise of Liem and the trust he placed. "I think Mr Liem has the ability to make [good] use of people. This is his strength."[20] During their discussions, Liem was sometimes accompanied by young Anthony, who had returned to Jakarta four years earlier. At the first meeting, Liem did all the talking. The presence of Anthony was an indication of how much confidence Liem placed in his youngest son. To see if trust would develop between Mochtar and Anthony, Liem produced a surprise one day when Mochtar arrived at the BCA office at Jalan Asemka for their meeting. Mochtar recounted:

> The father did not appear, but his son, Anthony, was there to meet me. He was young at that time... His hair was quite long. He had a little goatee, just some strands of hair from his chin. He was wearing flare pants and platform shoes, which went clickety-clack when he walked. I looked at him and felt so disappointed. I was upset. I thought to myself, Om Liem is making a joke [of me] ... or he really doesn't respect me.[21]

Liem corroborated Mochtar's account of the banker's meeting with Anthony:

> I sent Anton to discuss the details of Mochtar's joining; Anton had been back from England but he still looked like a hippie. He wore these heeled shoes that made a click-clock sound. Mochtar told me later he was thinking: *"Gi mana?"* ("What's this?") Why is this young boy being sent to talk to me?[22]

Mochtar initially feared his time would be wasted at that session. He recalled asking Liem's youngest: "Ok, Anton, what are you going to talk about?" and being taken aback when Anthony was prepared with the details of Mochtar's compensation package as well as subjects such as strategic plans for BCA. Towards the end of their discussion, Mochtar said, Anthony asked him whether he wanted to conduct due diligence on BCA. "I said: 'There's no need for due diligence.' He said: 'Why, are you sure? Or are you joking'?" And I replied: "the bank's assets are only $1 million ... why do we have to spend time and ask, say, Peat Marwick to do due diligence? Maybe their fee is much bigger [than the assets] ... It is not necessary. I trust you.' So, only after three hours, everything was finished. I entered the bank."[23] Mochtar said he came away from that meeting with a much altered opinion of the scruffy-looking interlocutor. He realized why Anthony became Liem's heir apparent. "He is not a joker. I understood why his father sent him and not his eldest brother Albert, or Andree. Anthony is the smartest."[24] Asked about their talk, Anthony acknowledged that the banker "couldn't take me seriously at first", but after a while, "we proceeded to talk the real things".[25]

THE BOOMING OF BCA

As soon as Mochtar came into BCA, the banker applied for a foreign exchange licence. The bank also absorbed Bank Gemari, a military-linked bank. Bank Indonesia granted the forex licence in 1977. That helped Mochtar accelerate moves to make BCA the king among privately owned financial institutions. True to his word, Mochtar used Liem's "golden keys" to good effect, opening the way to scores of new borrowers and fuelling spectacular growth for the bank. (For its corporate logo, BCA based the design on a clove stalk, a symbol of Liem's first "key", into the *kretek* business.) Mochtar targeted the customers of Liem's ventures — the cigarette manufacturers who needed to purchase his cloves, the users of the flour Bogasari produced, and the construction industry that used his Tiga Roda cement. All three industries were experiencing growth. Capacity at Liem's cement plants was steadily increasing. Although flour consumption was still small in the late 1970s, it was on a rising trajectory. While Bulog was technically the sole national distributor, the chain of milling-related businesses for Bogasari generated new clients for BCA. The stellar growth was reflected in the bank's numbers: from Rp998 million at the end of 1974, assets a year later — eight months after Mochtar joined — jumped to Rp12.8 billion. Within two years, the figure nearly doubled to Rp24.8 billion. By 1980, assets topped Rp100 billion. The growth trajectory continued, reaching Rp1 trillion by 1986; in 1990, the year Mochtar parted company with BCA, assets nearly topped Rp7.5 trillion.[26] Three years after he came on board, Mochtar reached his target of overtaking Panin as Indonesia's largest privately owned bank.

Important as they were, the "golden keys" were not the only factor behind BCA's boom. It took innovation, as in the 1970s and much of the 1980s, Indonesian banking remained a staid, state-dominated business that resisted rather than welcomed change; government-owned banks held more than 80 per cent of total assets. Mochtar pushed for changes that the far bigger but flat-footed state banks, more concerned about making politically correct loans than innovating, were years away from considering. The Liem family showed foresight in seeking new technologies and products. In 1980, BCA started issuing credit cards. Over a period of many years, the bank invested heavily on computerization and was the first Indonesian bank to link branches and other Salim businesses with a satellite VSAT (very small aperture terminal) communications system, made possible with government assistance. To help modernize its systems, BCA scouted for consultants from afar, preferring mid-sized U.S. and other foreign banks to banking giants which charged hefty fees. BCA found good people from far-flung places such as M&I (Marshall and Ilsley) Bank in Milwaukee, in the United States.[27] BCA was not the first bank to introduce the automated teller machines (ATM) — Bank Bali was — but BCA was the leader in aggressively installing hundreds of ATMs, another way to boost the bank's reach in the archipelago. By making it easier for people around the country to withdraw cash, BCA attracted big numbers of new customers happy to deposit their spare cash, giving the bank a strong low-cost funding franchise. Besides Mochtar, Liem's middle son

Andree Halim and Anthony also played important roles in building the franchise. Andree was considered an excellent people manager, and highly regarded by the bank's employees, while Anthony was a driving force for innovation. Bondan Winarno, a journalist commissioned to research the history of BCA for its fiftieth anniversary in 2007, credits Anthony's foresight for pushing the ATM network. Its rapid development "could not have taken off without Anton", says Winarno. He also said it was Anthony who tweaked the details of a savings-account programme called Tahapan (short for *Tabungan Hari Depan*, meaning savings for the future) that Mochtar introduced. Anthony "was the one who said Tahapan would not fly unless you had ATMs everywhere. And he was proven right; now a lot of mom-and-pop stores use them."[28]

By adding services and convenience, Mochtar helped come up with ways to leverage on BCA's growing customer base to increase income. He said in 1983 that "for every dollar a client takes from your bank, you can make three, or four, not even counting the interest. It's simple [from selling insurance, leasing arrangements etc] … there's no limit really, if you keep on expanding the services range, as your niche dictates."[29] The niche was growing. More than fifteen finance-industry businesses were created. In insurance, there was a build-up of old PT Asuransi Central Asia Raya, expanded with a life insurance company in 1976. In 1974, the year before Mochtar entered, BCA co-established a finance company called PT Multinational Finance Corp., or Multicor, and Mochtar helped expand it with the Royal Bank of Scotland, the Long Term Credit Bank of Japan, Jardine Fleming and Chemical Bank as shareholders.

SPREADING WINGS ABROAD

Soon after Mochtar entered BCA, he wanted a presence in Hong Kong, Asia's financial centre. He had first done business in Hong Kong in 1969, when the colony was still feeling the effects of the Cultural Revolution in China. By 1975, Hong Kong had rebounded and was enjoying a growth spurt. Many foreign banks were opening branches there but Mochtar did not have that option. BCA didn't have a foreign exchange licence yet, and even if it had, Indonesia's central bank at that time did not allow non-state banks to open branches outside the country. But Hong Kong regulations allowed individuals to set up what were called deposit-taking companies to get a presence in the colony, and that's the route Mochtar pursued while at the same time BCA applied for, and received, a foreign exchange licence.

Mochtar wasted no time getting moving outside Indonesia. Within months of his joining BCA, Central Asia Capital Corporation Ltd. (CACC) was registered in Hong Kong, with a paid-up capital of HK$12.5 million and a small office in Wanchai. According to the original company registration, Liem owned 35 per cent of the shares while Mochtar held 17.5 per cent, just like his BCA stake. In the registration, each was identified as a "banker", and each listed apartments in Hong Kong's Causeway Bay shopping district for a Hong Kong address. Holding the remaining 47.5 per cent of CACC was Anchor Development Ltd of Hong Kong, a Liem vehicle. Anchor's main figure was a Hong Kong man named Chan Ah Foo, Liem's point person there for clove imports from Zanzibar. CACC acted as a Hong Kong beachhead for BCA, and it helped Salim obtain foreign loans for its cement plants in Indonesia. (It was in Hong Kong in 1977 that Anthony met future partner Manny Pangilinan.) Having a flag to fly in Hong Kong was important for Mochtar, who networked easily there with global bankers, and that suited the Salim family, which began building its own businesses in the colony.

In 1977, Mochtar and Liem's overseas expansion reached the unlikely location of Little Rock, Arkansas. It followed an unsuccessful bid by Mochtar to buy a stake in a Georgia bank, partly owned by then-President Jimmy Carter's Budget Director Bert Lance. The Arkansas connection came from a friendship made during the failed Georgia purchase earlier the same year. Mochtar was one of the parties trying to buy some of the 16 per cent stake that Lance had to sell in the National Bank of Georgia to avoid a potential conflict-of-interest. (For many Indonesian businessmen, the concept of "conflict-of-interest" was an alien one.) Mochtar's Georgia move was typical of the bold ones that would mark the banker's career; The *Asian Wall Street Journal* said at the time he had already "acquired a reputation as a shrewd and aggressive financier."[30] Media reports in the United States of Mochtar's bid contributed to scuppering the deal, which was blocked by Indonesian monetary authorities in any case. But the key advisor to Lance, Jackson Stephens, became a friend and business partner of Mochtar and opened the door for a high-profile U.S. network for the Riady family.

Jackson Stephens came from a family of major financiers from Arkansas led by his older brother Witt. Jackson and Mochtar bonded, and each was eager to do business on the other's side of the Pacific Ocean. The American, six years older, teamed with Mochtar to open Stephens Finance in Hong Kong in the late 1970s. In 1983, they bought Seng Heng Bank in Macau (eventually sold to gambling magnate Stanley Ho) and a year later, the pair jointly paid HK$337 million for the Hong Kong Chinese Bank, which gave the Riady family its own banking beachhead in Asia outside Indonesia. Stephens, who died in 2005, told Forbes magazine in 1987: "I became entranced with the way they do business in Asia. It was very freewheeling with very few rules. However, you must have a good partner."[31] In the United States, the friendship with Stephens put Mochtar — and later Liem's son Andree — into banking in Arkansas and over time built a friendship between the Riady family and a young governor named Bill Clinton. (Liem and his wife, together with Mochtar and James, met the future U.S. president in Arkansas in 1983. Clinton later autographed a photo of that meeting with Liem.) In 1977, Mochtar's ambitious middle son James, then only twenty years old, went to Little Rock as an intern with Stephens Inc. Seven years later, Mochtar bought 14 per cent of Worthen Banking Corp., which came to own about a dozen Arkansas banks, and James returned to Little Rock, to work there. Also in 1984, Worthen director C.J. Giroir sold his 5.4 per cent stake in Worthen to a Delaware investment company, Balder Corp., whose principal shareholder was Andree.

The Worthen investment did not work out well for the Riadys. In April 1985, Worthen lost about US$52 million from the collapse of a New Jersey securities firm in which it had invested. After two Worthen officers resigned due to that case, James got more responsibilities; he told the *Asian Wall Street Journal* "we're here for the long-term".[32] In August, the U.S. Comptroller of the Currency cited Worthen for allegedly violating the law with questionable loans to companies controlled by the Stephens brothers and Mochtar. The comptroller also said the bank's international operations posed a "significant risk" of losses. A Worthen spokesman said the bank took steps to ensure compliance with the law.[33] In September 1986, Worthen announced that Mochtar's Lippo Holdings, with nearly 15 per cent, and Andree's Balder, with 9.9 per cent, were selling their stakes to unidentified institutional investors. The next month, James resigned from Worthen and in 1987 Mochtar left the board. James said his family was "just refocusing our investment strategy to concentrate on New York and California financial companies".[34] The Riadys did not have any banking presence in New York, though in 1985 BCA had opened there the first branch in the United States of a private Indonesian bank. Through his family's interests in Hong Kong, Mochtar bought a small bank in California, Bank of Trade (later renamed Lippo Bank and eventually sold to Bank of America). In 1982, Salim's First Pacific, in which Mochtar had no role, bought California's Hibernia Bank. So during the time Mochtar and Liem were together in BCA, both developed banking interests outside Indonesia — sometimes together, sometimes not.

TROUBLED TIMES

While Mochtar's years at BCA were ones of rapid growth and gains, it was not always smooth sailing for the institution or its captain. The year 1984 proved a particularly bumpy one for the bank. It found itself on the receiving end of negative attention from its close links with Suharto. That year, the president was pushing through his completely pliant parliament a law to make all organizations — from political parties to apolitical civic groups — pledge allegiance to Pancasila, the non-denominational state ideology — as their core philosophy. This would allow Suharto to use the law as a control mechanism for suppressing dissent and for deterring any attempted use of Islam as a political tool. Both Sukarno and Suharto had crushed Islamic separatist movements, but there were still extremist groups pushing for Indonesia to become an Islamic state, and the proposed law was aimed at squashing any such sentiments.

Suharto forced the one political party associated with the Muslims, known as the PPP, to capitulate and support the bill. Still, there remained some Muslims who wanted Islam to have an overt political role the president wouldn't allow. A few hardline Islamic preachers, opposed to Suharto's move, started giving anti-government, anti-Chinese and anti-Christian sermons.[35] One strongly Islamic enclave in Jakarta was the port area of Tanjung Priok, a stone's throw from Liem's Bogasari flour mill. It was largely populated by dock-hands, other poorly paid workers, and a fair number of unemployed young men. An academic, writing in 1993 about what later was called the "Tanjung Priok riots" noted that the area was known for drunkenness and gambling, and where gang fights between different ethnic groups were frequent. "The national police chief said that the area was unique in the nation for the extent of its labour disputes, narcotics, smuggling, counterfeiting, thievery, arson and violent crime", he cited a report as saying.[36]

Earlier in the year, the effects of a recession in the industrialized world were already being felt in prices of ordinary commodities and with oil prices down, government subsidies for daily necessities were slashed. The depressed state of affairs was compounded by a reorganizing of the stevedoring sector, which put more business in the hands of Chinese-owned companies and some labourers out of work.[37]

The smouldering fires of dissent were stoked. At the end of August 1984, a firebrand preacher attracted a large crowd with an incendiary speech, denouncing the Chinese as "the scoundrels of Indonesia" and accusing the Christians of poisoning the minds of the Muslims. Several other speeches followed over the course of the next weeks, some targeting Liem's link with Suharto. A young Chinese whose shophouse was near a mosque reported that one speaker proclaimed "Liem Sioe Liong is a Chinese running dog", and demanded, "Why do the Chinese have money but we do not? We will not take any goods from their stores, but take their lives."[38] The *Far Eastern Economic Review* wrote that "the Suharto-Liem link has been subjected to increasingly vitriolic attacks, which were much in evidence in Tanjung Priok on offending posters and in the fiery religious lectures".[39]

Anti-government slogans appeared on a wall in a mosque in Tanjung Priok. On 7 September, two policemen entered the mosque and ripped the slogans off the wall. Word quickly spread that the mosque had been defiled — one officer did not remove his shoes before entering, while the other allegedly smeared gutter water on the slogans. Angry protesters gathered the next few days. An ensuing confrontation with the police led to the arrests and detentions of several activists. On 12 September, a meeting at the mosque to discuss the police action featured strident anti-government speeches, after which a crowd of about 1,500 people, carrying banners and shouting "Allahu Akhbar" (God is great), started to march to a police station to demand release of the detainees. The military was called in to end it, and did so by firing live ammunition into the crowd.

"The Tanjung Priok Incident", as the government-constrained Indonesian media called it, was the strongest challenge to Suharto since the Malari riots in 1974. At the scene that night, Armed Forces Commander Gen. Benny Murdani, who had by then succeeded Ali Murtopo as Suharto's top henchman, put the death toll at nine. The official figure was later raised to eighteen, but no one believed that. Some observers said at least sixty-three people were killed, with hundreds wounded and many others missing.

Rumours circulated that hundreds had been massacred that one night. Jusuf Wanandi, in his memoir, wrote that ninety dead "was possible".[40]

The brutal suppression might have successfully ended the riots that September evening, but the anger at the government and resentment of the Chinese raged on. It didn't help that Murdani was a Catholic. In carrying out his duties, he was fast gaining a reputation as being as ruthless, if not more, than Ali Murtopo. At the same time, economic hardship fuelled resentment of Liem's wealth. An assessment of the Tanjung Priok incident nineteen years later, written by Goenawan Mohamad, the editor of *Tempo* magazine at the time of the violence, said that perceived inequities "exacerbated anti-Chinese racism among the lower classes. Liem became a symbol of 'Chinese-ness' and therefore, an emblem of the New Order's injustice. Such inequity, set in a social context where freedom of choice and expression are stifled, provided the spark that ignited violence in the economically-pressed and politically-marginalised Muslim community that night."[41]

Shortly after the deaths in Tanjung Priok, trouble erupted elsewhere in Jakarta. On 4 October, small bombs exploded outside two BCA branches in Glodok, Jakarta's Chinatown, killing two and injuring at least twenty. A third bomb went off outside a Chinese-owned grocery store. The crude but lethal bombs exploded within about 20 minutes of each other. It was not clear who was behind the bombing. The *Far Eastern Economic Review* reported Jakarta was, as usual, filled with speculation ranging from "simple explanations to labyrinthine conspiracy theories based more on imagination than evidence".[42] Authorities arrested seven men — including sixty-four-year-old Mohammed Sanusi, a minister in Sukarno's last cabinet and Suharto's first, who had joined a meeting held without a police permit on 18 September to protest the Tanjung Priok killings. The former Light Industries Minister was accused of financing the bombing plot. There was widely considered to be no real evidence of involvement, and many assumed Sanusi was blamed because he was an outspoken Suharto critic and one of the "Petition of 50" group, comprising former generals and prominent figures, whose statements were banned from being reported in the domestic media. (In May 1980, the signatories had submitted a "Statement of Concern" to parliament questioning Suharto's use of power.) Referring to Sanusi's case, a 1993 study on Indonesia published by the U.S. Library of Congress said the people jailed for the 1984 violence included one "whose real crime was association with the Petition of 50 group".[43]

At his trial the following year, Sanusi was convicted and sentenced to nineteen years in jail. In a separate case later that year, he was sentenced to twenty years for alleged involvement in the January 1985 bombing of the magnificent eighth-century Buddhist temple Borobudur in Central Java. But that conviction was overturned on appeal. In 1994, after serving nine years for the BCA bombings, he was released by Suharto. (Three months after Suharto's 1998 resignation, President B.J. Habibie awarded the country's second highest honour to Sanusi, for "special service". A Home Affairs official explained that the charges against Sanusi were "engineered" and never proved.[44])

Other incidents in late 1984 continued to rattle nerves. On 22 October, a fire of unknown cause destroyed Jakarta's best-known department store, state-owned Sarinah. A week later, residents in south Jakarta were subjected to a night of terror when munitions at a marine corps depot exploded. Fifteen people were killed and twenty-six injured in that episode that terrified many residents who thought a war had broken out. An American journalist who lived nearby wrote that rockets, mortars and tracers "rained down… Tons of projectiles screeched, whistled and roared into the night, turning the sky into a roiling orange hue, as metal thudded into roofs, yards and roads."[45] Some 1,500 homes were destroyed or damaged. The official explanation was that a fire, which was an accident and not arson, started detonating stockpiles of ammunition. As often happened in Indonesia, given the government's low credibility and Suharto-era restraints on the press, many people dismissed the official version, instead offering an array of conspiracy theories. One popular theory blamed the explosions on elements of the marine corps who were diehard Sukarnoists and not loyal to Suharto. (A respected retired marine general and former Jakarta governor, Ali Sadikin, had signed the Petition of 50 that enraged Suharto.) Bomb threats at office buildings belonging to Liem's family forced periodic evacuations over the next few weeks. Although BCA was not seriously affected by the October bombs, the bank had a bad year, by the standards of its rapid growth. Assets grew only 20 per cent in 1984, to Rp465 billion, compared with growth rates of 60 per cent or more in preceding years. The following year, the bank was able to get back on a better track, with assets rising 52 per cent.

In the mid-1980s, BCA faced another kind of problem; this was an internal one that fed Jakarta's active rumour mill but was not reported in the media and was not verifiable at the time. Bankers said that BCA suffered a sizeable foreign exchange loss stemming from trading done by Mochtar's eldest son Andrew, a director at the bank. Mochtar's decisive action in dealing with his son shocked Jakarta's business circles, including his boss, Liem, but it was a demonstration of the banker's professionalism. Instead of protecting his son as many Indonesian corporate bosses were wont to do, Mochtar fired him from his position. Some Indonesian business owners have simply refused to acknowledge their children ever made mistakes. Suharto was like that, too. Asked about the subject more than twenty years later, Mochtar would not disclose the details of the case but confirmed that he removed his son as a BCA director due to the speculative trading. Mochtar took his son's risky forex trading very seriously. "I told him to leave", Mochtar confirmed to the authors in 2007, "A banker cannot speculate." He said that Liem and Anthony then "came to see me and said 'how can you do this? It's too cruel.' I said this is dangerous...[it's] very serious, like gambling." In 1990, after Bank Duta suffered a huge forex trading scandal, as discussed later, Mochtar said that "Om Liem saluted me" for the way he handled the problem at BCA.[46]

PROPELLED BY JAKARTA'S BIG BANG

In the mid-1980s, Indonesia's fortunes were closely tied to oil prices; when the price of crude fell below US$10 a barrel from around US$45, the country was badly hit. While many businesses suffered, Mochtar and others hoped that the lousy oil price and depleted government revenue would increase the chance Suharto would deregulate the state-shackled economy. In banking, some wanted a "big bang" reform like other governments had done, and they got their wish in 1988.

The economic woes did prompt the president to push ahead with deregulation, except in areas and ways that would hurt his family and friends such as Liem. Until 1988, there had been a decade-long freeze on issuance of new banking licenses, and while BCA was growing very quickly, there were still restraints on the growth of privately owned banks, who weren't allowed to tap state company deposits or open branches freely. Suharto baulked at some economic reforms because they would end or reduce privileges of his family and pals; in banking, there was a way to produce widespread benefits and help his circle expand at the same time. Indonesia's "big bang" was dubbed "Pakto", a contraction for October packet. It triggered a proliferation of new banks, many of which imploded a decade later. The new rules dramatically changed the landscape; now practically any significant businessperson could — and many did — open a bank and as many branches as desired. Getting a bank licence required only capital of Rp10 billion (then about US$5 million), tiny by world standards. And to foster competition with state banks, Indonesia's hundreds of state-owned companies were now permitted to put up to 50 per cent of their deposits in privately owned banks, and up to 20 per cent in a single one.

There are no records or evidence, but it's likely that due to the reforms, state commodity regulator Bulog started keeping deposits in BCA. For sure, thanks to Pakto, BCA spurted ahead. During 1989, the first full year after the reforms were announced, BCA's assets soared 81 per cent, reaching Rp4.17 trillion. Loans rose even faster, at 86 per cent that year and then in 1990 they grew a stunning 114 per cent. At the end of 1989, BCA had 173 branches, compared with 50 a year earlier. The bank opened a staggering 148 branches — nearly three per week — over the course of 1990. Rapid-pace banking deregulation produced serious problems later. But it is significant that the policy greatly stimulated industry competition. In banking, unlike flour-milling, Salim never had an effective monopoly; it could say that BCA grew faster than others because of its services, its marketing success and other factors. And indeed, other private banks grew very rapidly after October 1988. The state definitely aided BCA's growth, but in this case government policy did not impede the chance of others to compete.

As it turned out, the banking reforms that boosted BCA's spectacular growth also led to another consequence — the departure of the "banking doctor" who nurtured the bank for fifteen years. Mochtar and his son James had already started their LippoBank, with the blessing of Liem, who also took some equity in it. Pakto's "big bang" opened the way for BCA and LippoBank to both cooperate as well as compete. In May 1989, BCA and LippoBank began jointly marketing the successful Tahapan savings programme, which mushroomed by offering lotteries for depositors, whose chances increased with larger deposits. Over time, many vehicles from Indomobil, Salim's auto business, were given away as prizes. For BCA, the prize was a flood of cash from customers. Its annual report for 1989 said the bank started Tahapan "proved to be a powerful weapon for deposit gathering". In the first three months of the launch, BCA attracted Rp162.53 billion of new deposits from 214,563 customers.

During the time Mochtar was at BCA, he basically ran the bank, though he never took the title of president. Instead, he was called "Chief Executive Director". BCA's president-directors were *pribumi* and often were retired central bank senior executives. For much of Mochtar's tenure, the position was held by Abdullah Ali, who worked thirty-one years at Bank Indonesia, becoming a deputy director there, and who knew Liem since 1957. Before Ali accepted the post, he said he told Mochtar "if you want me to be *presdir* (president-director), I want to be the real *presdir*. Not a toy."[47] According to Ali, Liem sometimes sent him the kind of notes that bank presidents often got from big shareholders: he received *"harap dipikirkan"* ("Please consider this") messages, and Ali said Liem liked to later ask "Why was this refused?" The answer, Ali said, was that the bank's top management made the case why something should not be done, which Liem accepted. Ali, who died in 2005, said working for Liem was attractive. In the same interview, he insisted that BCA was "pure professional" and did not get any government "facilities"; with the two Suharto children who had BCA shares, Sigit and Tutut, "there isn't any business at all", Ali said.[48]

Salim effectively capitalized on its ties to Suharto, helping BCA attain its spectacular growth. One example was satellite use for enhancing its internal communications systems. Salim was permitted to push ahead of rivals in getting VSAT technology because of its proximity to power. As Schwarz wrote about, in 1990 there was a monopoly on supplying such services, but it was very pricey. To avoid the monopoly, that year Salim won permission from Telecommunications Minister Soesilo Sudarman to lease a channel on Indonesia's state-owned Palapa satellites — something competitors couldn't obtain.[49] The services were provided to BCA by a Salim company, PT Rintis Sejahtera. In late 1990, as Mochtar's tenure was ending, the bank was a leader in technology in Indonesia and was performing strongly.

MOCHTAR'S EXIT

At the end of the 1980s, Mochtar was in the middle of rapidly expanding banking activity; he still ran BCA, but at the same time, he was becoming increasingly involved at the smaller institution that his family controlled, LippoBank (later renamed Bank Lippo). Although his dual role might be construed as a conflict of interest, it wasn't viewed that way in Indonesia, and certainly not in the heady days for the banking industry as the decade came to a close. Still, the gossip mill in the banking community was speculating that Mochtar was preparing to leave BCA to concentrate on his own bank. The rumour might have been precipitated by the return around that time from the United States of Mochtar's son, James, who had a brief stint at BCA in the late 1970s, when he was in his early twenties.

The Riadys' inroad into bank ownership — one where they controlled a bank rather than owning a minority interest — came in 1982, seven years after Mochtar entered BCA, when he bought 49 per cent of a small bank named Perniagaan from a businessman, Hashim Ning. The Minangkabau from Sumatra was one of the few *pribumi* businessmen from the Sukarno era who continued successfully in the New Order. Ning, born in 1916 to a trading family, had been a close aide to Mohammad Hatta, Indonesia's respected first vice-president from 1945 to 1956.[50] He had interests in the auto industry, but his roots in banking went back to the time the new republic was formed and was battling to get the Dutch out. The leaders of the republic wanted to set up Indonesian banks to cut reliance on Dutch institutions, and Bank Perniagaan (meaning commerce) was established in the late 1940s in Yogyakarta. Ning was made a director of the bank. Later, sometime in the 1960s, he bought the bank. As with many privately owned banks of its time, Perniagaan languished until the government deregulated banking in 1988. Ning, like Liem, found Mochtar a desirable candidate to partner. When the banker bought into Perniagaan, the bank was still small, with only about Rp13 billion in assets, compared with BCA's Rp241 billion.[51] James, then age twenty-five, was named president of the bank, even though he was then spending much time in the United States. By the time of the banking deregulation, Perniagaan was under Riady family control, and soon after, a burst of activity took place at the bank. It bought a smaller bank, Bank Umum Asia, changed Perniagaan's name to LippoBank, obtained a foreign exchange licence and got listed on the Jakarta Stock Exchange — all within about fifteen months. Mochtar became LippoBank's executive chairman while he was still an executive director at BCA; until the 1997–98 financial crisis, Indonesia's central bank allowed a person to hold a management post at one bank and board position at another. Perniagaan's rebranding as LippoBank presaged Mochtar's move to channel his energy and attention into it.

At the time of Mochtar's purchase of Perniagaan, Liem said he was fine with it. He recalled saying to his partner: "Pak Mochtar, I heard you bought a bank. He replied, 'yes, my son wanted to work…' And I said, 'no problem... We [should] marry banks and not cause them to break up'."[52] (Such a "marriage" did take place, as Liem's family took a 15 per cent stake in LippoBank, which put Anthony on its board of commissioners.) But in the months following, Mochtar's increasing attention to LippoBank was not universally welcomed at BCA. Some senior executives at the Salim bank grumbled privately about LippoBank's aggressive tactics and wondered whether Mochtar's loyalty would be split. Their concerns reached Liem, who became somewhat conflicted himself. In his 1990 rare interview with the press, published in March, the Salim boss was asked about speculation of a conflict between Mochtar and himself. Liem replied by noting that the banker had served fourteen years at BCA and had built it into a healthy, big bank. Mochtar's children, he said, now had their own bank, and that Mochtar could help lead them. Then he added, "according to me, it's not good if Pak Mochtar holds two flags. That's our policy."[53]

At the end of the 1980s, coinciding with the Riadys' activity at LippoBank, Mochtar had a heart problem. Although it meant he needed to undergo heart surgery — a triple bypass (uncommon in those days) — it provided a convenient exit for him, one which would not set off too many tongues wagging in the banking community. He broached Liem in early 1990 about his intention to leave BCA, saying he had surgery scheduled in Sydney with the renowned Chinese-Australian cardiac surgeon Victor Chang, who had done bypass surgery on long-time New Order minister Radius Prawiro as well as other well-known personalities. (Tragically, the fifty-four-year-old Chang was shot dead in Sydney the following year during a botched extortion attempt by a Chinese gang.) The parting was amicable. Mochtar had kept his end of the bargain in growing the bank, and Liem had benefited greatly from having the banker on board.

From Liem's point of view, it was best to accept Mochtar's decision to leave as being precipitated mainly by health reasons. Speaking to the authors in 2006, Liem said he accepted the banker's explanation for leaving. When Mochtar told him of the scheduled triple bypass operation, Liem said he told the banker, whom he respected greatly, "There's no need for you to separate from us. You take care of the operation; I will wait for you to return. Mochtar was touched. He thanked me, and he wept."[54] Anthony's version of his mentor's departure tallied with his father's: "The splitting up was because Pak Mochtar wanted to undergo [heart] bypass and would like to settle things before the surgery. That was the main reason."[55] The parting, he said, was "simple... [it] probably took only one or two days" to work out. Mochtar's employment at BCA didn't formally end until December that year. Aside from citing his surgery, Mochtar never publicly commented on speculation that other factors might have added to his decision to leave BCA. Asked by the authors in 2007 for his real reasons to part company with the Salims, he demurred, only commenting that Liem was upset to hear about his departure plans but said he "fully understood".[56] For sure, after Mochtar's departure, the two men continued to hold each other in high regard. Quite often, partnerships between big Indonesian businessmen end badly; this one did not. The two men quickly agreed to terms of separation that included eventually paring their cross-shareholdings. "We swapped equity," Mochtar said. "His Lippo shares were transferred to me; and I gave my BCA shares back to him."[57] This was a process, as Liem's family retained some shares in LippoBank for at least two more years. Anthony remained a commissioner at LippoBank until May 1992. At the time Anthony relinquished that post, LippoBank Managing Director Laksamana Sukardi told reporters there was no issue between Anthony and the Riadys' bank. "Anthony Salim says merely he is too busy. Perhaps he feels uncomfortable because he can never attend a meeting and therefore chooses to resign," Laksamana was quoted as saying.[58]

Mochtar's surgery was a success, and upon his recovery, he focused on the building of his Lippo Group. It was clear he had big ambitions for the group, which would certainly benefit from his full attention. At the start of the 1990s, Lippo was splashing its logo — a double-infinity sign — all around Jakarta. (The name Lippo came from the Chinese words *li*, meaning strength, and *bao*, which means treasure. *Li* was also Riady's Chinese surname, although written as a different character.) In a 2011 interview with a Singapore paper, Mochtar, who by then had become a well-known philanthropist to several universities in the nation-state, said that between 1970 and 1990 (which he considered the third phase of his business career), he began looking at "how I could turn Lippo into a globalised business". He said he did something radical for an Indonesian businessman, hiring 86 Americans to introduce modern management methods: "This was the globalization of human resources."[59] Mochtar long had investments in banks outside Indonesia and it was not surprising that he developed banking interests at home outside BCA. For one thing, it was common for Indonesians who owned part of one bank were often looking for another. For another, it was extremely common for Indonesian

CEOs to have multiple businesses. In Indonesia, few executives had just one position or business activity. Mochtar, who long possessed a worldview that reached far corners of the globe, had an advantage over Totok entrepreneurs — he spoke English and had already established contacts across the world, not just within the Chinese diaspora. The Riady family, Harvard Business School professor Rosabeth Moss Kanter wrote in the mid-1990s, "are masters of the principles of global networking". Mochtar, she commented, "has created an international financial network out of nothing more than his personal drive, ethnic ties and skills as an innovator and collaborator".[60]

During his time at BCA, Mochtar was deft enough to avoid being drawn into the Cendana circle, although there was no avoiding the fact that the two older Suharto offspring were significant shareholders of the bank — they already jointly held 30 per cent equity when Mochtar entered. The banker said he had no issues personally with Sigit and Tutut, the two shareholders. In fact, he said, he was "pleased" with them; they were, in his opinion, "quite ok... [they were] reasonable". According to Mochtar, Sigit tried to get him to join their business, but the banker said he politely declined: "I said I have no money; this [at BCA] is the bank's money. I am a professional banker. I don't know anything about business."[61] Mochtar said he preferred not to get too close to the leadership and consistently tried to maintain an arm's length; he was once quoted as saying that to link banking with politics was "very dangerous. Political power does not last long, so I always keep my distance."[62] (Perhaps the Riadys were able to keep an arm's length from the leadership in Indonesia during Suharto's New Order period, but in the United States, where the Riadys remained friends with Bill Clinton, they did not exactly keep a distance from political power. In 2001, James paid a record US$8.6 million fine for violating U.S. campaign financing rules.)

In the 2007 interview with the authors, Mochtar indicated his unease with Salim's strong links with the Suharto family. Asked how important it was for the growth of BCA to take deposits from Suharto-related foundations, Mochtar replied: "No, one cent I don't take. I'm strongly against money from Pak Harto's side, also from government side, but they [the Liems] prefer to get money from *yayasan* (foundations), the children's companies. No, I said. I don't want it."[63] Mochtar asserted that he did not want to be "disturbed by big money" that was "unstable" as it might quickly move in and out. He cited an Indonesian saying that to build with a solid base, "you first need sand, and then you add the pebbles, finally the big boulders. Then it will be a strong foundation. Otherwise it will be shaky. We had to build with sand first... [we] can't use big money."[64] Asked whether Liem ever called to say, for example, he could get a US$50 million deposit without specifying the source, Mochtar replied: "He has, but I told him no, please don't persuade me. I told him the reason. He is a very wise man, he says he understands."

Mochtar was never considered a Suharto crony, although he was careful not to "wrong-foot" the president and his family. Anthony confirms Mochtar's unease at the Liem family's close ties with Cendana. He recalled Mochtar suggesting that Liem step down as BCA chairman. "It was a good intention and good notion [on Mochtar's part] ... but we said this cannot be changed. Even if my dad stepped down, the attachment to Suharto will never be different. So might as well go ahead and face it; we don't hide the relationship." In any case, Anthony added, it was not possible to be separated from the president as "we had to have both feet on the accelerator ... how can you move away when all the major industries of the country are with you?" Included, Anthony noted, were "food, banking, construction — the nerve and muscle".[65] The path Salim took to move away from a total reliance on the strong bond with Suharto was to diversify business activity and invest outside the country. It did this through First Pacific, though that included Suharto foster-brother and fellow "Gang of Four" member Sudwikatmono.

Mochtar was Anthony and Andree's guru in banking. His departure, even though it was not sudden move, left the Liems "in a little bit of shock", admitted Anthony. [66] Even though Mochtar had more than fulfilled his vow to make BCA Indonesia's largest private bank and had installed a capable team of professionals, Anthony said the family was not fully prepared to lead the bank. "We didn't manage banks before", he said, "and suddenly we inherited the bank leadership; so we had to undergo some soul-searching ... we asked ourselves, what we are going to do next? It took us probably half a year to find our feet." Largely taking over BCA's operations was Anthony's brother Andree, who was a popular boss with many long-time bank staff. "Andree was very good with people ... cared about them", one said.[67]

About post-Mochtar BCA, Anthony commented that the Liem family had developed some banking expertise and "once we decided, ok, we'll proceed from here, I think we did quite well". Helped greatly by Indonesia's overall business boom and the expansion of Salim ventures in the first half of the 1990s, BCA's assets grew at an even faster pace than before. Anthony paid credit to his mentor:

> Pak Mochtar made a very good foundation for BCA ... very good first, second, third floor ... but the growing of the upper floors, which is much simpler, given the good foundation, good structure, good system ... we just capitalised on that. The basement, the foundation ... all the organisation system of BCA — that has to be credited to Pak Mochtar. So we're just building from Floor 5. We were very lucky ... we had the advantage of learning from Mochtar.[68]

Mochtar, in the 2007 interview, said he had no regrets about leaving BCA when he did. He pointed out that the bank's assets were close to US$3 billion, compared with US$1 million when he came in. "I think I am proud to be able to get out smoothly, [it was] OK ... not many bankers can get out smoothly...you can get in, but it's not always easy to get out — that's always a problem."[69]

Notes

1. Gunardi, who was an Indonesian citizen, retained some equity in the bank and following a dispute with Liem, wrested the bank back in 1966. The following year, Liem managed to buy it back.
2. *State Gazette* 1957, No. 965.
3. Yuri Sato, "The Salim Group in Indonesia: The development and behavior of the largest conglomerate in Southeast Asia", *Developing Economies* XXXI, no. 4 (December 1993), p. 416.
4. Ibid., p. 415.
5. Amitabha Chowdhury, "Mochtar Riady: The master builder of an Asian banking empire", *Asian Finance*, 15 September 1983, p. 67.
6. Interview with Mochtar Riady, 24 January 2007.
7. Ibid.
8. Leo Suryadinata, *Prominent Chinese Indonesians: Biographical Sketches* (Singapore: Institute of Southeast Asian Studies, 1995), p. 136.
9. Interview with Mochtar, 24 January 2007.
10. Li Wen Ming, in *hanyu pinyin*.
11. Interview with Mochtar, 24 January 2007.
12. Confidential interview in Jakarta, 10 August 2006.
13. According to Mochtar, Liem also had a third bank at the time, but during our interview, he did not recall its name. He could be referring to Bank Sarana

Indonesia, which was bought in January 1973, and later got merged into BCA.

14. Interview with Mochtar, 24 January 2007.
15. Ibid.
16. Ibid.
17. Interview with Anthony, 3 December 2006.
18. Interview with Liem, 9 December 2006.
19. Interview with Mochtar, 24 January 2007.
20. Ibid.
21. Ibid.
22. Interview with Liem, 9 December 2006.
23. Interview with Mochtar, 24 January 2007.
24. Ibid.
25. Interview with Anthony, 3 December 2006.
26. Figures from table in Sato, "The Salim Group in Indonesia", p. 417.
27. M&I was bought over by Bank of Montreal in 2010 and is now known as BMO Harris Bank.
28. Conversation with Bondan Winarno, 6 December 2007.
29. Chowdhury, "Mochtar Riady".
30. Raphael Pura, "Indonesia Banker Shelves Plan to Buy Lance's Bank Stock", *AWSJ*, 9 September 1977.
31. Stanley Angrist, "East meets Little Rock", *Forbes*, 6 April 1987.
32. Steven Galante, "Two Financiers, From Indonesia and Arkansas, Discover that in Banking, East Does Meet West", *AWSJ*, 29 April 1985.
33. Edwin Finn, Jr., "Worthen Is Cited by Comptroller's Office Over Loans to Three Holders' Companies". *Wall Street Journal*, 22 August 1985.
34. "Group plans to boost stake in Worthen banking to 31%", Dow Jones Newswires, 24 December 1987.
35. See Bill Tarrant, *Reporting Indonesia: The Jakarta Post Story, 1983–2008* (Singapore and Jakarta: Equinox, 2008), p. 77.
36. John Bresnan, *Managing Indonesia: The Modern Political Economy* (New York: Columbia University Press, 1993), p. 220.
37. Jusuf Wanandi, *Shades of Grey: A Political Memoir of Modern Indonesia, 1965–1998* (Jakarta: Equinox, 2012), p. 221.
38. Ang Peng Hwa, "Party Leaders Assess Jakarta Bombings", *Singapore Monitor*, 7 October 1984.
39. Susumu Awanohara, "Indonesia: Bombs in Chinatown", *FEER*, 18 October 1984.
40. Wanandi, *Shades of Grey*, p. 222.
41. Goenawan Mohamad, principal author, *Celebrating Indonesia: Fifty Years with the Ford Foundation* (Jakarta: Ford Foundation, 2003), p. 142.

42. Awanohara, "Indonesia: Bombs in Chinatown".

43. William Frederick and Robert Worden, eds. *Indonesia: A Country Study* (Washington, D.C.: U.S. Library of Congress, 1993).

44. Susan Sim, "Habibie confers honours on wife, Ex-minister", *Straits Times*, 15 August 1998.

45. Tarrant, *Reporting Indonesia*, pp. 73–74.

46. Interview with Mochtar, 24 January 2007.

47. Saudi Hambali, "Abdullah Ali: I am not a toy president-director", *Eksekutif*, August 1989.

48. Ibid.

49. Adam Schwarz, *A Nation in Waiting: Indonesia's Search for Stability*, 2nd ed. (St Leonards, NSW: Allen & Unwin, 1999), p. 112.

50. Ning's grandfather was Hatta's stepfather. Ning and several of his *pribumi* partners were beneficiaries of political patronage, being close to leading politicians in the 1950s. After independence, Ning secured Velodome Motors from the Dutch and in 1952, he was appointed President Director of state-owned auto plant ISC, which imported and assembled Dodge trucks and other vehicles. He partnered Sukarno-era *pribumi* businessmen Agus Dasaad in PT Daha Motors which got the sole agency for import of Fiat cars; when the Japanese autos entered the market, Daha saw a decline in sales. He was also a partner with Ibnu Sutowo in Chrysler sole agency, Jakarta Motors; by the 1980s, he was in joint ventures in hotels, electronics imports and assembly, construction, brewing and tourism. (Richard Robison, *Indonesia: The Rise of Capital* [Sydney: Allen and Unwin/Asian Studies Association of Australia, 1986], pp. 54–55, 332.)

51. BCA's 1982 assets given in Yuri Sato, "The Salim Group in Indonesia", p. 417.

52. Interview with Liem, 9 December 2006.

53. Fikri Jufri, "Liem Bicara Lagi: 'Saya Masih Kuasa Penuh'" [Liem Talks Again: 'I still have full power'], *Tempo*, 10 March 1990, pp. 76–77.

54. Interview with Liem, 9 December 2006.

55. Interview with Anthony Salim, 4 March 2007.

56. Interview with Mochtar, 24 January 2007.

57. Ibid.

58. "Banker says interest rates too high", *Suara Karya*, 6 May 1992. Translated and disseminated by Foreign Broadcast Information Service, U.S. Department of Commerce, 30 June 1992. Accessed 5 June 2011.

59. Vikram Khanna, "Banker, empire builder", *Business Times* (Singapore), 8–9 October 2011.

60. Rosabeth Moss Kanter, "Using Networking for Competitive Advantage: The Lippo Group of Indonesia and Hong Kong", *Strategy + Business*

magazine, 1996, Quarter 3, <http://www.strategy-business.com/article/17609?gko=17096> (accessed 15 November 2010).

61. Interview with Mochtar, 24 January 2007.
62. William Mellor, "Why This Billionaire Wants to Quit", *Asia Inc*, April 2000.
63. Interview with Mochtar, 24 January 2007.
64. Ibid.
65. Interview with Anthony, 4 March 2007.
66. Ibid.
67. Private conversation, Jakarta, 20 March 2007.
68. Interview with Anthony, 4 March 2007.
69. Interview with Mochtar, 24 January 2007.

11

BROADENING THE HOME BASE

Liem was not afraid of taking risks and venturing into territory he didn't know much about. His modus operandi was to find the right partner who could run the new venture for him. Liem's talent laid in sussing out capable and experienced people who could help grow his stable of businesses. Mochtar Riady led the charge in banking for nearly fifteen years. Robert Kuok was "instrumental" in building up flour milling, while in cement Liem got start-up help from a Taiwanese partner introduced by Bangkok Bank's Chin Sophonpanich. Another area where Liem forged a beautiful friendship was in property, where he teamed with savvy developer Ciputra, who spearheaded property developments through a company partly owned by the Jakarta government, PT Pembangunan Jaya, and through Ciputra's PT Metropolitan Development.

PARTNERING A PROPERTY KING

Born Tjie Tjin Hwa, Ciputra rose from very simple roots to become Indonesia's best-known property developer. He seemed to possess the *"tangan dingin"* — the kind of "magic" business touch that Riady and Liem had. Ciputra, who started using that name at age twenty-five, was born in 1931 in the small town of Parigi in central Sulawesi (then known as Celebes). His father was from a different part of Fujian than Liem's village. He was brought to Sulawesi at age ten by Ciputra's grandfather who had migrated earlier and was a shopkeeper in the northern Sulawesi town of Gorontalo. Ciputra's father, a coconut trader, had married a woman who was part-Chinese, part-*pribumi*; their son did not have any Chinese education. As a child, Ciputra recalls he had to walk seven kilometres each way between his primary school and home. One day, when Ciputra was twelve, during the Japanese Occupation, his father disappeared. The family found out much later that he died in a prisoner-of-war camp. After the war, Ciputra went to high school, where he did well enough to win a place at the prestigious Bandung Institute of Technology (ITB) in West Java. The institute, where Sukarno studied, admitted very few Chinese students at the time. While studying architecture in Bandung, Ciputra showed strong entrepreneurial instincts; he sold baskets and hats made from palm trees, traded batik, and designed and sold furniture.

After graduation, he went to Jakarta, lured by the prospects of the capital. There, he found work in property development, which gave him important contacts in the city government. In 1971, at age forty, he won a contract to build the Horison Hotel on Jakarta's coast, near the Copacabana Casino and also the Ancol recreation area, built with the Jakarta government. The casino, one of three then in the capital, was owned by businessman Atang Latief, who funded the hotel's construction. Gen. Ali Sadikin, Jakarta's governor from 1966 to 1977, permitted the operations of the casinos and used them to raise substantial funds to build the city's infrastructure. But there was a chorus of complaints from Muslim groups about the casinos, which were a magnet for prostitutes, and in 1981 Suharto shut them. Latief, hurt financially by the closing of the Copacabana, later sold another of his businesses, which assembled Suzuki motorcycles, to Liem. Meanwhile, Ciputra's work on the Ancol area helped him gain a reputation for delivering what he promised. According to Ciputra, not far into the 1970s, Liem asked to meet him. "Liem came to see me with Djuhar [Sutanto]", Ciputra recalled. "He proposed a project in Sunter [a district in northeast Jakarta]. I told him: 'Sunter no good. I have a better project: Pondok Indah [meaning beautiful cottage].' He said: 'I will provide the money'." Ciputra also said the two men were a natural fit as "he's already rich, and I don't have money". They quickly made a plan for building a luxury housing development south of Jakarta. Ciputra described the deal, settled with a handshake, as "50-50, and he lent me my 50." The developer said he borrowed Rp300 million, then worth about US$1 million, from Liem.[1]

Pondok Indah was to become one of Jakarta's most highly sought-after addresses. At the time, however, the land was home to some rubber trees and tappers. Asked if there was any problem relocating the rubber tappers, Ciputra replied: "Of course we had a problem", but did not elaborate. Over time, the lavish development, with private golf courses, took shape for members of Jakarta's elite. Ciputra, Liem and Sudwikatmono each purchased homes there. For the principals, the development proved a big winner. "One, the buyers made profit, [they] feel happy. Two, we make a lot of profit," added Ciputra, who said he repaid Liem, with interest, out of the profits.[2] Ciputra used more than Metropolitan Development to develop his business and become a brand in property. Separately, he had a role in Pembangunan Jaya, which had its roots in the Benteng programme in the 1950s that tried, without real success, to nurture *pribumi* entrepreneurs. Liem was not part of Pembangunan Jaya. Ciputra got close to Gen. Sadikin, who later became critical of Suharto and joined the "Petition of 50" group. After Sadikin's tenure, Ciputra proved he was able to work with a series of governors. A book about the property developer quoted him as saying, "I have the philosophy that I am a horse and the jockey is the Jakarta governor. If I want to be used, I have to be a horse that's good."[3] The developer had a fondness for horses and liked to compare himself to one. "I am like a horse", he declared to some journalists, "a good horse will be used by any master".[4] His property projects often featured statue of horses at the main entrance.

Indeed, Ciputra was a work-horse and was regarded by many Indonesians as a real entrepreneur. His political links were heavily with local-level politicians; it was Liem who had the alliance with Suharto and the money. Liem's excellent networking skills also brought in other investors. For a key project in the 1970s, Liem attracted three regional figures — Singapore-based developers S.P. Tao and Henry Kwee (a fellow Hokchia born in Indonesia who founded Pontiac Land in Singapore) plus Simon Keswick from Jardine in Hong Kong. The three, Ciputra recounted, were "looking to build an office tower in Jakarta" and it only took an hour for the parties to decide on the formation of PT Jakarta Land. Ciputra, who later joined Tao in developing Marina Square in Singapore, built Wisma Metropolitan, the first of many towers along Jakarta thoroughfare Jalan Sudirman. Ciputra credited his foreign partners with teaching him to undertake international projects. Much later, with Salim as a partner, he launched a housing development in Vietnam and one in India. Liem and Ciputra built a strong bond and broadened their relationship by working together in the Prasetiya Mulya foundation, started in 1980. The foundation opened a management school to train middle managers. For a period, Liem was general chairman and Ciputra was foundation president.

Not everything the two men did together was a great success. In the early 1980s, Liem brought Ciputra into PT Cold Rolling Mill Indonesia Utama, for a plant that Liem agreed to build for Suharto to boost national steel-making capability. Later, the facility resulted in more cost than gain for steel-users, and the state eventually bailed out Liem and Ciputra. The CRMI episode did not hurt Ciputra, who in the boom of the late 1980s was building his brand and getting a listing for a property company bearing his name: Ciputra Development. Years after Liem retired, Ciputra remained full of praise for his business partner, saying in 2007: "He has the vision. This man is special."[5]

GEARING UP IN AUTOS

Indonesia's auto business never was a monopoly or duopoly, though it had complex regulations and local-content rules that made it daunting for new parties to enter. At the start of the New Order, among those in the sector were Pertamina, the army and private companies with bosses linked to government figures (some were Old Order people). Liem got into the auto business in 1971 with PT Central Sole Agency, which imported the Swedish auto Volvo and when changing government policy dictated it, started assembling them in Indonesia. Liem assigned his oldest son Albert to run PT Salim Jaya Motor, which assembled two Volvo models.

Suharto opened Liem's joint venture with the Swedish car maker in 1975, and it supplied vehicles to top officials and high-ranking military officers. However, the company struggled to make a profit — in large part because the government was a major customer. As a business consultant who was friendly with the Liem family noted, "How do you collect money from the generals? They expect the government to pay for them, while the government may not have the budget. Yes, there were a lot of Volvos for the senior bureaucrats, but Salim wasn't making money out of them."[6]

A Jakarta banker made a similar assessment in 1978, telling a reporter "so many Volvos were sold to high officials in the army, police and government but never paid for."[7] It was not too surprising, then, that the Volvo assembly was a losing business. This rankled Albert, who obviously did not fancy association with a loss-making business. Many years later, he asserted that it was extremely difficult to make money selling Volvo at that point in time.[8] Anthony agreed that the Volvo business faced financial problems. "There wasn't enough of a critical mass at the time, and it was a high-end luxury car; it wasn't diversified enough," he reflected.[9] For Salim, it was motorcycle assembly — entered into later — that became a money-maker.

Liem also held the BMW agency for Indonesia, but at the end of 1970s, it was a tiny business that he sold to Astra, which was Toyota's Indonesian partner and miles ahead of Salim in the automotive industry. Salim's expansion in autos got underway in 1980 when it bought the agencies for Mazda cars, Hino trucks and Land Rover from Hashim Ning.[10] A chance for Liem to get bigger — and into motorcycles — came as Suzuki's Indonesia partner, Atang Latief, needed money after his lucrative casino business was closed. Latief controlled two Suzuki-related companies that bore names some people wrongly assumed, due to the "Indo" use, were Salim businesses from the start: Indomobil Utama and Indohero Steel & Engineering. Running Latief's Suzuki business was Soebronto Laras, a *pribumi* executive who was a friend of Anthony's from when both studied in the United Kingdom — though they were not at the same institution. Salim bought Indomobil, on terms that were not disclosed, but which Soebronto later said included his agreement to stay on. With the casino gone, "we had the need to hug a big group, and they [Salim] needed to find a partner who'd already developed well... [Liem] had already tried [automotive], yes, but not developed it," Soebronto once explained.[11]

After Indomobil developed some critical mass, Salim added Datsun (later renamed Nissan) and other marques. Eventually, Indomobil had about ninety subsidiaries and even had a car dealership in southern California. In Indonesia, it garnered about 20 per cent of the market, still far behind Astra International, king of the road with about 50 per cent, thanks largely to its Kijang vans. In 1993, owing to an unexpected development, Salim became an Astra shareholder, putting it in a curious position of being shareholders in two competing auto firms.

SALIM ENTERS ASTRA

Anthony liked to describe the Salim Group as "opportunity-driven". In late 1992, one such instance came, thanks to the dramatic fall of another business family, the Soeryadjayas. A financial crisis inside the family forced the Soeryadjayas to sell their controlling stake in Astra, the company that assembled Toyota vehicles and Honda motorcycles, and which had brought William Soeryadjaya and his family wealth and high regard. After the collapse, Salim got a small but important stake in Astra, which came in handy years later when Salim was on the ropes. At the end of the 1980s, Astra was regarded as a poster child for what was encouraging about Indonesian business. It was family-controlled but won kudos for being run by professionals. Its initial public offering, in February 1990, was more than twenty times oversubscribed. Indocement's IPO, three months earlier, was just barely sold.

A big factor in building positive feelings about Astra was its chief, William Soeryadjaya, a Peranakan Chinese whose grandfather migrated to Java from Fujian. William was not considered a crony of Suharto, and for that, he was admired by some. His father was an entrepreneur, starting a transport company and other businesses. William attended a Dutch missionary school. According to a 2002 authorized biography, William said his father's motto was "Think big, do big, grow big".[12] Both of William's parents died by the time he was twelve. The biography says that in 1947, his younger brother Tjia Kian Tie won a scholarship to do a master's degree in economics in the Netherlands, and William tagged along, taking a tannery course and making a living by selling *kretek* cigarettes brought from Java. He returned to newly independent Indonesia in 1949, and became a supplier of provisions to state agencies.

In 1957, William and his brother renamed a trading company they had started as Astra International. A deal to import General Motor trucks led Astra into the auto business. In a joint venture with the government in 1967, it fixed up a moribund plant for vehicle-assembly; Suharto attended its 1969 opening. That same year, Kian Tie got some help from his friend Trade Minister Sumitro Djojohadikusumo for Astra becoming sole agent for Toyota.[13] Through the years, Toyotas sold well, although there were setbacks such as the 1974 Malari riots in which rampaging youths targeted Japanese products and hundreds of vehicles were destroyed. In the 1970s, William embarked on a property venture with Pertamina to build

luxury houses in Jakarta's Kuningan district. Astra used US$20 million
from cashflow of its main motorcycle unit and collected US$40 million in
Pertamina promissory notes. Unfortunately for William, the oil company's
debt debacle in 1975 meant the notes were never honoured. According to
the biography of William, he had to sell his own house to cover debts.
Property, the author wrote, "held a fatal fascination for William."[14] After
the blows, William sought to depend less on political links. As academic
Shin observed:

> William already learned in the Malari affair the benefits and potential costs
> of personal clientage, the lesson that political ties gave high yields, but
> would damage the longevity of his wealth. Turning himself away from
> almost total dependence on political power for his initial accumulation
> of capital, he now bet on the market force, entrepreneurship and, no less,
> the state's protectionist policy. As a competent Chinese businessman,
> Soeryadjaya could have gained easy access to another patron. But he
> seemed to have seen the limits of personal patronage and political risks
> looming larger.[15]

Astra's growth was aided by state tariffs and other policies that limited
competition in the auto sector, though it had rivals — including Salim.
When deregulation in the mid-1980s spurred more diversified growth, Astra
was well positioned to invest in other areas the state was promoting, such
as timber and palm oil. In Shin's view, while "Astra responded actively
and positively to industrial policies the state formulated, the Liem group
colluded with the state through joint ownership of companies".[16] Shin said
there was a perception that "Soeryadjaya made efforts to be accepted by
the *nation* at large while Liem purchased various kinds of realistic, political
insurance".[17] In 1985, William's older son Edward — whose debts would
cause the family to later lose Astra — told Shin: "We could be 10 times
bigger by now, if my father had accepted every government project Pak
Harto [Suharto] offered." He took a swipe at Salim, asserting that when
"Tuan" Liem got such offers, he always replied to the president, "Yes, thank
you, Sir."[18] To Shin, it wasn't that William stopped seeking patronage, rather
he steered toward an "inclusive and institutional patronage" in contrast
to Liem's "adherence to an exclusive and personal patronage". Astra's
strategy had merit "in protecting its companies from possible political
turmoil in the future", the academic noted. Liem, on the other hand, "seems
to believe that his negative image in Indonesian minds is irreversible",

so no effort was made to change it. There was no doubt who would come out better financially while Suharto was in power. "This study of two cases shows clearly that Liem's strategy is by far superior to Astra's in rapidly accumulating capital in the New Order", he concluded.[19]

Shin's dissertation was submitted in 1989, before the Soeryadjayas faced financial calamity. Astra would survive and indeed thrive, but it would be minus the involvement of the founding family, a hitherto unthinkable scenario. The family's woes were rooted in Edward's quest to build a wider empire beyond the auto business, which his younger brother Edwin was on track to run. "Being the eldest son and being a good son to my father, I have to assume the responsibility of furthering my father's dream", Edward once declared.[20] There were stark personality differences between the brothers, born less than two years apart. Edward embraced risk while Edwin was more cautious in nature. Edward was forward, Edwin circumspect.

For Edward, funding was not a problem as the Soeryadjaya name opened doors. "Every time I approached a bank, I came away with a credit line of between US$500,000 and US$1 million," he once declared.[21] In 1988, just before Indonesia started issuing new bank licences, Edward bought a small bank called Bank Agung Asia. The following year, he changed the name to Bank Summa, and undertook breakneck expansion. By the end of 1990, Bank Summa was among the ten biggest private banks, with Rp1.76 trillion in assets — nearly seven times its level two years earlier, and the Summa Group had gone on a global buying spree. Asked if his bank was growing too quickly, Edward replied: "You either grow very big or you stay small."[22] As a consequence of many Indonesian banks growing too quickly, the economy was overheating. To cool it, the Finance Ministry in June 1990 ordered state banks to withdraw US$4 billion from the system and put it in central bank certificates. That made rupiah interest rates shoot up from less than 15 per cent to around 30 per cent. Many half-built property projects came to a screeching halt, and at the time Summa was one of the biggest lenders in the sector — and in a serious bind. In July 1991, banking authorities internally classified Bank Summa "unsound" and started pressing the family to put in more capital.

Speculation was rife in Jakarta that Summa needed a bailout. Many Indonesians concluded that Suharto refused to allow state funds to be used for a rescue, allegedly displeased that William didn't join the previous year's US$420 million bailout of Bank Duta, which was controlled by foundations chaired by the president. It was also believed that the president was unhappy with Edward for trying to undertake a banking venture with the Islamic group Nahdlatul Ulama, led by scholar Abdurrahman Wahid (Gus Dur) — who Suharto disliked due to his independence, criticism and advocacy of democracy. (Wahid in 1999 became the country's fourth president.) However, there's no evidence that Suharto ordered the central bank not to render help to Summa. Bank Indonesia did not want to aid a private bank after reiterating, in the wake of the Bank Duta scandal, there would be no state bailouts. The Soeryadjayas were backed into a corner: William made what must have been the most heartbreaking decision in his life — to sell the family's 76 per cent ownership in Astra International, his crown jewel and at the time Indonesia's second largest conglomerate. In May 1992, William injected Rp300 billion (nearly US$150 million) into the bank and announced that his family faced a "calamity" because of Summa's debts. But he promised the family would resolve the problem, with no losses for Astra shareholders as "it is beyond our thought to run away from our responsibilities".[23] While William was commended for his pledge, he did not admit that Edward had made errors. Of Edward's property gambles, William commented: "If there had been no economic downturn, we think Edward would become a hero, for his purchases would bring a good profit."[24]

The capital injection was insufficient, and the next month, William announced he would inject another Rp250 billion into Bank Summa and bring in a management team from Panin Bank, as the central bank had ordered. At the end of July, William stepped down as Astra chairman to concentrate on Summa, and named his friend Sumitro Djojohadikusumo, the former trade minister, to succeed him. But William resisted selling a chunk of the family's Astra holdings, which later precipitated the loss of the whole stake. Family associates and friends painted a picture of a father "unwilling or unable to steer his son off a path clearly headed toward disaster... whether out of stubbornness, paralysis or an unwillingness to recognize their predicament, the Soeryadjayas didn't cut their losses".[25] In November, there was a run on Bank Summa. Withdrawals were so large that the next day, the central bank suspended Summa from its clearing operations, effectively shutting the bank. (It reopened later for two weeks, but only so depositors could withdraw a maximum Rp10 million.) The bank needed a saviour, but what took shape instead was a suitor for the Soeryadjayas' Astra stake. In early December, Prajogo Pangestu (the boss of timber company Barito Pacific, who was close to Suharto daughter Tutut) emerged as point-person for a group of potential buyers, most of them linked to the Prasetiya Mulya Foundation. Liem, as foundation chairman, would have some role in the consortium, but not take the lead, as Salim had a rival auto business, Indomobil.

The Soeryadjayas were not enamoured of the Prasetiya Mulya courtship. Frantic behind-the-scenes proposals were considered over the next few harried days, and a competing bid was announced from Sumitro's son, Hashim Djojohadikusumo. William made it known he favoured Hashim's offer as it included a buyback option. But there were doubts about the financial viability of the Hashim plan, and it wasn't going to look good if Sumitro blocked a competing bid so his son's could win — which Sumitro fully realized. Still, the Soeryadjayas signed a memorandum of understanding (MOU) with Hashim on 10 December. But then the tussle over Astra, like some other disputes, went to a final arbiter — Suharto. On the night of 11 December, Prajogo, Liem and Anthony met Suharto at Jalan Cendana, and afterwards, associates of Prajogo told William that the government was poised to revoke Summa's banking licence. The die was cast. Soon after, the Soeryadjaya family signed an agreement with Prajogo.[26]

So now, the Soeryadjayas had said yes to both bidders. On 12 December, the family met Bank Indonesia Governor Adrianus Mooy, who pushed them to make a final decision. The family said they decided on Prajogo, but noted that this needed Sumitro's endorsement — which Mooy demanded by 11 a.m. on 14 December. It never came, and Sumitro later said the family did not tell him of the deadline. When the deadline passed, the central bank revoked Summa's licence, which triggered a default on a Rp500 billion loan the Soeryadjayas owed local banks — for which they pledged a 40 per cent stake in Astra as collateral. Now, those shares went to the creditors. Sumitro, caught in the high drama, soon resigned as chairman, and commented that the sequence of events would be "amusing if it weren't tragic".[27] Bank Indonesia said Summa, which had not published accounts for 1991, lost Rp591 billion (US$288 million) that year and now had nearly three times as much in liabilities. The pulling of Summa's licence triggered mini-runs on other banks rumoured to be overstretched — including two controlled by Sudwikatmono, Bank Surya and Subentra.

At this stage, there was still was no deal on Astra shares. About the Prajogo group, the *Economist* magazine wrote that bankers "are as doubtful

as Toyota about some of Astra's potential buyers, including Liem Sioe
Liong, mainly because they are a secretive lot who will make the company's
affairs far murkier".[28] But the Prajogo group had the backing of the most
powerful figure in the country — Suharto — to nail a deal. It did so on
15 January 1993, after ten days of negotiations that involved the central
bank, and a changing line-up of buyers. At one point, Sudwikatmono was
going to be part of the group, but then was not, probably so the Salim
component would not look too large. Bank Indonesia's main concern was
having a sale that would best help Summa depositors. But it rejected as
unacceptable one plan under which the Prajogo-led buyers would get a
chance to refloat the bank.

In a final deal, a sixteen-member consortium bought 31 per cent of
Astra from the Soeryadjayas for US$364 million; the per-share price was
Rp10,000, an 11 per cent premium over the latest closing. The net result
of changes since late 1992 left government-controlled bodies with 27
per cent of Astra, the public with 15 per cent and the rest split among
a large cast. Prajogo held 6.2 per cent. Salim — through Bogasari Flour
Mills — had 4.1 per cent, Sinar Mas boss Eka Cipta Widjaja 2.05 per
cent and former BCA boss Mochtar Riady had 0.2 per cent. Astra ended
its history as the Soeryadjayas' main vehicle, and became Indonesia's
first truly public company, with no dominant shareholder. On 22 June,
Toyota confirmed it was buying an 8.3 per cent block reserved for it,
and the deal was a good one; Toyota paid the same Rp10,000 a share
the consortium paid in January, while the market price now had shot up
to Rp13, 275. Back when the Prasetiya Mulya group of potential buyers
was taking shape, Sumitro declared that Toyota opposed Astra's sale to
it because of Salim's competing Nissan franchise, but Toyota spokesman
Eji Hirabayashi said about the new Indonesian shareholders: "We think
we can go well with them."[29]

The central bank's priority on getting money into the hands of angry
Summa depositors was understandable. It could not handle contagion
if rumours spawned hefty withdrawals from many banks, and two big
events were approaching in March 1993 — the big Islamic holidays and
a presidential election. Members of the Prajogo consortium said they
were worried that anger over Summa losses could be directed at ethnic
Chinese. Some depicted the buying of Soeryadjaya shares as acts of help,
not business. Eka of Sinar Mas called helping Summa depositors a "holy
task". Liem said of his participation in the buying consortium: "I'm only

expressing my solidarity." The Astra transaction, he asserted, was "purely based on the solidarity to help".[30] Salim did not have to worry about anti-trust rules — Indonesia had none — but it was a passive participant inside the consortium buying the Soeryadjayas' crown jewel.

THE "GROWTH TRIANGLE"

At the end of 1980s, as Indonesia was booming, Salim joined a business endeavour that strengthened Jakarta's ties with Singapore and further boosted Liem's ties to the Suharto family. The venture also broadened a Salim link with a brother of influential minister B.J. Habibie, which came in handy a decade later when the Liem family was imperilled during the financial crisis. Salim's business involvement with the Suharto children began in the 1970s, when Sigit and Tutut entered BCA. But for some years afterwards, there were not all that many linkages with the Suharto progeny — Salim's ties to Cendana were heavily through Sudwikatmono. This changed in the late 1980s as the economic "cake" was getting bigger, and Suharto's children were aggressively demanding, and receiving, bigger slices. Salim, naturally, was looking for larger pieces too. In some cases, they ended up jointly pursuing projects, with Salim putting up the money for a Suharto child's stake. In a media interview, Anthony in 1994 proclaimed he was "happy" and "comfortable" having businesses with the children. "If I partner with A and B, why not the children of Pak Harto?" he asserted. "I have known them since their childhood."[31] At the time, Anthony showed no worry about what might happen to Salim in the post-Suharto period. "Why is everybody pessimistic?" he shot back when asked about the issue of presidential succession. When that time arrives, Anthony acknowledged, it would pose a difficult test but he added: "We already go through so many tests" and Indonesia has a "system" that would work.[32]

Besides BCA, Salim at the end of the 1980s was linked up with Tutut through an Indocement stake in her toll-road company, Citra Marga Nusaphala Persada. CMNP was one of the early cases that stoked unhappiness with Suharto's family, and showed that the president was making the state "privatization" programme into one of "personalization". The Jakarta expressway that her company built and managed was needed, but CMNP was awarded a disproportionately high share of the tolls. No tender was called for the project given to CMNP — formally incorporated the same day in 1987 that it signed a twenty-two-year agreement with the state toll-road operator for a major highway through parts of Jakarta. Salim also formed multiple business links with middle Suharto son Bambang, including a sugar plantation in Sumatra and production, with a Korean partner, of food additive monosodium glutamate (MSG). In the late 1980s, Salim partnered Bambang for development projects in the Riau Islands, near Singapore. The biggest effort, part of moves to have a "Growth Triangle" made up of the Indonesian islands, Singapore and Malaysia's southernmost Johor state, involved Batam island, 20 kilometres from Singapore. At the time a Salim-Bambang venture took shape, nearly every business on Batam had some kind of Habibie family involvement. Suharto long viewed Batam as a potential competitor to Singapore and then — after that strategy was not working — as the city-state's development partner. In 1971, Suharto appointed Ibnu Sutowo to oversee Batam's development but after the oil honcho's fall from grace, the task was given to Habibie.

Eventually, Indonesia and Singapore agreed to cooperate in Batam, which had a few advantages over Singapore, such as ample land and low labour costs. The "Growth Triangle" idea never came to fruition, as Malaysia had no interest in integrating Johor, but links between Singapore and the Riau islands increased greatly, with a push from the two governments. During talks in October 1989, Suharto agreed to Singapore Prime Minister Lee Kuan Yew's proposal for Indonesia to allow 100 per cent foreign ownership of Batam investments, with the condition that 5 per cent be divested to Indonesians after five years. "It was not as attractive as what Singapore offered, but enough to draw some factories in Singapore that were feeling the pressure of our higher costs to move to Batam", Lee wrote.[33] Suharto's concession made Batam more attractive than the rest of Indonesia, where ownership rules introduced after the 1974 Malari riots were not foreigner-friendly.

On the Indonesian side, the key official for Batam was Junior Industry Minister Tunky Ariwibowo, who had worked with Salim on the cold-rolling mill it built at Suharto's request. In 1989, Suharto gave Tunky the additional job of deputy head of the Batam Industrial Development Authority. Tunky pushed plans to put in Batam a joint Indonesia and Singapore-backed industrial estate in which the Indonesian developers were private, not state, entities. For the first time, Suharto agreed to let a private company own an industrial estate. (In a tribute to the late

Tunky, then Singapore Deputy Prime Minister Lee Hsien Loong wrote
he was "a visionary, pioneer and innovator who contributed immensely
to Indonesia-Singapore bilateral relations".[34]) Not surprisingly, the main
player on the Indonesia side was Salim, which already had investment in
the islands. Salim was the main investor in a pig farm on Bulan Island, a
short boat ride from Batam. The farm, which Salim established with Sinar
Mas to supply pork to Singapore, was run by PT Sinar Culindo Perkasa.
Minority shareholders included Harry Murdani, a brother of onetime
Army Commander Gen. Benny Murdani, and Habibie's youngest brother
Timmy. The firm also operated an adjoining crocodile farm; pigs that died
were fed to the crocodiles, whose skin was exported.

Plans for the Batam industrial estate were unveiled in January 1990,
three months after the Suharto-Lee meeting. They featured a 500-hectare,
S$400 million estate at which multinational and other tenants would churn
out non-oil exports, tapping Singapore's service strengths. The investors
in Batam Industrial Park, or Batamindo, were potent. The Singapore
government tapped two state-owned companies, Singapore Technologies
Industrial Corp. (with 30 per cent) and Jurong Environmental Engineering
(10 per cent). For the 60 per cent Indonesian stake, Suharto steered it to
Salim, who took Bambang, then thirty-six years old, as its main partner,
in a company named Herwido Rintis. Bambang's Bimantara Citra, was
booming, helped by licences handed to it by the government, like for
Indonesia's first privately owned television channel. Bambang, Anthony
told the authors, was the Suharto offspring he preferred as a business
partner, as they shared "the same basic philosophy".[35]

At the time of the 1990 Batam announcement, the Indonesian media did
not identify Bambang and his siblings as Suharto's children — Bambang
was simply identified as a "young entrepreneur". The Singapore *Straits
Times* report on the industrial estate-signing named Bambang as Herwido's
president-commissioner (chairman) and also did not connect him to
Suharto, nor did it connect director Timmy Habibie to his brother. But
the report noted that Herwido president-director Anthony Salim was
Liem's son.[36] After the signing, things moved at lightning-speed. On
28 February, Lee Hsien Loong, then Singapore's Trade and Industry
Minister and Deputy Prime Minister, joined Ministers Habibie and
Tunky at a ceremony to lay Batamindo's foundation stone. Lee called the
estate a "concrete demonstration of the excellent bilateral relationship"
between Singapore and Indonesia, saying it reflected "the outward-

looking economic strategy to which both governments are committed".[37] In August 1990, Lee Hsien Loong's father, Prime Minister Lee Kuan Yew and President Suharto officiated at a topping-out ceremony. In less than a year, the first tenants, French and Japanese electronics companies, were churning out components. Within a few years, Batamindo had scores of tenants who, at one stage, together had 74,000 employees. Batamindo's growth encouraged others to plan industrial estates in Batam, though few of those proceeded.

For Salim, Batamindo was one part of expansion on three islands close to Singapore — Batam, Bintan and Bulan. On Bulan, the pig farm was expanded and an orchid farm added, for exports mainly to Japan. On much-larger Bintan, Salim put up an industrial estate and was a partner for developing a multi-hotel beach resort. The idea for a resort area came to Anthony, his staff said, once while his flight from Jakarta was approaching Singapore's Changi Airport. When he spotted an undeveloped stretch of white sand that was Indonesian territory, Anthony started mulling the possibility of developing it. The land, in fact, was used by the Indonesian Marine Corps for training. But Suharto agreed to a plan for developing the area as a beach complex geared towards Singapore residents and tourists. A consortium of Singapore government-linked and private companies built a ferry terminal in Bintan, a forty-five-minute ride from Singapore. Club Med, Banyan Tree and others came in. In 1995, in a move to help the Bintan resorts, Suharto suspended collection of value-added tax and sales tax on some goods brought to the island. "We are creating the Growth Triangle", Salim group executive director Judiono Tosin once declared.[38] The cooperation with Singapore helped Salim broaden its footprint and expand regional ties.

OLEOCHEMICAL EXPLOSION

In connection with Salim's rapid growth in noodle-making — the subject of Chapter 14 — the group expanded its oil palm estates through the 1980s and early 1990s. By 1992, Salim had 210,000 hectares of oil palm under cultivation on Sumatra and other islands. Most of the oil was refined to become cooking oil and used in making noodles, but having its own palm oil production positioned "opportunity-driven" Salim to enter a new industry and expand quickly in it by the first half of the 1990s: oleochemicals, which are oil- and fat-based specialty chemicals used for making detergents, soaps, cosmetics, pharmaceuticals and food additives. Dominating global production were giants such as Procter & Gamble and German chemical company Henkel. Salim had something those multinationals lacked, which was its own supply of crude palm oil.

Johannes Kotjo, a senior Salim executive, spearheaded a foray into oleochemicals that became, for him, like a battle to get as big, or bigger, in the field as his former employer Henkel. Kotjo had studied chemistry in Berlin and stayed on to join the German company. He returned to Indonesia in the early 1980s, and was working as Henkel's country manager when Anthony and his brother Andree, through a mutual friend, approached him to join Salim. Anthony, Kotjo recalled, "talked about the philosophy, not the business, and said he wanted a corporate structure". No specific title was offered him, just to join Salim. Kotjo said he asked what they wanted him to do. "Anthony replied, 'I don't know. There are so many things to do'."[39] Kotjo said he was hesitant to join as the group "seemed real Chinese." Kotjo, an ethnic Chinese himself, said he was comfortable at Henkel. But the opportunity at Salim was appealing, and "Anthony is very good in convincing people". In April 1983, at age thirty-one, he joined Salim.

Kotjo's presence and the high profile he had somewhat undercut public perceptions that Salim was a typical Chinese family business with the patriarch making all the decisions and outsiders having no say. Anthony knew Salim needed non-family executives, especially to conduct business on a broader stage. Prior to Kotjo's entry, Salim hired a fresh accounting graduate, Judiono Tosin, who became Indocement's finance director. Tosin and Kotjo, as directors, made themselves accessible to the press, unlike Anthony and others, and this provided credence to the view Salim gave responsibility to professionals and trusted them. In 1991, *Institutional Investor* magazine noted that Anthony "has brought in professionals and cut the ad hoc, opportunistic, ties with other business groups that were the hallmark of his father's operating style".[40]

After Kotjo joined Salim, he first worked with packaging and glass operations, and then assumed responsibilities in palm oil and chemicals. By the end of the 1980s, he was chief executive officer of PT Unggul Indah Corp. (UIC), a company started in 1983 and Indonesia's only producer of alkylbenzene, a basic material for making detergent. Unggul Indah was controlled by Salim and Sinar Mas, and both stayed in as partners after the groups' palm oil divorce by the start of 1991. Another shareholder, over time, was an Indonesian family surnamed Katuari that owned the Wings Group, which after Suharto's fall became a significant competitor with Indofood in instant noodles.

Given Kotjo's Henkel background, it was natural for him to get involved in chemicals, and the niche business of oleochemicals became the target. Kotjo once said: "In petrochemicals, we would be a small fish in a big ocean. But in oleochemicals we are a bigger fish in a smaller pond."[41] Salim opened an office in Dusseldorf and bought an oleochemical plant in western Germany, then went shopping in defunct East Germany, where an agency of the newly unified German government, called Treuhand, launched a giant fire-sale to offload thousands of antiquated, largely dysfunctional state factories. A Salim executive at the time, Noke Kiroyan, recalled that checking out the array of East German plants "felt like a kid going into a Toys R Us for the first time — oh, there are lots of toys!"[42] In May 1991, Salim paid a token DM1 for an oleochemical plant in Rodleben on which the German agency had put a value of DM270 million. Some conditions were attached to purchasing Deutsche Hydrierwerke GmbH Rodleben: Salim pledged to spend at least DM70 million on it by 1994 and to keep at least 700 people employed until mid-1992.

Salim, perhaps the only Asian entity to buy an East German plant, got a package deal that was beset with problems. Kotjo said the technology was good, but there were woes embedded by decades of controlled-economy management and a focus on what could be made rather than sold. Also, the plant was grossly overstaffed, once having 17,000 employees. Treuhand slashed the number to 1,600, but that was still several times the need. When Salim came in, it found the factory seemed to produce more paper than anything; monthly reports that meticulously detailed meagre production ran to hundreds of pages. A Salim executive in Dusseldorf cut those to twelve pages. Another hurdle was that the factory land was contaminated, as chemical wastes had been dumped there. An additional problem reflected naiveté and inexperience in corporate public relations back at Salim's Jakarta headquarters. Because the Salim name was not known in European chemical circles, the German operation asked the head office to send some promotional material to let potential customers see the range of Salim businesses. When the brochures arrived, the German executives were shocked to find that the section on agribusiness included a picture from Bulan Island that showed two pigs copulating. The brochures were destroyed.

The plant was a financial drain from the start. European Chemical News reported in 1993 that it was losing DM2 million a month (more than US$1.2 million), which sent Salim back to Treuhand to renegotiate its deal. Under a revised pact, Salim was given until 2000 to make its refurbishment investment, and the number of jobs Salim had to have that year was set at only 190.[43] Eventually, Salim gave up operations at the plant. Germany was not the only place outside Indonesia where Salim made oleochemical investments. In 1991, it bought 50 per cent of Albright & Wilson (Australia) Ltd. Salim held talks about buying the organic chemicals division of W.R. Grace & Co. of the United States, but it did not proceed, partly because of questions about the cost — and who would pay — to clean up an old Grace plant.

At home, Salim raised its capacity by building Batamas Megah, a large plant on Batam that made fatty alcohol for use in detergents, cosmetics and other consumer products. In February 1994, Suharto officially opened the facility. Chemical Week of the United States said at the time that Batamas Megah was "sending ripples through the worldwide fatty alcohols business".[44] Batamas Megah, which roughly tripled Salim's annual production of fatty alcohol in Indonesia, was estimated to cost US$230 million. A Jakarta banker recalled that when the plant was being built, a visiting industry analyst expressed surprise about the price tag and remarked "So two plants are getting built, right?"[45] Salim executives denied there was any of what Indonesians called "mark-up" in Batamas Megah's construction. Critics of Indonesian business practice assert that mark-ups are routine: If a plant could be built for US$50 million, the estimated cost is sometimes deliberately overstated — for example, to US$70 million — as the company would then be able to obtain an extra US$20 million in loans. This could be parked elsewhere or used for kickbacks and other payments. When some Indonesian businesspeople talked about a project's "IDC", they were not referring to the banking industry term "interest during construction" — but meant "income during construction". Project "mark-up" and "income during construction" were aspects of the corruption that was rampant in the Suharto period, and afterwards.

Boosted by production at Batamas Megah, Salim became a sizeable manufacturer of oleochemicals. In the mid-1990s, Salim set up an office in the U.S. state of Ohio, from which Salim Oleochemicals Inc. ran sales efforts in North and South America. According to Kotjo, from zero in 1984, revenue from chemicals in 1991 reached US$800 million, of which

US$300 million was from oleochemicals. He put total Salim revenue that year at nearly US$10 billion. In chemicals other than oleochemicals, Salim had two ventures with Dow Chemical to make petrochemicals on Java's west coast. Also, in the early 1990s there was a plan for a joint venture with Amoco Chemical to make purified terephthalic acid, or PTA, needed to produce polyester fibre for textiles. Kotjo said Salim chose to focus on oleochemicals, rather than invest in a crowded area like PTA. He cited Salim's pull-out to demonstrate that the group did not make all the investments it had a chance to. There were limits to Salim's expansion, he once acknowledged. "People say we are always buying companies, but we turn down 90 per cent of proposals we receive", he commented. "They don't fit with us."[46]

CORPORATE SPRAWL

When people ask many how companies are in the Salim stable, Anthony replies that he really does not know — and that is not surprising. Researchers and others have given or picked a number, like 600, but there's no way to be certain. Lack of transparency and problems obtaining corporate registrations pose obstacles. There are questions about how big of a shareholding would be a threshold for considering a business to be in the group, and issues because Salim deliberately never set up one holding company for its overall interests. The term "Salim Group" is more a convenience, for outsiders, rather than any actual or formal structure. (This was true, too, for most of the other Indonesian business "groups".) At one time, there was some speculation that Salim was using or planning to use a company called PT Salim Economic Development Corp., or SEDC, as a holding company or managing company for the group, but Liem and Anthony did not have SEDC or any corporate entity work that way. Researcher Yuri Sato concluded that SEDC, which she said was created in 1970, had no shareholdings in other companies and it "functioned in name only".[47]

Marleen Dieleman, in her 2007 dissertation on Salim, listed 536 companies in an annex of group companies.[48] The list includes companies that at one time were part of Salim, such as trading company Hagemeyer, in which offshore arm First Pacific held big stakes from 1983 until 1998. It also includes some companies whose shareholders were members of the Gang of Four or associates but not necessarily Liem or a Salim family member. But the list makes clear that Salim would have had, at one time or another, more than 500 units. The number may have been significantly higher, because the list is not exhaustive — it names "KMP" in Singapore, but there also were more than ten other companies in Singapore, besides KMP Pte Ltd, that had "KMP" in their names.

For the group, the number and reach became huge, both in terms of geography and activity. Like many businesses spanning multiple countries, Salim set up special purpose and shelf companies in different places, some of them with frivolous-sounding names: In Hong Kong, there's Frolic Pacific Development — a play on First Pacific — and Magic Success International, while one British Virgin Islands-registered firm is Rascal Holdings. Salim was involved in much more than the core businesses discussed in other sections. Indeed, there was real corporate sprawl. A 1996 group brochure published in English, for prospective foreign partners, cited twelve areas of significant activity (eleven sectors plus a heading of "international" that encompassed First Pacific). In an introductory note, chairman Liem stated "Our companies are intimately involved in the day-to-day lives of literally millions of Indonesian families." In the brochure text, Salim put combined annual revenue at US$20 billion; after its publication, Salim did not again give a figure for total turnover.

Here's a summary of Salim activities in several other businesses:

• *Coal*: The group started in coal in 1986, according to the brochure, through a company named Kitadin that had a 930-hectare concession in East Kalimantan. Later, Indominco Mandiri and other companies were started. After Suharto fell, Salim pledged its coal assets to the Indonesian Bank Restructuring Agency (IBRA) as part of its debt settlement, and they were sold to a unit of Banpu of Thailand for US$52 million. Subsequently, demand for Indonesian coal rose sharply, and Salim started to develop new coal and mining interests, through a company named Ithaca Resources.

• *Forestry*: Salim was a relatively small player in this big, lucrative business. Timber and plywood were the turf of giants in those specific industries like Suharto long-time friend Bob Hasan and more-recent Cendana friend Prajogo Pangestu. The Salim brochure said its Kalamur Group had a 500,000-hectare concession in Kalimantan, and was then producing 300,000 cubic metres of wood products a year. A researcher in forestry said that by size of concessions, in 1994/95 Salim was eighteenth largest in Indonesia, with 1,081,500 hectares. The largest, it said, was Prajogo's Barito Pacific, with 6,125,700 hectares, followed by Djajanti Group — in which Sudwikatmono had a small share — with 3,616,700 hectares.[49]

- *Distribution and Retail*: A Salim company, Indomarco, took over distribution of noodles and food items in 1992. About 20 per cent of Indomarco — the part not owned by Indofood — was pledged for settling Salim's post-1998 debt. It was sold in 2001 to Bhakti Investindo, whose boss Hary Tanoesoedibjo was viewed by many as a proxy for Anthony (both denied it). Indomaret, started in 1997, is a chain of mini-markets like 7-11. It became Indonesia's biggest chain of such retail outlets. In December 2013, there were 8,350 of them, mostly franchisees. In 1990, Salim became a partner in a venture with businessman Dick Gelael that had supermarkets and the Kentucky Fried Chicken (KFC) franchise for Indonesia. It got listed in 1993 as PT Fastfood Indonesia. A Salim unit, Megah Eraraharja, owned 36 per cent of Fastfood Indonesia, whose chairman was Anthony. By the end of 2012, there were more than 440 KFC outlets in Indonesia.

Another food product business that Salim entered was milk products, through Indomilk. This was another case where the "Indo" name was not a Salim original, but Salim got in and expanded the group. Indomilk was started by an early foreign investor in the New Order, Australian Dairy Corp. of Melbourne, which partnered with an Indonesian company named Marison, owned by a Sumatran trader who was the father of Akbar Tanjung, an important Golkar politician.

- *Television*: This is a field that shows clearly how Suharto, in the late 1980s, nurtured privatization that really was personalization. Television stopped being a state monopoly as licences for channels were given, without tenders, to private companies. The first ones were for the First Family, starting in 1987 with Bambang (for RCTI), followed by Sudwikatmono (SCTV) and then Tutut (TPI). The next licence went to the Bakrie Group (Anteve) and then Salim received a licence for Indosiar. That station, which became a good way to promote Salim products such as Indomie, began broadcasting in 1995. Indosiar was one of the companies that Salim relinquished control of when pledging assets to the state after Suharto's 1998 fall. Years later, Salim regained control but then relinquished it as part of a deal to get control of plantation company London Sumatra.

Notes

1. Interview with Ciputra, 19 March 2007.
2. Ibid.
3. Andreas Harefa and Eben Ezer Siadari, *The Ciputra Way — Praktik terbaik menjadi entrepreneur sejati* (Jakarta: PT Elex Media Komputindo, 2006), p. 106.

4. "Kami ini seperti kuda" [We are like a horse], *Tempo*, 16 July 1977.

5. Interview with Ciputra, 19 March 2007.

6. Private conversation, Jakarta, 14 February 2008.

7. Ian Verchere, "Liem Sioe Liong: Suharto's Secret Agent", *Insight*, May 1978, p. 15.

8. Conversation with Albert Halim, Jakarta, 4 December 2007.

9. Interview with Anthony, 23 December 2007.

10. Yuri Sato, "The Salim Group in Indonesia: The development and behavior of the largest conglomerate in Southeast Asia", *Developing Economies* XXXI, no. 4 (December 1993), p. 438. Separately, two Dutch academics wrote that Liem made good use of his contacts in the Hokchia community outside Indonesia, with a Hokchia businessman living in Japan helping make the contacts between Mazda and Salim; see Leo Douw and Peter Post, eds, *South China: State, Culture and Social Change during the 20th Century* (Amsterdam: Royal Netherlands Academy of Arts and Sciences, Verhandelingen, Afd, 1996).

11. "Bisnis saya memuka pasar" [My business is opening the market], *Eksekutif*, December 1986, p. 21.

12. Charlotte Butler, *Dare to Do: The Story of William Soeryadjaya and PT Astra International* (Singapore: McGraw Hill, 2002), p. 21.

13. Ibid., pp. 14–15.

14. Ibid., p. 33.

15. Shin Yoon Hwan, "Demystifying the capitalist state, political patronage, bureaucratic interests, and capitalist-in-formation in Suharto's Indonesia", Ph.D. thesis, Yale University, 1989, p. 406.

16. Ibid., p. 377.

17. Ibid., p. 390.

18. Ibid., p. 255.

19. Ibid., pp. 413–14.

20. Richard Borsuk, "Family Saga: How Son's Ambition Caused Disaster for the Soeryadjayas", *AWSJ*, 16 November 1992.

21. Ibid.

22. Ibid.

23. Richard Borsuk, "Astra chairman says son's debts won't hurt firm", *AWSJ*, 28 May 1992.

24. Ibid.

25. Richard Borsuk, "Family Saga".

26. Raphael Pura and Richard Borsuk, "Professor Placed in Eye of Astra Storm", *AWSJ*, 18 December 1992.

27. Ibid.

28. *The Economist*, "Indonesia's bankrupt Bank Summa".

29. Richard Borsuk, "Toyota Motor buys 8.3 per cent stake in PT Astra", *AWSJ*, 23 June 1993.

30. "The Chinese Factor", *Indonesian Business Weekly,* 29 January 1993.

31. Richard Borsuk, "Salim Group Steels Itself For Life After Suharto", *AWSJ,* 25 February 1994.

32. Ibid.

33. Lee Kuan Yew, *From Third World to First: The Singapore Story: 1965–2000* (New York: Harper Collins, 2000), p. 272.

34. Astuti Ariwibowo, comp., *Dalam Kenangan Tunky Ariwibowo: Pekerja Keras* [In Memoriam: Tunky Ariwibowo, a Hardworker] (Jakarta: Privately published, for his 1000th day memorial, 2005), p. 73.

35. Interview with Anthony, 21 January 2007.

36. "$400m Batam Deal Signed", *Straits Times,* 12 January 1990.

37. "Neighbouring nations should pool advantages", *Straits Times,* 1 March 1990.

38. Adam Schwarz, "Export Platforms: Indonesian Conglomerate Heads for Free Trade Zone", *FEER,* 18 October 1990, p. 77.

39. Interview with Kotjo, Jakarta, 23 March 2007.

40. Henny Sender, "Inside the Overseas Chinese network", *Institutional Investor,* August 1991.

41. Richard Borsuk, "Salim Group Targets Growth in Chemicals", *AWSJ,* 25 September 1992.

42. Interview with Noke Kiroyan, 23 April 2008.

43. *European Chemical News,* 26 February 1993, and *Europa Chemie,* 19 June 1993.

44. *Chemical Week,* 9 February 1994.

45. Private conversation, Jakarta, 24 February 1994.

46. Borsuk, "Salim Group Targets Growth in Chemicals".

47. Yuri Sato, "The Salim Group in Indonesia", p. 433.

48. Marleen Dieleman, "How Chinese are Entrepreneurial Strategies of Ethnic Chinese Business Groups in Southeast Asia? A Multifaceted Analysis of the Salim Group of Indonesia", draft Ph.D. dissertation, 2007.

49. David W. Brown, "Addicted to Rent: Corporate and Spatial Distribution of Forest Resources in Indonesia: Implication for Forest Sustainability and Government Policy", 1999, available at <http://www.reocities.com/davidbrown_id/index.html>, accessed 15 September 2010.

12

GOING INTERNATIONAL

At the time Suharto was solidifying the power wrested from Sukarno in 1966, Liem had little business outside Indonesia and was relatively unknown outside his Hokchia circle. Early in the New Order, though, Liem and his partner, fellow Hokchia businessman Djuhar Sutanto, established a beachhead for outside activity. On 31 March 1967 — less than three weeks after Suharto's handpicked assembly declared him acting president — Waringin Private Limited was registered in Singapore. Its principal activities, according to the registration, were "general wholesale trade" and "wholesale on a fee or contract basis (e.g. commission agencies)". The company registration papers listed Liem Oen Kian (Djuhar's Chinese name), as managing director, and Liem Sioe Liong as director. (Much later, Djuhar's role ended. In 2006, Liem owned 120 of the unlisted company's 300 shares, or 40 per cent, while unidentified nominees in Vanuatu held the other 180.)[1]

SINGAPORE BEACHHEAD

During the early Suharto years, the ability of Indonesian companies to export or import depended entirely on government licences. Dismantling stifling trade-controls was not an economic priority for Suharto, who had his focus on taming rampant inflation and getting money from the West. For sizeable Indonesian traders, it was good to have a presence in Singapore, whose port handled nearly all goods going to or from Indonesia. At this time, it was difficult for Indonesian traders to obtain letters of credit, a consequence of the economic mess the country was in at the end of Sukarno's tenure, and a Singapore firm would find it easier and cheaper to borrow from banks than an Indonesian one. In July 1968, Liem opened a second trading company in Singapore, Permanent Pte Ltd. That same month, he and others registered a textile business in Singapore, called International Spinning Mills Pte Ltd., to spin, weave and print yarns and fabrics. A co-shareholder was Indonesia-born businessman Henry Kwee, another Hokchia who later became a property king in Singapore. In the late 1960s, Singapore had a thriving textile industry but by the 1980s, the business had shifted to lower-cost countries. Liem sold the Singapore factory plot and moved the machinery to Indonesia. In 1981, Liem registered KMP Pte Ltd, which became his umbrella — not one for all of the Gang of Four — for Singapore ventures. Anthony said the initials stood for Keris Mas Patel. Keris Mas (golden *keris*, or dagger) and Patel were names of companies that were bought by Liem, but there was no special significance for using them. "We joked that KMP stood for 'keep making profit', or 'keep making problems'", Anthony said.[2]

At the start of the 1970s, Liem was not aiming to do business regionally, as opportunities in Indonesia were multiplying. Still, having some presence in the financial centres of Singapore and Hong Kong would prove important for growth. Four factors spurred an increase in Salim activity outside Indonesia. The first was Anthony's return to Jakarta from Britain. He was comfortable in English and had exposure to the outside world. Unusual for a "second-generation" entrepreneur, Anthony was even more of a risk-taker than his father. He also realized early that it would be wise to diversify geographically, given the history of enmity in Indonesia to ethnic Chinese. He told the authors in 2007, "We realised that things should not be in the same basket... So at an early stage we start to balance our portfolio."[3] The second factor was Liem's foray into cement. This import-substitution business would not offer much scope for exports, but expansion in the capital-intensive industry meant Liem increasingly needed ties to international debt markets — a place where private Indonesian groups could not go until then. The third factor was the 1974 Malari riots in Jakarta. Although Japanese businesses — not Salim — were targeted then, violence in Indonesia almost always hit the ethnic Chinese community, and the episode reminded them of their vulnerability.

Indonesia, unusual among developing nations, had no significant foreign exchange restrictions and allowed citizens to freely export money — this policy was one of the New Order's most surprising economic changes — and the Malari incident prompted Chinese Indonesians to think about putting eggs in baskets elsewhere. The fourth factor in Liem's move to set up shop outside Indonesia was the 1975 entry into BCA of Mochtar Riady. The two opened a Hong Kong deposit-taking company, Central Asia Capital Corp., which gave Liem a shingle in a place where most regional banking deals were done. In 1979, Liem created another foothold in Hong Kong, as he and Djuhar got control of a listed but barely traded finance company, Overseas Union Finance Ltd (no relation to Overseas Union Bank in Singapore). This little vehicle would come in handy when Salim wanted to plant a flag deep in the British colony. Liem's expansion in cement and the creation of a beachhead in Hong Kong had its roots in a friendship-turned-partnership that would give Salim global business interests.

A KEY COLD CALL

In 1977, a young U.S.-educated Filipino banker named Manuel V. Pangilinan went to Central Asia Capital's office in Hong Kong for an appointment with Anthony Salim. It was an introductory call, but it turned out to be the start of an important friendship. Later, after Manny established his status as a corporate chief, some Manila media referred to him by his initials, MVP, which also stood for "most valuable player". The son of a banker, Manny received an MBA when he was only twenty-two from the prestigious Wharton School at the University of Pennsylvania. He joined a Philippine finance house named Bancom International, which sent him to Hong Kong in 1976 to work for a joint venture with American Express Bank, Amex Bancom. At the time of his call on Anthony, who occasionally came to Hong Kong, Manny was thirty, a vice-president for merchant banking and thriving in Hong Kong's fast-paced environment. Anthony was twenty-seven, but already assuming heavy responsibilities given by his father. At Amex Bancom, Manny was looking for borrowers, and that was the reason for seeing Anthony. "Given the political clout of Mr Liem [Sioe Liong], they were a client any bank would like to have", Manny said nearly thirty years later in an interview. He recounted his first meeting with Anthony, saying "It was a typical merchant banker call". And a seemingly unsuccessful sales pitch, too, as Anthony "batted it back, saying 'we already have the money'. It wasn't a good start professionally," recalled Manny. "Afterwards, I said we'll never do business with these guys. I thought that was the end of it. Who are we [Amex Bancom]? — just too small, relatively unknown."[4] For the eager banker, though, the appointment had an upside. "We liked each other", he said of Anthony. The Filipino said he sensed that the Indonesian was "easy to deal with; you know where you are — which was nowhere, at that time."[5]

Later, though, Manny's effort bore some fruit. Anthony called to say he wanted to meet and introduce a Spanish cement plant contractor. Anthony still was not looking for money, but the contact produced some work with Manny. His bank got appointed to advise on structuring finance for a proposed petrochemical hydrocracker in Sumatra. The project turned into a complex saga. It was going to be partly owned by Salim but then evolved into a project owned by Indonesia's state oil company Pertamina. The Spanish contractors that Salim introduced, Technicas Reunidas and Centurion, got substantial work in Indonesia. Manny, at Anthony's invitation, went to Europe with him and the Spaniards to promote the Sumatra project. The trip enhanced the bonding already under way between the two young Southeast Asian executives. When the Dumai refinery was inaugurated in 1984, Amex Bancom was not a lender; far-larger J.P. Morgan arranged that financing. But Amex Bancom received fees for its early-stage work, and later did help finance Salim's cement production while Manny cemented ties with an important new friend.

Afterward, Salim appointed Amex Bancom to arrange a syndicated loan for the sixth production line at its cement complex near limestone supplies at Citeureup, between Jakarta and Bogor. To attract banks to join the loan, Amex Bancom had to prepare a standard "information memorandum" on the project. Up until then, Salim had not needed to make any information available — and it had not. Obtaining material from Salim for the info memo "was like pulling teeth", Manny said.[6] The memo got done and the loan was syndicated. For a signing ceremony at Hong Kong's Mandarin Hotel, Anthony — in a brief speech written by Manny — thanked lenders for their trust. A high degree of trust was getting built between the two, and in 1981 they joined hands in what became the flagship for Salim investments outside Indonesia — First Pacific. The teaming up of Anthony and Manny led to a pivotal partnership between the son of a chief crony and a Wharton graduate. First Pacific — and the relationship

— would experience some highs and a deep low. Anthony said that when he and Manny met, they "shared a lot of common base", including a passion to prove they were capable businesspeople. Both saw business as a global stage, and were keen to be on it. For Anthony, continuing to milk monopolies and protected positions could not prove his business acumen. On his part, Manny wanted to achieve more than just being a well-paid professional working for someone else.

Manny's family roots are in Pampanga, a province north of Manila. His grandfather was a public school teacher who, despite never finishing college, rose to be Philippine education secretary under President Elpidio Quirino (1948–53). Manny's father Dominador worked all his life in banks, starting as a messenger at Philippine National Bank and rising to its senior vice-president before retiring and then becoming president of Traders Royal Bank. The bank's main shareholder was sugar baron Roberto Benedicto, a friend of President Ferdinand Marcos, but Traders was not a crony bank. Unlike Anthony, who was not a fan of schools, Manny was a highly motivated student. He gained admission to the elite Ateneo de Manila University in his home country and hungered to do an MBA in the United States. His father would not pay for it, but Manny found a way to go, winning a national competition for a Procter & Gamble scholarship to the Wharton School. (In a 2006 speech to Ateneo graduates, Manny related how upon his return from Philadelphia, he had expected to be hired as a P&G manager, but was not accepted. After that, he took the first job offered, as an assistant to the president of Phinma [Philippine Investment-Management Inc]. Six years later, he itched to work abroad. There were the "usual reasons" of the glamour of being an expat in Hong Kong and the "stifling staleness" of his career at home, "but more importantly, I needed to find myself, to prove that I can stand on my own and succeed". At Bancom in Hong Kong, he said he "learned the dynamics of international finance from my Chinese colleagues, not from the Filipino executives".[7])

When Anthony and Manny were forging a friendship in the late 1970s, the Indonesian was on a fast learning track, accompanying his father in navigating through the opaque world of Jakarta business. But in the world of international finance, Anthony was a rookie and he found in Manny a tutor. "He's very articulate", Anthony recalled, "he's a Wharton grad [with] lots of knowledge… at that time, I'm not up to that standard. I was learning from him."[8] On starting First Pacific, Anthony said, it was a simple affair. "We're thinking, we're both young men. What do we want to do together?"

A third First Pacific founder was Robert Meyer, an American lawyer who had worked at Coudert Brothers. In 1978, the U.S. firm moved him from Tokyo to Hong Kong, where Asian loan syndication was booming. One Coudert client there was Amex Bancom, and Meyer had regular contact with Manny. Later, Meyer spent time with Anthony on the nitty-gritty of loan agreements and talking about many subjects. Meyer recalled that the Filipino and Indonesian "hit it off personally very, very well".[9]

THE BIRTH OF FIRST PACIFIC

In a video shown at a 2006 party for the twenty-fifth anniversary of First Pacific's creation, Meyer described First Pacific's roots: "One night, we're in the coffee shop of the Furama Hotel about 10.30 p.m., and I said to Manny, 'What are you doing with your life? It seems to me there is a great opportunity to link up with some of the big business groups in Asia'."[10] Manny had contact with a number of Asian groups, but Salim seemed the best possibility for working together. And while doing work with Salim, the idea had been floated. Manny's pondering about his goals intensified when Amex and Bancom decided to end their joint venture. Amex asked Manny to stay with the U.S. bank. He did, but said Anthony gave "hints about maybe I should leave Amex and set something up with them".[11]

At the end of 1980, Manny's boss transferred to London, and asked him to move there. It was time to talk seriously with Anthony, which led to the sketching of a rough plan and Manny's decision to quit Amex. "It was both a push and a pull" to team up with Anthony, he said. Manny felt he had proven he could succeed at an international bank "and anyway, I didn't want to move to London".[12] Negotiations with Salim took months, but Anthony and Manny's common interest in a pan-Asian investment company was strong. It was clear from the start that Manny and Meyer would be the pillars in Hong Kong. They complemented each other. "Manny and I were a very good team", Meyer acknowledged, adding: "He's a locomotive, he can forget some details; as a lawyer, I never forget details."[13]

The idea behind First Pacific was summed up by Thomas Yasuda, a San Francisco lawyer who joined in 1983 and later became an executive director and managing director. "The original concept was very simplistic; we would be a combination of financial services and trading investment group", Yasuda said in a Harvard Business School case study published in 1995. "We would be the Liems' window to the world and we would use their contacts in Indonesia. We would add value particularly in the areas of financial services and trading, e.g. trade finance and import and export."[14] In Meyer's view, "Anthony saw First Pacific as a lifeboat", he said, asserting that the prime motive was building up assets outside Indonesia, as a hedge against the country's risks for Chinese. "Salim couldn't run an international operation, and managers in Hong Kong couldn't run an Indonesian operation."[15]

To get First Pacific rolling, Manny wanted to hire a set of people but Anthony favoured starting small and growing incrementally. Before long, Manny won Anthony's okay to add two Filipinos who were Ateneo graduates and had worked at Bancom, Ricardo Pascua and Vicente Tinsay. According to Manny, the original idea for funding was to have half from the Liem family and half from Traders Royal Bank in Manila. But Traders shareholder Benedicto, not interested in a venture involving Hong Kong and Indonesia, nixed the idea. (Benedicto died in 2000; Traders Royal Bank later merged into Manila's Bank of Commerce.) Rather than seek a partner they might not know, the Indonesians decided to supply 100 per cent of the seed money. According to a 2006 video, the initial capital put in was a modest HK$4 million (about US$700,000 in 1981); another figure First Pacific used later was HK$7 million.[16] The shares were divided among the "Gang of Four" members, with the same percentages they used at the time in many ventures: Liem and Djuhar Sutanto each held 45 per cent, while Sudwikatmono and Ibrahim Risjad had 5 per cent apiece. Later, the breakdown for the four "Salim Investors" became 40-40-10-10. At the start, little was known in Hong Kong about the Indonesians — except that Liem was close to Suharto. So naturally, there was a wide assumption that First Pacific was a Suharto vehicle. Robert Meyer said that given Salim's ties to Suharto, "people joining First Pacific gave a big whiff-and-sniff test".[17] Anthony said that the Liem family never tried to hide what it was doing and wanted its investment in Hong Kong to be out in the open. In 1988, *Institutional Investor* magazine labelled First Pacific the "collective brainchild of a group of enigmatic Indonesian-Chinese financiers known as the Liem Investors", and it added that the Liems, with Suharto's blessing, "control much of Indonesia's economy".[18]

It was Manny who suggested the name First Pacific, and Overseas Union Finance was renamed First Pacific Finance (FPF). Manny was its managing director and Meyer was executive director and general counsel.

According to its annual report for 1981, the "First Pacific Group" was owned or controlled by Liem Sioe Liong and Liem Oen Kian "and their associates in Jakarta". That report, the first that used the name First Pacific, said that total assets of FPF increased from HK$157.3 million to HK$856.1 million in the two years ended 31 December 1981.

First Pacific Finance offered financial advisory services, and a Liem-related project was the first client. The work, obtained in November 1981, involved US$240 million in credit facilities for two new cement plants. The company acted as "advisor to the project promoters" of Liem's cold-rolling steel mill plus twin twenty-one-storey office towers to be constructed as the Indocement and BCA buildings in Jakarta. Later, that plan was amended, so the towers were not twins, and not identical structures; they were built about one kilometre apart along Jalan Sudirman, the prime location for office buildings in the city. In Hong Kong, in December 1981, FPF moved from Central Building to World-Wide House. The office used part of a floor Liem had bought; also on the floor was Central Asia Capital, the deposit-taking company Liem owned with Mochtar Riady.

For fledgling First Pacific Group, the early years featured a plethora of corporate moves in Hong Kong. These created some speculation about what Suharto crony Liem was up to. But early on, First Pacific won compliments for being open. A January 1983 cover story in the *Far Eastern Economic Review* declared that its moves had been done with a transparency that made the owners of mystery-shrouded Carrian business group "look like the powers of darkness".[19] (Property firm Carrian deliberately let the market keep guessing about whether it was backed by Philippine President Ferdinand Marcos or another controversial source. In Hong Kong's biggest corporate failure to date, Carrian collapsed in October 1983 with debts of at least US$1.2 billion.) Liem and his partners used a Liberian company they owned, First Pacific Investments Ltd., to take over a dormant firm, Shanghai Land Investment, in March 1982 and turn it into First Pacific Holdings.[20] This led to some wisecracks about Indonesians "shanghai-ing" a company that had halted commercial activity twenty-six years earlier after its twenty-seven land parcels in Shanghai were nationalized by the communists. Shanghai Land was incorporated in 1888 in Hong Kong and, before 1949, was publicly traded in Shanghai. Until it was bought by the Indonesians, the comatose company was partly owned by Hong Kong's powerful Kadoorie family.

In his first report to First Pacific Holdings shareholders in April 1983, chairman Liem began: "After more than 25 years of comparatively dormant existence following the cessation of your Company's activities in Shanghai in 1956, your Management has succeeded in breathing new life into First Pacific Holdings Ltd. (formerly, the Shanghai Land Investment Co. Ltd.)." He noted that management's mandate was to "transform" the company into "an investment holding vehicle for the acquisition of financial institutions located in the Asia-Pacific region."[21] In the video shown in 2006 at First Pacific's party, Meyer recounted that within two years of the May 1981 start, "we had acquired five publicly listed companies on three continents, and had put together what became the First Pacific Group".[22] In a short speech at the party, Anthony noted that First Pacific was aggressive in the early 1980s in its "quest to be active in the global area". Later on, he remarked, the company became "more deliberate" in its ways.

GOING DUTCH — AND AMERICAN

The founders wanted First Pacific to plant one leg in the United States and one in Europe. They wanted to own a bank in the United States, and hired Goldman Sachs to look for one. They sought a trading house as a marketing and distribution arm in Europe, and tapped Price Waterhouse for that search. The bank was secured first. At the end of 1982, First Pacific Holdings bought Hibernia Bank of San Francisco. For the European trading companies, Price Waterhouse shortlisted five candidates: Hagemeyer, Inchcape, Zuellig, Diethelm and East Asiatic Company. In 1983, First Pacific concluded a deal to buy Hagemeyer, a company born in Java during colonial days, but which was not one of the "Big Five" Dutch-owned international trading companies operating in the Dutch East Indies — Internatio, Borsumij, Geo. Wehry, Lindeteves and Jacobson & Van den Berg. (In 1991, First Pacific bought 43 per cent of Internatio-Mueller, the latest incarnation of the first firm, but it failed to secure majority control.)

In 1900, nearly four decades before Liem set foot in Surabaya, two Dutch brothers, Anton and Johan Hagemeijer (the Dutch spelling of Hagemeyer), started a trading business in the East Java port, which then had a population of about 150,000. The brothers, who sublet tiny premises from a print shop, incorporated Hagemeijer & Co. in 1904. According to a Dutch historian, a school exercise book that functioned as the small firm's financial record-keeper included a note from Anton, the younger brother, saying that the original capital was "2,000 guilders, being my wife's dowry".[23] The first business Anton did was importing cheese from a trader in his wife's hometown.[24]

From Europe, the brothers also brought cigars, watches and other luxury goods to sell in Java. The business flourished and a purchasing office was opened in New York in 1915. After Johan's death in 1918, the firm was reorganized and the spelling changed to Hagemeyer, which in 1937 was listed in Amsterdam. Just before the outbreak of World War II, a Dutch newspaper, *De Zakenwereld* (The Business World), opined about Hagemeyer in April 1940: "Not a bad investment for those who can be patient and who can carry the Dutch East Indies risk."[25] Through wars and revolution, Hagemeyer stayed in business in Indonesia until 1957, when Sukarno kicked out Dutch enterprises. However, the company was able to continue making profits for some years more from operations in Netherlands New Guinea, which remained a Dutch colony until Sukarno succeeded in making it part of Indonesia, renamed Irian Jaya, in 1963. Although chased out of the country where it began, Hagemeyer still had strengths, such as the links to Japan that it developed after World War II. The Dutch firm was the agent for Asia, outside Japan, for National, the brand name of Matsushita Electric products. After losing its Indonesia business, Hagemeyer started its own manufacturing, though that hurt the company's finances by the early 1980s — when First Pacific was looking to purchase a trading company.

Kwik Kian Gie, a Chinese Indonesian who in 1999 became President Abdurrahman Wahid's senior economics minister and then butted heads with Anthony over Salim's debts, claims some credit for putting Anthony together with Hagemeyer. Back in Jakarta at the start of the 1980s after fourteen years in the Netherlands, Kwik knew about Hagemeyer and its problems. He got an introduction to Anthony via a Salim lawyer and former Kwik classmate named Wardoyo. When they met, Kwik showed Anthony a Dutch newspaper article about Hagemeyer's money woes. According to Kwik, Anthony was excited to learn that Hagemeyer could be bought cheaply, and dispatched Kwik and a Price Waterhouse partner to Holland to gather information.[26] Later, Anthony and Manny went to Amsterdam, which was followed by negotiations with Hagemeyer in Singapore and Hong Kong.

Manny recalled that the negotiations stalemated, with a gap of 25 centimes (about 65 U.S. cents) a share between the two sides. Hagemeyer's chairman wanted 36.50 centimes a share, while Anthony offered 36.25 centimes. Manny, who had the title of First Pacific Managing Director, said he sealed the deal at 36.50 centimes. The difference was immaterial, he said, describing Hagemeyer as "the best investment we made".[27] First Pacific ended up paying about US$21 million for 51 per cent of the shares, and over time, it pumped in more than US$100 million. (Hagemeyer was sold in early 1998 for US$1.9 billion, which First Pacific calculated as providing a return of 24 per cent a year.) When the original purchases terms were set in early 1983, a Singapore newspaper quoted Hagemeyer's Asia director as saying that the deal came from its initiative. "We pursued the association because we saw advantages of being associated with the Liem Group", he claimed.[28] Anthony commented on purchasing Hagemeyer: "You were once Surabaya-based; you were in trouble and I can afford to buy."[29]

Hagemeyer had a coffee business, and First Pacific naturally hoped the trading company could boost exports of Indonesian commodities. But according to two Dutch historians, the Liem family didn't know at the time it bought in that "after internal debate Hagemeyer had just decided to terminate its coffee trade because of the large risks associated with commodity trading". Due to First Pacific's entry, Hagemeyer postponed its divestment plan.[30] In 1985, coffee stained Hagemeyer's results, as a wrong bet on price direction left a loss for the year. Owning Hagemeyer failed to boost Indonesian coffee exports.

The Salim Group was not the only party to show interest in the Dutch trading companies. American retailer Sears Roebuck & Co. had a subsidiary, Sears World Trade (SWT) that was exporting manufacturing products. Wishing to expand to Europe, SWT in 1984 approached Borsumij Wehry, but was rebuffed. In January 1986 SWT succeeded in buying 20 per cent of Hagemeyer.[31] While the Sears unit at the time of the purchase said teaming up with Hagemeyer "will help our performance measurably", it did not work out, and the U.S. company terminated the agreement only after nine months.[32] Later, Hagemeyer hired a CEO, Andrew Land, who remained until 1999, and greatly improved performance. Land complimented Manny as a "very professional man, an intelligent, hard-working sparring partner."[33] Land pushed his managers and staff to improve Hagemeyer's operations. In December 1992, Hagemeyer's staff magazine *Sagittarius* printed an item it labelled "the competitor's creed":

> Every morning when the sun comes up, the gazelle wakes, and he knows that he will have to outrun the fastest lion, or he will be eaten. When the sun comes up, the lion also wakes. He knows that he must outrun the slowest gazelle, or he will starve. In the end, it does not really matter

whether you are a lion or a gazelle. When the sun comes up, you'd better be running.[34]

Land saw a huge rise in Hagemeyer's market-capitalization, from 125 million euros in 1985 to 4.5 billion euros in 1997. "If shareholders stayed [in], they were paid 100 times", Land said.[35]

When First Pacific was still an infant, the partners went on a shopping trip in the United States, looking for a bank. They journeyed widely, even to Miami, which was quickly ruled out as too inaccessible and too different. "We were like gypsies, travelling around", Anthony recalled, about their search.[36] His preferred target was New York-based American Express Bank, co-owner of the merchant bank where Manny had worked and the international banking subsidiary of American Express. It could not collect deposits in the United States but had significant financial-services business in Asia. Anthony said a possible purchase was discussed but turned down by American Express CEO Sanford Weill.

The search narrowed to the West Coast, which was closer to Asia. Manny and Anthony started talking with the owners of San Francisco's Hibernia Bank. On 31 December 1982, Liem's full Gang of Four team was on hand in San Francisco for the formal completion of the deal. The buyers paid US$56 million and injected US$32.6 million into Hibernia, then California's twelfth largest bank with US$900 million in assets and thirty-five branches. Hibernia was part of San Francisco history and had some notoriety. Started by four Irish immigrants in 1859, it was the city's largest bank at the end of the nineteenth century and helped finance the city's famous Ghirardelli Chocolate Co. The bank's name once grabbed national attention because of crime news. In April 1974, two months after U.S. newspaper heiress Patty Hearst was kidnapped by a radical group calling itself the Symbionese Liberation Army, she took part in a robbery of a Hibernia branch; a picture from a security camera — published around the world — showed her cradling an M1 semiautomatic carbine. Ironically, the twenty-year-old granddaughter of legendary publisher William Randolph Hearst was friends with the daughter of the family that controlled Hibernia. Patty Hearst was later arrested, convicted of robbery and sentenced to thirty-five years in jail. She was freed after twenty-two months and, in January 2001, President Bill Clinton pardoned her on his last day in office.

When First Pacific came into Hibernia eight years after the robbery, the bank was losing money. For 1982, it reported a loss of US$15.3 million. Under the new owners, the position improved, and the bank made a net profit of US$2.5 million in 1983. New chief executive Carl Gustavson, a former Chase Manhattan executive in Hong Kong, won kudos. In January 1985, the San Francisco Chronicle said that guided by its new Asian parent, the bank had "undergone a metamorphosis during the past eighteen months, from sleepy community bank to aggressive international and commercial lender".[37] The paper reported that Hibernia had begun financing wheat exports to Indonesia worth about US$330 million a year. It did not note that the work stemmed from Salim's lock on flour-milling. The *American Banker* magazine also commended Hibernia, headlining a December 1985 profile: "Indonesian Owners, Ex-Chase Executive Turn the Once-Ailing Hibernia into a Winner".

However, for First Pacific, the bank did not prove a long-term winner. As a community bank for its first 120 years, Hibernia did not have a letters-of-credit department for international trade. The new managers started one, and Hibernia received some fees from financing trade, but the volumes were tiny. Also, Hibernia was still saddled with plenty of problems. First Pacific co-founder Robert Meyer later said the U.S. Federal Reserve kept urging that more capital be injected into Hibernia, which "was in worse shape than we thought" when buying it. "You just couldn't do much with this bank", Meyer said, describing it as "a flea among elephants, and in constant need of capital". He recounted that Gustavson, the Chase Asia veteran running Hibernia, reported to Hong Kong that the bank was "a can of worms" and later told Meyer even "the worms have worms".[38]

Also, Hibernia could not develop synergy with First Pacific's assets nor with Salim's Bank Central Asia. Under Indonesian law, BCA could not be injected into a foreign company even if the Liems had wanted to go that way, which they did not. (Until an IPO held after Suharto's fall and Salim lost BCA, the Indonesian bank did not have any foreign ownership.) That BCA did not mesh with First Pacific's financial interests outside Indonesia showed the lack of synergy between the Salim interests at home and outside during the Suharto era. Salim just wanted First Pacific as an offshore vehicle, and it didn't want First Pacific investing in the Gang of Four's home turf. Efforts by Hagemeyer and Hibernia to work with Liem's companies in Indonesia "went nowhere", Institutional Investor asserted in 1988, noting that "an elaborate web of family patronage spun by the individual Liem partners left little for First Pacific".[39] First Pacific never promised that Salim assets would be injected into the Hong Kong company, though that's what some securities analysts were keen to see.

Institutional Investor quoted Manny as saying "The Liem pipeline was a pipe dream". Anthony did not have any dream, at least not for many years, of putting Indonesian assets into what was his family's lifeboat. He told the U.S. finance magazine: "We recognize that First Pacific must be treated as a stand-alone business in order to grow and be treated as a true Asian multinational."[40]

Back in California, Hibernia stayed profitable, but just barely. In 1986, Hibernia bought troubled United Savings Bank, in San Francisco's Chinatown, a deal assisted by U.S. authorities promoting mergers. Still, Hibernia remained too small, and lacked any service or geographic advantage. First Pacific came to realize it could make more money on investments in Asia, and avoid the regulatory hassles that came with owning a U.S. bank. In June 1987, First Pacific started looking for suitors, and eight months later, Security Pacific Bank of Los Angeles agreed to pay US$160 million for Hibernia. First Pacific's Thomas Yasuda said it was better for shareholders to "redeploy" the money put into Hibernia.[41] Thus, First Pacific's U.S. bank investment lasted only five years. But First Pacific had achieved its goal of buying a bank and a trading company within two years of starting.

A SURPRISINGLY FREE HAND

After First Pacific bought Hagemeyer and Hibernia and other businesses, Meyer said he and Manny needed to check something with Jakarta. "We asked Anthony, 'Who's going to run all this?' And he replied: 'You'."[42] Indeed, as First Pacific got rolling, its Hong Kong-based principals found they had more freedom than they expected from an Indonesian family business. First Pacific was not going to literally run the trading company and bank, but Manny and Meyer in Hong Kong help set their courses. While Anthony would be involved, he conveyed early on that, contrary to how things traditionally worked with Asian owners, the party putting up the money would not be making all the decisions. In the twenty-fifth anniversary party video, photographs of Liem and Anthony were shown with text saying that First Pacific was founded with initial capital of HK$4 million and "the faith of the Salim Group".

In 2002, when Anthony and Manny got into a tussle over strategy in the Philippines, Meyer told the *Asian Wall Street Journal* that when he and Manny entered First Pacific, "we said we didn't want to create an Indonesian-cultured company, but one with an international and professional orientation... we wanted to be a little arms-length."[43] In fact, Jakarta did not extend its arms far or often. "They [the Liems] left us alone... Anthony never sent anybody from Jakarta," said Meyer, who gave Anthony "vast credit" for his hands-off approach and "daring step" for a Chinese-owned business.[44] He recalled just one proposed deal in the first decade — involving a Hong Kong bank — that Anthony vetoed. Manny agreed with Meyer about the long leash they had, remarking: "Anthony and Uncle [Liem] were unique as Asians and as Chinese in giving us a relatively free hand to run the enterprise."[45] The owners' faith helped earn First Pacific and Liem some favourable media coverage. Forbes once wrote that for all their moneymaking abilities, ethnic Chinese business clans "have a major weakness":

> They jealously keep decision-making within the family... This reluctance to share power or wealth limits the ability of many Chinese-owned businesses to grow and assures that many will suffer under inept heirs. Indonesian multibillionaire Liem Sioe Liong is a glaring exception to the rule.[46]

The *Far Eastern Economic Review* in 1983 complimented First Pacific for being transparent about its Hong Kong moves. The weekly noted that while others used their high-priced shares to acquire industrial assets, the Liem family's policy "has been to buy with their own hard cash... They then inject them into the public companies, subsequently asking minority shareholders to fund their share of the cost through rights issues." *FEER* said Liem could "go international" because of bringing in outsiders like Manny, and it gave this assessment:

> The Liems had the foresight to realize that the dynastic and nepotistic nature of traditional Chinese business does not lend itself to perpetuating a business empire as large and complex as theirs... They began looking offshore too — partly, perhaps, because they may have felt it healthier politically not to have all their assets onshore but also because they saw the opportunities for Indonesia to capitalize on activities like international trading and banking which have a natural connection with the group's domestic activities.[47]

But as seen, it turned out there were not natural connections in banking. As for trading, Hagemeyer stumbled with the one commodity where it should have had synergy with Indonesia, coffee. Yasuda, who had been with a San Francisco law firm that worked on the Hibernia purchase, told the 1995 Harvard Business School case study:

It became clear that the business synergies and contacts that were going to come out of Indonesia would not be as easy as expected. The Liem investors were not a monolithic block; they had different contacts and diverging interests. Although we had a large capital commitment from the Liems in the form of assets, we could not rely on flows coming out of Indonesia to support the growth. We realized that we would have to row our own boat and make our own way in the world.[48]

First Pacific rowed into many places. In the mid- and late-1980s, before the word "churn" came into use for frequent buying-and-selling of assets, that was what First Pacific did. Institutional Investor said it became an "organizational octopus" with a "cat's cradle of a corporate structure".[49] Among the scores of assets that First Pacific acquired and sold were distributor Berli Jucker in Thailand, dispensary chain Metro Drug in the Philippines, Hong Kong real estate partnership Davies Properties (which became First Pacific Davies), Hong Nin Savings Bank in Hong Kong (merged with Far East Bank and renamed First Pacific Bank), Indonesian pharmaceutical manufacturer Darya-Varia Laboratoria, Hong Kong retail chain Dragon Seed, meat processor Thai Pacific Foods, Imagineering Technology in Australia (renamed Tech Pacific) and China Telephone in Hong Kong (renamed Pacific Link). Another two were New York specialty food retailer Deluca Brands and a total of four gyms in Hong Kong and Singapore belonging to California Fitness.

Some investments came under First Pacific Holdings, an expanded version of First Pacific Finance, and some under First Pacific International. In 1988, First Pacific reorganized and merged the two into one new listed vehicle, First Pacific Co. The Liem Investors had about 58 per cent of the unified company. Asked what he expected to gain from the reorganization, Manny replied "Bigger numbers, for one thing... the optical effect of having one big company will be good... people don't realize how big we are. Now they will."[50]

In 1988, telecommunications accounted for a mere 0.8 per cent of turnover of US$1.13 billion. But during that year, this did not stop the company from making telecoms a new "core" business, to add to marketing and distribution, banking and real estate. For much of the 1980s and early 1990s, First Pacific frustrated analysts by periodically redefining its core areas. Manny once called the 1980s "a period of growing, testing and making mistakes. We shed some tears and some blood in terms of experience. But we learned lessons and now have the core businesses we're comfortable with."[51]

Some analysts applauded the 1988 reorganization, but scepticism remained due to the company's seemingly insatiable appetite for deals. "There still seems to be an inclination to trade assets rather than maximize returns and build on them", complained John Mulcahy, research director at Peregrine Brokerage. "Virtually anything in their portfolio is regarded as for sale at any time." Mulcahy also said while he did not doubt the company's vision, it could use "more managers and fewer deal makers".[52] The *Asian Wall Street Journal* wrote that despite profit growth of 44 per cent in 1989 and 26 per cent in 1990, investors "have largely dismissed First Pacific as an upstart hooked on the stock market for cash flow, an addiction reflected in the company's net debt-to-equity ratio of 40 per cent to 50 per cent". Until the late 1980s, the paper added, the company "appeared to jump from one investment to another with no obvious strategy".[53]

The 1995 Harvard Business School case quoted First Pacific executive James Ng as saying: "As we bought and sold, we did not present a clear identity. Manny and his team came from merchant banking and were deal driven. They tended to think that the more companies they bought and sold, the more deals they closed, the more value they would add." Executive director Ricardo Pascua put it this way: "We were investment bankers; we learned on the job. We made a lot of mistakes and we had to learn that we had to stop buying small companies that we arrogantly thought we could turn around. But we did make a few very good moves and thank God the good moves overwhelmed the mistakes."[54]

Shortly before the Harvard case study was published, First Pacific far outbid competitors to win rights to develop a former Manila military base, Fort Bonifacio, into a giant commercial complex. This deal, about which more is written later, was striking for multiple reasons, including the offer price — 33,283.88 pesos per square metre — significant because, according to the *South China Morning Post*, the numbers sounded like words in Cantonese meaning "business-business-easy-money-business-money-money."[55] Years later, Manny told BusinessWeek: "I just said 'Look, can we just construct the numbers to make it look like it's good *feng shui*'?"[56] Authors of a 1999 INSEAD study said First Pacific made "a number of ill-calculated investments that would return to haunt it".[57] The company paid a price for evolving into "Deal Pacific", as many analysts called it. But after the 1997–98 Asian financial crisis, Manny said, the company settled into focusing on limited parts of Asia rather than the world.[58]

SHOPPING SPREE IN SINGAPORE

By 1990, Liem was using two vehicles to extend his reach and size outside Indonesia. The first was First Pacific in Hong Kong. The second was his own business in Singapore, KMP, which operated separately from First Pacific. Thanks to a deal in 1990 making him the largest shareholder in Singapore property concern United Industrial Corp. (UIC), Liem turned into a major real estate player in the island state. As usual, Liem was deliberately low-keyed, yet becoming a major office landlord raised his profile.

As noted earlier, Liem set up trading companies in Singapore shortly after Suharto took power. While Singapore was an important networking point (Liem had a home there by the 1970s), it did not become a significant place for investment until 1990. There were modest investments in the 1970s and 1980s, such as the now-defunct Chong Gay theatre chain, or which involved Singaporeans who had a bigger public profile. Liem gained some attention with his investment in a large downtown development called Marina Centre, where office blocks and other hotels including Singapore's Mandarin Oriental were built, but he was part of a cast that included prominent Singaporeans. A 1979 Singapore newspaper article identified Liem, who at one stage had a 16 per cent stake in Marina Centre, as "reputed to be a financial advisor to President Suharto".[59]

Several factors contributed to increased Salim activity in Singapore from 1990, including its proximity to Batam and other Indonesian islands (less than an hour away by boat), where the group's investments were burgeoning. Another factor might be to draw attention to the group's move to diversification, compared with 1989, when the Jakarta IPO of Indocement was a focus. Also, 1990 was the year that Salim's divorce from Sinar Mas in plantations and edible oils was getting set; it was perhaps not a coincidence that by far the biggest Singapore deal of the year, at UIC, involved Salim buying most of the shares of Oei Hong Leong, a son of Sinar Mas founder Eka Tjipta Widjaja (Oei Ek Tjong).

Whatever the reasons, Liem ended 1990 with a hefty Singapore base after a dizzying buying spree. In April, KMP bought packaging company Lamipak Plastic Manufacturer for S$8.75 million. In August, it acquired 75 per cent of livestock feed manufacturer Gold Coin Singapore for S$10.7 million, a move linked with its pig farm on Bulan Island, close to Batam. In September, KMP purchased 19 per cent of Inno-Pacific Holdings, a listed company holding the Singapore franchise for Kentucky Fried Chicken.

In November, the property deal with UIC started to unfold, though not smoothly. It started with announcement of a complicated transaction under which Liem would pay S$201 million for 9 per cent of UIC, a detergent-maker that had diversified into property by taking over bigger Singapore Land, or SingLand. UIC's CEO and biggest shareholder was Oei Hong Leong, who long did business outside Indonesia from a Singapore base. Part of the proposed deal's complexity involved Liem's selling his shares in Marina City to SingLand while receiving 9 per cent of UIC to add to a small stake he already held. Liem offered a big premium for the UIC shares, leading a *Business Times* columnist to speculate that Salim likely "wants a listed entity to spearhead its expansion out of Indonesia, and is prepared to pay a premium to achieve this".[60]

But Liem was thwarted. UIC's minority shareholders rejected the plan, uncertain of its implications. Still, Liem's interest in UIC was piqued, and he starting buying shares in the open market, in competition with Oei. It was Oei who had spearheaded the transformation of lacklustre UIC through the SingLand takeover in April 1990. Then on 28 December, in a surprising development, Oei sold 17.8 per cent of UIC, most of his holding, to Liem. That took Liem's stake to 24.5 per cent, just below the 25 per cent level that, under Singapore rules, would force an investor to make an offer for all of a company. Liem paid a smaller premium than under the thwarted deal, but it was still hefty — 36 per cent more than UIC's last closing price. In total, Liem spent S$291 million. Oei stepped down as CEO.

Within days, Liem again received attention in the Singapore media, though this time not involving a corporate deal. On 2 January 1991, he visited a well-known Buddhist temple he frequented, Kong Meng San Phok Kark See Monastery, to pay respects to the late abbot, who had died on 25 December. The *Straits Times* reported that the tycoon pledged S$2 million towards construction of a Pagoda of 10,000 Buddhas in the complex. A decade earlier, Liem donated S$500,000 for a hall at the temple.[61] At one time, the temple's website said the late abbot had more than 280,000 disciples worldwide, and that Lin Shao Liang, as it rendered Liem's name in *pinyin*, was among "the more famous ones".[62]

Back in Jakarta, Liem's UIC investment sparked some criticisms about capital flight. It did not help that two months earlier, Liem had made his first trip back to Fujian in decades. He was quoted in *Tempo* as saying it was thirty years since he had *"pulang"* (returned), which was read by some Indonesians to mean "returned home". Shortly after Liem's UIC purchase, a member of Indonesia's parliament claimed that sources told him Indonesians had invested US$64 billion outside the country. He did not offer any evidence.[63] In Jakarta in February 1991, when Liem attended the opening of two battery factories owned by fellow tycoon and friend Sofyan Wanandi, reporters had a chance to corral Liem. The journalists tried to get him to admit that his overseas investments constituted capital flight. No, a somewhat testy Liem replied, expansion outside Indonesia supported domestic business operations, similar to Japanese companies investing outside Japan. The tycoon then asked reporters what he should do, given that he caught flak wherever he invested. "Where can I go?" Liem complained. "If I invest abroad, you call it capital flight; if I invest here, you say I want a monopoly."[64]

By the start of the 1990s, Salim had significant interests in both Hong Kong and Singapore, which looked like a kind of insurance policy for when Suharto was no longer president. Indeed, First Pacific would later play that role, helping Anthony keep control of Indofood in the post-Suharto period. The stake in Singapore's UIC came in handy, too, for raising cash in the wake of Suharto's fall.

Notes

1. Records on file at the Accounting and Corporate Regulatory Authority, Singapore.
2. Interview with Anthony, 9 March 2008.
3. Interview with Anthony, 2 January 2007.
4. Interview with Manny Pangilinan, Hong Kong, 20 April 2007.
5. Ibid.
6. Ibid.
7. Ateneo speech of 24 March 2006, <www.millionaireacts.com/569/manny-pangilinans-success-story.html>.
8. Interview with Anthony, 14 January 2007.
9. Interview with Robert Meyer, Hong Kong, 22 May 2006.
10. Video shown at First Pacific twenty-fifth anniversary celebration, Hong Kong, 25 May 2006.
11. Interview with Pangilinan, 20 April 2007.
12. Ibid.
13. Interview with Meyer, 22 May 2006.
14. Yoshino, Michael and Carin-Isabel Knoop, "First Pacific Company Limited: From Letters of Credit to Personal Communications Networks", Retired Case Study 9-396-139, HBS Archives, Baker Library Historical Collections, Harvard Business School, 1995, p. 2.
15. Interview with Meyer, 22 May 2006.

16. "Celebrating 30 Years" section of First Pacific's website, www.firstpacco.com, accessed on 4 September 2012.
17. Interview with Meyer, 22 May 2006.
18. Jonathan Friedland, "Pacific Overtures", *Institutional Investor*, May 1988.
19. Anthony Rowley, "Birth of a multinational", *FEER*, 7 April 1983.
20. Ibid.
21. First Pacific Holdings annual report for 1982.
22. Video shown at First Pacific celebration, 26 May 1986.
23. Keetie E. Sluyterman, "Hagemeyer — 100 years from colonial trading house to global corporate", from <www.hagemeyer.nl>, accessed 26 February 2008.
24. Jonker, Joost and Keetie Sluyterman, *At Home on the World Markets: Dutch International Trading Companies from the 16ᵗʰ Century Until the Present* (The Hague: Sdu Uitgevers, 2000), p. 216.
25. Ibid., pp. 225 and 250.
26. Interview with Kwik Kian Gie, 17 March 2007.
27. Interview with Pangilinan, 20 April 2007.
28. "Hagemeyer-Liem link will benefit local operations", *Straits Times*, 18 February 1983.
29. Interview with Anthony, 3 December 2006.
30. Jonker and Sluyterman, *At Home on the World Markets*, p. 351.
31. Ibid., p. 352.
32. "Sears Unit Will Buy Controlling Stake In Hagemeyer N.V. Distribution System", *Wall Street Journal*, 9 September 1985.
33. Interview with Andrew Land, 11 December 2007.
34. Jonker and Sluyterman, *At Home on the World Markets*, p. 365.
35. Interview with Land, 11 December 2007.
36. Interview with Anthony, 3 December 2006.
37. Gail Schares, "Hibernia Bank ready to test its new wings", *San Francisco Chronicle*, 14 January 1985.
38. Interview with Meyer, 22 May 2006.
39. Friedland, "Pacific Overtures".
40. Ibid.
41. "Security Pacific is Buying Hibernia", *San Francisco Chronicle*, 1 March 1988.
42. Interview with Meyer, 22 May 2006.
43. Matt Pottinger and Sara Webb, "At First Pacific, Boss's Woes Began with Homecoming", *AWSJ*, 12 June 2002.
44. Interview with Meyer, 22 May 2006.
45. Interview with Pangilinan, 20 April 2007.
46. Andrew Tanzer, "First Pacific's Pearls", *Forbes*, 13 February 1995.
47. Anthony Rowley, "Birth of a Multinational", *FEER*, 7 April 1983.
48. Yoshino and Knoop, "First Pacific Company Limited", p. 3.
49. Friedland, "Pacific Overtures".

50. Barun Roy, "The reincarnation of First Pacific", *Asian Finance*, 15 June 1988.
51. Robert Sherbin, "First Pacific is Converting Some Skeptics", *AWSJ*, 27 March 1990. Sherbin later joined First Pacific, becoming its spokesman from 1997 to 1999.
52. Ibid.
53. Steve Glain and Bob Hagerty, "First Pacific Pursues Diverse Purchases", *AWSJ*, 10 June 1991.
54. Yoshino and Knoop, "First Pacific Company Limited", p. 4.
55. "First Pacific's Numbers Hit the Metro Jackpot", *South China Morning Post*, 11 May 1997.
56. Michael Shari, "First Pacific: Take Two", *BusinessWeek*, 12 May 2003.
57. Keeley Wilson and Peter Williamson, "First Pacific Company: Building an Asian Conglomerate", INSEAD Euro-Asia Centre, 1999, Case 399-144-1, p. 3.
58. Interview with Pangilinan, 20 April 2007.
59. "Indonesian takes big stake in Marina complex", *Business Times*, 5 December 1979.
60. Lee Han Shih, "UIC likely to emerge the winner", *Business Times*, 3 December 1990.
61. "Liem pledges $2 million for pagoda", *Straits Times*, 4 January 1991.
62. Accessed on 15 January 2009, at <www.kmspks.org/kmspks/history.htm>. (The website was later revised and there was no more "History" section.)
63. Paul Jacob, "Indonesian tycoons defend their actions", *Straits Times*, 9 February 1991.
64. *Suara Pembaruan* and *Jakarta Post*, 8 February 1991, and *FEER*, 14 March 1991.

13

HELPING HANDS

On the night of 4 September 1990, Jakarta bankers were stunned by a press release from the central bank unlike any they had seen. In a terse statement, Bank Indonesia announced that the board of supervisors — including the chairman — and the board of directors at PT Bank Duta had been fired by its majority shareholders following "operational mistakes" and foreign exchange losses. Bank Duta, widely considered to be Suharto's bank as its dominant shareholders were three foundations chaired by the president, was Indonesia's fifth largest privately owned bank. The dismissed bank chairman was Bustanil Arifin, Suharto's close ally and a good friend of Liem. Bustanil, a retired general, was Minister of Cooperatives as well as head of Bulog. And the losses incurred at the bank involved a senior bank executive, who happened to be Bustanil's son-in-law.

BANK DUTA: THE "FAVOUR-EXCHANGE" BANK

Bank Duta's "operational mistakes" turned out to be serious gambles on currency movements that caused the bank to lose more than twice its total capital. The Duta scandal encapsulated many elements of the murky and sometimes wild Indonesian business environment. Duta was a publicly listed company, yet there was a complete absence of transparency about its financial position as well as a woeful lack of prudent banking regulation. In the handling of the scandal, what showed to be functioning well was Indonesia's version of the "Favor Bank", taking a term from American writer Tom Wolfe's 1987 novel *The Bonfire of the Vanities*. One character in the book, a lawyer, declares that "everything in the criminal justice system in New York operates on favors. Everybody does favors for everybody else. Every chance they get, they make deposits in the Favor Bank… It's saving up for a rainy day." People who make regular deposits in the Favor Bank, he explains, put themselves in position to ask politicians for big favors.[1]

Suharto's Indonesia operated as a kind of Favor Bank. Liem, who had given 30 per cent of BCA's shares to Suharto's eldest son and daughter, was arguably the biggest "depositor" in Jakarta's version. In June 1985, when Liem was squeezed by cement overcapacity and debt, the president returned the favour. At times, Suharto needed to call in favours, and Liem responded, as did others in the case of Bank Duta. The Salim Group reaped good dividends for providing needed deposits. At the time of the Bank Duta scandal, that institution was one of only two sizeable private banks (the other was Bank Niaga) that was not majority-owned by ethnic Chinese; Duta's owners and top managers were all *pribumi*. With Bustanil atop both the bank and Bulog, it was no surprise that Duta had significant links with the state commodity agency. Some Indonesians thought of Duta as a state-owned bank, as its shareholding appeared to guarantee it could not be derailed. The main shareholders were three of the Suharto-chaired foundations: Dharmais, Supersemar and Dakab.

In April 1990 — less than six months before the central bank's shocking statement — Bank Duta had joined the wave of companies getting listed on the Jakarta Stock Exchange. It sold 20 per cent of its shares in an offer that raised Rp220 billion (then US$119 million). After the offering, each foundation owned 24 per cent of the bank, so 72 per cent in total, compared with a joint 90 per cent before the IPO. Some fund managers and investors were wary of the share-offer because of a lack of transparency or other concerns. Others found the IPO appealing, as they thought they were buying a bank that should be politically safe and steadily profitable; the offering was oversubscribed. Naturally, the prospectus did not provide any clues that far from being any kind of unsinkable stock, Bank Duta, at the time underwriters were selling its shares, had already created its own iceberg and the bank was fast approaching it. It was hard to believe in contexts outside Indonesia, but central bank regulators were in the same boat as individual investors, that is, completely in the dark about Duta's true financial state-of-affairs.

It turned out that Bank Duta deputy president Dicky Iskandar Di Nata had started accumulating losses in off-the-books foreign exchange trading in the late 1980s. About four months after Duta's listing on the Jakarta Stock Exchange, the Bulog chief discreetly asked the central bank if it could lend Duta US$100 million to settle foreign exchange losses. Bank Indonesia refused; even if it wanted to, it could not as it had publicly stated earlier — with Suharto's endorsement — that the state would not bail out banks. (In the aftermath of the 1997–98 financial crisis, the central bank indeed did that. It took over scores of banks, including BCA and Bank Duta.) In the early 1990s, when the economy was growing well, Bank Indonesia was hoping to stick to its policy that if a commercial bank got in trouble, the owners would have to dip their hands into their own pockets — not the state's.

In the lead-up to Duta's share offer, its foreign exchange bets kept rising as Dicky tried feverishly to recoup the losses. At one point, apparently, he was forced to cut losses, which came to light in banking circles due to talk about the situation by foreign counterparties. The central bank, embarrassed about its ignorance of the giant hole at Duta, had to get Dicky (whose previous employment had been at Citibank) and the bank's top management out of office, hence the public statement issued on 4 September. Bank Indonesia continued to maintain that it was not bailing out Duta, and that was true; instead, it quietly asked Suharto, as chairman of the foundations owning most of the shares, to come up with the money. In turn, the president "mobilized the funds", in the words of a government official, by getting his cronies to cover the tab. One month after the central bank announcement, the public learned that the loss was far larger than bankers had guessed. During September, Bustanil denied the loss was as big as US$200 million, a figure that had been bandied around, but he would not provide the amount. On 4 October, at an extraordinary shareholders meeting, Bank Duta finally revealed the full size of the loss, US$419.6 million — huge by Asian standards at the time.

Before the full loss was publicly disclosed, the funds had already been injected into Duta, which never experienced a bank run. Shareholders and the public were never told who actually supplied the money. The official version was that the three foundations, fulfilling their responsibilities as shareholders, supplied US$419.6 million as a *hibah murni* (pure donation) to recapitalize the bank. No one believed that the foundations themselves came up with the cash. Soon after the 4 October shareholders' meeting, a cabinet minister told a few reporters that the tab was split by Liem and an up-and-coming crony, timber baron Prajogo Pangestu, who in recent years had become close to Suharto's eldest daughter Tutut. Prajogo denied he helped pay the bill.[2] A Salim executive, too, denied a role. But eventually, it was confirmed that Liem was a key player in the Duta bailout — as the public widely assumed to be the case.

The first public confirmation of Liem's role in the Duta rescue came only in May 1994, surprisingly from his partner, Sudwikatmono. Local media had been pressing Suharto's foster brother to confirm speculation that Salim would use US$500 million it had just raised from an international bond sale to inject into another troubled bank, state-owned Indonesian Development Bank (Bapindo, short for Bank Pembangunan Indonesia). In denying those rumours, Sudwikatmono remarked that it was logical for the government, and not a private group like Liem's, to help a state-owned bank. Then he added that Liem "is very loyal. Look at the Bank Duta case; Salim [Liem] was very responsive, wasn't he? Actually, he wasn't asked. It [the assistance] was done for smoothness."[3] Many years later, Anthony confirmed the Salim role. The group helped "in order to solve the problem. Otherwise it's going to be a big blow for the total banking industry," he said. But he denied the bill was split 50/50 by his father and Prajogo, saying that "several" people gave money to the foundations controlling Duta. "We were the main contributor. We shared a big chunk of it." He said the donation was made "in return for what we have accomplished."[4]

There's an intriguing tangent to the story of Duta's rescue. A cabinet minister at the time maintained that after the central bank revealed Duta's woes, "people at Cendana (Suharto's residence) told me that Liem wasn't welcomed there for about two weeks; it seems the president was irritated because he didn't pay his pledge (for Duta) right away. Then after Liem paid, everything (was) back to normal… I think that was the only time that Suharto not happy with Liem."[5] Anthony denied there ever was a period when his father was not welcome at Suharto's house on Jalan Cendana. He also maintained that Salim did not get repaid by Suharto for the Duta help with a specific favour, but Adam Schwarz, in his book *A Nation in Waiting*, had a different view. He wrote that in October 1990, the month when the size of Duta's loss was revealed, Suharto instructed Mines and

Energy Minister Ginandjar Kartasasmita to change existing plans and give Liem and Prajogo rather than *pribumi* businessmen a role in a planned oil refinery and a petrochemical project. A year later, those projects were delayed indefinitely, due to debt concerns, and they never were built. But the way the Chinese tycoons were inserted and indigenous businessmen cut out angered many people, according to Schwarz.[6]

While the Duta scandal should have been a cautionary tale for lenders to Indonesian banks and companies, given their opaqueness, it seemed to spawn more bemusement than worry. As Bank Duta's woes did not spark a bank run or any hint of panic, a "business-as-usual" mood prevailed until the 1997 Asian financial crisis, when confidence in Indonesian banking evaporated rapidly, with disastrous consequences. Further illustrating how Indonesian business was anything but transparent, Bank Duta never reported its massive loss in its publicly available accounts. In its financial statement for the first nine months of 1990, the bank reported a pre-tax profit of about US$12 million. The only hint of the loss was a footnote stating that the accounts reflected the bank's position after it received that "pure donation" of US$419.6 million from its majority shareholders. A foreign banker commented at the time: "Duta first made a loss, then announced the loss, but now it's not reporting the loss. No wonder there's a credibility problem."[7]

Only nine months after the public learned about Duta, another bank that Bustanil was involved in fell into trouble. Bank Umum Koperasi Indonesia, which was run by cooperatives and known as Bukopin, was strapped for cash. Again, there was no state bailout — and again, there was a white knight. Bustanil, who headed Bukopin's advisory council, told reporters on 1 May 1991 that Salim was depositing Rp15 billion (then about US$7.7 million) at rates extremely favourable to the troubled bank. At the time, normal rates for rupiah deposits were a whopping 24 per cent a year, while Bukopin paid Salim only a paltry 6 per cent.

Salim's friend Bustanil — so close he once joked that Liem was his boss — was tarnished by the scandal at Duta. So it was no surprise that when Suharto named his next cabinet, following his acclamation for a fifth five-year term as president in March 1993, he dropped his ally from the dual role Bustanil held ten years as Minister of Cooperatives and head of Bulog. That ended his twenty-year tenure as chief of the logistics agency. Still, Bustanil stayed close with the president, to the end. Years after Suharto resigned, Bustanil remained treasurer of the Suharto-led foundation that funded mosque construction. His strong link to the First

Family was on display when Suharto died; at the graveside in Central Java, Bustanil was standing right behind Suharto's children. Bank Duta, meanwhile, suffered big losses after Suharto's fall that no one was willing or able to cover. In 1999, the bank was taken over by the government and in 2000 it was merged, along with seven other insolvent ones, into Bank Danamon.

A CURIOUS JOB SHUFFLE

Around the time Salim helped cover the loss at Bank Duta, Mochtar Riady was clearing out at BCA and shifting his full attention to his family's Bank Lippo. Not far into the post-Mochtar period, there was an episode involving Indonesia's bureaucracy that seems to illustrate the potency of BCA's main owner. This episode is worth looking at for what it indicates about how policy could be set in Suharto's Indonesia, and also because it appears to be a case of where the president quietly did a favour for Liem. Because the way it was done did not flout existing rules, no one — not even the principal involved — could say something had been done wrong.

The subject was a personnel move — not at BCA, but at Indonesia's central bank. In early 1992, a respected Bank Indonesia career official named Binhadi, then Managing Director for Supervision and Bank Development, was suddenly moved to become BI's Managing Director for International Relations and Foreign Exchange. The unexpected shuffle caught Jakarta bankers by surprise, because Binhadi had only been bank supervision chief for eighteen months and was considered a good fit for that demanding post. Binhadi, who had worked in the supervision department for twenty-four years, was a stickler for rules. He had a reputation for incorruptibility and integrity, and did not play "let's make a deal" with bank owners. Also, the juncture at which Binhadi was transferred was a critical one. It had only been about twenty months since the central bank had been caught flat-footed by the Bank Duta scandal.

Unconnected with Bank Duta, BI was starting to implement newly enhanced "prudential regulations" aimed at keeping the country's rapidly mushrooming number of banks — which now topped 200 — stay on the rails. In February 1991, it announced "Further Provisions of Pakto Concerning Improvement of Bank Supervision". Officials used the term "PakFeb", short for *Paket Februari*, for this set of measures, while sceptics anxious about unbridled bank expansion dubbed them in English "Pakto Reconsidered". Indonesia had opened the floodgate to a stampede of banks without giving enough thought to the potential havoc irresponsible owners could wreak by making huge loans to themselves. Pakto of 1988 had set Indonesia's first "legal lending limits" meant to govern how much a bank could lend to businesses controlled by the same owner. It stipulated that no more than 20 per cent of a bank's capital could go to any single borrower, no more than 50 per cent could go to "any group of borrowers" and no more than 10 per cent of a bank's equity could be lent to shareholders or owners of the business.[8] But PakFeb said improvement was needed in the implementation of legal limits, as "there has been ambiguity that needs clarification" — a way of saying there was no enforcement. PakFeb did not change the percentages for lending limits — those would change later as the subject got increasing attention — but it spelled out much more clearly that loans to a bank's shareholders were subject to lending limits.

Binhadi's removal from his bank supervision post came after he had done much work on PakFeb and on a draft banking law which parliament approved. *Editor*, an Indonesian newsweekly, in March 1992 published an article on his transfer under the headline "BCA and a Rotation at Bank Indonesia". It suggested a link between Binhadi's transfer and his purported coolness to Salim-proposed changes in the ownership structure of the group's only listed company then, Indocement Tunggal Prakarsa, that would have involved some BCA funding. The article quoted an unnamed banker from a government-owned bank saying Binhadi "was shifted because he refused a request from BCA which wanted to do some engineering to resolve a problem with legal lending limit".[9] The article contained a denial from BCA President Abdullah Ali, who said "BCA doesn't have a problem with legal lending limit." Binhadi was quoted by the magazine as saying the transfer was "a normal thing at Bank Indonesia" and declined further comment. What the *Editor* article implied but did not state was that BCA's owners, Salim, had mentioned to Suharto that a central bank official was an obstacle, and the president had that person transferred. When it came to sensitive topics such as the exercise of power or the president's family in business, regular readers of Indonesian publications had ample practice reading between the lines. (There was no linkage to this 1992 report, but *Editor* was one of three publications that Suharto shut in 1994.)

Anthony Salim, asked by the authors years later about the *Editor* article, denied that Salim had applied pressure to get Binhadi transferred. Responding to a question about the group's ability, in effect, to affect personnel or policy decisions because of Liem's bond with the president, Anthony said "we may be contributing the influence, but we are not the factor to decide".[10] But a former high-level government official involved in banking in the early 1990s asserted that influence was brought to bear in the case. He confirmed the unstated thesis of the *Editor* article that Suharto wanted Binhadi moved. The president, according to this official, let it be known that one director at Bank Indonesia was too rigid; soon afterward, the central bank — at that time a direct part of the government and not independent — carried out a management "rotation".[11] Publicly, it could be called "normal" practice, as it was routine to move senior officials to broaden their experience. But in this particular instance, it reflected how powerful Suharto was, and how afraid ministers and senior officials were of him.

This was not the only case where the president's views were taken as an instruction to make a personnel change. In another case, people knowledgeable about it say, Finance Minister J.B. Sumarlin in the late 1980s told Suharto during a routine call who he intended to promote to director-general of customs to replace the retiring incumbent. The president expressed lack of enthusiasm for the candidate, which sounded the death-knell for the minister's proposal. Later, the individual whom Suharto wanted to run the notoriously corrupt customs service — but who the president had not directly suggested — got the post.

Many years after his transfer, Binhadi stated he still did not know the background to the job shuffle, which he continued to maintain was "very normal". He said he could confirm that Salim informally told Bank Indonesia of a plan to restructure links between BCA and Indocement. In an interview, Binhadi said he informed Anthony that he believed such moves would have tax implications and suggested that Salim talk with the director-general of taxation about that; it was a "very normal thing" for banks to informally raise ideas, and he was not aware of any follow-up to this one from Salim. Pressed on whether his transfer to international banking had any connection with his contact with Anthony on Salim's informal idea, or implicit instructions later from Suharto, the retired central banker would only say: "I can't confirm. I don't know."[12] To outsiders, this was an instance where it seemed that someone perceived as an obstacle was shifted from his position. David Cole and Betty Slade, who studied Indonesia's financial sector, wrote after Suharto's fall:

In the 1990s, the "Suharto connection" became the "guarantee" or collateral underlying the viability of many enterprises and financial institutions, most obviously in banking and securities. Any financial regulator who attempted to apply prudential rules to such connected financial institutions or transactions, for example Bank Indonesia Managing Director Binhadi in 1992... was removed from his position. Politics and connection dominated.[13]

A LITTLE (MORE) HELP FOR FRIENDS

Between the Bank Duta case in 1990 and the start of the Asian financial crisis in 1997, woes hit more Indonesian banks. BCA was not called on to help in all cases, though there were some instances where either the bank or the Liem family extended some form of assistance, thus plastering some cracks in the banking system and bolstering Suharto. (In the Duta case, the help didn't come from BCA itself.) The episode involving Bukopin, the bank run by cooperatives, has already been mentioned. On the state side, there was the near-collapse of Bapindo due to the Golden Key scandal (discussed later), while on the private side, there was the 1992 cancellation of Bank Summa's licence. BCA also played some role in resolving issues at other banks. It was part of the orchestrated takeover of a small, mismanaged institution in Medan and Jakarta, Continental Bank, in August 1994. In a far bigger case, Liem's BCA got involved when the Riady family's Lippo Bank got in a cash squeeze in late 1995 when it was unable to meet a temporary clearing obligation. Some bankers blamed problems at its property arm Lippo Land and others speculated the cause was heavy cash withdrawals by Lippo Bank customers trying to apply for shares in the IPO for state phone company Telekomunikasi Indonesia. Lippo Bank denied there was any problem or need to rescue it, though central bank officials said later there was an issue that had to be tackled to halt rumours. The central bank quickly allowed banks to use their holdings of Bank Indonesia Certificates, which are deposits with it, to meet clearing obligations.

Bank Indonesia did not say anything, but in a behind-the-scenes move approved by the central bank, BCA and three other large private banks concerned about possible ripple effects for the entire banking system moved to support Lippo Bank with a special short-term credit line. Along with the others, BCA helped Mochtar out, Anthony confirmed many years later. From his recall, the joint credit lines — which were fully repaid — came to US$700 million or US$800 million. "That gave a lifeline", Anthony said, adding that Liem organized the joint help. "My father called [others] and said 'why don't we help him'?"[14] The *Jakarta Post* said the rumours about Lippo Bank were short-lived, thanks to it acting rapidly to counter "irrational claims". The paper's editorial also thanked four banks who gave support for accelerating "restoration of the public's confidence." Had rumours lingered, the *Post* commented, there would have been a run on Lippo Bank that "could have affected the whole banking system."[15]

Until the Asian financial crisis began in mid-1997, BCA itself was seen as rock-solid and the bank best positioned to help others through bad spots. As written about later, the bank was the natural candidate to help Bank Yama, owned by Suharto daughter and BCA shareholder Tutut, when it began to flounder in 1997. But while BCA was the most able to help other banks, when Suharto was pulled down in May 1998, the behemoth itself would collapse, with stunning speed.

Notes

1. Tom Wolfe, *Bonfire of the Vanities* (New York: Farrer, Straus Giroux, 1987), p. 384.
2. Raphael Pura, 'Timber tycoon confronts his critics", *Asian Wall Street Journal*, 27 August 1993.
3. Richard Borsuk, "Salim official denies group is providing funding for Bapindo", *AWSJ*, 19 May 1994.
4. Interviews with Anthony, 7 March and 8 April 2007.
5. Conversation with confidential source, Jakarta, 26 April 2008.
6. Adam Schwarz, *A Nation in Waiting: Indonesia's Search for Stability*, 2nd ed. (St Leonards, NSW: Allen & Unwin, 1999), pp. 128–29.
7. Richard Borsuk, "Bank Duta posts profit, avoids citing losses", *AWSJ*, 25 October 1990. In 1991, Dicky was sentenced to ten years in jail for "damaging" Indonesia's economy.
8. Binhadi, *Financial Sector Deregulation, Banking Development and Monetary Policy: The Indonesian Experience* (Jakarta: Institut Bankir Indonesia, 1995), p. 314.
9. "BCA dan sebuah rotasi di BI" [BCA and a rotation at BI], *Editor*, 28 March 1992.
10. Interview with Anthony Salim, 9 March 2008.
11. Private conversation, Jakarta, 14 March 2008.
12. Interview with Binhadi, Jakarta, 25 April 2008.
13. David Cole and Betty Slade, "Why Has Indonesia's Financial Crisis Been So Bad?", *Bulletin of Indonesian Economic Studies* 34, no. 2 (August 1998).
14. Interview with Anthony, 6 April 2008.
15. "Lessons of Lippo", *Jakarta Post*, 14 November 1995.

14

NOODLE KING

After Suharto gained power, the United States provided aid to help him consolidate it. But Washington could not provide one thing the general wanted — big supplies of rice. The United States pressed Suharto to accept surplus wheat under the "Food for Peace" programme. But in the 1960s, Indonesians weren't keen on wheat, which they did not grow. Fifty years later, rice remained the essential staple, but the diet of many Indonesians included wheat products in the form of instant noodles, available in a dazzling assortment of flavours — and a Salim company, Indofood, was market king. Per capita consumption of wheat shot up from a miniscule 0.3 kilograms in 1966 to around 9 kilograms at the start of the 1980s and doubled to 18 kilograms in 2010.[1]

As noted by the U.S. Department of Agriculture in April 2011: "The price of instant noodles is currently cheaper than rice and many more middle to lower income consumers substitute instant noodles for breakfast or dinner."[2] Over the decades, "Indomie" noodles became the Salim product best known to the public, and noodles became Salim's "money machine", as described by *SWA*, a Jakarta business magazine, in 1994 — by which time Indofood was the world's largest maker of instant noodles, surpassing Nissin Food Products of Japan, whose founder Momofuku Ando invented the instant noodle in 1958.

MUSCLING INTO NOODLES

The story of how Salim became a noodle giant reflects the group's potency, not pioneering. For years after Bogasari began grinding wheat, Salim did not try to make anything with the flour it produced. Also of interest is that another man, not Liem, started Indomie, a contraction for "Indonesian *mie*" (*mie* is Indonesian for noodles). This case was similar to that of Indomobil, where a product with the "Indo" prefix was originally owned by another party. According to Anthony, Salim got into the noodles business by "accident", not design. Behind the famous Indomie name was an enterprising businessman from Medan, North Sumatra, by the name of Djajadi Djaja, who also started a distribution company, Wicaksana. He reluctantly entered a partnership with Salim and, over time, was bought out. After Suharto fell many years later, Djajadi sued Indofood and members of the Gang of Four, contending he had been forced to exit the joint venture and sell the now-famous Indomie name for a pittance. His lawsuit was fought up to Indonesia's Supreme Court, where it was rejected.

Although instant noodles — generally referred to in Indonesia as "*supermie*" or "*Indomie*" — is for the most part associated with Salim, its origins had nothing to do with the business group. In 1968, the year before groundwork was laid for Bogasari's construction, a company called Lima Satu Sankyu pioneered the production of the first brand of Indonesian-made instant noodles, which it named "Supermi" (*mi*, meaning noodles, is also spelled "*mie*"). Supermi's creator imported flour, as there was no domestic milling at the time, and received technical help from a Japanese company.)[3] Two years later, Djajadi set up PT Sanmaru Food Manufacturing, which started its own brand, named "Indomie". Nine years later Salim established PT Sarami Asli Jaya, which began production in the early 1980s. Its product was named "Sarimi" — meaning "the essence of noodles". According to Anthony, Salim's move into noodle production was prompted by a severe rice shortage in the late 1970s. In 1978, the government spent a hefty US$600 million on rice imports. At that time, government officials and soldiers were paid partly by rice rations. Salim entered the business intending to supply noodles to the military and civil servants, so there would be more rice available for the public. Bogasari stalwart Piet Yap affirmed that the government asked the miller to promote flour as a good substitute for rice. "We were encouraged to start advertising campaigns on television and in movie theatres, extolling the virtues of noodles and bread to the population", Yap wrote in his memoir. More use of wheat, of course, meant more business for Bogasari. After the danger of insufficient rice supply passed, Yap noted, "it was suggested that we should go slow with the media campaign".[4]

Salim's entrance into noodle-making was not smooth. In a typically ambitious move, it ordered twenty production lines from a Japanese supplier. Each line could churn out 100 million packets of instant noodles a year, for an annual capacity of 2 billion packets. Anthony told *Tempo* in 1984 that the plan to make noodles for the state, which he acknowledged "looked as if the flour man doubled as a noodle man", did not unfold as expected. "It turned out that we made the wrong calculation: rice production in Indonesia got better, and the government didn't want to buy noodles from us anymore", he recounted.[5] By 1984, good weather coupled with widespread use of fertilizers and pesticides helped Indonesia become self-sufficient in rice for the first time since Suharto came to power. (The president was proud of that achievement and pleased to be recognized with an award from the Food and Agriculture Organization the following year.) For Salim, however, its gambit to become a noodle producer was in jeopardy. Some of its purchased production lines were already in operation, and Anthony said he was unable to cancel orders for the others as letters of credit had already been issued.

Confronted with more production capacity than it could handle, Salim mulled its options. The best one, the group decided, was to approach the Indomie man. As related by Anthony: "So we went to Indomie [and said]: 'You are my customer [for flour]; we have extra lines ... can you do something about it? Because I don't want to compete with you'."[6] Djajadi, however, did not want the lines, which operated differently than his Indomie ones, so Salim's Sarimi went head-to-head with Indomie. Salim spent more than US$10 million to market its new brand, and priced it just below Indomie's. "In one year, we got 40 per cent market share... Because it was cheaper than anyone else's", Anthony noted. Djajadi was getting a taste of Salim's clout. Later, Salim again approached Djajadi to join forces. "Then he started to realize, if not [joining up], it would be a long battle", Anthony recounted.[7] Djajadi capitulated. In 1984, they created a joint venture, PT Indofood Interna. Djajadi's side held 57.5 per cent, Salim 42.5 per cent. The CEO was a Djajadi-side man, Hendy Rusli. Within two years of the "marriage" between Indomie and Sarimi, the joint venture was strong enough to acquire the other significant brand, Supermi.

For Salim, the journey from having no role in noodles to owning 42.5 per cent of a company controlling the three leading brands was a swift one. During the New Order, business rivals sometimes concluded it was futile to resist Salim overtures. Over a period of years following the formation of Indofood Interna, control shifted from Djajadi's hands into Salim's. During that transition, the company periodically increased capital. When asked how Salim got the majority, Anthony said some stakes shifted from Djajadi's group as "they had their own struggle and then we end up having the majority ... they had five or six people in a partnership and they could not get along ... the whole ball was falling apart so we picked up the pieces." Whenever either partner wanted to sell shares, the other had the right of first refusal, he added, insisting that the reduction in the Djajadi shareholding was "not initiated by us. We were lucky to pick up pieces."[8] One key person in the shifting sides was Djajadi's brother-in-law and erstwhile partner, Pandi Kusuma, who became a shareholder in a Salim-led company, PT Panganjaya Intikusuma, which in 1994 was renamed PT Indofood Sukses Makmur (ISM) and restructured to be listed.

In 1992, Djajadi was dealt another blow, as Salim stopped using his distribution company, Wicaksana, and gave the work to its own company, Indomarco Prima. *SWA* magazine, in a 1994 cover story on Indofood, asserted that Djajadi was "forced to sell to the Salim Group". The article maintained that Liem's group "snatched" Indomie, citing speculation that Salim pressured Djajadi's Sanmaru into a joint venture by cutting its supply of Bogasari flour. Salim denied the allegations. *SWA* quoted Indofood Sukses Makmur executive Hendy Rusli, an ex-Djajadi man, as saying there was good cooperation between Salim and Djajadi's companies, as shown by their creation of PT Indofood Interna.[9]

Djajadi, who did not respond to requests for inputs from the authors, kept silent about his experience with Salim while Suharto was in power. He would have judged, not unreasonably, that there was no upside in complaining about the president's close business ally. Several months after Suharto resigned, though, Djajadi aired his complaints, alleging that he and his partners were forced to sell their stakes in the joint venture after borrowing beyond their means from BCA. He told *Business Week*: "They'd lend and lend and lend, and then — pop! They'd make problems for the company and then say, 'I'll help you solve the problem', " Djajadi said.[10]

In December 1998, seven months after Suharto stepped down, Djajadi sued Indofood, Anthony and Liem's Gang of Four partners — Ibrahim Risjad, Djuhar Sutanto and Sudwikatmono. His lawsuit asserted that trademarks for Indomie and Chiki snack-foods were bought from him in 1984 at "unreasonable prices under duress" and claimed damages of Rp620 billion (US$68.5 million). A lawyer representing Djajadi said the businessman "was forced to sell 11 food trademarks to the defendants for only Rp30,000 and three of the brands were the most popular ones in the country at that time."[11] Court documents filed by Djajadi's lawyers alleged that Salim later obtained a majority stake through an increase in the paid-up capital of Sanmaru. "The strategy to increase the number of issued shares to 8,000 from 400 and to raise the paid-up capital to Rp1 billion from Rp50 million benefited the defendants because they were large investors and could afford to buy up a large portion in the company and become controlling shareholders," the plaintiff asserted. Djajadi claimed he was forced to sell Sanmaru and the brands to Indofood Interna at an "unreasonably" low price. As the brands belonged to him personally, he said, they should not have been sold along with the company, and the sale was extracted by force. His lawyers argued that the initial Salim purchase of a minority stake in Sanmaru was "part of their grand design to monopolise the noodle market in Indonesia".[12]

In February 2000, the South Jakarta District Court ruled against Djajadi. He appealed to the High Court, unsuccessfully. The Indomie founder then took it to the Supreme Court, which ruled in the defendants' favour in May 2002. Djajadi pursued one final avenue, asking the Supreme Court — made up of scores of judges — to review its ruling. While that request was pending, Indofood's then-CEO Eva Riyanti Hutapea was asked about Djajadi's battle. She replied:

> That is just an attempt by a certain party, which is not true. In 1994, before our IPO, we made an announcement in the media that anyone who had problems, such as debts or disputes with Indofood, should come to us and settle the matters. However, no one came and thus it was clear that there was no problem.[13]

Djajadi's request for judicial review was turned down in January 2006. His unsuccessful legal battle over Indomie lasted more than seven years. From the late 1980s, Salim aggressively deployed its growing marketing, capital and production strengths to turn Indomie and its other brands into national icons. (In 2012, Indofood's website declared "You can't claim to be an Indonesian if you haven't heard of Supermi."[14]) The Indonesian Commercial Newsletter took the view that after the Liem group's consolidation, noodle-consumption surged and Salim began to dominate the market. Several brands "disappeared one after another as a result of Indofood's strong promotional and marketing offensives".[15] A survey by the newsletter's publisher Data Consult in 1994, the year Indofood got listed, found Salim commanded nearly 80 per cent of the Indonesian market, through Indomie (60.3 per cent), Supermi (7.8 per cent), Sarimi (6.7 per cent) and other brands (4 per cent).[16] Of course, Salim had more than just growing economies of scale on its side; it was milling the flour that all Indonesian noodle-makers needed. The government and Salim continued to maintain the position that milling the flour itself gave Salim no advantage, as Bulog was the seller, distributor and price-setter of all flour. Still, being the miller provided an advantage, as a 1999 report commissioned by the U.S. Agency for International Development and an Indonesian government project concluded:

> Before deregulation of wheat flour, Bogasari may have been earning excess profits on its milling of wheat flour in its resales to Bulog. All noodle producers purchasing wheat flour from Bulog, including the Salim Group, had to pay the same price. To the extent the Salim Group profited on the sales to Bulog, it therefore had achieved a lower net price of the key ingredient, wheat flour; the more wheat flour that Indofood used, the more wheat that could be profitably imported and processed by Bogasari. The Salim Group's cost advantage may have allowed it to sell more noodles by lowering price and gaining sales.[17]

PALM OIL: A MARRIAGE, THEN DIVORCE

Salim's entry into noodle-making at the start of the 1980s generated an interest in vertical integration in food. This led to a desire to get into a business starting to boom: growing and refining palm oil for cooking and a myriad other uses, from cosmetics to plastics. As usual, partnering with others with proven capabilities was important. Salim Group's first linkage in palm oil was with Sukanto Tanoto, a brash young businessman. The eldest of seven boys, Sukanto was born in December 1949, two months after Anthony. His father, like Mochtar Riady's father, came from Putian in Fujian province. Settling in Medan, the father started a small spare-parts and services business, which when he fell ill, his resourceful teenage son took over and expanded it. Medan was a tough town, and some of the Chinese businessmen from there acquired a reputation for being aggressive and shrewd. Sukanto was both. When he was only eighteen, he entered the plywood business. Sukanto started calling his businesses the Raja Garuda Mas (RGM) Group in 1973. (RGM later changed to RGE, for Royal Golden Eagle.) By the end of the 1970s, ahead of many, Sukanto began growing oil palm through his Inti Indo Sawit Sejati (*sawit* means palm), which Salim subsequently entered. Together they bought a cooking oil refinery in Medan from Lam Soon of Singapore. Many years later, Anthony said it was Sukanto who taught him all about palm oil. Anthony once described Sukanto as being "smarter than me and very shrewd. He started from zero; [while] my dad was already rich... I had a lot of contacts, he started on his own."[18] (Sukanto was not without controversies; one industrial venture he started near Sumatra's Lake Toba was pulp and fibre mill Indorayon. Its construction stirred strong opposition from environmentalists. After Suharto fell, the mill was forced to halt operations, but some years later reopened under a new name.)[19]

While Sukanto was still working with Salim, Liem entered a partnership for palm oil growing and refining with a fellow Fujian migrant: Eka Tjipta Widjaja (Oei Ek Tjong), founder of the Sinar Mas (meaning "golden rays") conglomerate, which became one of the country's biggest groups in the 1990s. Eka, at age eighty-nine in 2012, was listed as Number Two in Forbes Asia's listing of Indonesia's "Wealthiest 40" list, with assets estimated at US$7.7 billion.[20] Eka was born in 1923 in Quanzhou (an important port in history), in southern Fujian and at age nine, was brought by his father to Makassar, on Sulawesi island. The father opened a provision shop and the young Eka was immediately put to work, selling sundries door-to-door. From a young age, he demonstrated entrepreneurial flair, starting a biscuit business at age fifteen.[21] He moved to Surabaya and then to Jakarta, where he started CV Sinar Mas in the early 1960s to export commodities and import textiles. In 1968, he established a coconut oil refinery, CV Bitung Manado Oil, which sold "Bimoli" cooking oil.

The Salim-Sinar Mas marriage in cooking oil represented an important alliance even though it only lasted eight years. Salim's alliance with

Eka was formalized in 1983, in PT Sinar Mas Inti Perkasa — a company with a name that academic Ahmad Habir noted could translate as "the golden-gleaming essence of bravery".[22] For a time, Sukanto teamed with both Liem and Eka, but later the Medan man shifted away from oil palm to focus to other businesses, particularly pulp and paper — a sector in which he and Sinar Mas became fierce competitors (and one that Salim didn't go into it). The chemistry between Sukanto's RGM and Sinar Mas wasn't good.[23] Luckily for the Salim-Sinar Mas palm oil venture, there was far better chemistry between Eka and Liem, who apparently met by 1970. Eka, who had many children from his wives, built a strong position in refining cooking oil and started cultivating oil palm. He also became a giant in pulp and paper manufacturing. As with Liem, he owned a bank, Bank Internasional Indonesia (BII). "We grew big, but not by special licence", Augusto Nilo, Sinar Mas' then-managing director, insisted in 1993. "We are good to the president, we are friends with everyone. You can't be isolated from the government."[24] Although SMIP, as the joint palm oil venture was known, bore the name Sinar Mas, Eka's side did not have a controlling stake: it had 45 per cent, as did Liem's side (which at the start included Sukanto). The other 10 per cent was in the name of Suharto's oldest son Sigit, a BCA shareholder, and included interests of Sudwikatmono, so that was seen by outsiders as giving Liem's side 55 per cent of SMIP but the holding company was jointly managed by Sinar Mas and Salim. Sudwikatmono was made president-director and Eka was chairman while Sigit and Liem were on the supervisory board. The Eka-Liem joint venture was one of those cases where there are different versions of a joint venture's origins. In 1989, Eka gave his side in a magazine interview:

Q: Did you get together with Om Liem because you needed increased capital, or something else?
A: No! It's like this. In 1983, the price of oils suddenly increased, exports declined. The reason was a drought that hit the world, and that resulted in the raw materials for making oils — like peanuts, soybean, coconut, oil palm — were short... Then I asked help of Om Liem, who I had known 20 years. I said to Om Liem: "this company really can be profitable, only I by myself can't *tahan* [handle] if always blamed from left and right." Then Om Liem entered, although my profit is reduced, because it must be split, but no matter, [company is] safe and peaceful. After that, we cooperated in planting palm.[25]

Businessman Sofyan Wanandi, who knew Liem and Eka well, told *Editor* magazine in 1991 that the two tycoons teamed up in SMIP because Eka was having financial problems "so he asked assistance from Om Liem".[26] However, Anthony denied this, attributing the partnership to a business proposal from the Salim side for pooling their resources and strengths.[27] Another theory on the origins is that Eka wanted the alliance with Liem not because he needed money, but because he wanted the Salim chairman's connections to Suharto. Eka had friends among senior military and government officials, but didn't have direct access to Suharto, and he might have feared that Liem's expansion in palm oil could be at Sinar Mas' expense; that seems to fit with Eka's comment about their alliance making SMIP "safe and peaceful".

SMIP expanded smoothly during the period the Sinar Mas side was headed by one of Eka's sons-in-law, Rudy Maeloa. Indra Widjaja, one of Eka's sons, once described Maeloa as his father's "right hand". Property developer Ciputra, a Salim partner in some real estate ventures, praised Rudy's knowledge and experience in the business, saying that in oil palm, Rudy was "Number One in Indonesia".[28] But in 1988, the well-regarded Maeloa, married to Eka's daughter Sukmawati, died from liver problems at age forty-two. Afterwards, the nascent Sinar Mas-Salim palm oil powerhouse became an unhappy house. Rudy was "the one that made solutions", Anthony commented, "After Rudy passed away, then things were different."[29] Tensions arose between the two groups, though not personally between Eka and Liem. *Editor* quoted Eka as saying "I have no problems with Uncle Liem. I'm not against him. And Uncle Liem also is not against us. Our staffs aren't compatible."[30]

The point person on the Salim side, Johannes Kotjo, said he got on very well with Rudy but "I had trouble talking with the others." Kotjo also said he believed some of Eka's children felt that the Sinar Mas–Salim cooperation would become competition. In the mid-1980s, "Sinar Mas was already dominant in this area, but afraid of Salim's growth. I think Sinar Mas saw that Salim was rising," Kotjo reflected.[31] A Sinar Mas executive, Jahja Sudomo, gave a different take, saying the joint set-up was not efficient, as executives of both groups had to approve moves and the ship "had two captains".[32] Eventually, the conglomerate captains decided to call the whole thing off. This was not a simple matter, because there was a complex web of cross-shareholdings to deal with when dividing up the assets under SMIP. At one stage, an informal arbiter whose accounting firm had done auditing for both Salim and Sinar Mas was brought in to help, and a deal was eventually struck to divvy up the palm oil interests, which included management of about 200,000 hectares. Anthony and Eka signed a "joint decision" for divorce in December 1990, and the agreement, which divvied up the assets, was signed in May 1991. An SMIP executive vice-president was quoted as saying that what was worked out "is not a split but a reorganization of the plantations by our side as well as by Salim".[33]

But it was a split. An earlier Eka proposal to change the shareholding inside specific assets to have a clear controlling party was discarded and units went to one group or the other. Some plantations moved into Sinar Mas' control, while Salim got others. Given a choice of keeping of its original and popular cooking oil brand Bimoli or cash equal to its then-valuation, Sinar Mas opted for the cash, which Anthony put at Rp20 billion.[34] So Salim ended up with well-established Bimoli brand, and also Simas margarine, as well as three cooking oil factories, including one near Jakarta. Sinar Mas came away with two brands of cooking oil, Filma and Kunci Mas plus a series of factories in East Java, plus the cash for expansion. Sinar Mas regrouped its oil and agribusiness interests under Sinar Mas Agro Resources & Technology (SMART), which it listed in 1992. The ending of the marriage showed how at Salim, Anthony was taking initiatives and assuming more responsibility. He did not want to continue an uncomfortable relationship. A split-up was in line with Anthony's character, given his preference to have control over operations. Eka, according to Adam Schwarz, had "lobbied strenuously against a complete split of the two groups' joint assets and proposed instead that each group retain a minority stake in the companies of the other. That motivation had nothing to do with the underlying business, Salim and Sinar Mas executives said at the time, but with Eka's fear of severing links with the politically powerful Liem."[35]

Sinar Mas and Salim remained partners in a few separate ventures outside of SMIP, including Indonesia's sole soybean crusher PT Sarpindo Soybean Industri, completed in 1987. Indonesia needed to import soybeans for food and animal feed. Like wheat, soybeans were controlled by Bulog. It gave a monopoly on crushing beans to a group led by Sinar Mas. A consortium of cronies and their friends owned Sarpindo. Salim was part of the group because of its alliance with Sinar Mas in the 1980s. Others in the cast were Suharto's golfing partner Bob Hasan and youngest son Tommy and music impresario Setiawan Djody, who with Tommy bought sports-car maker Lamborghini in 1994. Anthony acknowledged that the Sarpindo shareholders made good money.[36] Sarpindo also sparked public criticism as a glaring example of a monopoly that raised costs — in this case, for animal feed — which in turn hurt the domestic poultry industry.

For years, Suharto ignored the grousing and kept Sarpindo in business. Schwarz gave an illuminating account of the president's way of doing things: When the agriculture minister and other officials approached him in 1992 with a proposal to end Bulog's monopoly on importing soybean meal and the use of a sole domestic crusher to cut costs for agribusiness, Suharto merely replied: "If you want to kill Sarpindo, go ahead."[37] Officials got the message and the proposed reform was spiked. Sarpindo was a small business compared with Bogasari, whose arrangement with Bulog was untouchable in Suharto's eyes. Eventually, after a local-content scheme that made the industry buy at least some soybeans from the plant was dropped, Sarpindo quietly stopped milling.[38]

Going their separate ways following their divorce, Salim and Sinar Mas each made out well in palm oil. In the view of some Indonesians, they did too well, given the unofficial near-duopoly in the business. In 1996, when rising cooking oil prices were upsetting consumers and government efforts to reduce them were not working, the Indonesian Commercial Newsletter concluded: "The fluctuations in the price of cooking oil on the domestic market cannot be addressed through the Government's intervention in the upstream palm oil industry. This is because the cooking oil industry in Indonesia is monopolistic/oligopolistic in nature with Sinar Mas Group and Salim Group as the only cooking oil producers and, hence, as the only buyers of CPO (crude palm oil). Therefore, these two groups can determine the price of CPO on the domestic market."[39] In 1997, Sinar Mas' land bank consisted of 582,208 hectares, of which 211,713 hectares had been planted, while Salim had 275,000 hectares, of which 125,000 were under cultivation.[40] Salim never was no. 1 among private Indonesian oil palm growers, but oil palm was an area in which the group expanded after Suharto's fall.

SHUFFLING ASSETS

In June 1992, Indocement unveiled the country's largest corporate transaction to date, a three-part asset shuffle that some investors welcomed and others criticized. The idea was to turn the cement company into a cement, food and property business. What some fund managers liked was access, for the first time, to Salim's food assets. But others strongly opposed the mixing of assets, as they could not see natural synergies between cement and noodles. The cost of the package that Indocement shareholders were asked to approve was about US$845 million. The plan's biggest part was injecting into Indocement the operations and assets of Bogasari Flour Mills. A second part had Indocement buying 51 per cent of each of nine companies, all involved in food-making, in what Salim then called the "IndoFood Group". The third part was the purchase of the twenty-three-storey tower housing Indocement headquarters and many Salim offices. A circular to shareholders said Bogasari and IndoFood both have "an indomitable leadership in their respective food sectors with strong growth prospects... the company will become an unsurpassable leader in the basic industries of cement and food in Indonesia in the foreseeable future."[41]

In noodles, Salim's position was already unassailable. It owned nine of the country's twelve main producers of instant noodles, accounting for about 90 per cent of the 5 billion packets made in Indonesia in 1992. The proposed deal drew attention to Bogasari, Salim's most controversial asset, which already had received flak as a monopoly that raised costs for consumers. Salim largely ignored the criticism. As long as Suharto was strong and civil society was weak, the flak was the equivalent of pebbles tossed at a tank.

Salim's planned asset shuffle was announced less than two weeks after the 1992's once-in-five-years parliamentary elections, a ritual that Suharto sardonically called a "festival of democracy". The Parliament, known as the DPR, had no power to initiate legislation, and Suharto appointed 100 of its 500 members to represent the military. He also vetted candidates for the other 400 seats. By design, New Order elections were always won handily by Golkar, which civil servants had to support. Suharto refused to call Golkar a "party". The two other permitted, tightly-controlled parties had to subscribe to the national ideology. In the 9 June 1992 vote, Golkar won 68 per cent, compared with 73 per cent in 1987. Vote results did not matter as the president never considered ending his monopoly on power, but 1992's drop in Golkar's vote percentage signalled growing unhappiness with the regime. That year, the economy grew about 7 per cent, and that meant Suharto saw no need for more economic deregulation. Yet much of the economy remained shackled, and Suharto's refusal to hurt family and friends carried hefty costs. One week after the 1992 election, economist Mari Pangestu, in a commentary, zeroed in on food as high on deregulation's to-do list. She argued that restrictions on imports of foods other than rice...

> don't benefit farmers overall, because proceeds from the higher prices tend to go to Bulog, and simply increase costs to consumers. Wheat, for example, is imported by Bulog and then sent to a privately owned wheat mill that has a monopoly. The wheat flour is in turn sold by Bulog. By controlling both imports and sales, Bulog has effective control on the amount of price of wheat flour. The situation benefits Bulog and the wheat mill, which can name their prices. It doesn't help Indonesian farmers, because they don't grow wheat. And it doesn't help consumers; in 1991, Indonesians paid an estimated 35 per cent to 40 per cent above world prices for wheat flour.[42]

Before Salim injected Bogasari's operations into Indocement, it got confirmation that the status quo would be maintained, according to Adam Schwarz, who quoted Bulog chief Bustanil as saying that Salim "signed an agreement with me that the monopoly will stay in place after the Indocement acquisition. So for as long as I'm around, we won't be deregulating wheat imports."[43] Salim maintained that even if its cosy arrangement with Bulog ended, the future was still bright. With rising flour demand, utilization of the mills will increase and "this would further enhance Bogasari's competitiveness as a low cost producer", Indocement said in its circular to shareholders. Flour operations, it said, "would remain competitive even if the flour market would be deregulated". Indocement's circular contained the first financial information made public about Bogasari. It gave the operating profit in 1991 as Rp100.4 billion (about US$50 million then), double that from the year earlier. Sales of flour in 1991 amounted to Rp385.6 billion, a 19 per cent gain from the previous year.[44] Good as Bogasari's numbers and prospects may have looked, some analysts never warmed to the deal.

Why did Salim have a cement company acquire its food businesses? Indocement's answer was that this allowed the company to do something with the cash its business was generating, other than expand in cement. Years later, Judiono Tosin, Indocement's finance director at the time, said the company could have paid higher dividends, but under Indonesian law these were doubly taxed — once for the company and once for the recipients

— so Indocement did not want to go that route. So, Tosin contended, "the only choice at that time was growing — but grow where? In cement? That wouldn't be good for the market or for image…"[45] In 1992, Indocement had 52 per cent of the national market and was not looking to give critics more ammunition for attacking the group.

To some analysts and others, another motive was suspected: getting new tax breaks for Indocement. In the shareholders' circular, the company's financial advisors said that in 1992, Indocement was expected to "exhaust all its outstanding tax losses carried forward, amounting to Rp271 billion rupiah as of 31 December 1981".[46] The asset-shuffle, the *Far Eastern Economic Review* wrote, appears to be "at least partly driven by Indocement's desire to avoid paying taxes". It noted that that the deal will limit tax liabilities "through a substantial increase in depreciation and goodwill charges".[47] Tosin denied that tax breaks for Indocement were a key motive, though he noted that finding the lowest level of tax a company can pay is "the job of any chief financial officer".[48]

Critics of the shuffle also had concerns with valuations. One was the amount of "goodwill" Indocement shareholders were paying for 51 per cent of what was then called the IndoFood Group. That intangible accounted for 92 per cent of the Rp777 billion being paid, an amount many analysts found excessive, however bright the future of noodles. (The digits, by coincidence, added up to 21, Liem's lucky number.) Tosin maintained at the time — and reiterated the view sixteen years later — that the 1992 transaction was "a very good deal" for minority shareholders. "It was a very, very fair valuation", he asserted.[49]

The deal was to be financed with Rp400 billion from internal cash resources and Rp1.315 trillion of long-term borrowings. Repaying those borrowings would trim Indocement's profit in future, which was one reason some analysts didn't warm up to Salim's restructuring. There was some borrowing through promissory notes to sellers related to the substantial shareholders, and the remainder drawn from a facility of up to Rp800 billion from Salim's BCA. If there was any issue from this related to legal lending limits — the subject which *Editor* linked to the transfer of Binhadi at Bank Indonesia from heading banking supervision (discussed in Chapter 13) — it was not raised publicly at the time.

Whatever the objections, there never was doubt that Indocement shareholders would approve the asset-shuffle. To give the move more credibility, Salim individuals and related parties that controlled 58 per

cent of Indocement's shares opted not to vote, though they were allowed
to under Indonesia's stock market rules. (Afterwards, exchange rules were
amended due to complaints that majority shareholders could impose
major changes on powerless minority ones. New regulations barred
"related-party" shareholders from voting on major proposals — though
the will of a company's major owner would remain extremely difficult
to thwart.) In the Indocement case, the majority owners did not have to
worry about minority shareholders nixing their plan. The government,
holding 26 per cent equity, was not going to vote against the proposal
when a yes-vote was recommended by the state-owned securities firm.
When there was a show of hands at the 28 July extraordinary meeting,
no dissenting ones went up. When the chair asked if there were
abstentions, one middle-aged man put up his hand. He declined to talk
with reporters.

The big winners of the restructuring, to Australian commentator
Michael Backman, were the Gang of Four members. He asserted they
jointly collected more than US$300 million from cashing out Indocement
shares. Backman noted that the cashing out "occurred just prior to the
government's decision to soften the flour miller's monopoly, a move that
promised to reduce the company's future earnings and hence the total
value of the company."[50] The monopoly-softening he referred to was a June
1993 announcement that flour-milling was no longer closed for investment,
and that a once-announced stipulation that any new miller had to export
65 per cent of its output — which no party could comply with — was
scrapped. That 1993 mini-deregulation of wheat — Bulog's control was
not affected — did not dent Bogasari. However, it did pave the way for
other connected parties to enter the industry. Small mills in Java were later
started by Tutut and by the family of former Bulog chief Bustanil.

One person crucial to Bogasari's creation was not happy with the
1992 developments involving that company and Indocement: tycoon
Robert Kuok, who was pivotal to getting the mill started. Kuok was not
interested in being part of a cement company. Asked in 2010 about how his
involvement with Bogasari ended, he replied tersely that around August
1992, Anthony "with great persistence and insistence, made me accept
Indocement shares and thus flushed me out of Bogasari".[51] As it turned
out, the 1992 asset-shuffle was just the first round of restructuring. There
would be changes in the recipe sooner than many investors expected.

PUTTING INDOFOOD ON INVESTORS' MENUS

Just two years after Salim injected food assets into Indocement, it shifted most of them into a new listed company just for its food business. It involved the kind of corporate moves that had become a hallmark of the group and that annoyed some analysts. Bogasari was left inside the cement company — for a time — but the noodle industry was restructured. Plans were laid for a listing that would retire debt, provide funds for acquisitions that reduce tax liabilities and raise Indofood's profile in a way that being part of Indocement — where it provided at least 40 per cent of revenue — could not. "Psychologically, I think they've reached a point where they feel the need for the participation of the public", corporate researcher Wilson Nababan said.[52] Another reason may have been that Salim wanted to have a larger number of publicly traded companies, which let the public have a piece of more assets — but leave control with Salim. Basically, it could "unlock" value for shareholders in its first listed company, Indocement, while keeping a lock on control through the ownership structure.

Just as Indocement faced an obstacle to listing in 1989 — the fact that it was not profitable for two years before going public — Indofood faced a hurdle of a different type. In response to investor complaints about how expensive Indonesian share-offerings had become, market regulator Bapepam in November 1993 imposed a rule that newly issued shares could not be priced at more than thirteen times the current year's projected earnings. Around this time, the average price-to-earnings ratio of a listing on the Jakarta Stock Exchange was more than twenty-seven times. In January 1994, Bapepam responded to criticism by allowing companies to price shares at up to fifteen times, rather than thirteen times, the current year's earnings.

Even with the higher ceiling, the rule dented Salim's plans as an Indofood IPO could not be priced as high as the group wanted. Salim executives indicated they might price shares at around twenty times 1994's anticipated earnings, if they could, and they expected to raise at least US$500 million in an Indofood IPO. A banker from Union Bank of Switzerland, working on the Indofood fund-raising plans, was reported as predicting that if Salim "couldn't get away with a higher P/E than 15, they wouldn't go public at all".[53] But Salim really wanted to go ahead with an IPO, which would give it more leverage to borrow. Also, the Jakarta

Stock Exchange had had an excellent 1993, with the index soaring 115 per cent from the previous year.

Indofood was a sellable "growth story". By 1993, Indonesians were eating more than 5 billion packs of instant noodles a year, compared with 885 million packs in 1986. In 1993 alone, per capita consumption rose 42 per cent to 11.2 packs a year from 7.9 the previous year.[54] But while Indofood remained clearly the market leader, competition was increasing — which prompted Salim to raise money to add capacity. An Indonesian group named ABC, which made the interesting combination food sauces and batteries, entered the noodle business in 1993 with President Group of Taiwan. Another entrant was the Roda Mas Group, which in 1992 started a venture with Japan's Nissin Food, the original instant noodle manufacturer. Selling shares in Indofood would make another part of the Salim empire public while maintaining the family's dominance, as Indonesian rules allowed a listing company to offer less than 10 per cent of equity.

Salim was not going to let the market regulator's cap on IPO prices derail a listing. When Indocement's planned IPO hit a legal roadblock in 1989, the Finance Ministry gave it a waiver from compliance with a rule on past profitability. With Indofood, Salim did not seek a waiver; it found a way around the ceiling on P/E ratios. This was done by making its IPO tiny, selling only 2.75 per cent of Indofood shares, raising just US$60 million. But shortly before that IPO, Salim collected US$500 million by issuing, through a British Virgin Islands company, "mandatory exchangeable bonds" that could convert into Indofood shares in 1995. The bonds, sold in March 1994, carried interest of 3–4 per cent a year — on the low side — but were attractive because of the way they could turn into shares. The conversion would be at a price twenty-six or twenty-seven times Indofood's diluted 1994 earnings per share. At the time of Indofood's June 1994 IPO, in which shares were sold for Rp6,200 each (US$2.75), bondholders owned nearly half of the company.

To prepare for the bond issue and the IPO, Salim's food businesses were restructured. In February 1994, a unit named Panganjaya Intikusuma was renamed Indofood Sukses Makmur (ISM). Just one week later, newly created ISM was restructured to encompass eighteen food-processing firms in the informal "Indofood Group". In the process of restructuring ISM to go public, the Liem family spread ownership. When Panganjaya initially became ISM, it had only four shareholders: Indocement (51 per cent), Liem with 16.83 per cent and sons Andree and Anthony with 16.08 per cent each. After ISM's restructuring, the bond issue and the IPO, Indocement had 49.6

per cent of newly listed ISM and bond vehicle Global Mark International Ltd., the British Virgin Islands-registered entity, had 46.4 per cent. The public owned 2.75 per cent while seven individuals — the Gang of Four plus Andree, Anthony and Djuhar Sutanto's son Tedy — each had stakes of less than 0.15 per cent. Because the government at this stage continued to own 26 per cent of Indocement — the legacy of the 1985 bailout — the state held nearly 13 per cent of ISM (which the text will call "Indofood" from here on).

Just before the IPO, Indofood faced a public relations problem. Rumours started circulating that people in South Sumatra had been poisoned by eating its noodles; one version even alleged that there were deaths. The rumours, never substantiated, almost certainly were an effort to hit at Salim. Indofood's IPO was not affected, though noodle sales in some rural areas dipped. The company acted swiftly with a campaign to assure the public its noodles were safe — and gave away free packets to counter the rumours — and delayed a price increase widely anticipated after the IPO.

TOO BIG TO TOUCH

In February 1995, Salim reversed course by moving to take Bogasari out of Indocement thirty months after putting it there. The action, injecting Bogasari into Indofood, refocused attention on the flour-maker, whose virtual monopoly on milling wheat was still sacrosanct. Sudwikatmono explained that the reason for this latest shuffle, which brought Indofood tax advantages for depreciating Bogasari assets, was to let Indocement "have a business structure that is more focused on its core business — cement".[55] This was a 180-degree change from its 1992 rationale that Indocement should not just be a cement company. The 1992 decision had confounded and displeased some analysts, and three years later Salim basically was agreeing with them. Not surprisingly, some analysts remained cool to Salim and Indocement. A Smith New Court report in July 1995, which put a "sell" on Indocement both short term and long term, noted the company was owned by magnate Sudono Salim before remarking "Inter-group transactions between listed and privately-owned companies under his control have smeared his management's reputation."[56]

The strategy-switch that took food out of listed Indocement generated a new attack on Bogasari's unassailable position and Bulog's untouchable array of trade monopolies. Between 1992 and 1995, grousing about Suharto and how his family and circle were taking larger chunks of the economic cake had become louder. In the first half of 1995, as Salim staff were working out a price for transferring the mill to Indofood, the country's stalled deregulation effort came into the public eye in a way Suharto aides had to respond.

For Suharto, the main catalyst for deregulating was the annual meeting of Indonesia's donors, where billions of dollars of aid were pledged by foreign governments. The World Bank had been convening the annual sessions since 1992, the year a peeved Suharto kicked out the Dutch, who had hosted Inter-Governmental Group on Indonesia (IGGI) meetings since they started in 1967. (In a Sukarno-like step, Suharto told Holland to "go to hell" with its aid after a Dutch minister rapped Indonesia's human rights record and 1991 massacre in East Timor.) For a donors' meeting in July 1995, Suharto needed to sign off on a deregulation package by June. It had become standard for Jakarta to unveil measures shortly before meetings, so lenders could applaud Indonesia's ostensibly ongoing commitment to reform.

When donors had met the previous year, it was easy for them to maintain their applause due to one pro-foreign investment step just taken. Suharto signed a decree discarding rules put in after the 1974 Malari riots that forced foreigners to eventually divest to Indonesians 51 per cent of equity in most ventures. Peraturan Pemerintah (Government Regulation) No. 20 (PP 20) of 1994 was a strong move to help Indonesia compete with China, now drawing investors in droves. But Suharto never announced PP 20, whose existence was not known for two weeks, until Industry Minister Tunky Ariwibowo got the president's approval to tell the palace press corps.

Foreign investors warmly welcomed PP 20, but some enthusiasm waned within days. One of eight sectors that the regulation opened was "mass media", but Information Minister Harmoko said the president assured him that such investment "won't take place" as it was banned by a 1982 press law. This was typical of the mixed signals frequently sent out in Suharto's Indonesia. Such vague rules exasperated potential investors. Investment Minister Sanyoto Sastrowardoyo insisted there was no inconsistency. The opening of mass media to foreign investors, he said, was a "general government regulation. But if there's a special stipulation in a sector" such as the press law, that stipulation takes precedence.[57]

For Suharto, the relaxation on foreign ownership was a win-win situation; he won kudos from international donors for giving investors more scope. But the scope was not widened as much as it sounded, and businesses such as broadcasting remained in the hands of the state, his family and friends. Also, while allowing 100 per cent foreign ownership in some sectors was definitely welcome, not many investors went that route as they needed an Indonesian partner to cope with Indonesia's large bureaucracy, a labyrinth nearly impossible to navigate without paying bribes.

Despite PP 20, there was good reason to worry about deregulation — which was not moving forward. The World Bank sponsored a conference in April 1995, titled "Building on Success: Maximizing the Gains from Deregulation", aiming to convey to Suharto anxiety over "reform fatigue". "For various reasons, substantial parts of the economy remain in the grip of oligopolies", a bank paper said, noting the continuing plethora of restrictions. Included, it said, were "price controls, entry and exit controls, exclusive licensing, public-sector dominance, and ad hoc interventions by government in favour of specific firms and sectors".[58]

Suharto's technocrats were trying to foster change, but without success. In February 1995, they sent Suharto a proposal to end the special position of Bulog, which reported directly to the president. They could not publicly promote their proposals, for doing so would surely mean rejection; Suharto reacted sharply to people trying to force his hand. In fact, there was no way of changing Suharto's mind on Bulog. (His unyielding stance would only change during the 1997–98 financial crisis, when Indonesia became dependent on the IMF.) Still, in April 1995, optimism that the coming deregulation package would touch Bulog was sparked by a speech that agency chairman Beddu Amang gave at that World Bank conference. "Bulog is prepared to move towards a more open trading regime to help the Indonesian economy become more efficient and competitive", he declared. "Bulog does not want to be part of the high-cost economy." He noted that budget realities, World Trade Organization rules and major economic changes over twenty-five years have "refocused attention on Bulog's future mission".[59]

But Suharto liked Bulog just the way it was. The deregulation package he approved in May steered from touching it. Tariff reductions were made on 6,030 items, but this was a numbers game to camouflage that no meaningful deregulatory steps were taken. Even the Indonesian Chamber of Commerce and Industry (KADIN), which routinely applauded government moves, gave this package a thumbs-down. "We don't think the non-tariff import barriers on soymeal, wheat flour, sugar, clove and salt are justifiable", the chamber concluded. KADIN vice-chairman Iman Taufik said Bulog monopolies were okay if they are "truly aimed at protecting consumer interests. But what we cannot understand is why Bulog's monopolies on wheat flour and soymeal have been granted to private companies without clear-cut, transparent procedures" like competitive bids. Such monopolies have become a major component of Indonesia's "high-cost economy", he stated.[60]

In mid-June, the World Bank's annual report for the July donors' meeting gave some attention to Bulog and joined in describing Indonesia as "a high-cost economy" — one way of saying there was a great deal of corruption. It said manufacturing had a "very high" level of concentration and that, because of restrictions on competition, many industries were not globally competitive and featured "cartels". Suharto knew that such grouses would not translate into a cut in aid pledges. Indeed, the donors' meeting pledged US$5.4 billion, up from US$5.2 billion in 1994. The donor support bolstered Suharto's sense of confidence. The past year had been a good one, from his point of view. In 1994, GDP grew more than 7 per cent a year and foreign-investment approvals — aided by PP 20 — nearly tripled, to US$23.7 billion. On 10 August 1995, a beaming Suharto witnessed the first flight of Minister Habibie's homemade 35-seat plane, a project the technocrats loathed and the president loved. Along the way, and to the chagrin of some, Suharto had collected an unmerited credential as a free-trader when he hosted U.S. President Bill Clinton, Chinese President Jiang Zemin and others at the second-ever Asia-Pacific Economic Cooperation (APEC) summit in Bogor, in November 1994. Suharto proposed a vaguely worded resolution committing members to pursue free trade throughout Asia-Pacific by 2020. To cynical critics, this meant Bulog might have another 25 years as an "untouchable".

For its part, Bogasari said it welcomed deregulation, so it could sell flour not just to Bulog. Bogasari director Franky Welirang, Liem's son-in-law, interpreted deregulation as meaning "our flour will flood Asia. Our fixed costs are one-tenth of others."[61] But liberalization was definitely not on the cards. On 1 July 1995, Bulog raised Bogasari's fee for milling wheat for the first time in seven years, to Rp71.70 per kilogram of flour rather than Rp48.50. Analysts calculated the rise gave Bogasari nearly Rp55 billion more a year. The fee hike was announced about the same time as the pricing for Salim's plan to shift Bogasari from Indocement to Indofood, set at Rp1.86 trillion (US$835.4 million). To some, this was generous to

Indocement, which now wanted to expand capacity because Indonesia's boom meant cement shortages. While Indocement and Indofood's minority shareholders were highly likely to endorse Bogasari's transfer, they were courted by Salim, thanks to that stock-market regulation — put in after the 1992 shuffle — that let only minorities vote on major moves. Many analysts who didn't like the 1992 move were cool to this transaction, too, because of pricing or other factors such as belief that taking in Bogasari would trim Indofood's gross margins.

Just before the 30 June shareholders' vote, Investment Minister Sanyoto made a surprise announcement informing a parliamentary committee that Indofood would not get approval for applications to build four more factories as the government would block expansion for companies controlling at least 50 per cent of the market for a product; Salim then commanded nearly 90 per cent of the instant noodle market. It was unprecedented for an official to publicly say "no" to Salim, and here was a Cabinet minister taking on the best-connected conglomerate at a time when Indonesia did not have any anti-trust or competition laws.

At Indofood's shareholders meeting, where, unsurprisingly, no one voted against the Bogasari proposal, no one brought up Sanyoto's comment. Afterwards, though, Sudwikatmono rapped him. "I really regret the government's move to limit conglomerates from expanding their production capacity", he commented, adding that it "might cause them to invest abroad".[62] Sanyoto was forced to sing a different tune a few days later; he emerged from a meeting with Suharto stating that a policy limiting industry concentration will be enforced "on a case-by-case basis" and that groups were encouraged to expand production as long as most new capacity was for exports. In his clumsy retreat, Sanyoto suggested that Indofood get listed on Jakarta's stock exchange — which it already had, one year earlier.

While parliament was toothless during Suharto's tenure, some members nevertheless kept the topic of Bulog and its partners in the public eye. Over a three-month period in 1995, Bulog chief Beddu was called in twice to defend his agency. At the first session, he stated that Bulog's monopolies were necessary and transparent. "We are a non-profit monopoly and we cross-subsidize", he declared, "We don't look for profits."[63] Afterwards, the private Institute for Development of Economics and Finance accused Bulog of subsidizing wheat flour millers, meaning Salim, to the tune of about US$135 million a year. An editorial in the *Jakarta Post* blasted monopolies. It said Salim...

has been raking in high profits both from grain milling and from the below-market price of flour. No wonder the group succeeded in dominating the noodle market in just a few years. Even countries which pursue a liberal economy (free-fight capitalism) do not allow such flagrant market distortions and oligopoly from the upstream to the downstream industries.[64]

At Beddu's second appearance in Parliament, an MP suggested that Bulog halt subsidies to conglomerates "and channel them to cooperatives" instead. The Bulog chief replied: "We do not subsidize Bogasari or any other firm. Consumers are subsidized." Beddu contended that flour prices in Indonesia were lower than in many Asian countries.[65] After Beddu's second testimony, Suharto weighed in with his September 1995 talk at Tapos in which he defended his friendship with Liem. The business arrangements with Liem were undertaken for national interests, he said, adding that Salim was just a "tailor" who worked for the state. Suharto poked some fun at Liem's heavily-accented Indonesian. He told the audience that when Liem approached him to ask what he could do for the people, he referred to himself as a "working man" (which Suharto pronounced like "*olang kelja*" instead of "*orang kerja*"). Suharto told his audience: "Then I gave guidance (*petunjuk*). You don't just do trading to get profit, but also develop industry that the people require. What's an example? Food. We are producing but there are other food substances that are also still needed. Do you have other friends for coming up with capital?"[66] Noting that Liem replied in the affirmative, Suharto said he continued: "It's good if you can set up wheat flour ... because the government has assistance credits from America for [buying] wheat. But you only process [the wheat], the reins stay with Bulog."[67] That day in Tapos, the president indicated he didn't like people making Bogasari an issue. Soon after, Bulog disappeared as a hot topic in the domestic media, though two years later, it was back on a front-burner.

At the time of Suharto's remarks, Bogasari had begun a big-time expansion. The Jakarta mill's capacity was raised from 6,500 tonnes of wheat a day to 9,500 tonnes — nearly fifteen times its original size. The American trade journal *Milling & Baking* called the Jakarta facility "one of the miraculous growth stories of modern-day milling, in any part of the world".[68] With expansion, Bogasari's Jakarta and Surabaya mills, plus Berdikari's in Sulawesi, handled 17,000 tonnes of wheat a day. Even before the expansion, the Jakarta mill was already the world's largest at one site, covering 33 hectares. The trade journal said Bogasari's expansion "by any measure represents the largest flour mill building program carried out anywhere in the world". The unprecedented expansion, it added, was "on a dimension that boggles the minds of millers in lands where capital programs are carried out on a more modest scale". The journal reported that Bogasari general manager Piet Yap would not divulge the expansion's cost, which it estimated at several hundred million U.S. dollars. The article on Bogasari lavished praise on industry heavyweight Yap and "his amazing career", noting that he was known around the world for his leadership in developing the company into "a flour milling powerhouse".[69] Another trade magazine, *World Grain*, a few years later heaped more compliments, commenting: "The rise of Bogasari was driven by extraordinary leadership: Piet Yap has built an empire not so much by meeting market demand but by aggressively creating it — and has changed the eating habits of a nation in the process."[70] (Indonesian per capita consumption of wheat-based foods, at 15 kilograms in 1995, was still low by regional standards. At the end of the 1990s, Malaysia was 51 kilograms a year and Philippines was 31.[71]) Living up to its reputation for its confidence and aggressive expansion, Indofood commissioned its ninetieth production line for instant noodles in 1995, bringing its capacity to 8.9 billion packs a year. The company also looked at markets further afield, sending its first shipment to Brazil. The theme of its annual report for 1995 was "The Success Continues". The letter to shareholders trumpeted "a year of unprecedented success" and declared: "We see sustained success ahead."

Notes

1. "Rice Grain Marketing and Quality Issues: Selected Papers from the International Rice Research Conference", Seoul, 27–31 August 1990, and U.S. Department of Agriculture, April 2011.
2. "Indonesia Grain and Feed Annual 2011 Report", USDA Foreign Agricultural Service, 14 April 2011. Available from <http://gain.fas.usda.gov/Recent Publications> (accessed 23 July 2011).
3. Iskandar and Febriyani Witnoputri, "Pemetaan persepsi konsumen terhadap mie instan PT. Indofood Sukses Makmur Tbk. (Indomie, Supermie dan Sarimi) di Surabaya", Skripsi No. 02011910/MAN/2005, Universiti Kristen Petra (Surabaya), 2005, p. 28. Available from <http://dewey.petra.ac.id/jiunkpe_dg_2676.html> (accessed 18 August 2012).
4. Piet Yap, *The Grains of My Life* (Singapore: privately published, 2010), p. 64.

5. Fikri Jufri, "Liem buka suara", *Tempo*, 31 March 1984, pp. 68–69.
6. Interview with Anthony, 4 March 2007.
7. Ibid.
8. Ibid.
9. "Mesin Uang dan Citra Grup Salim" [The Money Machine and Salim Group's Image], *SWA* 4, no. 10 (July 1994).
10. Michael Shari, "A tycoon under siege", *BusinessWeek*, 28 September 1998.
11. Noel Fung and Edhi Pranasidhi, "Indofood and former officials face suit", *AWSJ*, 2 February 1999.
12. Ibid. See also "Indofood, former executives sued for unfair transactions", *Jakarta Post*, 30 January 1999.
13. "Indofood CEO sees bright future ahead for food company", *Jakarta Post*, 5 May 2003.
14. <http://www.indofood.com/product_noodles.aspx>.
15. "Indofood's domination of instant noodle business beginning to face significant challenge", Indonesian Commercial Newsletter, 22 July 1996.
16. Ibid.
17. "Report on Competition Policy in Indonesia", by Colleen Loughlin, S. Marks, Achmad Shauki and Ningrum Sirait, USAID Project No. 0497 0372. November 1999, p. 39 <http://unpan1.un.org/intradoc/groups/public/documents/apcity/unpan018024.pdf> (accessed 23 July 2011).
18. Interview with Anthony, 4 April 2007.
19. In January 2014, Indonesia's Attorney General said Asian Agri Group — a Sukanto palm oil business found guilty of evading tax — agreed to a timetable for paying about US$206 million in fines. (Reuters, "Indonesian palm oil firm Asian Agri to pay $206 million tax fine", 30 January 2014.)
20. The ranking was released in November 2012; Anthony Salim came in at no. 4. In 2011, rival publication Globe Asia listed Eka as Indonesia's richest man, with US$12 billion in assets; it did not rank Liem — long retired from active management — Anthony was listed as third richest, with US$8 billion.
21. Lensa ETF, November 2006, "Sukses Melalui Kegigihan" [Success through perseverance], posted in <http://ekatjipta.org> in 2010.
22. Ahmad D. Habir, "Conglomerates: All in the Family?", in *Indonesia Beyond Suharto: Polity, Economy, Society, Transition*, edited by Donald Emmerson (Armonk, NY: M.E. Sharpe with the Asia Society, 1999), p. 184.
23. As one aspect of the Sukanto and Sinar Mas competition, Sukanto's Asia-Pacific Resoures International Ltd. (APRIL) and the Widjajas' Asia Pulp & Paper both got listings in New York in the mid-1990s. During the Asian finance crisis, the share prices of both collapsed, and they were delisted.
24. Henny Sender, "Great on Paper: Indonesia's Sinar Mas group attracts close scrutiny", *FEER*, 8 April 1993.
25. Sigid Edi Sutomo, "Eka Tjipta Widjaja: 'Saya kerja keras'", *Eksekutif*, May 1989.

26. "Pecah Kongsi" [Broken partnership], *Editor*, 16 November 1991.

27. Interview with Anthony, 20 May 2007.

28. "Perginya nakoda group Eka" [The passing of the captain of Eka's group], *Tempo*, 23 April 1988.

29. Interview with Anthony, 20 May 2007.

30. "Culture, staff or money", *Editor*, 16 November 1991.

31. Interview with Kotjo, 23 March 2007.

32. "'Architect' of the Salim-Sinar Mas Divorce", *SWA*, August 1992.

33. David Chew, "Sinar Mas and Salim revamp plantation venture", *Business Times*, 30 March 1991.

34. Interview with Anthony, 8 June 2008.

35. Adam Schwarz, *A Nation in Waiting: Indonesia's Search for Stability*, 2nd ed. (St Leonards, NSW: Allen & Unwin, 1999), p. 114.

36. Interview with Anthony, 21 January 2007.

37. Schwarz, *A Nation in Waiting*, p. 134

38. George Fane and Peter Warr, "Indonesia", in *Distortions to Agricultural Incentives in Asia*, edited by Kym Anderson and Will Martin (Washington, D.C.: World Bank Publications, 2009), p. 177, <http://www.scribd.com/doc/15494394/Distortions-to-Agricultural-Incentives-in-Asia> (accessed 30 August 2010).

39. "Despite export taxes, investor interest in oil palm processing is still high", Indonesian Commercial Newsletter, PT Data Consult, 23 September 1996.

40. Anne Casson, "The Hesitant Boom: Indonesia's Oil Palm Sub-Sector in an Era of Economic Crisis and Political Change", Centre for International Forestry Research (CIFOR), 1999, p. 15.

41. Circular to shareholders of PT Indocement Tunggal Prakarsa, 30 June 1992.

42. Mari Pangestu, "An Economic Agenda for Indonesia", *AWSJ*, 16 June 1992.

43. Schwarz, *A Nation in Waiting*, p. 115. C. Peter Timmer, who long worked with Bulog, wrote in 2004 that some saw the agency's ability to stall deregulation in the early 1990s "as an early signal that the entire growth process was running off the rails into corrupt and distortionary cronyism". (Timmer, "Operationalizing Pro-Poor Growth: Country Study for the World Bank", 2005 <http://siteresources.worldbank.org/INTPGI/Resources/342674-1115051237044/oppgindonesiaMay2005.pdf> (accessed 21 September 2011).

44. Circular to shareholders of PT Indocement.

45. Interview with Tosin, Jakarta, 22 April 2008.

46. Circular to shareholders of PT Indocement.

47. Jonathan Friedland, "Feeding the giant: Indonesia's Salim Group beefs up Indocement", *FEER*, 2 July 1992.

48. Richard Borsuk, "Salim Group's Indocement Deal Gets Cool Reaction From Analysts", *AWSJ*, 27 July 1992.

49. Interview with Tosin, 22 April 2008.

50. Michael Backman, *Asian Eclipse: Exposing the Dark Side of Business in Asia* (Singapore: John Wiley, 1999), p. 115.

51. Written communication with Robert Kuok, 7 December 2010.

52. John McBeth, "Feeding time: Indonesia's Indofood appears ready for listing", *FEER*, 30 December 1993.

53. Adam Schwarz, "Don't choke", *FEER*, 31 March 1994.

54. Indonesian Commercial Newsletter, PT Data Consult, 27 June 1994.

55. "Indofood will acquire Bogasari from Indocement", *Jakarta Post*, 19 February 1995.

56. "Grey but never dull", Smith New Court report on Indonesian cement, July 1995.

57. Richard Borsuk, "Indonesia Does a Turnabout on Media Policy", *AWSJ*, 7 June 1994.

58. World Bank paper at Jakarta conference, 26 April 1995, as reported in *AWSJ*, 28 April 1995.

59. Maggie Ford, "Jakarta's plan to speed up farm reform may hit monopolies", *Business Times*, 28 April 1995.

60. "New reform package criticized", *Jakarta Post*, 27 May 1995.

61. "Indonesia's Bogasari to Discuss Flour Deregulation Tuesday", AP-Dow Jones News, 5 June 1995.

62. Raphael Pura, "Indonesians Debate Moves To Restrain Giant Firms", *AWSJ*, 4 July 1995.

63. K. Arasu, "Bulog head defends monopolies", Reuters, 26 June 1995.

64. "Flour floors consumers", *Jakarta Post*, 14 August 1995.

65. Arasu, "Indonesian agency defends wheat pricing policy", Reuters, 19 September 1995. In the post-Suharto period, Beddu was put on trial on corruption charges. He was jailed in 2004 after the Supreme Court rejected his appeal against a four-year sentence for his role in a 1995 Jakarta land deal with Suharto's son Tommy. "I am a former state official. I, as a subordinate, carried out two government policies", Beddu told reporters. ("Beddu Amang: 'I only carried out my superior's policies'", Antara News Agency, 17 January 2004.)

66. Various media reports, 25 September 1995.

67. Ibid.

68. *Milling & Baking News*, vol. 74, no. 40, 5 December 1995.

69. Ibid.

70. Suzi Fraser Dominy, "Bogasari Flour Mills: The Giant of the Milling Industry", *World Grain*, August 2003.

71. Jacinto F. Fabiosa, Westernization of the Asian Diet: The Case of Rising Wheat Consumption in Indonesia, Working Paper 06-WP 422, Center for Agricultural and Rural Development, Iowa State University, April 2006, <http://ageconsearch.umn.edu/bitstream/18335/1/wp060422.pdf>.

15

DARK CLOUDS

To get away from the political wrangling and daily grind of Jakarta, Suharto liked to retreat to Tapos, his 700-hectare ranch near Bogor, south of the capital. Originally part of a Dutch plantation taken over by the Indonesian state, it was "provided" for Suharto's use in 1974 by the governor of West Java and managed by a company owned by the president's children.[1] Set amid rolling hills and lakes, the ranch had an experimental station for breeding cattle and sheep. It even featured a go-kart track, where Suharto used to enjoy a few laps. He felt most relaxed there; as he wrote in his autobiography: "I feel very much at home in the environment of agriculture and animal husbandry."[2] He often invited friends on weekends for a barbeque and to chew the cud, so to speak. Liem, a frequent guest, recalled that steaks and *sate* (satay) were often on the menu.[3] On one Sunday in March 1990, the tycoon was present at the retreat, but the atmosphere that day was not that relaxing, and the presence of quite a few corporate bosses indicated the occasion had an agenda beyond that of a social event. Liem and some thirty other business chieftains had been summoned to Tapos to hear the president outline plans to deal with an issue receiving increased media attention. It was the thorny subject of income disparity, or social envy — *kecemburuan sosial* in Indonesian. It was no surprise that those present, except for two, were Chinese. Adding to their discomfort was the fact that the event was telecast nationwide as Suharto lectured them, urging them to take concrete action to help narrow the income gap. His solution to share the wealth: Make conglomerates shift a chunk of their equity to cooperatives.

ARM-TWISTED COOPERATION

In 1990, Indonesia was on a healthy growth track, but there were also increasing signs that Suharto, turning seventy in June the following year, was getting more out of touch, and dangerously overconfident his path was the right one. (Two years earlier, he blackballed think-tank CSIS when its director Jusuf Wanandi sent a memo suggesting that Suharto consider planning for political succession.) At this stage, he was given to surrounding himself with people less likely to question his judgements. He was also less inclined to accept advice from his economic technocrats. Deregulation had allowed the country to experience a growth spurt, but too many of the gains were garnered by those close to him — his children and groups such as Salim. Thus the fruits of the country's wealth were not being enjoyed by many and the unhappiness was being directed mainly at the Chinese tycoons, whose business successes were the subject of criticism. Crony capitalism was a mainstay in Suharto's economic system, and all the cronies and tycoons were at the ranch that day, except for Bob Hasan, who distanced himself from the Chinese magnates. Invitations for that event were issued through Prasetiya Mulya, the foundation set up by Liem and other ethnic Chinese bosses in 1980. Suharto was a strong advocate of cooperatives, which Indonesia's short 1945 Constitution described as a pillar of the national economy, along with the state and private business. From independence through the 1980s, though, cooperatives had a woeful management track record, but Suharto liked to hark back to his rural roots and talk them up. R.E. Elson, in his biography of Suharto, wrote that the president retained an "almost childlike attachment to the idea of cooperatives, remarking in the mid-1970s that the form of cooperative is the best economic form for Indonesia".[4]

When Indonesia began growing faster but less equitably, Suharto felt pressure to do something about the widely held view that a small number of Chinese were getting the lion's share of the gains. In his autobiography, Suharto wrote: "It is everyone's duty to foster the growth of cooperatives. Ultimately, cooperatives must be the main pillar of our economy".[5] Under Suharto, the government had a Ministry of Cooperatives, headed in 1990 by Bulog chief and Salim friend Bustanil Arifin, but there were never sustained efforts to make cooperatives viable, much less an economic pillar. Two months before the Tapos event, Suharto had served notice in his budget speech that the time had come for cooperatives to become a "national economic force" that should eventually own 25 per cent of the shares of "healthy companies." This part of his speech came right after he defended conglomerates, which had been under increasing attack. Suharto told his pliant parliament big businesses "should not be restrained because we can capitalize on them" to accelerate growth.[6] The mention of cooperatives unnerved foreign investors, who were unclear if they might have to sell a quarter of their shares to such organizations.

As usual, Suharto offered no clarifications. Radius Prawiro, the Coordinating Minister for the Economy, tried to allay concerns, saying he believed Suharto was "inviting pioneers" to start selling shares. Foreign companies will still be protected by investment laws and have options "but it will be appreciated" if they gave priority to selling stakes to cooperatives, he elaborated. That explanation, however, did not quell queasiness and with confusion spreading in the business community, Finance Minister J.B. Sumarlin reaffirmed that the government would use "persuasion, not coercion" to achieve the goal and emphasized that Suharto's call "is an appeal. There's no new policy or government decree or something like that."[7] With that, investors breathed a sigh of relief, assuming the president's statements were merely rhetoric. But after no companies volunteered as "pioneers", business leaders were summoned to Tapos that March day. It was not lost on TV viewers that almost all of the tycoons — wearing long-sleeved batik shirts — were Chinese. (This was not surprising, as non-*pribumis* control most of the country's top conglomerates.[8]) One of the two non-Chinese guests present was Liem's partner and Suharto kin, Sudwikatmono. Liem sat prominently in the front row. When Suharto finished his pitch, the brash boss of Sinar Mas group, Eka Tjipta Widjaja (Oei Ek Tjong) piped up, pledging that those present would respond positively to the president's request. The first act of a show on distributing some wealth was under way.

The spotlight on the Chinese tycoons at Tapos naturally drew attention to their role in the economy and position in the country. Lukman Harun, an official in the Islamic organization Muhammadiyah, was quoted as saying: "I'm not a racist. But the Chinese are a real problem in Indonesia. They control the economy, the big companies and the markets. They own big homes with lots of luxury cars, and send their children to universities abroad. All they talk about is money, money, money. They've got to give Indonesians a chance — and become more Indonesian themselves."[9] The fact there were many Chinese Indonesians who were barely eking out a living was conveniently ignored. Mely Tan, a University of Indonesia sociologist, commented later: "The stereotype that all ethnic Chinese are wealthy and that they have benefited most from 'facilities' made available by the New Order government and become big businessmen in the process has undoubtedly been reinforced by the event at Tapos."[10] Researcher Christian Chua took a different tack, saying the lecture "illustrated clearly the authority of the political elite, which capital could not oppose. However, Tapos disclosed at the same time that the tough stance against the capitalists was merely rhetorical and a means to sustain the pro-*pribumi* Robin Hood image of the government."[11]

The gathering at the ranch demanded at least a semblance of action to address the wealth imbalance, but there was no way the conglomerate bosses would give or sell, at concessional rates, 25 per cent of their businesses. Still, some follow-up was expected. In the following weeks, Prasetiya Mulya worked with Cooperatives Minister Bustanil and Suharto and a tacit agreement — one in which Liem was said to have played a vital role — was reached in which each participating tycoon would shift 1 per cent of one listed company to cooperatives that Bustanil's staff matchmade for them. As the cooperatives did not have money to buy the shares, they were supposed to pay for them over time, interest-free, through deductions of 75 per cent of the dividends they would receive. Under the rules set for the transfers, cooperatives couldn't sell the shares, but could use them as collateral for borrowing.

The "arranged marriage" between conglomerates and cooperatives from around the archipelago was performed at a ceremony on 27 July 1990, National Cooperatives Day. It was held at state-owned Hotel Indonesia (where scenes in the film "The Year of Living Dangerously" ostensibly took place; as the movie couldn't be made in Jakarta in Suharto's time, it was filmed in the Philippines.) For Suharto ally Bustanil, it was a huge night. (In a contribution for a book Tutut published the following year to mark the president's seventieth birthday, Bustanil wrote that Suharto's initiative to have companies sell shares to cooperatives at a nominal price was one example of how the president was "so full of brilliant and practical ideas."[12]) Amid glaring TV lights in the Hotel Indonesia ballroom, Liem, Astra chief William Soeryadjaya and other corporate bosses shook hands with their new shareholders. Salim gave 20,000 shares of Indocement to a

university-linked cooperative in Central Java. At the time, the shares were
worth about US$7.80 each, so the amount was US$156,000. Astra transferred
50,000 shares to a Sumatra cooperative comprising 366 rice farmers. Based
on the stock's value then, that worked out to around US$660,000. Altogether,
fifty-nine transfers were made that night, involving 46 million shares. Liem,
chairman of Prasetiya Mulya, read a statement expressing the foundation's
pleasure over the partnership with cooperatives. It was rare for Liem to
speak publicly at a media event, and some reporters present sniggered
at his heavily-accented Indonesian. Liem said businessmen "work for
profit" but that as Indonesians, they had a "duty to participate in building
this nation". He called on the cooperatives to be managed professionally.
Bustanil, in his speech, told the bosses their companies would not be
allowed to be an "industrial island enclave in a sea of backwardness". The
1 per cent transfers were a "stepping stone" to achieving more balance in
the economy, he declared.[13] During the New Order, many symbolic shows
were staged, and that evening was one. It is not known how many shares
stayed with the cooperatives, or were resold to the owners, though Liem's
Indocement shares remained with the cooperative. Suharto apparently felt
he was acting to contain the income gap, without impacting the tycoons.
Their growth — and favours — underpinned the New Order and him,
while they needed the protection he gave in return.

TOP SALIM LIEUTENANTS MOVE ON

With the rapid expansion of Salim Group activities, it was necessary that
outside professionals were hired to oversee the growth. Among them were
two top non-family executives Judiono Tosin and Johannes Kotjo. Both,
however, chose to exit the group not far into the 1990s. The departures
of the two senior executive directors generated some buzz, as outsiders
wondered whether there were push as well as pull factors. For an executive
of a group that deliberately wanted to keep a low profile, Kotjo at times had
been unusually outspoken. After their departure, both men commended
Anthony and their time at Salim. In the "go-go" first half of the 1990s, they
had plenty of business opportunities of their own to explore. Kotjo, who
with Anthony's blessing had already started a business while at Salim,
later teamed up with Suharto son Bambang. Tosin, who as Indocement's
finance director played a prominent role in its 1989 IPO, exited at the start
of 1994. He had been at Salim seventeen years, joining the group after
graduating from the University of Indonesia in accounting. He said his

starting pay at Salim, at Rp250,000 (then equivalent to US$600 a month), was "big money" for a fresh graduate. One of his early tasks was helping shift 40,000 spindles from a textile factory Salim was shutting in Singapore, International Spinning Mills, to PT Tarumatex in Bandung. He described work at Salim as "a very happy experience".[14] Like many Salim executives, Tosin stayed in the office until 11 p.m. many nights. After his departure, he remarked on the work ethic at the group, saying Salim people were willingly *"gila kerja"* (work-crazy), but said it wasn't because of money. "They have a feeling of internal satisfaction that can't be measured", the executive said.[15] After the 1992 group asset-shuffle, the executive, at age forty, wanted to find satisfaction elsewhere. "Already I'm on top, hard to go up [in Salim]", he said he was thinking. Also, "if I don't move [to do my own thing], will it then be too late?"[16] After his departure, Tosin set up a securities company with the former director of state investment fund PT Danareksa, lead underwriter for the Indocement IPO. Tosin also entered other businesses, including with Gang of Four member Ibrahim Risjad.

Johannes Kotjo had joined Salim from German chemical company Henkel. Unusual for a Salim executive, he was quite regularly accessible to the media — and sometimes spoke out of turn. In 1990, he upset Liem by casually telling *Tempo* magazine that the Salim founder and chairman basically had retired and had not been active in running the group for three or four years.[17] Liem reacted sharply, telling the newsweekly he definitely had not retired and remained in charge of policy-making as chairman. "People need to know I still have full authority", Liem stated. "If I say this can and that cannot, others [in Salim] cannot say anything. Anthony also can't."[18] A chastened Kotjo then clarified that he was just talking about day-to-day management, and insisted he wasn't disrespecting the founder. Many years later in an interview, Kotjo said: "Some people said it [his remark about Liem] was like a coup d'état, but it was no such thing." Referring to rumours that he was elbowed out by Salim, Kotjo described them as "nonsense". He remarked: "They tried to keep me."[19] According to Kotjo, he had submitted a resignation letter at the end of 1992, but it was only in mid-1994 — six months after Tosin's departure — before Salim allowed him to leave. Like Tosin, Kotjo wanted to do his own thing, saying: "I was successful working with a foreign company, and with Salim. I have to test myself."[20]

Kotjo continued to make headlines after leaving Salim. First, he tried to take over Kanindo, a debt-ridden textile maker. Kanindo chief executive Robby Tjahjadi had once been in prison for smuggling cars into Indonesia.

But Kotjo was thwarted by state banks and others who wanted a Kanindo takeover to involve a *pribumi*. Kotjo joined up with a potent *pribumi*, Suharto son Bambang, dropped the Kanindo idea and bought 70 per cent of another textile company, Mayatexdian Industry, headed by Tjahjadi. Again with Bambang, Kotjo aimed to build a US$1.5 billion privately owned oil refinery in East Java. Suharto wanted refining, a Pertamina domain, opened to private investors to give his children yet another area to enter. Two years before his departure from Salim, Kotjo had bought 13 per cent of a Singapore-listed marine engineering company, Van Der Horst Ltd., and became its chairman while Kuok Khoon Hong, a nephew of Robert Kuok and later boss of Singapore-listed agribusiness Wilmar International, bought about 11.5 per cent. Some media saw this as Robert Kuok's group and Salim themselves entering Van Der Horst, which wasn't the case. For a time, Van Der Horst flourished, and its share price rose more than sixfold. In early 1995, Bambang came in, getting 5.2 per cent. Kotjo was riding high until December 1995, when he was censured by the Singapore Stock Exchange for what it called "an inexcusable breach" of a rule by "creating a false market" for shares of United Pulp & Paper Ltd.[21] He was barred from assuming directorships of other listed companies in the island state for thirty months, and his Singapore involvement began to wane.

In place of the two directors who left, Salim promoted executives then in their thirties, Hartono Gunawan and Benny Santoso. Both were ethnic Chinese and also not related to Liem's family. Like Tosin, Gunawan joined Salim after graduating in accounting from the University of Indonesia. He became a Salim executive director in 1990 and president-director of listed detergent maker PT UIC in 1992. At the time Kotjo and Tosin departed, Benny was already a key lieutenant to Anthony. A native of Solo in Central Java, Benny studied business at Singapore's Ngee Ann College. After getting hired at Salim to work on finance matters, Benny came to the attention of Anthony, who was impressed by this eager young man. Once, when Anthony was taking his family to Hawaii on holiday, he invited Benny to join. Typically for Anthony, the holiday consisted largely of talking business, and his bond with the younger colleague — Benny is nine years younger — strengthened. A man with a pleasant countenance and the energy to keep up with his boss's demanding pace, Benny was given a series of directorships at Salim companies. After Kotjo's exit, to the extent Salim had a face to the outside world, it was largely Benny's. Unlike Kotjo, he never spoke brashly.

REFORM HOPES GO UP IN SMOKE

By the early 1990s, Suharto was in his political ascendancy. Increasingly imperious and convinced he possessed the divine right to rule, he depended less on the advice of his ministers and had long sidelined his early coterie of military advisors, including the staunchly loyal Benny Murdani. Gen. Murdani had been brought back from a diplomatic posting in South Korea after the 1974 Malari incident, after Ali Murtopo had been shunted aside. Murdani had earned the president's trust to the extent that he acted like a surrogate father figure to Suharto's children. When they came into adulthood and started their "rent-seeking" businesses, it spurred negative public reaction. Still, Murdani sought to rein them in. He was the only one who dared withhold the passport of eldest son Sigit to prevent him from travelling overseas to gamble. (Sigit was said to think nothing of blowing US$2 million a night on casino tables.[22]) Murdani's refusal to grant the Suharto children "lucrative military procurements" angered them, and as they grew older, they lobbied their father to alienate him.[23] Murdani, in the mid-1980s was the most powerful man in Indonesia next to Suharto. But the Catholic general had plenty of enemies. He had a potent one in Prabowo Subianto, then married to Suharto's daughter Titiek. The ambitious Prabowo thought his military career was stymied under Murdani and was said to have planted the idea in his father-in-law's mind that Murdani might have privately supported opposition to the president. In February 1988, the same year CSIS, the institution under Murdani's patronage, was ostracized, Suharto abruptly replaced Murdani as Abri (armed forces) chief. Murdani, who thought he had more to contribute to the country, came out of his meeting with Suharto "visibly shocked".[24] It was apparent that the president would not brook any criticism of his blatant favouritism to his children, even from a highly trusted aide.

Meanwhile, Cendana activity moved into higher gear in the 1990s. Soon after the 1990 Bank Duta mess, Suharto signed a decree that gave a company partly owned by Sigit and Sudwikatmono the sole rights to collect television licence fees for state broadcaster TVRI. After PT Mekatama Raya began work, complaints mushroomed, including from parliament speaker Kharis Suhud. TVRI had to drop Mekatama Raya as collection agent, but it was retained to provide "technical assistance".

The president wrapped up 1990 with a bang — or punch — that dashed hopes for economic reforms. Many years after the cessation of the clove-import duopoly involving Liem, the government created a broader monopoly to control the spice. The monopoly, which some economists called the death of deregulation, became one of the biggest sources of resentment of Suharto's children and the president. Suharto never publicly defended the policy. That fell to Trade Minister Arifin Siregar, who signed the 28 December decree and declared that while Indonesian policy was still to deregulate, "in some cases we must improve existing regulations".[25] The decree created the Clove Support and Trading Board, or BPPC after the Indonesian initials, to control the sale and transport of the spice needed for *kretek* cigarettes. As it did with cement when bailing out Salim in 1985, the government labelled cloves a "strategic" commodity. Chairing the new clove consortium was Suharto's youngest and favourite son, Tommy (Hutomo Mandala Putra), then twenty-eight.

BPPC was an egregious Suharto move that signalled some modification in his "favour bank" in the 1990s. The president directed that more favours be steered to his children than the Chinese cronies who put in deposits. Liem did not get many new favours in this period, though previous ones ensured he could continue to contribute. Sometimes, Salim's favours seemed to be in partnering with Suharto children. For the industrial estate in Batam, for example, son Bambang was brought into a joint venture with Salim and Singapore investors. Defenders of the patronage system could argue that when Liem was a beneficiary, such as with the 1985 Indocement bailout, he used it productively. In contrast, Tommy's clove venture reeked of blatant rent-seeking. BPPC's existence appeared to help only the board's participants and hurt everyone else, from the farmer to the *kretek* manufacturer, as well as the Indonesian taxpayer. The venture failed miserably. Suharto in 1991 made the central bank lend BPPC about US$350 million at concessional rates to start buying cloves. Then, because BPPC promised farmers a much higher clove price, they naturally responded by greatly increasing their planting. When that spawned a flood of cloves, Tommy recommended that farmers chop down 25 per cent of their trees to get BPPC's scheme on track. And if tree-cutting didn't work, he suggested that BPPC buy only half of the crop and farmers burn the other half "so nobody will try to make money from the unsold cloves".[26] Not surprisingly, his proposal stoked widespread anger. Asked at a parliamentary hearing if BPPC was repaying its loan from Bank Indonesia, Tommy replied that if the body was forced to pay back right then, "we have to repay in cloves." There is no evidence the loan was ever repaid. The clove monopoly lingered on until killed by the International Monetary Fund (IMF) package that Suharto acceded to in January 1998 as the economy was collapsing.

BPPC's birth demonstrated that when economic times were good, the influence of Indonesia's vaunted technocrats was extremely limited. The Berkeley Mafia had played a pivotal role when the New Order was younger and economically fragile. Much of the success was rooted in Suharto's relationship with the Mafia's dean, Widjojo Nitisastro, whose doctoral studies at the University of California-Berkeley were supported by the Ford Foundation. Widjojo, started his career at the University of Indonesia's economics faculty, and became its dean. In August 1966, he was invited to speak at an army seminar where he stated that economic moves by Sukarno's government were unwise and added to the country's difficulties.[27] Suharto, who at that stage was easing Sukarno out, was impressed by Widjojo.

Soon after he became acting president, Suharto tapped Widjojo and his team for advice. The economist, born in Malang, East Java, in 1927, was six years younger and an excellent tutor and policy-planner. Widjojo figured out early on how to play by Suharto's rules. Being Javanese, he knew when to tip-toe around thorny issues and when to lobby the president. A former minister, A.R. Soehoed, who battled Widjojo and the technocrats, once commented of the Berkeley Mafia: "They were very good at scaring the old man. They kept him on razor's edge and that's how they got their way. They told him that if he didn't follow their suggestions the people would be without food and clothes, or the economy wouldn't grow."[28] But as the New Order progressed, the technocrats lost more battles (or steered away from fighting them). Their list of opponents included the "nationalist" camp led by Suharto acolyte B.J. Habibie, long-time Research and Technology Minister, and cronies such as Liem. Visits by Liem and Anthony to Cendana to see Suharto at one stage were almost as frequent as Widjojo's, and both parties sometimes found themselves waiting for the other to finish their discussion with the boss.

Ultimately, the technocrats' most effective tool was bad times. When Pertamina honcho Ibnu Sutowo virtually bankrupted Indonesia in the mid-1970s, Widjojo was called on to help end his fiefdom. In the mid-1980s, Suharto agreed to many reforms proposed by the technocrats because the oil price had plunged below US$10 a barrel and Indonesia was in crisis. When the economy was better, Suharto was more prone to listen to Habibie or, increasingly, his children. That was why the technocrats, in 1990, were unable to dissuade the president from the clove monopoly. Their declining influence was illustrated by Suharto's 599-page autobiography, published in 1989; it mentioned Widjojo only twice and Habibie seventeen times.[29]

Some light on the dynamics between Suharto and the technocrats was shed in 2003 during a conference held by the Ford Foundation to celebrate fifty years of its Indonesia programme. Widjojo, who never previously talked publicly about working with Suharto, was a participant. Ford published one part of the transcript, quoting Widjojo and Saleh Afiff, chief economic minister from 1993 to 1998, and it showed how Suharto changed once he was confident he could handle everything:

> Widjojo: A question was raised whether President Suharto did not as much listen to us anymore at the time of the 1997-98 crisis. This question may also be correct. As (fellow technocrat) Ali Wardhana said, in the past President Suharto did not merely listen but also took notes... [Widjojo cites 1967 discussions about rescheduling Indonesia's foreign-debt]. At that time President Suharto was prepared to learn.

> Saleh Afiff: At one stage, Ali Wardhana and I had an audience with President Suharto to discuss deregulation. At first, he didn't even give us a chance to speak. He gave us a lecture... Indeed, in the past President Suharto took notes, later on we were the ones who took notes.[30]

The technocrats' waning influence on Suharto was apparent in the BPPC case. Ultimately it hurt Suharto too, as it bolstered the growing perception that the president increasingly put his children's interests ahead of national ones. The creation of BPPC reminded many that Bulog's market controls, which benefitted Salim, remained untouchable. So indirectly, the creation of BPPC undercut any Salim effort to show it could perform well in a competitive marketplace and not just make money off a privileged business position.

Also in the early 1990s came the "Golden Key" scandal. While it had no Salim link, it had an indirect impact on Chinese-led conglomerates by putting the Suharto government and one Chinese businessman in a very bad light. A little-known business group caused enormous losses for state-owned Indonesian Development Bank, or Bapindo. The bank had given a US$430 million letter of credit to the obscure figure behind Golden Key Group, a Hokchia businessman named Eddy Tansil, who had links to Admiral Sudomo, the influential head of the Supreme Audit Council and Suharto's Coordinating Minister for Politics and Security from 1988 to 1993. Tansil was the younger brother of a banker named Hendra Rahardja, who years later was convicted on corruption charges and sentenced to life in jail.[31] Sudomo wrote notes to bank directors recommending Tansil. The loans were ostensibly given to Tansil for three petrochemical plants, even though he had no background in the business and there was no study of his creditworthiness. He didn't provide any collateral and he didn't build the plants. Sudomo told the Indonesian media that Tansil, who once sold three-wheeled taxis, was a "loyal, highly dedicated businessman".[32] Tansil had another credential: Tommy Suharto was a shareholder in one of the three proposed plants. But coincidentally, before the Golden Key scandal became public, Tommy's share somehow shifted back to Tansil.

Tansil and several Bapindo officials were put on trial in proceedings that demonstrated how some high officials and potent individuals could act with impunity. Sudomo testified but wasn't pressed by prosecutors about his support for Tansil. Former Finance Minister J.B. Sumarlin, who some Bapindo officials testified had instructed them to help Tansil, wasn't called as a witness. Neither was Tommy. The witness who caused the biggest uproar was Tansil's wife, who wore to court a bright red dress sporting a large yellow dollar-sign on the front. She testified she knew nothing about finance, and just complied with her husband's instruction to write checks for about US$115,000 to each of two Bapindo executives. In August 1994, Tansil was sentenced to seventeen years in jail.

Less than two years later, his luxurious, air-conditioned "cell" in Jakarta's Cipinang prison — complete with satellite TV — was found empty one morning; he had flown the coop. Money did not just talk in Jakarta, it shouted. Naturally, jokes abounded that Tansil had a "golden key". Adding to the state's embarrassment, the escape came soon after Justice Minister Oetojo Oesman saw Tansil's cell, and ordered that the privileges end. Arief Budiman, a sociologist, commented after the escape that Jakarta executives knew that the fraud Tansil perpetrated at Golden Key "is a common practice. It is a system that people cannot avoid. Most businesspeople would tell you either you play within the system, or you will always stay at the bottom... the rent-seeking system has proved to be much stronger than any resistance to it."[33]

During the Tansil trial, hopes that Indonesia was becoming more open were dealt a severe setback as the Information Ministry shut *Tempo*, the country's boldest news weekly, and two other publications, *Editor* and *DeTik*. The ban on *Tempo* was prompted by a cover story about Minister B.J. Habibie's purchase of the antiquated ships of the former East German navy. Although touted as "a bargain" given a US$12.7 million price tag, the job to restore the crafts to seaworthiness was estimated to cost US$1.1 billion. *Tempo*'s report riled Habibie, whose special ties with the president dated to the early 1950s in Makassar, where Suharto was posted and said to have befriended Habibie's mother. The closures of the magazines shocked many who wanted to believe that Suharto was relaxing his grip. *Tempo*'s political reporting was long testing the limits, from Suharto's point of view; it had written boldly on many subjects, including the brutal 1993 rape and murder in East Java of a twenty-six-year-old woman labour activist, Marsinah — a crime widely suspected to have been carried out by government agents to halt a wave of strikes by exploited workers not allowed to have independent unions.

The June 1994 closures of news weeklies reconfirmed that Suharto would not allow any political deregulation to match the economic one — which itself was stalling. The muzzling of the media came only five months before President Bill Clinton and other leaders arrived in Indonesia for the APEC summit. But the media suppression didn't dent Suharto, who basked in having the world come to him. (On the sidelines of the summit, Suharto daughter Tutut's business horizons got expanded. While Philippine President Fidel Ramos was in Jakarta, a deal was signed for her company that developed toll-roads — in which Indocement was a shareholder — to build one in Manila.[34])

Buoyed by the boom years and how foreign capital was pouring into Indonesia, Suharto was not under pressure to allow any more political freedom or economic reform. "We will not change a system which has proven effective", he declared at an assembly of pro-government youth in 1996.[35] But it wasn't really a system: Instead of relying on institutions, Suharto depended on his monopoly on power. His political instincts were failing as he steadily became more king-like and even less receptive to feedback. Because Indonesia's "cake" was growing, he assumed that unhappiness over the increasing large slices going to his children and cronies reflected jealousy rather than anger that could not be hinted at by state-owned or state-regulated television, the most popular media in the largely oral Indonesian society.

As Suharto's children sought larger slices of the cake, some individuals who tried to contain that got pushed out of the way. In November 1995, the CEO of state-owned Merpati Nusantara Airlines was replaced after refusing to sign a contract under which sixteen planes from Habibie's factory would be leased through a company partly owned by Tommy. The removal of Ridwan Fataruddin was ordered by Transport Minister Haryanto Dhanutirto, a Habibie protégé. The following month, Haryanto found himself briefly in hot soup, as documents leaked to Jakarta papers alleged that flag-carrier Garuda Indonesia paid US$250,000 for shopping in Europe by his wife. Suharto, who periodically said corruption would not be tolerated, ordered a probe. It concluded there was some truth in the allegations, but Haryanto did not lose his job. The president just asked him to undertake "introspection" and improve his department's procedures.[36] So an airline chief with integrity lost his job while a minister who let the state pay for at least part of a private shopping spree received a meaningless reprimand.

Then an outspoken politician, Sri Bintang Pamungkas, went on trial on charges of insulting Suharto. Due to the president's prodding, Pamungkas already had been removed from parliament by his United Development Party. Now, he was in the dock for calling Suharto a dictator while speaking in Germany, ahead of a visit by the Indonesian leader. Suharto's visit was marred by raucous protests over Jakarta's human rights record. Pamungkas was sentenced to thirty-four months in jail. A Ph.D. in economics, Pamungkas had highlighted the rich-poor gap and lack of democracy. Back in the 1950s, he once said, Indonesia had democracy but no economic growth to help people live better. Now there was growth — he gave Suharto credit for this — but there was no movement towards democracy even though "we now have enough national assets" to support it. Asked in an interview if conglomerates should be cut down, he replied: "No, it's not that. The problem with our country is that we don't have good laws. I believe that in a democratic environment, we can produce laws like an anti-trust law so groups won't be so powerful." He also said "There is collusion between the conglomerates and government officials. This means corruption and inefficiencies... There are no rules of the game in Indonesia." On what changes he would make if he were a top minister, Pamungkas replied presciently: "With the concentration of power in the president's hands, you cannot do a lot. Change has to wait until after Suharto."[37] (Only days after succeeding Suharto in May 1998, President Habibie granted Pamungkas amnesty and released him from jail. In 2006, a new

Constitutional Court scrapped three articles of the Criminal Code, so "insulting the president" no longer was a crime punishable by up to six years in jail.)

Powerful as Suharto was, he could not stop criticism of the business activity of his close circle — particular his family — and the widening rich-poor divide. Five years after the fizzling out of Suharto's initiative to get Chinese-controlled conglomerates to transfer shares to cooperatives, it was time for him to try another tactic. In late 1995, yet another Suharto-led (and non-transparent) charity foundation was set up, a move that gave new proof that the president was increasingly reliant on a small circle of loyalists including Liem. The new effort's roots were a refresher course in Pancasila ideology that ninety-six top bosses, including Liem, Anthony and Eka Tjipta Widjaja of Sinar Mas, had to take in August 1995 in Bali. After the three-day course, a session on helping small businesses produced a statement on combatting poverty called the Jimbaran Declaration after the luxury beach resort area where the course took place. The unshy Sinar Mas boss, who owned a belt buckle spelling out "EKA" in diamonds, proposed that the tycoons donate 2 per cent of their net profits to a new fund to help the poor — an idea Suharto liked and would soon use as the basis for a new foundation, called Damandari. The president would tap Liem and Anthony to help promote it in the face of increasing resistance to him and his policies.

Notes

1. According to R.E. Elson in *Suharto: A Political Biography* (Cambridge, UK: Cambridge University Press, 2001, p. 210), Tapos was managed by a corporate body P.T. Rejo Sari Bumi-Unit Tapos, whose shares were owned by Suharto's children.
2. *Soeharto: My Thoughts, Words and Deeds; An Autobiography*, as told to G. Dwipanyana and Ramadhan K.H. (Jakarta: Citra Lamtoro Gung Persada, 1991), p. 295.
3. Interview with Liem, 9 December 2006. *Sate* is barbequed skewered meat — chicken, beef or mutton — served with a peanut sauce.
4. R.E. Elson, *Suharto*, p. 211, citing *Kompas*, 16 August 1981.
5. *Soeharto: My Thoughts*, p. 304.
6. AFP, as cited in *Straits Times* "Firmer oil prices lead Jakarta to boost Budget", 5 January 1990.
7. Richard Borsuk, "Indonesia Assures Firms Share Sales Won't Be Required", *Asian Wall Street Journal*, 12 January 1990.

8. Of the twenty-five top conglomerates, all except four were Chinese-owned, according to Hal Hill. Out of the three largest *pribumi* firms, two were owned by Suharto's sons (see Hal Hill, *The Indonesian Economy since 1966* [Cambridge: Cambridge University Press, 1996], p. 109).

9. Martin Cohn, "Chinese outcasts of Indonesia: Persecuted minority tries to be invisible", *Toronto Star*, 12 April 1990.

10. Mely Tan, "The social and cultural dimensions of the role of ethnic Chinese in Indonesian society", in *Indonesia* (special issue) (Ithaca, New York: Cornell University, 1991), p. 125.

11. Christian Chua, *Chinese Big Business in Indonesia: The State of Capital* (U.K.: Routledge, 2008), p. 45.

12. G. Dwipayana and Nazaruddin Sjamsuddin, eds., *Di antara para sahabat: Pak Harto 70 tahun* [Among Friends: Pak Harto's 70th] (English ed.) (Jakarta: Citra Gung Lamtoro Persada, 1993), pp. 203 and 205.

13. Richard Borsuk, "Indonesian firms transfer 1 per cent of equity to cooperatives in Suharto-backed move", *AWSJ*, 30 July 1990.

14. Interview with Tosin, 22 April 2008.

15. "Ingin risiko yang lebih tinggi" [Wanting to take on higher risk], *Editor*, 13 January 1994.

16. Interview with Tosin, 22 April 2008.

17. "Om Liem boleh bersenang-senang" [Om Liem can enjoy], *Tempo*, 10 March 1990.

18. Fikri Jufri, "Liem bicara lagi: Saya masih kuasa penuh" [Liem speaks again: I still have full power], *Tempo*, 10 March 1990.

19. Interview with Kotjo, 23 March 2007.

20. Ibid.

21. Conrad Raj, "SES bars Kotjo from more boards, including L&M's", *Business Times* (Singapore), 30 December 1995.

22. Jusuf Wanandi, *Shades of Grey: A Political Memoir of Modern Indonesia, 1965–1998* (Jakarta: Equinox, 2012), p. 233.

23. See R.E. Elson, *Suharto*, p. 259.

24. Michael Vatikiotis, *Indonesian Politics under Suharto: Order, Development and Pressure for Change* (London and New York: Routledge, 1993), p. 83, and Jusuf Wanandi, *Shades of Grey*.

25. Muklis Ali, "Indonesian Government Defends New Clove Monopoly", Reuters, 7 January 1991.

26. Richard Borsuk, "Indonesian Clove Farmers May Face Production Cut", *AWSJ*, 27 February 1992.

27. "Celebrating Indonesia: Fifty Years with the Ford Foundation, 1953–2003", Ford Foundation, 2003, p. 50.

28. Ibid., p. 51.

29. Ibid., p. 67.

30. Ibid., p. 59.

31. Hendra Rahardja fled Indonesia after his Bank Harapan Sentosa was shut in 1997 and he was arrested in 1999 while entering Australia. In 2002, Rahardja was convicted in Jakarta, *in absentia*, of stealing about US$217 million and sentenced to life in jail. He died in Australia in 2003 while still fighting extradition to Indonesia.

32. Richard Borsuk, "Official at Indonesian Bank Is Arrested in Loan Case", *AWSJ*, 17 February 1994.

33. Arief Budiman, "Why should bad guys always win?", *Jakarta Post*, 20 May 1996. Indonesian media periodically reported sightings of Tansil in China.

34 In late 1994, world leaders were not the only famous people visiting Jakarta. Three weeks before the APEC summit, Sylvester Stallone played golf with Suharto and Bob Hasan. Afterward, Bob boasted, "I told Rambo, 'I'm the king of the jungle.' — Raphael Pura, "Plywood Power: Bob Hasan Builds an Empire in the Forest", *AWSJ*, 20 January 1995. The next day, Stallone opened a Jakarta branch of Planet Hollywood. Sudwikatmono's daughter Martina was Stallone's Indonesian partner in the venture, which later failed.

35. *Straits Times*, "Political system will remain unchanged, Suharto vows", 13 June 1996.

36. Richard Borsuk, "Suharto rebukes, but keeps, minister", *AWSJ*, 27 December 1995.

37. Richard Borsuk, "The Asian Economist: An Interview on Regional Economic Issues", *AWSJ*, 16 December 1993.

16

THE SKY STARTS TO FALL

1996 — the year before the financial crisis hit the region — could be called Salim's high-water mark. Everything was progressing smoothly — business was booming and the sky looked to be the limit. In July 1996, *Asiaweek* magazine in Hong Kong put out its first annual list of people it labelled Asia's "Power 50", and Suharto and Liem proved their potency — the president topped the list, while his leading *cukong* was Number 5 (and the highest ranking businessperson).[1] That year, Salim published its first comprehensive corporate brochure, a forty-page full-colour production with a plain white cover featuring the group's logo — an embossed globe with the name Salim written across it. Chairman Liem's written message declared confidently that the group's "best years still lie ahead". What lay ahead instead was a traumatic plunge from power for Liem and his patron. In retrospect, the bucolic days of 1996 for Salim were somewhat akin to the maiden voyage of the Titanic before it struck the iceberg: there was celebration and partying on board, and passengers envisioned grand dreams for the future. It was the prophetic calm before the storm. For Suharto, 1996 portended the calamity that would follow. Having ditched his close military advisors and at the apogee of power, Suharto continued dispensing favours for his children's ventures, and indeed, extended it to the next generation as well. That year proved to be a turning point for the president when his wife — his pillar of support, and some say, the possessor of his *wahyu* — died.

HONOURED IN PHILADELPHIA

For Salim, though, 1996 was smooth sailing. There was a high point for Salim's offshore vehicle, First Pacific. In July, the company was named a "component stock" of Hong Kong's benchmark Hang Seng Index. Being part of the index boosted interest in First Pacific, whose shares were more than ten times higher than in 1991. The magazine *BusinessWeek* declared: "First Pacific's mix of East and West may be a model for the future."[2] It was a nice birthday present for FP chief Manny Pangilinan, who had just turned fifty and celebrated it with a big bash at the posh Shangri-la Hotel in Manila — he was now the head of a certified blue-chip company.

For Liem a more significant personal celebration came later in the year. In November, he travelled to the United States to accept a "Dean's Medal" conferred on him by the famous Wharton School at the University of Pennsylvania. Described as "the school's highest tribute", awardees, Wharton said, are "chosen for their contributions to the expansion of the global economy and to the improvement in the lives of people worldwide". According to the school, the dean selects individuals who "through excellence in management, have truly made a difference in the promotion of a peaceful and prosperous world". Among prominent awardees in Asia were Philippine President Fidel Ramos (1993), and former Thai Prime Minister Anand Panyarachun (1994). The Dean's Medal is not an honorary doctorate, which only the University of Pennsylvania itself can confer, but is considered as prestigious. Anthony had arranged for a US$1.6 million donation to the school, through alumnus Manny. It was to honour his father who only had a few years of informal schooling in his village but who always had high regard for education.

At the 15 November ceremony, Liem donned the cap-and-gown for the first time in his life. Wharton Dean Thomas P. Gerrity lavished praise on Liem, saying his enterprising nature was "the hallmark of his exceptional career". After noting that Suharto set out to rebuild Indonesia, Gerrity said: "Mr Liem has helped to lead the resurgence of the Indonesian economy through his leadership in private sector growth." As chairman of First Pacific, Gerrity added, Liem had become a "global business leader". After calling Liem to the podium to receive the medal, the dean declared: "I want to salute you for the exceptional role you have played in Indonesia's history and for the model of business and management leadership you offer." The medal's citation read: "Entrepreneur, Industrialist, Patriot and Patriarch — In Recognition of a Lifetime of Management Leadership, Achievement and Commitment to Family, Country and the Pursuit of Excellence."[3]

Reading a brief speech in Indonesian that Anthony then translated, Liem said that because of Indonesia's economic opportunities, plus support from friends and colleagues, Salim was involved in a spectrum of business activities in "many parts of the world... more than 225,000 jobs have been created". Liem described Salim's business philosophy as "honesty, hard work, integrity, prudence and open-mindedness". Achievements, he said, are only half of what's important, stating "The other half is to have a good, truly harmonious family, where my wife is my staunch companion and crutch."[4] Manny later described the ceremony as "a big occasion and quite rightly".[5] Wharton used the donation to create the Liem Sioe Liong/First Pacific Company Professorship. In a statement, Dean Gerrity described Liem as "a legend in Southeast Asia", and said the creation of the chair was "symbolic" of Wharton's growing internationalization and "the global nature of today's successful businesses".[6] The business school's associate dean for international relations, Jeffrey Sheehan, said that Wharton maintained "close relations" with Anthony Salim and Manny after the chair was established. "It is an honour for the school to have this professorship named for both a visionary business leader and a great company", he remarked.[7] Anthony said that for his father, receiving the Wharton medal was "something that is precious. It meant a lot to him." About establishing the chair, he said: "That is my gift to my dad."[8]

A TAX THAT WASN'T REALLY ONE

Suharto had always been proud of his efforts to bring development to the country, but one of the nagging social issues as Indonesia progressed was the wide income disparity. At the start of 1996, Indonesians learned of Suharto's new plan to elicit money from the well-off to help the poor. The last decree of 1995 — he signed ninety that year — stipulated that taxpayers with annual income of Rp100 million or more should give 2 per cent of their net income for social welfare programmes. The decree did not specify who would handle the payments.

On 15 January, this question was answered; the collector would be a new foundation called Dana Sejahtera Mandiri (or Prosperous Self-Reliant Fund), known as Damandiri. According to an announcement that day, the foundation would be chaired by Suharto "in his personal capacity". Many Indonesians winced at the creation of yet another *yayasan*, especially one backed by a presidential decree asking for money. Suharto made three inner-circle people vice-chairmen: Liem, Sudwikatmono and People's Welfare Minister Haryono Suyono. The president named his son Bambang Trihatmodjo treasurer and Anthony Salim assistant treasurer. Retnowati Abdulgani-Knapp, in her authorized biography of Suharto, called tapping Liem a "brilliant move", as he would undoubtedly rope in the heads of other conglomerates.[9] However, two academics threw cold water on the foundation, pointing out that its prominent figures "are not people normally associated with social welfare".[10] They said the foundation's establishment "gives every impression of being a cynical and desperate exercise intended to bolster the government's social justice credentials at a time of increasing popular anger directed at the rich in general — and at Suharto's family in particular. It shows that even the objective of social justice is subject to the politics of patronage." The academics quoted a member of parliament as saying the *yayasan* "was set up so the president and conglomerates could demonstrate they care about the poor. But that is bull — ... Poverty must be tackled through the state budget and government policies, not by a private foundation."

At Damandiri's launch, Sudwikatmono put it differently. "This represents a calling", he insisted. "We in Indonesia must work in harmony and in concert ... as businessmen, we call on our friends not just to talk but to implement as well."[11] Liem, hounded by reporters at the launch, said only that 2 per cent "is a small amount". Anthony acknowledged complaints but said the foundation was "probably the most realistic and effective way" to give seed capital for starting businesses to poor Indonesians not reached by the government. He said paying the 2 per cent was just a suggestion and did not affect big numbers of people.[12] Shortly after the launch, a booklet mailed to 11,000 people with incomes above the threshold contained a note addressed to "Affluent Taxpayers" that began: "You should consider yourselves fortunate to have been able to seize the opportunities presented during the overall development activities in this Land of Pancasila." Now, "you have the opportunity to carry out the noble task of poverty alleviation together with the government".[13] Later, the real arm-twisting would begin.

Later in the year, the president lamented that half of those approached had not contributed, ominously adding: "Perhaps they have difficulties. If they have difficulties, I can help… Perhaps in the assessment of their tax obligations, the director-general for tax can assist in the process."[14] Suharto, despite his power, could not unilaterally impose or raise taxes, but he could sign a decree aimed at twisting arms. Presidential Decree No. 92 of 1996, signed on 4 December, stated: "It is deemed necessary to intensify the realization of aid" to needy families. "Organizational taxpayers as well as individual taxpayers have an obligation (*wajib*) to provide aid" amounting to 2 per cent for companies or individuals with net income of more than Rp100 million. Like the earlier decree, the new one did not mention that a Suharto-chaired foundation was handling the donations.

Suharto even suggested vigilante-like action to get people to pay. He told villagers in Central Java that rich people would be "morally chastised" if they did not donate. "There's no need to lash out or be upset. Just mark their houses… with flags or whatsoever, they should be ashamed then." Also, he said businessmen "do not need to worry about how the funds will be channelled, because the mechanism to distribute them has been set up".[15] Suharto's effort to strong-arm people triggered new grumbling and showed the president's increasingly poor judgement. According to documents quoted by Kyodo News, Damandiri collected Rp4.56 trillion and one disbursement was Rp113 billion to shore up Bank Andromeda, shuttered in 1997, which was partly owned by Bambang, the foundation's treasurer.[16]

MORE FAVOURS FOR FAMILY AND FRIENDS

While Suharto was fretting about the poor response for his call to aid the poor, the number of his family members clamouring for a piece of the cake was growing. By early that year, a company partly owned by eldest grandson Ari H. Wibowo Hardojudanto (son of Sigit) was getting ready to start a rent-seeking plan guaranteed to rake in money — as well as raise the ire of tourists and beer suppliers to the country's main tourist draw, Bali. Ari's company received a licence from Bali authorities to issue stickers for every bottle or can of beer and alcohol sold, confirming that excise tax had been paid. This was ostensibly to combat smuggling, but it was not explained why tax authorities themselves could not handle the job. Naturally, contracting a private firm to do the job would incur mark-ups. Bali's governor appointed Ari's company, Arbamass Multi Invesco, to sell the Rp200 stickers for which distributors would pay it Rp600 for each. Indonesia's two main brewers, Bintang and Anker, showed surprising spine and resisted, saying they would pay Rp200 to the provincial government but not three times as much to Arbamass. When the sticker-system went into effect in January 1996, Bali went "dry". "I'm going beserk" from complaints, moaned Tommy Raka of the Indonesian Hotels and Restaurants Association, "If there's no beer, that's bloody terrible for a tourist destination."[17]

In this unprecedented case, anger from Bali and the national tourism industry derailed a terrible idea. Industry Minister Tunky Ariwibowo got the president's nod to have the monopoly spiked. Suharto, of course, never said anything. After meeting him on 1 February, Tunky said the government wouldn't allow private firms to collect official levies; all unofficial fees, he added, were a "burden to society". Beer started flowing again in Bali. But the derailment didn't stop the Suharto clan from widening their rent-seeking behaviour; the grandson was soon back in action, with levies involving birds' nest and imports of Chinese medicine. He even tried to force a "national shoe" for all Indonesian schoolchildren, but was tripped up by negative publicity. Then there was another case in which Bambang had exerted a monopoly on the transport of oranges in part of Kalimantan.

Despite the victory in Bali, 1996 produced a heavy dose of bad policy and governance news. One day, 19 February, turned out to be particularly damaging, with three developments. The first involved a new fund-raising drive by Suharto, who for the second time in two months became chairman of a non-state endeavour "in his personal capacity". He was spearheading efforts to raise money for Habibie's plan to build a 130-seat jet to compete with Boeing and Airbus. The plane was named the N-2130, and the company seeking US$2 billion in donations was PT Dua Satu Tiga Puluh (the Indonesian for two-one-thirty), or PT 2130, which would sell "shares" that didn't trade or pay dividends. At DSTP's 19 February launch at the Presidential Palace, attended by Sudwikatmono and other tycoons, Suharto described the jet as "vital".[18] The president thanked fifty-five businesses that had (been arm-twisted to) put in a combined US$50 million towards the first year's target of US$400 million. No details on the shareholdings were available.

For those who questioned the huge expenditure on what they perceived as a wanton project, this was not yet a time to be too vociferous in protests.

B.N. Marbun, a member of the Indonesian Democratic Party (PDI) struck one sour note, pointing out "there is no law that allows the head of state to head a private company". But to avoid trouble, he hastily added that DSTP was legitimate and praiseworthy.[19] An editorial in the *Jakarta Post* cheekily commented that DSTP "may have the most political clout of all private companies in Indonesia".[20] Noting how tough it would be to compete against the Boeing-737, the English-language daily said Suharto was "wise" to rule out using state money for the N-2130, adding that "his personal involvement will continue to be strategic in attracting private investors". While Indonesians were getting increasingly critical, at this stage few were willing to directly confront Suharto.

Still, people could vote with their wallets against Suharto's jet-promotion campaign, by ignoring his pitch. Redoubling efforts in March, he urged each one of the nearly 200 million Indonesians to give US$10, ominously adding that "all citizens must participate".[21] In June, Suharto told district chiefs and mayors "this is no white elephant, not at all … this is something we desperately need. And we have to build this before others do, so that we can secure the market… national pride doesn't come cheap. We have to pay for it."[22] But most Indonesians did not want to pay for Habibie's costly dreams and schemes, and Suharto paid a price by pushing for them.

The second of 19 February's three developments was the granting to son Bambang and his partners what the government earlier said they wouldn't get — tariff protection for a petrochemical project. Finance Minister Mar'ie Muhammad quietly signed a decree imposing a 25 per cent tariff on ethylene imported to make polyethylene, a policy that benefited ethylene-maker PT Chandra Asri. Mar'ie, who won kudos in 1995 for opposing such tariff protection, did not comment. Word of the decree only emerged in March, and from New York. The tariff move was a material development that U.S.-listed PT Tri Polyta Indonesia, which used ethylene, had to report. Tri Polyta made polypropylene, which already had a 40 per cent import tariff. Bambang, Sudwikatmono (who was the company's president-director) and Ibrahim Risjad were shareholders.[23]

The third policy move signed the same day would prove to be the most damaging. Again, it was done on the quiet and did not come to public attention for nine days. The "Presidential Instruction No. 2/1996 on the Development of the National Automobile Industry" was the innocuous title of the document that was to kick up a ruckus in the car industry and set off another wave of indignation at Suharto's blatant favouritism for his family's businesses. The "Instruction" had a stated goal of "continuing to strengthen the self-reliance of the nation", with the creation of a *mobil nasional* — "national car". What Indonesia got was a legal basis for son Tommy to get a stunningly unfair advantage over all auto assemblers, including Liem's Indomobil and Astra. The *mobil nasional* policy granted Tommy huge tax breaks for what essentially were fully assembled cars from South Korea. The fiasco did more than any other act to galvanize enmity to Suharto and his family.

At the palace on 26 February, the chairman of Kia Motors of South Korea, accompanied by Tommy, presented Suharto ten prototypes of Kia Sephia (with a couple of tweaks) that was called, strangely, the "Timor". Suharto donated the vehicles to Jakarta's police. Tommy told reporters Kia and he would invest $260 million in a joint venture. The full picture became clear two days later at an Industry Ministry press conference announcing Suharto's 19 February instruction and a host of decrees that gave Tommy and Kia special tax breaks. At one stroke, Suharto upset the auto industry, foreign governments who saw violations of World Trade Organization rules and growing numbers of Indonesians. Making a bad situation awful was how Kia could not immediately get production started in Indonesia. In June, that spawned Presidential Decree No. 42, in which Suharto permitted the first 45,000 "Timors" to be imported from Seoul tax-free and completely built-up; so the first batches of Indonesia's "national car" were in fact fully "Made in Korea".

The Industry Ministry tried, without success, to dislodge the view that Indonesia was re-regulating. It said the petrochemical tariff and the national car were exceptions to Jakarta's "steady and consistent" policy of deregulation. "As in all developing countries and even in the developed countries, conditions can arise that call for exceptional actions", the ministry asserted.[24] Suharto's exceptional favour to his youngest son hit even Salim, whose Indomobil unit was the second biggest auto assembler, after Astra. In 1990, Indomobil had tried and failed to sell a low-cost sedan — a modified Suzuki — called the MR-90 (for *mobil rakyat*, or people's car). The vehicle wasn't much cheaper than competitors, as it received no tax benefits, and Indonesian consumers apparently had no interest in a small (1300 cc engine) car to fight it out on the crowded roads. Indomobil and Astra were both upset by Suharto's "national car" policy but couldn't show it for fear of angering the ruler. Indomobil President-Director Soebronto Laras was quoted as saying it was lucky Indomobil also assembled motorcycles and trucks as the new policy would badly affect its sedans.[25] Later, when Tommy and Kia faced difficulties getting their factory built near Jakarta, Indomobil was leaned on to offer facilities for the "national car", though that never happened.

DEATH AND DESTRUCTION

The big cast riled by the national car policy went "in-house" — Tommy's brother Bambang, who had partnered another South Korean car manufacturer, Hyundai, lobbied for one of their car models to also be designated a "national car" and get similar tax breaks. Tension mounted on the home front. On 28 April, Ibu Tien died. Married for nearly fifty years, she had been Suharto's steadfast companion — "a dream partner and deep friend", as biographer R.E. Elson put it ... "patient, resourceful ... and a reliable source of commonsense and somewhat prudish advice".[26] The cause of her death was given as a heart attack. It happened after a family dinner. Jakarta's rumour mill went into overdrive, speculating that a row broke out between Bambang and Tommy over cars. In the most extreme version, one of the sons fired a shot and the bullet allegedly hit their mother. However, there is no evidence she died anything other than a natural death. The seventy-two-year-old had been suffering from several ailments, including diabetes, and it was reported that she died an hour or so after being admitted to hospital. Shortly after Tien Suharto's death was announced, Salim TV station Indosiar halted regular broadcasts and devoted all airtime to it for one week, with coverage of her life and charity activities. To cynics, Indosiar's blanket coverage was a way of thanking Suharto for being such a loyal friend of Salim. Tien's death marked the loss of the president's soulmate. Many Javanese believed her death robbed Suharto of his *wahyu*, or soul of being a leader, which they believed was derived from his wife. With her demise, many noticed, his power diminished. Indeed, for Suharto, things appeared to go downhill from there. Certainly, she was no longer around to curtail her children's excesses.

Less than a week after Tien's death, the government was embarrassed by the escape from prison of Golden Key boss Eddy Tansil. After that furore faded, attention shifted to the government's less-than-subtle manoeuvring inside the PDI to get Megawati Sukarnoputri, Sukarno's daughter, removed as chairwoman. This was rooted in Suharto's fear that upstarts in PDI, one of two parties he allowed to compete with Golkar in parliamentary elections, would get Megawati to make her group into a real opposition. Naturally, Suharto's own hand could not be seen in the supposedly internal agitation for Megawati's removal; it involved some retired military men who had joined her party, and got help from current officers. Megawati failed to thwart the move to toss her out at the party's June congress. Her successor was a former party leader, Suryadi, who Suharto quickly blessed.

Some Megawati supporters, angered by the blatantly engineered takeover, refused to vacate PDI's headquarters in central Jakarta. On 27 July, Jakarta police and men purported to be Suryadi-backers stormed the office, injuring about two dozen occupants. This prompted thousands of pro-Megawati demonstrators to descend on the office, and police used violence to break up the crowd. In the worst political disturbance in Jakarta in many years, at least three people were killed and more than fifty injured. The military, without any evidence or credibility, blamed the violence on alleged neo-communists wanting to overthrow Suharto. But the cause was the military's intervention in politics and desire for Suharto to have a smooth path to re-election in 1998.

Megawati's removal increased concerns about the country's stability and presidential succession. Many lenders to Indonesian companies weren't bothered by the Jakarta violence, as they saw Suharto remaining firmly on top and a tiger-like economy growing more than 7 per cent in 1996. But there were rising doubts. In a prescient commentary headlined "Is Indonesia Really a Tiger?" two weeks before the Jakarta violence, David Roche of Independent Strategy argued that the answer was definitely no. Indonesia's banks, he wrote, "are the weakest in non-communist Asia because of constant political interference over who gets access to domestic and foreign capital. The result is an overdependence on foreign capital to satisfy domestic demand growth and high foreign indebtedness." Roche also asserted that the government's mega-projects "play to none of Indonesia's natural strengths. The national-car project is an example of nepotism and irrational decision-making on a large scale" while airplane-making is "another flight of fancy in a domain where Indonesia has zero comparative advantage".[27]

BUSINESS — AND *"INTERVENSI"* — AS USUAL

The "national car" was the most egregious example of intervention in business by the government in 1996. But it wasn't the only instance in which Suharto undertook *intervensi* in the economy and the corporate world that year to get a result he wanted. The auto sector saw another big case, this one concerning top assembler Astra International and involving Salim. Since the collapse of the founding Soeryadjaya family four years earlier, Salim held slightly more than 4 per cent of Astra but it purposely remained a silent part-owner. 1996 brought tough times for Astra, thanks to the privileges accorded to Tommy. Still, *kretek* tycoon Putera Sampoerna made a bid to get into the driver's seat. That collided with the wishes of Suharto, who intervened to thwart Putera. His unsuccessful takeover was one of the last big cases of Suharto *intervensi* in business.

Putera's Chinese surname is also Liem (Lin, in *pinyin*) and his ancestors also hailed from Fujian province. His grandfather, Liem Seeng Tee, was born in 1893 in the tea-growing district of Anxi, north of Xiamen. He was five years old when his mother died, and the heartbroken widower brought the child to Surabaya. In 1913, Liem Seeng Tee, who died in 1956, started a provision stall in Surabaya at which *kretek* were rolled and sold. That root evolved to PT Hanjaya Mandala Sampoerna. After Suharto came to power and leaned on Chinese to Indonesianize names, family members started using Sampoerna (which means "perfect"). Through decades, PT H.M. Sampoerna innovated and thrived. In 2005, Putera sold the company to Philip Morris for US$5.2 billion. Born in 1947 as Liem Tien Pao, Putera (the Indonesian name means prince, or son) spent his formative years outside Indonesia. He graduated from the University of Houston, married a Chinese-American and, for some years, worked for the family business from Singapore. Low-profile Putera took PT Sampoerna public in 1990. He was viewed as an odd man out, neither *pribumi* nor really Chinese; to some, he was considered too Westernized (his mother was of Dutch heritage). Neither Putera nor his father, who died in 1994, was part of Prasetiya Mulya Foundation involving most Indonesian Chinese tycoons. In January 1993, Putera was not on the list of potential buyers when the Soeryadjayas needed to sell Astra.

But Putera saw much potential at Astra. In February 1996 — just before the national car policy was unveiled — Putera announced he had accumulated 1.5 per cent of Astra's shares, and he kept buying in the open market as the share-price slid due to Tommy's project and the July violence after Megawati's backers were forcibly dislodged from her party's headquarters. By late September, Putera had accumulated nearly 13 per cent and was moving toward the 25 per cent level that would trigger an offer for all shares. But his moves drew resistance from "Cendana" — the name used for Suharto's family. In October, *Kompas* newspaper revealed that a company led by the president's golf partner Bob Hasan would buy 10 per cent of Astra. Indeed, there was such a purchase by PT Nusamba Ampera Bakti, which was 80 per cent owned by three foundations that Suharto chaired, 10 per cent by son Sigit and 10 per cent by Bob Hasan. State Secretary Moerdiono then surprisingly announced that the government "expects Astra to remain a public company" with no single party owning a majority. Asked if the government was intervening in a private company, he replied, "It is the government's duty to intervene in a positive way".[28] According to people knowledgeable about Astra, Suharto communicated to Putera to stop trying for control of the car company; the cigarette executive was, in effect, told to back off and make way for Cendana-linked control.

Putera may have been on the verge of buying Astra when he got derailed. At the end of October, he disclosed that he personally had a 15 per cent stake while PT Sampoerna said that the company made and then cancelled a US$500 million plan to buy an additional 25 per cent through a tender offer. If this had been successful, that would have given Putera 40 per cent of Astra. PT Sampoerna said it dropped the plan due to coolness from shareholders, who did not want the *kretek* maker diversifying into cars. Concurrently, other Astra shareholding changes were made. Anthony ended up owning 7.4 per cent, up from less than 5 per cent, through PT Indo Artsa Bangsa. (Artsa is Astra spelled backwards.) Another Prasetiya Mulya backer, Usman Admadjaja of Bank Danamon, also had 7.4 per cent. In line with Moerdiono's comment about no one having a majority, Bob melded an informal (and uncomfortable) group of five men who together held more than 50 per cent: Bob (through Nusamba), Anthony, Usman, timber tycoon Prajogo Pangestu and Putera. Even though Putera had a bigger stake, Bob was now piloting Astra, and would soon become its chairman.

At a news conference at Bob's office, the five affirmed they would work together to "enhance" Astra's value. Anthony pledged that actions "will be in the best interests of Astra, not individual shareholders". Putera did not look buoyant, but when asked if he was happy to be part of the group, replied: "If I wasn't happy, I wouldn't be sitting here."[29] Anthony had a lot of exposure to presidential *intervensi* and accepted that Suharto wanted Bob atop Astra. Despite getting thwarted, Putera did emerge as a bigger player in corporate Indonesia. In March 1997, forming a partnership with Salim, he bought 5.6 per cent of Indofood. Commentator Christianto Wibisono said Putera's alliance would let him "increase his Chinese connections. With his Western education, Putera has never been as close to the Chinese tycoons as Anthony Salim is. But Putera is now positioned as an insider."[30] Around the time Putera was put in his place on Astra, another case of *intervensi* was unfolding: the Busang gold scandal. A battle over what was believed to be the world's biggest gold find pitted rival miners and Suharto children against each other. Salim played no role in this tale of greed and opportunism, but Bob did.

ALL THAT GLITTERS...

The Busang story revolves around Bre-X Minerals, a tiny Canadian company once unheard of outside the mining industry. The Calgary-based firm got listed in Toronto and on Nasdaq after obtaining rights to mine a remote part of Kalimantan. In early 1996, Bre-X claimed it had discovered a mother lode of gold, sending its shares skyrocketing. Opponents eyeing the trove thwarted Bre-X's path using the labyrinthine Indonesian bureaucracy. Given how the New Order's business environment was anything but transparent, this episode is worth highlighting. The Busang case was the first (and only) in which a foreign investor announced what it would pay a Suharto offspring to be on its side. Bre-X, afraid of losing rights to its trove, in October 1996 trumpeted a "strategic alliance" with a business group led by Sigit, who stayed out of the public eye.

Bre-X hired Sigit to help remove obstacles such as an Indonesian miner who claimed 40 per cent of its concession. A Bre-X release announced that "subject to the fulfillment of certain conditions", the Calgary company would pay Sigit's Panutan Group US$40 million for forty-months consulting work — US$1 million a month — to "assist in administrative, technical and other support matters". It also said Panutan would get a 10 per cent "carried interest", i.e., a free share, in two of Busang's three zones. A Canadian paper called virtually unknown Panutan "a powerful industrial concern with interests in energy, mining and telecommunications".[31] Bre-X Chairman David G. Walsh said he was "delighted to have formed an alliance with a strong Indonesian partner".[32] The lure of treasure was far too great to resist; Sigit's sister Tutut started helping Bre-X's bigger Canadian rival, Barrick Gold, try to snatch rights to the lode. In February 1997, Bob Hasan was called in to stave off a potentially nasty Suharto family brawl over Busang by fixing a deal that cut in Freeport McMoRan Copper & Gold, chopped Bre-X's stake and carved out 30 per cent for two Bob-led companies. But within three months, Freeport discovered that the mother lode was a hoax, saying there were at most "trace amounts" of gold in Busang. Bob, who didn't lose any money, shrugged off the world-class fraud. But the fiasco worsened the image of the Suharto family, and portrayed Indonesia as a place of great greed.

In the first quarter of 1997, there was another damaging state *intervensi*, involving a booming business, palm oil. The investment board (BKPM) announced it would not approve any more foreign investment in oil palm plantations. The move came while the board was weighing six applications, four by Malaysian firms. The U.S. and Foreign Commercial Service said the decision stemmed from a judgement that "foreigners had over-invested in oil palm plantations and there was a need to give a better chance to domestic firms". A cable from the service noted press speculation that the decision reflected lobbying by large Indonesian investors including "the Sinar Mas and Salim conglomerates, both controlled by influential ethnic Chinese businessmen with strong political connections".[33] Domestically, there were complaints about the ban. The *Jakarta Post* blasted it, saying that if big groups kept expanding, they would strengthen their grip on the industry. That, it said, "is not healthy for the long-term development of the sector, especially because two of the groups — Salim and Sinar Mas — also dominate the downstream palm oil industry."[34] Salim and Sinar Mas denied getting the ban imposed. In plantations, shutting the door to foreigners was one of many policies the IMF pressed Suharto to change when the Asian financial crisis enveloped Indonesia. In Presidential Instruction No. 6 of 1998, signed 21 January 1998, foreigners were again allowed to invest in palm oil. Following Suharto's fall, Guthrie of Malaysia bought the plantations that Salim surrendered.

THE STORM MOVES ONSHORE

May 1997 featured what turned out to be the last parliamentary election under Suharto. As usual, the president's well-funded Golkar — Liem remained a major donor — was guaranteed to win. But by now, the voting ritual designed to give Suharto's regime some credibility could not do it. People clamoured for reform and a say in politics, but Suharto stubbornly resisted. About two weeks before the 29 May election, Liem was called upon again to lend a helping hand to a business concern connected to the First Family. BCA was asked to stabilize a troubled small bank, Bank Yakin Makmur, known as Yama. The small bank had a big main owner — Suharto daughter Tutut, who was also a Golkar deputy chairwoman. As questions about the bank surfaced, Tutut was conveniently unavailable to answer them as she was out on the campaign trail. After Suharto's fall, it was revealed that Bank Yama had made hefty loans to Tutut's television station TPI. Substantial loans also went to Chandra Asri, the controversial petrochemical project involving her brother Bambang and headed by her friend, the businessman Prajogo Pangestu. The bank's plight should not have come as a surprise: As early as October 1995, Bank Indonesia (BI) flagged Yama's problems, saying the bank and Bank Pacific, run by Ibnu Sutowo's daughter, "need technical and management assistance from another bank in order to improve the management and operation".[35] The central bank appointed state-owned Bank Negara Indonesia to help, but the efforts were futile.

BCA's quick move to bolster Yama allowed Tutut to avoid the embarrassment of having the central bank take action against her bank. BCA president Abdullah Ali, chased by reporters to confirm rumours of BCA aid, acknowledged: "We are giving management and other assistance to Bank Yama to restore it to a sound condition."[36] However, it appeared to be a case of pouring good money after bad; Yama never got restored, even though BCA took a 25 per cent stake. In March 1999, ten months after Suharto's exit, authorities shut Yama. But from Suharto's point of view, Salim did a favour to shore it up so there was no run on the bank just before the 1997 elections.

Suharto wanted to ensure a big election victory, but the margin was arguably too big. Golkar churned out its biggest tally, 74 per cent, in an election that had the least credibility of any in the New Order because of the 1996 manoeuvres to remove Sukarno's daughter Megawati as leader of the PDI. It was evident that Suharto engineered the removal of "Ibu Mega" after observing with alarm her growing popularity. The Megawati-less PDI received a mere 3 per cent of votes, compared with 15 per cent in 1992 when the party was led by a man who was not popular. After the 1997 vote, the chairman of a non-government Independent Election Monitoring Committee, journalist Goenawan Mohamad, remarked violations of fair procedures "were systematic because the election was organized by government officials who have to maintain the single domination of Golkar".[37]

In commerce, it was business as usual. Less than ten days after the election, contracts were signed for two projects to privatize Jakarta's water supply, one involving Salim and the other Sigit. The deals were signed two years after Suharto told his public works minister to privatize Jakarta's water. Suharto instructed officials to give a contract covering half of Jakarta to Thames of the United Kingdom, with Sigit, and for the other half to Suez Lyonnaise of France, teamed with Salim, according to an investigation by journalist Andreas Harsono.[38] His report quoted a Thames official as saying "At the time, any company dealing with Indonesia would have to deal with almost some element of the Suharto family because of the way the government was set up. It was quite transparent." The previous year, Anthony had talked up plans to work with water-supply, saying "I wanted to do something new".[39] Asked about the flak Salim could receive for obtaining another Suharto favour if appointed for Jakarta water privatization, Anthony replied there were "so many other cities" where other companies could make proposals. But the Jakarta water authority opposed its privatization, and some Indonesians saw this as another case of "personalization", as there was no tender process. The government felt compelled to do something, as most Jakarta residents had no access to treated water, and too much underground water was being drawn from wells. Anthony defended the work and contracts. He said that based on a United Nations study on seawater intrusion, Suharto "asked if we had any solution for this". The president, he asserted, set a condition that Salim could not make money from the work. Anthony asserted that Salim was "wrongly implicated" by critics. He added that the city utility resisted privatization because some officials resisting change received money from suppliers of water-treatment chemicals. Regarding how Suharto ordered the Public Works Department to privatize Jakarta water, Anthony commented: "he has authority to do that. I follow the rules."[40]

Anthony also wanted to be a player in an ambitious Suharto plan to grow rice on the island of Borneo. The plan to convert a staggering one million hectares of swampy stretches into rice fields hit snags. The president, ignoring opponents, insisted his plan could restore the country to rice self-sufficiency. But environmentalists decried the scheme, maintaining rice-cultivation was not feasible in the swamps and would damage ecosystems as well as force indigenous people off their land. In a 1996 interview, Anthony said rice-growing in Kalimantan "makes sense" economically and the expected profit should be "not bad at all".[41] The rice proposal, however, did not move far forward — and neither did many other plans in mid-1997, due to the Asian financial crisis.

On 2 July 1997, Thailand shocked the financial world by abruptly devaluing the baht. Salim and nearly all others in Jakarta initially assumed this was a far-away storm that would not reach Indonesia. Complacency was bred by good economic numbers and false assumptions. Indonesia's pivotal import at the time was money, and it was still receiving plenty. Foreign donors, who had their annual gathering in early July, still wanted to believe reform was proceeding, even though a deregulation package completed before their meeting failed to impress; Bulog's monopoly on the import of raw sugar was ended, but that was relatively minor compared with the agency's role in wheat, where nothing was done. The amount pledged by donors totalled US$5.3 billion.

Just as currency turbulence elsewhere in Asia began to have some impact — on 11 July, Bank Indonesia widened the band in which the rupiah could trade — some attention in Jakarta was drawn to a surprise announcement by Salim. On 15 July, it unveiled plans to shift control of Indofood from Indocement, which then owned 60 per cent, to Salim's tiny Singapore-listed food company QAF, which once was Brunei-owned. This would make Indofood a foreign-investment company under Indonesian law rather than a domestic one. Academic Marleen Dieleman likened QAF buying Indofood to a dwarf buying a giant.[42] Like many Salim corporate moves, it was complex and controversial. Making their case, group executives argued that it would effectively mean a big new foreign investment in Indonesia. But because majority ownership of Indofood would move overseas, the proposal came under heavy attack as capital flight. Critics said it showed Salim was scared about its position in post-Suharto Indonesia. Salim executives sought to deny the proposal was tantamount to capital flight. Anthony contended the plan would stimulate lagging investor interest in shares of Indocement by making it the pure cement company it had started out as, while creating in QAF a potential "pan-Asian" food-product powerhouse.[43]

Economist Rizal Ramli blasted the restructuring as "a threat to national economic stability" and accused Salim of acting like a "peanut that has forgotten its shell".[44] (Some years later, Rizal renewed his attack on Salim, this time armed with greater ammunition as by then he had been appointed senior economic minister.) Djisman Simanjuntak, an economist involved in running Liem-supported Prasetiya Mulya's management school, said that with Asia falling into crisis, "this is the best possible time to remove the monopolies that up until now have been perceived as benefiting the [Salim] group".[45] Faisal Basri, an outspoken University of Indonesia economist, told Tempo Interactive — a website begun after Suharto shut the magazine in 1994 — that as Salim's business had been "assigned" by the president, it would be strange if the group's Singapore move lacked a green light from Indonesia's "superstructure". Basri commented: "I don't see Salim as a devil, because a crazier devil is right behind him." He also said he understood Salim's thinking for making Indofood a foreign-investment company. In the heated debate over Salim, "some people even say that Indofood should be taken over by the state, because it is now controlling the lives of the people at large", he said. "Which company can have peace with threats like these?" And, Basri noted, Singapore's corporate tax was only 20 per cent and companies do not have to pay bribes, whereas in Indonesia they faced 30 per cent tax plus the extras. Basri also tweaked Ramli, saying that because the critic of the Indofood plan "could not reach his shooting target, i.e. Suharto, he took on Salim. This makes me ask: Is it fair that we judge Salim as such [a peanut in a shell] while in the meantime the true target is unreachable? ... why is it that the grantor of the facility granted is never questioned? So who is the peanut and who is the shell?" To Basri, the issue was not Indofood's move, but Salim's monopolistic position in flour-milling. The government says it's ready to remove the monopoly, "so do that! The fact is that it is the government which is not ready. It is the government that continues to block here and block there."[46]

Some government officials were trying to end Bulog monopolies. Coordinating Economics Minister Saleh Afiff said: "If I have the full authority, I will slash them all, except for rice, our national staple, which I will not touch at all."[47] The statement was clear — but so was the fact Saleh Afiff had no authority. Sudwikatmono retorted: "we are happy" if the wheat-import monopoly ended.[48] This is because the flak over Bogasari would end, without any loss of business. Economist Didik Rachbini said it was already too late for dismantling the monopoly, as after decades of holding the exclusive rights to mill Bulog's wheat, "who can now challenge Bogasari's domination in wheat flour?"[49] Aside from Bogasari and the former Prima mill in Sulawesi that it controlled, the only other facility at this time was Tutut's small Citra Flour Mill in Central Java, and another being built that involved former Bulog chairman Bustanil Arifin.

Eventually, the government announced it had no issue with Indofood's Singapore proposal. State Secretary Moerdiono praised the way Salim laid out its plan as a "progressive step toward transparency, which I think should be followed by other companies". He apparently did not realize there was a legal obligation to inform Indofood's shareholders. Moerdiono dismissed assertions of capital flight, and said Suharto was "fully convinced that Salim will not have the courage to betray his trust".[50] In the end, Salim would scrap the heavily attacked restructuring plan. As the Asian financial crisis unfolded and share prices tumbled (QAF's fell more than 40 per cent in two months), the deal became increasingly unattractive. Salim had it fully underwritten by foreign banks, but it became harder to justify and sell.

STILL IN DREAMLAND

As the Asian financial crisis began to bite, Suharto was still preoccupied with helping family and cronies. On 6 August, he went to Kalimantan to open a US$1.3 billion pulp mill that Bob carved out of the jungle, complete with a landing strip. State banks coughed up more than US$400 million in loans, and Suharto ordered the state's forest replanting fund to lend US$100 million to Bob's company Kiani Kertas. (An environmental group sued to try to block that loan, but its suit was dismissed.) The mill still needed help, and Suharto supplied it with a decree reinstating a type of tax holiday that technocrats halted fifteen years earlier. Six projects involving Suharto friends, none by Salim, qualified for the holiday, with Kiani Kertas getting the longest one, eight years.

Less than a week after Suharto opened the pulp mill, he sent Moerdiono as guest-of-honour at a ground-breaking for a private project to build the world's tallest tower, in north Jakarta. The project was announced in 1995 by PT Indocitra Graha, which involved Sudwikatmono and others (but no Salim involvement). The planned 558-metre Jakarta Tower, with a revolving restaurant at the top, aimed to be 4.5 metres higher than Toronto's CN Tower, then the tallest structure. The cost was pegged at US$560 million. No money had been raised by the time of ground-breaking, at which Moerdiono said the tower would "elevate Jakarta's image on the international stage".[51] The next day, the Asian financial crisis started directly hitting Indonesia as the rupiah, facing the kind of pressure buckling other Asian currencies, broke through the trading band set by the central bank in July. On 14 August, Bank Indonesia Governor Soedradjad Djiwandono shocked the audience of a stock market conference by announcing that Indonesia was floating the rupiah. Corporate chiefs had happily and heavily borrowed offshore dollars — at interest rates far below rupiah loans — in the now-vanished certainty that Indonesia's currency would not weaken more than 3–4 per cent a year.

That day's flotation bombshell sank the rupiah 7 per cent, to 2,825 to the dollar. "I think we'll see the rupiah reassert itself", Salim executive Benny Santoso boldly predicted to reporters. The next day, Santoso said Salim intended to proceed with plans to list Indomobil by year-end and Bank Central Asia in 1998.[52] Several days later, with the rupiah and stock market reeling, it was sinking in that Indonesia could take a big hit. There started to be realization that distortions such as monopolies and interventions by Suharto in favour of family and friends counted more than economic indicators.

For a brief time, Suharto seemed fully aware of the dangers, stating in his National Day speech on 16 August that citizens had to "seriously understand new realities". He asked private companies to carefully choose projects, noting that businesses will find that foreign loans "are no longer easily and cheaply obtained like before the storm".[53] Yet just four days later, Suharto showed he did not grasp the "new realities", signalling again that his children's projects were laudable ones, no matter how little sense they made. The message was conveyed at a palace ceremony where he admired a model of what was billed the world's longest bridge, which middle daughter Titiek proposed to build linking Sumatra to Malaysia. Her intended partner was Renong, a conglomerate linked to Malaysia's ruling United Malays National Organization. "Mr Suharto strongly supports the idea to build the bridge", Titiek told reporters about the proposed ninety-five-kilometre link across the Straits of Malacca. She said funding would come from the stock market and foreign banks.[54] To some investors, the fact that Suharto could not see the harm of his massively mixed signals was as worrying as deteriorating conditions in Asia.

Entrenched on top for so long, Suharto remained convinced his path was right. It did not help that on 8 September, he was given a "Special Citation" by the United Nations Development Programme for Indonesia's "outstanding accomplishment and commitment" to alleviate poverty. It was Suharto's fourth U.N. award, after ones for rice self-sufficiency, family planning and education. His self-confidence was further boosted when visiting U.S. Assistant Secretary of State for East Asia and the Pacific Stanley Roth expressed confidence that Suharto's capable technocrats could keep the economy growing.

At this stage, Salim was still open to expansion. In mid-September, First Pacific bought 2 per cent of Philippine beer giant San Miguel for US$70 million. It indicated it wanted more, though that was stymied by San Miguel's shareholding structure, with a big stake sequestered by the Philippine government after Ferdinand Marcos was chased out in 1986. Back home, a company in which Anthony and U.S. company Enron were shareholders, PT East Java Power, signed a twenty-year agreement under which Pertamina would supply natural gas to a proposed US$525 million, privately owned power plant. The main promoter was former Salim director Johannes Kotjo; Anthony was to be a passive partner, along with Ibrahim Risjad and Bambang. The plan soon got axed by the government, which did not bother Anthony. Also halted was a proposed power plant whose partners included Sudwikatmono. Finance Minister Mar'ie Muhammad, citing worsening economic conditions, halted fifteen "mega" projects, including the Jakarta Tower. But to the dismay of many, the government did not postpone Tommy's "national car". That plan — for which the government leaned on banks to lend a sure-to-lose US$690 million — was untouchable. Also dismaying was how Suharto soon shortened the postponements list. Getting a green-light rather than a yellow (for "review") were power projects involving Bob and Tommy, plus a Surabaya toll-road for Tutut. In September, Suharto appointed 100 people to the 1,000-member People's Consultative Assembly (MPR) that would select the president in March. Part of the appointee list read like a family tree. Suharto named ten relatives, including four of his six children and two of their spouses. Also tapped were Anthony and Bob. After the swearing-in, Tommy gloated: "We are not just in business; we have socio-political roles as well."[55] At that same time, Indonesia was beset with fires, literally. Fires that were set to clear land for planting in Sumatra and Kalimantan, exacerbated by a fierce El Nino drought, were starting to choke Singapore, Kuala Lumpur and a swath of Southeast Asia.

The economy was getting burned, too. On 8 October, with the rupiah at 3,700 to the dollar, Suharto acceded to his technocrats and summoned the International Monetary Fund — not called on for nearly thirty years — to prepare an emergency package to stabilize Indonesia. At the time, the tumbling rupiah was battering companies who borrowed dollars heavily. Even money-machines such as Indofood were rattling. On the same day as the IMF announcement, Indofood tore up its forecast for a record Rp500 billion profit in 1997, and confessed it might not make any profit, due to far higher costs to service at least US$500 million in foreign loans. In a shock to some, the company admitted it had hedged only 15 per cent of its debt.[56] Scarily, Indonesian authorities did not know how much foreign debt was out there. There was a government rule requiring corporations to report debts "but compliance was loose", as then-central bank governor Soedradjad later put it.[57] He invited corporate chiefs to write down how much offshore debt they had.

Shortly after an IMF team arrived to negotiate a rescue package, Golkar held its last congress before the March 1998 presidential assembly. Harmoko, the obsequious former information minister and Golkar chairman, declared the nation would be lost without Suharto at the helm. On 16 October, he told the congress: "There is only one person wanted by the people... this is the people's wish. This is the aspiration of the democracy." The seventy-six-year-old Suharto, already thirty-one years at the helm, announced at the congress "If the people don't want me, there is no problem." Touching on the issue years later, Anthony told the authors that he tried to encourage Suharto to step down, but offered no evidence. Salim was irreversibly and inescapably bound to Suharto, who was very unlikely to step down unless compelled. In October 1997, with the IMF preparing a package, Salim shared Suharto's view that Indonesia could get back on track, with the long-serving president still on top.

TINDERBOX

The IMF routinely responded to members' calls for help by delivering a package containing cash and "conditionality". Some of Suharto's technocrats quietly wanted the IMF to set loan conditions to force the president to do what they could not get him to do, such as ending Bulog's monopoly on wheat. Suharto seemed to think — or wanted to think — that a package deal of cash-plus-conditionality was optional. He only wanted the cash. On 14 October, Moerdiono inexplicably announced the IMF would not impose any conditions in exchange for financial assistance — which could not have been the case. Asked to confirm that Indonesia wanted an IMF loan, he replied "That's right, we want to borrow money", adding that the government had its own programme.[58] Later, Suharto tried to make it look like Indonesia could raise enough money without the IMF; when neighbouring Singapore offered US$5 billion as part of an IMF-led programme, the president deliberately misrepresented the offer, putting it as twice as much, and indicating it was separate from the IMF effort. Suharto dismissed the idea that because Indonesia called in the IMF, therefore Jakarta "must do this, do that. That's mistaken."[59]

But it was Suharto who was badly mistaken. Indonesian negotiators knew Indonesia had to agree to major reforms and, with world pressure mounting, they got Suharto's sign-off on 31 October to a "Letter of Intent" with the IMF. (Eventually, Indonesia would sign sixteen such letters.) Point 41 stated that Jakarta "intends to phase out import and marketing monopolies and price controls on agricultural commodities, except for rice, sugar, and cloves, over the next three years. As a first step, wheat and wheat flour, soybean and garlic will be made freely importable." The exclusion of cloves was obviously a concession for Tommy, but at least some Bulog monopolies would end. "An impenetrable fortress has been breached", a World Bank official said.[60] One day later, the media largely forgot about the wheat deregulation — a significant move — as attention shifted to Indonesia's closure of 16 of its 239 banks, including some associated with the First Family. Finance Minister Mar'ie said the closures were ordered "to repair the health of our banking system". But instead, they made panicked crowds pull money out of other banks. There was political fallout, too; son Bambang owned 25 per cent of shuttered Bank Andromeda while the president's half-brother Probosutedjo owned another closed one, Bank Jakarta. Both began steps to sue Mar'ie. Bambang lambasted the Andromeda closing as "an attempt to sully our family name" so his father would not get another presidential term.[61]

Most damagingly, Bambang was able to quickly buy the licence of another bank, small Bank Alfa, from Liem's eldest son Albert Halim. (Bank Alfa's own assets and liabilities were transferred to Bank Risjad Salim International.) Then-BI governor Soedradjad later wrote that "very quickly, the government's actions [to close banks] were tainted" by Bambang's move.[62] Soedradjad defended BI's acquiescence to the Alfa purchase, saying that as there was no formal connection between Bambang and Andromeda's insolvency, the central bank could not deny his wish to buy Alfa "but of course the decision was perceived by foreign markets as showing the softening of the monetary authorities' stance". The lawsuits by Bambang and Probo, Soedradjad wrote, "tarnished" authorities "and the foreign market joined the domestic market in distrusting the Indonesian banking system". Had Suharto relatives "acted like responsible bankers to accept the bank closure, bank runs may not have followed and banking restructuring could have proceeded as planned. What happened was a self-fulfilling prophecy", he added.[63] On the same day as the bank closures, Suharto made a bad economic situation worse by signing a decree authorizing 15 of the 150 infrastructure projects which were halted six weeks earlier to proceed. The biggest was a Central Java power plant involving Tutut.[64] Also getting the green light was Tutut's plan for a new Medan airport. Markets saw the decree as "a blatant intervention by the President on behalf of the interests of his family and cronies", Soedradjad commented.[65] On 12 November, IMF Managing Director Michel Camdessus arrived in Jakarta to try to stop things from unravelling. He informed the media that Suharto "told me he is fully behind this programme". The IMF chief said he told the president that stabilizing the rupiah should not take long "but one should be careful. Don't believe that with a stable rupiah, everything is done — No!" Changes were needed in how business was done, Camdessus insisted, as "You must be transparent; you can't hide things."[66]

As the country stumbled, the rumour mill accelerated. On 14 November, rumours began in Medan that Liem had died and that BCA's Singapore branch had closed. (BCA did not have a Singapore branch.) The rumours spread to Jakarta, where some people started withdrawing money from BCA branches. Liem, in Singapore that day, returned to Jakarta early, and made it a point to appear on television that evening at Indomobil's launch of a motorcycle, an event he was not scheduled to attend. Before leaving Singapore, Liem told a reporter he was returning home "to show depositors I am still around. Please tell your readers I am still here."[67] At the Indomobil event, he told reporters: "Look at me, I am perfectly fine."[68] The run on BCA drained an estimated Rp500 billion (then US$147 million), President Abdullah Ali said. Former Army Chief of Staff R. Hartono, now the Information Minister (he had replaced Harmoko in that portfolio in June 1997), blamed the rumours on unnamed "irresponsible people". He chided panicked depositors, saying "Why did you instantly believe such rumours [on Liem]? ... It is impossible such a bad thing [as closure] would happen with a big bank like BCA."[69]

The economic crisis was presenting both opportunities and problems for Salim. On the day of the rumours of Liem's death, Anthony signed a memorandum of understanding to give the group an even bigger role in banking. In the deal, Salim would buy 19 per cent of BCA rival Bank Danamon for US$84 million and Credit Suisse First Boston (CSFB), which did investment banking work for Salim, agreed to consider later buying 10 per cent of the 700-branch bank. Danamon was controlled by businessman Usman Admadjaja, a supplier to Pertamina who went into banking in the 1970s. After the 1988 deregulation, he listed the bank and expanded it at lightning speed. In late 1997, Danamon was stretched by its overseas borrowings. A Danamon release said Usman "invited Salim to develop a strategic alliance" and become "an equal partner" with his family, which then owned 48 per cent of Danamon. At a joint press conference, Usman said he and Anthony were "old friends" after co-investing in Astra years earlier. Anthony also put a positive spin on the deal in which Salim was to give Danamon essential support. Salim is putting in money "not because (Danamon) is *jelek* (bad or spoiled), but because it's good".[70] He called it a "pure business decision". The "marriage" with Danamon was never consummated, as events spiralled rapidly downward. On 4 April 1998, Danamon was one of seven banks put under the Indonesian Bank Restructuring Agency (IBRA) after receiving cash injections more than five times its capital. Two days later, Salim and CSFB announced that the Danamon plan was cancelled due to "recent developments".

While BCA took a small hit from rumours of Liem's death, perceptions that the bank was too big and too well-connected to fail allowed it to gain deposits after the closure of sixteen banks. As of 31 December 1997, BCA had Rp43.4 trillion of deposits, compared with Rp38.7 trillion at 30 September. BCA also remained the place to go for some people in a pinch. One example was property honcho Ciputra, who partnered Liem in the 1970s. He recounted being squeezed in late 1997 as he borrowed dollars but had revenue in rupiah. "One day I needed money, so I went to see Om Liem", Ciputra said. "He gave me Rp60 billion, without getting a guarantee." Years later, he remained full of praise for Liem, stating "This man is special."[71] In late 1997, the public couldn't know how unlisted BCA was faring, but investors could see Indofood and Indocement were doing badly; shares of Indofood slid more than 55 per cent in rupiah terms, and about 70 per cent in dollar terms, in the first eleven months of the year. On 26 November, Indofood announced a one-time charge of Rp900 billion for foreign exchange losses and reported a Rp456 billion loss for the first nine months. Given how close Salim was to Suharto, some securities analysts were baffled that Indofood had not bought "forward cover" — secured future supply of dollars — for repaying heavy offshore borrowings prior to July 1997. Marleen Dieleman quoted an unnamed person close to Salim as saying Anthony's financial advisors told him to hedge "but he calculated that it would cost him in the area of US$80–$100 million and he considered this too much. Then the crisis came and it turned out he made a mistake."[72]

Anthony told the authors that when the crisis came, the group's borrowings were about half in rupiah and half from offshore dollars. Overseas loans were not hedged "because we were so confident at that time" that the rupiah would depreciate slowly, he said.[73] In July 1997, when the crisis began, Anthony was expecting to raise money through the Indofood-QAF deal, as QAF would have had rights issues, in dollars, to buy the Indofood stake. The inflow of dollars, he maintained, would have bolstered Salim's finances. Then when the rupiah was floated — Anthony insisted he had no advance notice — "we didn't want to be part of the problem" of Indonesian companies pushing the rupiah down more by rushing to buy dollars... "When people asked me about hedging, then I instructed strictly not to hedge... If we started to move [to buy cover], the market might move in the wrong direction. So we don't want to be the cause of it. That's one; number two, in fact we were trying to help in order to stabilize," he asserted.[74] He also said "if I started to engage on the conversion, dollar to rupiah, or start [going] short in rupiah, long on dollar and try to buy a lot [of cover] ... it will be recorded in the central bank, then I will be in trouble. My hands were tied."[75]

REALITY BITES

Cumulatively, Indonesian companies had taken tens of billions of dollars of unhedged loans from foreign banks that freely shelled it out. The central bank was still trying to get a grip on how much debt Indonesian companies had. For Governor Soedradjad, December 1997 was particularly painful. A mysterious fire on 8 December burned three floors of a new Bank Indonesia tower, killing fifteen people; the rumour mill claimed it was set to destroy papers on key debtors. Then eleven days later, Suharto sacked four of the central bank's seven managing directors without consulting the governor. With the dismissals, Suharto reminded Indonesians he was still in charge — something the public had reason to start to doubt. The president had disappeared at the end of November after a twelve-day, 28,500-kilometre trip that took him to Africa, Canada and Saudi Arabia. Suharto did not appear in public for more than two weeks, and obviously was sick, though officials maintained he just needed rest. He cancelled an Iran trip for an Islamic summit. Then Moerdiono announced Suharto would go to an ASEAN summit in Kuala Lumpur on 15 December but that too was axed; Moerdiono insisted the president had been "refreshed" by rest "however, the freshness needs to be maintained".[76] With government credibility badly shot, the rupiah fell 11 per cent on the "freshness" remark, to 5,225 to the dollar, while the Jakarta Composite Index tumbled 7.6 per cent.

On the weekend of 13–14 December, two weeks after his last appearance, Suharto was shown on TV making brief comments from home saying his doctors had advised him to rest "but now I am healthy and in good condition". He was shown tending to his talking parrot and inspecting his Harley-Davidson motorcycle.[77] On 22 December, his first day in the presidential palace in three weeks, he summoned sixty businesspeople — including four of his children — for an economic pep talk. Suharto assured the assembled group the government had enough money for the budget plus food and fuel subsidies. He did not talk about soaring money supply and inflation as the central bank was injecting heaps of cash, called "liquidity assistance" into strapped Indonesian banks. (Salim was eventually the biggest recipient of such funds, which reached a staggering Rp52 trillion.)[78] To deal with private debt issues, Suharto appointed former economic coordinating minister Radius Prawiro to represent the government on a "contact committee" with foreign lenders screaming for repayment. The president also appointed Anthony as one of three businessmen to "liaise" with Radius. There were grumbles about Anthony's appointment, rooted in suspicions he'd seek a better deal for Salim than others could get. Radius raised a few eyebrows on 29 December when he urged Indonesian companies to be market-oriented. "I call on entrepreneurs, if they want to be strong, not to dream of getting subsidies, protection, special treatment or facilities from the government, similar to what they had received in the past", the former minister said.[79]

For Salim, a drama-filled 1998 began with confirmation that the group would not go ahead with the plan unveiled in July to inject Indofood into Singapore-listed QAF. The proposed rights issue by QAF to finance it — and raise lots of new dollars — was unsellable with Indofood shares down nearly 65 per cent. Salim, UBS Jakarta research head Stephen Rogers said, "will have to learn to restrain itself" and put expansion on hold "for the foreseeable future".[80] Worryingly, however,

Suharto continued to show he was still in serious denial. For the annual budget speech to Parliament on 6 January, his first public function in five weeks, he looked alright but his projections were riddled with wildly unrealistic assumptions. Earlier that day, the rupiah hit 7,000 to the dollar, yet Suharto insisted the rate would average 4,000 during the fiscal year to start on 1 April. He projected that GDP would grow 4 per cent. (It shrank more than 13 per cent.) He said government spending would rise 32 per cent, which would mean zero chance of meeting an IMF requirement of a budget surplus.

Suharto's in-dreamland budget scared markets, which tanked the next morning. The rupiah tumbled 8 per cent and one day later, it got uglier, plunging a further 20 per cent to an unprecedented 10,200 to the dollar amid a chorus of complaints that Suharto was snubbing the IMF, who was paying Jakarta's bills. On Thursday, 8 January, panicked middle-class Jakarta residents grabbed goods off supermarket shelves after rumours that debt-laden food companies such as Indofood would halt production and staples would be rationed. (Indofood said it had no problems.) As the rupiah was dropping like a rock, Anthony and Radius were in the Singapore offices of UBS, telling a group of international creditors private-sector borrowers could not pay their debts in coming months. Back in Jakarta, a parade of world leaders or their representatives arrived to try to get Suharto back on the same page with the IMF. Its chief Camdessus signalled that he would come to sign a new deal. U.S. Treasury Secretary Lawrence Summers was dispatched to Jakarta and President Bill Clinton called Suharto. On 10 January, it looked like the president made some concessions, with announcement of a new Suharto decree stopping the fifteen infrastructure projects that two months earlier he had allowed to proceed, including Tutut's power plant and Medan airport.

Salim, too, had to get real. In Hong Kong that same day, First Pacific announced plans to sell its most profitable asset, 40 per cent of Dutch-based trading company Hagemeyer, and other assets to raise about US$2 billion to get cash and pay down debt. Hagemeyer was one of First Pacific's first purchases and, through waves of asset-trading, one it wisely kept. Explaining the sale, Manny Pangilinan of First Pacific said "The name of the game for the next year or two in Asia is cash."[81] Selling Hagemeyer showed how First Pacific, like many Asian companies, lived on debt. When times were good and loans repayments were modest, profits soared. That's what happened in 1996, when First Pacific reported a net profit of US$204 million. In 1997, it was a different tune. A main factor causing First

Pacific's stock to tumble was worries about debts for its Fort Bonifacio project in Manila, for which it had paid top dollar in 1995. Metro Pacific, First Pacific's Manila unit, had taken on a bigger share of the property when its own plans to borrow offshore were stymied.

On 23 October 1997, when spiking Asia worries knocked 10 per cent off the Hang Seng Index, shares of First Pacific plunged 27 per cent. The stock, which hit an all-time high of HK$12.85 in August 1996, plunged a total of 70 per cent in 1997, to HK$3.75. In early December, First Pacific sold its 65 per cent stake in Pacific Link Communications, a Hong Kong cellphone operator, to Hong Kong Telecom, netting US$341 million. Even after that deal, First Pacific was carrying nearly US$800 million in debt, compared with US$118.5 million two years earlier, and its debt-to-equity ratio had soared from 16 per cent to 85 per cent in that time, according to the *AWSJ*.[82] There was also worry First Pacific would try to acquire San Miguel (it was tempted, but did not), or pay a dividend to its cash-stretched Indonesian shareholders (it did not).

Around the time First Pacific announced its Hagemeyer exit, Indonesia's New Order was showing cracks as prominent figures were lobbying Suharto to end the monopolies which had helped him stay in the saddle more than thirty years. On 13 January 1998, as IMF Deputy Chief Stanley Fischer was pressuring the president, the central bank called a meeting of business leaders including Liem to secure support for whatever new IMF deal was reached. With Camdessus on the way, Suharto finally agreed to whatever conditions the IMF wanted to impose, including ending Tommy's unpopular "national car" programme and dissolving his clove monopoly. It all sounded too good to be true, and it was. In a move meant to show 100 per cent support for the new letter of intent, to be signed on 15 January, Suharto agreed to sign it himself. The ceremony went badly. As the president leaned down to sign the document on a table, Camdessus stood behind him, with arms folded across his chest. The photo showing the two became etched in the Indonesian psyche and formed a lasting image from the Asian financial crisis. While Camdessus did not mean anything (he said later his posture was the one he naturally took while standing), many Indonesians cringed and felt insulted. The picture conveyed the impression of a colonial master watching a submissive subject comply with an order.

In the new agreement, Suharto acceded to limiting Bulog to just one monopoly, for importing rice, and to ending Bob's plywood-exporting cartel. Controls on the pricing of cement, where Salim was the biggest producer, were also scrapped. The changes meant that distribution of flour, along with import of wheat, would become open to anyone. Overall, this did not create problems for Salim, whose real problem was the collapsing rupiah and teetering economy. Far-reaching as the new IMF deal was, it only strengthened markets for about an hour, reflecting well-founded doubts that Suharto would really do what he agreed to do. The first post-signing moves augured poorly. Within hours, an unusually animated Suharto held a rare press conference with Indonesian reporters, at which he sounded like Malaysian Prime Minister Mahathir Mohamad in blaming the financial crisis on foreigners. "We have 30 years' experience building a strong foundation. Then, in six months it collapses, not because of an internal crisis but because there is manipulation of [our] currency," he declared.[83] He also signalled that Bulog's role would not diminish as comprehensively as detailed in the new pact. On monopolies ending, Suharto effectively cocked a snook at the IMF, remarking ominously "we'll wait and see how that develops".[84]

Less than a week later, Suharto upset already-traumatized markets anew by saying his next vice-president should have mastery of science and technology, a clear sign he was poking a finger in the IMF's eye by choosing Habibie, anathema to technocrats. Immediately following his statement, the rupiah plummeted to an all-time low of 17,000 to the dollar, making the currency's collapse — from 2,300 in August — one of the most rapid ever. Virtually all borrowers were stiffing their foreign creditors, and Indonesians themselves were scared of holding the currency. To try to bring some order and avoid a calamity, the government on 27 January guaranteed all bank deposits and creditors of Indonesian banks. At the same time, it created IBRA to repair the mess that the banking industry was becoming. During this period, Anthony was devoting time to helping Radius try to quantify the country's debt load. Before a meeting of debtors and creditors in February, Radius put the total at US$137.42 billion as of 31 December 1997, of which US$63.46 billion was owed by the government and state companies, and US$73.96 billion by private ones. (At the end of 1997, he gave the private total as US$65.6 billion.)

For Indonesian policy-makers, precious time in early 1998 was wasted on a distraction promoted by Suharto's two eldest daughters: a proposal for a currency board that would establish a fixed rupiah-dollar rate. The idea was advocated by Steve Hanke, a Johns Hopkins University economics professor brought to meet Suharto through Tutut, who had started an "I Love Rupiah" campaign. Several major businesspeople endorsed the Hanke plan. Anthony was not among them, and he did not want to get on the wrong side of the IMF, which considered Hanke's idea calamitous. Central bank Governor Soedradjad was cool to the proposal. That was a major (and unstated) factor in Suharto in mid-February unceremoniously sacking Soedradjad, whose wife was a sister of Gen. Prabowo, only two weeks before the governor's five-year term was to end.

In early 1998, the country was becoming increasingly unhinged. Social tensions were already high in January, when the collapsing rupiah caused prices of essential goods to rise, badly hurting the growing ranks of the poor. They had to struggle extra hard to meet basic needs while their safety net, the home village, was hurting too, due to the fierce El Nino drought that cut crop output. The mood in January should have been buoyant for the coming holidays at the end of the Ramadan fasting month, but many workers in Jakarta went home bearing fewer gifts and less cash than usual. A growing number of people wanted to hit out at somebody, and that usually meant Chinese shopkeepers, historically the scapegoat in bad times. Such attacks were sometimes encouraged by security forces, who wanted the Chinese — and Suharto — to remain dependent on them. Also heating up the political scene in early 1998 were the disappearances of some dissidents, kidnapped by military operatives.

By February, with hardship mounting, Indonesia was a tinderbox — and matches got lit. In the worst violence to date, hundreds of Chinese-owned shops were set afire in Jatiwangi, 240 kilometres east of Jakarta, on 12 February. Riots broke out the next day in seven other West Java towns. Trouble spread to Lombok, the island east of Bali, where soldiers opened fire on rioters, killing two. Suharto ordered a clampdown on unrest. His attention, however, was on the Jakarta assembly, opening on 1 March, to give him a seventh term and make Habibie his vice-president. As riots spread across the archipelago, some Chinese tycoons including Liem started a small-scale food giveaway programme. (About this time, Liem again topped an annual Finance Ministry list of the largest taxpayers. On the list for 1996, Anthony moved up to fifth place from eighth in 1995.) Astra too made donations for the needy. In Jakarta, Indofood gave 100,000 packets of basic commodities to the governor's office to distribute through mosques. In Bandung, it gave 25,000 packets. Each contained 5 kilograms of rice, a 40-unit box of noodles and a litre of cooking oil. Indofood said the donations were worth about Rp2.8 billion rupiah (US$320,000 then). "This donation is to help people to fulfil their daily needs and in line with a government appeal to businessmen to smooth the supply of basic commodities", the company said.[85]

Strife spiked again in late February, as the MPR session neared. For the first time in decades, campuses were bubbling with protests, and not just in Java. Calls by students and others for Suharto to step down were getting more strident. The MPR definitely did not offer a path out of trouble; it was a scripted recrowning of an ageing political monarch who was bordering on delusional. Hopes that Indonesia could emerge from the crisis without violence were sinking.

A LAST, HOLLOW HURRAH

The deployment of 25,000 soldiers in the middle of Jakarta ensured that the Parliament building hosting the MPR would be an enforced sea of tranquillity for the 1–11 March session. What would unfold inside was one of the few things that Suharto could still control. Still, nothing was left to chance. To avoid any possible repeat of a 1988 assembly incident when a military delegate got on a microphone to complain about Suharto's choice of vice-president, no microphones were set up at delegates' seats. In Indonesia's top-down politics, Suharto remained at the top — for now. During the New Order, assembly practices were set in stone. The standing joke was that delegates just had to follow four Ds: *datang* (come), *duduk* (sit), *diam* (stay silent) and *duit* (collect money). The only time delegates' voices were essential was to declare *"Setuju!"* (Agreed) when, on the tenth day, a motion was read to confirm Suharto, the sole candidate, as president for the next five years. For the 1998 session, there was some pre-meeting intrigue as Berkeley Mafia member and former Environment Minister Emil Salim bravely announced he wanted to be nominated for vice-president to compete with Habibie, but it was 100 per cent certain no delegate would support him.

The session's backdrop was dramatically different from the last one in 1993. On the first day of the 1993 meeting, the government had issued a new Rp50,000 note depicting a beaming Suharto, "the Father of Development". At that time, it was worth US$24.30. On 1 March 1998, that banknote bought US$5.40. In his opening day "accountability" speech, Suharto gave an assurance he was "fully committed" to the IMF programme, but then contradicted himself by saying he sought a "more appropriate concept" he dubbed "IMF Plus". One day earlier, currency-board promoter Steve Hanke used that phrase when telling the media Suharto told him the IMF programme was a failure. The president told the MPR he was "carefully and cautiously contemplating the possible adoption" of a currency board. Hours after his speech, Suharto received a visitor at his Cendana home — Walter Mondale, Jimmy Carter's vice-president from 1981 to 1984 and now President Clinton's envoy. Later, Mondale recounted the frustrating session, saying Suharto "gave a long speech about how well he had done in the past" and described the reforms the IMF and the United States wanted as "suicide".[86] Another visitor that same day to Cendana received a warmer welcome: Thai Prime Minister Chuan Leekpai, who donated 5,000 tonnes of rice.

Five days later, on 6 March , the IMF announced it was delaying a US$3 billion instalment of its bailout until at least April, in part because the government had not fulfilled the "basic conditions" of the pact Suharto signed in January. Naturally, this threatened a rupture with the president. Chillingly, the president on 8 March told Golkar leaders that the measures he had agreed to in January would "violate" Article 33 of Indonesia's constitution, which said the economy should be managed on a "family principle" including cooperatives. Playing on nationalistic sentiments, Suharto's children started knocking the IMF. Middle daughter Titiek was quoted saying, "We do need the IMF, yes, but not if we are continually being repressed with this-and-that conditions. We are a sovereign nation and we have our dignity."[87]

Speaking of repression, the MPR session restored to Suharto unlimited "emergency powers" he once had, but which he hadn't seen the need to renew in 1993. "Nobody knows what these special powers entail", Golkar member Marwah Daud Ibrahim confessed, adding, "We feel it is necessary to give the president more power to deal with any situation that can threaten national unity."[88] The decree, endorsed on 9 March, gave Suharto "the special duty and privilege to take steps deemed necessary". The next day, it was time for the last hurrah. The assembly called out *"setuju"* (agreed) acclaiming Suharto as president until 2003. Demonstrators on campuses, whose ranks were rapidly swelling, howled in protest. On 11 March, Habibie was confirmed as vice-president. That night — on the thirty-second anniversary of gaining control from a besieged Sukarno — Suharto was sworn in for a seventh term. On the same day, leaked news crushed any hope that Suharto could restart the economy. Aides revealed that Suharto golfing partner Bob Hasan would be Trade and Industry Minister, replacing Tunky Ariwibowo, who was working well with the IMF. Bob's appointment was a huge snub to the IMF. Suharto seemed to have the bizarre notion that Indonesian Chinese and markets would like his choice of Bob, the first ethnic Chinese in a Suharto cabinet. But Bob, a convert to Islam who distanced himself from his roots, was anything but popular with the Chinese. There had been strong rumours that Suharto wanted to make Anthony a minister, but the Salim chief took himself out of consideration earlier by telling Suharto not to consider him.

The new team, announced on 14 March and immediately dubbed the "crony cabinet", was a poke in IMF's eye. Daughter Tutut was appointed Social Welfare Minister, which bolstered the view Suharto wanted to position her to become president. Bob promptly pronounced that monopolies are acceptable "if they are in the public interest".[89] The day before the cabinet was sworn in, Japanese vice finance minister Eisuke Sakakibara, nicknamed Mr Yen, had lunch with Bob, new Economics Coordinating Minister Ginandjar Kartasasmita, a few other new ministers and Anthony. The lunch reflected how Anthony was in the middle of efforts to deal with Indonesia's woes and how Japan was trying to head off an irreparable Suharto-IMF rupture that could exacerbate the Asian financial crisis. Tokyo had a chance, which the United States and others did not. Japan was Indonesia's biggest aid donor, creditor and investor. Also, Prime Minister Ryutaro Hashimoto pleased Suharto by coming to Jakarta right after his re-selection. Japan achieved some measure of temporary success in easing the row. Two days after the power lunch, Ginandjar said Indonesia was dropping the currency board idea "for now" as Jakarta lacked the foreign exchange to make it work. That was essential to staying on civil terms with the IMF, whose top Asia official Hubert Neiss held talks the next day with the new economic team in a small group that again included Anthony. Over time, the relationship between Neiss and Anthony — which developed into a friendship — would be significant.

It was no surprise that Anthony was at the table; it fit with his position on the committee on debt woes and his link to Suharto. Salim, despite some diversification, had everything at stake in Indonesia. "It's as if you're sitting on the Titanic. If Indonesia sinks, all the corporations will sink," Anthony told *BusinessWeek*. The article, titled "Can Anthony Salim get out of this corner? Drowning in debt, a Suharto pal scrambles to save his empire", described the Salim Group as imperilled with shares in its listed units now "virtually worthless".[90]

The day after being in the group that met with Neiss, Anthony was appointed by Suharto to an official position. Presidential Decree No. 47 of 1998 made Anthony secretary-general of the National Economic and Financial Resilience Council, succeeding Widjojo Nitisastro. The Berkeley Mafia dean became vice-chairman — Suharto remained chairman — of the council created in January to implement the revised IMF agreement signed that month. Anthony was also made secretary of the council's new daily economic management group, whose chairman was Ginandjar. *BusinessWeek* quoted an unnamed executive saying that Anthony was "effectively Prime Minister now", though this was an exaggeration.[91] But the Salim CEO was in the middle of trying to keep the IMF programme alive and Suharto in power. Getting along with the IMF was critical, as the economic situation was turning desperate; according to the International Labour Organization, four million jobs had already been lost in construction and manufacturing.[92] In late March, Indonesia jacked up interest rates, to adhere to IMF prescriptions. IMF and Indonesia agreed on realistic targets for 1998, including reining in inflation to no more than 45 per cent and keeping shrinkage of gross domestic product to only 5 per cent, compared with the wildly unrealistic target Suharto set in January of 4 per cent growth.

As the new cabinet was starting to work, the government did a second round of bank clean-up. On 4 April, it froze the operations of seven "unsound" banks including two controlled by Sudwikatmono — Bank Surya and Bank Subentra. Sudwikatmono, unlike Suharto's half-brother Probosutedjo the previous November, did not make any fuss. The government also took over management of seven bigger banks, including Bank Danamon, the one Salim made a plan to enter. Four days later, the IMF and Indonesia agreed on a third Letter of Intent (LOI) to replace the January one — and this time, Suharto did not personally sign. The 177-item LOI included new commitments to end crony deals and plans for the government to issue more than $18 billion in bonds to recapitalize ravaged banks. It was the first LOI to include corporate foreign debt as an agenda item. Confirmation of the new deal — the only one in Suharto's truncated final term — temporarily boosted the rupiah, to 7,800 to the dollar from 8,500. Meanwhile, a Suharto decree on 8 April ordered private borrowers to stop stalling and report their full debts within fourteen days to let the country find a "fast and accurate" solution. But penalties for late reporting, just US$65 a week, were not exactly punitive or compliance-inducing.

At the same time — and in time for a meeting of debtors and foreign creditors in New York — Bank Indonesia put total foreign corporate debt for end January at US$80.2 billion. Attending the 15–16 April talks at Chase Manhattan's headquarters were Radius, Anthony and representatives of thirteen international banks, led by Chase, Bank of Tokyo-Mitsubishi and Deutsche Bank. Most Indonesian companies wanted creditors to take "haircuts" of at least 30 to 40 per cent on their debts, and the banks — who historically made big money on Indonesia loans — naturally balked. Participants in New York agreed to talk again in May in Tokyo. Back in Jakarta, Indonesia fulfilled one IMF requirement — to pass a new bankruptcy law to replace an antiquated Dutch one. But the economic picture continued to deteriorate amid mounting protests. At the end of April, Indofood and Indocement reported huge losses for 1997. Indofood, blaming "unforeseen" devaluation of the currency, said it lost a staggering Rp1.2 trillion, compared with a profit of Rp351 billion a year earlier. Indocement, which made Rp551 billion in 1996, reported a Rp378 billion loss for 1997. (The 1998 loss ballooned to Rp1.05 trillion.)

Meanwhile, protests against Suharto escalated, and public order was unravelling. On 1 May, Suharto riled many by promising political change, but added it would have to wait five years, until the MPR session in 2003. His thumbs-down to change raised already-sizzling temperatures, and the weekend of 2–3 May brought some of the worst violence yet. In Medan, scores of buildings were damaged. On 3 May, Suharto went back on TV, ostensibly to explain why Indonesia still needed to work with the IMF, but instead he vigorously defended Tommy while talking about the IMF's ending of his son's clove monopoly. Still confident that he was in full control, the president saw no reason to cancel plans to go to Egypt on Saturday, 9 May for a Group of 15 meeting hosted by his friend President Hosni Mubarak.

On Monday, 4 May, the gloomy Indonesia picture brightened slightly as the IMF reopened the tap and paid US$1 billion to the government. Indonesia was moving ahead on a "credible, well-balanced" programme, IMF chief Camdessus said in Singapore, adding, "I had no hesitation in recommending to the executive board to approve the first disbursement."[93] But within twenty-four hours, Indonesia began moving toward a cataclysm.

Notes

1. In that first *Asiaweek* list, second through fourth place were given to Chinese President Jiang Zemin, Taiwan President Lee Teng-hui and Malaysian Prime Minister Mahathir Mohamad, respectively. (*Asiaweek*, 5 July 1996.)

2. Mark Clifford, "The New Asian Manager", *BusinessWeek*, 2 September 1996.

3. Texts provided by Wharton.

4. Ibid.

5. Interview with Manny Pangilinan, Hong Kong, 20 April 2007.

6. "A New Chair at Wharton Honors the Asian Tie", *University of Pennsylvania Almanac*, vol. 42, no. 31, 7 May 1996.

7. E-mail from Jeffrey Sheehan, 12 July 2007.

8. Interview with Anthony, 28 October 2007.

9. Retnowati Abdulgani-Knapp, *Soeharto: The Life and Legacy of Indonesia's Second President* (Singapore: Marshall Cavendish, 2007), p. 269.

10. David Bourchier and Ian Chalmers, "Privatising social justice", *Inside Indonesia*, Edition 50, April–June 1997, Melbourne. Posted on <www.insideindonesia. org/edition-50/privatising-social-justice> (accessed 2 June 2010).

11. Paul Jacob, "Body to help distribute money to Indonesia's poor", *Straits Times*, 16 January 1996.

12. Richard Borsuk, "Salim Moves Into Basics: Water and Rice", *AWSJ*, 28 February 1996.

13. Margot Cohen, "Twisting arms for alms", *FEER*, 2 May 1996.

14. Paul Jacob, "Suharto Calls on Companies to Honour Pledge To Help Needy", *Straits Times*, 17 November 1996.

15. "Suharto warns businesses which fail to donate", *Jakarta Post*, 23 December 1996.

16. "Suharto's money: Where it came from, where it went", Kyodo News Service, 30 August 2000.

17. Richard Borsuk, "Storm brews in Bali over beer levy", *AWSJ*, 26–27 January 1996.

18. "Suharto leads firm to finance N-2130 jet project", *Jakarta Post* , 22 February 1996

19. "Legislators hail funding for jet plane project", *Jakarta Post*, 23 February 1996.

20. "Financing jet development", *Jakarta Post*, 26 February 1996.

21. "Suharto to mobilize nation to fund plane construction", Kyodo News, 28 March 1996.

22. "Regents told to raise funds for national plane project", *Jakarta Post*, 14 June 1996.

23. In Tri Polyta, Sudwikatmono was also teamed with timber tycoon Prajogo Pangestu; some of the shareholders were also in the controversial Chandra Asri project. Tri Polyta in July 1994 was the first Indonesian company listed in New York. Asian depository receipts that were sold for US$21 each in the offering jumped 32 per cent on the first day of trading, to US$27.75. But for investors who held Tri Polyta throughout 1997, the journey proved calamitous; the shares plunged 89 per cent that year to end at US$0.6875. One month after Suharto stepped down in May 1998, Sudwikatmono, who owned 5.3 per cent of the company, quit as Tri Polyta's president-director and Bambang resigned as chairman. In 2000, the New York Stock Exchange delisted Tri Polyta because its shareholder equity and market capitalization had both fallen below the minimum-required US$50 million.

24. Richard Borsuk, "Indonesia fights protectionist label on trade", *WSJ*, 18 March 1996.

25. Richard Borsuk, "Indonesia sets plan to assemble a national auto", *WSJ*, 1 March 1996.

26. R.E. Elson, *Suharto: A Political Biography* (Cambridge: Cambridge University Press, 2001), p. 282.

27. David Roche, "Is Indonesia Really a Tiger?", *AWSJ*, 12 July 1996.

28. S.N. Vasuki, "Astra should stay a public company", *Business Times*, 24 October 1996.

29. Richard Borsuk, "Astra's Informal Group Unveils Its Plans", *AWSJ*, 27 November 1996.

30. Jay Solomon, "Burning Ambition: Can Putera Sampoerna join Indonesia's big leagues?", *FEER*, 24 April 1997.

31. "Bre-X Finds Powerful Friend", *The Financial Post*, 29 October 1996.

32. Richard Borsuk, "Bre-X Allies with Sigit's Panutan Group", *AWSJ*, 29 October 1996.

33. Unclassified cable of 11 March 1997 of the U.S. Foreign and Commercial Service, cited in International Markets Insight Report.

34. "Palm oil investment", *Jakarta Post*, 24 March 1997.

35. "BNI assists two banks", *Jakarta Post*, 4 October 1995.

36. "Bank Central Asia helps salvage Bank Yama", *Jakarta Post*, 17 May 1997.

37. "Violations rampant — poll watchdog", *Jakarta Post*, 31 May 1997.

38. Andreas Harsono, "Water and Politics in the Fall of Suharto", The Center for Public Integrity, Washington D.C., 10 February 2003.

39. Richard Borsuk, "Salim Moves into Basics: Water and Rice — 'Opportunity-Driven' Group Says It Can Profit while Nurturing Indonesia", *AWSJ*, 28 February 1996.

40. Interview with Anthony, 18 November 2007.

41. Borsuk, "Salim Moves into Basics".

42. Marleen Dieleman, *The Rhythm of Strategy: A Corporate Biography of the Salim Group of Indonesia* (Amsterdam: ICAS/ Amsterdam University Press, 2007), p. 90.

43. Raphael Pura, "Salim Group Unveils Broad Restructuring", *AWSJ*, 16 July 1997.

44. "Interview with Faisal H. Basri: Well, who's the peanut, who's the shell?", Tempo Interaktif, Edition 22/02, 30 July 1997; <www.tempo.co.id/ang/min/02/22/utama1.htm> (accessed 13 September 2010).

45. Jim Erickson and Keith Loveard, "Hot Noodle Take-Away", *Asiaweek*, 22 August 1997.

46. "Interview with Faisal H. Basri", Tempo Interaktif.

47. "Govt's plan on Bulog hailed", *Jakarta Post*, 22 August 1997.

48. Ibid.

49. Ibid.

50. "Govt okays Salim's maneuvers", *Jakarta Post*, 31 July 1997.

51. "558-meter-high tower to 'lift Jakarta's image'", *Jakarta Post*, 13 August 1997.

52. "Many firms hedged for forex losses", Dow Jones, 14 August 1997; and "Salim to float Indomobil soon, BCA next year", *Jakarta Post*, 16 August 1997.

53. Richard Borsuk, "Suharto Urges Calm as Float Prompts Fears", *AWSJ*, 18 August 1997.

54. S.N. Vasuki, "Suharto okays Indon-M'sia bridge", *Business Times*, 21 August 1997.

55. Jim Della-Giacoma, "Indonesia's new parliament includes 10 Suharto kin", Reuters, 1 October 1997.

56. "Indofood sees 1997 net zero or negative", Reuters, 8 October 1997.

57. Soedradjad Djiwandono, *Bank Indonesia and the Crisis: An Insider's View* (Singapore: Institute of Southeast Asian Studies, 2005), p. 106.

58. Raphael Pura, "Indonesian Markets Play Waiting Game", *AWSJ*, 20 October 1997.

59. Richard Borsuk, "Singapore Said to Offer Aid of $10 Billion to Indonesia", *AWSJ*, 31 October 1997.

60. Private conversation, Jakarta, 31 October 1998.

61. Raphael Pura and Richard Borsuk, "Suharto's Son Lashes at Finance Minister", *AWSJ*, 5 November 1997.

62. Djiwandono, *Bank Indonesia and the Crisis*, p. 133.

63. Ibid., p. 136.

64. Richard Borsuk,. "Suharto Gives Go-Ahead to Some Projects", *AWSJ*, 7 November 1997.

65. Djiwandono, *Bank Indonesia and the Crisis*, p. 153.

66. Richard Borsuk, "IMF Chief Upbeat on Indonesia's Future", *AWSJ*, 13 November 1997.

67. Lee Han Shih, "Me dead? Here I am — Liem", *Business Times*, 15 November 1997.
68. "Om Liem — I say white, you write red", *Bisnis Indonesia*, 24 November 1997.
69. "Rumors Spread by Irresponsible People — Hartono", *Jakarta Post*, 18 November 1997.
70. Press briefing on Salim-Danamon agreement, 16 November 1997.
71. Interview with Ciputra, 19 March 2007.
72. Dieleman, *The Rhythm of Strategy*, p. 91.
73. Interview with Anthony, 22 April 2007.
74. Ibid.
75. Interview with Anthony, 24 June 2007.
76. Susan Sim, "Suharto scraps Asean trip, and rupiah crashes", *Straits Times*, 13 December 1997.
77. "Indonesia's Suharto receives ministers at residence", Reuters, 15 December 1997.
78. Kevin O'Rourke, author of the book *Reformasi*, points out that cash in circulation soared 50 per cent between end-October 1997 and end-January 1998 (p. 60).
79. "Firms told not to rely much on govt's help", *Jakarta Post*, 30 December 1997.
80. Jay Solomon and I Made Sentana, "Salim Postpones Planned Restructuring", *AWSJ*, 5 January 1998.
81. Jon Hilsenrath, "First Pacific to Sell Stake in Netherlands' Hagemeyer", *AWSJ*, 12 January 1998.
82. Jon Hilsenrath, "First Pacific's Debt Load Makes Analysts Nervous", *AWSJ*, 15 December 1997.
83. Raphael Pura, "Suharto Plans to Supervise IMF's Economic Programme", *AWSJ*, 16 January 1998.
84. Ibid.
85. "Indonesia's Chinese Wage Public Relations Campaign", *Reuters*, 19 February 1998.
86. David Wessel and Bob Davis, "Limits of Power: How Global Crisis Grew Despite Efforts of a Crack U.S. Team", *Wall Street Journal*, 24 September 1998.
87. "IMF loan delay upsets legislators", *Jakarta Post*, 10 March 1998.
88. Derwin Pereira, "Suharto to be given extra powers to handle emergencies", *Straits Times*, 7 March 2010; and "Suharto given new security powers to counter unrest", 10 March 1998.
89. "Global ties vital, says Hasan", *Jakarta Post*, 17 March 1998.
90. Michael Shari, "Can Anthony Salim get out of this corner?", *BusinessWeek*, 9 March 1998.

91. Michael Shari, "Suharto gives a little — and gets a lot", *BusinessWeek*, 6 April 1998.

92. Richard Borsuk, "Millions in Indonesia Lose Jobs, Poverty Ranks Grow Amid Crisis", *AWSJ*, 25 March 1998.

93. "IMF's Camdessus recommends payments to Indonesia", Reuters, 4 May 1998.

17

GÖTTERDÄMMERUNG[1]
OF THE NEW ORDER

On 4 May 1998, Liem left for Hong Kong enroute to the United States, where he was scheduled to undergo cataract surgery. A couple of days earlier, he stopped by Jalan Cendana, to inform Suharto about his departure, as was customary before he made any extended overseas trips. The political tension was palpable in recent weeks; the IMF was just about to reopen the critical money tap but the economy was in dire straits while calls for Suharto's resignation were getting more strident. Despite signs that all hell could break loose, Suharto maintained a typically calm Javanese demeanour. "He said to me, *'semua beres'* [everything's in order]," the *cukong* recounted. He said the president told him he was leaving for a trip himself — to Cairo. (Suharto was scheduled to attend the eighth Summit of the Group of 15.) But the president added as an afterthought that it was probably a good idea for his old friend to be away for a while as even he "was unable to protect me".[2] Little did the two men know that they would not see each other for years, and when they met again, Suharto was no longer president and Liem was no longer living in Indonesia.

MAY "MADNESS"

Even with the IMF back on board, the picture in Indonesia was far from in order. To get the IMF money flowing again, Suharto made additional concessions in late April, including consenting to raise domestic energy prices to cut the state subsidies that had kept fuel prices among the lowest in the world. On 30 April, Coordinating Minister for the Economy Ginandjar Kartasasmita said that energy prices would rise by early June "at the latest". In fact, action came faster than the IMF asked for or expected. On the afternoon of 4 May, Suharto directed his energy minister, Kuntoro Mangkusubroto, to announce whopping price rises effective at midnight. Petrol was jacked up a massive 71 per cent. The percentage increase for kerosene, the fuel most used by poor Indonesians, was smaller, but still a painful 25 per cent. Jakarta bus fares were raised 67 per cent, to Rp500. Although that seemed paltry, equivalent then to about 6 U.S. cents, it was a hardship for the growing numbers of poor struggling to feed their families. The jump in fuel prices was bound to fan social tensions.

Many people in Jakarta automatically assumed that the scale and timing of the fuel price hikes was mandated by the IMF, which that same day agreed to give Indonesia a fresh injection of US$1 billion. But IMF officials maintained this wasn't true, and they were caught off guard by the sharp increases. A 2003 report by the IMF's Independent Evaluation Office said: "Internal documents indicate that the decision to accelerate the fuel price increase was against the advice of the IMF, which had agreed a gradual approach with the economic team."[3] After Suharto's fall, one conspiracy theory circulating in Jakarta was that the hikes were a ploy by allies of Vice-President Habibie wanting to pressure Suharto to step down. However, few bought this line. The IMF evaluation cited a senior Indonesian official as saying the fuel price move reflected Suharto's "renewed confidence that he was fully in charge of the economic and political situation".[4] Anthony Salim, who was involved in policy discussions given his position as secretary-general of the government's "economic stabilization council", said it was Suharto himself who set the fuel rates, adding: "It was suggested [to raise prices] in stages, but Pak Harto at that time decided to go [to the new levels] in one go."[5] In Anthony's view, expressed a decade later, Suharto was likely driven by "over-confidence" that he remained firmly in control. Suharto's approach to raising oil prices was to "get it over with and see what happens", he added.[6]

What happened was disaster. Petrol stations were swamped by motorists, jostling to refuel before the hikes took effect. In the north Sumatran city of Medan, violence broke out. The city had already been tense due to rising unemployment and hardship. The night that the fuel hikes kicked in, thousands looted shops and burned cars. Domestic media reported that up to six people were killed. When Jakarta financial markets opened on Tuesday (5 May), the good news that the IMF had resumed loans to Jakarta was negated by ugly news-pictures from Medan. In Jakarta, about 200 students showed growing boldness by gathering in front of Parliament House and calling for Suharto's ouster. The police seemed to be losing their toughness, and refrained from chasing away protesters from the main gate of Parliament. In Medan, the situation remained grim enough that Armed Forces Commander Gen. Wiranto, a Suharto loyalist and former aide-de-camp, rushed there along with army reinforcements. Upon his return to Jakarta, he raised eyebrows by saying reform had become "a national agenda" and that the military was prepared to discuss reforms and implement them, but with a caveat that they should be implemented "gradually and constitutionally".[7]

LOSS OF A HOME

The price hikes undoubtedly accelerated the unravelling of the New Order. Suharto's belief that he was firmly in control sparked intensifying feeling that he had stayed too long and was incapable of introducing meaningful, needed change. From the palace in Jakarta, the president blamed the growing instability on the foreign media, which was "always reporting that Indonesia is insecure".[8] Suharto himself should have been feeling insecure as some long-time sycophants were now changing their tunes dramatically. The Association of Indonesian Muslim Intellectuals (ICMI), set up in 1990 in part to embellish the Islamic credentials of now-Vice President B.J. Habibie, declared that the government's reform efforts were "vague, too little and too late". The following day, Golkar chairman and former information minister Harmoko announced that Golkar would push at the next MPR session in 2003 to amend the constitution to allow only two terms for future presidents.

The spreading unrest prompted some foreigners to cancel trips to Indonesia. The venue for a meeting of foreign creditors on 8–10 May, which involved Anthony, got switched to Tokyo as some participants were afraid to come to Jakarta. Not surprisingly, the meeting produced no breakthroughs. The post-session statement said terms of any deals on restructuring loans had to be set by individual debtors and creditors but it was agreed that the framework would be voluntary and not require debt forgiveness. Participants agreed to continue discussions on 26 May in Frankfurt, a meeting that never happened.

Suharto, aiming to show the situation was under control, left for Cairo on 9 May as scheduled to attend a summit of the Group of 15, a body started in 1989 by members of the Non-Aligned Movement as a response to the Group of 8 (G-8) leading Western nations. Suharto was a key figure in the G-15, whose members included India, Iran and Brazil. Given the heated situation at home — akin to a volcano about to erupt — many Indonesians thought he should skip the Cairo summit altogether. However, Suharto didn't want to appear unduly alarmed. The president, Anthony said later, was "so confident at that time things will be OK. But things were not OK."[9] Asked if he had any inkling that violence would hit Jakarta in Suharto's absence, Anthony replied: "If I knew, Pak Harto would not be leaving for Cairo. And he has better information than we do."[10] If Suharto's intelligence services had any clue that trouble was brewing, they didn't share it with the president. Hardly had his flight left Jakarta when new violence broke out. In Bogor, 50 kilometres south of the capital, a police intelligence officer who had infiltrated protesters' ranks was beaten to death. Also while Suharto was still in the air, students at an East Jakarta teaching institute held a mock trial and burned an effigy of him as police just stood by and watched.

On 12 May, while Suharto was at the Cairo summit, the lid blew off in Jakarta. Mysterious snipers on a highway overpass shot dead four students taking part in an anti-Suharto rally at nearby private Trisakti University. It wasn't clear who ordered the snipers to shoot at demonstrators spilling out from the campus. A line had been crossed, and the shooting deaths of the middle-class students galvanized anti-Suharto feeling to boiling point. Trisakti rector Adi Andoyo, a former Supreme Court judge who had been dismissed after alleging corruption among judges, said the students were "just shot down like pigs… now it's clear that Suharto must go."[11] To former U.S. Ambassador to Indonesia Paul Wolfowitz, visiting Jakarta that day, it was becoming clear there were "elements within Indonesia's military that are out of control".[12]

The slaying of the students ignited a fuse. The morning of Wednesday, 13 May, there was an emotional memorial service for the Trisakti students.

Speakers included opposition leaders Megawati Sukarnoputri and Amien Rais, who had catapulted from a little-known lecturer in Jogjakarta to national prominence through his blunt demands for Suharto to quit. Amien told the army, "Don't sacrifice the Indonesian people just to defend the limited interest of a family." It was a message that found increasing resonance. In the afternoon, arsonists set fires in several parts of the capital including Jakarta's central Monas Square. One branch of Liem's BCA got torched. It remains unclear whether anti-government protesters or provocateurs or others with their own agenda had set the fires. At one point, anti-Suharto demonstrators briefly blocked Jalan Thamrin, a Jakarta thoroughfare, but they dispersed without incident. The government announced that Suharto was shaving a day off his Cairo stay — the G-15 meeting was already over — and would leave Egypt on Thursday. (Ironically, the day Suharto sliced off his schedule was largely for spending time with President Hosni Mubarak, who in 2011 — like Suharto in 1998 — was forced out of power after more than three decades.)

In Jakarta that Wednesday night, spasms of violence erupted around Chinatown. Groups of youths smashed storefronts and started fires. Badly outnumbered police generally did not try to stop the marauding bands, who took that as an invitation to spread mayhem. Into the first hours of 14 May, gangs targeted heavily ethnic Chinese residential areas and began terrorizing residents. The army, Suharto's iron fist throughout the New Order, was conspicuous by its absence. Terrified Chinese started fleeing town, swarming Soekarno-Hatta Airport to try to get a ticket out. By coincidence, among visitors in Jakarta when the rioting began was a group of students from the Wharton School in Philadelphia, which gave Liem a medal in 1996. The group arrived in Jakarta on 12 May — the day the Trisakti students were killed — to learn about the operations of Indofood. Early on the morning of 14 May, Indofood got the Wharton team to the airport by bus before gangs blocked the toll-road and, in some instances, dragged Chinese-looking passengers out of cars. (The Wharton group's riot-shortened Jakarta adventure featured in a *New York Daily News* article that described Suharto as "an old man, filthy rich through stealing". The *Daily News* summed up his career by saying he grabbed power with U.S. help in 1965, then killed 500,000 suspected communists and installed "a regime of kleptomaniacal shoplifters".[13])

When the Jakarta riots erupted, nearly all members of Liem's family — with the exception of Anthony — were away from Indonesia. Liem was in Los Angeles for eye surgery, together with his wife and daughter.

Anthony's wife and children were in Singapore (where his children attended Singapore American School). Anthony said that prior to 13 May, he suggested to Andree to shift his family in case there was violence. Some senior Salim staff and their families had already been evacuated to Singapore.

Since shortly after moving to Jakarta in 1952, Liem lived in the northern part, about five kilometres east of Glodok, considered the Chinatown district. A family compound contained multiple houses, including one that Anthony lived in. For many years, Anthony's weekday routine was to leave home in the late morning for Wisma Indocement, and not get back from the office till very late at night. Every morning, he exercised at home; when Liem was still able, father and son regularly took walks around the grounds of an Indomobil facility near their Jalan Gunung Sahari compound. On the night of 13 May, Anthony did not go straight home from Wisma Indocement. Instead, he followed the advice from his lieutenant Benny Santoso to spend the night at the nearby Shangri-La Hotel, which Salim partly owned. But in the middle of the night, Anthony decided it was safe to shift home. At daybreak on 14 May, a security man working for Salim advised Anthony to leave his house as the situation was increasingly dangerous in that area and other parts of north Jakarta. Anthony promptly left for his office and encountered no issues as the roads he used remained open at that point.

Within hours of reaching Wisma Indocement, Anthony got a call from home. A few trucks had disgorged groups of menacing-looking youths, armed with cans of fuel and tools, intent on destruction. They were at the compound gate and demanding entry to Liem's mansion. Anthony decided that trying to block the squad from coming in was not an option. "I told our guards not to resist", he said. "Better that [the house get burned] than bodily harm... If somebody got killed, it's much worse... if blood was spilled to protect the house, then the rest of the city could become even more violent."[14] The mob was allowed into the compound by a family member, Sutoyo, a relative of Liem's wife who was keeping an eye on the compound together with some security guards. Although he looked Chinese (and was one), the bespectacled Sutoyo mustered all the courage he had, retreated to the back wall separating the new mansion from the old bungalow house and blocked the gangs from getting to that section of the compound. It didn't much matter to the mob. They evidently came to make a show and there was enough to make a dramatic scene. They systematically set about burning the cars in the garage, then entered the mansion and set fire to furniture. They ripped paintings off the walls and ransacked rooms. No one was hurt during the attack. In Liem's home, "basically, there was nothing to loot", said Anthony. Once the house was set ablaze, "the peak [of emotion] was already reached", he added.[15] To leave evidence that the home of Suharto's biggest crony had been successfully attacked, the men dragged out into the street a large portrait of Liem and his wife, and with some fanfare, slashed it and paraded around with the mangled frame. Pictures of the scene were transmitted widely. Someone painted on the front gate the words *"Anjing Soeharto"* (Suharto's dog). Then, the men piled back into the trucks and drove off. Anthony said it was fortunate his parents were not there at the time: "Usually, my mom is always home. If that happened at the time, there would been more worries." According to him the only real loss to the family was "a lot of photos...the albums, the history, all finished, got burnt with the house... it was traumatic."[16]

Just as many questions linger about what happened in Jakarta in late 1965, when tumult began that led to Sukarno's downfall, some remain about the May 1998 violence. The biggest unknowns are whether there was one mastermind who planned the riots and, if so, who that person was. Among many offshoot questions are who ordered the sacking of Liem's house, and whether the assailants would have harmed Liem or family members if they had been home. Suharto's Indonesia had a history of rent-a-mob activity, and members of vigilante-type groups were active during the New Order, sometimes for debt-collection and to provide private security. It's highly likely that the ruffians who ransacked Liem's house were hired for the job by what Indonesians call *pihak ketiga*, a "third party".

While his father's house was burning, Anthony was in the Wisma Indocement building, about eight kilometres to the south, monitoring the increasingly chaotic situation. From his office on the nineteenth floor, which looks north to Merdeka Square and Chinatown, he literally could see how quickly the situation in Jakarta was deteriorating. During normal times, on a clear day, he could see the Java Sea past the teeming cityscape. But in the late morning on 14 May, the sky was clouded from proliferating fires. Panic was fast spreading to other parts of the metropolis as word of the fires and looting in the north travelled. (Reports on assaults of Chinese women began to circulate well after the riots.) Foreign embassies and multinational companies frantically arranged to put citizens, staff and families on any available flight out to Singapore, Bangkok and beyond. Some chartered airplanes. Among the many foreigners evacuating the beleaguered city were people working on the IMF programme. Offices and schools shut abruptly, sending hordes frenetically attempting to get home.

For Anthony, home would not provide safety as the compound might be targeted again; the realization he would have to flee Jakarta was sinking in. Anti-Suharto sentiment was building into a crescendo and Salim was a natural target. "After the house burnt, we got a bit worried the next target must be the office", he said.[17] Already, thousands filled the main road near Parliament and were moving towards Semanggi, a pivotal junction of two crucial arteries about two kilometres south of Wisma Indocement. The mood was getting decidedly ugly. Access to Soekarno-Hatta Airport, to the northwest, which growing numbers of often-panicky Chinese and foreigners were trying to reach for flights out, was now cut off from central Jakarta, as zones of anarchy widened. Gangs of youths set up their own private toll-gates, checking the identities of passengers in the vehicles, and pulling out some who looked Chinese. They were then robbed and sometimes savagely beaten. With the police nowhere in sight, mobs ruled the main roads.

In his office, Anthony came to the decision the time had come for him to leave. But instead of Soekarno-Hatta, he needed to get to the old Halim airport, in east Jakarta, the former international facility now used mainly for private flights. (From late Thursday through Saturday, hundreds of emergency evacuation flights chartered by foreign companies would depart Halim for Singapore.) On Halim's tarmac sat an old but refurbished Boeing-727. In early 1997, Salim and Suharto's daughter Tutut had bought the plane, once owned by Ford Motor. Tutut had used it when campaigning for Golkar in that year's parliamentary election. Prior to 14 May, Anthony had not flown in it.

By that afternoon, getting to Halim was becoming risky, but vehicles were still able to reach that airport — as long as passengers paid gangs who had commandeered the roads to lift their human toll-gates. Contrary to what might be assumed, Anthony did not have the option of leaving Wisma Indocement by helicopter, as there was no helipad on the roof. When the building was constructed in the early 1980s, apparently no one considered the possibility the owners might someday want to avoid the roads.

Anthony said it was the crowd massing along Jalan Sudirman, effectively cutting off Jakarta's main thoroughfare, which triggered his decision to join the exodus. "We didn't want to be caught" in a crowd, Anthony said.[18] The "we" included chief lieutenant Benny Santoso, whose family was already in Singapore. The two men left Wisma Indocement in a van convoy, accompanied by bodyguards. On a normal weekday mid-afternoon, the roughly 10-kilometre trip from Wisma Indocement to Halim Airport, much of it on a toll-road, could be made in 30 minutes. Anthony recalled that his trip took about two hours, because his vehicle had to stop multiple times for negotiations at the human roadblocks. Asked if he ever thought he might not make it to Halim if somebody recognized him, he replied "I think there was a risk, but at that particular moment, [I] just had to go."[19]

The Salim executives carried a critical commodity — cash. They were armed with stacks of the then-largest banknote, for Rp50,000 featuring "Father of Development" Suharto.[20] Anthony guessed they were carrying roughly Rp10 million, converting to about US$870 due to the plunge in the rupiah's value. The rupiah had started trading that day at about 11,500 to the dollar — far better than the 17,000 nadir in January when Suharto signalled he wanted Habibie as his vice-president. Carrying a stash for paying their way past obstructions was "very helpful", Anthony said. At the roadblocks — Anthony said he doesn't remember how many they faced — his bodyguards did the bargaining. He estimated that the trip to Halim required about Rp5 million. After he and Benny reached the terminal, they were soon on the 727 and then up into Jakarta's smoke-filled air to Singapore, where they turned the KMP office into a crisis centre.

LOSS OF A PATRON

Some hours after Anthony flew out of a smouldering Jakarta, Suharto was in the air too, returning home from Egypt. On his last night in Cairo, Suharto told a group of Indonesians that if he was no longer trusted to be president, he would become a *pandita* (sage) and "I will spend my time to guide my children, so they become good people."[21] He arrived at Halim just before dawn on Friday, 15 May, to a completely different Jakarta. It seemed he was meeting his Armageddon. The usual bustling capital was now virtually a ghost town; terrified residents bolted their doors and cowered inside. The army had finally moved late Thursday, clearing major thoroughfares so mobs were replaced by tanks and soldiers. Sizeable parts of northern Jakarta were still smoking. When Suharto arrived — in stark contrast to when he left Jakarta six days earlier — it seemed like the unthinkable might actually happen — that his long rule was about to end, though it was unclear when or how it would come about.

The morning Suharto returned, officials reported a soaring death toll from the riots as the charred remains of hundreds of people — some burnt while they were looting — were found trapped in a collapsed shopping centre that had been set on fire. More than 500 were dead, and more than 5,000 structures destroyed or damaged. There was almost no commerce, as shops, banks and offices remained shut. Of the few vehicles on the road, most were taking people to Soekarno-Hatta — now more easily accessible, after army tanks and vehicles finally moved in — or to Halim for flights out.

Tension remained high over the weekend of 16–17 May. Parts of the city resembled a war zone, with burned-out buildings. Most people did not venture out, unless in search of food. On Monday, some businesses reopened partially, if they could. Among them was BCA, one of the hardest hit in the riot. In a statement on Monday, the bank said it reopened whatever Jakarta locations it could; all told, 122 branches were reported damaged by fire and vandalism — later specified as seventeen branches burned down, twenty-six damaged and looted, and seventy-nine damaged but not looted. Also at least 150 ATMs were wrecked and the cash inside stolen. "Total financial losses due to looting from ATMs could reach Rp3 billion", BCA said. At the few fully functioning branches and ATMs, long queues formed. This was a kind of preview of the run on BCA that Suharto's resignation four days later spawned, but some of the people who queued for hours on 18 May could have thought that after the violence Suharto and those close to him would be going down. Throughout that Monday, there were at least 1,000 people in line outside Wisma BCA, the bank's headquarters. Withdrawals were limited to Rp500,000 for regular customers, or Rp1 million for holders of premium ATM cards. The ceiling changed periodically. "It depends on the number of people in line", a BCA spokesman said.[22]

Among Salim businesses, BCA suffered the most riot damage, but Indofood took hits as well. One factory near Solo, in Central Java, was looted and burned, causing a loss that CEO Eva Riyanti Hutapea put at Rp42 billion.[23] Also targeted was a distribution centre in Tangerang, an industrial area 25 kilometres west of Jakarta, where attackers caused an estimated Rp2 billion in damage. According to one news report, troops called in to stop theft at that Indofood facility ended up helping looters instead, out of sympathy for their plight. It quoted an Indofood marketing manager as saying that soldiers asked rioters to line up for merchandise, telling them "Once you've got enough, please go outside and give other people their chance."[24]

Meanwhile, people broadly sensed for the first time the vulnerability of Suharto; he was losing his mandate and could not begin to restore the stability and growth that had been his hallmarks. Not only was money now gone from the country — billions of dollars had been transferred offshore — but many corporate chiefs, like Anthony, and much of the foreign business community had evacuated too. (A few days after fleeing to Singapore, Anthony came back to Jakarta for part of a day; he didn't go to the family compound to see the ruins of his father's house.)

After the riots, there was a chorus, reported in a greatly emboldened domestic media, calling for the badly tarnished Suharto to step down. The day after Suharto's return, respected Islamic intellectual Nurcholish Madjid called for new parliamentary elections. Amien Rais, by now a hero among students for demanding Suharto's ouster, announced that on Wednesday, 20 May there would be a rally at Merdeka Square and he promised to get one million people there to tell the president to quit. The dramatic way in which Suharto's ship was sinking was emphasized on Monday afternoon when his chief apologist jumped off. At Parliament Golkar chairman Harmoko read a statement saying he and the deputy speakers — all seated with him, including the military faction's leader — called on the president to resign immediately. Only seven months earlier, it was Harmoko who declared that the entire country wanted and needed Suharto to serve another term. It wasn't certain what sparked Harmoko's resign-now call, but some Indonesian editors — who were forced to get along with him when he had the power to shut their publications — said that his home in Solo had just been burned during riots there. Harmoko's abandonment of his boss sparked euphoria among protesters, sensing that the end of Suharto's tenure was at hand. But that subsided within hours, when Armed Forces Commander Wiranto told reporters that Harmoko's call "has no legal basis".[25]

With Wiranto publicly backing him, Suharto stalled for time. At Cendana on Tuesday, 19 May, the president met Nurcholish Madjid and other Islamic figures (Amien Rais was not invited), and told them he was willing to step down, but only after existing laws were overhauled and new parliamentary elections held. In other words, he intended to hang on to his office for a long time. In line with what he called "the people's wishes", Suharto said he would install a "reform council" that would propose change in the laws on political participation, as well as for fighting monopolies and corruption.

By that time, however, Suharto's comments had no credibility. In any case, Nurcholish and the others refused to join the council, and bluntly advised the president to resign. In increasing desperation, Suharto tried another tack to deter them from pushing for his resignation. He noted he would be succeeded by Habibie and ironically added "there is a question of whether the vice-president is capable".[26] That strategy did not work. (It succeeded in infuriating Habibie, who was hurt that his long-time mentor apparently thought so little of him.) Later that day, pressure on Suharto intensified as protesters swarmed into the grounds of Parliament, facilitated by sympathetic local security commanders. Giant banners calling for Suharto's ouster were unfurled from the roof.

Starting Tuesday evening, there began a thirty-hour period of almost non-stop meetings at Jalan Cendana as Suharto made a last-ditch attempt to stay on while Gen. Wiranto, one of his last remaining loyalists, tried to find an exit strategy that would not look as though the army pushed the president out in a coup. Such a move might look like how Suharto gained power in 1965–66, and would undermine Wiranto's effort to check the ambitions of Suharto's son-in-law Gen. Prabowo Subianto, who many accused of having some hand in fuelling the riots (which Prabowo denied). Wiranto did not seek the kind of blank-check authority that Suharto forced from Sukarno in 1966. While Wiranto shaped a strategy, he headed off possible violence by getting Amien Rais, at dawn Wednesday, to call off his planned million-person anti-Suharto protest in Jakarta that day. Another jolt was delivered to Suharto later that day, when his chief economics minister Ginandjar announced that he and thirteen other ministers would not serve in a new Suharto-led cabinet. This effectively ended Suharto's plan to put together a new cabinet, as there would not be enough people to serve in it. Through all of Wednesday night, meetings continued, with people talking with the sullen president.

In the wee hours of Thursday, 21 May, word began to spread that Suharto had decided to resign rather than face the likelihood of being removed — and would be making the announcement to the nation in the morning that he was stepping aside. (Suharto initially thought that Habibie, as his vice-president, would step down together with him, but that didn't happen, much to Suharto's chagrin.) At 9.05 a.m. Thursday — one week after riots engulfed parts of Jakarta — the autocrat announced his resignation in a live telecast from the Istana that stunned many Indonesians. In a brief statement that he read out, Suharto made reference to his plan for a reform committee, which, he noted, had met with "no adequate response". Thus, his proposal to change the composition of his Cabinet was "no longer necessary". Given the circumstances, the president continued, "it would be very difficult for me to implement in a good manner, duties governing the State and in development. Therefore, in line with Article 8 of the 1945 Constitution ... I have decided that I have ceased to be president of the Republic of Indonesia as of the time I read this on this day, Thursday, 21 May 1998."

Then a hastily summoned member of the Supreme Court swore in Habibie as Indonesia's third president. In a blink, the Suharto era and one-man rule were over. Dewi Fortuna Anwar, a political scientist who became a key Habibie advisor, commented: "Nothing moved for 32 years, and then in three days everything happened."[27]

LOSS OF A BANK

While many Indonesians were jubilant about Suharto's resignation, his family, cronies and associates naturally worried and wondered what would befall them. Indeed, they had reason to be concerned. Significant public attention and emotion shifted to taking down those who had been closely associated with him. Salim was obviously in a bad position as a long-time pillar of support for the strongman. Another cause for apprehension was the new president; Liem and Anthony were not exactly ardent backers of Habibie. The volatile Habibie knew that Anthony had tried to get Suharto in early 1998 to retain Gen. Try Sutrisno as Vice-President. The newly installed president was mindful of the rising tide of anti-Suharto sentiments, and he could get a boost from joining the backlash against Salim and other cronies. Not surprisingly, as soon as Suharto stepped down, moves against Salim began.

The first and biggest action was a massive run on BCA, which toppled with stunning speed the behemoth that earlier had commanded 12 per cent of all bank deposits. In the days after 21 May, queues began to form at BCA branches. It didn't matter how strong the bank had been for decades, as many people knew — or were told — it was the Suharto family's bank. As of May 1998, his two eldest children still owned a combined 30 per cent. With Suharto's fall, his crony Liem and the bank they jointly owned was going to be next, so the reasoning went. Already on tenterhooks from the riots and widespread violence, many customers wanted their money out. Referring to the lines forming, a security guard at a BCA branch told a reporter, "People are all here because they are convinced Liem is finished in Indonesia."[28] The bank was not prepared for the enormous run that took place.

Salim executives maintained the run was an orchestrated campaign to drain BCA. Like many events that happened in Indonesia, it's not possible to know for certain, but the theory that the run on BCA stemmed partly from *rekayasa* (manipulation) seems plausible. It didn't take much: Some of those in the queue to withdraw money were what Indonesians call "jockeys" — people who got hired to hold a place in the queue, and who immediately rejoined the line after they pulled out money. This triggered the anticipated panic in many bank depositors, who as they watched the lines getting longer outside Wisma BCA and branches elsewhere, started to worry about their savings in the event of a bank collapse.

In Anthony's mind, there was no question the bank run was politically motivated. Frustratingly for the bank's executives, there was no way to stop it. Suharto's family was "still there, so it was an obvious target", Anthony conceded.[29] The bank wanted to pay out whoever wanted out, and that meant needing to borrow trillions of rupiah from the central bank. Anthony said the problem of meeting cash demands became "so huge" that to handle them all, even for the central bank "the legal tender is probably not available". He described the draining of BCA as a "traumatic experience".[30]

On Monday, 25 May, a rumour started that Liem had died. However, unlike in November the previous year when a similar rumour spread, this time Liem could not be put on TV; he was recuperating from eye surgery in California. Also, even if Liem was able to appear on television, it would not have changed anything, as Suharto's fall had changed everything. BCA president Abdullah Ali denied Liem had died and told reporters he would return to Jakarta the following week (which was not the case). Ali joined the central bank in denying rumours that BCA would be liquidated, and said Anthony would be adding Rp1 trillion (about US$92 million) in capital.[31] BCA's president also asked depositors wanting their money to be patient. "It takes a lot of time to obtain money from the central bank now", he explained.[32]

The next day, Bank Indonesia Governor Sjahril Sabirin said the central bank would inject funds in BCA "up to a certain limit", which he didn't specify. He followed up a day later with the pronouncement that BCA was still "healthy" and added that it would remain so "just as long as [the rush] does not carry on for too long". With BI putting in money and the Salim family commitment to increase capital, depositors "should not worry", he added.[33] But no amount of state reassurances could put doubts to rest, and heavy withdrawals continued unabated. On Wednesday, ABN Amro Hoare Govett's global research head Eugene Galbraith, an experienced Indonesia observer, was quoted as saying "BCA is to the financial system what Mr Suharto has been to Indonesia's political system. There is great determination [in the country] to pull it down."[34]

That same day, with the bank run continuing at full tilt, executives of four other private banks — including the Riady family's Lippo Bank — met to see if there was a way they could help BCA out. They concluded there was not. One participant said BCA was "too big to be helped by us. It's too heavy."[35] By Thursday, 28 May, the prolonged bleeding had indeed become too heavy, and that evening, the government announced that the Indonesian Bank Restructuring Agency (IBRA) was taking over BCA. This was necessary, by law, because the central bank had injected a sum equivalent to at least 200 per cent of BCA's capital. At the announcement of BCA becoming a "BTO" (Bank Taken Over), Bank Indonesia Governor Sjahril would not give a figure for BCA, but said that since 14 May the central bank had provided liquidity credits totalling Rp20 trillion to Indonesian banks. The government said that for the time being, BCA would be managed by executives from state-owned Bank Negara Indonesia and Bank Rakyat Indonesia. The latter's CEO, D.E. Setiyoso, was named chairman of a new board to replace the dissolved Salim-led one. After the government took over BCA, the legal and other work to be completed on Salim's loss of BCA (including the exit of Tutut and Sigit) would take a few months to complete.

With that brief announcement, BCA was finished as a pillar of the Salim Group. Some years after BCA flourished under new owners, the history of the bank as listed on its website stated matter-of-factly that while the Asian monetary crisis had "a tremendous impact on Indonesia's entire banking system, in particular it affected BCA's cash flow and even threatened its survival. Panic rush forced the bank to seek assistance from the Indonesian government."[36] On his part, Liem, who was not often given to expressing feelings publicly, lamented the takeover as unfair, saying that given more time to settle the debts, "we could have saved it".[37]

The way Salim lost BCA only one week after Suharto's resignation reflected the strong public backlash against his circle. Already, in the days between Suharto's resignation and the BCA takeover, actions directly or indirectly affecting other Salim interests were under way. On 26 May, government officials said they were restructuring cooking oil distribution in Jakarta, ending Bulog's role. That sparked speculation that Salim could see all its work with Bulog halted. The biggest piece was the effective monopoly on milling wheat, but the IMF programme had already decreed the end of that prior to Suharto's resignation.

The following day, the combination of bad news — about Jakarta cooking oil, the unstoppable run on BCA and speculation about other moves against Liem's interests — caused Indofood's share price to plunge 31 per cent to Rp1,675 (15 U.S. cents) on the Jakarta Stock Exchange. While Indofood said there was no reason for investors to dump shares, many did. Meanwhile, just two days after Suharto quit, Jakarta Governor Sutiyoso — a retired lieutenant-general who got his post due to Suharto's backing — moved to get the city out of the privatization contract its water authority had signed with Salim in June 1997, as well as another with a company owned by Sigit. The water-work, in fact, had just begun and no real money had been invested yet. Sutiyoso signed a decree putting under "review" the management deal between Salim unit Garuda Dipta Semesta and French partner Suez Lyonnaise. This was misreported as cancelling the contract, which the governor could not do, but it was the first step towards getting Salim out. Suez Lyonnise took quick pre-emptive action, announcing on 2 June that it had moved to "terminate its partnership with the Salim Group" by buying its 60 per cent stake in the joint venture.[38]

With the backlash against Suharto's cronies producing some results, some observers predicted that Salim would be badly crushed if not annihilated. A Dow Jones report began: "Salim Group, the most prominent of Indonesia's powerful conglomerates, is rapidly dissolving into a shadow of its former gargantuan self." The article added, though, that analysts felt the current crisis was "unlikely to spell the death of the Salim empire" as its interests are "too far-flung and include a huge financial presence in Hong Kong."[39]

At the end of May, meanwhile, Liem remained in California, recuperating from eye surgery while Anthony camped in Singapore, staying out of Jakarta until he could be sure he would not be detained upon his return by Habibie. Not surprisingly, the responsibilities that Suharto had given Anthony on economic policy ended abruptly, which freed him to work full-time on trying to save parts of the empire. Anthony was no longer a participant in talks between the Indonesian debt team and foreign banks. Hours before the state took over BCA, Habibie signed a decree that dropped Anthony from the National Economic and Financial Resilience Council. The decree changed the body's composition: Widjojo Nitisastro remained the main point person, and another long-time technocrat, Ali Wardhana, was retained. Anthony was replaced as secretary-general by Planning Minister Boediono (who in 2009 was elected Indonesia's Vice-President on Susilo Bambang Yudhoyono's ticket) and the new private-sector member was Aburizal Bakrie, chairman of the Indonesian Chamber of Commerce and Industry. Those personnel changes were announced on 1 June by Habibie's state secretary, Akbar Tanjung, an important Golkar politician whose family was partnered with Salim in PT Indomilk.[40]

Among the many things Habibie did after becoming president was a pledge to punish the masterminds and perpetrators of the May riots. Pressure to do this intensified because of assertions by non-government organizations that violence directed at the Chinese community included rape. In fact, no prosecutions for the Jakarta mayhem were ever made. In the case of the attack on Liem's house, police at one point said they had a suspect and hauled in for questioning an ethnic Chinese crime lord-turned-Islamic preacher. The forty-year-old man, born as Tan Hok Liang, was only age thirteen when convicted of a murder. While in jail, he took the name Anton, but there were three prisoners with that name in his block, and guards dubbed him Anton Medan, after his hometown. Medan swore he gave up being a crime boss after losing US$4.2 million and nine homes due to a gambling binge in Las Vegas. The suspect denied any connection with the destruction of Liem's house, protesting "I don't even know where he lives". Medan asserted that on the morning of 14 May, he was on the streets in Chinatown, just trying to maintain peace and safeguard shops and houses. The police released Medan, saying they had no evidence for charging him. He told a newspaper that the masterminds of the 14 May riots had to be high-ranking military officers, rather than civilians such as himself. Military officers, Medan asserted, "can manage and control the unrest systematically and simultaneously".[41]

Anthony had pressing matters on his mind. These certainly did not include asking the new government to find and punish the mastermind behind the house-burning. Now that the family had lost a patron and its pivotal bank, Anthony was focused on surviving and keeping the backlash against Suharto's circle from ending Salim's entire role in the Indonesian economy.

Notes

1. *Götterdämmerung*: A collapse (as of a society or regime) marked by catastrophic violence and disorder; broadly: Downfall, as in: the Götterdämmerung of Communism, <http://www.merriam-webster.com/dictionary/g%C3%B6tterd%C3%A4mmerung>.
2. Interview with Liem, 6 May 2006.
3. "The IMF and Recent Capital Account Crises: Indonesia, Korea, Brazil", Independent Evaluation Office of the IMF, 2003, p. 16. <www.imf.org/external/np/ieo/2003/cac/pdf/all.pdf>. Accessed on 8 November 2010.
4. Ibid.
5. Interview with Anthony, 2 November 2008.
6. Ibid.
7. "Indonesian military chief says no Medan deaths", *Reuters*, 7 May 1998.
8. Richard Borsuk, "Asia Weighs Risk of Renewed Turmoil", *AWSJ*, 8 May 1998.
9. Interview with Anthony, 20 May 2007.
10. Ibid.
11. Richard Borsuk, Jay Solomon and Kate Linebaugh, "Security Forces in Jakarta Fire on Crowd of Student Protesters, Killing at Least 4", *AWSJ*, 13 May 1998.
12. Ibid.
13. Jim Dwyer, "U.S. Students Witness Indo Chaos", *New York Daily News*, 17 May 1998.
14. Interview with Anthony, 20 May 2007.
15. Ibid.
16. Ibid.

17. Ibid.
18. Interview with Anthony, 22 April 2007.
19. Ibid.
20. The year after Suharto lost power, he was replaced on the Rp50,000 note by the late W.R. Soepratman, composer of the national anthem.
21. "If I'm no longer trusted, no problem — Soeharto", *Jakarta Post*, 14 May 1998.
22. Barry Porter, "Rush for cash at Jakarta banks", *South China Morning Post*, 19 May 1999.
23. Dow Jones Newswires, 28 May 1998.
24. Joel Manuel Tesoro, "People Power", *Asiaweek*, 28 May 1998.
25. "Students swarm parliament to demand Suharto go", Reuters, 19 May 1998.
26. Peter Waldman, Raphael Pura and Marcus Brauchli, "Suharto's final days were a shadow play of shifting loyalties", *Wall Street Journal*, 22 May 1998.
27. Ibid.
28. Jay Solomon, "On the outs: Salim Group's Suharto ties make it target of retaliation", *AWSJ*, 28 May 1998.
29. Interview with Anthony, 22 April 2007.
30. Ibid.
31. "Indonesia's Bank Central Asia receives injection", Reuters, 25 May 1998.
32. "Salim keeps BCA majority stake", *Jakarta Post*, 25 May 1998.
33. Intania Fajar, "Central bank ready to provide assistance to Indonesia's beleaguered BCA", AFP, 27 May 1998.
34. Solomon, "On the outs". (In 2002, Galbraith was named BCA's president-commissioner, or chairman. He was selected by the new owners, the U.S. fund Farallon and the family owning cigarette-maker Djarum. In 2011, he became BCA's deputy president-director.)
35. Ibid.
36. "The First Five Decades" <http://www.klikbca.com/individual/silver/company.html> (accessed 15 November 2010).
37. Interview with Liem, 12 August 2006.
38. Richard Borsuk, Michael Casey and Grainne McCarthy, "European Groups cut ties to Suharto-Linked firms", *AWSJ*, 3 June 1998.
39. Michael Casey, "Indonesia's Salim Group falls victim to Post-Suharto purge", Dow Jones Newswires, 27 May 1998.
40. Akbar Tanjung, one of fourteen cabinet members who jumped off Suharto's ship on 20 May 1998, remained a power broker in the early post-Suharto period. While Golkar chairman and speaker of the House of Representatives, he was convicted of misusing US$4 million in Bulog funds in 1999 — in a case called

"Bulog-gate" — and sentenced to three years in prison. He remained House Speaker while appealing the conviction, which the Supreme Court eventually overturned. Akbar unsuccessfully ran for president in 2004.

41. Jay Solomon, "Unorthodox Cleric: Riot Suspect in Jakarta is a Man of Many Convictions", *AWSJ*, 28 July 1998.

18

SURVIVING

After Suharto's resignation, the *"reformasi"* movement brought pressure for significant change in the political system. For many Indonesians who had lived under the repressive regime of the autocrat, the hope for reform was palpable. A liberated domestic media embraced its new role. In business, meanwhile, rivals of Suharto-assisted groups were sharpening their knives, eager to slash the privileges accorded to Salim and the favoured few. Many people wanted the Salim Group to pay heavily for buttressing Suharto. Some politicians saw a chance to get control of valuable assets and ensure Anthony was crushed in post-Suharto Indonesia. "They could go after him for everything", Indonesian agricultural economist H.S. Dillon remarked. "He would be a very good symbol to crucify. He is the most vulnerable of the cronies."[1]

Exacerbating Salim's situation was that Indonesia's new president, B.J. Habibie, was no friend. Habibie was an unpredictable, hyperactive man who, during Suharto's time, pushed grandiose nationalistic plans at great cost to the country. He was distrustful of Salim and saw Liem competing for favoured status with Suharto. Anthony, however, stayed on good terms with Habibie's younger brother Timmy (Suryatim), with whom he had business in Batam. But that cut little ice with Habibie who, Anthony acknowledged, "hated me like hell" because the Salim CEO had urged Suharto in early 1998 to give Gen. Try Sutrisno a second vice-presidential term.[2] Habibie had surrounded himself with advisors who were deemed nationalists and not particularly friendly to the *cukong* culture. Liem confirmed that he also weighed in on the vice-presidential appointment, warning the president that the German-trained engineer was "like a tiger … he will get you when you are down."[3] Anthony added that when Habibie became president, he wanted to "change the total picture of the players".[4]

SHEDDING WEIGHT TO STAY ALIVE

Confronted with a sea change, some Salim executives were not confident about the future of the group. Andree Halim wanted out of Jakarta, as the May riots, the loss of BCA, and the enmity shown after Suharto's exit made him want to stop working in Indonesia. (Andree declined to meet the authors.) The fight to keep Salim afloat was solely on Anthony's shoulders. He was determined to see it survive but given the political situation, it was far from a sure bet. He began shaping a strategy that would require finding a way to get on with Habibie while keeping the anti-crony backlash from wrenching away all assets. From the start, Anthony pursued a path under which he would surrender many assets but safeguard a base and maintain enough cash flow to stay in business. In early 1999, he told the *New York Times*: "The most important thing is to weather this period — not to be wiped out by the big wave coming in."[5]

"I only thought about survival", he said years later, and referring to how bleak the situation was for him at one stage, remarked, "I was (down) in basement four." But asked if he ever thought Suharto's fall would mean the end of Salim, Anthony said "No. I never even think about it." From a "crisis centre" in Singapore, he focused on his return to Jakarta and pursuing survival. "Once you have progress, 5 per cent, 10 per cent, the rest can fall into place", he said. The most important things, Anthony said, were achieving the first 5 per cent to maintain spirit and to keep Salim's structure intact. "Without organization, it's impossible to face the task", he said.[6] After Suharto's fall, Anthony remained in Singapore for about two weeks, and then returned to Jakarta when he felt confident he could go without facing arrest. While in Singapore, Anthony met Timmy, who acted as a bridge to Habibie. Anthony sought to show that he intended to work with the new government to resolve huge debt issues stemming from the money, called liquidity credits, that the central bank had pumped into BCA. On 11 June at the Indonesian embassy in Singapore, Anthony signed a guarantee to work on resolving Salim's debts.

Upon Anthony's return to Jakarta, he was immediately confronted with pressure on the liquidity credits and on inter-group lending at BCA that violated Bank Indonesia rules. And with Indonesians now free to speak, the flak against Suharto, his family and cronies came thick and fast, with even trade magazines joining the chorus. An article in shipping publication *Lloyd's List International* began: "Never in history has one family so dominated the economic affairs of a nation to the extent that former president Suharto did with Indonesia." It said he, his children and circle had a "vise-like grip on how things were done."[7] The article quoted the Indonesian Shippers Association president complaining that Anthony controlled Bulog's rice imports, which arrived in foreign rather than domestically owned ships. (Anthony said the rice was bought on a cost, insurance, freight basis to speed the food imports, and in CIF deals, it was the seller, not buyer, who stipulated the shipper.[8])

In Jakarta the cry for rooting out "KKN" — for *"korupsi, kolusi dan nepotisme"* (corruption, collusion, and nepotism) — was in full throat. Some quickly responded to the changing tides. By mid-June, the two Suharto offspring who were BCA commissioners, Tutut and Sigit, had resigned and their joint 30 per cent equity was transferred to the state. Sudwikatmono lost one of his non-Salim cash cows when Pertamina terminated contracts with Permindo Oil Trading, a company that received an allocation of oil for export and which was a toll-gate for well-connected individuals. Indirectly through another company, Sudwikatmono held a 13 per cent share in Permindo, whose other shareholders included Bambang, Tutut's husband Indra Rukmana and Nirwan Bakrie, younger brother of businessman Aburizal Bakrie.

Habibie was trying to make political change and stay in his new seat. On 30 June, he removed Anthony, Bob Hasan, a group of Suharto relatives and others from the People's Consultative Assembly (MPR) and appointed forty-one new members. "The measure is designed to clean the MPR of corruption, collusion and nepotism", said its deputy chairman Abdul Gafur, a former Suharto minister who abandoned him in May.[9] Habibie, despite his long association with Suharto but sensing the widespread revulsion to the former strongman, made it a priority to set himself apart from some repressive symbols of the New Order regime. Aside from freeing the press, Habibie released prominent political prisoners. Under pressure from donors, he agreed to bring forward parliamentary elections to 1999 (from 2002). Stunningly, he made the monumental decision to let people in East Timor vote on whether to stay in Indonesia. Habibie naively assumed the East Timorese would happily agree to stay, while any non-government visitor to the disaffected territory knew a free vote would go overwhelmingly against Jakarta. Habibie also revoked Suharto decrees that compelled civil servants to give monthly contributions, from their pay, to the ex-president's foundations.

In the name of *"reformasi"*, there was also intense lobbying of Habibie to dismantle Suharto-era conglomerates run by Chinese, starting with Salim, and distribute assets to *pribumis*. Unlike his predecessor, Habibie did not surround himself with Chinese businesspeople. His inner circle included fervent nationalists such as Adi Sasono, named Cooperatives Minister. Sasono had long advocated cutting down conglomerates, and worried many Chinese with talk about a populist approach he called "the people's economy". He also publicly questioned the loyalty of the Chinese community. In what was seen as a broadside against the Chinese, Sasono in July told an audience which included Habibie that during the May riots, cooperative members "did not flee abroad but stayed in their country. They also love the rupiah and not the U.S. dollar."[10] Habibie contributed to the continuing anxiety among the Chinese by his seeming indifference to the trauma they suffered during the riots and the aftermath. At one point, he remarked: "If the Chinese community doesn't come back because they don't trust their own country and society, I cannot force them. But do you really think that we will then die? Their place will be taken over by others."[11] At the time of his remarks, sizeable chunks of the food distribution networks, run by Chinese Indonesians, had not yet resumed normal operations, contributing to high prices and, in some areas, even malnutrition. Other parties were trying to take up the role traditionally played by Chinese, but not making headway.

Habibie met the Young Indonesian Entrepreneurs Association (HIPMI), a *pribumi* group whose chairman Bambang Wiyogo reported that the president wanted it to help solve the food crisis by filling gaps in distribution chains. Wiyogo said he asked Habibie for "more balanced and just economic policies", for in the past "too big of a chance with unlimited facilities was given to the non-indigenous group".[12] But HIPMI lacked the capital, network and skills. To the chagrin of some, there was no viable alternative to Chinese businesses. Richard Robison, who wrote in the 1980s about Suharto's dependence on Chinese business, was quoted in 1998 as saying: "The Chinese are not good or bad at business in Indonesia. They are business in Indonesia."[13]

The president was forced to modify his position, given pressure from international donors to show Indonesia was moving past the May trauma and reopening for business. He toned down his rhetoric and began to woo those who had fled to return, asserting that his government could guarantee there would be no repeat of the riots. In late July, the president met a group of Chinese bosses — Anthony was not among them — and talked about protecting and re-involving the Chinese community. "This is their home, they should come home, and continue their work and contribute as they used to contribute to sustainable economic growth", he said a media interview afterwards.[14] (After Liem returned to Singapore from a long stay in the United States and Hong Kong following his eye surgery, Habibie invited the *cukong* to meet. This was still during the time when some were clamouring for the dismantling of the group and urging the prosecution of conglomerate bosses who had violated the country's banking rules. Following the president's invitation, Liem made a day trip to Jakarta by private jet after receiving reassurances that he would not be harmed. He said that at their meeting, Habibie assured him: "I am not a bad person'."[15])

Habibie wanted it both ways: to gain popular support by promoting a "people's economy" while getting needed Chinese capital and skills back to work. In an August speech, he rapped Suharto economic policies as "neglecting distribution of wealth" while encouraging conglomerates to expand.[16] On 4 August, Habibie summoned Anthony and other big oil-palm investors for a meeting and announced that as cooking oil was in short supply, he was assigning cooperatives instead of Bulog to handle distribution in some areas. It did not happen. Less than three weeks later, Habibie fired long-time Bulog chief Beddu Amang, who some considered close to Salim. At the time of his removal, Beddu — later jailed for corruption in a land deal with Tommy Suharto — was organizing the first tenders for contracts, which Bulog traditionally just awarded to connected parties. Before Beddu's firing, the *Far Eastern Economic Review* noted, he "had been under pressure from some of Habibie's ministers to channel future rice imports through favoured ethnic-Indonesian businessmen — a change from the Suharto days, when shipments were the preserve of the Salim Group".[17]

Hoping to get a slice of the Bulog action was the Bakrie Group. Aburizal Bakrie complained that his group could not win contracts in Suharto's time as Salim "was authorized for commodity transportation monopolized by Bulog".[18] During the New Order, according to the *Indonesian Commercial Newsletter*, "it seemed like an impossibility to unseat the Salim Group as the partner of Bulog."[19] H.S. Dillon told *BusinessWeek*: "You can rightfully say that Bulog worked for Anthony."[20]

Indonesia needed the world's money — and this tempered plans by politicians to shift assets from Chinese to other hands. In early July, Habibie's economic czar Ginandjar Kartasasmita asked the international community for another US$4 billion to US$6 billion to fund a safety net for the estimated 80 million Indonesians who remain mired in poverty. Donors complied, but delivered an explicit message that Habibie had to stick with the IMF programme, plus an implicit one that policies discouraging Chinese capital from returning were unacceptable. The conglomerates were under political pressure to pay their debts, and the government needed money so that it was not wholly living off IMF loans. Naturally, the nationalist camp around Habibie was unhappy with the IMF programme and conditionality. But the cash-strapped government had no alternative to taking the IMF medicine. It had promised the IMF to unveil a plan for rebuilding Indonesia's broken banking system by 21 August. The plan was to be administered by the Indonesian Bank Restructuring Agency (IBRA), which in May took over BCA. Among IBRA's many tasks was negotiating with Salim and other groups on repayment of debts. IBRA hired Lehman Brothers and J.P. Morgan plus government-owned securities firm Danareksa to advise it. In August 1998, staff of Lehman and IBRA began to meet regularly with Anthony to negotiate. The *Wall Street Journal* wrote that at a session on 11 August, Anthony bluntly told IBRA officials and their advisors "If you want to kill us off, fine, but you'll lose 100,000 jobs."[21]

Many people wanted to take apart Salim, but not those on the other side of the table. The IBRA team wanted to strike a deal that could, over time, get the state repaid and keep businesses running. It was impossible at that stage to get full cash repayment from Salim or from any debtor, so the government decided to work towards getting control of assets judged to be worth what the groups owed. IBRA vice-president Dasa Sutantio related: "Some ask, 'Why are you letting Salim Group off the hook?' But it's a question if we want cash or justice. It's a fine line we walk."[22] Dasa added that many in the government "simply wanted blood. But if you give them blood, you might hurt an entire generation." A senior banker involved in the negotiations with Anthony commented: "We needed to set an example that the government wasn't anti-Chinese, but wasn't bailing out Salim Group either... A fair, unbiased agreement was critical."[23] No one put it this way publicly, but Salim was too big — and post-Suharto, still too connected in the bureaucracy — to fail. On 21 August, the government announced the national banking reconstruction plan, which included merging the four big state banks. That was also the day Liem and his sons formally lost their flagship bank. Officials indicated that at least half of BCA's loans had been found to be inter-group, well above the permitted 20 per cent level. IBRA chief Glenn Yusuf said only that an audit by an international accountant found there was a "gross breaching" of legal lending limits (LLL).[24] Yusuf, who rarely spoke to the media, later told *Fortune* magazine: "The Salims created a truly remarkable money-gathering machine through BCA. But they also broke the law."[25] The same article quoted D.E. Setijoso, a highly regarded banker brought from state-owned Bank Rakyat Indonesia to run BCA, as saying the Salim Group was overconfident of its business acumen: "They thought the best borrowers in Indonesia were their own companies."[26] In 2000, the *Wall Street Journal* put the share of BCA's inter-group loans at 70 per cent[27] and others thought the level was even higher.[28]

Liem was given until 21 September to sign agreements on how to settle the loans Salim companies had taken. At the announcement, the IMF resident representative in Jakarta, Kadhim Al-Eyd, expressed confidence the government would fully recover what Salim owed, saying "These guys have long-term interests in this country."[29] That same day, economics minister Ginandjar talked tough on getting conglomerates to settle their debts. "If their cash is not enough, we will take their assets and if even that is not enough, we will seize their assets ... they will not get away just like that," he pronounced.[30] For Salim, he specified Indofood, Indocement and Indomobil as possible candidates. But his threat was not carried out, unsurprisingly as the IMF would not have allowed it. Also, there would have been a practical question of who would run nationalized Salim companies. Indofood was too big to stop producing, and its managers were well respected. After IBRA took over BCA, it changed the board of directors, and left in place many of the managers or operations people who helped the bank recover.

Right after the bank reconstruction announcement, Salim intensified negotiations with IBRA. As expected, Anthony pushed for a debt settlement that gave stakes in Salim companies, and not cash. At that time, he said later, nobody in Indonesia had substantial cash. Salim had control or stakes in hundreds of companies, though only a few were listed and had a market value that did not need to be negotiated. Due to Indonesia's near-collapse, the value of the listed businesses had dropped calamitously. Indofood became like a penny stock in June 1998, and around August when Anthony was negotiating with IBRA, the market capitalization was well less than US$500 million, compared with the peak of US$4.4 billion just fourteen months earlier.

To reach an agreement on debt settlement, according to Anthony, there was an understanding that "it should be commercial [negotiation], it cannot be a politically-driven negotiation". Anthony said later he told government negotiators that he would list all his assets, and the team could confirm the list's veracity. According to Anthony, the government side found that Salim "told not a single lie". His approach, Anthony said, was: "anything you want to take, as long as it still belongs to the [Liem] family, we can negotiate".[31] But he pushed to keep assets that were already pledged to banks out of play, unless IBRA repaid the loans underpinning them — which naturally it wouldn't want to do. This strategy helped him retain control of Indofood, most of whose shares were pledged as collateral for loans given before 1998. In the end, Anthony only ceded 2.5 per cent of Indofood to IBRA. (By contrast, Anthony gave IBRA all of the 22 per cent he then controlled in Astra International.) People at IBRA said they sought, without success, a bigger pledge of Indofood and that Anthony — later labelled a "cooperative" debtor — complied in providing other, unlisted assets in his settlement. The debt negotiations were testimony of Anthony's prowess; this was reaffirmed by several participants, including an unnamed IBRA employee, quoted by Dutch academic Marleen Dieleman in her 2007 study of the Salim Group:

> Anthony Salim laid down his cards on the table, but it was still a poker game. He is smart. Asks us for our conditions first. We would like to have the liquid assets, like Indofood shares, but it turns out that there is a condition, that if he has less than 51 per cent ownership, his bank loans become immediately payable. Obstacles arise. Instead he offers Indomobil. Anthony Salim is very tough to negotiate with.[32]

Asked by the authors if he ever loses in a negotiation, Anthony replied: "A lot, but on average, it's okay."[33]

As Anthony and IBRA worked feverishly to meet the 21 September deadline set by the IMF, pressure was building up for Suharto and his other cronies. Bob Hasan, half-owner of shuttered Bank Umum Nasional, was questioned twice for hours by police. Suharto, amid calls in the Indonesian media and parliament to investigate his wealth, appeared on Tutut's television channel on 6 September to declare he was not a crook. "I don't have one cent of savings abroad, I don't have accounts at foreign banks... I don't have any shares in foreign firms, much less hundreds of billions of dollars," he read from a prepared statement.[34] Shortly before Salim's deadline, Ginandjar told *BusinessWeek* that the group had been "too dependent on government support. Of course, now that has become a liability for them." The conglomerate, he added, "should not expect the treatment they got in the past". But Ginandjar was not involved in the IBRA negotiations. For those talks, some analysts were sure Anthony would emerge with significant interests intact. Wilson Nababan, president of business researcher CISI Raya Utama, described Anthony as "the most intelligent and resourceful businessman in Indonesia".[35]

Salim proposed to pledge a particular asset and provided its estimate of the value, then IBRA and its advisors calculated their own. This process was complicated for the unlisted companies that formed the bulk of Salim's list. On 21 September, an agreement on pledged assets was reached. Anthony and Finance Minister Bambang Subianto signed a Master Settlement and Acquisition Agreement (MSAA); Salim pledged assets in 104 companies that the agreement valued at Rp48.6 trillion, more than US$5 billion at the time. (In 1999, in a supplemental agreement to the MSAA, the total value was raised to Rp52.6 trillion, as liabilities were added through Ibrahim Risjad's Bank Risjad Salim International, and some additional liabilities of Salim itself. IBRA's financial advisors said these were settled by a transfer to Holdiko Perkasa — the organization IBRA set up to sell Salim assets — of additional shares in companies already pledged plus shares of companies not previously pledged. The number of companies in which Salim pledged some shares eventually rose to 108.) Among the stakes Anthony proposed to surrender to IBRA to cover Salim's debts were 13 per cent of Indocement and 5 per cent of First Pacific. The First Pacific stake reduced the Liem family's holding in the Hong Kong conglomerate to 26 per cent from 31 per cent. ("Gang of Four" members, known for the purposes of First Pacific as "the Liem Investors", retained 49 per cent.) As an indication of how stock valuations had changed, shares of First Pacific had plunged to about HK$2.30 in mid-September 1998 from around HK$8 in October 1997, as the Asian financial crisis was intensifying, and a peak of HK$12.85 in August 1996.

According to documentation reviewed by the authors, Salim itself put the total value of its pledged stakes at Rp127.605 billion, whereas the "settlement value" — what IBRA and the Lehman-led advisors negotiated it down to — was Rp48.650 billion, or 62 per cent less.[36] A letter the advisors sent IBRA stated that the valuations were made in line with Ministry of Finance requests, including that they incorporate "normalized economic and political scenarios"; in other words, without any crises raging. The text said that each valuation used "the assumption that the Indonesian economy would rebound during the next few years" and that Salim's valuations were adjusted to "develop cash flow projection and discount rates more conservative than the original shareholder case".[37] The valuations, it also stated, weighed nine factors including competition, demand, distribution and management. According to an appendix, the largest settled value for a company, at Rp3.37 trillion, was for unlisted PT Buana Megawisatama, the investor in resorts and developments on Bintan Island near Singapore. Salim had itself proposed a value nearly eight times larger, at Rp25.69 trillion.

Brian O'Connor, Indonesian representative of Lehman Brothers, said at the time of the agreement signing that "the valuations of the companies were extremely rigorous".[38] Soon after the Salim settlement — and others were set with Sudwikatmono and Gajah Tunggal boss Sjamsul Nursalim — IBRA chairman Yusuf said the agency's valuations of the pledged company stakes were "extremely conservative. We will have no problem recovering the government's debts in full, not to mention a healthy return premium."[39] As it turned out, this was not the case, causing many complaints about the original agreements. At the time the pacts were set, there was already criticism about management control staying with the original conglomerate owners in many cases, though the government had no means to run the businesses better than the indebted founders. IBRA boss Yusuf, a well-regarded former Citibank executive who had led state-owned securities firm Danareksa, defended the strategy, saying that "minimising the government's involvement ... is key to maximising the government's recovery and helping to rebuild the real economy... This isn't nationalization of bank shareholder assets. It is a secured repayment programme to ensure Indonesia gets its cash back."[40]

Just as the deal was sealed, Habibie — living up to his reputation for being unpredictable — threw a spanner in the works by insisting that groups pay 100 per cent of their debts with cash, and within one year.

Habibie advisor Frans Seda, who from 1966 to 1968 was Suharto's finance minister, announced to the palace press that Habibie had just told him "one year should be enough" for conglomerates to raise the cash they owed by selling assets.[41] Such a deadline and requirement might have spelled the end of Salim. But it would have been an unrealistic goal for the government, which badly needed more money from asset sales than could be raised by quick deals at a time Indonesia was unstable and unattractive. Fortunately for Salim, Habibie got steered off his "100 per cent cash within a year" plan. It was the IMF that came to its aid.

Habibie's demand for cash repayment came just as the IMF and Indonesia were negotiating a new letter of intent that would spark a fresh US$1 billion injection. On 18 October, IMF Asia-Pacific director Hubert Neiss wrote Habibie a note that did not specifically mention the one-year, 100 per cent cash idea but made clear he thought it was a bad one. There was a need for "flexibility" over the debtors' repayment period, Neiss wrote, adding "If all assets were dumped in a 'fire-sale' under presently depressed economic conditions, the return to the government would be very small." Also, the letter said that quick sales "could cause serious disruptions in the management of the companies sold, with undesirable effects on the economy".[42] The Neiss letter did not mention this, but the IMF also wanted to derail a proposal to hand to cooperatives some IBRA assets; Cooperatives Ministry director-general Deswandhy Agusman had said he wanted 20 per cent of the companies transferred to his ministry because "wealth should be distributed to the people".[43] Seda, the Habibie advisor, acknowledged that the president was under pressure to "do something for the cooperatives" but added "we don't want to give the impression to foreign investors that assets are being nationalized".[44]

Habibie backed away from his full cash, one-year demand, and the conglomerates were given four years to settle their debts. Asked a decade later about the IMF's intervention, Neiss commented on Habibie's plan: "This idea was very disruptive. It would have been a setback." Neiss played down the IMF role in derailing the plan, saying that Habibie "wouldn't have pursued that course, whatever I said". As to whether the affected business groups would have been crushed by a one-year payback stipulation, Neiss said: "I don't know. But for the economy, recovery would have been delayed if Salim and other groups were crushed. That was the rationale." The retired IMF executive, who joined Deutsche Bank as Asia chairman in 2000, denied suggestions he had saved Salim. "My intention wasn't to save any specific group", Neiss said. To say that he saved Salim was a "simplification and misleading", he asserted, as in all actions "I tried to remove any policy obstacles, to enable an economic recovery".[45]

For his part, Anthony in 2008 acknowledged that it was "lucky" the Fund was involved, as otherwise settlement of the group's debts — its overall fate — "becomes [a] totally domestic agenda".[46] With MSAA, in Anthony's view, it was between the government and the IMF to settle how to recover the debt. Regarding the move by some parties to get hold of the assets Salim pledged to IBRA, Anthony reflected: "We were basically the chicken on the plate." If other parties got control of the assets, then these could not be used to raise money for the state budget, and then "of course the IMF is not happy". And the IMF, which was providing essential funds for the government, could respond by halting money injections, he said. Some people believed the IMF's lobbying against the Habibie plan was not sufficient to stifle it, and allege that Salim gave money to key individuals to take pressure off it. Questioned about this, Anthony replied this was "100 per cent not true".[47]

Following the debt talks, Finance Minister Bambang Subianto on 10 November confirmed that the government had ratified the deals with Salim and four other groups to recover their debts over four years. The debtors, he said, had to repay 27 per cent of their total in the first year. To sell the assets, IBRA set up holding companies; the one for Salim was named Holdiko. Assessing the debt settlement negotiations between the government and Salim and other debtors, scholars Richard Robison and Vedi Hadiz commented: "There was little doubt that the conglomerates had the upper hand. The opaque nature of corporate governance prevented a clear picture of corporate assets."[48] For Salim, getting acceptance of non-listed businesses already was a big victory, as it helped let Anthony retain Indofood. Allowing Liem to hand over a package of chunks of more than 100 companies, Robison and Hadiz said, "made due diligence appraisals a nightmare". By their reckoning, surrendering Indofood, Bogasari and television station Indosiar "would have covered all debt".[49]

Although Adi Sasono's efforts to get some Salim assets into cooperatives' hands were blocked, other initiatives to build up small business continued during Habibie's presidency. In late 1998, Golkar unveiled a "People's Economy" programme. "In the Suharto era, a small group of cronies received virtually all of the wealth", complained Fadel Muhammad, a *pribumi* businessman and Golkar's economic commission chairman. "Now we're seeking to create 10,000 mid-size businessmen in their place."[50] While Salim was shifting assets to IBRA at home, the family's most viable asset outside Indonesia, First Pacific, was moving to add one that would have a big impact. In late 1998, it used proceeds from selling Hagemeyer to buy a state-controlled stake in Philippine Long Distance Telephone (PLDT). As Indonesia's traumatic 1998 drew to a close, Anthony had plenty of worries at home. Although the group's bank was gone, he had succeeded in keeping Salim going despite the backlash following Suharto's fall. "Surviving" is how he regularly replied when people asked how he was doing, and indeed he was doing okay in an Indonesian version of "Survivor". A top goal for 1999 was ensuring that Indofood, the most precious asset, stayed under Salim's wings.

SECURING SUSTENANCE, VIA INDOFOOD

Salim's empire was built on three pillars — banking (BCA), construction materials (Indocement) and food (Bogasari and Indofood). Suharto's fall in May 1998 imperilled all three, and the banking pillar collapsed shortly after the ruler did. The cement pillar crumbled more slowly. But Anthony found a way to preserve its third pillar, food, and that allowed the group to remain a major player. Anthony strove to "hang on to Indofood more than the others", said Benny Santoso, his chief lieutenant. "Anthony loves this line of business so much."[51]

There was a compelling reason to keep a grip on Indofood — cash flow. While the crisis cut consumption, people still needed to eat and instant noodles were now in the diets of millions. While the economy shrank a 13 per cent in 1998, Indofood's cash flow "remained strong" that year, First Pacific said later. When Anthony was calculating what assets to cede to settle Salim's debts to Indonesia's central bank, he did not put any of his family's stake in Indofood on the table. IBRA and its advisors tried to get it included, but in the end got only 2.5 per cent, which left Salim with more than 50 per cent. (At that stage, the Indonesian government owned 10.18 per cent of Indofood, from when Indocement had majority-ownership of Salim food businesses.)

Keeping most shares away from IBRA did not guarantee they would stay with Salim. Some politicians badly wanted to pry them away. Also, Indofood's sizeable debts — US$989 million as of December 1998 — were a heavy burden. Salim needed a capital injection, and many in the market expected it would come from related party First Pacific, which might be pressed to shore up its Indonesian owners. When all hell seemed to be breaking loose in Jakarta in 1998, First Pacific said it couldn't do anything but watch. During the week in May between the Jakarta riots and Suharto's resignation, Managing Director Manny Pangilinan directly ruled out a Salim bailout. "We will have to hold off considering, as a general matter, any investments in Indonesia. Whether it is Indofood or any other possible investment, we can't proceed," he said. Manny added that it would not be in the interest of the Salim family to force a bad deal onto First Pacific: "If I were in their shoes, this is my viable lifeboat, isn't it? If I were to load it with undesirable [investments], it is not going to help."[52] Later that year, First Pacific Chief Operating Officer Michael Healy, who described Salim as in "utter disarray", reiterated Hong Kong's stance: "We have not — and cannot — give or lend money to the Salims. It's against the rules of the Hong Kong stock exchange."[53]

Manny recognized that Indofood could eventually be a good investment — if priced fairly for First Pacific shareholders. He was quoted as saying in late 1998, "If you abstract from — I know you can't, but if you abstract from — the political situation in Indonesia, and you look at Indofood purely as Indofood, it is a wonderful company."[54] Manny said First Pacific was talking with Salim and a "strategic partner". That turned out to be Japan's Nissin Food Products. The courtship made sense. Nissin founder Momofuku Ando was the inventor of instant noodles.[55] With the Japanese market already mature, Nissin was looking to boost *ramen* sales overseas. Company president Koki Ando, Momofuku's son, in 1997 described Indofood as "our biggest rival globally". Explaining Nissin's aim to expand in noodles rather than diversify into other foods, Koki Ando declared: "*Ramen* is like air or water. People can't live without it anymore because it's convenient and good."[56]

For Anthony, Nissin seemed a natural fit. He needed cash and it craved growth outside Japan. Nissin salivated at the prospect of getting into an Indonesian powerhouse at a crisis-slashed price. Anthony negotiated a structure that would get the Japanese in while keeping Indofood — then 63 per cent owned by Salim — pretty much in his family's hands. In mid-December, a deal for doing that was announced: Nissin and First Pacific would each pay US$285 million and each get 30 per cent of Indofood. Their combined 60 per cent would be held through a joint venture. The proposed deal would give Nissin a big role in steering Indofood, something Salim was not wild about, but the plan looked like a life-saver. "We really needed to raise money... we signed an agreement out of necessity", Benny

Santoso said later.[57] Koki Ando called the move "very important for our global strategy". At the time, Nissin made about 4 billion packs of noodles a year at twenty-three plants in eight countries; Indofood's capacity was 13 billion packs at seventeen factories in Indonesia. The deal was based on an Indofood share-price of Rp3,950, which valued it at US$950 million. Indofood's top manager Eva Riyanti Hutapea thought the buyers were getting too good a deal. Not one shy to express her opinion, she was quoted as saying: "If I were standing in the position of Pak [Mr] Anthony, I would not release it [Indofood] at that price."[58]

One day in January 1999, Indofood's share price plummeted 18 per cent on fears — later dissipated — that Indonesia's planned anti-monopolies bill could hit the company, which many viewed as nearly a monopoly. But Nissin did not worry, and some analysts said reducing Salim ownership could be a way to undercut moves against Indofood. Nissin was particularly keen on the Indofood deal because it expected to take the helm. An Indofood extraordinary general meeting on 25 January 1999 approved board changes contingent on completion of the Nissin deal. Shareholders endorsed allowing Indofood to have majority foreign ownership. Also, there was a plan to have Koki Ando become chairman in place of Liem, who held that post since Indofood went public in 1994. Other intended moves, subject to Nissin's entry, were to put Momofuku Ando on the board of commissioners and make a Nissin man a company vice-president director in place of Anthony. In the end, none of these changes materialized, because Nissin failed to get into Indofood.

In February, minority shareholders of First Pacific approved the purchase, together with Nissin, of 60 per cent of Indofood, but that didn't make it a sure thing. As time passed, Anthony found a way to raise needed money and maintain control in Indofood. The money came through selling a major Singapore asset, his family's 23 per cent stake in big Singapore office landlord UIC. On 9 March, Salim's KMP announced the sale to Hong Kong property company HKR International for US$179 million. But the deal fell through; HKR cited a "breach" of proposed terms when UIC's profit in 1998 fell more than 35 per cent. Analysts speculated that the real reason the buyer pulled out was chemistry issues between HKR chief executive Payson Cha and UIC's other main shareholder, United Overseas Bank chief Wee Cho Yaw.

The aborted UIC sale presented a headache, but Salim quickly found another buyer: a resourceful Philippine tycoon whom Liem had not met before. John Gokongwei got interested in the Singapore opportunity when he learned the Salim-HKR deal didn't proceed. He agreed to pay Salim the same price. Gokongwei, nine years younger than Liem, was born near Xiamen. When he was one year old, his father took him to the Philippines, where Gokongwei's grandfather had settled. When Gokongwei was thirteen, his father died, and the youth started showing his entrepreneurial flair by selling soap and candles at a Cebu stall. While World War II brought great hardship, Gokongwei once said he looked back at the period "with the fondest of memories... It was the great equalizer. Almost everyone I knew had lost big and small fortunes... we all started at ground zero."[59] Gokongwei became one of the Philippines' wealthiest men, with interests in food, retail, property, petrochemicals, cellphones and airline Cebu Pacific.

In April 1999, the bridge that formed between Gokongwei and Salim had nothing do with common Fujian roots. "I heard they were in trouble", Gokongwei recounted later about the Salim family. "I called Goldman Sachs, who talked to Anthony." The deal to buy UIC, he recalled, was done "in 2–3 days. It was a listed company, easy." Through the transaction, Gokongwei said he developed respect for Liem. "I didn't know the Salims before", he said. "We got to be quite close friends."[60] At a dinner after the UIC purchase, according to Gokongwei, Liem thanked him for rescuing the property deal. "He said, 'You helped me. Without you, we would have been dead'."[61]

Shortly after the UIC stake was sold, the deadline for the proposed sale of 60 per cent of Indofood to Nissin and First Pacific passed, and the plan was cancelled. First Pacific said the transaction died "following the inability of the companies to secure consents and waivers from Indofood's creditor banks."[62] In Jakarta, Indofood announced: "After exhausting all efforts to obtain ... consents and approvals, the parties have decided that is in their best interests not to proceed with the acquisition in the structure and form previously announced."[63] First Pacific spokesman Robert Sherbin said Nissin's entry "would have brought certain advantages but I don't think Indofood needs lessons on how to sell instant noodles."[64] In Tokyo, a Nissin spokesman was quoted as saying the issue "involved confidential matters between Indofood and First Pacific".[65]

The nixing of Nissin's planned entry was good for Salim, which had seller's remorse. Also, thanks to Gokongwei's Singapore purchase, Anthony did not require the cash he earlier felt was needed. For Salim, the plan's axing just meant it paid a US$25 million non-completion fee to Nissin. Earlier, Salim viewed the deal as helping anchor the group in Indofood. "In case the government of Indonesia tries to grab Indofood, at least you [would] have Japan to go to", Anthony said about it.[66] But then Salim's political and financial problems seemed more manageable, and the group believed it could cope and avoid having Nissin in Indofood's cockpit. "We let it [the deal] expire", Anthony said, acknowledging that Nissin was not happy, as the company was "hoping to buy this".[67] For Salim, paying a US$25 million scuttling fee was a small price to pay for retaining control of Indofood. It was becoming clear Indofood could make good money again. Despite rocky political times, the company reported an initial net profit for 1998 of Rp150 billion (later restated as Rp458 billion; the 1997 loss, originally reported as Rp1.2 trillion, got restated as Rp910 billion). In the tumultuous year of 1998, when political uncertainty and riots wreaked havoc, sales rose 76 per cent, in rupiah terms, to Rp8.8 trillion.

With the Nissin deal dead in the water, it also meant First Pacific did not enter Indofood. But unlike Nissin, First Pacific was sure to get another chance. Right away, First Pacific said it would keep seeking a stake in Indofood. Managing Director Thomas Yasuda — who had succeeded Manny, now the chairman — said buying 30 per cent "and possibly more would be extremely positive for our company".[68] After Nissin's effort failed, another suitor, Philippine beer giant San Miguel, had tried to come in. But this was stymied by Anthony's insistence that no foreign buyer — except for related party First Pacific — could get more than 30 per cent. Benny Santoso explained that San Miguel "required some degree of control; we couldn't reach agreement ... We want to keep Indofood within the [Salim] group."[69]

A plan in which First Pacific alone would enter Indofood was unveiled in June. It was to buy 40 per cent, in two transactions, for US$650 million. The first covered the purchase of 30 per cent, on similar terms to what First Pacific and Nissin were going to pay in the scuppered deal, and the second was for 10 per cent, on different terms. The deal was structured to undercut any contention that First Pacific was bailing out Salim. Terms were adjusted from December to account for Indofood's now-stronger position; the share price on 21 June 1999 was Rp11,900, or 81 per cent above the 15 December 1998 level of Rp3,950. (During the six months, the rupiah had strengthened slightly; Indofood's share price on 21 June worked out to US$1.66, compared with US$0.52 in mid-December.) First Pacific's share price, since December, had risen 90 per cent to HK$6.65 from HK$3.50. Salim wanted to make sure the proposal won approval from minority shareholders, as required by Hong Kong rules.

The first part of the proposed transaction called for First Pacific to pay US$150 million — the same amount of cash as before — and to issue 264 million new shares at HK$4.00 each. This worked out to paying the equivalent of Rp5,000 for each share of Indofood, a 48 per cent discount to its average close over the previous ten days. The second transaction involved First Pacific issuing another 81 million new shares, and a note of US$50 million that could get converted into First Pacific shares, at HK$8.40 each. In total, the 40 per cent of Indofood that First Pacific would buy cost it an average Rp6,432 a share, a 33 per cent discount to its average closing price over the preceding ten days.

Indofood's Eva Riyanti Hutapea again spoke bluntly about the pricing, asserting, "It's unreasonably cheap … I don't know why the Salims are so generous to First Pacific shareholders… But if Mr Salim wants to sell, I cannot say anything. If I got involved, I would get more emotional and ask a higher price."[70] First Pacific's Yasuda, who called the original deal with Nissin good for his company, described the revised one as "great". The *Asian Wall Street Journal* agreed it was great for Salim, as it "provides the family with cash to pay off debt and maintains the family's controlling stake in First Pacific".[71] It quoted David Chang, head of research at Jakarta's Trimegah Securities, as saying shifting control to Hong Kong "will shield Indofood from any political repercussions" from a change of Indonesian government.

One day later, Salim said it would sell about 12.5 per cent of its remaining stake in Indofood to "international investors" by a private placement. The shares were sold in July at Rp8,300, raising US$284 million. The transactions with First Pacific and the private placement reduced the Salim family's direct stake in Indofood to just more than 10 per cent, from 62.7 per cent. It was time for a formal change of Indofood leadership. At its annual meeting on 29 June, Liem did not offer himself for re-election as chairman and Sudwikatmono stepped down as president-director. In October, First Pacific chairman Manny was approved to succeed Liem while Hutapea, *de facto* chief executive and "Vice President Director II", was formally appointed president-director and CEO. Anthony relinquished his post of "Vice President Director I" and joined the board of commissioners. In Indofood's annual report for 1999, Manny lauded

Liem and Sudwikatmono for "their invaluable guidance in creating and shaping Indofood into the success that it is today".[72] On 11 August, 99.9 per cent of First Pacific's minority shareholders approved the Indofood deal, which closed in September when the Salim shares were sold to CAB Holdings in Mauritius, wholly owned by First Pacific. Around the same time, Indonesia again came into world headlines in a bad light, due to the destruction that Jakarta-backed militias wreaked after East Timor, forcibly annexed in 1977, voted overwhelmingly for independence from Jakarta. Yasuda was quoted as saying that when Indonesia settles down politically, Indofood "will be seen as the best acquisition First Pacific has ever made".[73]

NEW OWNERS FOR THE OTHER OLD PILLARS

Before looking at Holdiko and its sales of assets Salim pledged to IBRA, it is worth summarizing what happened to BCA and Indocement, whose post-1998 paths were not made by Holdiko. The Indocement case is intriguing because Salim thought it could still set the course, but a minister who wanted to cut the crony to size snatched the reins away. Here's a review of what happened to these group pillars.

1. Bank Central Asia

After the massive run that led the government to take over BCA a week after Suharto's resignation, efforts got under way to rebuild and recapitalize it. Because the public was assured that the bank would not close, money pulled out in May 1998 began to return; BCA said that by December, deposits had returned to the "pre-crisis" level. By May 1999, with BCA fully recapitalized, most of the loans the government had given were swapped with government bonds. The Suharto children were gone as shareholders, and Salim had lost most of its stakes. IBRA owned 92.8 per cent of BCA. The other 7.2 per cent remained with Liem's family and, according to BCA's annual report on 1999, included the following:

Anthony Salim: 2.894 per cent
Soedono Salim (Liem): 2.147 per cent
Andree Halim: 2.147 per cent
Albert Halim: 0.005 per cent

While BCA's recapitalization was under way, the government shaped a plan to sell much of it, making it a public company with a new private, main owner. But there were many problems getting to new ownership during the bumpy early post-Suharto period. It took nearly four years to find a new controlling owner, during which Indonesia had three presidents: B.J. Habibie, Abdurrahman Wahid and Megawati Sukarnoputri. Anthony harboured hopes that some year, somehow he could get back a key stake, but there was no way it was going to happen. Understandably, there was strong public sentiment against the government allowing owners of banks that flouted lending rules and received central bank injections to get back into them. Also, Anthony's priorities were survival, and hanging onto Indofood. BCA was gone — a price Salim paid for being so closely wrapped to Suharto.

It took a long time to get an IPO for BCA off the ground. Proceeding with those plans was impossible during Habibie's tenure, which ended in October 1999, thanks in large part to political turmoil that sapped interest among potential investors. When Abdurrahman Wahid was president, IBRA pushed ahead an IPO for the bank that agency deputy chairman Jerry Ng described as "the best franchise in the country".[74] BCA, at this stage, had very few non-performing loans because all the bad inter-group ones had been removed. Thanks to reconstruction, the bank was not large at this stage — at the end of 1999, it had loans of Rp3.78 trillion. (At 30 September 2013, loans amounted to Rp298.93 trillion.) For 1999, BCA had a net profit of Rp641.3 billion, compared with a staggering 1998 loss of Rp28.40 trillion, according to the bank's annual report for 1999.

Putting aside Indonesia's woes — impossible to do at the time the government initially wanted to sell shares — BCA was attractive for investment, given its countrywide reach with nearly 800 branches and about 2,000 ATMs. It had roughly 8 million account holders and a highly sophisticated computer system. In Singapore in May 2000, on a roadshow for the public offering, IBRA chairman Cacuk Sudarijanto said investor response in Indonesia was "overwhelming as the people know that BCA is the crown jewel of the country's banking system".[75] Still, BCA remained a tough sell. The offering price was set at Rp1,400, at the lower end of the planning range of Rp1,350–1,750, and only 22 per cent of the bank, rather than the hoped-for 30 per cent, was sold. The issue was just 1.2 times subscribed, and the first day's trading on 31 May 2000 provided no spark for Indonesia's feeble exchange. The stock closed at its IPO price.

Plans to follow up the IPO with a block sale to a "strategic" investor had plenty of twists and turns. Implementation sparked friction between the government of Abdurrahman Wahid, who became president in October 1999, and the IMF. At the end of 2000, the Fund delayed a US$400 million payment in part because a BCA block sale had not proceeded. Squared off against the IMF was Wahid's Coordinating Minister for the Economy Rizal Ramli, who had been vocal in criticizing Salim's 1997 plan to have foreign parties own a majority of Indofood. Slowly and unsurely, sale of a block of BCA shares got done. There were fears that several interested parties were proxies for Anthony, who insisted he wasn't trying to get in, though doubts lingered. In March 2001, Finance Minister Prijadi Praptosuhardjo vowed that a Salim buyback "is not allowed".[76] At the end of June, IBRA confirmed there were two bidders for a 30 per cent stake, who it did not name but domestic media knew to be Newbridge Capital of the United States and a consortium involving Bhakti Investama of Indonesian businessman Hary Tanoesoedibjo, who denied speculation he was a Salim proxy. But the prices offered were disappointing, and no sale went ahead. To get some cash while it called a new tender, the government sold another 10 per cent of BCA in a second public offering.

One reason the BCA divestment proceeded so slowly was the growing wobbliness of the Wahid administration, which had many ramifications including abrupt changes in IBRA leadership. While some of Wahid's ministers were taking a tough line with Salim, the stroke-impaired president was personally quite friendly with Anthony, in contrast to Habibie. But Wahid's presidency was dogged by management woes and corruption allegations called Bulog-gate about use of the commodity agency's money. On 23 July 2001, in a move in the works for months, the People's Consultative Assembly (MPR) impeached Wahid, and Vice-President Megawati became president.

By late August, Megawati's cabinet negotiated a new letter of intent with the IMF, who reopened the money tap. In it, Jakarta agreed to sell a 51 per cent stake of BCA by the end of 2001. That deadline, like others, was broken but by December the number of contenders for BCA was cut from fifteen to nine. Indonesian media speculated that at least several finalists were Anthony's proxies. In January 2002, about 75 people organized by an unknown party demonstrated outside Wisma BCA, demanding that the bank be given to the "people" rather than sold, arguing that it had been built on collusion between Liem and Suharto.

An effigy of Liem was burned. Sentiment against Salim perhaps was increased slightly by media reports in late 2001 that Bank Indonesia officials wanted the Liem family to give up its remaining 7.2 per cent stake in BCA to increase pledged assets, which Salim initially refused to do. "This shows that the central bank is powerless against Salim", a commentary in the *Jakarta Post* opined.[77] But the Liem family stake was reduced, to less than 2 per cent.

Meanwhile, serious BCA suitors were cut to four. These were a group led by Standard Chartered Bank (whose partners included the Government of Singapore Investment Corp., or GIC); U.S. investment firm Farallon (partnered with the Hartono family, owners of *kretek*-maker Djarum); an Indonesian consortium led by a cooperative of batik-makers; and Bank Mega, a little-known institution headed by businessman Chairul Tanjung. Some Indonesian media speculated that Anthony, after he lost BCA, invested in Bank Mega, and was using Chairul as a proxy. Both men, who were on friendly terms, denied this. It was not surprising that Anthony had some association with the young *pribumi* businessman, who gained attention and size in the post-Suharto period. Born in 1962, Chairul studied dentistry but was more interested in business, creating a partnership in trading that won state banks' backing. This expanded into the Para Group, which in 1996 got permission to take over small Bank Karman in Surabaya, renaming it Bank Mega. It emerged unscathed from Indonesia's 1997–98 crisis — as did Chairul. In the post-Suharto period, Chairul expanded the bank and went into retailing (main shareholder of Carrefour's Indonesia operation), media (Trans TV) and property, building an indoor theme park called Trans Studio in Makassar, Sulawesi's biggest city. In 2005, after BCA's new owner was in place, Chairul and Anthony made a small investment together in a Singapore company. In a 2008 newspaper profile, Chairul reiterated that he was Anthony's partner, not proxy, and he said their links were rooted in help Bank Mega gave BCA and loans that Chairul's bank made to a couple of Salim outfits.[78] Anthony told the authors he didn't think the BCA part was correct, but Salim companies were clients of Bank Mega and he was very happy to have Chairul as a business partner.[79] Asked if Chairul was particularly close among his post-1998 partners, Anthony merely smiled, saying: "We associate with everybody post-Suharto."[80]

In the contest for BCA, Bank Mega did not get into the final round of competition. Bank Indonesia, after conducting financial "fit and proper" tests, short-listed Standard Chartered and Farallon. Some analysts thought StanChart had an advantage because it was a bank, and had long sought to enter an Indonesian bank. But Farallon had a plus factor: Deutsche Bank was a technical advisor to the consortium and former IMF top Asia official Hubert Neiss, was now chairman of its Asia operations. The bitter battle for BCA included a tussle between IBRA chairman I Putu Gde Ary Suta and Minister of State Enterprises Laksamana Sukardi over who had the power to pick the winner. Media leaks said that StanChart was offering Rp1,800 a share versus Farallon's Rp1,775 but StanChart's offer came with conditions such as keeping 15 per cent of its purchase payment in an escrow account to guard against any problems from taking control of BCA. After the leaks, IBRA said it would let the contenders amend their final bids, which made Farallon threaten to withdraw. Some staff at BCA demonstrated against feared lay-offs, a protest that targeted StanChart as a foreign bank. Amid growing contention, Laksamana ended the contest by naming the winner: the Farallon consortium, which bid about US$530 million. BCA definitely did not move back into Salim's hands. The main owner became the Hartono family. The late founder of Djarum, father of Michael Bambang and Robert Budi Hartono, had been a friend of Liem's from shared Kudus days, but their sons were not close. Under the new owners, BCA prospered, producing strong results. As of 30 September 2013, the Hartono's vehicle FarIndo Investments (Mauritius) had 47.15 per cent of BCA while 51.09 per cent of the shares traded publicly. Anthony retained 1.76 per cent equity.

Years after the loss of BCA, Liem remarked that it was "very sad for us".[81] Anthony was philosophical about the loss, and a little wistful. "We are a painter; we always can paint", he said. "You can paint a masterpiece, but next time maybe [what] you paint [is] less of a masterpiece."[82]

2. Indocement

Salim had wanted to hold onto Indocement, a building block of Liem's empire. But efforts to keep control were thwarted by Rizal Ramli. At the time of Suharto's fall, PT Mekar Perkasa, a company held 50/50 by the Liem and Djuhar families, owned 58 per cent of Indocement. Another Salim-linked company had 4.4 per cent while the government, from its 1985 bailout of Salim, held 26 per cent and the rest was publicly owned. Salim pledged 13 per cent of Indocement for the MSAA, from its Mekar Perkasa holding, and later gave the state another 6 per cent. Indocement was in a bad way in mid-1998, with about US$1 billion in foreign debt and tumbling domestic sales. In July, the company announced a debt "stand-still", meaning repayments stopped, and then there was no choice but to seek a new investor. Three European companies checked out Indocement: Lafarge of France, Holderbank (renamed Holcim) of Switzerland and Heidelberg Cement of Germany. Salim's plan was to sell a maximum 30 per cent, so the foreign stake would not be larger than the biggest Indonesian one. Heidelberg was given exclusive bidding rights, and negotiated with Anthony.

In 2000, Heidelberg and Salim agreed on a plan giving each equal stakes through a joint venture. But the plan angered senior economics minister Ramli, who was intent on yanking Salim out of Indocement's driver's seat. In October 2000, after Holdiko sold a Salim stake in QAF in Singapore to Salim-linked parties, Ramli had a government financial-policy committee bar the group from further bidding for any of its assets unless it had fully settled its debts. The minister pushed Heidelberg top management to drop their plan with Anthony. Marleen Dieleman, in her Salim study, threw light on what happened at Indocement. A Heidelberg manager related to her:

> The government finally told me, we are in control and even though we know you have a deal with Anthony Salim, we don't want you to enter into a 50/50 partnership with him, because he is no longer very much liked in Indonesia. Make it a minority share. I told them I needed a local partner with knowledge. So finally I ended up, against my wishes, buying 65 per cent of the company, with Anthony Salim owning 13 per cent.[83]

Also, an unnamed former Indonesian minister confirmed to Dieleman that the Indonesian government got involved to derail the agreement between the Germans and Anthony. He was quoted as saying:

> we contacted Heidelberg's management and told them that if this was true (about the arrangement with Anthony), they would have to pay a fine. They responded by telling us that they had a 50/50 agreement, where Salim would manage it. I told Heidelberger that cement is not high technology, and that they can manage it themselves. So they cancelled the deal with Salim.[84]

A revised deal that brought Heidelberg into the company, tied up with how parts of Indocement's debt were restructured, was completed in April 2001. After buying a combined 19 per cent from Holdiko and IBRA, and getting more through a rights issue, a Heidelberg vehicle named Kimmeridge emerged with 61.7 per cent of Indocement. A Heidelberg executive was made president-director in place of Sudwikatmono, who was moved to deputy chairman, while another Heidelberg person succeeded Liem as chairman. For a time, the main shareholdings were:

Kimmeridge: 61.7 per cent (Heidelberg)
Indonesian government: 16.9 per cent
Mekar Perkasa: 13.5 per cent (Salim interests)
Public: 6.1 per cent

The German entry in 2001 was widely welcomed. One Jakarta press comment said Indocement now "will be run to generate shareholders' value, in contrast to the old practices of subjecting the company to various dodgy inter-company transactions".[85] Indocement's shareholdings later changed as the government sold its stake. Heidelberg's holding topped 65 per cent at one point, then it sold 14 per cent to raise money for dealing with the debts of its parent, which took over rival Hanson of the United Kingdom. By the end of 2010, the shareholdings were:

Kimmeridge: 51 per cent
Mekar Perkasa: 13.03 per cent
Public: 35.97 per cent

With the loss of Indocement, Liem's time as Indonesia's cement king ended, and he was no longer a banking king. But Anthony had been able to keep the food pillar from being pulled down, meaning Salim would survive — and have the chance to thrive again.

Notes

1. Mark Landler, "Year of Living Dangerously for a Tycoon in Indonesia", *New York Times*, 16 May 1999.
2. Interview with Anthony, 24 June 2007.
3. Interview with Liem, 3 June 2006.

4. Interview with Anthony, 8 February 2008.
5. Landler, "Year of Living Dangerously".
6. Interviews with Anthony, 22 April 2007 and 12 April 2009.
7. "Indonesia post-Suharto: Shipping industry desperate for reform", *Lloyd's List International*, 19 June 1998.
8. Interview with Anthony, 14 December 2008.
9. "Habibie purges 41 assembly members including Suharto cronies", AFP, 30 June 1998.
10. "President reminds people of cooperatives mission", *Jakarta Post*, 13 July 1998.
11. Keith Richburg, "Indonesia Sliding Toward Economic, Social Chaos", *Washington Post*, 22 July 1998.
12. "Young entrepreneurs to fill void left by Chinese Indonesians: Habibie", AFP, 7 July 1998.
13. Christine Hill, "The Chinese Dilemma", *Institutional Investor*, 1 July 1998.
14. Richard Borsuk and Reginald Chua, "Habibie courts Ethnic Chinese as 'ally'", *AWSJ*, 4 August 1998.
15. Interview with Liem, 3 June 2006.
16. "Habibie vows not to repeat mistakes of his predecessor", *Jakarta Post*, 11 August 1998.
17. John McBeth, "Grains of Truth", *FEER*, 10 September 1998.
18. "Bakrie Group hoping to win Indonesian grain supply tender", *Antara News Agency*, 7 September 1998.
19. "The Bakrie Group: Relying on agribusiness", *Indonesian Commercial Newsletter*, 27 January 1999.
20. Michael Shari, "Indonesia: A tycoon under siege", *BusinessWeek*, 28 September 1998
21. Jay Solomon, "Second Wind: A Tycoon nearly sunk by Indonesia's straits lands on solid ground", *WSJ*, 12 January 2000.
22. Ibid.
23. Ibid.
24. S. Karene Witcher and Jay Solomon, "Repay loans, Indonesia tells three big banks", *AWSJ*, 17 August 1998.
25. Neel Chowdhury, "A crony capitalist bounces back", *Fortune*, 10 May 1999.
26. Ibid. Setijoso, a graduate from the Bogor Agriculture Institute, remained as BCA's president-director until 2011, when he became its chairman.
27. Solomon, "Second Wind".
28. Eugene Galbraith, who in 2002 became chairman of BCA, said that when loans to Suharto family companies were included, the level would be more than 90 per cent (Joe Studwell, *Asian Godfathers: Money and Power in Hong Kong and South-East Asia* [London: Profile Books, 2007], footnote on p. 218).

29. Grainne McCarthy, "Salim Group can't keep BCA control", *Dow Jones Newswires*, 21 August 1998.
30. "Indonesia moves to clean up ailing banking sector", AFP, 21 August 1998.
31. Interview with Anthony, 14 December 2008.
32. Marleen Dieleman, *The Rhythm of Strategy: A Corporate Biography of the Salim Group of Indonesia* (Amsterdam: ICAS/ Amsterdam University Press, 2007), p. 94.
33. Interview with Anthony, 20 May 2007.
34. Suharto reiterated that message when suing *Time* magazine in Jakarta for a May 1999 cover story, "Suharto Inc.", saying he and his family had amassed US$15 billion. A lower court decided in Suharto's favour, but Indonesia's Supreme Court in 2009 — the year after he died — overturned that ruling.
35. Michael Shari, "Indonesia: A tycoon under siege".
36. Letter of IBRA's financial advisors, Bahana-Danareksa-Lehman Brothers, to IBRA, 6 January 2000.
37. Ibid.
38. Jay Solomon, "Indonesia is set to be repaid by 2 concerns", *AWSJ*, 23 September 1998.
39. "Indonesia to decide on Salim, Gajah Tunggal sales by Oct 31", Dow Jones, 1 October 1998.
40. Gde Anugrah Arka, "New Indonesia deadline for banks seen missed", Reuters, 1 October 1998.
41. Grainne McCarthy, "Jakarta sees full recovery of debt from 2 big groups", *AWSJ*, 2 October 1998.
42. Jay Solomon, "Habibie's plan for asset sales worries IMF", *AWSJ*, 27 October 1998.
43. Ibid.
44. Ibid.
45. Interview with Hubert Neiss, 13 June 2008.
46. Interview with Anthony, 8 February 2008.
47. Ibid.
48. Richard Robison and Vedi Hadiz, *Reorganising Power in Indonesia: The Politics of Oligarchy in an Age of Markets* (London: Routledge Curzon, 2004), p. 194.
49. Ibid.
50. Jay Solomon, "Proposal aims to boost Ethnic-Indonesian business — plan perceived as reaction to Chinese Dominance", *AWSJ*, 11 November 1998.
51. Interview with Benny Santoso, 9 March 2009.
52. Jon E. Hilsenrath and Douglas Appell, "Despite slump, analysts alter views on First Pacific", *AWSJ*, 18 May 1998.
53. John Goff, "Life during Wartime: Can finance chief Michael Healy help First Pacific survive the Asian economic siege?", *CFO Asia*, November 1998.

54. Rigoberto Tiglao, Kathy Wilhelm and Joanna Slater, "After years of fast-paced mergers and acquisitions, First Pacific's Manuel Pangilinan says it's time to buy big and hold", *FEER*, 17 December 1998.
55. Ando was born in Taiwan during Japan's occupation of the island, and was alive at the time of the negotiations on Indofood; he died in 2007, age 96.
56. "Nissin Food will continue focus on noodles", Dow Jones, 28 March 1997.
57. Interview with Benny Santoso, 9 March 2009.
58. Riyandi and Dandy Koswaraputra, "Salim Group makes efforts to escape from onslaught", *Jakarta Post*, 28 December 1998.
59. Raju Gopalakrishnan, "Crusty Chinese trader in midst of PLDT deal", Reuters, 5 June 2002.
60. Interview with John Gokongwei, 10 September 2006.
61. Cris Prystay, "Philippine tycoon can cap a career with PLDT Deal", *AWSJ*, 7 June 2002.
62. Richard Borsuk, "Nissin shelves deal with Salim over Indofood", *AWSJ*, 28 April 1999.
63. "Indofood back in black but deal off", Reuters, 27 April 1999.
64. Borsuk, "Nissin shelves deal".
65. "Japan's Nissin Foods confirms it scrapped deal for 30% of Indofood", Dow Jones, 28 April 1999
66. Interview with Anthony, 12 April 2009.
67. Ibid.
68. First Pacific press release, 27 April 1999.
69. Richard Borsuk, "Salim rejects bid for stake in Indofood", *AWSJ*, 18 June 1999.
70. Louise Lucas and Sander Thoenes, "First Pacific to pay $650m for Indofood stake", *Financial Times*, 23 June 1999; and Sander Thoenes, "Indofood chief finds $650m deal a little hard to swallow", *FT*, 24 June 1999.
71. Richard Borsuk and Jon Hilsenrath, "First Pacific to buy 40 per cent of Indofood for $650 Million", *AWSJ*, 23 June 1999.
72. Indofood Annual Report, reporting on 1999.
73. Kenneth Wong, "Indofood to be First Pacific's Best Purchase", Dow Jones Newswires, 6 September 1999.
74. Jay Solomon, "Jakarta Delays Its Offering of BCA Stock", *AWSJ*, 13 March 2000.
75. "BCA offer gets on the road", *Straits Times*, 6 May 2000.
76. "Jakarta says Salim cannot buy back BCA", Reuters, 1 March 2001.
77. Riyadi Suparno, "Intricate BCA sale racing against time", *Jakarta Post*, 24 January 2002.
78. Laurel Teo, "Man with the Midas touch", *Business Times* (Singapore), 26 January 2008.

79. Interview with Anthony, 8 February 2008.
80. Interview with Anthony, 24 June 2007.
81. Interview with Liem, 18 November 2006.
82. Interview with Anthony, 22 April 2007.
83. Dieleman, *The Rhythm of Strategy*, p. 100.
84. Ibid.
85. Hidayat Jati, "Learning lessons from IBRA's asset sales", *Jakarta Post*, 27 October 2001.

19

ASSETS: LOST AND FOUND

Seven months after Liem's home was torched, a company was created for
the sole purpose of disposing Salim assets in order to repay the outstanding
debts. Holdiko Perkasa was formed in December 1998 by IBRA. An
information memorandum said Holdiko was established "in relation to the
settlement between the Salim Group and the Indonesian Bank Restructuring
Agency with regard to liquidity credits provided to BCA and the affiliated
loans which exceeded the Legal Lending Limit given by BCA to Salim
Group affiliated companies."[1] Office space for Holdiko was created in
Wisma Indocement, seven floors below Anthony Salim's nineteenth storey
office. Cynics viewed it as literally "being under" Anthony. But by then,
Salim had lost some of its vaunted clout, and Holdiko worked hard to be
credible, keeping more than an arm's length away. Its efforts won kudos
as well as criticism. Holdiko worked a lot better than four similar bodies
set up by IBRA to sell assets pledged by other debtors.

GETTING STARTED AMID TURBULENCE

Technically, Holdiko was owned by two Salim companies, Gemahripah
Pertiwi and Carakasubur Nirmala. But all their shares were pledged to
IBRA along with all of Holdiko's in the Salim-pledged assets, and the

information memo noted it was "under the effective control of IBRA", which appointed Holdiko's management and directed its work. IBRA said it would have "hands-off management but hands-on oversight".[2] Salaries and Holdiko expenses were paid out of sales of Salim assets, not by IBRA. Salim was meant to have nothing to do with Holdiko's operations, but not surprisingly, there were serious doubts that Anthony could be kept at bay. By design, there were two Salim people among Holdiko's directors, but the pivotal person was an American investment banker, Scott Coffey, who had a reputation for solid integrity and no Salim links. Coffey came to Jakarta in 1990 with Citibank and later worked at state-owned Bahana Securities. IBRA chairman Glenn Yusuf hired Coffey, who had a power-of-attorney to act for IBRA. Holdiko's small professional staff — fewer than twenty — included largely young bankers, as they were perceived to be less likely to be steeped in Indonesia's corruption-tainted ways. Holdiko took possession of pledged Salim assets and prepared procedures for selling them.

Some outsiders assumed that even with Suharto gone from power and a backlash raging against cronies, Anthony could easily bully or outmanoeuvre any government-appointed official, including a foreign hired hand. But the American had solid credentials, credibility and character, plus important allies in Yusuf and the IMF, which was calling a lot of the shots in Indonesia because it was paying a lot of the bills. Still, Coffey had to prove he wasn't intimidated by Anthony and had to elicit from Salim the kind of detailed financial information that many Indonesian businesses habitually hide from outsiders. The relationship didn't get off to a great start. "I hated him like hell in the beginning", Anthony confessed about Coffey. It wasn't because he couldn't manipulate or work around the Holdiko director, the tycoon said, but because Coffey questioned him intensively and extensively about the operations of the assets Holdiko was charged with selling, and the grillings seemed endless. Coffey was "trying to squeeze out every single detail", Anthony recounted. "He was a pain... I was so squeezed ... I just hated him."[3] Coffey put it differently, describing his relationship with Anthony as starting off "quite tenuously". To Coffey, this was to be expected as Salim was "a very professionally run organisation that didn't need nor want outside interference in their company affairs — particularly with a target of selling off their prized companies". Building the kind of working relationship both men needed in order to meet the asset sales targets was a challenge, acknowledged Coffey, adding there was "a lot of tension between Holdiko and the Salim Group."[4]

Contention bred familiarity and respect. In working together, the loathing and wariness gave way to mutual appreciation. The credibility that Coffey gave Holdiko translated to giving Anthony credibility for complying with requirements on him. Coffey was "very professional and very credible", Anthony later conceded, adding that the Holdiko chief's intense questioning and high standard proved good for Salim. "This has been helping me in order to answer all the queries at the end, when we queried by government and officials, because he [Coffey] put up a very good standard."[5] In Coffey's view, the tension eased as Holdiko and Salim worked through issues and focused on implanting the goals of Holdiko and IBRA. In the process, Coffey said, "we gained a tremendous amount of respect for each other's professionalism and developed a strong, close relationship that saw us through those exacting years".[6]

IBRA, and not Holdiko, handled the sale of two central assets that Salim lost or relinquished after Suharto's fall — BCA and a stake in auto assembler Astra. (Anthony pledged 22 per cent of Astra to Holdiko as part of his debt settlement agreement, which was put together with other stakes that IBRA sold as a 40 per cent block.) Before a look at Holdiko operations, it is worth touching on the political picture and IBRA's priorities as Holdiko was laying groundwork for asset sales. For IBRA, the 40 per cent of Astra was a natural asset to get out the door early to promote needed corporate rebuilding. But in 1999, Indonesia was still reeling from the May 1998 riots, and IBRA was already experiencing operational problems, so any sale done hastily would surely have meant poor returns for the government.

But there was surprisingly positive political news in May 1999, as the first post-Suharto parliamentary elections went smoothly. The results were not good for President Habibie and Golkar, which fared poorly now that Indonesians had a free choice and wanted to show anger towards Suharto and his close associates. Golkar garnered only 20 per cent of the vote, compared with 74 per cent in the last New Order elections in 1997. The winner, with 33 per cent, was Megawati Sukarnoputri's newly formed PDI-P. The winning performance by her party — which reclaimed the hijacked "Indonesian Democratic Party" name and added "perjuangan", for struggle — seemed to give her a good chance of defeating Habibie when the MPR, which elects the president, convened in October. But Habibie won credit for making significant changes from the Suharto era, such as promoting decentralization through giving more autonomy to the provinces. He also loosened the shackles on the domestic media, freed some political prisoners and ended a system where Indonesia's president was perceived as an imperial ruler. But Habibie could not provide Indonesia the stability to get back on a good growth track. He was saddled with immense baggage from the past. For one thing, he was from Golkar, which millions of Indonesians wanted to punish. Also, the new president was a protégé of Suharto's and with whom he had long and close ties — indeed, he said on several occasions he considered Suharto as a father. Furthermore, he was associated with extravagant projects like domestically made aircraft that Indonesia couldn't afford.

In a bid to break from the Suharto mould, Habibie made a politically bold decision — which would come back to hurt him. The president agreed to hold a referendum in East Timor to let its people decide their future. In doing so, Habibie naively assumed the East Timorese would choose to stay in Indonesia. When they voted overwhelmingly for independence, Jakarta-backed militias, in vengeful and outrageous rampages, inflicted casualties and destroyed what little infrastructure the impoverished territory had. Conservative Indonesians were angered by Habibie's referendum, which they saw as potentially triggering a split-up of Indonesia, while the rampages reinforced the impression that the country was badly governed. Then Habibie was tainted by a scandal dubbed "Baligate", because it involved Bank Bali, a privately owned bank. The scandal put Habibie, Golkar and IBRA in a very bad light. Bank Bali, in order to get a payment due from IBRA for a debt from another bank, had to pay a huge fee to a businessman who was linked to Golkar and raising funds for it.[7]

In October 1999, the MPR rejected the president's state-of-the-nation report — called the "accountability speech" — and that ended Habibie's candidacy for a full five-year term. (The same MPR session amended the constitution to limit a president to two five-year terms.) Immediately after the speech, the unpredictability of post-Suharto politics was demonstrated, as a series of surprises resulted in blind Muslim leader Abdurrahman Wahid running for president and, in a vote on 20 October, defeating his erstwhile ally Megawati 373 to 313, angering her supporters and triggering violent protests in some places. The next day, following intense manoeuvring that saw two candidates withdraw from the race, Megawati defeated an Islamic party leader, Hamzah Haz, for Vice-President by 396-284. Wahid, who led the large Islamic organization Nahdlatul Ulama (NU), was widely respected for his tolerance and strong commitment to racial and ethnic harmony, and many welcomed his election. Ethnic Chinese were particularly enthusiastic about Wahid — the liberal grandson of a cleric who founded NU — taking over from Habibie. On Wahid's first foreign trip, to Singapore, less than three weeks after becoming president, he sought to reassure Indonesian Chinese they were needed and welcome. He told hundreds of executives that getting Indonesian Chinese money to return home was a top priority. In the audience at the Shangri-La Hotel were dozens of Indonesian Chinese, though not Liem and Anthony; they were in a room upstairs, where they met Wahid after the speech. Anthony said later that he assured the new president that Salim remained "a player" at home and wanted to "comply with the [government] policy". Wahid, he said, was "very receptive".[8]

Back home, Wahid's honeymoon as president was extremely brief. The agenda was huge. Hobbled by health problems including an earlier stroke that had left him effectively blind, he struggled to show he was in charge. Much energy went into a showdown with the still-powerful military, with Wahid eventually sacking top commander Gen. Wiranto, whom human rights activists wanted punished for the destruction in East Timor. During Wahid's only full year in office — 2000 — efforts to prosecute Suharto on corruption charges were initiated. (Habibie had blocked calls to bring his mentor to trial.) In August 2000, a trial on charges of embezzling of state funds through Suharto's foundations opened. But the following month, court-appointed doctors declared Suharto unfit to stand trial. Wahid's government appealed, but in February 2001 the Supreme Court ruled that Suharto was too ill to go on trial — so the former strongman never entered a courtroom.

During this period, one Suharto crony found he was no longer untouchable. Golfing partner and plywood godfather Bob Hasan was arrested in March 2000 on charges he corruptly gained from US$75 million the Forest Ministry paid for satellite mapping services. He was convicted and sentenced to two years jail in February 2001. (Bob was put in Nusakembangan, a Dutch-built island prison south of Java, which in the past harboured many political prisoners. His sentence was increased to six years, then cut to less than four years for good behaviour.) In October 2000, Suharto's favourite son Tommy was convicted on a corruption charge involving Bulog, but when jailers came to collect him, he had fled, and it took until November 2001 to find him. Then Tommy was sentenced to fifteen years in prison for masterminding the murder of the judge who had found him guilty in the Bulog-linked case. That sentence was reduced to ten years, on appeal, and Tommy was freed after only four years. Indonesians had no confidence that the largely dysfunctional legal and justice systems of the New Order were getting any better in the post-Suharto period.

Exacerbating Indonesia's already-poor reputation for justice were judgements against foreign creditors who took debtors to court. One egregious case involved insurance company Manulife. The Canadian investor's deal to buy more shares in its local affiliate was torpedoed by manoeuvring that included a court declaration that Manulife was bankrupt and the jailing of an Indonesian executive who faced no charges. (He was freed only three weeks later, after Canadian Prime Minister Jean Chretien wrote to Wahid.) There were growing complaints from businesses about having to pay off more people for fewer results. A Manulife executive in 2001 commented in a column: "Doing business today in Indonesia is significantly riskier than it has been for generations."[9]

IBRA looked like part of Indonesia's myriad of management and other problems. The chairmanship became a revolving door and a nightmare for most of its heads. "The complexity of the problems here is probably more than anywhere," sighed respected Edwin Gerungan — the third IBRA chief in less than twelve months.[10] World Bank country manager Mark Baird felt sorry for the former Citibanker, saying "He's got the toughest job in town. It's not a job to get attached to."[11] Gerungan did not have a chance to get truly settled; two months later, he was sacked by Wahid, who said he wanted faster asset sales. (Wahid, impeached the following month, fired three IBRA chiefs during his twenty-one-month presidency.) Some of IBRA's problems stemmed from conglomerates trying to maintain powerful positions. The initial post-Suharto governments were particularly weak, which made it hard for IBRA to be tough on conglomerates with links to Suharto-era officials who were still in the bureaucracy. In January 2000, Finance Minister Bambang Sudibyo told legislators the government was less potent than other forces, so authorities were not sure they had the "real political power" to jail powerful business figures who messed up the banking system. "Legitimacy is just one source of power. Money, weapons and experience can also create power", he said.[12] University of Indonesia economics professor Sri Mulyani Indrawati, who years later won kudos as a gutsy finance minister fighting for reform, saw a simple reality: "The conglomerates don't want to give up."[13]

Wahid had a chief economics minister who tried to take on the conglomerates. Kwik Kian Gie, the first ethnic Chinese in a post-Suharto cabinet, had long been active in Megawati's party. As written about earlier, Kwik had played a role in getting Anthony interested in having new First Pacific buy Dutch trader Hagemeyer in 1983. In the late 1980s, Kwik sold his ailing television assembly business, Altron Panorama Electronics, to Salim, which later halted the business. While Kwik got along with Anthony, he regularly blasted conglomerates in his front-page economic commentaries in the 1990s in the national daily paper *Kompas*. After his appointment as minister, Kwik maintained his negative view of big business. On 8 December 1999, he told Parliament that conglomerates had a history of setting up banks to finance their businesses and "they also marked up the value of their projects and put the extra funds overseas". Kwik said a full crackdown on corruption was not possible, as that would cause economic activity to "grind to a halt" because "most businesspeople" would end up in jail.[14] Six months later, Kwik caused a furore by saying "If I were a foreign investor, I wouldn't come to Indonesia."[15] He caught flak for talking Indonesia down, but Kwik insisted he was just being realistic about what investors face as "the law enforcement is not there. But not only that, the whole thing is so confusing. How can you come here?"

Kwik's comments came at a critical time, when some foreign investors were taking a chance on Indonesia, and finding prices attractive. IBRA scored a needed success in selling 40 per cent of Astra for US$506 million. Winning the Astra competition was a consortium led by Jardine Matheson's Singapore-listed affiliate, Cycle & Carriage. The Astra sale took place shortly after Wahid fired the well-respected Glenn Yusuf and installed Cacuk Sudarijanto, former CEO of the state telephone company Telkom, atop IBRA with explicit orders to speed up asset sales. But Indonesia, still mired in political turmoil, faced years of few transactions that raised only a modest amount to plug yawning holes in the government budget. In 1999, Holdiko completed its first three transactions. In the first, long-time partner Dow Chemical bought out Salim's stake in their 50/50 polystyrene joint venture Pacific Indomas Plastics Indonesia for Rp37.2 billion. Later, there were several other cases in which an existing foreign partner purchased Salim's shares. This raised no issues as revised rules now often allowed 100 per cent foreign ownership, and Indonesia was getting so little investment that such transactions were welcomed.

What was not welcomed, understandably, were moves by Salim to repurchase its assets at an attractive price. There was strong opposition to the conglomerates trying to do this, and for good reason given the Bank Indonesia liquidity credits that banks, like Salim's, had received. At the time that Holdiko began operating, there were no rules in place about who was allowed to bid, so the possibility was there of Salim itself or linked parties buying pledged assets. In late 2000, this caused a furore because of one deal involving QAF, the small Singapore-listed company that Salim in mid-1997 had failed to make the main owner of Indofood. Holdiko was given a free hand to dispose assets through share placements, asset sales, initial public offerings or strategic sales. "Cash is king", declared Coffey, who was initially Holdiko's finance director before becoming CEO. His goal was to create competition "to achieve the highest possible price regardless of who the buyer is.... And we always sell our companies to the highest bidder."[16] In some cases, it was not completely certain whether the buyer had links to Salim, or whether it was a proxy rather than a principal.

LET'S MAKE A (PACKAGE) DEAL

In 2000, the mechanism the government set up with Holdiko and four other IBRA-controlled companies to sell assets of debt-ridden tycoons did not look like it would produce substantial revenue for the state budget. After the Astra sale, there were no other individual assets that could be sold for US$500 million or more. So a search began for ways to get the pledged assets to produce cash more quickly. IBRA chief Cacuk, who announced he wanted more and faster sales, took a liking to the idea of selling a swath of assets at one time. In May, he made the surprising statement that the Quantum Fund of George Soros had expressed interest in buying all of Holdiko assets but then changed its mind. It is not clear that Soros gave the idea any serious consideration; no due diligence on Salim assets was done.[17] But the idea of a block sale stuck in Cacuk's mind, and he subsequently went to Kuala Lumpur to try to interest Malaysian Finance Minister Daim Zainuddin in having his country's sovereign wealth make a bid. It did not. A potential package deal to sell all or much of Holdiko had two main opponents: the World Bank and Kwik, the senior economics minister. On 26 July, the Bank wrote to Cacuk to say it saw "many risks in such a complex transaction". In particular, it worried whether the approach would be viewed as favouring Salim, who would have knowledge of the assets that outsiders did not. The letter also asked if it "will be acceptable to the public" for Salim to potentially be allowed to reclaim its assets.[18]

Indeed, Anthony was interested in a package deal and maintained he had a right to buy back assets, under the MSAA. Media reports said he and some financial advisors, including Credit Suisse First Boston, had talked with government officials. Anthony, who didn't have a direct line to Wahid (the way he and his father had to Suharto) and used an intermediary, had promoted the idea with the president. Wahid later acknowledged he met Anthony seven times to talk about the tycoon's debt, defending the meetings as necessary as the tycoon was a big debtor.[19] From those discussions, Anthony might have been close to getting a green light.

But Kwik was dead-set against any idea of a buy-back. All Indonesian conglomerates were trying to buy their assets or debt back at bargain prices, and there was no reason to think Salim would bring another approach. In 2000, Kwik had an audit done that estimated the total value of the Holdiko assets — valued in September 1998 at Rp48.5 trillion, based on "normal" economic conditions — was now Rp20 trillion. He said that at one point, he saw a letter from banks he believed to be working with Anthony that offered Rp20 trillion for a package deal.[20] In addition to opposing a package deal that offered far less than the September 1998 asset valuations, Kwik opposed all the MSAAs, which he felt were going to make the state suffer big losses because the pledged stakes would raise far less than the agreements' valuations. In Anthony's view, the MSAA was legal and binding, and the reason only lesser values could be realized was Indonesia's weak investment conditions at the time that IBRA was selling assets. (Well beyond 2000, Anthony's contention that Salim companies were fairly valued had merit, as some assets pledged in 1998 thrived and had far greater value, as written about later.)

On 31 July 2000, as Jakarta signed a new letter of intent with the IMF, Kwik said he would not try to cancel the MSAA pacts but he wanted to improve the terms "to make them fairer and more accountable, and to maximize the debt payback".[21] At the time Kwik was talking tough about debtors, there was particular attention on one pledged asset — from Gajah Tunggal Group controlled by Sjamsul Nursalim — that had been valued at about US$1.8 billion and now, according to Kwik, had negative equity. The asset was a huge shrimp farm in southern Sumatra. In 2007, the farm was bought from IBRA's successor, the State Asset Management Co., for US$76 million — roughly 4 per cent of the valuation IBRA accepted in 1998 — by the Indonesian unit of Thai agribusiness giant Charoen Pokphand.

Kwik resigned from Wahid's fractious cabinet in August 2000 to facilitate a reshuffle that ostensibly would give more day-to-day executive power to Vice-President Megawati. Kwik did not get reappointed, and economist Rizal Ramli, who similarly took a tough line on Salim, succeeded him. Kwik soon was sniping at the new economic team, warning that the government "is starting to flirt with tycoons", whom he described as "unscrupulous". Also, Kwik alleged that he and Finance Minister Bambang Sudibyo were ejected from the last cabinet as they were a threat to tycoons.[22] In October, on a visit to Singapore, Ramli complained that what Salim had pledged in the MSAA was "not the money machines of the group".[23] A short time later, Ramli ordered Salim — as well as Bob Hasan and Sjamsul Nursalim — to surrender additional assets or face legal proceedings. "In return, the government will agree to extend the repayment period of their obligation", he said. Two days later, though, Attorney General Marzuki Darusman indicated there was no legal case to bring against Salim and said the group was the only one observing provisions of the MSAA agreement it signed in 1998. Bambang Sudibyo, the former finance minister, told Antara the same day that except for Salim, the conglomerates had been uncooperative and had not shown goodwill to settle their debts.[24]

Still, Salim came under new pressure following the appointment of yet another IBRA chairman. President Wahid replaced Cacuk with former Citibank executive Edwin Gerungan, who demanded that Salim and the others provide new personal guarantees by 15 November for handing over more assets. They complied. Meanwhile, the IMF again seemed to be of some help to the tycoons. On 14 November, chief Jakarta representative John Dodsworth said the Fund was concerned about "legalities" of demanding billions in additional assets. He supported tough action by IBRA, but said efforts at amending MSAA agreements need "to be firmly based on legal evidence of non-compliance".[25] At the same time, IBRA vice-president Dasa Sutantio said the agency found "certain misrepresentation" and "non-compliance" with requirements by conglomerates, none of whom he identified.[26] After further negotiations, Anthony and IBRA agreed on settling the "misrepresentations" and Anthony handed over some more assets, including part of his remaining BCA stake.

RAISING CASH AND QUESTIONS

In the second half of 2000, Holdiko found its footing and the pace of asset sales accelerated. Some of the transactions, though, sparked unhappiness. This section looks at several deals that raised significant cash or questions.

The first, involving an overseas Salim company, prompted a policy change.

QAF

In 1997, QAF was the small food-manufacturing company in Singapore that Salim tried unsuccessfully to make a major shareholder of Indocement. Rizal Ramli, then a private consultant, had been highly critical of Salim's proposal. Now, in 2000, he was top economics minister and QAF gave him a fresh reason to blast the group. Stakes in QAF and First Pacific were the only Salim assets listed outside Indonesia that were pledged to IBRA in the MSAA. QAF made Gardenia bread, popular in Singapore and Malaysia. The company, which at one time owned a Singapore supermarket chain, had other food-making, processing and trading businesses in Southeast Asia. Salim had ceded 19.44 per cent of QAF to IBRA, and the stake was transferred to Holdiko to sell. In July 2000, QAF announced plans to buy two Salim-linked edible oil processing plants in China, to be paid for by issuing S$41.6 million in bonds. Some analysts criticized the deal, which hit the share price. Then, on 3 November, IBRA and Holdiko announced they had sold their shares in QAF — IBRA had a 4.76 per cent stake separate from Holdiko's — through a "market placement agreement", getting S$36 million. The shares were sold at 45 Singapore cents each, a discount of nearly 20 per cent to QAF's last market price. An IBRA official was quoted as saying "This has been a difficult disposal to conduct on the back of among others, the overhang in the market, QAF's recent corporate announcement on their plans to acquire two Salim edible oils factories in China, and also the fact that its traded volume of shares is historically relatively small."[27]

Then it was reported in the media that many of the shares were bought by QAF's chairman Didi Dawis (a Hokchia friend of Liem's family), and by a unit of Salim's KMP, Qualif. These purchases raised no legal issues, but there was consternation among some in Jakarta that Salim had in effect bought back some of its shares — which it could do legally, as no IBRA rule barred it. Minister Ramli conceded that Salim had not broken any law but called the group-related purchases "unethical". Salim had not settled its debt, he complained, "but in reality, they have the money to buy assets".[28] *Tempo* magazine in Jakarta asserted that in the QAF case, IBRA was "duped again". It quoted IBRA's Dasa Sutantio as saying "we only found out that the Salim Group was involved in the purchase through the news wires". *Tempo*'s view: "It seems as if, even in as difficult a situation as this, the Salim Group is incapable of ridding itself of the greedy reputation that the group has been stuck with for a long time now."[29]

The QAF case spurred Ramli to impose rules stipulating that owners of pledged assets, and parties related to them, could not buy from Holdiko or IBRA. From now on, any bidder had to give a written undertaking saying it did not have any Salim links, and that it would not resell the asset to Salim or a related party for two years. In the murky Indonesian business environment, such a commitment would be easy to circumvent, but the rule-change was significant. Ramli put it into immediate effect by getting Salim ruled out as a possible buyer for its biggest pledged asset, oil palm plantations.

Oil Palm Plantations

The sale of pledged stakes in plantations was Holdiko's biggest single deal of Salim assets, with Guthrie of Malaysia buying them for about US$350 million. (Selling 40 per cent of Astra brought the government US$506 million, but the Salim-pledged portion accounted for just over half of the shares sold by IBRA, together with others the agency controlled.) The oil palm transaction, which had many twists, took months to complete. It covered 25 plantations, controlled by four Salim companies, with a total of nearly 270,000 hectares in Sumatra, Kalimantan and Sulawesi. Guthrie, founded in 1821 as a British colonial company, obtained far more oil palm acreage than the 110,000 hectares it then had in Malaysia. During the competition for Salim's stakes, seven bidders were short-listed, including one that raised eyebrows — Indofood. In the past, these plantations provided palm oil for Indofood, which needed large quantities. The rule Ramli imposed amid the QAF case spawned complaints about Indofood being a contestant. Indofood maintained it was a public company, not a Salim company. But a government committee on finance policy quickly scratched Indofood from the short-list of bidders. IBRA's Dasa Sutantio told reporters: "In principle, debtors are not allowed to buy. Salim has debts [to the government] … it is not allowed [to bid for the plantations]. This includes Indofood."[30]

In late November 2000, IBRA declared Guthrie the winner. The path to closing the deal, though, was strewn with obstacles. Some analysts thought Salim had a hand in setting up a few, which the group denied. Vice-President Megawati's PDI-P party decried the deal because the winning suitor was Malaysian, which displeased some of party members who held the patronizing view that Malaysia was a younger brother to Indonesia. (Megawati never publicly criticized Guthrie's selection, but she stayed silent when party members asserted that she opposed it.) Then some farmers who worked on the plantations contended that Salim had long ago taken their land without adequate compensation, and they demanded it now. IBRA's view that the sale was a done deal finally prevailed and, on 13 March 2001, Guthrie signed and paid. Ramli said the Malaysian entry showed the "foreign investor-friendly environment" that the Wahid government was encouraging.[31] But what the episode also showed was how weak the government was, and how newly empowered legislators could delay state plans and policies. Even after the Guthrie signing, Finance Minister Prijadi Praptosuhardjo threw another spanner in the works by proposing creation of a team to review the sale. Failure to close the deal, a Singapore media commentary warned, would "destroy whatever confidence investors still have in the government".[32] Finally, the imperilled Wahid government got ministers on the same page, and public attention shifted back to "Bulog-gate", a scandal involving the president's masseur, that in July prompted Wahid's impeachment and replacement by Megawati.

Oleochemicals

Anthony pledged to IBRA Salim's significant business in oleochemicals, the raw materials for making detergents, toiletries and other products. Salim had manufacturing and trading assets in several countries, and controlled Indonesia's only production of natural fatty alcohols, which came from palm and other oils. When Holdiko offered the combined oleochemical assets for sale in late 2000, there was real competition from about ten parties. The two finalists were a group led by Bhakti Investama, a finance company, and one involving Tira Austenite, a diversified business active in construction materials and industrial gases. The Bhakti group won, offering Rp1.23 trillion (about US$130 million).

At the time of the bidding, little was known about Bhakti's thirty-five-year-old president Hary Tanoesoedibjo, which fuelled speculation he was a proxy for Anthony. Hary, an up-and-coming businessman in post-Suharto Indonesia, had some financing from George Soros's Quantum Fund.

Born in Surabaya in September 1965, Hary had BA and MBA degrees from Canadian universities. On his return to Indonesia in 1989, he started stockbroker Bhakti Investama just as the nation's stock market was stirring. The brokerage went public in 1997 and, for a short time, a company owned by Suharto's middle daughter Titiek was a small shareholder. Hary's father had converted to Islam, and from links in East Java — the base for Wahid's Nahdlatul Ulama — the family knew the cleric who was president from October 1999 until July 2001. Hary and Anthony were friendly, but Hary regularly denied that he was the Salim CEO's proxy. In April 2001, after Hary won another Salim asset, the company owning convenience-store chain Indomaret, he was asked again by *Tempo* magazine whether he was backed by Salim. His reply:

> Show me proof that this backing actually exists. You have to remember that not everyone is happy with what we are doing. It's all just rumours from people who aren't happy.... The truth of the matter is that the Salim Group is not behind us. We should be given an award because while everyone else is too frightened to invest, at Bhakti, we have even invited foreign investors to get involved.[33]

When the *Tempo* reporter persisted, saying there were reports that Hary had Salim money "to the tune of $1 billion to buy everything up", Hary retorted: "Salim is not backing us. I don't know anything about these reports. So, as I don't know anything, it means they can't be true, doesn't it? ... That's enough, I really don't like listening to stories that aren't true."[34]

Anthony also denied Hary was a proxy. They made some co-investments, he acknowledged, such as a building that later housed Indofood headquarters. Anthony clarified that Hary had helped him make a connection when Abdurrahman Wahid, whom Anthony did not previously know, became president. Wahid, widely known as Gus Dur, had a brother named Hasyim who got appointed an "expert advisor" to IBRA, and Anthony had contact with the brother. The brother's presence at IBRA naturally sparked complaints of nepotism, which Wahid denied. However, following a row between Wahid and Hasyim, the brother's appointment at IBRA ended. That left Anthony without a channel to the president. "When Gus Dur split with his brother, then I was outside the circle. And Hary helped explain my case to Gus Dur. So I owe him on that count," Anthony explained.[35] After his consortium bought Salim's oleochemical assets, Hary said in a media interview:

This is the end for the Salim empire, but it is a great opportunity for the younger generation to establish something for the future ... you have to admit that most Salim assets are good assets, they are diversified and of good quality, so it is easier to resell them later.[36]

Hary, in fact, soon resold oleochemicals to two of his bid partners. He focused on building a multi-media empire after a 2002 move to take over Suharto son Bambang's company, Bimantara Citra, whose name Hary changed to Global Mediacom. Anthony called Hary "very smart", adding "You have to respect people who can build things from nowhere."[37] One of the two parties who had teamed with Hary for the oleochemicals bid was Wings, a maker of detergents and household goods owned by the Katuari family and which later emerged as a significant rival to Indofood in noodles. The other was Lautan Luas, a chemicals company. A later entrant was Djarum, the *kretek*-maker whose owners bought control of BCA. The name Salim Oleochemicals was changed to Ecogreen Oleochemicals, which was owned by Wings (47.7 per cent), Lautan Luas (33.3 per cent) and Djarum Group (19 per cent).

Although Wings was a serious competitor with Salim in noodles, they were partners in a separate venture to manufacture alkylbenzene, the key ingredient in making detergent. The venture with the Katuari family, PT United Industrial Corporation, in 1999 was renamed Unggul Indah Cahaya. This was not the only case in Indonesia where competitors in one business could team up in another. "We always have competitor-and-partnership relationships", Anthony once remarked, saying that Indonesian business is something like batik and "not like a Burberry [design], which is very clear-cut ... the batik motif here is always rather dark."[38]

Indomobil

In late 2001, Holdiko completed a series of sales that allowed it to attain its revenue target for the year — and stirred controversy. Many analysts believed that at least some sales were made to Salim proxies, thus helping the group to reassemble chunks of its empire. Particular unhappiness was generated by the speedy sale of 73 per cent of PT Indomobil Sukses Internasional, for a much lower price than the value assessed in the MSAA. Salim had retained 27 per cent. The winner was a consortium led by Trimegah Securities. In January 2002, some legislators called for an inquiry into the Indomobil deal. Alvin Lie of the National Mandate Party said "The Salims are shrewd business people, but this is no longer just about business but also about politics. There is a great sense of injustice in allowing large debtors to repurchase their former companies at a cheaper price."[39]

By any measure, the deal was wrapped up rapidly; bidders had just days to conduct due diligence. Many final bidders were expected, because of Indomobil's business, especially in Suzuki motorcycles, but there were only three. One involved Hary Tanoesoedibjo's Bhakti Investama, which was not successful. One member of the winning consortium was Lautan Luas, a part of the successful team Hary had led in the bidding to get Salim's oleochemical assets. The Rp625 billion winning price for Indomobil was a 4 per cent premium to the last day's share price of Rp600, but the winning bid was rapped as small compared with the MSAA's valuation of Rp1.85 trillion for the auto company's stake.

The sale was probed by Indonesia's new Business Competition Supervisory Commission, set up under a law enacted as part of a commitment Habibie made to the IMF. Law Number 5 of 1999, titled "Concerning the Prohibition of Monopolistic Practices and Unfair Business Competition", created the commission, known by its Indonesian initials KPPU.[40] In rulings announced in May 2002, the KPPU did not cancel the Indomobil transaction, as the money had been already put into the state budget. But the commission, exercising its powers, fined Holdiko and five other parties a total of Rp268.5 billion (then about US$30 million) for "irregular practices" and causing losses to the state. The fines were intended to be equivalent to the extra money that the commission calculated the government would have received from a proper auction. All of the penalized parties denied wrongdoing and appealed the rulings. (Decisions of the KPPU, which was not a court, could be appealed in a court.) Holdiko, which was then in the process of selling Salim's stake in a property business, announced suspension of further asset-sales until the legal ramifications of the KPPU ruling became clear.

A major problem with the Indomobil sale was that Holdiko telescoped the timeframe for completing it. "First they put it at six months and then they changed it to two weeks. That was discrimination against potential bidders", KPPU member Pande Radja Silalahi said, adding that it ensured that only parties already familiar with Indomobil were able to put in a bid.[41] Holdiko chief Scott Coffey, defending the transaction, noted that speeding up the sale was a request by IBRA's chairman to meet 2001 budget targets, and that the trade-offs of doing this were explained to the government. Coffey said: "We said the minuses were less transparency; we said the minuses were less price. We laid all this out and said 'What do you want to do?' And they said sell it."[42]

When district courts started giving verdicts on the suits brought by those KPPU fined, all of them rejected the anti-trust agency's decision. Given the lack of credibility of Indonesian courts, this did nothing to allay public suspicions that a Salim proxy had bought Indomobil — and that Salim still exercised substantial influence even after its patron was gone. A *Jakarta Post* commentary said the court judgements reversing the KPPU findings seem to "have only confirmed the public's perception of the court system as a grossly incompetent and corrupt institution". The hurried Indomobil sale, the paper said, meant a "disastrously low price" as only "insider parties" made final bids as others were not able to make proper assessments. Also, it said Pricewaterhouse Coopers had in 2001 assessed a value for the Indomobil stake of between Rp850 billion and Rp1.1 trillion, above the Rp625 billion the winner paid.[43]

In the case against Holdiko, a district court ruled against KPPU, nixing its fine. The KPPU appealed that decision to the Supreme Court while Holdiko resumed selling its sales. On 2 January 2003, the Supreme Court ruled on a series of appeals stemming from the KPPU's fines over Indomobil. On a legal technicality, the court rejected both the KPPU fines and the lower court decisions. The Supreme Court did not assess the substance or legality of the KPPU's rulings. It focused on a technicality that the KPPU put at the top of its Indomobil decision a wording that prefaces all Indonesian court judgements — and which the highest court said the KPPU had no authority to use. The wording the court took issue with was "In the Name of Justice, Based on the Belief in One Supreme God". Two weeks after the Supreme Court's ruling — which was not announced — one of its judges revealed it by talking to a legal affairs news portal. "KPPU is not a legal body, so it does not have the right to include this statement in its ruling", Judge Paulus Effendy Lotulong said.[44] After getting its Indomobil decision and fines tossed out because of the first phrase in a 114-page text, the KPPU did not use that wording again.

Meanwhile, it turned out that the CEO of Trimegah Securities, leader of the winning Indomobil business, did not want to stay in the business for a long time. He sold those shares while Lautan Luas, who was friendly with Salim, stayed in Indomobil. After the two-year "no sale to Salim" period ended, Salim acquired more shares, as it had the right to do. Moving ahead to 2011, Indomobil was restructured to encompass more than just automotive businesses. After a rights issue, a Salim unit, Tritunggal Intipermata, owned 24 per cent of the company. Later, that stake would decline but Salim would buy majority control of Indomobil back. Giving credit to successful Astra International, Anthony said he aimed to make Indomobil into a "mini-Astra".[45]

Other Sales of Note

A number of other Holdiko transactions raised eyebrows — and sometimes sparked heckles — because the buyer was a new company or one whose bona fides were unknown. One was the November 2000 sale of 49 per cent of Salim's listed television station, Indosiar. The sale raised about US$72 million, and the per-share price was a 19 per cent premium to the last trading level. Still, many analysts thought the price should have been higher, and nothing was known publicly about the winner, TDM Asset Management, which had been incorporated only five months earlier with assets of US$96,000.[46]

One intriguing asset sale involved the Sulawesi flour mill built by Prima of Singapore, which in 1982 was forced to sell to Indonesian state interests who, in turn, made Salim a 40 per cent shareholder. In December 2001, Holdiko sold Berdikari Sari Utama Flour Mills for US$21.5 million to a U.S. company named ATS. After more ownership changes, the mill in 2005 became half-owned by Pacific Agrifoods of Australia, a joint venture involving Salim, and it was renamed Eastern Pearl Flour Mills.

One Holdiko sale, of Salim sugar growing and milling interests in Sumatra, prompted a long legal dispute. In 2001, the assets were sold for Rp1.161 trillion (US$130 million). The buyers said they found they were then unable to get use of a plantation they had purchased, as it was the subject of a land dispute. The *Jakarta Post* quoted Gunawan Jusuf, leader of the buyers, as saying "It's like buying a car. It's impossible to buy a car without the engine." The buyers sued Anthony, Liem and dozens of other parties, including IBRA. Anthony, who denied wrongdoing, was questioned for seven hours in 2007 as a case witness at the National Police headquarters in Jakarta. According to Supreme Court documents, Indonesia's highest court in 2010 overturned judgements the plaintiff had won in provincial courts. Years later, related cases remained in litigation.

HOLDIKO'S RECORD

Holdiko's performance featured definite disappointments and shortcomings, but also successes. Holdiko did not dismantle chunks of the Salim empire, but that was not its brief. The assignment was to receive assets and sell them in a competitive and transparent way for as high a price as possible to put money in the state budget. After some sales were completed, the Wahid government in 2000 imposed a rule, not there at the start, that Salim and its affiliates could not bid for Holdiko assets. Salim did effectively regain control of some assets by using what looked to be proxies, stoking public unhappiness, but there were also cases where the group got blocked from repurchasing its former companies. Another state-set rule imposed on Holdiko sales forbade buyers from selling them to Salim for two years. Over time, though, there was no practical way to keep Salim from regaining an asset it wanted to regain. (Some assets sold by the early 2000s later became worth far more than before, thanks to their success and better economic and business conditions in Indonesia.)

One widely held critical view is that Holdiko's performance is part of a larger scheme, starting with the MSAA, that helped Salim stay in business and then let rebuild parts of its empire at attractive prices. At the other end of the spectrum, Holdiko is seen as achieving far more than could have been expected, given Indonesia's corrupt business environment and its then-chaotic conditions, Salim's clout and links with the bureaucracy plus a scramble among political parties to raise money. During Holdiko's four-plus years in operation, the average tenure of the IBRA chairmen was less than six months.

Holdiko produced far better results than the other four other holding companies IBRA set up for assets of other tycoons. Nearly all the money the state got from indebted conglomerates came from Holdiko. "At least Salim delivered the assets and didn't stand in the way of their being sold", Holdiko president-director Scott Coffey once commented.[48] Holdiko's sales collected about 38 per cent of the Rp52 trillion-plus that Salim owed the government. Again, there are many different views of that result, from caustic to favourable. Holdiko's brief included disposing of assets quickly, which some people (including Anthony) point to as a major reason the sales netted far less than MSAA valuations. Early on, Holdiko had Pricewaterhouse Coopers do a valuation of the agency's portfolio, which concluded the pledged assets were worth about Rp21 trillion — roughly the amount Holdiko did, in fact, raise.

There was unhappiness with the valuations that IBRA and its advisors accepted in 1998 for the assets that Salim pledged in the MSAA, and there was unhappiness with the process and winning prices for some Holdiko sales, most notably the 73 per cent stake in Indomobil. There were also cases where Holdiko got a price above what the market expected. Asset values can gyrate wildly, as Indonesia before and after Suharto's fall illustrates. Indofood, in mid-1997, had a market capitalization of more than US$4 billion. It plunged to less than US$400 million after Suharto's fall, while at the end of 2010, it was above US$5 billion. The valuations accepted by IBRA for the MSAA used the assumption of reflecting "normal" conditions, rather than chaotic ones, like in 1998, when many Indonesian firms were technically bankrupt.

It is true that years after Holdiko was wrapped up, some of the pledged Salim assets had far greater value than they did when they were sold off in 2000 or 2001. One example is listed Astra, of which Anthony surrendered Salim's 22 per cent. In 2000, IBRA sold it (and another 18 per cent) for a better-than-market price of Rp3,700 a share; at 30 December 2010, shares of Astra were at Rp54,550 rupiah, worth nearly 15 times as much. At the end of 2010, a year in which the Jakarta benchmark index gained 45 per cent, Astra had a market capitalization of Rp221 trillion, or about US$24.5 billion — so a 22 per cent stake was worth about US$5.4 billion, compared with less than US$280 million when IBRA sold it in still-shaky 2000.

Another example of sharp valuation changes is the coal business that Salim pledged to IBRA. The agency sold it for US$45 million in March 2001 to a unit of Banpu of Thailand. Later, demand and prices boomed and Indonesia became the world's top exporter of thermal coal. In 2007, there was an IPO for PT Indo Tambangraya Megah, Banpu's Indonesian unit. In late 2010, Indo Tambang had a market capitalization of about US$1.5 billion and was Indonesia's fourth biggest exporter. Anthony mourned the loss of coal interests, though in later years he developed new ones. Another area where he lamented losing was the oil-palm plantations that, after Indofood was forced to drop a bid, went to Guthrie of Malaysia. In that area, too, he eventually rebuilt an interest, gaining control of a company more than a century old, London Sumatra.

Indirectly, diverging views on how Holdiko performed reflect differences on how much influence Anthony was able to exert on it. Some observers felt he wielded a lot of influence, and was able to accomplish what he wanted — not unlike the decades when Suharto was still in power. A commentary in Jakarta Post said that during IBRA's operation, there was no way to guarantee any Salim buy-back would be thwarted: "The same old tycoons and the corporate interests still reign supreme, and that the public can only seethe with resentment."[49] There was still ample scope for "*rekayasa*" (engineering) by powerful individuals. While Salim virtually always got its way in Suharto's time, this was not true at Holdiko; one consultant to IBRA estimates Anthony only got what he wanted 50 per cent of the time.

"Contrary to popular belief, Anthony Salim didn't buy back most of the assets that Holdiko has sold", *BusinessWeek* wrote in assessing the body's performance in 2003. It concluded that while IBRA had some success in selling tycoons' assets, the effort "won't truly shake up the powerful families at the heart of the Indonesian economy".[50] Coffey was quoted in the article as saying about Anthony: "He has felt pain through the sale of a number of his assets, half of which went to foreigners. However, he continues to be a formidable businessman in Indonesia." Asked years later about Anthony, Coffey replied: "No matter how challenging those (Holdiko) years were, I've always felt that I've never worked with anyone as talented as Anthony Salim and it was an honour to work with him throughout the duration of Holdiko Perkasa."[51]

Notes

1. Holdiko Preliminary Information Memorandum, December 1999, p. 5.
2. Noel Fung, "IBRA Sets up Five Holding Companies", *AWSJ*, 9 July 1999.
3. Interview with Anthony, 12 April 2009.
4. E-mail communication with Scott Coffey, 29 November 2011.
5. Interview with Anthony, 12 April 2009.
6. E-mail with Coffey.
7. For a fine account of Baligate, see Kevin O'Rourke, *Reformasi: The Struggle for Power in Post-Soeharto Indonesia* (London: Allen & Unwin, 2002).
8. Interview with Anthony, 8 February 2008.
9. Chris Bendl, "Indonesia — Waiting for Godot?", *Asia Insurance Review*, 15 March 2001.

10. Warren Carragata, "One Lousy Job", *Asiaweek*, 15 February 2001.

11. Mark Landler, "For Indonesia, Solvency is Political", *New York Times*, 20 April 2001.

12. "Government assesses 'powers' to nail corrupt tycoons", *Jakarta Post*, 27 January 2000.

13. Carragata, "One Lousy Job". In 2010, then-Finance Minister Sri Mulyani drew the ire of a conglomerate, the Bakrie Group, and President Susilo Bambang Yudhoyono helped arrange for her to leave her post to become deputy managing director of the World Bank.

14. I Made Sentana, "Indonesia Corruption Crackdown Would Halt Econ Activity", Dow Jones News Service, 8 December 1999.

15. Simon Montlake, Grainne McCarthy and I Made Sentana, "Rupiah Falls Sharply After Minister's Remarks", *AWSJ*, 12 May 2000.

16. Richard Borsuk, "Jakarta's Holdiko Faces Criticism on Asset Sales", *AWSJ*, 4 January 2002.

17. Grainne McCarthy and I Made Sentana, "IBRA considers selling companies as a whole", *AWSJ*, 10 May 2000.

18. Jay Solomon, "Jakarta Begins to Sell Salim Assets", *AWSJ*, 1 August 2000.

19. "Gus Dur admits having often met three business tycoons", Antara News Agency, 25 January 2001.

20. E-mail communication from Kwik, 14 February 2009.

21. "Indonesia's Kwik says won't cancel corporate debt deals", Dow Jones News, 31 July 2000.

22. "Economic team 'flirts' with unscrupulous tycoons — Kwik", *Jakarta Post*, 16 September 2000.

23. "Indonesia wants more of Salim Group jewels pledged", Reuters, 8 October 2000.

24. "Salim Group 'obeys' MSAA agreement", *Jakarta Post*, 22 September 2000.

25. Jay Solomon, "IMF Expresses Concern with Jakarta's Demands", *AWSJ*, 15 November 2000.

26. Ibid.

27. "Indonesia Investment Highlights", *PT Data Consult*, 1 November 2000.

28. "Repurchase of QAF shares by Salim 'unethical'", *Jakarta Post*, 10 November 2000.

29. "Salim Group Fools IBRA — Again", *Tempo*, 20 November 2000.

30. "Jakarta blocks Indofood's plan to buy IBRA assets", Reuters, 10 November 2000.

31. Richard Borsuk, "Jakarta's plantations sales may boost investment", *AWSJ*, 14 March 2001.

32. "Settle the Indon oil palm deal", *Business Times* (Singapore), 3 April 2001.

33. "New Taipan, Old Money?", *Tempo*, 23 April 2001.

34. Ibid.

35. Interview with Anthony, 24 June 2007.

36. Shoeb Kagda, "Bhakti hits the limelight with Indon asset deals", *Business Times* (Singapore), 17 January 2001.

37. Interview with Anthony, 24 June 2007. In 2011, Hary joined a political party, Nasdem, and later he switched to Hanura, which said he would be its 2014 vice-presidential candidate on a ticket led by former general Wiranto.

38. Interview with Anthony, 24 June 2007.

39. Shoeb Kagda, "Salim Group set to reclaim Indon dominance", *Business Times* (Singapore), 7 January 2002.

40. The Komisi Pengawas Persaingan Usaha was created to check monopolistic practices and unfair business competition.

41. Timothy Mapes, "Jakarta Sticks with Plan for Giant Bad-Debt Sale", *AWSJ*, 13 June 2002.

42. Ibid.

43. Vincent Lingga, "Courts overturn antitrust body's rulings", *Jakarta Post*, 30 July 2002.

44. "KPPU loses legal battle in Indomobil case", *Jakarta Post*, 17 January 2003, which quoted the judge from <www.hukum-online.com>.

45. Interview with Anthony, 3 April 2011.

46. "As Indonesia sells Salim assets, few clues to buyers", Bloomberg, 28 January 2002.

47. "Acquisition of Salim asset in question", *Jakarta Post*, 24 January 2003.

48. Sadanand Dhume, "Indonesia hopes to close books on bank bailout", *AWSJ*, 6 January 2003.

49. Riyadi Suparno, "IBRA — a case of too much politicking", *Jakarta Post*, 28 December 2001.

50. Michael Shari, "Indonesia's Bailout Plan: A Partial Success", *BusinessWeek*, 10 March 2003.

51. E-mail communication with Coffey.

20

MOVING AHEAD

As Holdiko was selling pledged assets, Anthony was consolidating control over what was left of the Salim empire. Not one to sit around licking his wounds, he was already looking beyond the remnants of the group and exploring new growth possibilities. Through the first ten years after Suharto's fall, the Salim story featured twists and turns, low points and highs, as the group lurched ahead. One striking low point — rooted in First Pacific's expansion in the Philippines — was a bruising, public spat between Anthony and his long-time partner at First Pacific, Manny Pangilinan. Fortuitously for both men and for First Pacific, the relationship was repaired and the partnership flourished again. An important albeit low-key high point was Anthony getting a document from Indonesian authorities called a "release and discharge" statement saying he had discharged his obligations from debts owed to the state in the wake of Suharto's fall. After receiving this legal all-clear, Anthony decided to become CEO of Indofood, so he was directly running a big listed company for the first time. Anthony's business interests expanded at home and elsewhere. Moves to grow on new turf did not always succeed, most clearly in an effort to get a beachhead in India, which went badly. But on the whole, the Salim Group — or what now should be considered the Anthony Salim Group — was again on the move.

STRESS TEST AT FIRST PACIFIC

The severe backlash against Salim that began as soon as Suharto was forced to step down made the group relieved it had created First Pacific. However badly things went for Salim inside Indonesia, the Hong Kong-based company gave Anthony a tool away from home. First Pacific had cash, thanks to completion of the big sale of Hagemeyer two months before the May 1998 Jakarta riots. Some First Pacific shareholders fretted about the possibility of the Hong Kong-listed company being prevailed upon to come to the rescue of the sinking Salim ship in Indonesia. In mid-1998, they saw its biggest owner imperilled and Asia in crisis while First Pacific's most profitable investment, Hagemeyer, was gone. The May 1998 events pummelled First Pacific's share price. Earlier in the year when things were getting shaky in Indonesia, some shareholders fretted that Salim might use First Pacific as a crutch, and Manny sought to reassure them: "We want to avoid the impression we are the banker of last resort to any shareholder... If we are perceived as a milking cow for the Salims, that's the end of First Pacific."[1]

When announcing the Hagemeyer sale, First Pacific had said it would focus on Asia, and the company was paying increasing attention to Manny's native Philippines. In late 1997, it had bought 2 per cent of San Miguel and then gave up trying to get more as regional economic conditions deteriorated. First Pacific made another Philippine move, with a far smaller quarry; in April 1998, it bought 55 per cent of shipping company Negros Navigation via Manila unit Metro Pacific. The investment did not fit the strategy then of four core businesses: telecoms, property, banking and marketing. Manny explained that First Pacific was now "focusing more on country-specific strategies... In some ways we should relax the four main sectors."[2]

Through the unhappy summer of 1998, the trampling of First Pacific shares continued. In August, while Anthony was working on pledging assets to IBRA, the stock plunged more than 20 per cent. It could be argued that First Pacific was now a bargain — but investors were not buying that argument. Bear Stearns analyst Scott Benesch commented that the international investment community "is really having a tough time. They know the shares are cheap and want to buy into the stock, but they are finding it difficult to overcome the risk of the Salims."[3] The assets that Anthony pledged to IBRA in September included a 5 per cent stake in First Pacific. That would reduce the total Gang of Four's ownership to 49 per cent from 54 per cent, but allowed it to maintain control. Manny, meanwhile, was eyeing a big telecoms deal in Manila. First Pacific had entered the Philippine telecom industry five years earlier by taking, together with affiliate Metro Pacific, a 40 per cent stake in mobile network provider Smart Communications. Back in 1995, First Pacific brought Japan's NTT into Smart. To be a player in telecoms, Manny wanted to get into the one-time state monopoly fixed-line firm, Philippine Long Distance Telephone (PLDT). Getting into notoriously inefficient PLDT was tough, but a block of shares tied to Marcos era disputes came into play, and Manny worked frenetically for months to pull it off. During one helicopter trip south of Manila for an appointment, the engine failed and the aircraft crashed. Manny escaped with just bruises. "I almost died for this deal", Manny declared when his pursuit of PLDT succeeded in November 1998.[4]

First Pacific paid US$749 million for 17.2 per cent of PLDT — 5.9 per cent bought in the open market plus 52.7 per cent of a company that held 21.5 per cent of PLDT. Combining that 17.2 per cent with interests held by Smart, Manny now had PLDT's reins, controlling 27.4 per cent. He became the president and CEO, replacing a member of a Cojuangco family that had run the monopoly for thirty years. Manny inherited a problem-ridden company with a woeful billing system and collection. Many analysts thought the Filipino had overpaid for a dysfunctional, untameable utility. Between mid-September and late November, as Manny was working to come in, PLDT's share price rose from less than 700 pesos to more than 1,000 pesos due largely to his pursuit. In the end, First Pacific paid 1,420 pesos a share, a 31 per cent premium to the 24 November closing of 1,085 pesos.

Thanks to Manny's ambitious moves, first with Fort Bonifacio in 1995 and then PLDT in 1998, First Pacific ended up with about two-thirds of its assets in the Philippines. No one else was anywhere near as bold or aggressive in Manila, especially following the election of movie star Joseph Estrada as president in May 1998. Manny's pursuit of PLDT led the *Far Eastern Economic Review* to comment that First Pacific "has once again shown its willingness to swim against the tide in its effort to become one of Asia's leading companies". The article remarked that First Pacific was often praised for unusually transparent management while garnering criticism for a "scatter-shot approach to investing" and for staying "in transition virtually since the Salims founded it."[5]

The Indonesia crisis and the Manila move led to line-up changes at a First Pacific shareholders meeting in February 1999. Liem, executive chairman since the start, relinquished that post to become honorary chairman and advisor to the board. Succeeding Liem was Manny. A statement explained that by being chairman rather than managing director, Manny could "devote himself more fully to overseeing First Pacific's substantial investments in the Philippines".[6] Taking over as MD was Thomas Yasuda, the San Francisco lawyer who joined First Pacific after working on its purchase of Hibernia Bank. Exiting from the board together with Liem was his long-time partner Sudwikatmono, also named an "advisor". Manny dropped anchor in Manila and threw himself into resuscitating PLDT, in which First Pacific's own stake became nearly 25 per cent. The year 2000 — when the dotcom bubble burst — brought some cheer for First Pacific, as PLDT had strong growth in cellular service and Indofood paid its first dividend since 1996. But the upbeat developments were buried by a 63 per cent tumble of First Pacific's share price, compared with just an 11 per cent slide for the Hang Seng Index. The following year, First Pacific was dropped as a component in the benchmark index. For 2001, the stock plunged 57 per cent while the Hang Seng slid 25 per cent.

Financially, First Pacific was haemorrhaging due to the Fort Bonifacio property that Manny had paid top dollar for in 1995, and the debt-load of PLDT and First Pacific's holding unit in the Philippines, Metro Pacific. To get cash, First Pacific sold some small assets in other countries. Divestments included controlling stakes in a profitable Thai consumer products distributor, Berli Jucker, for US$125 million, and Indonesian pharmaceutical company Darya-Varia Laboratoria, for US$35 million. Some analysts questioned why First Pacific was selling profitable companies to support loss-making ones, and the company insisted it wanted a few big investments, no longer a grab bag of smaller ones. The asset sales were not sufficient to service debt. During 2001, ING Bank arranged a HK$1.56 billion (US$200 million) loan for First Pacific.

First Pacific was burdened "because we have two big items [Fort Bonifacio and PLDT], about US$1.4 billion exposure ... there's not enough cash flow, just [enough] to foot some of the expense and interest. And the market has crashed," Anthony recounted years later.[7] "You have to dispose one of three — Fort Boni, PLDT or Indofood, and Indofood we will never sell. Then I told Manny, as management you have to choose one [of the two Manila assets] to dispose. Because we are short about 150 million bucks." Manny was trying to buy time for all the investments to be digested, Anthony said, adding that the need to cut Philippine exposure had been discussed for almost a year.[8] Manny's long-time colleague Ricardo Pascua, president of Metro Pacific, resigned in January 2002 after trying unsuccessfully to organize a buyout of First Pacific's interest in Fort Bonifacio. Manny assumed leadership of debt-ridden Metro Pacific, which had said it could not repay a US$90 million advance from a First Pacific unit, Larouge. Metro Pacific announced a loss for 2001 of 23.185 billion pesos (about US$453 million) including a 19.2 billion peso asset impairment provision — the bulk of that for Fort Bonifacio. Metro Pacific had debts of 12 billion pesos to service.[9] A few days after Metro Pacific reported its dire straits, First Pacific announced a 2001 loss of US$1.8 billion, more than the profits of the preceding fourteen years. It took massive write-downs in asset values, including 88 per cent for Metro Pacific and 63 per cent at Indofood. Manny still produced a positive spin, declaring: "When viewed in its totality, 2001 was a year of achievement and progress."[10]

In early 2002, Anthony was in Beijing, where he joined a Citibank event to celebrate operating in Asia for 100 years. At the party attended by tycoons from across the region, a conversation became the root of a revolt that nearly ended Anthony's twenty-year partnership with Manny. During the banquet, the future of First Pacific's Philippine assets turned out to be on the menu. Anthony strolled to another table to greet fellow guest John Gokongwei, the Philippine business honcho who after Suharto's fall had helped cash-strapped Salim by buying Liem's 23 per cent in Singapore office-landlord UIC. Later recounting their chat, Gokongwei said that when he inquired about how First Pacific businesses in the Philippines were doing, Anthony asked if he was interested in the Fort Bonifacio project (for which Gokongwei had bid far less than Manny in 1995). "I said no, the business is lousy", Gokongwei recalled. "So he [Anthony] said, 'how about PLDT?' I said 'Ah, we can always talk'."[11] Next, the two men arranged to fly together to Shanghai and set in motion a proposed deal in which Gokongwei would buy two-thirds of First Pacific's Philippine telecom and property interests. Anthony, at one stroke, would slash the Philippine exposure that Manny had built up. Gokongwei would move from a tiny player to a big one in the country's cellphone business. Size mattered to Gokongwei, who was nicknamed "Big John" by Filipinos. "Why PLDT?" he mused. "It's big. I love huge things."[12]

Under the proposal they sketched out, Gokongwei and First Pacific would form a joint venture to buy First Pacific's 24.4 per cent stake in PLDT and its controlling interest in Bonifacio Land Corp. Gokongwei would pay First Pacific US$616.7 million for a 66.7 per cent shareholding in the joint venture as well as assume two-thirds of a US$105 million Metro Pacific loan. So it seemed that Anthony had found a way that could put new cash into First Pacific and chop Philippine debt. Meeting Gokongwei "was just accidental", Anthony said later. "It was not by plan."[13] Meantime, not looped into the Anthony-Gokongwei planning was Manny, who had been involved with virtually every detail at First Pacific. Anthony's proposal sparked an unprecedented, out-in-the-open tussle with Manny, who was furious at being blind-sided. Manny vociferously opposed letting Gokongwei into PLDT. Most outsiders assumed Anthony would seek to remove Manny for his resistance, but he kept his jobs and control of PLDT. The bond between Anthony and Manny was severely tested yet it survived. Years later, Manny said that after Anthony first told him about largely exiting PLDT, he responded "Oh my god" and "Why didn't we talk?" Manny also recalled saying "I won't endorse the position to sell. He [Anthony] said 'you have to stay [and] you have to support.' I said I was willing to resign. He said he didn't want that."[14]

Manny's anger was understandable. He had spearheaded the pivotal investment in PLDT, and he was working feverishly to improve the company. To him, the proposed sale "couldn't have come at a worse time" as PLDT was in the middle of restructuring its debt. He naturally was upset that Gokongwei, a rival in the telecom sector, would be allowed to call the shots at PLDT. Anthony, circumspect years later, said he understood why Manny was "very mad".[15] In pursuing an arrangement with Gokongwei, Anthony contended he followed procedures that were "100 per cent correct".[16] Because First Pacific was a public company, and approval was needed from the company's board and shareholders, Anthony did not seal a pact; he signed an MOU (memorandum of understanding) with Gokongwei that was subject to First Pacific board and shareholder approval. On 30 May, the outlines of the plan were reported in the Philippine media. "In effect, the low-key Salims have decided to cut their losses and agreed to sell their crown jewels in the Philippines to an offshore company controlled by Gokongwei", a columnist in the *Philippine Daily Inquirer* wrote. He added: Overexposure to the country had "driven a wedge" between Anthony and Manny "despite MVP [Manny] and his band of Filipino executives having parlayed First Pacific from an obscure investment house ... into a regional though ailing powerhouse that it is now."[17]

PLDT and Manny scrambled to find ways to block the entry of Gokongwei, whom First Pacific had not publicly identified as the prospective buyer. One justification for resistance was that Gokongwei was a competitor with PLDT, as he owned a small cellphone service named Digital Telecommunications. Opponents of the proposed deal aimed to portray it as a hostile takeover by Gokongwei, even though the biggest shareholder of First Pacific was on very good terms with Gokongwei. In Hong Kong, the battle over PLDT began at a board meeting on 3 June, which lasted seven hours. Anthony sought the board's endorsement, but Manny effectively derailed that by ensuring there was not unanimous agreement. Separately, Manny and Anthony had a two-hour session that day. Nine months later, Manny told reporters that he told Anthony "to solve your problem I'm prepared to resign from First Pacific" and that when Anthony asked for his support for selling PLDT, an aggrieved Manny replied, "No, I cannot do that, it is against my conscience".[18]

Speaking to waiting reporters after the tense board meeting, Manny did not say so explicitly but left no doubt he opposed the Gokongwei deal. Manny only announced that the board had agreed to "proceed with negotiations" on a possible transaction, without naming any names. Then he exited abruptly as reporters fruitlessly fired questions. A Salim executive in Jakarta insisted there was a "collective" decision by the board to move ahead with Gokongwei and "monetize" some Philippine assets. Anthony "has finally lost patience with Manny after 20 years", the Salim person said.[19] The next day, First Pacific and Gokongwei signed but did not release a "memorandum of agreement" (MOA) on creating a joint venture that would take stakes in PLDT and Bonifacio Land. After the 3 June meeting, Manny returned to Manila, where PLDT held an emergency board meeting that approved a motion to defer any action on implementing the sale of First Pacific's stake.

The next day, First Pacific identified Gokongwei as the intended buyer of PLDT while giving some details of the 4 June memo with him. First Pacific announced that as part of the deal, US$187 million of Gokongwei's money would pay down debt, an unspecified amount would go to new investments, and it planned to channel a to-be-determined sum to pay First

Pacific shareholders a dividend. So there would be money going to the Indonesian owners. First Pacific said that the Liem Investors — the Gang of Four, then holding 43 per cent of the Hong Kong company — would abstain from voting on any pay-out. Thus, the company said, other First Pacific shareholders would have "the ability to approve or disapprove any proposed dividend arrangements".[20] The proposed deal with Gokongwei would leave First Pacific with 8.1 per cent of PLDT. At this time, PLDT shares were around 450 pesos, roughly one-third of the 1,420 pesos First Pacific paid in November 1998.

What came next seemed tantamount to a corporate mutiny. On 5 June, PLDT's board declared it would protect the phone company from "direct or indirect competing and antagonistic interests" and vowed it would not make available information that Gokongwei needed to perform due diligence.[21] Firing back, First Pacific said its board was denying Manny — its own chairman — access to confidential information about the sale of its PLDT stake and ordered him not to be involved in any activities at PLDT or Metro Pacific related to the Gokongwei proposal due to potential conflict of interest. Within days, Manny snubbed that by voting all of First Pacific's proxy votes to re-elect the Metro Pacific board instead of transferring them to First Pacific in line with Hong Kong's order. Some First Pacific executives viewed that as "rogue" behaviour, but they could not guide, much less control, Manny's actions on his home turf. PLDT staff feared a Gokongwei takeover might bring job cuts. Outside PLDT's annual general meeting, where Chairman Antonio "Tony Boy" Cojuangco and eleven other board members who backed Manny were unanimously re-elected, a group of employees displayed "We Love MVP" placards. Addressing shareholders, Manny did not mention the proposed deal, but Manila newspaper accounts said he grinned when an elderly woman shouted "I can't let the competitor, Gokongwei, enter." Manny noted that no deal had been done yet. He told the crowd "I will see all of you — more of you — again next year".[22]

In Hong Kong, First Pacific Chief Operating Officer Michael Healy told a reporter that Manny should have pulled the plug sooner on the Philippine investments. "We tried to engage Manny in conversations about our strategy. His view always seemed to be that we should give it more time", Healy said. "Everyone knew what the problems were, but he didn't come up with an alternative strategy."[23] While some viewed Manny's action as insubordination at First Pacific, he asserted he was fulfilling his duties to PLDT, of which he was CEO. Anthony clearly misjudged how intensely Manny wanted to remain atop PLDT. Some of Anthony's associates wondered why he did not remove Manny as First Pacific's executive chairman. It is not clear whether Anthony had the option of doing that, but he thought it best to do nothing, apparently in the belief there would be a resolution that left intact their long partnership. There was minimal contact between the two while the turbulence swirled. The Manny-Anthony dispute provided good grist for Manila's press, parts of which were unabashedly rooting for Manny.

Before easing, the dispute intensified as PLDT filed a complaint in a U.S. court against First Pacific. Both PLDT and First Pacific had New York-listed American depositary shares, which is why the Philippine company Manny led could file suit in New York against the Hong Kong company he chaired. The suit alleged that First Pacific did not make full disclosure, in a Securities and Exchange Commission document, of its 4 June memorandum of agreement with Gokongwei. *FinanceAsia* magazine described the suit as "surely the first instance in Asian history of a company suing its own major shareholder".[24]

PLDT succeeded in getting First Pacific to make available to Philippine regulators and PLDT the text of its June 4 agreement with Gokongwei. This provided new ammunition for Manny, because it showed Gokongwei's listed company, JG Summit Holdings, as a party to the agreement although Gokongwei had said it was not involved. A First Pacific statement clarified the reference to JG Summit, saying it was "purely descriptive in nature and was not intended to make JG Summit a party to the MOA". First Pacific headlined a press release "First Pacific Focuses on Substantive Merits of Proposed Transaction rather than Collateral Obstacles".[25] PLDT communications vice-president Butch Jimenez shot back, "Do they expect us to base our decision on press releases, bits and pieces of information, and a hastily drafted MOA full of imperfections for which we had to sue just to obtain a copy of?"[26]

Time was on PLDT's side. Anthony and Gokongwei's memo said the proposed deal had to done by 30 September, and that was impossible. On 23 September, First Pacific acknowledged the deadline could not be met, and blamed PLDT for blocking due diligence. On 1 October, Gokongwei formally pulled out, writing to First Pacific that the decision stemmed from his conglomerate's "inability to perform" the terms of their 4 June agreement. A Gokongwei statement cited "open resistance" from PLDT

management. Anthony declined to comment about the failure, though a
Salim executive in Jakarta called it "very bad for the Philippine corporate
sector. There was a willing seller and a willing buyer."[27] On 2 October,
confirmation of the collapse knocked 6.9 per cent off First Pacific's share-
price, to HK$0.81, and two weeks later, it reached an all-time low of
HK$0.69. Shares of PLDT, battered throughout the fight, in October hit
an eleven-year low of 209 pesos.

Six weeks after the deal formally lapsed, Manny defended his actions in
a speech. He told the Rotary Club of Manila an enterprise "is accountable
to all its owners and not just one — even if he owns the biggest chunk of
shares". Manny also asserted that the proposed deal would have violated
PLDT's by-laws by subjecting it to having as a board member, prior to
purchase, a party from a "competing or antagonistic business".[28] PLDT's
decisions during the episode "were not the unilateral act of one 'rogue
executive' out to protect his job, but reflected the unanimous approval of
the board, including its independent directors and government appointees",
he declared.

Tensions between the two strong-willed corporate bosses prevailed
well into late that year. Intermediaries promoted quiet efforts to repair
their bruising breach. Before the fight formally ended, the pair appeared to
reach an understanding to stick together. Achieving an accommodation was
helped when Metro Pacific sold 50.4 per cent of the Fort Bonifacio Global
City project to the Ayala Group, the Philippines' largest conglomerate, in
late November. As part of the deal, Ayala and a partner paid the US$90
million loan that Metro Pacific owed a First Pacific unit, Larouge. The
Wall Street Journal calculated that Ayala got into Fort Bonifacio property
at 5.6 per cent of the cost, in dollar terms, of what First Pacific paid in
1995.[29] But Manny cut Philippine debt and exposure, so achieved the goal
Anthony was pushing. "At the end of the day, they [Metro Pacific] sold
Fort Boni... [Manny] solved First Pacific's problem", Anthony said years
later, adding "Things calmed down, and we go ahead... the rhythm of
management is already back on track." Anthony acknowledged the value of
Manny's strategy, as the telcom company produced "very good" dividends.
"It's better to keep telecoms than property — property you can invest in
everywhere, telecom you cannot", Anthony said.[30]

Both men suffered losses: Anthony let go of the Gokongwei deal, and
Manny let go of a major Philippine asset. But both men didn't want to lose
more, and they had much vested in continuing their partnership. Anthony

needed Manny to manage and grow the business in the Philippines. Anthony had steered Indofood into the hands of First Pacific, which was important to Manny for the Hong Kong flagship. After the spat between Anthony and Manny, PLDT did deliver highly profitable years, which boosted the Filipino's standing and laid the groundwork for expansion in the Philippines. Anthony recalled that during the tense months of 2002, his father asked him, "Why are you having a problem with Manny?". Despite media speculation, the Salim CEO just bided time. He said later: "You cannot just dismantle [things] because of one anger... See things as a journey; you have to absorb and make a cool, right decision."[31] With the Bonifacio transaction, Anthony and Manny could each say they got what they wanted: for Anthony, a reduction in Philippine debt, while for Manny, continuing control of PLDT. In February 2003, when a Manila reporter asked about the state of his relationship with Anthony, Manny replied: "It's OK. We talk once in a while."[32] A month later, there was concrete evidence that the two men were back on the same page, as PLDT appointed Benny Santoso, Anthony's right-hand man, to an advisory board. This move, formally approved by PLDT's directors in June, let Anthony have a direct link with Philippine developments and was a sign he and Manny had restored the confidence to work together again.

The battle at First Pacific produced multiple casualties. Manny lost protégé Ricardo Pascua, who had been at Bonifacio. First Pacific lost top executives. In May 2003, First Pacific said COO Michael Healy, with the company since 1994, and general counsel and company secretary Ronald Brown, since 1986, had resigned. The two, involved in trying to manage the proposed Gokongwei deal, had incurred Manny's enmity. On 2 June 2003, First Pacific's AGM approved major boardroom changes. Manny relinquished the title of executive chairman, which Anthony assumed. This was no blow to Manny, who got back the post of managing director (relinquished when he became chairman in 1999) and was also named CEO. The company said the changes were made to implement the Hong Kong Stock Exchange's recommended practice for a company to have one person as chairman and another as CEO. After the meeting, Manny told Manila reporters "I'm relieved and happy ... relieved that everything is back to normal here in Hong Kong. I actually welcome coming back to my old post. Anthoni [First Pacific uses this spelling] should really be chairman, anyway. We talked about it yesterday. It's fine with me; it's fine with him."[33]

Meantime, First Pacific produced greatly improved financial results. For 2002, it recorded a net profit of US$40 million, compared with 2001's US$1.8 billion loss. But the company still carried heavy debts, and it had to use some Indofood shares to underpin high-yield bonds sold for debt-refinancing. *FinanceAsia* magazine in 2003 called First Pacific "a company with two good assets (Indofood and PLDT) but with very bad cashflow (a situation which will only improve when PLDT starts paying dividends)."[34] In 2005, PLDT did pay dividends for the first time since 2001, following bumper 2004 net profit of 28.04 billion pesos (about US$512 million). Cellphone subscribers jumped 48 per cent that year to 19.2 million.

After relations were again fine with Manny, Anthony in 2006 initiated a reorganization of the holdings in First Pacific by the "Liem Investors" who included the Gang of Four and some of their children. Anthony bought from some of the others control of two holding companies, one in the British Virgin Islands and one in Liberia, which held blocks of shares in the Hong Kong conglomerate. With those purchases, Anthony emerged with control of 44.5 per cent of First Pacific, and the other Liem Investors had small stakes. A statement from Manny said the reorganization of the interests "consolidates Mr Salim's position and demonstrates his personal commitment to the First Pacific Group".[35] Under rules of the Hong Kong stock market, Anthony had to next make an offer for all shares of First Pacific, as he had accumulated more than 30 per cent. But he did not want to acquire 100 per cent, so he deliberately made an offer that others would reject. Anthony offered to pay existing owners 32 per cent below the stock's last trading price. As intended in this kind of "compliance offer", there were no takers.

Anthony's reorganization of the Indonesian interests was completed just before a glittering party in May with more than 500 guests at Hong Kong's Four Seasons Hotel to mark twenty-five years since First Pacific's creation. "The hottest ticket of the year was definitely the supremely elegant, completely dazzling and meticulously planned First Pacific's 25th anniversary", noted a Manila columnist who writes about social scenes. He gushed about the gala where guests feasted on *foie gras* and wagyu beef. "The hotshot namedroppables who jetted in from all over the globe were enough to make you snap to attention."[36] Joining from Jakarta was a frail Liem, walking slowly with assistance, plus Sudwikatmono and Ibrahim Risjad. Guests from Manila included former President Cory Aquino and the archbishop of Manila. It was really Manny's party and for the event, he brought in a large cast of top-tier Filipino singers and musicians. Manny and Anthony looked completely reconciled and happy together, toasting each other. Speeches were short. In his remarks, Anthony summed up First Pacific's journey: "We have had our share of ups and downs ... there may have been shortcomings on our part, but we ran amid [them] resilient and flexible throughout. With Manny at the helm, and with the support of the Salim Group, we have weathered the storms and become today a respected business."[37]

Accolades were heaped on Manny. In a video made for the night, Cory Aquino remarked: "It's truly amazing what has happened to PLDT since Manny Pangilinan took over ... It's good there are people like Manny, who can make things happen ... show the best side of Asians, in particular Filipinos. So I hope there will be more Filipino businessmen like Manny."[38] Philippine Ambassador to the U.S. Albert del Rosario — also a First Pacific non-executive director — presented a state service award to Manny from President Gloria Macapagal Arroyo.[39] The Filipino performers kept the ballroom rocking until past midnight and then, according to the Manila social columnist, "everyone" partied in Hong Kong clubs till 5.30 a.m. except for Manny, who was in the office "bright and early the next morning, ready to chart the next twenty-five years" for First Pacific.[40]

In April 2007, when asked about relations with Anthony following their tussle five years earlier, Manny replied: "Things have changed, but there's a good deal of love and affection and respect for each other." After that episode, "it's different and, at the same time, it's the same".[41] Soon after those comments, Anthony strongly came to Manny's defence when a London fund manager sought to replace him as CEO at First Pacific's annual general meeting on 1 June. Jeremy Hosking of Marathon Asset Management, whose clients held about 6 per cent of First Pacific, wrote to shareholders: "We have become convinced that he is not the right person to take the firm through the next several years due to his determination to pursue an acquisition oriented growth strategy as a means of boosting firm value and lowering the share price discount." The Marathon man was unhappy that his proposal for First Pacific to buy back some shares to raise the price was "rebuffed in a most cursory manner".[42] Anthony, as First Pacific chairman, wrote to shareholders to express disagreement with Hosking and declared he would be casting his 44 per cent for Manny's re-appointment as CEO. "First Pacific's share price has risen by more than 320 per cent over the last five years, significantly outperforming the

Hang Seng Index which rose 75 per cent over the corresponding period",
Anthony pointed out, adding that the 2006 dividend payout was 83 per
cent higher than the previous year. Re-electing Manny was in everyone's
best interests, Anthony contended, as "Mr Pangilinan and his team have
been instrumental in achieving the considerable enhancement in value
and performance demonstrated by the company that has benefited all
shareholders".[43] At the AGM, where Manny needed more than 50 per cent
of shareholder votes to get three more years as CEO, he received 83.4 per
cent.[44] Marathon remained a shareholder.

Long after the temporary split with Manny, Anthony was full of praise
for a business partner whom he said worked thirty-six-hour days. "First
Pacific would never have become what it is today if Manny is not there…
From HK$6–7 million of capital to become that big, he put his life there…
First Pacific without Manny is nothing — zero," said Anthony. He felt their
relationship had moved far from 2002's rockiness and now, communication
was "much better. We communicate well. We're very close."[45] With the
conflict now history and businesses in the Philippines growing, sticking
together with Manny "turns out to be better, right?" observed Anthony,
with a smile.

CLEARED TO CARRY ON

Under the debt settlement agreement that Salim signed in 1998, all provisions
were meant to be carried out within four years. In mid-2002, with the
deadline looming, the state-of-play with Salim was getting significant media
attention in Jakarta. The MSAA agreements were not made public, but
some Indonesians believed that fulfilling the document's provisions meant
Salim would pay back the full Rp52 trillion it owed the state. But sales of
the pledged Salim assets were on track to raise only about Rp20 trillion.
This spurred a common view that the MSAA had been a bad deal for the
government. From Anthony's point of view, Salim had fully complied with
the stipulations of MSAA by delivering to IBRA and Holdiko the assets
he pledged. The fact that sales of the assets raised less than 40 per cent of
their assessed worth was not Anthony's fault. In his view — which the
governments led by Megawati Sukarnoputri and Susilo Bambang Yudhoyono
confirmed — Salim had met all its obligations. To Anthony, the recovery
rate of around 38 per cent reflected the speed at which pledged assets were
sold when economic and political conditions were poor. "All was done in
line with the [MSAA] settlement conditions", Anthony asserted.[46]

In early 2002, the level of grumbling escalated when Indonesian newspapers reported that a Jakarta law firm, hired by the government to make an independent review of the MSAAs, concluded they were seriously flawed. Tumbuan Pane Law Firm said the pacts should have included provisions for debtors to add more assets if the value of those already sold was lower than expected. It was "unreasonable and inequitable" for all the downside risk to be on IBRA, the review concluded.[47] That news story came out at a time IBRA had put forward a plan to give some debtors — not including Salim — six more years to fully settle up. After flak from the public, Megawati's government in March 2002 said it would stick to the existing debtors' agreements.

Salim and all debtors under IBRA had as their goal obtaining from the government a "release and discharge" statement, which they expected to ensure they would not face any criminal charges after the accepted settlement — not the same thing as full repayment — of their debts. Salim's path to collecting that clearance was slowed at times by frustration with the disappointing amount that sales of its assets raised — and how some were carried out. But there was no reason to doubt Salim would get a "release and discharge", especially after economic ministers who had taken a tough stand against the conglomerate — Kwik Kian Gie and Rizal Ramli — were no longer in office.

At one point, IBRA officials leaked word that the agency had concluded there were some "misrepresentations" in the valuation of some Salim assets, and some Indonesian media reported that the group would need to pledge an additional Rp2.2 trillion. Salim disputed that figure, and in July 2002 there was an agreement with IBRA that it would top up nearly Rp960 billion, of which Salim would pay about Rp230 billion in cash. *Tempo* called the "misrepresentation" matter a "stone in Salim's shoe".[48] The magazine reported that an IBRA official cited as an example Salim's pledge of shares in Bumi Serpong Damai, a Jakarta suburb developed with Ciputra and Sinar Mas. The shares should have been valued on a net basis (total amount of land minus road area), but instead were done on a gross basis, with the roadway included, *Tempo* wrote. In July 2002, IBRA chairman Syafruddin Temenggung — the body's seventh and last head — announced that Salim had agreed to pay the balance of about Rp730 billion within three months. Asked about the additional Rp2.2 trillion figure that had come out before he entered IBRA, Syafruddin replied: "According to the Oversight Committee, the figure is only Rp729.4 billion. That's all I have received. Where did this figure of Rp2 trillion come from?"[49]

A month later, Syafruddin said he wanted to complete the settlement with Salim by October, when the Rp729.4 billion was due. Anthony settled that in part by reducing the Salim's remaining 7.2 per cent stake in BCA to about 2 per cent. In November, Syafruddin announced that Salim had settled up. "We just reported it [Salim's status] and declared it settled", Syafruddin told reporters.[50] In mid-December, the government's Financial Sector Policy Committee approved IBRA proposals to grant "release and discharge" status to four debtors including Sudwikatmono and Ibrahim Risjad, but not yet Salim. The committee was still reviewing the Salim case, which Syafruddin said involved only "technicalities".[51] The government may have wanted to look as if it was giving Salim a harder time than others, but at this stage, no one in Megawati's cabinet took a really tough line with Salim.

On 30 December, Megawati signed Presidential Instruction No. 8 of 2002. Its title was a mouthful: "The giving of legal certainty to debtors who fulfilled their obligations, or legal action to debtors who did not fulfil their obligations as based on completing obligations as shareholders". By contrast, the text was brief, saying debtors who did what they were supposed to do in MSAA contracts should be cleared and those who did not should be taken to court. In a year-end speech the next day, Mega referred to the decree, saying that without government action, protracted debt problems could trigger difficulties in "other areas". She insisted that "release and discharge" was part of the government programme agreed to with the IMF and in line with state guidelines. "We can't let this problem drag on", Megawati announced. "That's why in December, I ordered a thorough resolution, while at the same time providing legal guarantees for debtors who have settled their obligations."[52]

Megawati's instruction came as she announced that the government had to triple some fuel prices, which would hurt the country's poor. Both statements coincided with Jakarta media reports about a lavish sixtieth birthday party in Bali for the president's husband, Taufik Kiemas. The *Jakarta Post*, which felt that conglomerates had been let off too easily, noted that the president's debt policy "has been strongly criticized by many parties who say it violates the people's sense of justice". A columnist for the paper wrote that Megawati's instruction made a few "problematic" conglomerates — naming Liem and Sudwikatmono — the recipients of "her most gracious New Year gift of all" as she had "pardoned their past banking crimes without trial".[53] A different view on the presidential declaration came from the IMF representative in Jakarta, David Nellor, who was quoted as saying the government showed it is willing to honour contracts signed with businessmen, which he called "critical to rebuilding the economy".[54] In February, the Indonesian Legal Aid Foundation unsuccessfully petitioned the Supreme Court to annul Presidential Instruction No. 8, which the group complained was "legally flawed" and violated earlier laws.

IBRA was supposed to cease operations at the end of February 2004, but it was still in existence on 11 March when Syafruddin signed a *surat keterangan lunas* (settlement confirmation letter) addressed to Liem and his sons Anthony and Andree. It stated they had "fulfilled their obligations" to IBRA as shareholders of a bank (BCA), and thus were given "release and discharge" (*pelepasan dan pembebasan*) in order to have "legal certainty" (*kepastian hukum*).[55] Grumbles that Salim got off the hook resurfaced in subsequent years, but state agencies, including the National Audit Agency (BPK) reiterated that Salim had complied with requirements of its MSAA agreement.

In 2004, eighteen years after academic Richard Robison wrote insightfully about Indonesian conglomerates in "The Rise of Capital", he wrote about the post-Suharto period with political sociologist Vedi Hadiz. About the IBRA period, they concluded "In the end, it became clear that the government possessed neither the capacity nor the will to enforce a rigorous programme of debt-restructuring". To an important extent, they argued, "business had largely forced the government to carry the burden of much of its debt".[56]

After getting his "release and discharge" letter, Anthony was in a good position. The document came in time for his family to mark a significant milestone. In April 2004, there were lavish celebrations at the luxurious Shangri-La Hotel in Singapore marking Liem and his wife's sixtieth wedding anniversary. To accommodate about 2,000 guests, from Jakarta and elsewhere, the party took place over two nights. Liem and his wife rode into the ballroom on trishaws. Attendees included several Suharto-era cabinet ministers. Suharto daughters Titiek and Mamiek attended. (The former president never left Indonesia after his resignation.) A video tribute shown at the diamond jubilee made no mention of Suharto. Of the traumatic events of 1998 that brought down the long-time patron, there was only one line describing it as a time of "uncertainties and tribulations". Two much earlier incidents were mentioned, however. After noting that Liem survived the 1949 car accident which killed his fellow passengers, and how Mrs Liem nearly lost her life after getting shot at home in Jakarta, the narrator said that "life for Mr and Mrs Liem was never short of miracles".[57]

NEW BOSS AT INDOFOOD

In June 2004, two months after Liem's sixtieth wedding anniversary, Anthony became CEO of Indofood. This was a significant development that, a year earlier, no one in Jakarta expected. Although Anthony has been calling the shots as head of the Salim Group, he had never been CEO of a listed company. Prior to his confirmation at an Indofood AGM, the company had been led through the post-Suharto period by Eva Riyanti Hutapea, who had risen through the company ranks from the audit department after graduating in accounting from the University of Indonesia. Her husband Bunbunan Hutapea was a career official at Indonesia's central bank, and in 2002 was promoted to be a deputy governor.[58] Eva Riyanti had played a major role in Indofood's growth before the 1997–98 crisis, and after it, she was looking again for ways to expand, though some proposals did not work out. One was to buy the joint venture the Salim family and a local partner had in Saudi Arabia to make noodles there, Pinehill Arabia Food. In May 2001, Indofood launched a US$173 million bid to buy 30 per cent of Golden Agri, a plantation company owned by Sinar Mas. The idea was for Indofood to get more of its own palm oil supply after most of the holdings Salim pledged to IBRA were sold to Guthrie. But then Golden Agri's auditors said they could not express an opinion as to whether that company's financial statements gave a true and fair picture; Indofood scrapped the bid, saying it was having difficulty doing due diligence because of missing information.[59] Eva then expressed interest in plantations owned by Astra or others.

Earlier, Indofood shareholders had approved a plan that Eva opposed, to sell miller Bogasari. As competitors were now free to mill their own flour or import it, unlike in Suharto's time, Bogasari had less attractive margins. Also, there were foreign parties including the Australian Wheat Board and Cargill who were interested in buying the giant mill. Indofood management, however, wanted to retain vertical integration, so it backed off from plans to sell it. "We don't want to lose control of Bogasari", Eva explained.[60] In the early 2000s, despite significant profits, Indofood's share price languished, and Indonesia's political turmoil was only part of the reason. *Forbes* in March 2002 published an article titled "The Salim Discount" that blamed the low price on the Salim family, which indirectly controlled Indofood through First Pacific. "Investors shy away because of the opacity of the Salim family's plans for the company", *Forbes* argued. It quoted a Singapore analyst saying Indofood "is seen as a vehicle for Salim, which we feel is not appropriate". The article, which did not have a comment from Salim, included Eva saying Indofood could best answer its critics in a few years' time. "I have full authority to run the company. Our challenge is to convince investors that Indofood is run by professionals", she said.[61]

In 2003, more challenges arose, as margins narrowed, net profit declined and competitor Wings was stepping up pressure. Wings introduced a product called "Mie Sedaap", or Delicious Noodle ('*sedaap*' had an extra *a* to fit how Indonesians could stretch out pronunciations; later, Indofood put "*sedaaap*", with three *a*'s, on some Supermi packages.) As 2003 was ending, Eva, who basically ran Indofood for a decade, surprised the market by submitting her resignation. The Indonesian daily that first reported it, *Koran Tempo*, said she was leaving because of conflicts with Anthony.[62] After a meeting the same day as the news report, Indofood's board expressed regret that Eva had resigned, thanked her for big contributions and said that until shareholders approved a successor, Anthony would "provide the board with all assistance it may require".[63] So Anthony became, at least temporarily, de facto CEO. Eva, who was usually accessible to the press, didn't speak to reporters that day. A few days later, in an article in *Kompas* newspaper, she talked about wanting to contribute to society. Asked by *Kompas* if she had big differences with Salim Group after working there twenty-two years, she replied, "There are no big differences between me and Pak Anthoni. Differences are normal."[64] Eva's exit caused much buzz; during her tenure, Indofood had won a clutch of awards and in 2002 a *Far Eastern Economic Review* survey named it Indonesia's best-managed company. The *Jakarta Post* praised Eva for "erasing the company's negative image as a money-making machine of the former Suharto regime".[65]

Years after Eva's departure, Anthony said she "had a different concept of what to do with the company".[66] One executive knowledgeable about Indofood's operations said that Eva may have become overconfident that her course was the right one. There was speculation that Eva and Anthony disagreed over strategy, over how much to pay for oil palm production and other issues. After First Pacific bought into Indofood and Manny became its chairman in October 1999, succeeding Liem, associates said that Eva told colleagues that Manny, and not Anthony, was her boss. The "management discussion" section of First Pacific's annual report on 2001 included a question about Anthony's involvement in Indofood's "strategic and operating decisions". Eva replied:

> Mr Salim is the head of Indonesia's largest conglomerate, which owned businesses throughout the world prior to the Asian economic crisis. As such, he has a wide range of experience and, as a Commissioner and founder of Indofood and a Non-executive Director of First Pacific, he has developed extensive expertise in the Indonesian food and plantation businesses. So, although he has no involvement in the day-to-day operations of Indofood, he makes a very valuable contribution to the company's overall strategy.[67]

Three months after Eva submitted her resignation, media reports quoting Anthony's brother-in-law confirmed disagreements between Anthony and her. Franky Welirang, who ran Bogasari, told an interviewer that Eva was leaving in part because of a dispute over what the mill charged to supply Indofood's noodle operations. Welirang also signalled other issues at Indofood, saying Anthony "is convinced that management was not deep enough... Anthony wants a management that drills down the line." The flour mill chief also said that Anthony was disappointed Eva had not gone into other segments of consumer foods. Indofood, Franky said, "could have been managed better".[68] Welirang, according to the *Financial Times*, was a leading candidate to replace Eva. But it turned out that Anthony, who received his "release and discharge" statement in April 2004, wanted to stay in charge.

On 25 June, shareholders approved Anthony's appointment as president-director. At the meeting, which Eva attended, Anthony reiterated Eva's resignation was a loss — and made clear changes were coming. Afterwards, Anthony told reporters Indofood was "a big ship that needs to be restructured"[69] and that every company "needs to revitalize itself in order to face tougher competition".[70] But in a bid to sound conciliatory, Anthony also said that Indofood "will really miss" Eva. But asked by a reporter if it was true that Eva resigned of differences with him, he replied:

> The fact is there were differences. What is important is that differences are either constructive or not. In fact, we are looking for constructive differences in order to strengthen ourselves. It is better to gather opinion

from 10 people than from one person in order to take efficient and effective steps to solve problems. I've said the departure of Eva is a big loss to Indofood".[71]

One newspaper cited legislator Hakam Naja as saying Anthony becoming CEO showed Liem's family felt that it was fine to have a public profile again. The debt settlement clearance from IBRA, Naja said, was the "main reason why they have decided to come out from their hiding places". Anthony remarked to reporters after becoming Indofood CEO, "I have always been out in front, not hiding behind a screen."[72]

As CEO, Anthony bore into details, a passion for him. He altered Indofood's distribution system and other facets of operations. Some critics accused Anthony of micro-managing, though he stabilized the company's market share in Indonesia for noodles at around 70 per cent. The greater political stability that followed Susilo Bambang Yudhoyono's election as president in September 2004 was a major factor promoting gains in the economy, in turn helping draw positive attention to Indonesia and its stock market. Indofood no longer claimed to be the world's largest maker of instant noodles — China player Tingyi had surging sales because of that nation's growth — but the Indonesian company was growing and drawing attention from fund managers even though its share price was at times roller-coaster like. At the end of 2004, the share price was unchanged from the end of 2003 (Rp800) even though Jakarta's benchmark index rose 45 per cent that year. In 2007, Indofood surged 91 per cent (to end at Rp2,575), far outperforming the index's 52 per cent gain. Then the 2008–09 global financial crisis whacked Indofood, taking its shares as low as Rp840 in March 2009. But then they rallied to end 2009 at Rp3,575, a gain for the year of 281 per cent (against the Indonesian market's 87 per cent rise). In 2010 and 2011, when there was a second Indofood listing, Indofood Sukses Makmur (INDF) underperformed the Jakarta index. It outperformed in 2012 and 2013, and ending the later at Rp6,600 — higher than the previous year's close of Rp5,850, but lower in dollar terms because the rupiah weakened more than 20 per cent during 2013.

Anthony expanded oil palm acreage, which helped recreate one part of Salim's empire. In 2005, there was an attempt, through First Pacific, to buy into pineapple plantations in the Philippines. That failed, which did not bother Anthony, whose main interest was palm oil to supply

Indofood.[73] To get more, Anthony injected into the listed company some pieces of plantation land that his family had, including 60 per cent of a British Virgin Islands company he owned named Rascal Holdings Ltd. Then, in late 2006, he started a chain of convoluted moves that injected into a listed company affiliated with Indofood some already-producing Indonesian acreage, via a reverse takeover in Singapore. In the first step, Indofood bought a small listed Singapore interior design company, ISG Asia, which was then renamed City Axis. It then became the vehicle for buying 64.4 per cent of London Sumatra, one of Indonesia's oldest plantation companies, from several parties. City Axis then was renamed Indofood Agri Resources, or IndoAgri. It paid about US$1 billion for London Sumatra, which vastly increased Anthony's land bank in Indonesia to about 387,500 hectares from less than 225,000. IndoAgri said that owning London Sumatra, started in 1904 by Britain's Harrisons & Crosfield, would eventually allow the Indofood group to be self-sufficient in crude palm oil.

In another move, Anthony in 2009 shifted the noodle and food ingredient businesses from Indofood into a new unit, Indofood CBP Sukses Makmur ("CBP" for Consumer Branded Products). In late 2010, Indofood CBP had Indonesia's largest initial public offering in two years, selling 20 per cent of its shares for about US$700 million. Now there were two listed Indofood companies in Jakarta, and another in Singapore. "Salim Rises Again" is how a *Tempo* headlined an article written just before the London Sumatra purchase. *Tempo*, which blasted Salim at times, said the majority of Indofood shares had been "astutely sold" to First Pacific and now "it seems as if the wheel of fate has turned a complete circle once again". Even though the group lost pillars after May 1998, Salim was rising again, the magazine concluded, "because it controls businesses that are closely connected to people's stomachs: noodles and flour."[74]

In 2009, Anthony's middle child and elder son Axton was appointed a director of Indofood. Born in 1979, Axton received a bachelor's degree in business administration from the University of Colorado and his first job was at Credit Suisse's investment banking unit in Singapore. In 2004, he joined Indofood as marketing manager of its joint venture with Frito-Lay of the United States. Axton became the youngest member of Indofood's board, and his appointment prompted speculation that Anthony was grooming him to run the company. Anthony just noted that Axton was "coming along" in learning about business.[75]

Outside of Indofood, another food investment at home involving Anthony expanded. This was in the mass-making of white bread and other "Sari Roti" baking products by PT Nippon Indosari Corpindo, which was formed in 1995. The company, which got listed in Jakarta in 2010, had six factories by the end of 2011. At that point, Anthony and the family of former Bogasari executive Piet Yap each owned 34 per cent of the company that also had Japanese investors.

EXPANDED ACTIVITY OVERSEAS

Before Anthony Salim received his "release and discharge" letter in March 2004, the group completed a transaction that opened a new avenue in China. In Jakarta, this spawned criticism on the grounds that if Salim had money to expand overseas, it had cash to settle its debts. (Salim's view was that it was meeting all the terms of its 1998 MSAA pact.) Businesswise, it was logical for Salim to grow in China, which was becoming increasingly important to companies globally.

1. China

Investing in China was far from new for Salim, but in the past, it was often carried out with partner Djuhar Sutanto, in both infrastructural and charitable projects in Fujian. To aid the arid area, Liem put money into many projects including construction of a dam, reservoir, port and irrigation viaducts around Fuqing. After a falling out between Liem and Djuhar in the post-Suharto period, their tie-up in Fujian ended. Anthony told the authors that Salim "decided to go into Shanghai, not expanding further in Fujian".[76] Going into Shanghai meant getting a potential springboard so "we can invest anywhere in China". For Liem, putting money in China meant his home province, for emotional reasons. For Anthony, who did not have sentimental ties to Fujian, and did not grow up speaking Mandarin at home, China was about business, and developing it in Shanghai was a logical way to go. "China is so exciting", Anthony once enthused.[77]

The property arm of state-owned China Ocean Shipping Co. (Cosco) became Anthony's vehicle. In September 2002, Cosco officials confirmed a report in a Shanghai weekly that a Salim family investment company had bought 45 per cent of Cosco Property Group.[78] They did not confirm the reported price of US$500 million, which sounded far too high. Later, Anthony said only that the price was lower. The buyer was a British Virgin Islands-registered firm named Success Medal International Ltd. The real estate company's name was changed to Cosco Salim Property, and the Salim stake was put under a Shanghai-registered firm named Salim Wanye (meaning 10,000 enterprises). One of the company properties was a Hainan island hotel and convention centre that hosted the Boao Forum for Asia, which China launched in 2001 as a kind of Asian equivalent of the World Economic Forum's annual Davos meeting.

In 2005, Chinese government policy made Cosco divest non-core businesses and concentrate on shipping. It moved to list, in Shanghai, Cosco Development, which held Cosco's remaining 55 per cent in Cosco Salim Property. Salim Wanye was the buyer, and Chinese media put the price at 958 million yuan (US$119 million). In addition to Salim Wanye, Anthony got another tool in China in Huili Building Materials, a smaller listed company. In 2006, Salim Wanye became the main shareholder of another Salim-linked company in China, Guangdong Jiangmen ISN Float Glass Co., one of the assets Salim pledged to IBRA. (The factory was bought by a company that was, in effect, a Salim proxy and had outbid a competitor, Taiwan Glass.) Through Salim Wanye and other companies, Salim started to make ambitious China plans. One did involve his father's home province of Fujian, where Salim was given a role in developing a coal-import terminal, which fit with a move by Anthony in Indonesia back into coal exploration.[79]

Liem made several trips to China after 2005, one of which put him in Beijing at the time of the 2008 Summer Olympics. He received VIP treatment and access to very high echelons of the Communist Party. In Beijing in April 2007, father and son made a call on then-rising Commerce Minister Bo Xilai, whose star crashed and burned in 2012. (In 2013, he was sentenced to life for corruption and other charges.) The Indonesians also called on old friend and party ascendant Xi Jinping, who was appointed vice-president in 2008, and in November 2012 was made Communist Party chief, confirming him as China's top leader. Xi had spent years in Liem's home province of Fujian, where he held various party positions including governor of the province and had courted investment from overseas Chinese. While in Fujian, Xi developed ties with Liem. In September 1991 — only thirteen months after China and Indonesia normalized their long-frozen diplomatic relations — Xi visited Jakarta, during which Liem showed him Bogasari and Indocement. When then-Vice-President Xi visited Singapore in 2010, three generations of the Liem family — Liem, Anthony and Axton — met him.

2. Australia

In 1989, Salim obtained Australian exposure through First Pacific's investment in a computer-software distributor, Imagineering Technology. Manny Pangilinan later called the company "a dog" that Anthony had pushed to acquire.[80] First Pacific pumped money in, took it private and changed the name to Tech Pacific. During the Asian financial crisis, it sold the company. In 2003, Salim got reconnected to Australia. Agricultural company Futuris announced an alliance with Salim and Japan's Nissho Iwai to build an Australian grain export business. Salim, which Futuris described as "a leader in food processing and distribution in Indonesia, the Philippines and Malaysia" took a 5 per cent share and invested A$46 million through a company named Droxford International. Anthony became a director of Futuris and its unit Elders Australia.[81] In October 2009, Anthony did not seek re-election as a director of Elders, as Futuris was called by then, but he remained a shareholder. In April 2004, Salim entered an alliance with CBH Group (Cooperative Bulk Handling) for a 50-50 owned company, Pacific Agrifoods. Seven months later, it bought 67 per cent of a firm named Interflour that operated four flour mills in Malaysia plus a grain terminal in Vietnam. CBH took one-third interest in Berdikari Sari Utama Flour Mills, the facility in Sulawesi that Suharto made Prima Ltd of Singapore sell out of in 1982. In 1998, Salim had pledged its 40 per cent stake in Berdikari Sari to IBRA. Later, investments with CBH got Salim back into part-ownership of that facility, renamed Eastern Pearl Flour Mills.

3. Singapore

Salim made several moves in Singapore in the mid-2000s, some of which involved KMP. In 2003, it registered a company called Gallant Venture, into which assets in the nearby Indonesian islands of Batam and Bintan, including shares in resorts and industrial estates, were put. Salim had pledged most of its assets in the islands to IBRA in 1998. Some were sold to Singapore interests and, as allowed by IBRA after two years passed, were resold to Salim-connected companies. In 2006, Gallant Venture got listed in Singapore, and in late 2012, Salim held a 53 per cent stake, while state-linked SembCorp Industries of Singapore had 24 per cent. Gallant had a nice stretch of beach-front property in Bintan, a popular getaway for Singaporeans. Its claim to the land was disputed in a case that went to Indonesia's Supreme Court, where Gallant won. In 2013, Gallant paid US$809 million to acquire 52 per cent of Indomobil in Jakarta. Indomobil, now revived and diversified, was fully back in Salim hands.

Years earlier, Anthony made several small investments in Singapore. In 2006, he bought 22 per cent of listed Food Empire, which sends packages of MacCoffee (not connected to McDonald's) and other instant beverages to Russia, Eastern Europe and Central Asia. But he showed no inclination to try to connect it with his Indonesian food empire. Another investment in Singapore was of interest because Anthony partnered with rising Indonesian businessman Chairul Tanjung of the Para Group — later renamed CT Corp — who denied being a proxy for Salim. In 2005, as partners in a Singapore company named Grandiflora, they bought 28 per cent of AsiaMedic, a health services provider, for S$13 million.

Anthony surprised the Singapore stock market with his quick response to a California short-seller's attack on a Singapore-listed, Fujian-based vegetable processor in which Indofood owned 29 per cent. Anthony made a general offer at nearly three times the price the short-seller's action dropped the stock to. That drew takers, and Indofood gained control of China Minzhong Food at an attractive price.

4. Middle East and Africa: The Long Reach of Indomie

In the 2000s, consumption of Indomie, Indofood's best-selling instant noodle, stretched across growing parts of the Middle East and Africa. The first production in Middle East was by Pinehill Arabia Food in Saudi Arabia. Salim's partner in Jeddah-based Pinehill was Said Bawazir Trading Corp. (SBTC), which has affiliates in other Mideast countries. In Syria, Indomie was made by Salim Wazaran Brinjikji, or SAWAB, in a factory at Adra, about 40 kilometres northeast of Damascus. (As of end-2013, it remained in production when it could receive needed raw materials while the civil war raged.) In Egypt, the maker was Salim Wazaran Abu Elata (Egypt). These companies, according to First Pacific annual reports, are "associates" of Anthony's. Indofood collects fees for licences sold to the companies to use the "Indomie" brand. Some flavours are the same as those sold in Indonesia; some are different as they are adjusted for local tastes. (Indofood tries to cater to a raft of taste preferences at home; in late 2011, there were 113 varieties of its noodle products on sale in different parts of Indonesia.) In Africa, Indomie is well-known in Nigeria, the most populous nation. De United Food Industries, or Dufil, started making Indomie in 2004. In 2011, its website claimed that Indomie "has grown to become a household name across the country".[82] Dufil is a joint venture involving Salim and the Singapore-based Tolaram Group, which is controlled by an Indian family whose patriarch migrated to East Java in the early twentieth century. The family had textile factories in Surabaya and Malang, and expanded into other businesses. Indomie is also sold in South Africa and other African nations.

INDIA: FAILED EXCURSION

While Suharto was in power, Salim paid scant attention to India, which wasn't yet an investment hotspot and where apprehensions about foreign investment remained high. Salim had a corporate logo that showed its name written across a globe, but it had never tried to do business in heavily populated South Asia — and understandably, as it had so many opportunities at and near home. After surviving the early post-Suharto years, the situation was different. Salim was open to looking at India, and one relationship that had developed in Jakarta led Anthony to put on his radar a country that otherwise would not have been there. Although India became a possible new frontier, Salim never planned to put into India anywhere near the billions of dollars some media said it intended to invest. In the end, it learnt how tough the Indian terrain was; in money terms, it lost little.

Salim partnered with an Indian-born, Singapore-based businessman named Prasoon Mukherjee, whose activities included having the franchise in Southeast Asia for Outback Steakhouse, a U.S. chain of Australia-themed restaurants. Mukherjee had worked in Jakarta for a company that ran an amusement park. While there, he became friends with Benny Santoso, Anthony's lieutenant. Mukherjee started a company called Universal Success Enterprise, and he had ambitions for his home state of West Bengal. He became the bridge between Salim and the state's chief minister, Buddhadeb Bhattacharjee. From 1975 to 2011, West Bengal's government was controlled by a left-wing coalition led by Bhattacharjee's Communist Party of India (Marxist) — which was different from the

Communist Party of India. But Bhattacharjee, who became chief minister in 2000, was a Marxist who wanted to tap international capital to industrialize his state. To some, he was West Bengal's Deng Xiaoping, whose famous maxim for a changing China was "To get rich is glorious". For his pragmatism, Bhattacharjee won accolades from Prime Minister Manmohan Singh and others.

In 2003, the chief minister told Mukherjee he wanted an international-style satellite town near Kolkata. Mukherjee took the idea to Santoso, and later plans were laid for such a project, with roles for Salim and Ciputra, the property mogul Liem worked with thirty years earlier in Jakarta. So Kolkata West International City, for which Bhattacharjee laid a foundation stone in 2006, began to take shape. In 2011, a Ciputra website showed a front gate that featured statues of horses, which the developer liked. The website post, taken down later, described the residential project as a "masterpiece of creation" and said the space "provides harmony and beautiful living!".[83] However, the project did not proceed beautifully, and the Indonesians exited when only a fraction of the planned units were moving ahead. Mukherjee later found new Indian investors.

The West Bengal chief minister — called Buddha for short — wanted Salim's participation in building an industrial estate similar to the one put up on Indonesia's Batam Island. Meantime, Bhattacharjee's government envisioned a New Kolkata International Development (NKID) that included a 100-kilometre expressway to reach a special economic zone that would be expanded to have a petrochemical hub, a medical-services town and other projects. In August 2005, Bhattacharjee travelled to Indonesia and Singapore to encourage investment in his state. In Jakarta, he met Salim executives and saw motorcycle assembly at Indomobil. *The Telegraph* of Kolkata reported that Anthony gave a presentation on Batam and said West Bengal's zone could be better as the state had "such a large pool of university graduates".[84] The article noted there was irony in the chief minister working with Salim, because (according to the newspaper) when the regime of its patron Suharto was "killing tens of thousands of communist", young Marxist Bhattacharjee was joining rallies in Calcutta to protest "the massacre of the Indonesian comrades". The *Telegraph* commented that Anthony had the credentials to be Bhattacharjee's "man of all reforms".[85]

While in Jakarta, Bhattacharjee signed an MOU with Salim for West Bengal to lease 5,100 hectares to it for developing an industrial estate.

The chief minister declared it was "a historical day for Bengal and the happiest of my life".[86] But back home, critics attacked him for promoting capitalism. To some hostile questions at a press conference on his return, Bhattacharjee insisted West Bengal had to "reform, perform or perish" and added "I don't see the colour of capital. The only investment I will not accept is black money and the money of smugglers." When asked how he, as a Marxist, could accept money from an Indonesian business group closely linked to the staunchly anti-communist Suharto, the chief minister retorted, "It is nonsense to rake up such past issues. Why then are Vietnam and China inviting American capital?"[87]

Some Indian media reported that Salim planned to invest US$10 billion in West Bengal, and that figure was widely repeated in the Indonesian press. Even if everything had gone well, that figure was a wild exaggeration. Salim's own investment would have been relatively small, for setting up infrastructure for industrial estates; if big investors had been found, particularly for capital-intensive petrochemical projects, then conceivably the total spent by all parties could have reached US$10 billion. One Jakarta media report that Salim would invest US$3 billion led a member of Indonesia's parliament to comment that the group "has made its money in this country. Hence, I think it is morally obliged to pay back by investing in the country. But of course we can't force them."[88] Salim ignored the flak; it was not investing billions in India or anywhere outside.

Back in West Bengal, the job of picking a site for a Salim-prepared industrial area, and evicting dwellers from it, fell to the state government. Authorities selected a swath of farmland southwest of Kolkata, around Nandigram. This drew fierce resistance from residents, and from the opposition Trinamool Congress, which saw a chance to hit at Bhattacharjee. When Benny Santoso visited Kolkata in October 2005 to talk about implementing the MOU, Trinamool's vocal leader Mamata Banerjee tried to get him surrounded by protesters, first at the airport and then his hotel. The efforts failed, as he arrived earlier than planned and switched hotels. She blasted the state government for giving misleading information on Santoso's visit; Bhattacharjee dubbed her group's protests a "circus".[89]

On 31 July 2006, an agreement was signed between the state's Bengal Industrial Development Corp. and New Kolkata International Development Pvt Ltd. The latter included Salim and Mukherjee's Universal Success Enterprises. NKID was to encompass a chemical hub at Nandigram and a range of projects. But none of this came to pass, as Bhattacharjee's dreams got violently disrupted. Land acquisition and the displacement of farmers became a boiling hot issue in the state, not just for NKID but also for auto maker Tata, which gave up trying to open a factory there to produce its "people's car", the Nano. In the NKID case, opponents began an aggressive campaign against the chief minister's acquisition efforts, culminating in violent clashes and deaths in 2007. The population in Nandigram lobbied for independence from West Bengal. Residents barricaded the road into Nandigram with logs and rocks, making it a no-go zone for outsiders. Bhattacharjee persisted, telling farmers they would benefit from having an industrial zone on land where their poor families grew crops for generations. "It is not agriculture versus industry, it is agriculture to industry", the chief minister asserted in February 2007 as violence was escalating. He predicted that "finally good sense will prevail, but it will take some time".[90]

The chief minister was wrong. On 14 March, there was a spasm of violence; police frustrated at their inability to access the area fired on opponents, and at least fourteen people were killed. Nandigram immediately became a name throughout India and, for many, a rallying cry. Opponents of Bhattacharjee called a series of crippling strikes in Kolkata and strife continued for months. Bhattacharjee gave up relocating people from Nandigram, and his hopes for NKID were dead. In August, he met Santoso and Mukherjee, and they decided to look for a new site for a scaled-down project that would not uproot farmers. One was found, on an island off India's east coast, Nayachar. That immediately drew protests from environmentalists. Meanwhile, ferment and resistance continued at Nandigram, where some villagers and politicians did not believe the state government had abandoned the industrial zone plan. Overall, at least thirty-four people were killed around Nandigram during 2007. In later local elections, the Communist Party of India (Marxist) lost the area, for the first time in decades, to the Trinamool Congress.

In June 2008, Anthony arrived in Kolkata to discuss the situation with Bhattacharjee, who was still chief minister. The Salim chief reiterated the group's interest in investing in West Bengal and said any timeframe was okay with him. Santoso brought the same message in September. In February 2009, India's national government — not the state one — approved a chemical hub for Nayachar, for which an MOU with Mukherjee's company was signed that year. In early 2011, Mukherjee said development of the island would go ahead, partly for petrochemical projects and partly for ecotourism. Before state elections in West Bengal in May 2011, the Trinamool Congress said only ecotourism was okay. That became the state government's view when Trinamool trounced Bhattacharjee's party in the voting that made Mamata Banerjee chief minister. This was fully expected, as the Nandigram deaths crippled the incumbent, who lost his own seat by a landslide. The state's new industry minister, Partha Chatterjee, said there would be no petrochemical project because of pollution concerns.[91] In November 2011, the state government and Mukherjee signed a new "project development agreement" for development of ecotourism and a thermal power station on Nayachar.[92] There was no role for Salim, now gone from India.

So the world's second most populous nation did not become a new frontier for Salim. By coincidence, Liem Sioe Liong once told the authors — before the violence in Nandigram — that he had a bad dream about India, causing him to feel it would be a mistake for Salim to make major investments there.[93] Told this, Anthony remarked in May 2007 "we are not going in a big, big way" and investing there might produce "some success, some failure".[94] In this case, there was no success.

GETTING BIGGER ON FAMILIAR TURF

This century, First Pacific has been a much different company than in the 1980s or 1990s. Instead of a wide array of scattered assets, it has kept two big ones — majority ownership of Indofood and effective control of PLDT. There were no assets in Hong Kong or China, unusual for a business based in Hong Kong. Rather than seek new turf, First Pacific was largely sticking to the birthplaces of its key figures Manny and Anthony. A new phase of expansion at Manny's home began after resolution of the spat with Anthony. Through First Pacific affiliate Metro Pacific, Manny moved into power generation, water supply, mining, toll-roads and hospitals. In October 2008, First Pacific bought a 20 per cent stake in gold and copper producer Philex Mining, the country's largest miner, for US$131 million. Manny became chairman in June 2009, and in December, First Pacific raised its stake to 31 per cent.

Also in 2009, PLDT unit Pilipino Telephone Corp. bought 20 per cent of Manila Electric Co., known as Meralco, and Manny later became its president and CEO. In 2011, Metro Pacific Tollways Corp. operated two expressways, and aimed to do more. Health was another area in which

Metro Pacific grew rapidly. By late 2011, it had become the Philippines' largest hospital operator, with five facilities including the Makati Medical Center in Metro Manila. For Manny and PLDT, an intriguing and important deal was a telecom one turning a one-time foe and competitor into a partner. In March 2011, PLDT announced a plan to buy out John Gokongwei's Digital Telecommunications Philippines (Digitel), whose cut-rate Sun Cellular brand was pinching market share from PLDT and the second biggest mobile provider, Globe Telecom, owned by Ayala Corp. and Singapore Telecommunications (SingTel). It was Gokongwei who, to Manny's chagrin, had made a pact with Anthony in 2002 to gain control of PLDT to alleviate First Pacific's debt burden. Now, nine years later, a marriage was shaped in which Manny joined hands with a pesky competitor and Gokongwei's group gained a coveted seat on PLDT's board. The announced US$1.6 billion deal, in which PLDT would get 51.55 per cent of Digitel, was the largest corporate takeover in the Philippines.

Critics complained that the deal would create a duopoly, and that PLDT would emerge with 70 per cent of the national market and Globe Telecom the rest. But a regulatory agency eventually endorsed the deal, and PLDT and JG Summit were now partners. PLDT became majority owner of Digitel, which made Manny its chairman. JG Summit got 8 per cent of PLDT. The animosity of the 2002 episode involving First Pacific was gone; JG Summit chairman James L. Go said the new transaction "ensures that Digitel remains in good hands".[95] As the deal got completed, Manny was looking to increase his involvement in Philippine infrastructure. Similar to how Salim Group, by the 1990s, had made itself part of the everyday life of millions of Indonesians, Manny and First Pacific had come to supply services such as cellphones, water and power to growing numbers of Filipinos.

When Manny turned sixty-five in July 2011, he showed no sign of losing interest in doing deals. Earlier he told a reporter: "Well, it is infectious I must say; when you get into a deal mode, it's like a slippery slope."[96] Anthony, who turned sixty-four in October 2013, remained addicted to doing business. He once said, "I won't ever retire. I don't want to talk to fish."[97]

THE FADING OF THE GANG

The aftermath of the financial crisis, called *krismon* in Indonesian (for *krisis moneter*), saw some casualties in long-standing relationships.

Liem's "Gang of Four" was one. Although the quartet had stopped making new joint investments long before 1998, and each man went his own direction, they remained friends. But in the post-Suharto period, the core friendship between Liem and fellow Hokchia Djuhar Sutanto ended, unhappily. Disagreement over Anthony's debt settlement with IBRA led to the Djuhar family taking Salim to court in Jakarta, though the lawsuit was soon withdrawn. Despite that case, some Salim-Djuhar business ties remained in place. Djuhar still retained some shares in First Pacific but he did not seek re-election to the board in 2010, when his son Tedy Djuhar was re-elected. Tedy also remained vice-president director of Indocement, where a Salim-Djuhar company, Mekar Perkasa, retained a 13 per cent stake. In Wisma Indocement in Jakarta, Tedy's office remained on the same floor with Anthony's.

Of the four "Gang" partners, Djuhar was by far the least publicly visible in Indonesia. In 1995, Forbes — in an item incorrectly describing him as Liem's distant relative — wrote that Djuhar "is as mysterious as he is rich".[98] From the late 1980s, Djuhar was often in Singapore, where he had an office, and in Fujian, where he and Liem had joint projects and individual ones. In Fujian in 1987, they began an industrial estate called Yuan Hong, named after their fathers, to attract investment by overseas Chinese to the poor province where Djuhar was born in 1928 and Liem in 1917. Among Yuan Hong's businesses was a flour mill. In a rare instance where Djuhar was quoted in the media, a 1997 article in the South China Morning Post on overseas Chinese helping China reported him saying: "When we started in 1987, Fuqing had no factories and no industrial workers. Now it has 500 factories and 60,000 industrial workers, with GDP in 1996 of 20 billion yuan, 50 times the level of 1987."[99]

After the falling-out between Djuhar and Liem, it affected Yuan Hong, which passed to Djuhar. In a 2005 hagiography about Djuhar, which doesn't mention Liem Sioe Liong's name, the author tells of Djuhar complaining about missed opportunities. Citing the time he got Taiwan plastics king Y.C. Wang (Wang Yung-qing) interested to jointly invest in a project in Fujian, he indicated that Liem nixed the idea. The text quoted Djuhar as asserting that his unnamed partner opposed working with another big Chinese business name, allegedly telling Djuhar: "One mountain cannot have two tigers. I came here, how is it possible for Wang Yung-qing to also come?"[100] The book lavishly praised Djuhar for attaining success as an enterprising overseas Chinese who became wealthy then deployed funds to build up a poor part of China. About Djuhar's relations with Liem, the Chinese language book said:

> A significant portion of Lin Wen Jing's assets is the "Salim Group", the business group that he started with a person that he refers to as his father's friend. This uncle is 11 years older than Lin Wen Jing. He is also from Fuqing originally, and is a friend of Lin Wen Jing's father. Like him, he had been forced by poverty and lack of opportunity to leave his newly married wife to travel to Nanyang [Southeast Asia] to work. This partner is also a person with a strong "home town" connection. He supported Lin Wen Jing's decision to return to Fuqing to help it develop and get out of poverty. He told Lin Wen Jing: the hometown is so impoverished that it makes us rich sons overseas feel shameful. He allowed Lin Wen Jing to give up all his work in the Salim Group, so that he [Wen Jing] can remain in Fuqing on a long-term basis, and concentrate on the work of helping his home town to get rich. After more than ten years, the assets that Lin Wen Jing handed over to his partner had evaporated mysteriously. There were people who reported to Lin Wen Jing that the reason why his partner had allowed him to remain in China was to lure him away, so that he could take over his assets. But Lin Wen Jing would rather think that it was the love for the country and his hometown that drove this partner to allow him to remain in China. More and more people made reports to him, but he kept saying: this cannot be the case. He is my father's friend![101]

While Djuhar had ties with Liem that went back a long time, he did not develop a strong bond with Anthony, and that became apparent after the collapse of Indonesia's economy and the fall of Suharto. Action by Anthony involving one property company that Gang of Four members helped set up, PT Metropolitan Kencana, sparked the dispute that resulted in Djuhar going to court. On 8 October 2002, lawyers for Djuhar filed a suit in South Jakarta District Court against Liem, Anthony, his older brother Andree Halim, IBRA, Holdiko and two other defendants. The suit sought damages as well as the halting of Holdiko's planned sale, for about 600 billion rupiah, of 47.5 per cent of Metropolitan Kencana, the developer of the luxury Pondok Indah estate. Anthony had pledged the 47.5 per cent under Salim's MSAA agreement. The Djuhar family maintained it owned

10 per cent of Metropolitan Kencana, through a company of Tedy's named PT Grandwood Buana. Salim, it contended, only had the rights to 37.5 per cent and Anthony had appropriated an extra 10 per cent. Anthony denied the accusation, saying he acted legally in pledging the 47.5 per cent to IBRA.

A battle in Indonesian court between two long-time partners might have featured juicy revelations. But it did not unfold, as right after the suit was filed, efforts began to settle the conflict outside of court. Businessman Sofyan Wanandi sought to mediate. He told *Tempo* magazine the dispute's root cause was "calculations still being incomplete when the Salim assets were transferred to IBRA."[102] The two families agreed to cease hostilities, apparently at a meeting in Singapore. In attendance were members of two generations of each family. By the end of November, the lawsuit was withdrawn. According to Jakarta media, Djuhar's law firm said in a letter to the court there was a resolution through *musyawarah* (deliberations) carried out in "a family atmosphere". According to *Koran Tempo* newspaper, Djuhar lawyer Denny Kailimang said the dispute "was resolved in a peaceful manner".[103]

Years later, Anthony declined to discuss details of the lawsuit while Tedy Djuhar declined requests by the authors to meet. With the suit dropped, Holdiko proceeded to sell the 47.5 per cent Metropolitan Kencana stake, which was acquired by Jakarta businessman Murdaya Poo. Anthony said in 2007 his family was upset at being taken to court. "My father never initiated any court action [against any one] ... there was no problem splitting with Mochtar Riady, [or] with Eka [Sinar Mas boss Eka Cipta Widjaja]", he remarked.[104]

Nearly eight years after the suit, there was a reunion of sorts at the luxury Capella Hotel in Singapore for the Gang of Four, though with Anthony standing in for his frail father. The occasion, in August 2010, was a party with hundreds of guests — many of them prominent businessmen from Jakarta — to celebrate the wedding of seventy-six-year-old Ibrahim Risjad, who remarried after his wife died. Sudwikatmono came from Jakarta. Djuhar and Anthony politely exchanged greetings. For one night, the gang was by and large again all there. There would not be another occasion like it: Sudwikatmono died less than five months later, age seventy-six, and Risjad died in February 2012, age seventy-seven.

Notes

1. David Lanchner, "Playing political angles", *Global Finance*, 1 March 1998.
2. Jon Hilsenrath and Douglas Appell, "Despite slump, analysts alter views on First Pacific", *AWSJ*, 18 May 1998.
3. Jon Hilsenrath, "First Pacific's stock endures gyrations", *AWSJ*, 25 August 1998.
4. Jon Hilsenrath, "PLDT sells dominant stake to First Pacific", *AWSJ*, 25 November 1998.
5. Rigoberto Tiglao, Kathy Wilhelm and Joanna Slater, "After years of fast-paced mergers and acquisitions, First Pacific's Manuel Pangilinan says it's time to buy big and hold", *FEER*, 17 December 1998.
6. First Pacific press release, 25 February 1999.
7. Interview with Anthony, 8 February 2009.
8. Ibid.
9. "Philippine MetroPac sees hope after huge '01 loss", Reuters, 1 March 2002.
10. First Pacific press release, 4 March 2002.
11. Cris Prystay, "Philippine tycoon can cap a career with PLDT deal", *AWSJ*, 7 June 2002.
12. Ibid.
13. Interview with Anthony, 8 February 2009.
14. Interview with Manny Pangilinan, 20 April 2007.
15. Interview with Anthony, 8 February 2009.
16. Ibid.
17. Victor C. Augustin, "MVP fights for survival", *Philippine Daily Inquirer*, 31 May 2002.
18. "PLDT sees sharply higher 2002 income", Reuters, 26 February 2003 and "First Pac executive chairman ready to quit if causing HK group woes", Dow Jones, 26 February 2003.
19. Private conversation in Jakarta, 3 June 2002.
20. First Pacific release, "First Pacific and Gokongwei Group partner in joint venture arrangements", 5 June 2002.
21. Gil C. Cabacungan Jr. and Doris C. Dumtao, "Executives, taipans, solons gang up on Gokongwei", *Philippine Daily Inquirer*, 6 June 2002.
22. "Defiant chief ignores instruction to lie low at meeting", *South China Morning Post*, 12 June 2002.
23. "HK's First Pacific looks beyond Philippines, eyes China", Reuters, 13 June 2002.
24. Steven Irvine, "Crossed wires continue in PLDT debacle", *FinanceAsia*, 19 July 2002.
25. First Pacific press release, 24 July 2002.

26. "PLDT: HK First Pac unclear on details of Gokongwei deal", Dow Jones, 25 July 2002.

27. James Hookway and Matt Pottinger, "Suitor drops bid for PLDT stake", *AWSJ*, 3 October 2002.

28. The *Philippine Daily Inquirer* published the speech text the next day, 8 November 2002, under the headline "Ethics, sound business practice go together".

29. James Hookway, "Buying former base is a gain for Ayala, loss for First Pacific", *AWSJ*, 2 December 2002.

30. Interview with Anthony, 8 February 2009.

31. Ibid.

32. Manolette P. Tabingo, *BusinessWorld* (Manila), "Salims not likely to divest PLDT stake — Pangilinan", 27 February 2003.

33. Dennis Serfino, "First Pac back in MVP hands", *Manila Standard*, 3 June 2003.

34. Steven Irvine, "Nice assets, shame about the cashflow", *FinanceAsia*, 11 July 2003.

35. First Pacific press release, "Liem Investors Reorganize Their Interests in First Pacific", 1 May 2006.

36. Maurice Arcache, "Pacific-wide party for Asia-Pacific conglomerate", website of *Philippine Daily Inquirer*, <http://showbizandstyle.inquirer. net/lifestyle/lifestyle/view/20060622-6100/Pacific-wide_party_for_Asia-Pacific_conglomerate> (accessed 18 December 2010).

37. Text of Anthony Salim's remarks at First Pacific's 25th anniversary party, Hong Kong, 25 May 2006.

38. Video at First Pacific's 25th anniversary party, Hong Kong, 25 May 2006.

39. Del Rosario resigned from the board of First Pacific after President Benigno Aquino made him the Philippines' Foreign Secretary in 2011.

40. Arcache, "Pacific-wide party for Asia-Pacific conglomerate".

41. Interview with Manny Pangilinan, 20 April 2007.

42. First Pacific posted Hosking's letter of 16 May 2007 on its website <www. firstpacific.com>, and it remained there in late 2012.

43. First Pacific Board letter to shareholders, 26 May 2007.

44. First Pacific press release, 1 June 2007.

45. Interview with Anthony, 8 February 2009.

46. Interview with Anthony, 8 February 2008.

47. "Review spots faults in Salim's MSAA", *Jakarta Post*, 26 January 2002.

48. "Stone in Salim's Shoe", *Tempo*, 16–22 July 2010.

49. Ibid.

50. "Salim may avoid criminal charges", *Jakarta Post*, 27 November 2002.

51. "Former bank owners not to be subject to criminal charges", *Jakarta Post*, 13 December 2002.

52. "Megawati defends 'release and discharge' policy", *Jakarta Post*, 2 January 2003.

53. Kornelius Purba, "Mega's risk government by making dubious decisions (*sic*)", *Jakarta Post*, 9 January 2003.

54. Sadanand Dhume, "Indonesia hopes to close books on bank bailout", *AWSJ*, 6 January 2003.

55. Letter of 11 March 2004 from IBRA Chairman Syafruddin Temenggung to Soedono Salim, Anthoni Salim and Andree Halim.

56. Richard Robison and Vedi Hadiz, *Reorganising Power in Indonesia: The Politics of Oligarchy in an Age of Markets* (London: Routledge Curzon, 2004), pp. 196 and 199.

57. Video shown at celebrations in Singapore of the Liems' 60th wedding anniversary, 15–16 April 2004.

58. In 2009, Bunbunan Hutapea and three other former Bank Indonesia deputy governors were jailed after being convicted of misappropriating funds from a foundation linked to the central bank. Hutapea's four-year sentence was reduced to three years on appeal, and then he was paroled in 2010.

59. Tom Wright, "Indofood scraps deal to buy Golden Agri from Asia Food", *AWSJ*, 13 August 2001.

60. Simon Montlake, "Indonesia Indofood seeks to buy Salim Saudi noodle plant", Dow Jones, 25 May 2000.

61. Justin Doebele, "The Salim Discount", *Forbes*, 4 March 2002; available at <http://www.forbes.com/global/2002/0304/045.html> (accessed 27 October 2010).

62. "Eva Riyanti ajukan penunduran diri dari Indofood" [Eva Riyanti submits her resignation from Indofood], *Koran Tempo*, 16 December 2003.

63. "Indofood CEO resigns over internal dispute", *Jakarta Post*, 17 December 2003.

64. "Antara Saya and Anthony Salim" [Between me and Anthony Salim], *Kompas*, 20 December 2003.

65. Rendi Witular, "Indofood CEO resigns over internal dispute", *Jakarta Post*, 17 December 2003.

66. Interview with Anthony, 18 March 2007.

67. First Pacific, Annual Report 2001, p. 8.

68. Shawn Donnan, "Adding new ingredients", *Financial Times*, 16 March 2004.

69. "Indofood to pay modest dividend, names new chief", Reuters, 25 June 2004.

70. Rendi Witular, "Salim in driving seat at Indofood", *Jakarta Post*, 26 June 2004.

71. "Keberangkatan Eva Riyanti Kehilangan bagi Indofood" [The departure of Eva Riyanti is a loss for Indofood], *Koran Tempo*, 26 June 2004.

72. Witular, "Salim in driving seat at Indofood".

73. First Pacific sought to buy 40 per cent of Singapore-listed Del Monte Pacific for US$164 million. If that had succeeded, it would have triggered a mandatory offer for the other 60 per cent. But a rival bidder, connected to First Pacific rival San Miguel, made a higher offer and First Pacific withdrew.

74. "Salim rises again", *Tempo*, 9 April 2007.

75. Interview with Anthony, 14 November 2009.

76. Interview with Anthony, 14 October 2007.

77. Ibid.

78. "Indonesian Salim Grp buys 45 pct stake in China's COSCO Property", Dow Jones, 26 September 2002.

79. "Fuqing City in southeastern China to build a large coal wharf", Platts International Coal Report, 12 September 2011.

80. Tiglao, Wilhelm and Slater, "After years of fast-paced mergers and acquisitions".

81. Futuris statement to the Australian Stock Exchange, 4 March 2003.

82. <www.dufil.com> (accessed 27 January 2011).

83. <http://www.ciputra.com/?url=housing/index/27> (accessed 15 January 2011). On 26 August 2012, the same website did not contain any India content. The only overseas projects listed were for Vietnam and Cambodia.

84. "Buddha's Man of All Reforms", *The Telegraph* (Calcutta), 27 August 2005.

85. Ibid.

86. "Salem (*sic*) township: A tale of two Howrahs", *Hindustan Times*, 21 April 2006.

87. Ravi Velloor, "India's Marxist-capitalist chief minister riles party", *Straits Times*, 31 August 2005.

88. "Salim Group's $4.7 billion deal in India slammed", *Straits Times*, 12 August 2006.

89. "Mamata claims moral victory despite investor's arrival", *Hindustan Times*, 20 October 2005. (That article, and many in the Indian press, wrongly identified Santoso as Salim's CEO.)

90. "Indian communists turn sickles into hammers", Reuters, 5 February 2007.

91. "Bengal scraps Nayachar petrochem project", *The Hindu*, 20 August 2011.

92. "Govt signs Nayachar agreement", *The Statesman*, 4 November 2011.

93. Interview with Liem, 19 August 2006.

94. Interview with Anthony, 20 May 2007.

95. PLDT press release, "PLDT completes acquisition of Digitel in landmark telco transaction", 26 October 2011.

96. Mary-Ann Li Reyes, "MVP sets goals before retirement", *The Philippine Star*, 24 May 2011.

97. Interview with Anthony, 14 November 2009.

98. "New Names This Year" section of "The International 500" list of the richest people outside the U.S., *Forbes*, 17 July 1995, p. 140.

99. "Overseas fortunes help out the motherland", *South China Morning Post*, 6 April 1997.

100. Xiao Liu, *Lin Wen Jing: Ta gai bian le jia xiang* [He Changed His Home: Fuqing's Lin Wen Jing Returns After 18 Years] (Hong Kong: Takungpao Publishing, 2005), p. 100.

101. Ibid.

102. "The End of the Friendship", *Tempo*, 11 November 2002.

103. "Kisruh Metropolitan Kentjana Selesai, Keluarga Djuhar Cabut Gugatan Terhadap Salim" [Disruption at Metropolitan Kentjana is over, Djuhar family withdraws accusation against Salim], *Koran Tempo*, 28 November 2002.

104. Interview with Anthony, 18 March 2007.

21

TWILIGHT

In the years after the downfall of his patron, Liem spent most of his time in Singapore, leading a mostly sequestered life far removed from his days as one of the most recognized faces in the Indonesian corporate world. Unlike in Jakarta where he was constantly hounded, he was able to move around in the island republic scarcely disturbed. Unaccustomed to being at home much of the time, he kept up the habit of going to the office, only this time it was to the office of Permanent Pte Ltd usually every afternoon, except Sundays, when he would go to the KMP office at the forlorn-looking Fook Hai Building in Chinatown, which was Anthony's base. No real business had been conducted at Permanent for years, but Liem felt that in keeping with its name, the office should remain open. Sometimes, visitors from China dropped by to see him. It was Anthony's habit to be in Singapore on weekends when he was not travelling elsewhere on business. He would brief his father about the latest business developments. Liem continued to make occasional trips to China as long as his health permitted. He particularly enjoyed going to his hometown, Fuqing, which welcomed him with open arms. Before his health declined to the point he could no longer travel, Liem also made the occasional short trips to Jakarta, and whenever possible he would stop by at Jalan Cendana to visit his old friend Suharto.

A "HOMECOMING" IN CHINA

Liem regarded Indonesia as his home, but there always was a special place in his heart for his native town in China. When he was able to return to his village of Niuzhai, he would pay respects to his ancestors at their simple graveyard. He was much loved as a philanthropist in Fuqing, credited with leading the charge in transforming the provincial backwater into a modern city. Here, he was simply called *"laoban"* — the Boss — and the one who was instrumental in providing seed money that enabled Fuqing to have roads, bridges, shopping malls, hospitals, schools, industrial areas and even a port. In his ancestral home, Liem was accorded demigod status. It was evident during one visit he made during Chinese New Year in February 2006. The reception he received was nothing short of adulation. Everywhere he went, the red carpet was rolled out — from the moment his chartered jet from Singapore touched down at the airport in Fuzhou, the capital of Fujian province. High-ranking Communist Party officials led the welcoming committee, and firecrackers heralded the return of Fuqing's wealthiest and perhaps most famous son. Liem had come to attend a congress of the World Fuqing Association, which he founded and was life chairman. The venue was at the vast atrium of a shopping mall he had developed. His entourage stayed at the city's four-star hotel, called Rongqiao,[1] which he had built. On his arrival at the hotel, a hundred or so staff members lined the lobby and reception area, applauding him, looking genuinely delighted and in awe to see him. A few days later, he visited a high school he helped fund; hundreds of students welcomed him enthusiastically.

Residents of Fuqing compare Lin Shaoliang (Liem's name in *hanyu pinyin*) to Mi Le Fuo, the bodhisattva sometimes referred to as the Laughing Buddha. In Haikou, there is a gigantic statue of Mi Le Fuo. Carved from a single huge boulder, the centuries-old statue has been accorded "national treasure" status. Mi Le Fuo is also known as the Maitreya Buddha; the word *"maitri"* being Sanskrit for "universal loving-kindness" and is often represented by a statue of a rotund Buddha with a broad smile and a paunch. He is believed to bring happiness and hope. Rubbing his belly is thought to bring good luck. In the 1990s, Liem donated more than RMB13 million towards the upkeep of the statue and the temple area where it is located. But Liem is revered in Fujian not just because of his enormous wealth, but because of his lifelong efforts in developing the region.

It was because of him that the dire conditions that blighted Fuqing and its environs have become a thing of the past, Communist Party officials say. Starting in the 1980s, Liem and his business partner, fellow Hokchia Djuhar Sutanto, invested heavily and donated generously to multiple projects in Fujian, especially around Fuqing. Thanks to a reservoir and irrigation system, Fuqing no longer is a victim of drought and flooding that historically plagued the area. They also put substantial money into manufacturing facilities and a 5,000-hectare industrial park that bears the combined names of their fathers — Yuan Hong. The partners also built a port capable of handling ships of up to 30,000 tonnes. The list is long. A taboo subject back in Jakarta, the philanthropists preferred not to reveal the extent of their money pumped into China, but reports estimate the amount to be well over RMB400 million.

The population of Fuqing prefecture has multiplied twelve times to 1.2 million in 2006, from the early 1980s, said former Fuqing mayor Qiu Yuqing. Now retired, the former Communist Party official first met Liem in the 1980s and couldn't say enough good things about the man he also calls "*laoban*". In a chat at the Rongqiao Hotel in 2006 with the co-author, he said "*Laoban* is a shining example of someone who *ai guo, ai xiang* (loves his country and his village)".[2] Listing the infrastructural developments that bore Liem's donations, he said Liem had led the way in transforming Fuqing from a provincial backwater into a modern city. "You can see that now people can afford to host as many as 50 to 100 tables for a wedding dinner; one table costs around RMB1,500! Just look at the number of buildings coming up! And we have achieved this, all thanks to *laoban*," Qiu said, adding "*Laoban* has a saying he abides by: 'Plant the seed with which you can grow more.' I liken him to a mother hen laying eggs ... then letting them hatch. *Laoban* never forgot his roots. As long as he is around, Fuqing will continue to thrive. We hope he lives forever!"

Liem was already an adult when he left China. His first trip back to his home village since leaving was in 1961, twenty-three years later. Sukarno was in power and Liem had to use a "back door" to leave Jakarta as he was not yet an Indonesian citizen and did not have a passport. On that occasion, he was accompanied by his wife, who was meeting her mother-in-law and Liem's China-born wife for the first time. After Indonesia suspended diplomatic relations with China in the aftermath of the 1965 abortive coup, Liem was not able to visit again until 1983 when he received special permission from Suharto to go. On that occasion, officials in Fuqing declared the day of his arrival a public holiday so crowds could line the streets to get a glimpse of the already well-known son of the soil. Liem's contributions also helped areas of education, health and culture. He made possible construction of the city's first modern hotel, Rongqiao, 17 kilometres from the village where he grew up. It features a marbled lobby replete with Indonesian artefacts and batik artwork.

Marking a Chinese New Year in Fuqing

Liem's February 2006 trip was all the more special as it coincided with the Chinese New Year period. At his suite at the Rongqiao Hotel, he was inundated with requests for private meetings. A deluge of letters arrived, seeking assistance and favours, from financial help to recommendations for promotions. Some "petitioners" arrived with letters they had drafted, and addressed to officials — all they sought was Liem's signature. It was like a scene from *The Godfather*, minus the violence. The following days were filled with meetings, lunches and dinners, with local and regional officials and bureaucrats all wanting to toast *laoban*. The finest and most expensive dishes Fujian had to offer appeared at meal times, including the famous "Buddha Jumps over the Wall" — a soup stewed for days with the most expensive ingredients such as shark's fins, abalone, ginseng and sea cucumber. (According to legend, the dish got its name when a Buddhist monk, unable to resist the delicious and tempting aroma wafting from the other side of the wall where it was being cooked, leapt over to get a taste.) Fine wines flowed freely, and every guest approached Liem to offer a toast to his health. Every now and then, the eighty-nine-year-old barely ambulatory magnate cracked a joke, and his audience would laugh uproariously. He appeared energized by the warm reception that awaited everywhere he went. He had a full programme, with light entertainment in the evenings usually featuring Fuqing's finest and prettiest singers and dancers.

Liem's return to his home village of Niuzhai was met with high anticipation. Excitement was palpable among the villagers. Security men had to cordon off his home from villagers who swarmed around, trying to get close to its most famous son. He had paid for the asphalt paving of the road to the village, lined pleasantly by rows of willowy trees. As his car approached, firecrackers were thrown in a noisy welcome. His old house, completely renovated into a two-storey structure featuring flush toilets, is nothing ostentatious, but large by village standards, and well maintained. At the family altar, large portraits of his parents and other family members cast benign looks on visitors. A traditional Min opera had been commissioned to perform for several nights at the village. Liem, a big fan, covered the costs. He had become a substantial backer of the troupe, which he had sponsored for performances in Singapore and Indonesia. Before the evening performance, all the main artistes lined up to greet him and at the end of the receiving line, a family member handed each one a *hongbao* — a red envelope, with cash in it. For the show, a few rows of VIP seats were set up close to the stage; tea, oranges and snacks were served to Liem and his entourage. The scene was a far cry from his childhood days, when he had to sneak off to watch opera and was once caned by his father for returning home late. The next day, Liem, accompanied by his youngest sister who lives in Hong Kong, and other relatives, paid his respects at the grave of his ancestors, located on a hillside, overlooking the village. The gravestone of his father and grandfather were simple small slabs in the ground, almost inconspicuous unlike the elaborate tombstones of rich Chinese seen all over Southeast Asia. Some would expect more imposing burial plots for the ancestors of the region's wealthiest tycoon. But this would not happen. "*Laoban* doesn't want to change their tombstones", a family friend explained, "he doesn't want to risk disturbing the *fengshui*."[3]

DEATH OF THE PATRON

Belief in the supernatural or in things that cannot be fully explained in the rational world — this was what Liem was accustomed to and grew up with. He and Suharto believed in mysticism. Why risk angering the spirits; why tempt fate? There is a widely-held Javanese belief that says when two people are very close, after one of them dies, the other may soon follow.[4] Thus when Suharto died at age eighty-six, on the afternoon of 27 January 2008, Liem was not told about it. Aware of the Javanese saying, Liem's family deliberately kept the news from him. (Liem would outlive his patron by nearly four and a half years.) For weeks before his death, Suharto laid gravely ill in Jakarta's Pertamina Hospital. Since mysticism was so entrenched in Suharto's background, the rumour mill in Jakarta was abuzz with speculation that magic needles called *susuk*, said to ensure power and longevity — believed to have been implanted in the strongman's body long ago by a *dukun* or Javanese mystic — must have remained inside the ex-president. People who had such *susuk* implanted needed to get them removed by the same *dukun* if they wanted those powers to end. In Suharto's case, it was said, the *dukun* had died years earlier.

Suharto's death sparked a host of commentaries on his life and legacy. Journalists, politicians and observers, both foreign and domestic, weighed in on the good, the bad and the ugly of the Suharto presidency. As befitting his controversial legacy, obituaries proffered diverse views of the autocrat — some defending him as a nation-builder, others decrying a greedy despot. Former Australian Prime Minister Paul Keating mourned him as a friend and viewed him a white knight who saved Indonesia from economic ruin.[5] Other headlines summarized opposing sentiments: "Exit Suharto: Obituary for a mediocre tyrant" was one that accompanied Cornell University academic Benedict Anderson's piece in the *New Left Review*; and "Poor man, rich man, thief" headlined journalist David Jenkins' contribution in the *Sydney Morning Herald*. Anderson, who had been banned by Suharto from Indonesia in 1973 for expressing views on the 1965 abortive coup which were contrary to the government's, was understandably critical. By the end of Suharto's tenure, he noted, "bitter local wits" had changed the president's title Bapak Pembangunan (Father of Development) to Bapak Pembangkrutan (Father of Bankruptcy).[6] Both Anderson and German-born naturalized Indonesian Jesuit priest Franz Magnis-Suseno recalled Suharto's offer — widely received as insincere — to step down in October 1997 if people no longer wanted him. Using an expression from the Javanese *wayang*, Suharto had said he was prepared to *lengser keprabon ngadeg pandita* — which translates to abdicating his throne and becoming a sage (and give advice to his "children", which could mean Indonesians in general).[7] But then, Suharto was assured by his toadies that the populace still clamoured for his leadership, and he went on to accept the MPR nomination for his seventh five-year term in March 1998. Suharto's "proclamation" that he was ready to make way for someone else was nothing new. It was typically Javanese — not to be seen craving the position, but stepping up to the plate at "popular behest". It was a routine repeated every election cycle since 1988 (the year he fired his staunchest supporter in the armed forces, ABRI commander Gen. Benny Murdani).

The journalist David Jenkins, author of the 1984 work *Suharto and his Generals* and widely regarded as an astute observer of Indonesian politics, noted in his piece that the country's second president gave Indonesia a second chance after the political, economic and social chaos of the Sukarno years. His obituary credited Suharto with bringing major social benefits and growing the economy at an average annual rate of 7.5 per cent over the thirty years to 1998 despite corruption and mismanagement. Suharto's New Order period, he noted, gave the country new roads, health centres, schools, universities, harbours, airports and factories. "Suharto transformed Indonesia, building a modern economy on the ruins left by his predecessor, improving the lives of tens of millions of people. For that, he deserves much praise." But all this was done, Jenkins pointed out, against a backdrop of violence, excesses and abuses exacted on the population in consolidating his grip on power.[8]

In his later years, Suharto's indulgence of his children — the principal beneficiaries of his cronyism when they came of age in the mid-1980s — grated even long-time supporters, including some in the top echelon in the military. Theodore Friend noted in his book *Indonesian Destinies* that as the president grew more powerful, he "increasingly used the Javanese maxim *tut wuri andayani,* suggesting he was the all-seeing parent guiding children in learning how to walk".[9] Friend pointed out that between 1988 and 1996, when World Bank estimated that Indonesia received more than US$130 billion in foreign investment, was the time of "the most intense politico-entrepreneurial activity of the six Suharto children".[10] Many political observers agree that had Suharto stepped down earlier, his legacy could have been a good one — he would have been remembered more for his accomplishments in lifting the country out of dire poverty than for the egregious favours dished out to his family. Some speculated that he might have felt he had to remain in the post to ensure his children's business opportunities could be enhanced. The president bristled at murmured criticisms that his progeny and family members — brother, cousin, in-laws — were receiving too many favours from the government. He viewed it as an entitlement. Bustanil Arifin once told reporters that on one occasion, Suharto said to him: "If my children cannot run a business because I am president, then it would be better that I not be president."[11] Suharto's half-brother Probosutedjo claimed the president never gave his family special treatment, but said that "our success is due to Pak Harto's position and our hard work". Probo added that his success was due to his half-brother's *sawab* — meaning "good fortune" in Javanese — "but that *sawab* didn't include getting government favours".[12]

Still, Suharto's brazen indulgence of his children whittled support for his regime, and with time, he alienated many in the armed forces as well as his senior advisors. He grew more confident and more "sultanistic", as Edward Aspinall put it, until towards the end of the New Order he was visibly ageing, ailing, and "increasingly more remote from his subordinates, and beyond challenge".[13] Wrote Aspinall:

> The internal sultanistic element in the regime was most obvious in the role of the first family, whose business interests were promoted with increasing disregard for legal nicety or public sensitivity. Bizarre schemes were devised to increase the family fortune, and the president increasingly openly intervened on his children's behalf. Their greed was far outstripping that of other elite families. [Suharto's] children also acquired growing political influence.

The wealth of Suharto's family will long be debated. Transparency International alleged in 2004 that it had embezzled between US$15 billion and US$35 billion during Suharto's thirty-two-year presidency.[14] In 1999, *Time* estimated the total at US$15 billion, which prompted Suharto to sue the magazine in Jakarta.[15] Start-and-stop efforts by post-Suharto governments to find and retrieve Suharto money concentrated on the dozens of so-called charitable foundations, or *yayasan*, linked to his family. When prosecutors filed corruption charges against Suharto for misuse of state funds by foundations, the Supreme Court ruled that he was too ill to go on trial. The indictment for those charges stated that some foundations — including some chaired by Suharto — had received state money; in 1978, for instance, a Finance Ministry decree ordered the central bank and state banks to pay 2.5 per cent of the net profits to Supersemar, the first *yayasan* Suharto set up after he became president. It was established in May 1974, after the Malari incident, with the goal of giving scholarships to bright but needy students. The indictment also said recipients of foundation largesse included son Tommy's failed Sempati Air, getting Rp17.91 billion from Dakab foundation (seen as a Golkar money machine) and Rp13.17 billion from Supersemar, while nearly Rp450 billion went from Damandiri foundation, meant to help alleviate poverty, went to two banks partly owned by Suharto's son Bambang.[16] It was also found that the Trikora foundation, set up in 1963 to give scholarships to children of soldiers killed in the campaign to wrest Papua from the Dutch, gave Rp3.5 billion to a museum located at Taman Mini built to "commemorate Suharto's lifetime achievements". Called Purna Bhakti Pertiwi (the Sanskrit-based name means "perfect service given to the motherland"), the museum took five years to complete and was opened in time for Tien Suharto's seventieth birthday in 1993. The US$19 million structure housed gifts and expensive *objets d'arts* given to the president over the years.[17]

In 2008, the South Jakarta District Court found Supersemar guilty of using part of the donor funds to finance businesses of Suharto's cronies and children, and in 2010 the Supreme Court ordered the foundation to pay Rp3.7 trillion — which at the end of 2013 had not been paid.[18] Much of the money acquired by many of Suharto's *yayasans* had been milked from the president's cronies, of whom Liem was one of the primary sources. Naturally, the *cukong* viewed his patron from a very different perspective. Asked about what he thought of Suharto, Liem replied that he regarded the president "like family"; saying "we were extraordinarily close".[19] Quite a few people would not share Liem's opinion of the general whose icy stare could intimidate the severest general, as the *cukong* described his patron as "a nice and caring person" devoted to bringing development to his people. "He has *gan qing*" [feelings], Liem said.[20] His view is echoed by Suharto's authorized biographer, who wrote: "Once he [Suharto] comes to know and trusts someone, he emerges as an open and warm person."[21]

The regional leader who best knew the strongman was Lee Kuan Yew, long-time leader of Singapore, who was prime minister from 1959 until 1990. Lee developed a close bond with the Indonesian leader after overcoming a rocky start in their relationship when Suharto was upset that Singapore hanged two Indonesian Marines convicted of placing a bomb that killed three civilians in a Singapore office building in 1965, during Sukarno's *Konfrontasi*. Lee became a firm ally and supporter of Suharto. Two weeks before Suharto died, Lee visited him in hospital. The former president was already on a ventilator and showing signs of multiple organ failure. Lee emerged from the hospital visibly saddened, and told reporters he was "dismayed" that the former general was "reaching the end of his life without being given full dues for his instrumental role in Indonesia's development". He pointed out that many people did not recall that it was "Mr Suharto who had pulled Indonesia from the brink of disaster 40 years ago and put the fledgling nation onto the gradual path to prosperity."[22] He added:

He [Suharto] gave Indonesia progress and development. He educated the population. He built roads and infrastructure. And from (Indonesia's first president) Sukarno's *Konfrontasi* and other foreign policy excesses, he stabilised international relations, cooperated with ASEAN, made ASEAN more successful than SAARC (the South Asian Association for Regional Cooperation) ... Today, we have a stable South-east Asia. So I want to pay this tribute to him and I came here. Yes, he gave favours to his family and his friends, but there was real growth, real progress. One had only to compare the starkly different fates of Myanmar and Indonesia to realize how much Mr Suharto had done for his country.

As for the rampant corruption associated with the New Order, Lee had this to say:

At the same time in the 1960s, Burma had the same coup with General Ne Win taking over. He did not have this team of economists. He did it his own way ... Compare. Who's better off? Who deserves to be honoured? What's a few billion dollars lost in bad excesses? He built hundreds of billions of dollars' worth of assets.[23]

In his declining days, Suharto shunned those whom he felt betrayed him. One prominent person who got the cold shoulder was his former protégé Habibie, his last Vice-President who was once so close they were like father and son. Some observers speculated that Suharto had expected Habibie to also tender his resignation on 21 May 1998. Instead, he was sworn in to succeed his mentor. The ex-president was said to have been particularly riled when Habibie failed to quash investigations into the wealth of the Cendana family. Abdurrahman Wahid, who succeeded Habibie as president, said he believed Suharto was adamant he had done nothing wrong, "nothing for which he should apologize or seek forgiveness".[24] Instead, the former strongman continued to blame others for bringing the country to its knees. Fuad Bawazier, his last Finance Minister, wrote that Suharto believed his own economic team destroyed the economy, singling out two individuals — a former Finance Minister and a Bank Indonesia Governor. Bawazier cited Suharto's insistence that a currency board system (promoted by his children) could have saved Indonesia, but was convinced otherwise by his economic team.[25]

Due to declining health (he suffered several strokes in the nearly ten years between his downfall and his death), Suharto never once entered a courtroom despite the attempts to prosecute him. In the months that followed his resignation, Suharto must have been reeling from the rapid unfolding of events and shell-shocked by his abandonment by his coterie of loyal supporters. Suharto's isolation perhaps prompted him to reach out to a once-close aide that the leader had cut links with — Gen. Benny Murdani. In an account related by Jusuf Wanandi, Suharto asked why he had not heard from Murdani, the former ABRI chief who was once one of his staunchest military backers but whom he fired in 1988. Murdani noticeably had kept silent in the years following his abrupt ouster from his powerful post. In December 1998, Tutut arranged for the once-feared general to visit her father. Suharto, wrote Wanandi, had only one question to ask of his former henchman: "Ben, how could this happen?" And Murdani spent the next hour and a half releasing his pent-up frustration, saying in effect: "You didn't trust us [meaning ABRI]. We were the base of your power, but in the end, you didn't trust us, and instead you trusted Habibie and ICMI…[when] actually we were very supportive of you. And loyal."[26]

The fall of Suharto was sudden and unexpected: three years after being named the most powerful man in Asia by *Asiaweek* in 1996, Suharto presented a very different picture to the public; as biographer R.E. Elson wrote, the former leader appeared "sunken and sallow of face … his political achievements destroyed, his economic triumphs maligned, and the object of hatred and derision by his own people."[27]

WINDING DOWN

During Liem's Singapore years, there were two big social events that the family hosted at the Shangri-La Hotel, owned by old friend Robert Kuok, marking significant milestones in Liem's life. One was his sixtieth wedding anniversary in 2004, celebrated with a two-day bash, and the other was for his ninetieth birthday in September 2005, also marked on two consecutive nights to accommodate the number of guests. On that occasion, the stage was decorated to resemble imperial China, and Liem rode into the grand ballroom in a trishaw, to thunderous applause. The event featured one of his favourite singers, Singapore's Kit Chan, who serenaded the audience with some of the late Teresa Teng's hits, including the popular "Moonlight represents my heart", Liem's personal favourite. Liem read a message thanking guests for their friendship and help. As a souvenir, guests were given a 5-gram gold bar with the inscription of the Chinese character for longevity "*shou*" and his name, in Chinese characters as well as Soedono Salim on one side, and the Salim corporate logo on the other.

It was in 2006 and 2007 that Liem conversed with the authors. Much of the time, he was in good humour. Although he had lost his vision, his hearing was good. He walked with assistance, but spent much of the time in a wheelchair. He greeted visitors with a firm handshake. He still enjoyed good food and perked up when talking about his past. Told of a co-author's visit to Kudus, the central Java town where he first got started in business, he smiled broadly and asked if the *soto* was still good, and whether she had a chance to ride in a *becak*. On a few occasions, though, Liem appeared to be in a somewhat sour mood. He would be reticent and withdrawn, complaining about how his rest the night before had been disturbed by spirits. The night visitations so bothered him, he insisted that his male nurses, and sometimes, a nephew, sleep in his room, to act as "ghostbusters" when needed.

Much of the time the ageing tycoon preferred to avoid subjects that made him unhappy, such as how Salim Group had teetered on the brink of collapse, and how some people deserted him in those dark days. Asked how he felt when his house was targeted by rioters in May 1998, Liem professed not to hold any grudges against the perpetrators. However, he did not want the badly damaged house to be fixed up, so it would be testimony to those sad events that drove him out of the country he felt he had a role in building. (Eight years after the riots, the burnt cars still sat in the garage, and the charred walls had not been repainted. More recently, the cars were cleared so it didn't look too much like a junkyard.) He preferred to recall the happier times he had in Indonesia, which he maintained, had been good to him, as it offered great business opportunities. For making money, he commented, Indonesia was "Number 1".[28] Despite his enormous wealth, Liem tried to abide by his parents' motto — to be humble and helpful. His donations to charities and organizations were not highly publicized. Loyalty mattered to Liem — he said he respected the ousted general Benny Murdani who never publicly said a bad word about his former boss. Friends may have abandoned him as well as his protector, but Liem stayed loyal to Suharto to the end. He recalled a visit to Cendana in late 2006, one of the last times he saw the ex-president: "We said goodbye at the door", Liem said, "and Pak Harto cried".[29]

Notes

1. Meaning "Overseas Chinese".
2. Interview with Qiu Yuqing, Fuqing, 10 February 2006.
3. Private conversation in Fuqing, February 2006.
4. Mari Elka Pangestu, for seven years Trade Minister in President Susilo Bambang Yudhoyono's cabinet, recounted that her father, the respected economist

J. Panglaykim, passed away very soon after the death in 1986 of his close friend, Maj. Gen. Sudjono Humardani, Suharto's close advisor and Javanese mystic. Although Panglaykim was a Chinese and a Catholic, he had a strong bond with Sudjono. Both were involved in the think-tank, CSIS. According to Mari Pangestu, her father had breakfast almost every day with Sudjono and the two men enjoyed many deep and wide-ranging conversations.

5. Paul Keating, "Soeharto's unsung legacy", *The Age*, 2 February 2008.

6. Ben Anderson, "Exit Suharto", *New Left Review*, Mar–Apr 2008.

7. Ibid., and see also Franz Magnis-Suseno, "*Lengser keprabon*: New Order leadership, Javanese culture, and the prospects for democracy in Indonesia", in *Post-Soeharto Indonesia: Renewal or Chaos?*, edited by Geoff Forrester (Singapore: Institute of Southeast Asian Studies, with Australian National University Research School of Pacific and Asian Studies, 1999), p. 214. Just before Suharto resigned, political commentator Wimar Witoelar, who later became presidential spokesman for Abdurrahman Wahid, remarked that it was better for Suharto to retire and "be a *pandito*' [variation of *pandita*] instead of being a 'bandito'". "Swift on His Feet, Wimar the Satirist Needles Suharto — Not Directly, That's Risky, But Indonesian Audiences Get the Point of the Barbs", by Peter Waldman, *Wall Street Journal*, 12 May 1998.

8. David Jenkins, "Poor Man, Rich Man, Thief", *Sydney Morning Herald*, 29 January 2008.

9. Theodore Friend, *Indonesian Destinies* (Cambridge, Mass.: Belknap Press of Harvard University, 2003), p. 253.

10. Ibid., p. 251.

11. In "Suharto di-antara sahabat" [Suharto: among his friends], excerpted in *Editor*, 15 June 1991, and reported in *Straits Times*, 21 June 1991 by Paul Jacob.

12. Steven Jones and Raphael Pura, "All in the family", *Wall Street Journal*, 24 November 1986.

13. Edward Aspinall, *Opposing Suharto: Compromise, Resistance, and Regime Change in Indonesia* (Stanford: Stanford University Press, 2005), p. 205.

14. Transparency International, The Global Corruption Report 2004 <http://www.transparency.org/research/gcr/gcr_political_corruption>.

15. In April 2009, Indonesia's Supreme Court overturned a lower court ruling that had found *Time* guilty of libelling Suharto and had awarded him Rp1 trillion in damages.

16. "Suharto's funds: where money came from, where they went", *Kyodo News*, 30 August 2000.

17. Margot Cohen, "Have a walk through Indonesia's wedding album", *AWSJ*, 8–9 October 1993.

18. Erwin C. Sihombing, "Attorney General Compiles Inventory of Supersemar Foundation Assets", *The Jakarta Globe*, 10 June 2013.

19. Interview with Liem, 29 April 2006.

20. Interview with Liem, 13 March 2007.

21. Retnowati Abdulgani-Knapp, *Soeharto: The Life and Legacy, Indonesia's Second President* (Singapore: Marshall Cavendish, 2007) pp. 336–37.

22. Laurel Teo, "Suharto deserves full glory, says MM Lee", *Business Times*, 14 January 2008.

23. Ibid.

24. R.E. Elson, *Suharto: A Political Biography* (Cambridge: Cambridge University Press, 2001), p. 295, citing *Detik*.

25. "Suharto's two sides", Special report in *Tempo*, 29 January–4 February 2008.

26. Jusuf Wanandi, *Shades of Grey: A Political Memoir of Modern Indonesia, 1965–1998* (Jakarta: Equinox, 2012), pp. 279–80. ICMI stood for the Association of Indonesian Muslim Intellectuals.

27. Elson, *Suharto*, p. 297.

28. Interview with Liem, 3 June 2006.

29. Interview with Liem, 18 November 2006.

22

END OF AN ERA

FAREWELL TO A TYCOON

Liem died on 10 June 2012 at Raffles Hospital in Singapore, just short of his ninety-fifth birthday.[1] By the Chinese lunar calendar, it was the twenty-first day of the fourth leap month; a date that some considered coincidental as the figure 21 had always been special for the tycoon. Liem was buried at the Choa Chu Kang Cemetery in Singapore on 18 June, a date chosen by Buddhist monks. Despite the fact that he regarded Indonesia, where he lived for sixty years, as home, it was decided that the island state was the most appropriate place to hold his funeral and burial at this time. The long-term plan was to have his remains eventually moved to Java where he and his wife, who in June 2012 was too frail to travel, would eventually be buried. (A burial plot in land-scarce Singapore is only guaranteed for fifteen years, with the government exhuming multiple cemeteries to make way for development.)

Liem's death sparked a send-off rarely seen in Singapore for a non-political figure. A parade of people from all over the region attended his week-long wake. The demand for wreaths was so great there was a shortage of fresh flowers in the country for a few days. Friends and business associates flooded Indonesian and Singapore newspapers with condolence announcements. First Pacific issued a statement on the death of its long-time chairman, noting that while retired from active involvement, Liem "stood at the peak of a long and distinguished career... His career culminated in the unofficial title, Indonesia's first industrialist."[2]

At the wake, air-conditioned tents were set up, and the Mandarin Orchard Singapore hotel, controlled by Mochtar Riady's Lippo Group, provided five-star catering for guests. Mourners covered the myriad of people whose lives had been touched by the *cukong*, including politicians, industrialists, businessmen, fellow clansmen and schoolchildren — beneficiaries of his philanthropy.[3] Visitors from Indonesia included former President Megawati Sukarnoputri, whose family ties with Liem began with her grandfather Hasan Din, as well as Suharto's two youngest daughters, Titiek and Mamiek — the two among the six Suharto progeny that Liem once told the authors he felt the most affinity with. Titiek's ex-husband, 2014 presidential aspirant Prabowo Subianto (whose late father as Trade Minister in the early New Order was sometimes a thorn in Salim's flesh), was also among those who turned up at the Mount Vernon funeral hall. Tourism and Creative Economy Minister Mari Pangestu, one of a few Chinese Indonesians to serve in a Cabinet, also paid her respects. She described Liem as the pioneer in private sector entrepreneurship and business in Indonesia. "He was there right at the start of Indonesia's economic development in the late 1960s and 1970s, at a time when Indonesia needed to start the industrialization process and the food supply business," she was quoted as saying.[4]

Many tributes were read during the funeral. Representing the Salim group's more than 200,000 strong staff (and "more than one million indirect workers") in Indonesia was Daddy Hariadi, a long-time executive. Starting his eulogy with a few lines from Wordsworth's famous ode "Intimations of immortality", Hariadi described his late boss as a "visionary" and a "great leader who was compassionate and who smiled very often". He praised Liem as a down-to-earth person who never sought recognition but yet had given "a great contribution to Indonesia's economic development".[5] Manny Pangilinan, CEO and managing director of First Pacific, spoke on behalf of the group's overseas staff. He offered this salute:

> In retirement, we saw a man with the gentleness and dignity of a quintessential Mandarin.... he believed in discipline and determination. He believed in loyalty to the company and his friends. He believed in serving Indonesia by building the iron need to start its industrialization.

> Oom Liem carried himself, even at the height of his power, with attention to small kindnesses. He was gentle and considerate — slow to anger, not inclined to slight or embarrass others. He was a people person. In business, strong passions are the norm. He was a strong man. He was shrewd. He was decisive. I have seen him make decisions that could determine the fortunes of a business. Those were his finest hours.[6]

Effusive eulogies came from China, especially the contingent from Liem's native province of Fujian, who viewed the late tycoon as the epitome of the ideal emigrant. Not only did a villager become wildly wealthy in his new country — beyond most dreams — he also always held his ancestral roots close to his heart and continued to contribute and invest in his "homeland". In life, unreserved tributes from China might have become fodder for Salim critics in Indonesia, but at Liem's death, the extent of appreciation showered on him was fulsome. A eulogy read by He Yafei, Deputy Director of the State Council's Overseas Chinese Affairs Office said, in part:

> Mr Liem Sioe Liong was a man of diligence and industriousness who carved out a spectacular career in business with extraordinary courage and talent and made outstanding contributions to economic growth and social development in Indonesia. He actively protected legitimate interests of the ethnic Chinese population, helped Indonesian Chinese to integrate socially, full heartedly facilitated the friendship between China and Indonesia and played a key role in boosting bilateral economic and trading relations, which earned him great respect in Indonesia and people in the Chinese community. Mr Liem cared about and participated in the economic development and public welfare causes such as education and charity work in the country of his birth and hometown, where he is much loved and highly admired.[7]

Two former mayors from Fuqing and Fuzhou, Lian Zhixuan and Song Kening,[8] enumerated the extensive contributions made by Liem in an essay published by the Liem family in conjunction with a Fuqing association. "Vast sums" had been poured in over the years, earmarked for schools and infrastructure, including RMB20 million in 1991 to build the Yuanzai Bridge. As far back as September 1986, before diplomatic relations were restored between China and Indonesia, Liem and his partner Djuhar Sutanto "contributed jointly to the construction of the first modern highway in Fuqing — a 7-kilometre concrete road that stretches from the city to Honglu. To ensure that future generations will always remember their hometown, Mr Liem and Mr Djuhar named this road 'Yuanhong (元洪) Road', deriving the Chinese characters from the middle character of their respective fathers' names," the officials noted. They wrote:

> The people of Fuqing love Mr Liem Sioe Liong not because he was a world-class character or one of the world's richest, but more because he was a flag and symbol of the Fuqing character — one that represents the ability to withstand hardship, courage to fight, and dedication of the majority of overseas folks who have become rich but not forgotten their homeland.

Another ardent admirer of Liem's was former mayor of Fuqing, Qiu Yuqing, whose ties with "*laoban*" dated to the 1980s. He recounted that in 1991 Xi Jinping — later Communist Party chief and China's President — "personally led a delegation" to Jakarta to discuss with Liem about developing a 50 square kilometre tract of land into an industrial park. Diplomatic ties between the two countries had just been restored the year before. Xi, at the time a standing member of Fujian Provincial Communist Party Committee as well as Fuzhou Municipal Communist Party Committee secretary, developed a cordial relationship with Liem. Their 1991 discussion led to the development of the Yuanhong Investment Zone in Fuqing, again named after the fathers of Liem and Djuhar. Qiu's tribute detailed Liem's role in the development of Fuqing:

> Mr Liem's fine example by action ignited the unwavering passion of Fuqing clansmen around the world to care for, love and develop their hometown. They have invested and set up factories, industries and welfare facilities in their hometown with great enthusiasm. Having made the largest donation to hometown in terms of monetary value, number of projects, scope and span of donation to the hometown, Mr Liem is undoubtedly the most significant figure in the history of contribution among overseas Chinese originated from Fuqing. Incomplete statistics indicate that Mr Liem donated more than RMB430 million to his hometown to build road, bridge, water conservancy facility, school, hospital and cultural projects and to help alleviate poverty.... A man of great kindness, Mr Liem Sioe Liong donated for the betterment of hometown continuously for over thirty years since his first donation arrived in 1979.[9]

Tributes were more muted in Indonesia, but the sentiments of Liem's fellow Hokchia clansmen were reflected in a remembrance piece by Didi Dawis, as recounted by a reporter. Dawis, president of the Indonesia Jakarta Fuqing Association, hailed the indomitable fighting spirit of the man he called his mentor. He recalled his first meeting with Liem, which was in 1980. The tycoon encouraged him to follow his conscience. "Do not worry about what others may say or be afraid that they may defame you as only man proposes and only heaven disposes", Dawis quoted Liem as saying. The tycoon had to bear the brunt of diatribes over the years due to his close association with Suharto, but has learnt to deal with adversity calmly. Liem's unflappable demeanour was helped by the maxim he held to: "It is not possible for a snake to transform into a dragon. It would remain a snake after it has molted. I do not mind if others speak ill of me. Genuine gold is not afraid of being heated."[10]

There were two commentaries published in the *Jakarta Post* after the tycoon's passing, which captured Liem's character and his contribution to Indonesia. One was written by Jusuf Wanandi, who together with his brother Sofyan, had a long relationship with the *cukong*. Wrote Jusuf:

> He has always been pro-Indonesia, although he never forgot that he was of Chinese origin and was born in China. He knew his bread was buttered in Indonesia and he adopted it as his new "motherland". More than that, he got his luck in Indonesia and became the greatest among Indonesian entrepreneurs. Of course, he received help from President Suharto like other tycoons did — the "robber barons" of their time. But it has been widely acknowledged that Uncle Liem managed to turn all those given facilities and privileges into real economic and business entities and corporations that not only survived the Suharto regime change, but even thrived and developed regionally and globally.

Liem's greatest achievement, according to Jusuf, was his willingness to lead a group of conglomerate bosses to found Prasetiya Mulya Management School in 1982, which "opened up opportunities for both indigenous residents and Chinese Indonesians to study together". (Jusuf was school chairman in 2012.) Since its inception, the school has produced nearly 4,000 MBAs. Jusuf described the man widely considered the "godfather" of the Chinese *cukongs* as "an extraordinary character... He was a giant with a big heart: humble and generous."[11] Endy Bayuni, former editor-in-chief at the *Jakarta Post*, commented: "For good or for bad, Liem is very much part of the nation's history, just as Suharto is." He concluded:

> The real test of the resilience of the Salim Group came after it lost all privileges, including access to power, with the departure of Suharto. Now in the hands of the second and third generations of the family,

the Salim Group may no longer be the wealthiest family business in the country, but its Indofood is still one of the largest and most profitable producers of food products in the country... It is probably a moot point to ask whether Liem would have prospered as much without the special relationship he had with Suharto. He just happened to be the right man, at the right place and at the right time, and used this historical destiny well in building his business empire.[12]

A LUCKY MAN

Bayuni's assessment hit the nail on the head. Liem himself once acknowledged: "I am lucky. They say that if you are not lucky, whether you are clever, a professor, nothing will become of you. I worked and I grew. If I were in Africa, the Middle East, how could I work? Time, place, and good luck ... these things cannot be dodged."[13] This belief in the element of luck playing a central role in business endeavours is generally shared by many Chinese tycoons through the ages. Many of them consult *feng shui* masters to pinpoint auspicious times or the positioning of their buildings. Another well-known Indonesian Chinese tycoon, arguably the country's first industrialist, was Oei Tiong Ham (1866–1924), who lived in the Dutch colonial era. He, too, was a big believer in luck. The legendary sugar king, as he was often referred to, took over his father's company, Kian Gwan (later loosely called the Oei Tiong Ham Concern), and launched a sprawling business enterprise, that succeeded in beating well-established Dutch companies at their own game.[14] Though generations apart, comparisons have inevitably been made between Liem and Oei. The Semarang-based Oei operated without the political patronage that Liem enjoyed, but he was wise not to antagonize Dutch officials, and kept them plied with expensive gifts and food.

Oei and Liem were considered outstanding entrepreneurs of their time. Although both men emphasized traditional family values, they were open to new ideas. Oei in the nineteenth century forsook his father's conservative traditional management practice and, unheard of in those days, abandoned the Chinese reluctance to sign written contracts. He insisted on documenting business deals (using the best Dutch lawyers in the Dutch East Indies) and was not shy to take legal action for infractions. He came to own several sugar mills that way. Both tycoons relied on their instincts to judge character. (Liem believed in physiognomy — he could tell, he claimed, by looking at someone's face, whether the person could be trusted or not.) And Oei, like Liem, believed that without luck, one could not get very far. In a 1943 autobiography, his daughter Oei Hui Lan, who married renowned Nationalist Chinese diplomat Wellington Koo, wrote about her father:

> He was always alert for new ventures in which to invest his money and he had a remarkable flair for choosing brilliant up-and-coming associates. He believed in "hunches" and played them for all they were worth. He stressed luck and often told me that if he were given the choice between a dozen intelligent men and one lucky man he would take the lucky one every time.[15]

Liem, who became Suharto's *cukong extraordinaire,* was the Indonesian leader's go-to guy, especially in the formative years of the New Order when the president favoured import-substitution policies. Perhaps Suharto was just as lucky to have Liem, who supported him unquestioningly. Having Liem as a pillar was a big asset for the strongman. As the late Australian academic Jamie Mackie, a keen observer of Indonesian developments, concluded: "Suharto was very lucky to have a man of Liem's calibre at his right hand — sure, he was a rent-taker and crony, but he built an empire."[16]

CONTRIBUTIONS

Liem could be called the capable crony. Charming in manner, he was personable and generous — qualities that enabled him to get on with nearly all of Suharto's family, generals and top bureaucrats. He was capable of seeing the larger picture and did not begrudge others their perceived "dues". Liem brushed off criticisms that cronies helped perpetuate the corruption endemic in the New Order. His role was as a participant in the "favours-for-favours" situation. Besides, he was not unfamiliar with cronyism, connections and corruption, which existed in Chinese society since time immemorial. It was no different under the communists. Likewise, nepotism and pay-offs are common in Indonesia, so the mutual back-scratching was not limited to Suharto era politics. Writing about the culture of returning favours, an academic, citing a Harvard professor, described it as a cultural norm of "*pao*" (reciprocity); "the term *pao* has a wide range of meanings, that which is most relevant to social relations in China is 'response' or 'return'."

> The Chinese believe that reciprocity of actions (favour and hatred,
> reward and punishment) between man and man, and indeed men and
> supernatural beings, should be as certain as a cause and effect relationship,
> and therefore, when a Chinese acts, he normally anticipates a response
> or return. Favours done for others are often considered what may be
> termed "social investments", for which handsome returns are expected
> … In China the principle is marked by its long history, the high degree of
> consciousness of its existence, and its wide application and tremendous
> influence in social institution.[17]

When Suharto thought Liem was suitable to work with, the Chinese
businessman confidently told the general he could muster the financial
backing to help achieve his development goals. Of course, Suharto helped
make sure the ventures, whether they were the early import monopolies
(such as cloves) or wheat milling, were profitable. A strongman such as
Suharto was going to tap and lean on favoured, cosseted business partners
who gave major financial support without posing any political threat.
Suharto skillfully used Chinese businessmen like Liem as he did not trust
their *pribumi* counterparts, who might use accumulated wealth to build
a political base. Liem posed zero potential threat as the Chinese were
excluded from politics in the New Order. An academic once noted the
political vulnerability of the Chinese "offered fertile soil for pre-contractual,
semi-institutional patron-client arrangements between the political elite,
backed by state power and their Chinese clients".[18]

Rizal Ramli, who as a *Reformasi* era minister thwarted some efforts by
Anthony to rebuild the empire, noted later that Salim's size stemmed from
the structure of Suharto's Indonesia. "Liem was at the apex, a godfather",
Ramli asserted. "He supported Suharto and got political maintenance. It
was a win-win game for them, but it created an uncompetitive business
pattern that closed opportunities for others."[19] Given Liem's political
backing, which made him unchallengeable in business, "godfather" was
a fair description.[20] Liem was viewed and treated as the most senior and
respected among the Chinese *cukongs*. He was accessible and many people
turned to him for help. Money was a tool for him, to solve problems and
win friends.

Liem offered both skills and connections. Former senior Salim executive
Judiono Tosin, who thinks enmity towards Salim was rooted in jealousy,
asserted that Liem and his group thrived not just because of "facilities"
from Suharto, but capabilities. "No matter how well connected you are,

you couldn't do it without hard work and smarts", he said.[21] Liem's foremost talent lay in his ability to choose the right partners. Whenever he undertook a business he had scant knowledge or experience in, he would seek out the best and gauge if he could partner them. Liem always maintained that however good a businessman you were, you could not develop to the fullest potential if you did not have the right people working with or for you.

It's a credit to Liem's personality that for the most part, his former partners still had good things to say about him years after they separated. Banker Mochtar Riady maintained high respect after he split from Bank Central Asia. Ciputra, the property magnate who used Liem's capital to develop Jakarta's elite Pondok Indah project, said: "I really admire his spirit ... he has the spirit of Overseas Chinese — to reach for the sky ... not many people have the ideas he had, like Bogasari. He has the vision." To Ciputra, Liem also "possessed the sixth sense; he can see it, read it". The property baron saluted Liem for believing in "win-win, give and take... He's loyal to friends."[22]

Liem's approach to doing business was based on trust, a buzzword for him. Asked by the authors what qualities were important to him, he replied: "In business, you have to be honest; don't lie or cheat. If people are good to me, I'll always remember it. But I don't like it when people are not honest with me. If you are not straightforward, it can be troublesome."[23] He won and retained trust, called *xinyong* in Chinese, a quality highly valued among overseas Chinese businessmen in Southeast Asia. Liem once told an interviewer: "Trust comes first, then capability."[24] Mochtar Riady recalled that Liem took time sizing him up, then he "trusted me 100 per cent, and never interfered".[25] Piet Yap, long-time head at Bogasari, wrote of Liem, "When he says 'we work together', he keeps his word and is loyal to you. He truly is a man of principles."[26] Asked in 1978 about his management philosophy, Liem said it was based on hard work, perseverance, planning and an appreciation of other points of view: "I have a strong management team and they see the opportunities, but choosing the right people and believing in professionalism is my underlying approach. You see, I believe in teamwork and not dictatorship."[27]

Liem was seen by many of his staff as an exemplary, considerate boss. He helped put countless children of employees through school and seldom turned down requests for assistance. He was a big believer in karmic laws — he had reaped the good karma from his ancestors, and he had to do good deeds so his descendants would likewise benefit. As a staunch Buddhist, he contributed to temples in China, Indonesia, Singapore and even the United States. Ego was never a driving force for him. At his funeral, eldest son Albert, flanked by Anthony's daughter Astrid and Andree's son David, read a thank you message in Chinese, Indonesian and English. Of their father and grandfather, they said: "He taught us to be humble, honest, disciplined, diligent, hardworking, also being wise, big-hearted, respecting of others and always keen to learn."[28]

LIEM AND THE CHINESE COMMUNITY

Liem was not universally liked in Indonesia's Chinese community. Naturally, the power that came with being Suharto's No. 1 *cukong* begot respect among some businesspeople, but also jealousy and scorn among others. To some, he was a symbol of the cronyism that was a hallmark of the New Order that contributed to the bad image of a rich Chinese who paid off powerful people in exchange for privileges and protection. In their view, he made the overall community more of a target and a scapegoat in a country with a history of anti-Chinese sentiment and sporadic violence. In the eyes of the critical Chinese, Liem's cozy relationship with Suharto reinforced a stereotype that Indonesian Chinese were rich and corrupt, when in fact many were struggling to make a living. This downtrodden class had no means to contend with the discrimination they faced during the Suharto period — certainly not through any political representation. (Indonesian Chinese — whose identity cards marked them as Chinese — were natural targets for extra payments when seeking services from government offices.) They faulted Liem for not using his position to advance the status of the community while benefitting enormously from his relationship with the president. Liem's insider status with Suharto did not lead to any obvious improvements in the welfare of the Indonesian Chinese community, in this view. Liem did not lobby Suharto to allow celebrations of Chinese New Year nor did he seek the reopening of Chinese-language schools that Suharto's government shut. After blaming the 1965 abortive coup attempt on Beijing, Suharto faced a dilemma in dealing with the "Chinese issue". In 1967, his government urged resident Chinese to change their names to make them more "Indonesian-sounding".

But unbeknown to many, Liem quietly — in line with his mode of operation — made a valuable contribution on the position of the stateless Indonesian Chinese. Many Chinese who were born in China and their born-in-Indonesia children faced major problems obtaining Indonesian citizenship. Unlike many other problems in Indonesia, where solutions could be found by paying sizeable bribes, the issue of the "alien" status of hundreds of thousands of Chinese remained intractable. Not having an official identity card, issued to citizens, meant being unable to own a business, start a company or even attend school. With the ghost of the 1965 abortive coup still lingering, especially after Suharto accused Beijing of backing it, the Indonesian military was opposed to giving ethnic Chinese citizenship. Suharto's ambivalence towards the Chinese was captured by Jusuf Wanandi, who wrote in his 2012 memoir:

> We remained discriminated against in many fields, from education to employment. We were never really well assimilated. This, I think, was in large part because of the attitude from the top. Suharto, A.H. Nasution and other top military brass never recognized the contribution of the ethnic Chinese. Suharto made use of us. He used businessmen like Liem Sioe Liong to get money. He asked the cronies to help his family with business. He asked for our support on political issues. But he would never recognize us ... if the Chinese were attacked [Suharto] never said anything; it was only Benny [Murdani] and Pak Ali [Murtopo] who came out and condemned such incidents. It wasn't racism; his closest friends and cronies were all Chinese.... he used them but did not want to acknowledge that because it could become a political liability for him...
> It was sadly fitting that the New Order should later collapse amid the rubble of anti-Chinese riots. We were treated as minor wives, enjoyed but not recognized.[29]

Indonesia's Chinese community did not have a single leader, but as commerce was the main activity open to it — careers in the civil service, military and government were for *pribumi* — it is natural that many saw the biggest businessman as its de facto leader. Liem always wanted a low profile, but he was under scrutiny whether he stayed out of the media or not. Occasionally, the spotlight was turned on him because he was active in the Prasetiya Mulya Foundation.[30] Sofyan Wanandi, also a Prasetiya Mulya founder, rejects the common notion that Liem rendered little assistance to Indonesia's Chinese. "Liem did a lot for the community, especially for the Totok (those born in China)", said Sofyan, asserting that at least 500,000 stateless Chinese got their Indonesian citizenship because of Liem. The *cukong* worked with Suharto to cut through red tape and political resistance to deal with the stateless Chinese. "He made everything smooth. This is a very big contribution to the Chinese," Sofyan affirmed.[31] Of his father's role in getting Suharto to agree to grant citizenship to the stateless Chinese, Anthony Salim said:

> My father was probably the centrepiece. We have converted (to citizens) almost probably close to 800,000 Chinese who were stateless; it was not an easy job... We tried and tried until he (Suharto) agreed; at the time, we convinced him that these (people) were Indonesians too; we said, "if you would like them to vote... they will be supporters of the government".[32]

Anthony said his father long worked to persuade Suharto that granting citizenship would be the first step to helping them integrate. They would have the legitimacy to stay, he had argued, and get their children educated and growing up as Indonesian citizens. According to Anthony, Liem's work was not limited to persuasion; he also paid for the needed administration work. When it was pointed out that not many people knew of his father's behind-the-scene effort, Anthony replied: "It doesn't matter. Because we did it not to take credit; we did it for the deed." To a comment that some young Indonesian Chinese have a negative impression of his father, whom they associated with cronyism, he shrugged, "Yeah, yeah. It's only about the bad things." He tacitly acknowledged there was no way to dislodge the view that Chinese became a bigger target during the New Order — clearly targeted in the May 1998 riots — because a small group of them became very rich. "We cannot change history", Anthony responded.[33]

DIFFERENT LANDSCAPE

Fifteen years after Suharto's fall amid cries for *reformasi*, many things had changed in Indonesia. It had moved far, from an authoritarian regime to a democratic system, albeit still a fragile and flawed one. The military was removed from parliament. Citizens directly elected a president, and term limits now meant someone could lead a maximum ten years (two five-year terms). Power was no longer concentrated in the presidency. The domestic press was now vibrant and free, and often blasted the performance of the legislature, the president and others. There was an independent body to investigate and prosecute cases of alleged corruption, and eventually its performance gained credibility and public support.

For sure, quite a lot of the "old" Indonesia remained. Corruption remains rampant, and arguably worsened by political decentralization that created new layers of decision-makers away from Jakarta. Chunks of the national bureaucracy remained venal. Also, the legal system remained sorely in need of reform — the court system continued to suffer credibility issues, and implementation of rules stayed weak. In 2010, a report by CLSA Asia-Pacific Markets, done with the Asian Corporate Governance Association in Hong Kong, stated that in Indonesia "judges can almost always be had for a price".[34] In the 2012 edition of the same two groups' "CG Watch" on corporate governance, Indonesia moved back into last place in Asia, a year after it had climbed out of that and above the Philippines.[35]

But there were encouraging developments, including positive changes for the Chinese, which benefitted the community and boosted integration. In 2000 and 2001, while Abdurrahman Wahid was president, long-standing discriminatory rules were scrapped. Public celebration of Chinese New Year including lion dances was permitted. The teaching of Chinese in schools was once again allowed. Imports of Chinese-language publications were no longer banned, and some local television channels have Mandarin programming — unthinkable in Suharto's time.

In 2013, there was not a single, near-dominant businessman such as Liem who was the business pillar to political power. Also, monopolies geared to benefitting Suharto's circle had long been dismantled. Although commodity supply agency Bulog still exists, it no longer controlled a broad sweep of commodities. Economic power, along with political power, was dispersed now, and not dominated by the president. This was a factor in Indonesia's economy in 2011–13 growing close to or above 6 per cent a year — rates not seen since the mid-1990s when Suharto was strong — at a time when the global economy was tepid. More *pribumi*-led conglomerates sprouted in this period, and foreign investors — who faced obstacles like nationalist economic policies — no longer felt compelled to partner with the leader's children and circle. The era of conglomerates is not entirely over but the scene is different because there are more players. Business tycoons, who used to be centralized under Suharto's patronage, are now "liberated, in the sense that they are now more motivated to create their own political networks", political analyst Fachry Ali was quoted as saying in the *Jakarta Post*.[36] "But many Chinese-Indonesian moguls, who enjoyed the 'glorious' New Order years, did not disappear; they merely shifted their methods in influencing power," he said, adding "Their capital posed significant attractions to political groups, which have become increasingly

more diverse today. The richer a political party is, the greater its influence
and ability to gain support."

SALIM'S NEW LIFE

The Chinese have a saying — *fu bu guo san dai*, meaning: wealth doesn't
last more than three generations,[37] and many scions of rich business
dynasties in Asia have sought to prove that wrong. Liem, who was fully
aware of the popular adage, gave opportunities early on for each of his
three sons to have some role in the group's businesses. "If a son just eats
and plays, the wealth will be finished", he once commented.[38] Liem was
wise not to blindly follow the Confucian norm to bestow to the eldest
offspring the responsibilities of leadership. Over the years, he quietly
groomed Anthony, who proved he was the most capable. Anthony picked
up the baton and, in the aftermath of Suharto's fall, lived up to his Chinese
name and managed to save Salim from near-death. Liem saluted his
youngest son's efforts, remarking in 2006: "If not for him, we won't still
be here today."[39] Long before 1998, Anthony acted as Salim's bridge to a
globalized business world. Some observers opined that he made Salim a
bigger target for opponents through pushing for expansion outside the
country. But he also made it possible for the group to survive, a process
aided greatly by having control of Hong Kong-listed First Pacific, which
post-1998 became Indofood's biggest shareholder. Liem stood by his son's
decision, and credited Anthony with having the wisdom and foresight to
move beyond Indonesia's shores. He remarked: "How to succeed, if you use
old-fashioned thinking? Anton is not traditional …"[40] In 1998, Anthony's
job was guiding Salim through uncharted territory, fending off those who
wanted to kill the group and strip its assets. He was not only able to stay
in business in the post-Suharto period, but to thrive.

To some critics, Salim's business trajectory in the *Reformasi* period post-
1998 continued in much the same way as earlier. While Anthony negotiated
with IBRA and protected the core asset of Indofood, Trisakti University
economist Bob Widyahartono opined that Salim "will never change its
business style. The group's dealings will remain as sly as ever."[41] But one-
time vociferous Salim critic Rizal Ramli said of the group: "After the crisis,
they proved they can operate without patronage. It's a credit to Anthony
Salim." He added: "They [now] understand that competition should be
the rule of the game… Of course, the group made a ton of money before,

because of patronage; it (Salim) was the Suharto franchise."[42] Indonesia finance sector analyst Lin Che Wei, who often rapped Salim along with other conglomerates for their business practices, in 2004 said of the group: "To most bankers, Salim's reputation is much better than other conglomerates, and they are willing to lend … I have to admit that the Salims actually know how to build a business and create value."[43]

On his part, Anthony says Salim had moved far from its origins, from "connections to non-connections". Asked his reaction to those who still describe Salim as a crony and heavily dependent on connections for success, Anthony shrugged and remarked:

> It doesn't matter; it's up to people to decide whether Louis Vuitton or Bata are good shoes; we don't care, frankly speaking … Our philosophy is that we probably do more right things than wrong things. And we believe in what we are doing, that's why we are able to survive until today. We've been tested so many times. And today we are thriving better than before, and we adjusted ourselves with the situation. From my father's generation, from my generation … the way we do business is probably much more structured than before.[44]

Forbes Indonesia in 2013 put Anthony as number 3 on its list of the fifty wealthiest Indonesians, with an estimated US$6.3 billion in assets, up from US$5.2 billion the previous year, when he ranked number 4. Occupying top spot, as in the previous year, were brothers Budi and Michael Hartono of *kretek* maker Djarum, who became the main owners of BCA in 2002. *Forbes* estimated the Hartonos' net worth at US$15 billion. However much money Anthony was thought to have, long after Suharto's fall, he had moved into a position that perhaps was the best he ever had. While Salim Group did not have the assets it did in the late Suharto period — with BCA gone, and Indocement under control by others — Anthony could maintain that all his businesses faced competition. Flour is an example of how the group — now really the Anthony Salim Group — was in a tough-to-assail position long after Suharto's exit. Salim was able to remain the dominant miller, but it no longer caught flak for having a monopoly as many others had entered the market. But while there was free entry, no competitor could come anywhere close to Bogasari; Salim had tremendous "first-mover" and economies-of-scale advantages. In instant noodles, new competitors kept Indofood on its toes, another healthy development. In spite of serious competition, especially from the Wings Group, Anthony managed to keep Indofood's market share at more than 70 per cent. "We welcome competition", Anthony asserted, when asked about others giving Indofood a run for its money.[45]

One unanswered question was future leadership for Indofood and Salim. In 2009, Axton, the elder of Anthony's two sons was made an Indofood director and daughter Astrid is also working in the group. Side-stepping queries on whether the reins can be kept in the family, Anthony replied: "They will have to prove themselves."[46] Geographically, Anthony was working on a wider map, regularly travelling to other continents. While he continued to occupy a prominent position in Indonesian business, the Salim name no longer engendered fear. The post-Gang of Four Salim Group is now just another big business group, and not *the* dominant one that was backed directly by political power.

In the past, Anthony liked to suggest that people view the Salim Group as a moving picture, not a snapshot. For a long time after Suharto consolidated power, the picture was unambiguously one of a crony getting ahead through mutual-benefitting opportunities provided by the strongman. In 1991, Anthony defended Salim's development to a journalist this way:

> We don't deny we had good access to capital in the early days. But credit shouldn't just be given to capital formation. The important thing is what happened after that. At the time, there were plenty of other people who had the same access to capital we had, but they didn't manage it properly. Capital is only one thing, but the management is another thing and business vision is another thing... The monopolies that we were granted were like a glass of water that gets the machine going. Admittedly, the first glass of water is the most important, but relative to the size of Salim's revenues today, the [monopoly-derived] revenues are reasonably moderate.[47]

The monopolies and the 1985 bailout in cement were more like a twenty-year supply of water rather than a glass, and it's doubtful that "plenty" of others had the same access to capital. But after that bailout, the Salim Group largely expanded its industrial base without new favours, and grew some businesses helped by its own acumen. The combination of Liem's savvy and Anthony's smarts propelled the group. Although Liem referred to his son as the savior of the conglomerate, Anthony was quick to acknowledge Liem's role:

His contribution is maybe 80 to 90 per cent; mine only 10 per cent ... because I studied [overseas] and had the luxury of understanding the world through my education and language while my father didn't; he started from zero. So 90 per cent is his credit. The foundation was all built by him, not me. I just capitalized on the pillars, the foundation; I try to thrive based on the strength.[48]

In his later years, Liem sometimes fell pensive when asked about his past. In 2007, a few months before his ninetieth birthday, he told the authors that he was successful because things had fallen into place for him: he had been at the right location, at the right time and had the right connections. He added that he tried to abide by the principles he learnt and valued, one of the foremost being to act with integrity.[49] On another occasion, he mulled about his achievements and cited the saying by Mencius, a disciple of Confucius, that there had to be harmony between the weather, terrain (geography) and people (*tian shi di li ren he* 天时地利人和) for success to be ensured. Asked in 2006 if he had any regrets in life, Liem replied, "No. I worked hard. When I was younger, if I saw someone rich, I thought to myself: 'I want to be richer.' But I will be honest. Only now, people understand our intentions were good; heaven knows I was doing the right thing."[50] Asked how he would like to be remembered, the near-nonagenarian smiled and half-jokingly replied: "I want to be remembered as a rich man; without money you are nothing."[51]

Anthony, who shared his father's belief that luck was an important element in business, agreed too that the other factors mentioned by Liem have to fall into place for one to become successful. Indonesia offered the family a "big opportunity". If his father had ended up in Singapore rather than Java, Anthony mused, "maybe he would only have [had] three *becak* [pedicabs]; we don't know."[52]

Notes

1. The family obituary listed his age as 97, based on his officially recorded birth year and the tradition of adding a year when a baby is born.
2. First Pacific statement of 13 June 2012, on <www.firstpacific.com>.
3. Liem was a generous donor to educational institutions. The students at the funeral were from a Singapore school affiliated with the Singapore Futsing (Fuqing) Association, of which Liem was the permanent honorary president. Singapore media noted that Liem donated S$1 million to the school in 2003 and the same amount in 2010.

4. "Tycoon who profited from Suharto links", *Financial Times*, 11 June 2012.
5. Text provided by the Salim Group, and subsequently published in the private publication entitled *Liem Sioe Liong: Memorial Album in Commemoration of the permanent Honorary President of the International Association of Fuqing Clansmen Limited* (Hong Kong: The International Association of Fuqing Clansmen Limited, 2013).
6. Ibid.
7. Ibid.
8. Lian Zhixuan is former secretary of Fuqing Municipal Communist Party Committee, Fuzhou Mayor and Chairman of Fuzhou Municipal People's Congress; Song Kening is identified as Former Fuqing Mayor, secretary of Fuqing Municipal Communist Party Committee and incumbent Director of Foreign Affairs Office of the Fujian Provincial Government. The statements were provided by the Salim family.
9. *Liem Sioe Liong: Memorial Album*, pp. 94–101.
10. Ibid., pp. 68–69.
11. Jusuf Wanandi, "In Memoriam: Uncle Liem Sioe Liong", *Jakarta Post*, 15 June 2012.
12. Endy Bayuni, "Uncle Liem leaves a lasting legacy in Indonesian business", *Jakarta Post*, 12 June 2012.
13. "Om Liem — I say white, you write red", *Bisnis Indonesia*, 24 November 1997.
14. He beat the Dutch heavyweight trading companies of the day, dubbed the Big Five. Two Dutch researchers noted that Kian Gwan had a capital of three million guilders in 1892, rising to no less than 15 million guilders twenty years later — double the capital of then leader of the Big Five trading firms in the Dutch East Indies, Internatio. See Joost Jonker and K. Sluyterman, *At Home on the World Markets: Dutch International Trading Companies from the 16th Century Until the Present* (The Hague: Sdu Uitgevers, 2000), p. 211.
15. Koo Hui Lan, *Madam Wellington Koo: An autobiography, as told to Mary Van Rensselaer Thayer* (New York: Dial Press, 1943), pp. 57–58.
16. Conversation with Jamie Mackie, Singapore, 25 April 2006.
17. Wang Yeu-Farn, "Chinese entrepreneurs in Southeast Asia: Historical roots and modern significance", Stockholm University Centre for Pacific Asia Studies, Working Paper 34, May 1994, citing Lien-Sheng Yang of Harvard University, p. 9.
18. Ibid., p. 8.
19. Interview with Rizal Ramli, Singapore, 11 January 2011.
20. The term "Asian Godfathers" was used by Joe Studwell for his book about business tycoons in Asia. (*Asian Godfathers: Money and Power in Hong Kong and South-East Asia*. London: Profile Books, 2007.)
21. Interview with Judiono Tosin, Jakarta, 22 April 2008.

22. Interview with Ciputra, Jakarta, 19 March 2007.

23. Interview with Liem, 3 June 2006.

24. Fikri Jufri, "Liem buka suara", *Tempo*, 31 March 1984.

25. Interview with Mochtar Riady, Singapore, 24 January 2007.

26. Piet Yap, *Grains of My Life* (Singapore: Privately published, 2010), p. 45.

27. Ian Verchere, "Liem Sioe Liong: Suharto's secret agent", *Insight*, May 1978.

28. Text provided by Liem family, and subsequently published in *Liem Sioe Liong: Memorial Album*.

29. Jusuf Wanandi, *Shades of Grey: A Political Memoir of Modern Indonesia, 1965–1998* (Jakarta: Equinox, 2012), pp. 126–27.

30. In 2009, the foundation named Liem, Astra International founder William Soeryadjaya and Sinar Mas founder Eka Tjipta Widjaja as "honorary lifetime leaders". One of the buildings on the campus was named after Liem.

31. Interview with Sofyan Wanandi, Singapore, 17 September 2006.

32. Interview with Anthony, 22 July 2007.

33. Ibid.

34. Corporate Governance 2010 , from CLSA Asia-Pacific Markets, in collaboration with ACGA, p. 74; accessed at <https://www.clsa.com/assets/files/reports/CLSA-CG-Watch-2010.pdf> on 24 December 2010.

35. <http://www.acga-asia.org/public/files/CG_Watch_2012_ACGA_Market_Rankings.pdf> (accessed on 1 December 2012).

36. Bagus BT Saragih, "Chinese tycoons join politics for survival", *Jakarta Post*, 24 January 2012.

37. The first generation establishes the business; the second generation makes the money; the third generation loses it.

38. Interview with Liem, 23 September 2006.

39. Ibid.

40. Interview with Liem, 23 September 2006.

41. "Born Sly", *Indonesian Business*, 18 September 2000. The magazine later ceased publication; this item as posted on website <http://www.library.ohiou.edu/indopubs/2000/09/18/0012.html> (accessed on 15 September 2011).

42. Interview with Rizal Ramli, 11 January 2011.

43. Michael Vatikiotis, "Tycoon is back, with a hunger Salim rebuilds crumbled empire". *International Herald Tribune*, 20 November 2004.

44. Interview with Anthony, 3 April 2011.

45. Interview with Anthony, 24 June 2007.

46. Ibid.

47. 13 February 1991 interview with Anthony Salim by Adam Schwarz, in Schwarz, *A Nation in Waiting: Indonesia's Search for Stability*, 2nd ed. (St Leonards, NSW: Allen & Unwin, 1999), p. 113.

48. Interview with Anthony, 3 April 2011.

49. Interview with Liem, 13 March 2007.
50. Interview with Liem 23 September 2006.
51. Interview with Liem, 19 August 2006.
52. Interview with Anthony, 3 April 2011.

GLOSSARY AND ABBREVIATIONS

Apkindo	Asosiasi Panel Kayu Lapis Indonesia (Indonesian Plywood Association).
Aspri	Asisten Pribadi; personal assistants to Suharto in the early New Order.
Banpres	Bantuan Presiden (Presidential Assistance Scheme); Banpres money is spent by Suharto himself as he pleased.
Bapepam	Badan Pengawas Pasar Modal (Capital Market Supervisory Agency).
Bappenas	Badan Perencanaan Pembangunan Nasional (National Development Planning Board).
BKPM	Badan Koordinasi Penanaman Modal (Investment Coordinating Board).
BLBI	Bantuan Likuiditas Bank Indonesia (Bank Indonesia Liquidity Support); funds the central bank pumped into commercial banks in the 1997–98 financial crisis.
BPPC	Badan Penyangga dan Pemasaran Cengkeh (Clove Marketing Board); set up in 1990 as part of Tommy Suharto's monopoly on clove sales.
BULOG	Badan Urusan Logistik (National Logistics Agency).
Cendana	the street in Menteng, Jakarta where President Suharto lived; the name became synonymous with the president's family and cronies, as in "the Cendana clique".
CSIS	Centre for Strategic and International Studies.

cukong	term for a Chinese businessman who is protected by a powerful official in return for a share of the profits; taken from Chinese dialect.
desa	village.
DPR	Dewan Perwakilan Rakyat (People's Representative Council).
dukun	traditional healer or seer.
Finek	finance and economic planning divisions in the military.
Golkar	Golongan Karya (Functional Groups); Suharto's main political vehicle.
Hankam	Ministry of Defence.
Hanyu pinyin	romanization of Chinese characters.
Hokchia	people or dialect from the Fuqing area in Fujian province, China.
Holdiko	the company that received and sold assets that the Salim Group pledged to IBRA as part of its 1998 debt settlement contract.
IBRA	Indonesian Bank Restructuring Agency (BPPN in Indonesian).
ICMI	Ikatan Cendekiawan Muslim se-Indonesia (Association of Indonesian Muslim Intellectuals).
IGGI	Inter-Governmental Group on Indonesia; the consortium of international donors set up during the New Order.
Inpres	Instruksi Presiden (Presidential Instruction); funds were channelled through this for development aid.
IPTN	Industri Pesawat Terbang Nusantara (State Aerospace Corporation).
Jamsostek	state-owned insurance company for employees.
Kabupaten	regency or district.
Kadin	Kamar Dagang dan Industri (Chamber of Commerce and Industry); Indonesia's largest business association; enjoys a quasi-corporatist relationship with the government.

KAMI	Kesatuan Aksi Mahasiswa Indonesia (Indonesian Student Action Front).
KAPPI	Kesatuan Aksi Pemuda dan Pelajar Indonesia (Indonesian Youth and Student Action Front).
kebatinan	innerness; a comprehensive term for Javanese spiritualism.
kejawen	adherence to Javanese tradition.
kepercayaan	belief in Javanese mysticism.
Kolognas	National Logistics Command (precursor to Bulog).
kongsi	an informal business partnership between friends that was common in the old days among the overseas Chinese community.
Kopassus	Komando Pasukan Khusus (Special Forces Command); also referred to as the Red Berets.
Kostrad	Komando Cadangan Strategis Angkatan Darat (Army Strategic Reserve Command).
KPK	Corruption Eradication Commission; set up in the post-Suharto period.
KPPU	Supervisory Committee for Business Competition.
kretek	clove-scented cigarette.
Laoban	Chinese for "Boss"; what Liem was often called in Chinese circles.
Malari	Malapetaka Lima Belas Januari; acronym coined from Indonesian for the 15 January 1974 violence in Jakarta.
Mobnas	contraction of *mobil nasional*, or national car; Suharto's youngest son Tommy got his father to declare his "Timor" venture to assemble Kia cars a national car, to avoid taxes, but the cars were imported fully assembled from Korea; critics changed it to *mobil buatan negara asing*, meaning "a car made in a foreign country".
MPR	Majelis Permusyawaratan Rakyat (People's Consultative Assembly); operates like an Upper House of Parliament.

MSAA	Master Settlement and Acquisition Agreement; the contracts that the government signed with big debtors spelling out how they would repay liquidity injections made to their ailing banks, which were taken over by IBRA.
New Order	the period associated with Suharto's presidency, from 1966 to his downfall in 1998.
Nusamba	short for PT Nusantara Ampera Bakti; business group headed by Bob Hasan, formed in 1982, with investments in timber and tea plantations, and monopolies in tin plate and oil sector insurance. Suharto's son Sigit is a shareholder.
Opsus	Operasi Khusus; Special Operations group, headed by Suharto henchman Gen. Ali Murtopo.
PDI	Partai Demokrasi Indonesia (Indonesian Democratic Party).
PDI-P	Partai Demokrasi Indonesia-Perjuangan (Indonesian Democratic Party for Struggle); breakaway party led by Megawati Sukarnoputri.
Peranakan	an assimilated Chinese, usually multiple generation descendant of migrants settled in Indonesia; may also have married *pribumi*.
Pertamina	Pertambangan Minyak dan Gas Bumi Nasional (State Oil and Gas Company), which for many years was headed by Ibnu Sutowo.
PL480	Public Law 480; a "Food for Peace" assistance programme initiated by the United States.
PNI	Partai Nasional Indonesia (Indonesian National Party).
Prasetiya Mulya	management institute set up by Liem and other wealthy Indonesian Chinese businessmen to train and develop local managers; means "noble vow".
preman	bandit/gangster; thug.
pribumi	indigenous Indonesian.
PRRI	Revolutionary Government of the Republic of Indonesia, based in Padang, Sumatra, declared in

	February 1958 to stage a revolt against Sukarno; it was said to be backed by the CIA.
Repelita	Rencana Pembangunan Lima Tahun (Five Year Development Plan).
sandang pangan	clothing and food programme; in 1959, Sukarno promised adequate supply of clothing and food to the people within two years.
singkeh	(also spelled *singkek*, also *xinke*); literally, newcomer; a newly-arrived Chinese migrant.
Spri	Staf Pribadi; personal staff, appointed by Suharto.
Taman Mini	Taman Mini Indonesia Indah; "Beautiful Indonesia" park, an initiative of Mrs Tien Suharto, opened on 20 April 1975, on 100-hectare (later expanded to 150 hectares) land in East Jakarta; it has attractions representing all the provinces in the country.
Tanjung Priok incident	riots that broke out in the port area of Jakarta on 12 September 1984.
Totok	pure-blooded Chinese (usually China-born migrants who adhere to Chinese traditions and speak Chinese dialects).
yayasan	charitable foundation.

SELECTED BIBLIOGRAPHY

Abdul Rahman. "Investor Terbesar Tanpa Holding Company" [Biggest investor without a holding company]. *SWA*, April 1995, pp. 12–14.

Abdulgani-Knapp, Retnowati. *Soeharto: The Life and Legacy of Indonesia's Second President*. Singapore: Marshall Cavendish, 2007.

Abdullah Ali. *Liku-liku Sejarah Perbankan Indonesia: Memoar A. Ali, Presiden Direktur Bank Central Asia* [The vagaries in the history of Indonesian banking: Memoirs of A. Ali, President Director of Bank Central Asia]. Jakarta: P.T. Grasindo, 1995.

Aditjondro, George. "A new regime, a more consolidated oligarchy, and a deeply divided anti- Suharto movement". In *The Fall of Soeharto*, edited by Geoff Forrester and R.J. May. Bathurst: Crawford House Publishing, 1998.

Alagappa, Muthiah, ed. *Political Legitimacy in Southeast Asia: The Quest for Moral Authority*. Stanford: Stanford University Press, 1995.

Ali, Fachry. *Beras, Koperasi dan Politik Orde Baru: Bustanil Arifin 70 tahun* [Rice, Cooperatives and New Order Politics; For Bustanil Arifin's 70th birthday]. Jakarta: Pustaka Sinar Harapan, 1995.

Anderson, Benedict. "Exit Suharto: Obituary for a mediocre tyrant". *New Left Review*, no. 50 (Mar–Apr 2008).

——— and Audrey Kahin, eds. *Interpreting Indonesian Politics: Thirteen Contributions to the Debate, 1964–1981*. Ithaca, NY: Cornell Modern Indonesia Project, Southeast Asia Program, Cornell University, 1982.

Anderson, Kym and Will Martin, eds. *Distortions to Agricultural Incentives in Asia*. Washington, D.C.: The World Bank, 2009. Available from <http://siteresources.worldbank.org/INTTRADERESEARCH/Resources/544824-1146153362267/Asia_e-book_0209.pdf>.

Angrist, Stanley W. "East meets Little Rock". *Forbes*, 6 April 1987.

Arifin, Alwin. *Mengelola Dengan Hati: Pelajaran Sederhana Seni & Praktik Manajemen Bustanil Arifin* [Managing with a heart: Simple lessons from Bustanil Arifin in the art and practice of management]. A book written and published by Bustanil's family to mark his 85th birthday. Jakarta: Privately published, 2009.

Ariwibowo, Astuti R., compiler. *Dalam Kenangan Tunky Ariwibowo: Pekerja Keras* [In Memoriam: Tunky Ariwibowo, a Hardworker]. Jakarta: Privately published, for his 1,000th day memorial, 2005.

Arndt, H.W. "Economic disorder and the task ahead". In *Sukarno's Guided Indonesia*, edited by Tan Tjin-Kie. Brisbane: Jacaranda Press, 1967.

——. "PT Krakatau Steel". *Bulletin of Indonesian Economic Studies* 11, no. 2 (1975).

Asiaweek. "The Quiet Billionaire". 26 May 1989.

Aspinall, Edward. "Opposition and elite conflict in the fall of Suharto". In *The Fall of Soeharto*, edited by Geoff Forrester and R.J. May. Bathurst: Crawford House Publishing, 1998.

——. *Opposing Suharto: Compromise, Resistance, and Regime Change in Indonesia.* Stanford: Stanford University Press, 2005.

——, Herb Feith and Gerry van Klinken, eds. *The Last Days of President Suharto.* Clayton, Vic.: Monash Asia Institute, 1999.

Awanohara, Susumu. "Indonesia: Bombs in Chinatown". *Far Eastern Economic Review*, 18 October 1984.

——. "Krakatau's production is coated in confidentiality". *Far Eastern Economic Review*, 23 June 1983.

Backman, Michael. *Asian Eclipse: Exposing the Dark Side of Business in Asia.* Singapore: John Wiley, 1999.

Basri, M. Chatib and Pierre van der Eng, eds. *Business in Indonesia: New Challenges, Old Problems.* Singapore: Institute of Southeast Asian Studies, 2004.

Bayuni, Endy. "Uncle Liem leaves a lasting legacy in Indonesian business", *Jakarta Post*, 12 June 2012.

Binhadi. *Financial Sector Deregulation, Banking Development and Monetary Policy: The Indonesian Experience.* Jakarta: Institut Bankir Indonesia, 1995.

Blusse, Leonard. "The Role of Indonesian Chinese in Shaping Modern Indonesian Life: A Conference in Retrospect". In a special issue of the same title, edited by Audrey Kahin, published by Ithaca, NY: Cornell University Southeast Asia Program,1991.

Borsuk, Richard. "Jakarta's Steel-Mill Rescue Sparks Dispute". *Asian Wall Street Journal*, 5 July 1989.

——. "Indonesia's biggest-ever share offering succeeds but falls below expectations". *Asian Wall Street Journal*, 17 November 1989.

——. "Indonesia Assures Firms Share Sales Won't Be Required". *Asian Wall Street Journal*, 12 January 1990.

——. "Japanese group, Jakarta banks join in credit". *Asian Wall Street Journal*, 31 May 1990.

——. "Suharto son, partners form plastics firm". *Asian Wall Street Journal*, 20–21 July 1990.

———. "Indonesian firms transfer 1 per cent of equity to cooperatives in Suharto-backed move". *Asian Wall Street Journal*, 30 July 1990.

———. "Bank Duta posts profit, avoids citing losses". *Asian Wall Street Journal*, 25 October 1990.

———. "Indonesian Clove Farmers May Face Production Cut". *Asian Wall Street Journal*, 27 February 1992.

———. "Astra chairman says son's debts won't hurt firm". *Asian Wall Street Journal*, 28 May 1992.

———. "Salim Group's Indocement Deal Gets Cool Reaction From Analysts". *Asian Wall Street Journal*, 27 July 1992.

———. "Salim Group Targets Growth in Chemicals". *Asian Wall Street Journal*, 25 September 1992.

———. "Family Saga: How Son's Ambition Caused Disaster for the Soeryadjayas". *Asian Wall Street Journal*, 16 November 1992.

———. "Toyota Motor buys 8.3 per cent stake In PT Astra". *Asian Wall Street Journal*, 23 June 1993.

———. "The Asian Economist: An Interview on Regional Economic Issues". *Asian Wall Street Journal*, 16 December 1993.

———. "Official at Indonesian Bank Is Arrested in Loan Case". *Asian Wall Street Journal*, 17 February 1994.

———. "Salim Group Steels Itself for Life After Suharto". *Asian Wall Street Journal*, 25 February 1994.

———. "Salim official denies group is providing funding for Bapindo". *Asian Wall Street Journal*, 19 May 1994.

———. "Indonesia Does a Turnabout on Media Policy". *Asian Wall Street Journal*, 7 June 1994.

———. "Plantations deal raises profile of 3 investors". *Asian Wall Street Journal*, 30 September 1994.

———. "Market Reform: Slowing of deregulation hurts progress in Indonesia". *Asian Wall Street Journal*, 28 April 1995.

———. "Suharto rebukes, but keeps, minister". *Asian Wall Street Journal*, 27 December 1995.

———. "Storm brews in Bali over beer levy". *Asian Wall Street Journal*, 26–27 January 1996.

———. "Salim Moves Into Basics: Water and Rice". *Asian Wall Street Journal*, 28 February 1996.

———. "Indonesia sets plan to assemble a national auto". *Wall Street Journal*, 1 March 1996.

———. "Indonesia fights protectionist label on trade". *Wall Street Journal*, 18 March 1996.

———. "Bre-X Allies with Sigit's Panutan Group". *Asian Wall Street Journal*, 29 October 1996.

————. "Astra's Informal Group Unveils Its Plans". *Asian Wall Street Journal*, 27 November 1996.

————. "Suharto Urges Calm as Float Prompts Fears". *Asian Wall Street Journal*, 18 August 1997.

————. "Singapore Said to Offer Aid of $10 Billion to Indonesia". *Asian Wall Street Journal*, 31 October 1997.

————. "Suharto Gives Go-Ahead to Some Projects". *Asian Wall Street Journal*, 7 November 1997.

————. "IMF Chief Upbeat on Indonesia's Future". *Asian Wall Street Journal*, 13 November 1997.

————. "Millions in Indonesia Lose Jobs, Poverty Ranks Grow Amid Crisis". *Asian Wall Street Journal*, 25 March 1998.

————. "Asia Weighs Risk of Renewed Turmoil". *Asian Wall Street Journal*, 8 May 1998.

————. "Markets: The limits of reform". In *Indonesia Beyond Suharto: Polity, Economy, Society, Transition*, edited by Donald Emmerson. Armonk, New York: M.E. Sharpe with The Asia Society, 1999.

————. "Reforming business in Indonesia". In *Post-Soeharto Indonesia: Renewal or Chaos?*, edited by Geoff Forrester. Singapore: Institute of Southeast Asian Studies with Australian National University, 1999.

————. "Tougher times loom for Hasan, others". *Asian Wall Street Journal*, 4 February 1999.

————. "Nissin shelves deal with Salim over Indofood". *Asian Wall Street Journal*, 28 April 1999.

————. "Salim rejects bid for stake in Indofood". *Asian Wall Street Journal*, 18 June 1999.

————. "Jakarta's plantations sales may boost investment". *Asian Wall Street Journal*, 14 March 2001.

————. "Jakarta's Holdiko Faces Criticism on Asset Sales". *Asian Wall Street Journal*, 4 January 2002.

————, Michael Casey and Grainne McCarthy. "European Groups cut ties to Suharto-Linked firms", *Asian Wall Street Journal*, 3 June 1998.

———— and Reginald Chua, "Habibie courts Ethnic Chinese as 'ally'". *Asian Wall Street Journal*, 4 August 1998.

———— and Jon Hilsenrath, "First Pacific to buy 40 per cent of Indofood for $650 Million". *Asian Wall Street Journal*, 23 June 1999.

————, Jay Solomon and Kate Linebaugh. "Security Forces in Jakarta Fire on Crowd of Student Protesters, Killing at Least 4". *Asian Wall Street Journal*, 13 May 1998.

Bourchier, David and Ian Chalmers. "Privatising social justice". *Inside Indonesia* (Melbourne), Edition 50, April–June 1997. <www.insideindonesia.org/edition-50/privatising-social-justice> (accessed 2 June 2010).

Breman, Jan and Gunawan Wiradi. *Good Times and Bad Times in Rural Java*. Leiden: KITLV; Singapore: Institute of Southeast Asian Studies, 2002.

Bresnan, John. *Managing Indonesia: The Modern Political Economy*. New York: Columbia University Press, 1993.

————. "Economic recovery and reform". In *Indonesia: The Great Transition*, edited by John Bresnan. Lanham, Maryland: Rowman & Littlefield, 2005.

————, ed. *Indonesia: The Great Transition*. Lanham, Maryland: Rowman & Littlefield, 2005.

Brown, David Walter. "Why governments fail to capture economic rent: The unofficial appropriation of rain forest rent by rulers in insular Southeast Asia between 1977 and 1999". Unpublished dissertation, 2001. <www.reocities. com/davidbrown_id/Diss/DWB.fintext.doc>.

Brown, John Murray. "Commodities and agriculture: The politics of Indonesian cloves". *Financial Times*, 20 August 1987.

Brown, Rajeswary Ampalavanar, ed. *Chinese Business Enterprise in Asia*. London: Routledge, 1995.

————. *Chinese Big Business and the Wealth of Asian Nations*. New York: Palgrave, 2000.

————. "Conglomerates in contemporary Indonesia: Concentration, crisis and restructuring". In *Southeast Asia Research* 12, no. 3 (November 2004).

————. *The Rise of the Corporate Economy in Southeast Asia*. London: Routledge, 2006.

Butler, Charlotte. *Dare to Do: The Story of William Soeryadjaya and PT Astra International*. Singapore: McGraw Hill, 2002.

Castles, Lance. *Religion, Politics and Economic Behavior in Java: The Kudus Cigarette Industry*. New Haven: Yale University, 1967.

————. "The fate of the private entrepreneur". In *Sukarno's Guided Indonesia*, edited by Tan Tjin-Kie. Brisbane: Jacaranda Press, 1967.

Chalmers, Ian. "Domestic Capital in the Evolution of Nationalist Auto development Policy in Indonesia: From Instrumental to Structural Power". Working Paper No. 30. Perth: Murdoch University, 1994.

———— and Vedi Hadiz, eds. *The Politics of Economic Development in Indonesia: Contending Perspectives*. London: Routledge, 1997.

Chan, Anthony B. *Li Ka-shing. Hong Kong's Elusive Billionaire*. Hong Kong: Oxford University Press, 1996.

Chan Chao Peh. "Fuqing's call to home". *Asia, Inc.* September–October 2006.

Chan Kwok Bun, ed. *Chinese Business Networks: State, Economy and Culture*. Singapore: Prentice Hall, 2000.

———— and Claire Chiang. *Stepping Out: The Making of Chinese Entrepreneurs*. Singapore: NUS Centre for Advanced Studies and Prentice-Hall, 1993.

Chapman, Ross. "Indonesian Trade Reform in Close-Up: The Steel and Footwear Experiences". *Bulletin of Indonesian Economic Studies* 28, no. 1 (1992).

Charney, Michael, Brenda Yeoh, and Tong Chee Kiong, eds. *Chinese Migrants Abroad: Cultural, Educational, and Social Dimensions of the Chinese Diaspora*. Singapore: Singapore University Press, 2003.

Chin Sophonpanich: In memoriam, 1910–1988; the man and his dream. Bangkok: Business Review (*The Nation*), 1988.

Chowdhury, Amitabha. "Mochtar Riady: The master builder of an Asian banking empire". *Asian Finance*, 15 September 1983.

Chowdhury, Neel. "A crony capitalist bounces back". *Fortune*, 10 May 1999.

Chua, Christian. "Defining Indonesian Chineseness under the New Order". *Journal of Contemporary Asia* 34, no. 4 (2004): 465–79.

———. "Business as usual: Chinese conglomerates in post-Soeharto Indonesia". In *Democratisation in Indonesia after the fall of Suharto*, edited by Ingrid Wessel. Berlin: Logos Verlag, 2005.

———. "The survival of business groups in Indonesia: Two case studies". *Journal of Asian Business* 21, no. 3 (2005).

———. *Chinese Big Business in Indonesia: The State of Capital*. U.K: Routledge, 2008.

Clifford, Mark. "Question of Loyalty: Indonesian capital spending in China sparks controversy". *Far Eastern Economic Review*, 29 April 1993.

———. "Hard Times Ahead". *Far Eastern Economic Review*, 3 November 1994.

———. "The New Asian Manager". *BusinessWeek*, 2 September 1996.

Cole, David and Betty Slade. "Why Has Indonesia's Financial Crisis Been So Bad?". *Bulletin of Indonesian Economic Studies* 34, no. 2 (August 1998).

Colmey, John and David Liebhold. "Suharto Inc.: The family firm". *Time*, 24 May 1999.

Coppel, Charles. "Patterns of Chinese Political Activity in Indonesia". In *The Chinese in Indonesia: Five essays*, edited by Jamie Mackie. 1st published by The Australian Institute of International Affairs. Hong Kong: Heinemann, 1976.

———. *Indonesian Chinese in Crisis*. Kuala Lumpur: Oxford University Press, 1983.

———. "Liem Thian Joe's Unpublished History of Kian Gwan". In *Oei Tiong Ham Concern: The First Business Empire of Southeast Asia*, edited by Kunio Yoshihara. Kyoto University: The Center for Southeast Asian Studies, 1989.

Cribb, Robert and Audrey Kahin. *Historical dictionary of Indonesia*. 2nd ed. Lanham, Maryland: Scarecrow Press, 2004.

Crouch, Harold. "Generals and business in Indonesia". *Pacific Affairs*. August 1975.

———. *The Army and Politics in Indonesia*. Ithaca, NY: Cornell University Press, 1978.

———. "Patrimonialism and military rule in Indonesia". *World Politics* 31, no. 4 (July 1979): 571–87. Reprinted in *The Political Economy of East Asia 3: Singapore,*

Indonesia, Malaysia, The Philippines and Thailand, vol. 1., edited by John Ravenhill. Aldershot, UK: Edward Elgar, 1995.

Cushman, Jennifer and Wang Gungwu, eds. *Changing Identities of the Southeast Asian Chinese since World War II*. Hong Kong: Hong Kong University Press, 1988.

Dagg, C.J. "The 2004 elections in Indonesia: Political reform and democratization". *Asia Pacific Viewpoint* 48, no. 1 (April 2007).

Daud, Teuku Mohamad. "Recollections of My Career". *Bulletin of Indonesian Economic Studies* 35, no. 3 (December 1999): 41–50. Reprinted in *Recollections: The Indonesian Economy, 1950s–1990s*, edited by Thee Kian Wie. Singapore: Institute of Southeast Asian Studies, 2003.

Dewanto, Nugroho. "Misrepresentation Threat for Salim?". *Tempo*, 5–11 November 2002.

——— and Levi Silalahi. "Rise and Fall of a Friendship". *Tempo*, 5–11 November 2002.

———, L. Tanjung, Levi Silalahi, and Agus Hidayat. "The End of a Friendship?". *Tempo*, 5–11 November 2002.

———, Wenseslaus Manggut, Gita Laksmini, Agus Hidayat and Dwi Arjanto. "Salim's homecoming targets Holdiko". *Tempo*, 3 September 2000.

Dick, Howard. "Survey of Recent Developments". *Bulletin of Indonesian Economic Studies* XXI, no. 3 (December 1985).

———. *Surabaya, City of Work; A socioeconomic history, 1900–2000*. Athens: Ohio University Center for International Studies, 2002.

———, James Fox and Jamie Mackie, eds. *Balanced Development: East Java in the New Order*. Singapore: Oxford University Press, 1993.

———, Vincent J.H. Houben, J. Thomas Lindblad and Thee Kian Wie. *The Emergence of a National Economy: An Economic History of Indonesia, 1800–2000*. Crows Nest, NSW: Allen & Unwin, with Asian Studies Association of Australia, 2002.

Dieleman, Marleen. "The Salim Group: The art of strategic flexibility". Case study. Leiden University School of Management, 2003.

———. "Co-evolution of generational and regime changes with strategy of ethnic Chinese conglomerates: The case of the Salim Group of Indonesia". Leiden University Working Paper, February 2006.

———. "How Chinese Are Entrepreneurial Strategies of Ethnic Chinese Business Groups in Southeast Asia? A Multifaceted Analysis of the Salim Group of Indonesia". Draft of Ph.D. thesis, Leiden University, February 2007.

———. *The Rhythm of Strategy: A Corporate Biography of the Salim Group of Indonesia*. Amsterdam: ICAS/Amsterdam University Press, 2007.

———. "Reluctant internationalization: The case of the Salim Group". In *Ethnic Chinese in Contemporary Indonesia*, edited by Leo Suryadinata. Singapore: Chinese Heritage Centre and Institute of Southeast Asian Studies, 2008.

———. "Continuous and discontinuous change in ethnic Chinese business networks: The case of the Salim Group". In *Chinese Indonesians and Regime Change*, edited by Marleen Dieleman, Juliette Koning and Peter Post. Lieden: Brill, 2011.

——— and Wladimir Sachs. "Economies of scope and economies of connectedness: Illustrated by the Salim Group of Indonesia". Leiden University Working Paper, Version July 2005.

——— and Peter Post. "Punctuations in emerging markets: Regime change and family firm responses". *Economics and Finance in Indonesia* 57, no. 1 (2009): 25–46.

———, Juliette Koning and Peter Post, eds. *Chinese Indonesians and Regime Change*. Lieden: Brill, 2011.

Djiwandono, Soedradjad. *Bank Indonesia and the Crisis: An Insider's View*. Singapore: Institute of Southeast Asian Studies, 2005.

Djojohadikusumo, Sumitro. "Recollections of my career". *Bulletin of Indonesian Economic Studies* 22, no. 3 (December 1986): 27–39. Reprinted in *Recollections: The Indonesian Economy, 1950s–1990s*, edited by Thee Kian Wie. Singapore: Institute of Southeast Asian Studies, 2003.

Donnan, Shawn. "Adding new ingredients at Indofood. Interview with Franciscus Welirang". *Financial Times*, 16 March 2004.

Douw, Leo. M. and Peter Post, eds. *South China: State, Culture and Social Change during the 20th Century*. Amsterdam: Royal Netherlands Academy of Arts and Sciences, Verhandelingen, Afd, 1996.

Drysdale, Peter, ed. *Reform and recovery in East Asia: The role of the state and economic enterprise*. London: Routledge, 2000.

Dwidjowijoto, Riant Nugroho, ed. *Manajemen Presiden Suharto: Penuturan 17 Menteri* [Suharto's Management: Narratives by 17 Ministers]. Jakarta: Yayasan Bina Generasi Bangsa, 1996.

———, ed. *Sudwikatmono: Sebuah Perjalanan di antara Sahabat* [Sudwikatmono: A Journey Among Friends]. Jakarta: Yayasan Pendidikan Hanurita, 1997.

Dwipayana, G. and Sjamsuddin, Nazaruddin, eds. *Di antara para sahabat: Pak Harto 70 tahun* [Among Friends: Pak Harto's 70th]. Jakarta: Citra Gung Lamtoro Persada, 1991. English ed., 1993.

Eksekutif. "Sepak Terjang: The Gang of Four" [The Gang of Four's tactics and manoeuvres]. September 1996, pp. 122–29.

Elson, R.E. *Suharto: A Political Biography*. Cambridge: Cambridge University Press, 2001.

———. "Time, timing, and the 'historical moment' in Suharto's politics". In *The Inclusive Regionalist: A Festschrift dedicated to Jusuf Wanandi*, edited by Hadi Soesastro and Clara Joewono. Jakarta: Centre for Strategic and International Studies, 2007.

Emmerson, Donald K., ed. *Indonesia Beyond Suharto: Polity, Economy, Society, Transition*. Armonk, NY: M.E. Sharpe with the Asia Society, 1999.

England, Vaudine. "Brother-in-law rejects magazine's report of $116b haul". *South China Morning Post*, 20 May 1999.

Fane, George and Peter Warr. Indonesia chapter in *Distortions to Agricultural Incentives in Asia*, edited by Kym Anderson and Will Martin. Washington, D.C.: The World Bank, 1999.

Feith, Herbert. "Politics of economic decline". In *Sukarno's Guided Indonesia*, edited by Tan Tjin-Kie. Brisbane: Jacaranda Press, 1967.

Finn, Jr., Edwin A. "Worthen Is Cited by Comptroller's Office Over Loans to Three Holders' Companies". *Wall Street Journal*, 22 August 1985.

Forrester, Geoff. "A Jakarta Diary, May 1998". In *The Fall of Soeharto*, edited by G. Forrester and R.J. May. Bathurst: Crawford House Publishing, 1998.

———. *Post-Soeharto Indonesia: Renewal or Chaos?* Singapore: Institute of Southeast Asian Studies, with Australian National University Research School of Pacific and Asian Studies, 1999.

——— and R.J. May, eds. *The Fall of Soeharto*. Bathurst: Crawford House Publishing, 1998.

Frederick, William and Robert Worden, eds. *Indonesia: A Country Study*. Washington, D.C.: U.S. Library of Congress, 1993.

Friend, Theodore. *Indonesian Destinies*. Cambridge, MA Belknap Press of Harvard University, 2003.

Fung, Noel. "IBRA Sets up Five Holding Companies". *Asian Wall Street Journal*, 9 July 1999.

Glassburner, Bruce, ed. *The Economy of Indonesia: Selected Essays*. Cambridge, MA: MIT Center for International Studies, 1971.

———. *Indonesia's New Economic Policy and Its Sociopolitical Implications*. Cambridge, MA: MIT Center for International Studies, 1974.

Gottschalk, Earl. "Sutowo defends role at Pertamina's helm, retreats on Rappaport". *Asian Wall Street Journal*, 14 February 1977.

Greenhouse, Steven. "A secret emperor of oil and shipping". *New York Times*, 4 February 1988, p. 16.

Habir, Ahmad D. "Conglomerates: All in the family?". In *Indonesia Beyond Suharto: Polity, Economy, Society, Transition*, edited by Donald Emmerson. Armonk, NY: M.E. Sharpe with the Asia Society, 1999.

———, E. Sebastian and L. Williams, eds. *Governance and Privatization in Indonesia*. Sydney: University of Sydney, Institute for Asia and the Pacific, 2002.

Habir, Manggi. "There's no business like go-go business." *Far Eastern Economic Review*, 17 April 1983.

———. "Fears of a feudal divide: Indonesia wants to boost private-sector investment in plantations but baulks at the possible consequences. [Salim and palm oil]". *Far Eastern Economic Review*, 29 December 1983.

———. "Only a few brave the public arena". *Far Eastern Economic Review*, 19 April 1984.

———— and Anthony Rowley. "The extended (corporate) family of Liem Sioe Liong". *Far Eastern Economic Review*, 17 April 1983.

Hambali, Saudi. "Abdullah Ali: 'Saya bukan presdir pajangan'." [Abdullah Ali: "I am not a toy president-director"]. *Eksekutif*, August 1989, pp. 18–24.

Handley, Paul. "Onward business soldiers". *Far Eastern Economic Review*, 24 October 1985.

Hanusz, Mark. *Kretek: The Culture and Heritage of Indonesia's Clove Cigarettes*. Jakarta: Equinox, 2000.

Harefa, Andreas and Eben Ezer Siadari, "The Ciputra Way — *Praktik terbaik menjadi entrepreneur sejati*" [The best practice to become a true entrepreneur]. Jakarta: PT Elex Media Komputindo, 2006.

Hawkins, Frank. "Indonesia's own military-industrial complex". *Bangkok Post*, 28 January 1971.

Hering, Bob. *Soekarno: Architect of a Nation, 1901–1970*. Leiden: KITLV Press, 2001.

————. *Soekarno: Founding Father of Indonesia, 1901–1945*. Leiden: KITLV Press, 2002.

Hewison, Kevin, Richard Robison and Garry Rodan, eds. *Southeast Asia in the 1990s: Authoritarianism, Democracy and Capitalism*. New South Wales: Allen and Unwin, 1993.

Hidayat, Yopie. "Ekspansi, Lagi Ekspansi" [Expansion, and more expansion]. *Tempo*, 10 March 1990, pp. 71–73.

Hill, David T. *Journalism and Politics in Indonesia: A critical biography of Mochtar Lubis (1922–2004) as editor and author*. London: Routledge, 2010.

Hill, Hal. *The Indonesian Economy since 1966*. Cambridge: Cambridge University Press, 1996.

————. "The Indonesian economy: The strange and sudden death of a tiger". In *The Fall of Soeharto*, edited by Geoff Forrester and R.J. May. Bathurst: Crawford House Publishing, 1998.

Hilsenrath, Jon and Douglas Appell, "Despite slump, analysts alter views on First Pacific". *Asian Wall Street Journal*, 18 May 1998.

Holloway, Richard, ed. "Stealing from the People: 16 studies of corruption in Indonesia". Vol. 3. *Foreign Aid, Business and State Enterprise: Counting the Cost*. Jakarta: Aksara Foundation, 2002.

Human Rights Watch Report. "Wild Money: The Human Rights Consequences of Illegal Logging and Corruption in Indonesia's Forestry Sector". 2009.

Hutabarat, Winfred, Her Suharyanto and Savitri Setiawan. "The Chinese factor: The next generation". *Indonesia Business Weekly*, 4 February 1994, pp. 4–7.

"Ibrahim Rishad: 'Dalam international trade, saya masternya' " [Ibrahim Risjad: "In international trade, I am the master"]. *Eksekutif*, April 1990, pp. 20–28.

Ikhsan, Mohamad, Chris Manning and Hadi Soesastro, eds. *Ekonomi Indonesia di era politik baru: 80 tahun Mohamad Sadli* [Indonesian economy in the era of new politics: commemorating Mohamad Sadli's 80th year]. Jakarta: Kompas, 2002.

Indonesia in the Soeharto Years: Issues, Incidents and Images. Jakarta: The Lontar Foundation, 2005.

Indonesian Cement Directory. Jakarta: Asosiasi Semen Indonesia, 1999.

Indonesia's Economy: Entering the Third Millennium. London: International Quality Productions, 1997.

Jackson, Karl D., ed. *Asian Contagion: The Causes and Consequences of a Financial Crisis*. Singapore: Institute of Southeast Asian Studies; Boulder, CO: Westview Press, 1999.

Jakarta Post. "Big Names Probed for Alleged Abuse of Forestry Funds". 17 February 2000.

Jenkins, David. "Suharto: A decade of deeds and dilemmas". *Far Eastern Economic Review*, 20 August 1976.

————. "The politics of corruption". *Far Eastern Economic Review*, 20 August 1976.

————. "Power of the Mystic Lobby". *Far Eastern Economic Review*, 31 March 1978.

————. "Giving credit where it is due". *Far Eastern Economic Review*, 21 September 1979.

————. "The traders who came to stay". *Far Eastern Economic Review*, 21 September 1979.

————. "The Jakarta solution". *Far Eastern Economic Review*, 21 September 1979.

————."Military Budgets: The Military's Secret Cache". *Far Eastern Economic Review*, 6 February 1980.

————."The quiet, bald moneymaker of Jakarta's elite". *Sydney Morning Herald*, 10 April 1986.

————. "Family ties, Jakarta to Washington". *Sydney Morning Herald*, 16 October 1996.

————. "Poor Man, Rich Man, Thief". *Sydney Morning Herald*, 29 January 2008.

————. *Soeharto and his Generals: Indonesian military politics 1975–1983*. Ithaca: Modern Indonesia Project, Cornell University, 1984. Republished by Equinox, Singapore, 2010.

Jones, Steven. "Suharto's kin linked with plastics monopoly". *Asian Wall Street Journal*, 25 November 1986.

————. "Monopoly on plastics enriches Indonesian leader's kin". *Asian Wall Street Journal*, 26 November 1986.

———— and Cheah Cheng Hye. "Indocement Replaces US$120 Million Loan". *Asian Wall Street Journal*, 15 July 1985.

———— and Raphael Pura. "All in the family: Indonesian decrees help Suharto's friends and relatives prosper". *Asian Wall Street Journal*, 24 November 1986.

———— and Raphael Pura. "Suharto-linked monopolies hobble economy". *Asian Wall Street Journal*, 24 November 1986.

————, Christopher Hunt and Richard Borsuk. "Fund officials cool on Indocement offering". *Asian Wall Street Journal*, 8 November 1989.

Jonker, Joost and Keetie Sluyterman. *At Home on the World Markets: Dutch International Trading Companies from the 16th Century Until the Present*. The Hague: Sdu Uitgevers, 2000.

Jufri, Fikri. "Liem buka suara: Orang banyak salah sangka" [Liem speaks: People have many wrong ideas]. *Tempo*, 31 March 1984, pp. 68–69.

————. "Liem Bicara Lagi: 'Saya Masih Kuasa Penuh'" [Liem Talks Again: "I still have full power"]. *Tempo*, 10 March 1990, pp. 76–77.

Kagda, Shoeb. "Bhakti hits the limelight with Indon asset deals". *Business Times* Singapore, 17 January 2001.

————. "Salim Group set to reclaim Indon dominance". *Business Times* (Singapore), 7 January 2002.

Kahin, Audrey, ed. *Indonesia: The role of the Chinese in shaping modern Indonesian life*. Ithaca, New York: Cornell University Southeast Asia Program (special issue), 1991.

Kahin, George McT. *Southeast Asia: A Testament*. London and New York: Routledge, 2003.

Kanter, Rosabeth Moss. "Using Networking for Competitive Advantage: The Lippo Group of Indonesia and Hong Kong". *Strategy + Business magazine*, Quarter 3, 1996. <http://www.strategy-business.com/article/17609?gko=17096> (accessed 15 November 2010).

Khan, Mushtaq and Jomo K.S., eds. *Rents, Rent-Seeking and Economic Development, Theory and Evidence in Asia*. Cambridge: Cambridge University Press, 2000.

Khanna, Vikram. "Banker, empire builder: Raffles conversation with Mochtar Riady". *Business Times* (Singapore), 8–9 October, 2011.

Kompas. "Presiden bicara soal kolusi dan monopoli" [President discusses issue of collusion and monopoly]. 25 September 1995.

Koo Hui Lan. *Madam Wellington Koo: An autobiography as told to Mary Van Rensselaer Thayer*. New York: Dial Press, 1943.

————. *No Feasts Lasts Forever*. NY: Quadrangle, 1975.

Kuntjoro-Jakti, Dorodjatun. "The Political economy of development: The case of Indonesia under the New Order government, 1966-1978". Ph.D. thesis, University of California at Berkeley, 1980.

Landler, Mark. "Year of living dangerously for a tycoon in Indonesia". *New York Times*, 16 May 1999.

Lee Han Shih. "Singapore government unveils first major investment in China". *Business Times* (Singapore), 8 November 1992.

Lee Khoon Choy. *Indonesia: Between Myth and Reality*. Singapore: Federal Publications, 1977.

———. *A Fragile Nation: The Indonesian Crisis*. Singapore: World Scientific, 1999.

Lee Kuan Yew. *From Third World to First: The Singapore Story: 1965–2000*. New York: Harper Collins, 2000.

Legge, J.D. *Sukarno: A Political Biography*. 3rd ed. Singapore: Archipelago, 2003.

Legge, John. *Indonesia*. 2nd ed. Sydney: Prentice Hall, 1977.

Lev, Daniel S. *Making Indonesia: Essays on Modern Indonesia in Honor of George McT. Kahin*. Ithaca: Southeast Asia Program, Cornell University, 1996.

Liddle, William. *Leadership and Culture in Indonesian Politics*. Sydney: Allen & Unwin, 1996.

———. "Indonesia's unexpected failure of leadership". In *The Politics of Post-Suharto Indonesia*, edited by Adam Schwartz and Jonathan Paris. New York: Council on Foreign Relations Press, 1999.

Liefer, Michael. *Dictionary of the Modern Politics of Southeast Asia*, 3rd ed. London and New York, 2001.

Liem Sioe Liong: Memorial Album in Commemoration of the Permanent Honorary President of the International Association of Fuqing Clansmen Limited. Hong Kong: The International Association of Fuqing Clansmen Limited, 2013.

Lindsey, Tim, and Helen Pausacker, eds. *Chinese Indonesians: Remembering, Distorting, Forgetting*. Singapore: Institute of Southeast Asian Studies, 2005.

Lipsky, Seth. *The Billion Dollar Bubble and Other Stories from the Asian Wall Street Journal*. Hong Kong: Dow Jones, 1978.

Lloyd, Grayson, and Shannon Smith, eds. *Indonesia Today: Challenges of History*. Singapore: Institute of Southeast Asian Studies, 2001.

Lopez, Leslie. "Guardians of a hydra-like business empire". *Business Times*, 24 November 1995.

Loughlin, Colleen, S. Marks, Achmad Shauki, and Ningrum Sirait. "Report on Competition Policy in Indonesia". USAID Project No. 0497 0372. November 1999.

Luthfie, Nukman. "'Kerajaan' Dwi di luar Grup Salim" [Dwi's "kingdom" outside the Salim Group]. *SWA*, April 1995, pp. 26–32.

Maarif, Syamsul. "Competition Law and Policy in Indonesia". Jakarta, 28 March 2001 <http://www.jftc.go.jp/eacpf/02/indonesia_r.pdf>.

MacIntyre, Andrew. *Business and Politics in Indonesia*. Sydney: Allen & Unwin, with Asian Studies Association of Australia, 1990.

———. "The dynamics of economic transformation in Indonesia". New York: Council of Foreign Relations Asia Project Working Paper, July 1995.

———. "Funny money in Indonesia". In *Rents, Rent-Seeking and Economic Development, Theory and Evidence in Asia*, edited by Mushtaq Khan and Jomo K.S. Cambridge: Cambridge University Press, 2000.

Mackie, Jamie. "The government estates". In *Sukarno's Guided Indonesia*, edited by Tan Tjin-Kie. Brisbane: Jacaranda Press, 1967.

———. "The commission of four report on corruption". *Bulletin of Indonesian Economic Studies* VI, no. 3 (1970).

———, ed. *The Chinese in Indonesia: Five essays*. Hong Kong: Heinemann, 1976 (first published by The Australian Institute of International Affairs).

———. "Changing economic roles and ethnic identities of the Southeast Asian Chinese: A comparison of Indonesia and Thailand". In *Changing Identities of the Southeast Asian Chinese since World War II*, edited by Jennifer Cushman and Wang Gungwu. Hong Kong: Hong Kong University Press, 1988.

———. "Property and Power in Indonesia". In *The Politics of Middle Class Indonesia*, edited by Richard Tanter and Kenneth Young. Clayton, Victoria: Centre for Southeast Asian Studies, Monash University, 1990.

———. "Towkays and Tycoons: The Chinese in Indonesian Economic Life in the 1920s and 1980s". In *Indonesia: The role of the Chinese in shaping modern Indonesian life*, edited by Audrey Kahin, pp. 83–96. Ithaca: Cornell University Southeast Asia Program (special issue), 1991.

———. "Changing patterns of Chinese big business in Southeast Asia". In *Southeast Asian Capitalists*, edited by Ruth McVey. Ithaca: Cornell Southeast Asia Program, 1992.

———. "Overseas Chinese Entrepreneurship". *Asian-Pacific Economic Literature* 6, no. 1 (May 1992): 41–64.

———. "Soothing Indonesia's Resentments". *Asian Wall Street Journal*, 10 September 1998.

———. "Tackling 'the Chinese problem' ". In *Post-Soeharto Indonesia: Renewal or Chaos?* edited by Geoff Forrester. Singapore: Institute of Southeast Asian Studies, with Australian National University Research School of Pacific and Asian Studies, 1999.

———. "Five Southeast Asian Chinese Empire-Builders: Commonalities and Differences". In *Chinese Migrants Abroad: Cultural, Educational, and Social Dimensions of the Chinese Diaspora*, edited by M.W. Charney, B. Yeoh, and Tong Chee Kiong. Singapore: Singapore University Press, 2003.

Magiera, Stephen L. "The Role of Wheat in Indonesia's Food System". U.S. Department of Agriculture, Foreign Agricultural Economic Report, No. 170, Economic Research Service, 1981.

———. "Grain Quality as a Determinant of Wheat Import Demand: The case of Indonesia". U.S. Agency for International Development, Jakarta, April 1993 <http://pdf.usaid.gov/pdf_docs/PNACM520.pdf>.

Magnis-Suseno, Franz. "*Lengser keprabon*: New Order leadership, Javanese culture, and the prospects for democracy in Indonesia". In *Post-Suharto Indonesia: Renewal or Chaos*, edited by Geoff Forrester. Singapore: Institute of Southeast

Asian Studies and Australian National University Research School of Pacific and Asian Studies; Leiden, KITLV Press, 1999.

Mallaby, Sebastian. *The World's Banker: A Story of Failed States, Financial Crises, and the Wealth and Poverty of Nations*. New York: Penguin (Council on Foreign Relations Books), 2006.

Malley, Michael. "Soedjono Humardani and Indonesian-Japanese Relations, 1966–1974". *Indonesia Issue* (Cornell), No. 48 (October 1989): 47–64.

———. "A political biography of Major General Soedjono Hoemardani, 1918–1986". MA thesis, Cornell University, 1990.

Mandal, Sumit. "Strangers who are not foreign". In *The Chinese in Indonesia*, by Pramoedya Ananta Toer, English edition, translated by Max Lane. Singapore: Select Publishing, 2007.

Manguno, Joseph. "Suharto denies taking payoffs on arms deals". *Asian Wall Street Journal*, 23 July 1980.

———. "Indonesian-run Firm Buys Flour Mill, Stirs Controversy". *Asian Wall Street Journal*, 12 March 1982.

———. "Half brother of Suharto wins project". *Asian Wall Street Journal*, 20 September 1982.

——— and S. Karene Witcher. "Suharto relatives, officials gain control of Indonesian flour trade". *Asian Wall Street Journal*, 23 November 1981.

Mapes, Timothy. "Jakarta Sticks with Plan for Giant Bad-Debt Sale". *Asian Wall Street Journal*, 13 June 2002.

Maroef, Taufik M. "The Shareholder Settlement Programme: A pragmatic resolution to confront a systemic banking crisis in view of the dysfunctional legal system and tradition of the Republic of Indonesia". Ph.D. dissertation, Leiden University, 2010.

Masud, Didin Abidin, Paulus Pandiangan, and Umniyati Kowi. "Jalinan Lobi dan Bisnis Sudwikatmono" [Sudwikatmono's Interwoven Lobby and Businesses]. *SWA*, April 1995, pp. 15–21.

Matsumoto, Yasuyuki. *Financial Fragility and Instability in Indonesia*. New York: Routledge, 2007.

May, Brian. *The Indonesian Tragedy*. Singapore: Graham Brash, 2001. (Originally published in 1978, Routledge & Kegan Paul.).

McBeth, John. "Grains of Truth". *Far Eastern Economic Review*, 10 September 1998.

McCarthy, Grainne and I Made Sentana. "IBRA considers selling companies as a whole". *Asian Wall Street Journal*, 10 May 2000.

McDonald, Hamish. *Suharto's Indonesia*. Australia: Fontana, 1980.

McGregor, James. "Fujian gets boost from Overseas Chinese — Flood of investment tied to ancestral roots yields economic boom". *Asian Wall Street Journal*, 4 June 1992.

McLeod, Ross. "Indonesia's crisis and future prospects". In *Asian Contagion: The Causes and Consequences of a Financial Crisis*, edited by Karl Jackson. Singapore: Institute of Southeast Asian Studies, and Boulder, Colorado: Westview Press, 1999.

———. "Government-business relations in Indonesia". In *Reform and recovery in East Asia: The role of the state and economic enterprise*, edited by Peter Drysdale. London: Routledge, 2000.

———. "Suharto's Indonesia: A better class of corruption". *The Indonesian Quarterly* 28, no. 1 (2000): 16–27.

——— with George Fane. "Banking Collapse and Restructuring in Indonesia, 1997–2001". *Cato Journal*, 2001.

———. "After Suharto: Prospects for reform and recovery in Indonesia". Canberra: Australian National University, Department of Economics, Research School of Pacific and Asian Studies, Working Paper 10, 2003.

McVey, Ruth. "The Beamstenstaat in Indonesia". In *Interpreting Indonesian Politics: Thirteen Contributions to the Debate, 1964–1981*, edited by Ben Anderson and Audrey Kahin. Ithaca, NY: Cornell University, 1982.

———, ed. *Southeast Asian Capitalists*. Ithaca: Cornell Southeast Asia Program, 1992.

Mellor, William. "Why This Billionaire Wants to Quit". *Asia Inc.*, April 2000.

Menkhoff, Thomas. "The impact of the new Asian realism on Chinese business networks in Asia-Pacific". University of Bonn; Department of Southeast Asian Studies Working Paper 5, 1999.

Michener, James. "Chinese success story". *Life*, 31 December 1951.

Milton, Giles. *Nathaniel's Nutmeg: How One Man's Courage Changed the Course of History*. London: Hodder & Stoughton, 1999.

"Mochtar Riady: Pioneer of modern retail banking". *Globe Asia* 1, no. 6 (July 2007).

Moh. Arsjad Anwar, Aris Ananta and Ari Kuncoro, eds. *Tributes for Widjojo Nitisastro by friends from 27 foreign countries*. Jakarta: Kompas, 2007.

Mohamad, Goenawan (principal author). *Celebrating Indonesia: Fifty Years with the Ford Foundation*. Jakarta: Ford Foundation, 2003.

Montlake, Simon, Grainne McCarthy and I Made Sentana. "Rupiah Falls Sharply After Minister's Remarks". *Asian Wall Street Journal*, 12 May 2000.

Muhaimin, Yahya A. *Bisnis dan Politik: Kebijaksanaan Ekonomi Indonesia, 1950–1980* [Business and Politics: Indonesian Economic Policy, 1950–1980]. Jakarta: LP3ES, 1991.

———. *Perkembangan militer dalam politik di Indonesia, 1945–1966* [Military expansion in Indonesian politics, 1945–1966]. 2nd ed. Yogyakarta: Gadja Mada University Press, 2002.

Mulcahy, John. "On the expansion trail". *Far Eastern Economic Review*, 16 April 1987.

Mulder, Niels. *Mysticism in Java: Ideology in Indonesia*. Amsterdam: Pepin, 1998.

Mulholland, Jeremy and Ken Thomas. "The Price of Rice". *Inside Indonesia*, No. 58, April–June 1999.

Multatuli. *Max Havelaar, or the Coffee Auctions of the Dutch Trading Company*. London: Penguin, 1987 (first published 1860).

Nuranto, Nobertus. "The evolution of Chinese business under the New Order in Indonesia: Four case studies". MA thesis, Cornell University, 1990.

O'Rourke, Kevin. *Reformasi: The Struggle for Power in Post-Soeharto Indonesia*. London: Allen & Unwin, 2002.

Onghokham. "Reforming a diffuse and profiteering martial elite". *Far Eastern Economic Review*, 24 October 1985, pp. 28–29.

———. "Chinese capitalism in Dutch Java". *Southeast Asian Studies* (Kyoto University) 27, no. 2 (September 1989).

———. *The Thugs, the Curtain Thief, and the Sugar Lord: Power, Politics, and Culture in Colonial Java*. Jakarta: Metafor, 2003.

———. "Soeharto and the Javanese tradition of monarchy". *Indonesia in the Soeharto Years: Issues, Incidents and Images*. Jakarta: Lontar, 2005.

Overseas Chinese Business Networks in Asia. Department of Foreign Affairs and Trade, East Asia Analytical Unit. Canberra: Australian government, 1995.

Pabotinggi, Mochtar. "Indonesia: Historicizing the New Order's legitimacy dilemma". In *Political Legitimacy in Southeast Asia: The Quest for Moral Authority*, edited by Muthiah Alagappa. Stanford: Stanford University Press, 1995.

Pan, Lynn. *Sons of the Yellow Emperor: A History of the Chinese Diaspora*. New York: Kodansha, 1990.

———, general ed. *The Encyclopedia of the Chinese Overseas*. Singapore: Chinese Heritage Centre, 1998.

Pangestu, Mari. "The role of the private sector in Indonesia: Deregulation and Privatisation". Jakarta: Centre for Strategic and International Studies, November 1990.

———. "An Economic Agenda for Indonesia". *Asian Wall Street Journal*, 16 June 1992.

Panglaykim, J. and I. Palmer. "Entrepreneurship and Commercial Risks: The Case of a Schumpeterian Business in Indonesia". Singapore: Institute of Business Studies, Nanyang University Occasional Papers 2, 1970.

Pearson, Stuart. *Bittersweet: The Memoir of a Chinese Indonesian Family in the Twentieth Century*. Singapore: National University of Singapore Press, 2008.

Plunkett, H.H., W.E. Morgan and J.L. Pomeroy. "Regulation of the Indonesian Cement Industry". *Bulletin of Indonesian Economic Studies* 33, no. 1 (April 1997).

Pomeroy, Jacqueline. "Measuring costs and benefits of soymeal deregulation in Indonesia, 1991–1994". Paper presented in seminar on Building on Success: Maximising the gains from deregulation, Jakarta, 26–28 April 1995.

Post, Peter. "On bicycles and textiles: Japan, South China and the Hokchia-Henghua entrepreneurs". In *South China: State, Culture and Social Change during the 20th Century*, edited by L.M. Douw and P. Post. Amsterdam: Royal Netherlands Academy of Arts and Sciences, Verhandelingen, Afd, 1996.

——. "The study of Chinese business in the modern history of Indonesia: Themes and Prospects". In *Zhongguo Shangye Shi* [Chinese Business History] Vol. 14, no. 2 (Fall 2004) <www.umassd.edu/cas/history/fall04cbh.pdf>.

——. "The Oei Tiong Ham Concern and the change of regimes in Indonesia, 1931–1950". In *Chinese Indonesians and Regime Change*, edited by Marleen Dieleman, J. Koning and P. Post. Lieden: Brill, 2011.

—— and Elly Touwen-Bouwsma, eds. *Japan, Indonesia and the War: Myths and Realities*. Leiden: KITLV, 1997.

Pour, Julius. "Benny Moerdani: Profile of a Soldier Statesman". Translated by Tim Scott. Jakarta: Yayasan Kejuangan Panglima Besar, 1993.

Pramoedya Ananta Toer. *Hoakiau di Indonesia*. Jakarta: Penerbit Garba Budaya, 1998. First published by Penerbit Bintang Press, Jakarta in 1960. English ed.: *The Chinese in Indonesia*. Translated by Max Lane. Singapore: Select Publishing, 2007.

Prawiro, Radius. *Indonesia's Struggle for Economic Development: Pragmatism in Action*. Kuala Lumpur: Oxford University Press, 1998.

Probosutedjo. *Visi dan liku-liku keberhasilan sebagai pengusaha nasionalis* [The vision and twists and turns of success of a national entrepreneur]. Jakarta: Gemah Ripa, 1999.

—— with Alberthiene Endah. *Saya dan Mas Harto: Memoir Romantika Probosutedjo* [Me and brother Harto]. Jakarta: PT Gramedia Pustaka Utama, 2010.

Prystay, Cris. "Philippine tycoon can cap a career with PLDT Deal". *Asian Wall Street Journal*, 7 June 2002.

Pura, Raphael. "Indonesia Banker Shelves Plan to Buy Lance's Bank Stock". *Asian Wall Street Journal*, 9 September 1977.

——. "Suharto Family Tied to Indonesian Oil Trade". *Asian Wall Street Journal*, 26 November 1986.

——. "Pertamina wins its legal battle over deposits". *Asian Wall Street Journal*, 4 December 1992.

——. "Timber tycoon confronts his critics". *Asian Wall Street Journal*, 27 August 1993.

——. "Stamina and Success Mark Fuzhou Chinese Diaspora". *Asian Wall Street Journal*, 8 June 1994.

——. "Plywood Power: Bob Hasan Builds an Empire in the Forest". *Asian Wall Street Journal*, 20 January 1995.

——. "Indonesians Debate Moves To Restrain Giant Firms". *Asian Wall Street Journal*, 4 July 1995.

———. "Salim Group Unveils Broad Restructuring". *Asian Wall Street Journal*, 16 July 1997.

——— and Richard Borsuk. "Professor Placed in Eye of Astra Storm". *Asian Wall Street Journal*, 18 December 1992.

——— and Richard Borsuk. "Suharto's Son Lashes at Finance Minister". *Asian Wall Street Journal*, 5 November 1997.

Purcell, Victor. *The Overseas Chinese in Southeast Asia*. Oxford University Press, 1980.

Purdey, Jemma. "Anti-Chinese violence in Indonesia, 1996–1999". Singapore: ASAA Southeast Asia Publication Series, 2006.

Rae, Ian and Morgen Witzel. *The Overseas Chinese of South East Asia: History, Culture, Business*. Basingstoke, New York: Palgrave Macmillan, 2008.

Raj, Conrad. "Singapore court battle looms for 2 prominent Indonesian tycoons". *Business Times*, 20 September 2001.

Ransom, David. "Ford Country: Building an elite for Indonesia". In *The Trojan Horse: A Radical Look at Foreign Aid*, edited by Steve Weissman, with members of the Pacific Studies Center and the North American Congress on Latin America, rev. ed., pp. 93–116. Palo Alto, California: Ramparts Press, 1975.

Ravenhill, John, ed. *The Political Economy of East Asia 3: Singapore, Indonesia, Malaysia, The Philippines and Thailand*. Vol. 1. Aldershot, UK: Edward Elgar, 1995.

Reid. Anthony. " 'Outsider' Status and Economic Success in Suharto's Indonesia". Paper presented at the workshop "Chinese Indonesians: The Way Ahead", Australian National University, Canberra, 15–16 February 1999.

"Risjadson Group: Expansion step blocked by crisis". Indonesian Commercial Newsletter, 27 April 1998.

Robertson-Snape, Fiona. "Corruption, collusion and nepotism in Indonesia". *Third World Quarterly* 20, no. 3 (1999): 589–602.

Robison, Richard. "Towards a class analysis of the Indonesian military bureaucratic state". *Indonesia*, No. 25. Cornell University Press, April 1978.

———. "Capitalism and the bureaucratic state in Indonesia, 1965–1975". Microfilm. Ph.D. thesis, The University of Sydney, 1979.

———. "The Liem Group: From domestic to international corporate operations in Asia". Paper presented at the Workshop on Indigenous Multinationals and the Role of the Family Firm in the Pacific Basin. Canberra, Australian National University, 1 September 1983.

———. *Indonesia: The Rise of Capital*. Sydney: Allen and Unwin/Asian Studies Association of Australia, 1986.

———. "Authoritarian states, capital-owning classes, and the politics of newly industrializing countries: The case of Indonesia". *World Politics* 41, no. 1 (October 1988): 52–74.

————. "Power and Economy in Suharto's Indonesia". *Journal of Contemporary Asia Publishers* (Manila and Wollongong), 1990.

————. "Industrialization and the economic and political development of capital: The case of Indonesia". In *Southeast Asian Capitalists*, edited by Ruth McVey. Ithaca: Cornell, 1992.

————. "Indonesia: Tensions in state and regime." In *Southeast Asia in the 1990s: Authoritarianism, Democracy and Capitalism*, edited by Kevin Hewison, Richard Robison and Garry Rodan. Australia: Allen & Unwin, 1993.

———— and Vedi Hadiz. *Reorganising Power in Indonesia: The Politics of Oligarchy in an Age of Markets*. London: Routledge Curzon, 2004.

————, Kevin Hewison and Richard Higgott, eds. *South East Asia in the 1980s: The Politics of Economic Crisis*. Sydney, London, Boston: Allen & Unwin, 1987.

Roeder, O.G. *The Smiling General: President Soeharto of Indonesia*. Jakarta: Gunung Agung, 1969.

————. "Chinese 'impudence'". *Far Eastern Economic Review*, 7 May 1973.

Roham, Abujamin. *Bustanil Arifin: Kaya hati, dermawan harta* [Bustanil Arifin: Generous and wealthy philanthropist]. Festschrift in honor of Bustanil Arifin, former Minister of Cooperatives and Head of National Logistics Agency. Jakarta: Privately published, 2003.

Roosa, John. *Pretext for Mass Murder: The September 30th Movement and Suharto's Coup d'etat in Indonesia*. Madison: University of Wisconsin, 2006.

Rosser, Andrew. *The Politics of Economic Liberalisation in Indonesia: State, Market and Power*. U.K.: Curzon, 2002.

Rowley, Anthony. "Birth of a multinational". *Far Eastern Economic Review*, 17 April 1983.

————. "Purchase by proxy: Indonesia's Liem Sioe Liong makes a low-profile move in to HK banking — with a strong US partner". *Far Eastern Economic Review*, 15 November 1984.

Rush, James. "Placing the Chinese in Java on the eve of the twentieth century". Cornell University Southeast Asian Studies. *Indonesia*. Special edition, July 1991.

Sacerdoti, Guy R. "Bulog archipelago under fire". *Far Eastern Economic Review*, 24 February 1978.

————. "A Made-in-Indonesia Controversy". *Far Eastern Economic Review*, 15 February 1980.

————. "High oil profits permit a change in financing strategy". *Far Eastern Economic Review*, 4–10 April 1980.

————. "Litigation: The revelations of a widow: The Singapore court case into who owns a former Pertamina's official fortune takes on a new turn — and the dispute promises to drag on". *Far Eastern Economic Review*, 1–7 August 1980, p. 112.

Sage, Lazuardi Adi. *Dari Wuryantoro ke sineplek: Biografi popular kisah sukses Sudwikatmono* [From Wuryantoro to cinema: A popular biography of Sudwikatmono and his success story]. Jakarta: Trendi Media, 1994.

Sastrosatomo, Soedarpo. "Recollections of My Career". *Bulletin of Indonesian Economic Studies* 30, no. 1 (April 1994). Reprinted in *Recollections: The Indonesian Economy, 1950s–1990s*, edited by Thee Kian Wie. Singapore: Institute of Southeast Asian Studies, 2003.

Sato, Yuri. "The Salim Group in Indonesia: The development and behavior of the largest conglomerate in Southeast Asia". *Developing Economies* XXXI, no. 4 (December 1993).

———. "The development of business groups in Indonesia: 1967–1989". In *Approaching Suharto's Indonesia from the Margins*, edited by Takashi Shiraishi, pp. 101–53. Ithaca, NY: Southeast Asia Program, Cornell University, 1994.

———. "Corporate governance in Indonesia: A study on governance of business groups". In *The Role of Governance in Asia*, edited by Yasutami Shimomura. Singapore: Institute of Southeast Asian Studies, with Japan Institute of International Affairs and Asean Foundation, 2003.

———. "Post-crisis economic reform in Indonesia: Policy for intervening in ownership in historical perspective". IDE Research Paper No. 4, September 2003.

———. "The decline of conglomerates in post-Soeharto Indonesia: The case of Salim Group". *Taiwan Journal of Southeast Asian Studies* 1, no. 1 (2004): 19–43.

———. "Bank restructuring and financial institution reform in Indonesia". *The Developing Economies* XLIII, no. 1 (March 2005): 91–120.

Sawitri, Isma. "Om Liem Boleh Bersenang-senang" [Om Liem can be happy]. *Tempo*, 10 March 1990, pp. 68–71.

Schuman, Michael. *The Miracle: The Epic Story of Asia's Quest for Wealth*. New York: Harper Collins, 2009.

Schwarz, Adam. "Wavering alliance". *Far Eastern Economic Review*, 25 October 1990.

———. "Empire of the son: Indonesian patriarch prepares to hand over reins of Salim Group". *Far Eastern Economic Review*, 14 March 1991.

———. *A Nation in Waiting: Indonesia's Search for Stability*. 2nd ed. St Leonards, NSW: Allen & Unwin, 1999.

——— and Jonathan Paris, eds. *The Politics of Post-Suharto Indonesia*. New York: Council on Foreign Relations Press, 1999.

Seagrave, Sterling. *Lords of the Rim: The Invisible Empire of the Overseas Chinese*. London: Bantam, 1995.

Sender, Henny. "Inside the Overseas Chinese Network". *Institutional Investor*, 1 September 1991.

———. "Eye of the scandal: What is Lippo? Not the bank its founder had in mind". *Far Eastern Economic Review,* 31 October 1996.

Shaplen, Robert. *A Turning Wheel: Three Decades of the Asian Revolution as Witnessed by a Correspondent for the New Yorker.* New York: Random House, 1979.

Shari, Michael. "Can Anthony Salim get out of this corner?". *BusinessWeek,* 9 March 1998.

———. "Suharto gives a little – and gets a lot". *BusinessWeek International,* 6 April 1998.

———. "A tycoon under siege: How Anthony Salim is fighting to save his family's assets — and clout". *Business Week,* 28 September 1998.

———. "Indonesia's Bailout Plan: A Partial Success". *BusinessWeek,* 10 March 2003.

———. "First Pacific: Take Two". *BusinessWeek,* 12 May 2003.

Sheng, Andrew. *From Asian to Global Financial Crisis: An Asian Regulator's View of Unfettered Finance in the 1990s and 2000s.* Cambridge: Cambridge University Press, 2009.

Sherbin, Robert. "First Pacific is converting some skeptics". *Asian Wall Street Journal,* 27 March 1990.

Shimomura, Yasutami, ed. *The Role of Governance in Asia.* Asian Development Experience Vol. 2. Singapore: Institute of Southeast Asian Studies, with Japan Institute of International Affairs and ASEAN Foundation, 2003.

Shin, Yoon Hwan. "Demystifying the capitalist state, political patronage, bureaucratic interests, and capitalist-in-formation in Suharto's Indonesia". Ph.D. thesis. Yale University, 1989.

———. "Role of elites in creating capitalist hegemony in post-oil boom Indonesia". In *Indonesia: The role of the Chinese in shaping modern Indonesian life,* edited by Audrey Kahin, pp. 127–43. Cornell University Southeast Asia Program, 1991 (special issue).

Shiraishi, Takashi, ed. *Approaching Suharto's Indonesia from the Margins.* Ithaca, NY: Southeast Asia Program, Cornell University, 1994.

Simpson, Bradley. *Economists with Guns: Authoritarian Development and US-Indonesian Relations, 1960–1968.* Stanford: Stanford University Press, 2008.

Siregar, Liston, and Susanto Pudjomartono. "Pulang Kampung, Setelah 30 Tahun" [Returning home, after 30 years]. *Tempo,* 24 November 1990, pp. 32–26.

Siregar, Sori Ersa and Kencana Tirta Widya. *Liem Sioe Liong: Dari Futching ke Mancanegara.* [Liem Sioe Liong: From Fuqing to Multinational]. Jakarta: Pustaka Merdeka, 1989.

Smith, Benjamin. "'If I do these things, they will throw me out': Economic reform and the collapse of Indonesia's New Order". *Journal of International Affairs* (Columbia University) 57, no. 1 (Fall 2003).

Smith, Roger M., ed. *Southeast Asia: Documents of Political Development and Change.* Ithaca, NY: Cornell University Press, 1974.

Soeharto: Pikiran, ucapan dan tindakan saya: Otobiografi seperti dipaparkan kepada G. Dwipayana dan Ramadhan K.H. Jakarta: Citra Lamtoro Gung Persada, 1989. English ed.: *Soeharto: My Thoughts, Words and Deeds; An Autobiography*, as told to G. Dwipanyana and Ramadhan K.H. Jakarta: Citra Lamtoro Gung Persada, 1991.

Soesastro, Hadi. *The Indonesian Economy: Recent Developments.* Jakarta: Centre for Strategic and International Studies, November 1990.

———— and Clara Joewono, eds. *The Inclusive Regionalist: A Festschrift dedicated to Jusuf Wanandi.* Jakarta: Centre for Strategic and International Studies, 2007.

————, Anthony Smith and Han Mui Ling, eds. *Governance in Indonesia: Challenges facing the Megawati Presidency.* Singapore: Institute of Southeast Asian Studies, 2003.

Soetriyono, Eddy. *Kisah Sukses Liem Sioe Liong* [Liem Sioe Liong's success story]. Jakarta: Indomedia, 1989.

Solomon, Jay. "On the outs: Salim Group's Suharto ties make it target of retaliation". *Asian Wall Street Journal*, 28 May 1998.

————. "Unorthodox Cleric: Riot Suspect in Jakarta is a Man of Many Convictions". *Asian Wall Street Journal*, 28 July 1998.

————. "Habibie's plan for asset sales worries IMF". *Asian Wall Street Journal*, 27 October 1998.

————. "Proposal aims to boost Ethnic-Indonesian business — plan perceived as reaction to Chinese Dominance". *Asian Wall Street Journal*, 11 November 1998.

————. "Second wind: Salim Group, Nearly sunk, now expands across Asia". *Asian Wall Street Journal*, 13 January 2000.

————. "When investing in Indonesia, don't forget perhaps the most important factor: Politics". *Wall Street Journal*, 8 May 2000.

————. "Jakarta Begins to Sell Salim Assets". *Asian Wall Street Journal*, 1 August 2000.

————. "IMF Expresses Concern with Jakarta's Demands". *Asian Wall Street Journal*, 15 November 2000.

Stern, Joseph. "The rise and fall of the Indonesian economy". Kennedy School of Government, Harvard Faculty research working paper series, June 2003.

Stiles, T.J. *The First Tycoon: The Epic Life of Cornelius Vanderbilt.* New York: Alfred Knopf, 2009.

Studwell, Joe. *Asian Godfathers: Money and Power in Hong Kong and South-East Asia.* London: Profile Books, 2007.

Sudwikatmono. "Manajemen 3 SA (Catatan Seorang Pengusaha)" [3 'SA' management]. In *Manajemen Presiden Soeharto*, edited by Riant Nugroho Dwidjowijoto, pp. LXXII–LXXIII. Jakarta: Yayasan Bina Generasi Bangsa, 1996.

Sukarno. *An Autobiography*: As told to Cindy Adams. Hong Kong: Gunung Agung, 1965.

Sumarkidjo, Atmadji. "The rise and fall of the generals". In *Indonesia Today: Challenges of History*, edited by Grayson Lloyd and Shannon Smith. Singapore: Institute of Southeast Asian Studies. 2001.

Sumarlin, J.B. "Ir. Tunky Ariwibowo: seorang pekerja keras, jujur, loyal dan tekun mengabdi tugas" [Tunky Ariwibowo: A hardworking, honest, loyal and diligent, dutiful 'servant']. In *Dalam Kenangan Tunky Ariwibowo*, edited by Astuti Ariwibowo. Jakarta: Privately published, 2005.

Sung Chek Mei. 林绍良传: *Lin Shao Liang Zhuan* [in Chinese]. "Who's Who in South East Asia: The career of Liem Sioe Liong — a prominent entrepreneur in contemporary Indonesia". Hong Kong: South East Asia Research Institute, 1988.

Suryadinata, Leo. "Chinese economic elites in Indonesia". In *Changing Identities of the Southeast Asian Chinese since World War II*, edited by Jennifer Cushman and Wang Gungwu. Hong Kong: Hong Kong University Press, 1988.

———. *Prominent Chinese Indonesians: Biographical Sketches*. Singapore: Institute of Southeast Asian Studies, 1995.

———. *The Culture of the Chinese Minority in Indonesia*. Singapore: Times Book International, 1997.

———, ed. *Southeast Asia's Chinese Businesses in an Era of Globalization*. Singapore: Institute of Southeast Asian Studies, 2006.

———, ed. *Ethnic Chinese in Contemporary Indonesia*. Singapore: Chinese Heritage Centre and Institute of Southeast Asian Studies, 2008.

———, ed. *Southeast Asian Personalities of Chinese Descent: A Biographical Dictionary*. Singapore: Institute of Southeast Asian Studies, 2012.

Sutriningrum, Indyah. "Om Liem — I say white, you write red". *Bisnis Indonesia*, 24 November 1997.

Tahija, Julius. *Horizon Beyond: Entrepreneurs of Asia*. Singapore: Times Books International, 1995.

Tan, Mely. "The social and cultural dimensions of the role of ethnic Chinese in Indonesian society". In *Indonesia*, pp. 113–25. Ithaca, NY: Cornell University (special issue), 1991.

Tan, Thomas Tsu-wee. *Your Chinese Roots: The Overseas Chinese Story*. Singapore: Times Books International, 1986.

Tan Tjin-Kie. "Sukarnian economics". In *Sukarno's Guided Indonesia*, edited by Tan Tjin-Kie. Brisbane: Jacaranda Press, 1967.

———, ed. *Sukarno's Guided Indonesia*. Brisbane: Jacaranda Press, 1967.

Tangkudung, Audrey. "Sudwikatmono: Becoming a giant through partnership". *Sunday Observer*, 11 January 1998.

Tanter, Richard and Kenneth Young, eds. *The Politics of Middle Class Indonesia*.

Clayton, Victoria: Centre for Southeast Asian Studies, Monash University, 1990.

Tanzer, Andrew. "First Pacific's Pearls", *Forbes*, 13 February 1995.

———. "The Amazing Mr Kuok". *Forbes*, 28 July 1997.

Tarrant, Bill. *Reporting Indonesia: The Jakarta Post Story, 1983–2008*. Singapore and Jakarta: Equinox. 2008.

Tee Ming San. *Lin Shaoliang chuan: Nanyang sou fu de teng fei he kun jing* [A biography of Lin Shaoliang: The rise and fall of Southeast Asia's wealthiest]. Hong Kong: Notable, 1999.

The Sampoerna Legacy: A Family and Business History. Conceived by Michelle Sampoerna; written and illustrated by Diana Hollingsworth Gessler. Privately published, 2007.

Thee Kian Wie. "*Reflections on the New Order 'Miracle'* ". In *Indonesia Today: Challenges of History*, edited by Grayson Lloyd and Shannon Smith. Singapore: Institute of Southeast Asian Studies, 2001.

———, ed. *Recollections: The Indonesian Economy, 1950s–1990s*. Singapore: Institute of Southeast Asian Studies, 2003.

———. "The Indonesian government's economic policies towards the ethnic Chinese: Beyond economic nationalism?". In *Southeast Asia's Chinese Businesses in an Era of Globalization*, edited by Leo Suryadinata. Singapore: Institute of Southeast Asian Studies, 2006.

Thomas, K.D. "Political and economic instability: the Gestapu and its aftermath". In *Sukarno's Guided Indonesia*, edited by Tan Tjin-Kie. Brisbane: Jacaranda Press, 1967.

——— and J. Panglaykim. "Indonesia's Development Cabinet, Background to the Current Problems and the Five-Year Plan". *Asian Survey* 9, no. 4 (April 1969): 223.

Timmer, Peter. "Wheat Flour Consumption in Indonesia". *Bulletin of Indonesian Economic Studies* (Canberra) 7, no. 1 (March 1971): 78–95.

Triyanto, Gatot, K. Karsadi and R. Wiranto. "Om Liem: Dari Tapos meluruskan isu kolusi" [Om Liem: Straightening out the issue of collusion from Tapos]. *Gatra*, 7 October 1995, pp. 70–71.

Turner, Sarah. *Indonesia's Small Entrepreneurs: Trading on the Margins*. London: Routledge, 2003.

——— and Pamela Allen. "Chinese Indonesians in a changing nation: Pressures of ethnicity and identity". *Asia Pacific Viewpoint* 48, no. 1 (April 2007): 112–27.

Twang Peck Yang. *The Chinese Business Elite in Indonesia and the Transition to Independence, 1940–1950*. Kuala Lumpur: Oxford University Press, 1998.

Van der Kroef, J.M. *Indonesia Since Sukarno*. Singapore: Asia Pacific Press, 1971.

Van Dijk, Kees. *A Country in Despair: Indonesia between 1997 and 2000*. Leiden: KITLV Press, 2001.

Vandenbosch, Amry. *The Dutch East Indies: Its Government, Problems and Politics.* University of California Press, 1941. First edition published by Wm. Eerdmans, 1933.

Vatikiotis, Michael. *Indonesian Politics under Suharto: Order, Development and Pressure for Change.* London and New York: Routledge, 1993.

———. "Indonesian Chinese". In *The Encyclopedia of the Chinese Overseas*, edited by Lynn Pan. Singapore: Chinese Heritage Centre, 1998.

———. "Tycoon is back, with a hunger; Salim rebuilds crumbled empire". *International Herald Tribune*, 20 November 2004.

Verchere, Ian. "Changing world of Robert Kuok". *Insight*, August 1978.

———. "Chin: Thailand's banking genius". *Insight*, June 1978.

———. "Liem Sioe Liong: Suharto's secret agent". *Insight*, May 1978.

———. "Mochtar Riady's Chinatown beat". *Insight*, April 1978.

Vickers, Adrian. *A History of Modern Indonesia.* Cambridge: Cambridge University Press, 2005.

———. "The New Order: keeping up appearances". In *Indonesia Today: Challenges of History*, edited by Grayson Lloyd and Shannon Smith. Singapore: Institute of Southeast Asian Studies, 2001.

Waldman, Peter, Marcus Brauchli and Jay Solomon. "Suharto family missed out on a fortune: Business blunders outweighed influence in attempts to amass wealth". *Asian Wall Street Journal*, 4 January 1999.

Wall Street Journal. "Indonesia Cement Plant Owners Line up $120 Million Bank Loan". 13 October 1981.

Waluyo, Dwitri. "Persahabatan empat decade" [A four-decade friendship]. *Gatra*, 7 October 1995, pp. 72–73.

Wanandi, Jusuf. *Shades of Grey: A Political Memoir of Modern Indonesia, 1965–1998.* Jakarta: Equinox, 2012.

Wanandi, Sofyan. "The Post-Soeharto business environment". In *Post-Soeharto Indonesia: Renewal or Chaos?*, edited by Geoff Forrester. Singapore: Institute of Southeast Asian Studies with Australian National University, 1999.

Wang, Yeu-Farn. "Chinese entrepreneurs in Southeast Asia: Historical roots and modern significance". Stockholm University Centre for Pacific Asia Studies, Working Paper 34, May 1994.

Warta Ekonomi. "Kami Besar Bukan Karena Dekat Dengan Pak Harto" [We are big not because we were close to Pak Harto]. 21 February 1994, pp. 43–54.

Weidenbaum, Murray and S. Hughes. *The Bamboo Network.* New York: Martin Kessler, The Free Press, 1996.

Weissman, Stephen, ed., with members of the Pacific Studies Center and the North American Congress on Latin America. *The Trojan Horse: A Radical Look at Foreign Aid.* Rev. ed. Palo Alto: Ramparts Press, 1975.

Wessel, Ingrid, ed. *Democratisation in Indonesia after the Fall of Suharto.* Berlin: Logos, 2005.

——— and Georgia Wimhofer, eds. *Violence in Indonesia*. Hamburg: Abera-Verl, 2001.

Widhardin, Irene, Deden Setiawan, J.B. Soesetiyo, R. Nurjaman, S. Merwanto and R. Noor. "Ambisi Salim kuasai bisnis makanan" [Salim ambition to dominate the food business]. *Warta Ekonomi*, 13 June 1994, pp. 14–17.

Willmott, Donald Earl. *The Chinese of Semarang: A Changing Minority Community in Indonesia*. Ithaca, NY: Cornell University Press, 1960.

Wilson, Keeley and Peter Williamson. "First Pacific Company: Building an Asian Conglomerate". INSEAD Euro-Asia Centre, 1999, Case 399-144-1.

Winters, Jeffrey. *Power in Motion*. Ithaca, NY: Cornell University Press, 1996.

Witcher, S. Karene and Joseph Manguno. "Suharto received kickbacks, affidavit charges". *Asian Wall Street Journal*, 17 July 1980.

Wolfe, Tom. *The Bonfire of the Vanities*. New York: Farrer, Straus Giroux, 1987.

World Bank East Asia Poverty Reduction and Economic Management Unit. "Combating Corruption in Indonesia: Enhancing Accountability for Development". Washington, D.C.: World Bank, 2003.

Xiao Liu. *Lin Wen Jing: Ta gai bian le jia xiang* [He Changed His Home: Fuqing's Lin Wen Jing Returns After 18 Years]. Hong Kong: Takungpao Publishing, 2005.

Yap, Piet. *The Grains of My Life*. Singapore: Privately published, 2010.

Yeung Yue-Man and David K.Y. Chu, eds. *Fujian: A Coastal Province in Transition and Transformation*. Hong Kong: Chinese University Press, 2000.

Yong, C.F. *Tan Kah-Kee: The Making of an Overseas Chinese Legend*. Singapore: Oxford University Press, 1987.

Yong Mun Cheong. *The Indonesian Revolution and the Singapore Connection: 1945–1949*. Leiden: KITLV, 2003.

Yoshihara, Kunio. *The Rise of Ersatz Capitalism in South-East Asia*. Singapore: Oxford University Press, 1988.

———, ed. *Oei Tiong Ham Concern: The First Business Empire of Southeast Asia*. Kyoto University: The Center for Southeast Asian Studies, 1989.

———. *Building a Prosperous Southeast Asia: From Ersatz to Echt Capitalism*. U.K.: Curzon, 1999.

Yoshino, Michael and Carin-Isabel Knoop. "First Pacific Company Limited: From Letters of Credit to Personal Communications Networks". Retired Case Study 9-396-139. HBS Archives, Baker Library Historical Collections, Harvard Business School, 1995.

INDEX

ABOUT THE AUTHORS

Richard Borsuk, a graduate in Asian Studies from the University of Wisconsin at Madison, has worked as a journalist in Asia for more than forty years. He was the *Asian Wall Street Journal*'s Thailand correspondent from 1981 to 1987 and its Indonesia correspondent from 1987 to 1998. After Suharto's fall in May that year, Richard moved to Singapore, where he held regional reporting and editing positions for the newspaper. In 2011, he joined Reuters as a news editor. A presentation he made at the Australian National University's 1998 Indonesia Update conference in Canberra became a chapter titled "Reforming business in Indonesia" in the book *Post-Soeharto Indonesia: Renewal or Chaos?*, published in 1999 by the Institute of Southeast Asian Studies. He also wrote a chapter, "The Limits of Reform", in *Indonesia Beyond Suharto*, published by M.E. Sharpe and The Asia Society the same year.

Nancy Chng is a graduate of the University of California at Berkeley. She co-founded Select Books, a Singapore bookshop and publisher specializing in Southeast Asia. In 1991, Select published the English translation of *Gadis Pantai* (The Girl from the Coast) by famed Indonesian author Pramoedya Ananta Toer, whose books were banned by Suharto. Nancy contributed a chapter and edited a book called *Questioning Development in Southeast Asia*. In 1979, she joined the *Straits Times* (Singapore) as a feature writer and was the newspaper's correspondent in Thailand from 1982 to 1986. She moved to Jakarta in 1987. Her interest in Indonesia had roots in the 1970s, when she was part of an informal study group on Southeast Asia whose members included some of Indonesia's most respected intellectuals: the diplomat Soedjatmoko, journalists Goenawan Mohamad and Mochtar Lubis as well as cleric Abdurrahman Wahid, who later became the country's president. Nancy, who had been a political analyst at a Jakarta securities firm, was a visiting research fellow at the Institute of Southeast Asian Studies, Singapore, from 2006 to 2007.

CPSIA information can be obtained
at www.ICGtesting.com
Printed in the USA
BVOW07s0905120717
489093BV00023B/143/P